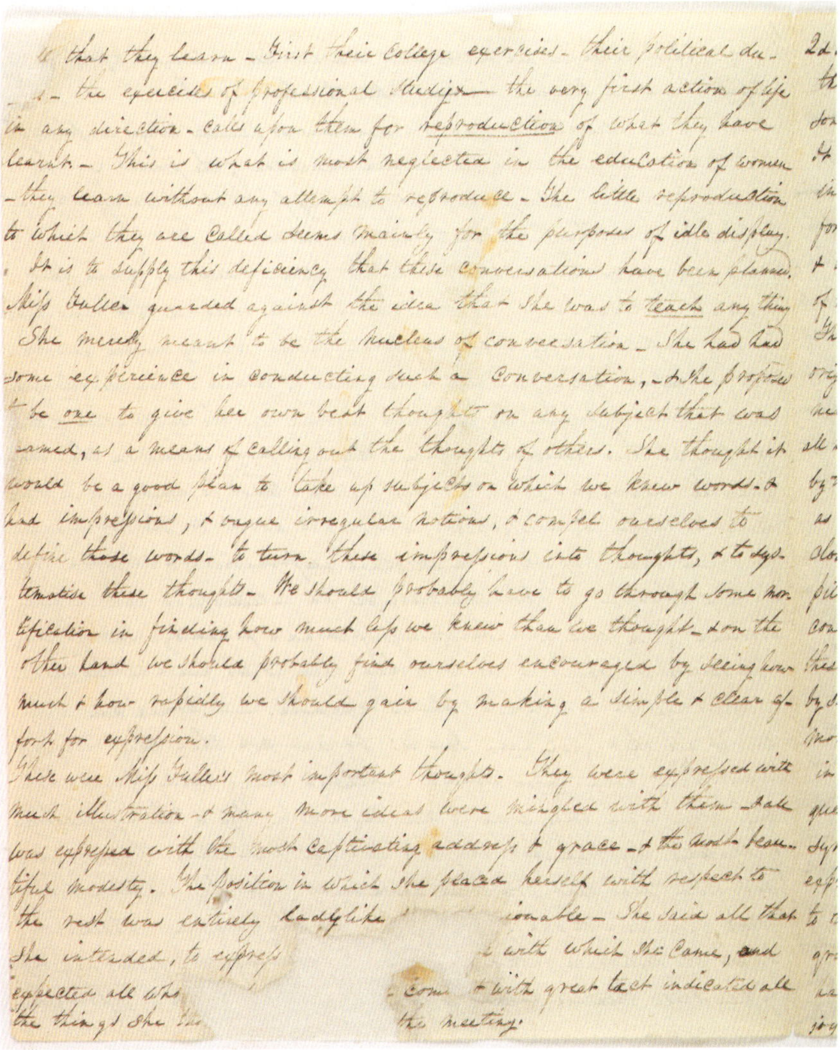
t that they learn – First their College exercises – their political du-s – the exercises of professional studies – the very first action of life in any direction – calls upon them for reproduction of what they have learnt. – This is what is most neglected in the education of women – they learn without any attempt to reproduce – The little reproduction to which they are called seems mainly for the purposes of idle display. It is to supply this deficiency that these conversations have been planned. Miss Fuller guarded against the idea that she was to teach any thing. She merely meant to be the nucleus of conversation – She had had some experience in conducting such a Conversation, – & she proposed to be one to give her own best thoughts on any subject that was named, as a means of calling out the thoughts of others. She thought it would be a good plan to take up subjects on which we knew words – & had impressions, & vague irregular notions, & compel ourselves to define those words – to turn these impressions into thoughts, & to systematise these thoughts – We should probably have to go through some mortification in finding how much less we knew than we thought – & on the other hand we should probably find ourselves encouraged by seeing how much & how rapidly we should gain by making a simple & clear effort for expression.

These were Miss Fuller's most important thoughts. They were expressed with much illustration – & many more ideas were mingled with them – & all was expressed with the most captivating address & grace – & the most beautiful modesty. The position in which she placed herself with respect to the rest was entirely ladylike [illegible]ionable – She said all that she intended, to express [illegible] with which she came, and expected all who [illegible] come & with great tact indicated all the things she [illegible] the meeting.

Bright Circle

Bright Circle

Five Remarkable Women in the Age of Transcendentalism

RANDALL FULLER

OXFORD
UNIVERSITY PRESS

OXFORD
UNIVERSITY PRESS

Great Clarendon Street, Oxford, OX2 6DP,
United Kingdom

Oxford University Press is a department of the University of Oxford.
It furthers the University's objective of excellence in research, scholarship, and education by publishing worldwide. Oxford is a registered trade mark of Oxford University Press in the UK and in certain other countries

Published in the United States of America by Oxford University Press
198 Madison Avenue, New York, NY 10016, United States of America

British Library Cataloguing in Publication Data
Data available

Library of Congress Control Number: 2024905338

ISBN 978–0–19–284363–0

DOI: 10.1093/oso/9780192843630.001.0001

Printed in the UK by
Bell & Bain Ltd., Glasgow

For Elizabeth Schultz

Table of Contents

	Introduction: Bright Circle	1
1.	Mary Moody Emerson among the Stars	11
2.	Elizabeth Palmer Peabody at 13 West Street	69
3.	Sophia Peabody in Cuba	128
4.	Lydia Jackson Emerson's Marriage of Heaven and Hell	192
5.	The Tempests of Margaret Fuller	245
	Epilogue: Circles	307

Acknowledgments 355
Abbreviations 357
List of Illustrations 359
List of Plates 365
Endnotes 367
Bibliographic Essay 395
Index 399

Introduction

Bright Circle

> As I sat there, my heart overflowed with joy at the sight of the bright circle, . . . for I know not where to look for so much character, culture, and so much love of truth and beauty, in any other circle of women and girls.
>
> —unidentified woman from Margaret Fuller's "Conversations"

1.

Elizabeth Palmer Peabody needed to earn a living. She had already devoted the better part of her thirty-six years to this task, writing histories, translating philosophical works from French and German, teaching in private academies from Massachusetts to Maine. Unfortunately, her career as a teacher was now officially over, the casualty of a scandal involving the transcendentalist Bronson Alcott's experimental school in Boston. Elizabeth had served for more than a year as an assistant teacher at the Temple School, chronicling Alcott's unusual teaching methods in a book she called *Record of a School.* But when Alcott borrowed her transcriptions for a second book that included references to human sexuality and circumcision, the work was deemed in such poor taste that one aggrieved lawyer purchased 750 copies to use as toilet paper. Elizabeth resigned her position at the Temple School before the offending book was published, but it was too late. Her reputation as a teacher was tainted by the association with Alcott. That part of her life was finished.

In the wake of this disaster, she hit upon the idea of opening a bookshop. She imagined a cozy, welcoming space where Boston intellectuals could gather and purchase hard-to-find books of philosophy and literature from Europe. Long fascinated by the writers and thinkers who had gathered half a century earlier in the small college town of Jena, Germany and fueled the Romantic revolution that soon changed the direction of English poetry, Elizabeth conceived of a bookstore that would be the first of its kind to sell books that were slow in reaching the young nation. She imagined a commonwealth of knowledge and aspiration, a shared universe located between the hardcovers lining her shelves.

The bookshop was located at 13 West Street—a short, narrow lane paved with cobblestones—across the street from a noisy livery (figure 1). On one end was Boston Common; on the other, Washington Street, then known as Publishers Row, where the city's burgeoning book trade thrived. Elizabeth's shop never boasted a formal name—it was commonly referred to as "Miss Peabody's Book Room"—but in the summer of 1840, when it opened its doors, making Elizabeth

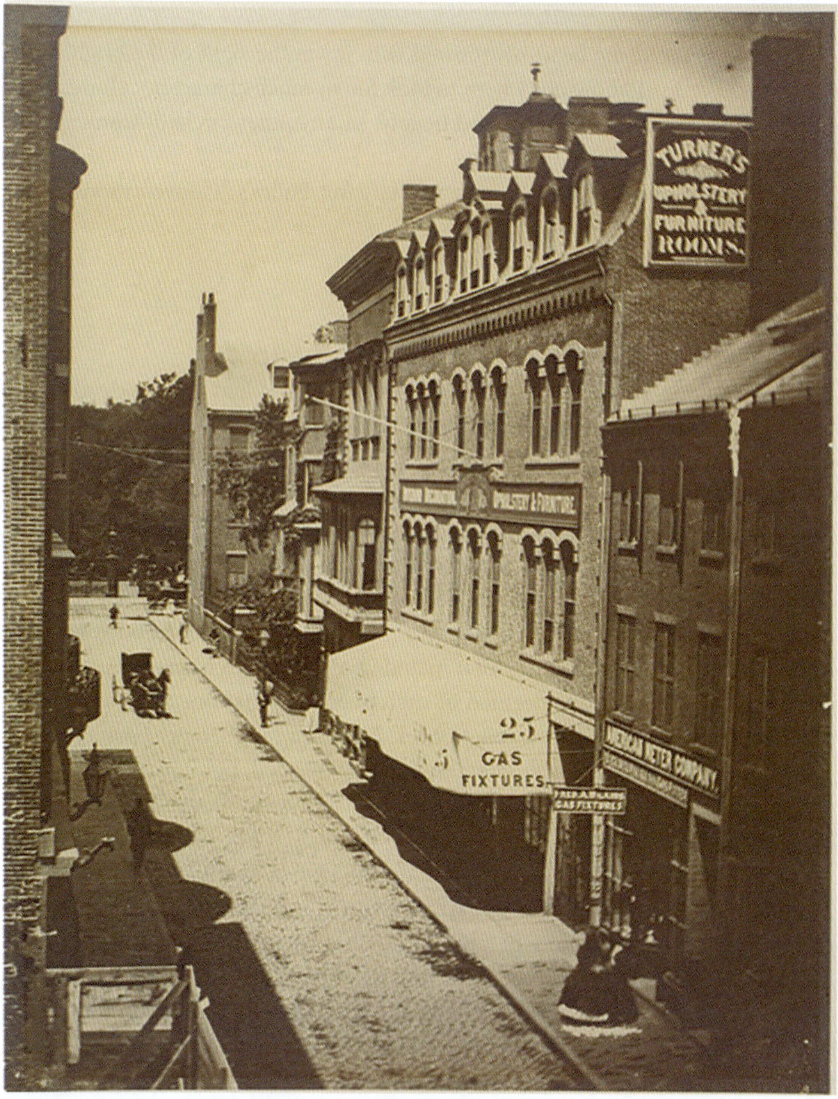

Figure 1. View of West Street looking toward Boston Common.

the only female bookstore owner in Boston, the front parlor of the Federal-style rowhouse quickly became an intellectual mecca, an "immense convenience" for a certain portion of "young Boston," which wanted "to keep more in the current flow of German and French life."[1]

Her customers were a group of eccentric philosophers and social radicals known as the transcendentalists. As the name rather vaguely implies, adherents of this movement were concerned with transcendence—with transforming everyday experience into something lofty, ideal, even godlike. The transcendentalists combined the notion of divinely inspired creativity they absorbed from Romantic poetry with New England's local preoccupation with the development of the self. To most people, these intellectual vagabonds seemed harebrained, if not a little dangerous to polite society. They loitered along the fringes of acceptable thought, trafficking in unpopular ideas such as the abolition of slavery and the need for women's rights. Some argued for communal property, equitable marriages, the end of market capitalism. Widely disparate in temperament and personality, they were nevertheless united in their desire to imagine new ways of living, new modes of being. As Elizabeth Peabody observed, the men and women who filled her bookshop in those days were people "who have dared to say to one another… Why not begin to move the mountains of custom and convention?"[2]

At the heart of transcendentalism was a new orientation toward the individual. The movement asserted that God existed in each human being. Its adherents therefore elevated the self to infinite worth. The only obstacle was society—a degrading force of conformity best resisted by immersion in nature. From this interlocking set of premises, transcendentalism became the first important literary and philosophical movement in Anglo-American history. While its critics ridiculed its pronouncements as absurd and impractical, its advocates believed they were participating in the nation's second great revolution—this one committed not to political freedom but to the spirit and its unfettered expression. Out of this revolution were forged some of the nation's first literary classics, including Ralph Waldo Emerson's essay on "Self-Reliance," Henry David Thoreau's *Walden*, and Margaret Fuller's *Woman in the Nineteenth Century*.

Most histories of transcendentalism locate it in the tiny village of Concord, Massachusetts. In this telling the energies surrounding the new movement were created in the cluttered study at Emerson's house and the tiny cabin Thoreau built on Walden Pond. But Elizabeth Peabody's bookshop was every bit as important to the development of the movement. "Here," remembered one of its patrons, "the 'Dial' was published. Here any one could subscribe a small annual fee, and carry home the last German or French review…. Here, when one looked in of a morning or afternoon, he met, as the chance might give, Mr. Allston the artist, Mr. Emerson, Mr. Ripley, Mr. Hawthorne, Mr. Hedge…or the three Misses Peabody."[3] Elizabeth's shop, in other words, was at the very center of tremendous cultural ferment. It was a place where belles lettres, freethinking religion, and social reform collided and mixed, combining to create something wholly new. As she later recalled of these heady times, "I came into contact with the world as never before. [A]ll...things were discussed in my book-store by Boston lawyers and Cambridge professors. Those were very living years for me."[4]

In Elizabeth's front parlor, the Transcendental Club met. Emerson, Thoreau, the radical minister Theodore Parker, and other luminaries sat at her hearth and debated the purpose of religion and the qualities of the soul. Editorial meetings of *The Dial* also occurred in the cramped, book-lined space, proof sheets spread out on the countertop and floor. Open houses were hosted in the evenings to discuss a range projects, including the utopian community known as Brook Farm. Here, too, Elizabeth printed works by Thoreau and Hawthorne on the little hand press she bought to create her own publishing house. And it was in the bookshop, on Wednesday mornings, that another series of momentous events occurred. These were Margaret Fuller's Conversations.

2.

Imagine the front parlor lined with makeshift shelves sagging with the weight of books. Books and periodicals are everywhere: stacked in corners, stacked in boxes, scattered on tables—many of them, those circulated through Elizabeth's lending library, wrapped in brown paper with their titles neatly inscribed in her flowing black script (figures 2 and 3). A long counter occupies one end of the room. Encircling the cramped parlor are twenty-five or so ill-assorted chairs, some of horsehair, some with faded upholstery, all of them borrowed by Elizabeth from friends and neighbors or salvaged from her years teaching school, so tightly crowded that there is hardly space to walk. Around ten thirty or so, women begin to arrive.

They range in age from thirteen to sixty. Most, though, are in their twenties and thirties. Many have walked or taken omnibuses from their homes in Beacon Hill or from rented apartments elsewhere in Boston. Others have traveled from as far away as Newton, Concord, and even New York. Today we would consider most of them privileged—by education, by the color of their skin, in some cases by wealth. (Several women hover around the margins of genteel poverty, however.) Their commitments are similarly wide-ranging: Some are abolitionists, some animal rights activists, some vegetarians, some utopian dreamers. Some are artists, poets, and writers, while others consider domestic work their primary occupation. For the next two hours, these distinctions will seem meaningless. To the assembled women, no other place in the world will feel quite so important, so vivid with life and ideas. They will discuss literature and history and other topics of conversation all too often considered beyond their prerogatives or grasp.

Figure 2. Books from Elizabeth Palmer Peabody's lending library.

We picture the life of the mind as solitary. The image, inherited from the Romantic era, is of a lone, passionate writer, hunkered over a desk, alone in a study, exorcising demons with pen and ink. But thought and creativity are *communal* endeavors. New ideas are shared and tested; sentiments are refined and modified through discussion, argument, collaboration. The women who frequented Elizabeth Peabody's bookshop were passionate about thought. They believed in that central tenet of transcendentalism: that ideas could transform the world. They wanted to create an extraordinary life for themselves, but they also believed that the individual came into radiant being best through community and interaction with others.

Although the Conversations are justly famous in the history of transcendentalism, comparatively little is known about them. Some participants remain anonymous. Many topics are elusive. Even the location of the first gatherings is somewhat mysterious. But we know for certain that by the summer of 1840, the meetings found their rightful place in the front parlor of Elizabeth's bookshop. Notes were taken for a handful of sessions, but most of the nearly one hundred Conversations that ran from 1839 to 1844 went unrecorded. Nearly two centuries later, we can glimpse the faintest glimmerings of what transpired. Yet the excitement they generated is palpable to this day. One unnamed woman described the "the earnestness and simplicity of the discussion as well as the gifts of the speakers."[5] Another wrote that only in the Conversations had she found anything approaching "real society."[6] Yet a third remembered feeling "all kindled" during

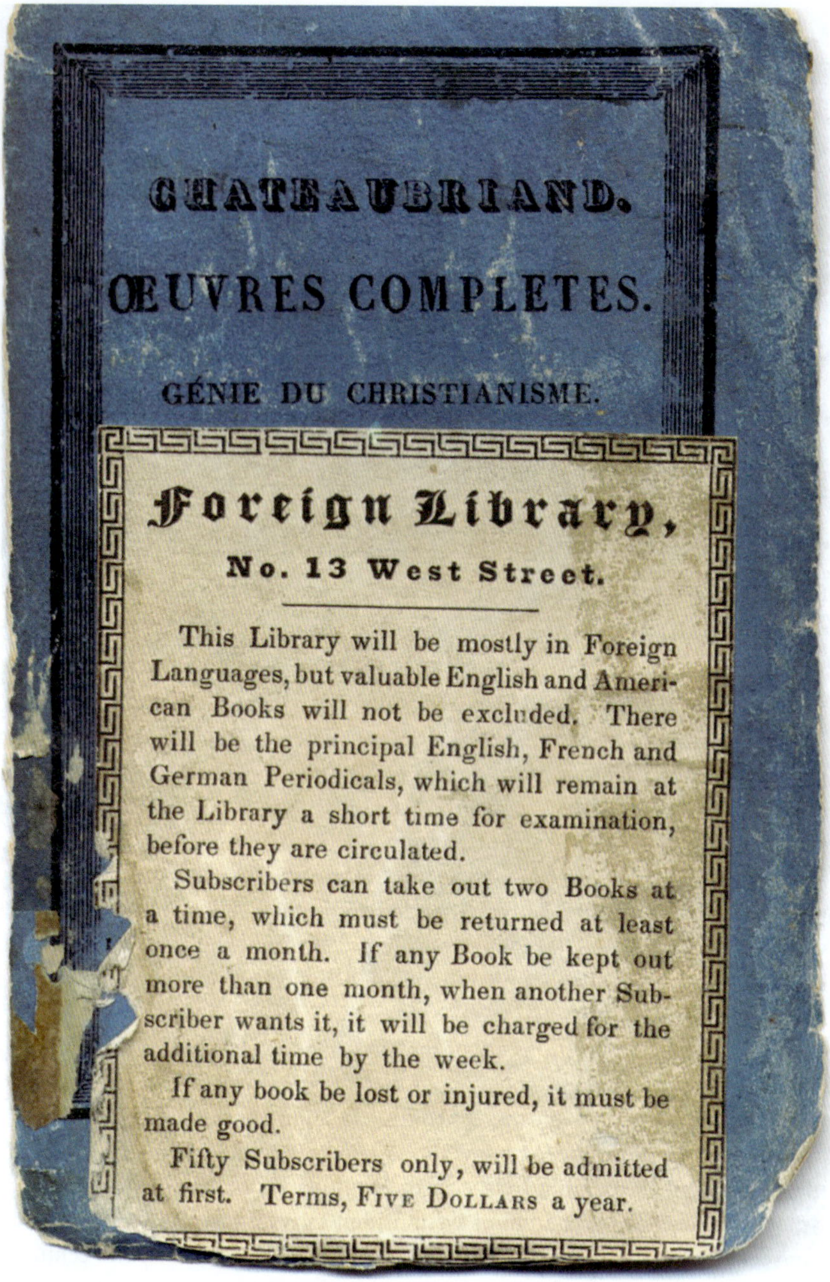

Figure 3. Bookplate from the lending library.

the meetings. When they concluded, she was suffused with a glowing sense that "none there could be strangers...."[7]

The Conversations offered an intellectual community that was otherwise unavailable to women in the first half of the nineteenth century. They provided an outlet for those who could expect nothing in the way of social or institutional support for their ideas. A cross between graduate seminar, professional symposium, and social network, they provided communion and growth to those fortunate enough to attend. They also served as something more: the foundation of what we now call the women's rights movement. In the intellectual headquarters of Elizabeth Peabody's makeshift bookshop, the Conversations opened a space for women who wanted to embark on the arduous process of thinking for themselves.

3.

Bright Circle chronicles the lives of five women who participated in one form or the other in Margaret Fuller's Conversations. For many years, the women of the Bright Circle (except for Fuller herself) were overlooked by scholars of transcendentalism. They were diminished as wives incapable of understanding the greatness of their husbands or described as poor writers and undisciplined, eccentric thinkers. This has changed in the last generation or so, as a collaborative and persistent effort to recover these and other women intellectuals has provided us with a richer understanding of their accomplishments. Each woman portrayed in this book had an aspiring nature, a sense of latent power. Each lived during a time when women were supposed to subdue that ambition, to channel their ego into obedience, to be seen and not heard. The conflict between these antagonistic forces is the backdrop against which the Conversations took place.

As a group, the Bright Circle was never particularly cohesive. The five women disagreed with one another almost as often as they agreed. In fact, it was their independence that enabled them to make brilliant—if often forgotten—contributions to the culture of the United States in the first half of the nineteenth century. They wrote some of the earliest works of transcendentalism, edited the first avant-garde magazine in the nation, contributed to a wide range of social causes that included the abolition of slavery, animal rights, and child education. They helped establish feminism in this country.

At their head was a magnetic former schoolteacher named Margaret Fuller. Her arrogance was legendary—but so was her talk. She was a virtuoso of conversation, a genius at off-the-cuff statements that perfectly crystallized what everyone else was struggling to formulate. When she spoke, people quickly forgot about her icy hauteur. In September 1839, at what was then considered the perilous age of twenty-nine years (one became a "spinster" at thirty), she came up with the idea for a women's discussion group. "Could a circle be assembled," she asked, "in earnest desirous to answer the great questions. What were we born to do? How shall we do it? which so few ever propose to themselves 'till their best years are gone by." Soon she was portraying the meetings as "a point of union to well-educated and thinking women, in a city which, with great pretensions to mental refinement, boasts, at present, nothing of the kind."[8] From the Conversations emerged her landmark work of early feminism, *Woman in the Nineteenth Century*, where she insisted that independence and meaningful occupation were the birthrights of women every bit as much as of men.

It is unlikely the Conversations would have come to pass without the energetic involvement of Elizabeth Peabody. Always at the center of any new trend or idea, a cultural entrepreneur who expended her prodigious energy organizing all sorts of events and gatherings, she transcribed the proceedings of the Transcendental Club, served as editor for several literary magazines, and involved herself in dozens of charitable causes. To the extent that she is remembered today, it is for the company—the *male* company—she kept. Over the course of her long life, Elizabeth befriended and promoted the work of Ralph Waldo Emerson, Nathaniel Hawthorne, and Henry David Thoreau, among others. But she was a remarkable thinker in her own right, often far in advance of her contemporaries. Among the first to absorb the new idealist philosophy emerging from Germany and England, she disseminated its teachings in essays and adult classes for women. More than anyone else, she helped solidify the new form of thought into a recognizable movement, which she was also the first to name: transcendentalism.

Her sister, Sophia, was in many ways her exact opposite. More artist than intellectual, more lighthearted than her older sister, Sophia was among the first women in the United States to earn an income from painting. Her "Cuba Journal," written while she lived in the Caribbean for her health, also broke fresh ground. It expressed a poetic nature-worship that prefigured the more famous rhapsodies of male transcendentalists. Circulated among a network of New England intellectuals and artists, the journal, written two years before Ralph Waldo Emerson's famous manifesto, *Nature*, was appreciated by dozens of readers for its aestheticized descriptions of the natural world. Sophia's many accomplishments are overshadowed today by her marriage to Nathaniel Hawthorne—an irony given that as a young woman she declared her intention never to marry. What changed her mind (in addition to the Byronically glamorous author) was the inner conflict she felt forging an artistic career. To be a serious female artist in the nineteenth century was to be an outlaw, a marginal figure. Sophia was all too familiar with the prejudices and loneliness experienced by her older sister Elizabeth, who never married or had a home of her own. If she ultimately chose to live a more conventional life, sacrificing her artistic career to raise three children and tend to her literary husband, she never relinquished her independent mind or creative vision.

Another woman who experienced the private battle between personal freedom and the expectations of marriage was Lydia Jackson Emerson, known in transcendentalist circles as Lidian. Widely considered the intellectual equal and foil of her husband Ralph Waldo Emerson, Lydia was a keener analyst of human behavior, a sardonic witness to the foibles of her contemporaries. This allowed her to perceive the limitations of transcendentalism more acutely than almost any other critic of the movement. Early on, she realized that if the individual was truly the source of preeminent value, it was impossible to locate greater meaning beyond the self. Lydia convinced her husband to redirect his rarefied philosophy toward the less fortunate, especially enslaved African Americans. And her "Transcendental Bible"—a barbed rewriting of the gospel she aimed at the reformers who visited her house—remains unparalleled in its skewering of transcendentalism's smug self-satisfaction.

These four women were inspired in various ways by a completely original precursor. Mary Moody Emerson, a generation older than the rest, was an omnivorous reader who recognized the importance of Romantic thought before almost anyone else in America. Mary dreamed of becoming a writer. After that dream was dashed, she turned her attention to the education of her nephew, Ralph Waldo Emerson, introducing him to Wordsworth and Coleridge, to German philosophy, and to an older Puritan piety marked by spiritual enthusiasm. She also instilled in him a love of nature. Above all, she provided him with a model of independent and uncompromising intellect. A remarkable thinker and writer, Mary Emerson's ecstatic visions of nature and the divine, which she chronicled in a voluminous spiritual journal she called her "Almanacks," are among the very earliest texts in America to anticipate transcendentalism. As a pioneering female intellectual, she inspired Elizabeth Peabody and Lydia Emerson.

The five women who make up this book were brilliant, original, prodigiously talented. They were also fallible, often conflicted. Each helped create transcendentalism. Each found in the movement a vision of the independent self that was enormously alluring. And each found that vision untenable, unsustainable—all but impossible for a woman living in the first half of the nineteenth century. Sitting together in Elizabeth Peabody's bookshop, they grappled with these ideas. They questioned the values of their culture as well as their place in it. They shared the rich complications of their lives, the profound complexities of their existence. The room they sat in crackled with their energy. The sparks and embers of conversation rose and swirled. The warmth of togetherness, of friendship, of shared purpose filled the room. Their example is an invitation for us to do the same (figure 4).

Figure 4. Doorway of 13 West Street.

1
Mary Moody Emerson among the Stars

1.

On the evening of November 4, 1804, a young woman named Mary Moody Emerson stepped outside the unpainted meetinghouse in Malden, Massachusetts and gazed at the heavens. She had just sat through an interminable sermon, delivered by a preacher she considered "Frivolous," a silly and inconsequential "Mr. G," who had failed, once again, to quench her thirsting and limitless soul. Outside, the night was clear: cold and crystalline. The brilliance of the stars swept over her like a revelation; for a shimmering moment, she felt engulfed in the living presence of God.

She was a thoroughly unusual person. The first thing most people noticed about Mary Emerson was her size. She stood at least two inches under five feet. But other features quickly asserted themselves—her eyes, for instance. There was a terrific blue flash in them, a piercing intelligence that stripped away fripperies and pretensions and seemed to bore straight into a person's very essence.[1] There was also her restless energy. She spun, her nephew Ralph Waldo Emerson once observed, "with greater velocity than any of the other tops . . . [and] would tear into the chaise or out of it, into the house or out of it, into the conversation, into the thought, into the character of the stranger."[2]

She was prickly, disputatious, unpredictable. Once, when asked whether she preferred tea, coffee, or chocolate, she replied, "*All.*" When her hostess inquired if she wanted them in separate cups, she answered, "*All together.*"[3] Another time, when she paid a visit to her longtime friend, Cynthia Thoreau (the mother of Henry David), she kept her eyes shut throughout their entire conversation. Only at the end did she venture to say, "Mrs. Thoreau, I don't know whether you have observed that my eyes are shut."

"Yes, Madam," was the reply, "I have observed it."

"Perhaps you would like to know the reasons?"

"Yes, I should."

"I don't like to see a person of your age guilty of such levity in your dress." She disliked the pink ribbons on her friend's new cap.[4]

These crotchets obscured a profoundly serious thinker. Always happiest when she was alone in the woods or writing by candlelight in her room, Mary resembled her Puritan ancestors, who had favored private intercourse with the Almighty to congress with the corrupting force of the world. But she was also a child of the Enlightenment, a self-taught polymath with wide-ranging interests in science, philosophy, and literature. An insatiable letter-writer, she left more than a thousand to posterity, a voluminous correspondence that surveys a remarkable range of topics, from Byron's poetry and Spinoza's philosophy to studious reflections on theological treatises and descants upon Wordsworth, Hume, and Goethe. She also wrote to friends about planetary revolutions and the lives of plants.

She was an anomaly. When Mary Moody Emerson was coming of age in early republican America, women were thought to have been expressly fitted by God for two mutually supportive purposes: to serve as wives and mothers. "[T]he great Province of a Woman," declared one writer (who happened to be a man), was "Economy and Frugality in the management of Family."[5] Another observer (who also happened to be a man) wrote that "it was sufficient for a woman to know enough to make a shirt and a pudding."[6] We should be careful about overstating the strictures applied to women during this period. There were certainly some who remained unmarried, widowed or determinedly solitary, some who managed to sustain themselves by opening shops or working in mills or doing piecework of all sorts. But these statements nevertheless represent a commonly expressed *ideal*, an ideology, that was meant to define and domesticate women.

As most of her acquaintances prepared for a home life, Mary determined to live beyond the restrictions of gender. She resolved to exist in "single blessedness."[7] And because her thoughts and feelings seemed as interesting to her as those of anyone else, she decided to experience as much as she possibly could. She rode her horse through blinding snowstorms and along the stony beaches of northern Massachusetts. She took solitary walks through the flat chill fields surrounding Malden. "Yesterday I walked 3 miles or more to Lynn," she wrote in November 1804, when she was thirty. "Never were emotions so animated & uninterrupted as those of my walk." Nature ever aroused her most intense feelings: "Why oh my God, are thy virtuous creatures ever unhappy! It is because they comprehend nothing of the wonders w'h surround them in the vast vol[ume] of nature—in the divine book of providence w'h nature unfolds, and which revelation writes with sun beams!"[8] (figure 6).

When she was not plunging through woods and pastures, she was reading. Once, as a child, she had carried an armful of books to the henhouse (she thought the creatures must be lonely) and read aloud to the perplexed creatures.[9] When she was twelve, she discovered a tattered old volume in her Aunt Ruth's attic. The cover and title page were missing, the pages torn, scuffed, and yellowed, but the author of the book seemed to have written his poem with her in mind. Mary Emerson read the book over and over, memorized its long, stately passages, its insistent iambic pulse. Only some years later, when she overheard her older brother discussing poetry with his college friends, did she realize she had been reading Milton's *Paradise Lost.*

As she grew older, her life became a never-ending quest to secure enough time and solitude to read: "I have been up 13 hours[,]" she confided in her journal. "Save 3 I have had them to myself." In those ten delicious hours, she perused Shakespeare's *Othello*, Cicero's letters, and John Aikin's *Letters from a Father to His Son on Various Topics Relative to Literature and the Conduct of Life.*[10] As this account makes clear, books were squeezed into the interstices of household chores: "Rose before light every morn; visited from necessity once, and again for books; read Butler's *Analogy;* commented on the Scriptures; read in a little book,—Cicero's letters,—a few; touched Shakespeare,—washed, carded, cleaned house, and baked."[11]

Reading, as is so often the case, provoked in her a desire to write. She called this her "mania for the pen."[12] Gathering loose sheets of stationary, which she folded and bound with thread and titled her "Almanacks," she produced a sprawling chronicle of the peaks and valleys of her spiritual life. You can see her in the tiny golden halo of candlelight, scrunched over her writing table, quill in hand, scribbling away, oblivious to the house beams creaking in the frosty winter night. Into the Almanacks she poured her inward adventures, filling its pages with her crabbed handwriting, adding as many digressions as appear in *Tristam Shandy* or some other eighteenth-century novel, impelled, always, by a "*something* that almost forces my pen along."[13] The result would grow to become a sprawling document: thousands of pages, an endless unspooling account of her quicksilver mind, the changeable climate of her soul. "This poor old memoir is as disconnected and collected in loose leaves as its Author," she once claimed. But this was

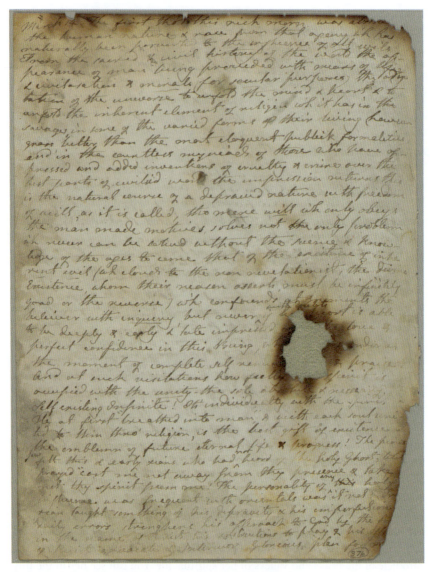

Figure 6. A page from Mary Moody Emerson's Almanacks.

false modesty.[14] The truth was simpler, more profound. The Almanacks, she insisted, are "my *home*—the only images of having existed."[15]

On the November night when she left the hard wooden pews of the Malden meetinghouse, she was in an exultant mood—a *writing* mood. Spirit seemed to course through the universe, through her, a pulsing excitement, a throb of awareness. She sensed, just beyond her fingertips, just beyond the cold skin of her cheek, something boundless, infinite. When she got home, she lit her candle and sat at her desk. "I trod on air," she wrote, "I danced at the musick of my own imajanation—it is well no one knows the frolick of my fancy, for they w^{d} think me wild unless they knew me."[16]

2.

She was born amid revolutions. On the morning of April 19, 1775, when British troops marched into Concord, Massachusetts to confiscate muskets from a rebellious citizenry, Mary Moody Emerson was less than two years of age. Her father, the upright and venerable Reverend William Emerson, pastor of Concord's First Parish Church, was awakened before dawn that day by the cry of a messenger on horseback. Pale, unshaven, he scurried from the house, tying on his lace neckcloth as he went, to join the ragtag collection of colonial militias gathering in the hills just outside of town. When the sun arose, he saw row upon row of English bayonets glittering along the meadow like the serrated teeth of some predatory monster. "Don't be afraid, Harry," the Reverend said to one trembling young man, patting him on the shoulder. "God is on our side"[17] (figures 7 and 8).

The first casualties of the American Revolution occurred just behind the tall gabled house the minister had built six years earlier. That house, noisy with children, filled with the smells of stewed meat and baked bread, stood next to an apple orchard that sloped gently toward the Old North Bridge. The bridge spanned a sluggish, weed-choked river once known by native peoples as Musketaquid, or "grass-grown water," the same name they had given to the land they inhabited. The river was called the Concord by colonial inhabitants. It was here, on its muddy banks, just a hundred feet or so from the orchard, that British and colonial soldiers fired muskets at one another, sparking a war between one of the world's great imperial powers and a loose confederation of frontier colonies. When the British grenadiers hastily retreated (they had expected little resistance and were surprised by the tenacity of their opponents), a rowdy band of minutemen chased them through the surrounding woodlots and meadows, pausing now and then to load their muskets and fire final, departing shots.

Half a century later, when the revolutionary hero General Lafayette returned to the United States to celebrate the nation's birthday, Mary Emerson attended his reception in Boston. The tall Frenchman arrived first in New York (where he is said to have picked up and kissed a five-year-old Walt Whitman) before traveling under cavalry escort to Boston. The city's church bells rang with welcome, and the streets were lined with crowds who waved flags and cheered his arrival. Mary Emerson, every bit as tenacious as her forefathers, plowed through the crush of people, pushing and straining until she reached the great man. When Lafayette bent toward her, she told him she had been "in arms" when the Battle of Concord

Figure 7. The Old Manse

erupted behind her father's parsonage. It was a joke: she had been in her mother's arms when the first shots of the war were fired.

The Reverend William Emerson joined the Continental Army at Ticonderoga as chaplain shortly after the Battle of Concord. He died less than a year later, of dysentery, in Vermont, when his impressionable daughter was only three. Mary's mother, Phebe Walker Emerson, now a widow with five small children, decided to send the girl to live with her paternal grandmother, who was also named Mary Moody Emerson, on a small, isolated farm sixteen miles away, in Malden. The reason for the banishment is a mystery. Was Mary exiled from home because Phebe Emerson was recovering from childbirth and needed help caring for her children? Was the three-year-old too unruly to manage? Or did the grandmother feel a special connection to her namesake? Regardless of motive, for the rest of her life Mary felt unwanted, deprived of family and home, burdened by a sense of dispossession and the stubborn suspicion she had been unloved—or worse, unlovable.

Years later, she explained that her father's death had meant for her a life "of poverty—of protracted sufferings...—w'h doom the helpless orphan to find

Figure 8. Mary Moody Emerson's father.

liberty & all that makes life valuable sunk in the beloved grave."[18] Her father's parsonage in Concord would forever hold a "gloomy association of my infant exile."[19] When Mary's grandmother died in 1779, just three years after the young girl moved to Malden, she was sent to live with a childless aunt and uncle, Ruth and Nathan Sargent, whose combined ill-temper and chronic poor health provided her, she later wrote, with "early lessons in fortitude."[20]

Despite the separation from her family, she preserved a deep attachment to her older brother, William, the only other Emerson child to share her intellectual interests (figure 9). William, who remained in Concord and was raised by Phebe, was tall and handsome. He brushed his thick hair into a pompadour and carried a gold-topped cane. Of his legs he was inordinately vain. (One acquaintance recalled that he invariably "placed one ankle on the other knee, for that showed his leg to best advantage.")[21] He graduated from Harvard in 1789, when Mary was fifteen and, soon after, entered the ministry, as six generations of Emersons had done before him. Eventually he married one of Mary's closest friends, Ruth Haskins. By the turn of the century, when the young couple moved to Boston, he was among the city's most prominent citizens: a Unitarian pastor at the city's First Church

Figure 9. William Emerson, Mary Moody Emerson's brother.

and the energetic founder of the Philosophical Society, the Anthology Club, and the Boston Athenaeum.

Mary's life could scarcely have been more different. While William attended Harvard, she kept Aunt Ruth's house in Malden, tending chickens and geese, scouring floors, plying "the needle, the flat iron, the porridge pot."[22] Then, in 1792, when she was seventeen, she left the Sargent household to live in the coastal town of Newburyport with her older sister Hannah, who had married a bookseller named William Farnham and required help caring for her growing family. Two years later, she moved again, this time to Concord, to look after her invalid mother, who in the intervening years had married the Reverend Ezra Ripley and thereby remained in the parsonage overlooking the apple orchard and river where she had first moved two decades earlier.

It was a cozy, well-appointed dwelling. There was creaky old colonial furniture, an enormous fireplace, and towering hemlocks that cast a purplish shade in the parlor. But for Mary Emerson, it was a place of toil. She hemmed and scrubbed and baked. She milked the cows and churned the butter. None of these tasks was so disheartening, however, as the woman's chore of caring for the sick. Each day she ascended the narrow, wainscoted stairs to spoon broth into her mother's trembling mouth. She bathed her frail body, carried out her chamber pot—tasks which elicited the same exclamation Hamlet made in the graveyard scene of Shakespeare's tragedy: "[T]he anatomy of one carcase ('pah! How it smells')," she wrote, "answers for a thousand."[23]

Yet Concord wasn't all illness and gloom. It was here that Mary overheard her older brother discussing Milton's *Paradise Lost* with his college classmates, and here, too, that William gave her a thick, four-volume set, bound in handsome leather, of Ann Radcliffe's gothic romance, *The Mysteries of Udolpho*, which told the gripping tale of an orphaned heroine who lived with her aunt and was inordinately fond of nature. ("My taste was formed in romance," Mary later acknowledged, referring to this book.)[24] While in Concord, she and William regularly exchanged their favorite poetry of the moment, whether by Thomas Gray or the "Ossianic" verse of James Macpherson or the works they discovered in a popular miscellany called *Elegant Extracts in Poetry*, which they discussed at the dining table or on walks along the river or during carriage rides to visit relatives in nearby villages.

Despite their shared interests, brother and sister were ill-matched. William thoroughly embraced the Enlightenment principles of his father's generation. He supposed that calm rationality should order one's life, and he scorned the evangelical fervor then fueling Methodist, Baptist, and other New Light denominations during the period. He gave public expression to these opinions at Boston's Fourth of July oration in 1802, telling a large assembly that when his father's generation had declared itself free from the tyrannical yoke of Britain, "They neither sought nor wished the freedom of an irrational, but that of a rational being; not the freedom of savages, not the freedom of anchorites, but that of civilized and social man."[25]

Mary did not share her brother's faith in human reason—at least not entirely. She valued the ardent religiosity, the upsurge of piety, that characterized her Puritan forbearers. She burned to feel the presence of God in her soul and craved nothing less than spiritual ecstasy. "How inrapturing the sight of the Heavens," she exclaimed, "exalt the sentiment."[26] Her mind, a restless, seething vortex, could certainly hold its own in reasoned debate. But Mary suspected that the transports of feeling she experienced were every bit as significant as any logical argument. She called these emotional peaks *enthusiasm*, investing the derogatory term for religious fanaticism with a positive connotation. She believed the insights she derived from them were as meaningful as any other form of knowledge.

Then as now, emotionalism and intuitiveness were ascribed to women to belittle them. But Mary seized upon these terms to claim power for herself. She insisted that inspired vision led to a deeper understanding of God and creation. They endowed her with religious authority, enabled her to dispense judgment on ministers and other spiritual leaders who failed to meet her standards. If strong emotions were the product of her difficult upbringing, they also allowed her to *feel* God's love, to experience divine love with soul-ravishing immediacy. As she put it in a letter from 1827, "[E]nthusiasm in all that is great is the best idea we have of Heaven."[27]

Enthusiasm also gave her insights that were unavailable to her older brother. William's university training, desirable as it was, had ill-prepared him for what was most important. "We are conscious of certain moral truths," Mary wrote in her Almanacks, "and [of] an intuitive belief of the Supreme, as we are of our own existence."[28] Developing a conception of religious knowledge that was grounded in intuition, she berated her brother's frosty rationalism. "You *will* talk of coolness and calmness in religion," she scolded him in a letter. "Let Angels and Seraphs be calm—let *man* struggle and agonize for truth..."[29]

Mary and William were children of the Revolutionary War, but their disagreements were rooted in another revolution—this one theological—that had begun a decade before their father's birth. In the winter of 1733–4, in the tiny village of Northampton, Massachusetts, the Congregationalist minister Jonathan Edwards had preached of God's inscrutable and absolute sovereignty. Soon the entire community was engulfed in a revival of faith. As Edwards described it in *A Faithful Narrative of the Surprising Work of God in the Conversion of Many Hundred Souls in Northampton* (1737), the people in his congregation felt their "hearts [had] been strongly impressed, and their affections greatly moved with a sense of the beauty and excellency of Christ."[30] The grace and salvation that visited his flock were less the result of an obedient acceptance of Christian doctrine than a surrender to powerful emotions, which Edwards described as rocking the foundations of the heart and permanently altering the lives of each church member (plate 1).

The Great Awakening permanently divided the churches of New England. In one camp were those who considered the religious revivals a welcome return to Puritan piety. In the other were moderates who believed such emotional outpourings threatened the social order. By the end of the eighteenth century, when William Emerson entered college, Harvard's divinity school had turned decisively away from Awakening theology to a more rational and liberal interpretation of Christianity. Unitarianism, as the new theology was called, stressed universal order and law. It denied the Calvinist doctrines of original sin and total depravity, and it argued that while Jesus was a savior, he was not God incarnate.

William aligned himself squarely with the new creed. He found his younger sister's views "Ascetick and censorious," aligned with a new wave of Protestant revivalism that would eventually be called the Second Great Awakening. Among Mary's faults, wrote William, was her evangelical enthusiasm, her "balloon-like" imagination, her effusions of fancy, and her writing style, which he considered both "bloated" and "obscure." From his well-appointed home in Boston, he lobbed at her the most odious word he could think of to describe her viewpoint: "Romantick."[31]

"Romantic" and "Romanticism" were not yet terms used to describe the visionary work of German philosophers and English poets. (That would happen several decades later.) But William's choice of the word was apt. The cultural upheaval that eventually came to be known as Romanticism had already reached Mary through the eighteenth-century English poets Edward Young and William Cowper, both of whom were inspiring a younger generation of writers on the other side of the Atlantic. Mary first read the popular Cowper in her early twenties and was given to quoting lines from his *Yardley-Oak*. She prized his fervent evangelism, his unabashed nature-worship, and the glamorous portrait he provided of the spiritual exile.

But it was Young who captured her strongest devotion. His *Night Thoughts*, one of the eighteenth century's most admired poems, never failed, as she put it, to rouse "the old jaded imajanation." A long work in blank verse, Young's poem stimulated the youthful Goethe with its emphasis on "moonlight and melancholy." It influenced the Romantic treatment of originality and genius. But for Mary, it was Young's description of the imagination that resonated most powerfully. She absorbed his portrait of the prophetic mind casting off its "Shackles" and mounting above "*Earth*'s Inclosure," and she especially admired his narrative of the imagination rising "Angelick, wing'd with Fire/To reach the distant Skies."[32]

Her own imagination sometimes stirred her so much that it interfered with her social obligations. "Never so good a day for... seeing my brother," she once confessed, "if in my walk my fancy had not run wild."[33] But it also enabled her to pierce the surface of everyday reality, to glimpse the radiant truth that lay, spread out, just beyond cognition. This was a sublime subjectivity, she thought, a realm in which the "instinct irresistably overpowers the difficulties of reason."[34]

While the learned men of New England remained tethered to heroic couplets and the Augustan conceits of neoclassical poetry, while they adhered to the strictures of reason and syllogism, Mary Emerson forged her own distinctive viewpoint. She fused the emotional intensity of New Light piety with Edwards Young's emphasis on the imagination. "The heart is the seat of holiness that is never inactive," she rhapsodized in her Almanacks.[35] By 1800, when she was scarcely twenty-five and had yet to discover Wordsworth or any other Romantic poet, she had already arrived at a strikingly original creed that mixed pious feeling, an appreciation of nature's sublime beauty, and her own stubborn refusal to discount the power of individual imagination. She had become, as her censorious older brother had suggested, America's first Romantic.

3.

To be a woman in the new nation was, by definition, to be dependent. It was to be reliant upon husband, family or, if these were unavailable, charity and an unhandsome fate. Single women typically lived with their families or hired themselves out as teachers, farmhands, seamstresses. Married women, laden with domestic chores and the often-endless task of childrearing, were granted few rights outside the domestic realm. A woman exercised no control over the property she earned or inherited. (According to Anglo-American law, only the so-called dowager's "thirds" was assured if a husband died.) She was prevented from attending college or entering the professions. Most egregiously, she was kept from changing her lot by the only path available in a democratic republic: voting. "In our present state of society," one reformer wrote, "woman possesses not; she is under possession."[36]

There were exceptions, of course. A widow could open her house to boarders or sell surplus butter and cheese at the market. A more fortunate woman might inherit an estate or acreage to lease. She might even inherit a business, affording her the chance to pursue a comparatively independent life. On the other end of the social spectrum, Black women and immigrant women worked as domestic laborers. But these exceptions only proved the rule: most women of Mary's class and upbringing relied on others for support.

At the same time, women were increasingly assured of their vital importance to the success of the young republic. A common trope in the years following the American Revolution was that a family was the nation in miniature. If sons were trained for roles in business and government, daughters were expected one day to run households of their own. Mothers therefore played an essential role in preparing children to participate in the world's first modern republic. "How should it enflame the desires of the mothers and daughters of our land," one preacher announced in 1802, "to be the occasion of so much good to themselves and others!"[37] Such platitudes emphasized the importance of women to the development of America. They also implied the need to educate women. And few argued more passionately or tirelessly for female education than Judith Sargent Murray, whose collection of topical essays on the subject appeared under her pseudonym "Constantia" (figure 10).

Mary Emerson's uncle Nathan Sargent, in Malden, was a distant relative of Judith Sargent Murray. But even without this family connection, the bookish young woman would have been aware of "Constantia's" prodigious literary output in New England's magazines. She would have read Murray's remarkable admission: "My desires are aspiring—perhaps presumptuously so. I would be distinguished and respected by my contemporaries... and I would descend with celebrity to posterity."[38] In a culture that prized modesty above nearly every other female virtue, this assertion bordered on the blasphemous. But it also enabled Murray to develop her main point: that women were every bit as intelligent as men.

Figure 10. Judith Sargent Murray.

Inspired by Mary Wollstonecraft's *Vindication on the Rights of Woman*, which was published in 1792, the same year her own essays began appearing in print, Murray argued that women were thought to be less intellectually inclined because they were prevented from acquiring a proper education. "Will it be said that the judgment of a male of two years old, is more sage than that of a female of the same age?" she asked. The problem was that once boys and girls grew older, "the sister must be wholly domesticated, while the brother is led by the hand through all the flowery paths of science."[39] Women's so-called intellectual inferiority was the product of cultural limitations.

Murray considered it a positive sign that the "province of imagination hath long since been surrendered to [women]." But she lamented that most women's creativity went no farther than cooking and sewing, gossip and fashion—which is to say, in preparations for marriage. "Our girls, in general, are bred up with one particular view, with one monopolizing consideration, which seems to absorb every other plan that reason might point out as worthy their attention: an establishment by marriage." This argument might have been pulled from the pages of Wollstonecraft, yet Murray's version had a distinctly national bent. Only by cultivating women's intellect and imagination could they expect to become full-fledged participants in the new republic. "Was I the father of a family," she declared, "... I would give my daughters every accomplishment which I thought proper, and to crown all, I would early accustom them to habits of industry, and order; they should be taught... to procure for themselves the necessaries of life, independence should be placed within their grasp, and I would teach them 'to reverence themselves.'"[40]

Mary Moody Emerson read Murray's remarkable essay "On the Equality of the Sexes," in which the author turned the tables on centuries of biblical commentary and defended Eve for being deceived by the serpent while Adam *knowingly* sinned by eating the forbidden fruit. Murray's essays contributed to Mary's growing determination to choose her own destiny in the face of her society. She, too, believed that steady intellectual development might eliminate "*that softness* in girls which lays a foundation for many future ills in their lives."[41]

She also shared Murray's skepticism about marriage. In 1805, William Emerson wrote that his younger sister was "combatting the attacks... of Cupid." Later, her nephew Ralph Waldo Emerson explained that "she was addressed and offered marriage by a man of talents, education and good social position, whom she respected."[42] Possibly she gave the proposal careful consideration. After all, marriage to a professional man—the suitor was a lawyer—would have altered her life immeasurably, providing financial stability and a secure position in society. But she declined.* She declined another offer in January 1807, when she thirty-three. (Nothing is known about this admirer.) After the second refusal, she scribbled in her Almanacks: "Promised never to put that ring on."[43]

Most of all, Mary found in Judith Sargent Murray a model of the woman writer. She began composing her Almanacks soon after the publication of *The Gleaner*, when she was around twenty and living in Concord to care for her mother. The journals quickly became a repository for her boldest and most confidential thoughts—a record, she later said, of "actions so pure as to be presented to the Infinite."[44] Entries penned in her spidery, crabbed handwriting were often dated "midnight" or "5 a.m.," as if written in secretiveness and haste. Much like Emily Dickinson—who stitched together booklets into which to store her private reflections—she waited until everyone else in the house was asleep before writing.

The Almanacks have been described by some scholars as the last authentic Puritan spiritual autobiography. Indeed, many of its entries describe a quest to experience and celebrate God's sovereign authority. "Lost in wonder & ignorance let us adore & admire & praise Him!!" Mary wrote in the winter of 1804. "That I love Him supremely I believe... [H]is will & approbation are ultimate when

* "[S]he refused it," wrote Waldo, "I know not on what grounds; but a few allusions to it in her diary suggest that it was a religious act..."

I contemplate ... the possible honors & pleasur of Heaven."[45] But to call Mary Moody Emerson a Puritan is to miss the rich and often contradictory strains of thought that course through her Almanacks. Because she believed that true religion was personal, intuitive, and emotional, she was far less concerned with charting the cycles of sin and grace so typical of Puritan writing. Instead, her Almanacks are filled with descriptions of vivid, passionate experiences. These experiences were religious *and* intellectual. They compelled her to develop an idiosyncratic vocabulary to account for them. She mixed the vernaculars of Calvinist piety, Enlightenment science, and something close to the worship of nature she was just beginning to find confirmed in German and English Romanticism. All these strains are evident in this glowing, gorgeous passage, written late in life, about the morning star:

> I am weak but God is eternal immutable and full of love. This morning the woods were inchanting, the crescent was brilliant—near it was the morning star, the east was reddened, the air was mild, I was wrapt, I prostrated my self, I promised my truth, my charity and love should resemble those benign planets. They are now my contemporaries—they move in radiant regular orbs and often oh often reproach me with their order and splendor—and they too shall shine on my grave.... But when that star *falls from Heaven* I, even this feeble emanation of light shall then exist—be beginning new periods of glory forming new plans of extending, perpetuating my knowledge and union to the *Head of all principality & power*!! Heavens! can I ever again find time to wish, to waste or even to *mourn*[?][46]

Ultimately, the Almanacks do more than chronicle Mary's quest to discover the divine. They also record her attempt find an authentic voice—to describe her life in a language that was commensurate to her experiences. In this sense, they are an experiment in what Samuel Taylor Coleridge was beginning to theorize as organic form. Poetry, for Coleridge, was neither an artificial nor a mechanical production. It was a living, growing organism, developed "from within, and the fullness of its development is one and the same with the perfection of its outward form."[47] Coleridge's friend and collaborator, Wordsworth, put a similar idea more succinctly: "poetry is the spontaneous overflow of powerful feeling."[48]

Mary's journals are an early example of this aesthetic ideal. Each entry develops organically, independently, unfolding precisely at the pace of her intellect. Over time, these entries create something like a comprehensive account of her relation to God and His creation. Her prose style, untaught, murky, often tangled, and always idiosyncratic, is nevertheless probing in its search for accurate expression. The Almanacks are supremely heterogeneous. They include digests of philosophical and theological texts; they alternate between reasoned argument, associative leaps, and outbursts of exaltation; they swoop from sibylline utterance to pithy aphorism, with long, sinuous sentences (often eccentrically punctuated) suggesting the way an active mind unspools its own thoughts. More than anything, the

Almanacks reveal their author's insatiable desire to record moments of direct perception.

That she ultimately did not publish these "prophetic and apocalyptic ejaculations" (her nephew's admiring term) suggests less about her than about her social milieu. As the English novelist Mary Brunton wrote around the same time, "To be pointed at—to be noticed & commented upon—to be suspected of literary airs—to be shunned, as literary women are, by the more unpretending of my own sex: & abhorred, as literary women are, by the more pretending of the other!—My dear, I would sooner exhibit as a rope dancer."[49] Despite her iconoclasm, Mary Emerson felt similar pressures. Later in life she declared that "not a scrap [of the Almanacks] is to see print as many deceased persons have had their papers."[50†]

Yet that is only part of the story. For again, like Emily Dickinson, she carefully stored the booklets that comprised her voluminous journal. She kept them in order. And toward the end of her life, she bequeathed them to a relative, hoping future generations would appreciate them. She harbored ambitions for them—and for herself. She wanted freedom, unshackled independence. She wanted the chance to determine her life's course. And she wanted to leave her mark on others. As she scrawled in the Almanacks, aged forty-three, "I want influence—agency,—this *this* is glory virtue wisdom!"[51]

4.

In 1803, while still living in Concord, Mary Emerson met the most extraordinary person she had ever encountered. Mary Van Schalkwyck, *née* White, lived a quarter mile from the old parsonage on Monument Street. She hosted teas and entertained a string of suitors from nearby Harvard College. In her spare time, she managed to work on "a translation from the French, on the subject of the imagination."[52] She was pious and irreverent—a combination Mary Emerson always found irresistible. And at age twenty-three, she was already the survivor of a tumultuous, event-filled life (figure 11).

In many ways, the two Marys were quite similar. Van Schalkwyck was noted for her "strength of mind[,] . . . very perceptible at an early age." As a child she had been a voracious and untutored reader, devouring novels like plum cakes. She could recite the plot of *The Mysteries of Udolpho* in such gruesome detail that decades later, her younger cousins recalled the shivers she produced in them. Like Mary Emerson, she was a connoisseur of the emotions: "The language of the *heart* is the language of *nature*," she wrote a friend, "it is easily spoken and easily

† The Almanacks remain unpublished in their entirety. Fortunately, a continuing online project to present authoritative transcriptions of them can be found at Women Writers Project, https://wwp.northeastern.edu/research/projects/manuscripts/emerson/index.html.

Figure 11. Mary Van Schalkwyck.

understood, and I would give more for five lines of it than for five pages of the cold, methodical labours of the head."[53]

But there the similarities ended. For Van Schalkwyck had married at twenty—and was a widow a year later. The story of her marriage was as harrowing as it was dramatic, involving a young French planter from the West Indies, a landowner and enslaver named Antoine Van Schalkwyck. Soon after their marriage, the couple set sail for Guadeloupe, in the Lesser Antilles, where Antoine promptly died of yellow fever and Mary Van Schalkwyck found herself alone in a nation rocked by earthquakes and slave rebellion. "Every day I heard horrors," she wrote her parents, "every night retired to my chamber with an expectation of being assassinated before morning." As days passed, the violence intensified. Villages were burned. Battles raged through the night. At one point, the biracial leader of the rebellion, Louis Delgrês, retreated to a house in the mountains with dozens of his followers. They emptied barrels of gunpowder and blew up their small army rather than surrender to French forces. Because the only ships bound for the United States were on the opposite side of the island, Mary was carried in a sedan chair over the mountainous interior, at last reaching the harbor of Basse-Terre. After nearly ten months, she had escaped from what she called a "theatre of horrors," returning to her parents' home in Concord.[54]

Mary Emerson was twenty-nine when she first met the young woman. She was drawn to her for much the same reason she had been drawn to Radcliffe's heroine in *The Mysteries of Udolpho*—for the penumbral glamor of her misfortune. Van Schalkwyck, on the other hand, was delighted to meet someone who valued intellectual life more than domesticity. The two met during sleety November afternoons in the parlor of the Ripley parsonage, where they discussed Radcliffe's Gothic masterpiece or Mary Wollstonecraft's *A Vindication of the Rights of Women*. Both admired the idealized account of Wollstonecraft presented in *St. Leon*, a novel written by her husband, William Godwin. Van Schalkwyck was also particularly fond of Thomas Gisborne's *An Enquiry into the Duties of the Female Sex*, published in 1801; she approved of the author's refusal "to make [women] either *Amazons* or *babies—goddesses* or *idiots*. He appears to me to have given the female character nearly the dignity and energy of Mary Wollstonecraft, with far more amiability and sweetness."[55]

Discussing some of the earliest defenses of women's rights written in English, the two friends tried to make sense of a world that had left them both feeling banished and bruised. Each woman felt vulnerable and dependent on family. Each knew that by reading Wollstonecraft they appeared to others as selfish, even immoral. But they insisted that women were neither "*goddesses* [n]or *idiots*," that both labels were attempts to marginalize them. Together they felt invincible, rebellious, on the cusp of a new world.

They loved to talk. Mary Emerson would later speak of her interactions with Elizabeth Palmer Peabody as "conversation that makes the soul," referring to the way in which intimate discussions enlarged her sense of self.[56] She considered her long, lively talks with Van Schalkwyck among the earliest "soul-making" events in her life. The two women shared stories, swapped opinions, reveling in the unpredictable, often serendipitous exchanges that resulted. During their conversations, Van Schalkwyck noticed something about Mary Emerson that most people missed: she longed for companionship. Beneath her prickly demeanor and her ferocious desire to act on her own was a deeply-felt need for others. Years later, her nephew would remark on her compulsion to wound the very people she loved, observing that "if she finds anything dear or sacred to you, she instantly flings broken crockery at it."[57] But Van Schalwyck discerned, beneath the volatile exterior, a shy woman who continued to think of herself as abandoned and unloved: an orphan in the universe.

She noticed other qualities, as well. "Courageous in correcting, and generous in commending," she said of Mary, "she stimulates her friends to the pursuit of excellence, by every motive and every method that piety, good sense, and affection can suggest."[58] And there was something else she soon learned about her friend: Mary Emerson longed to become an author. Early in their friendship, Mary gave Van Schalkwyck portions of the Almanacks to read, allowing her friend a glimpse into her most private musings. Evidently, she asked Van Schalkwyck for a response, for there soon followed a letter that mixed admiration with exasperation: "My dear Mary writes too much like other great people to be always legible; and she will not be surprised when I acknowledge I have not enjoyed the whole of her valuable manuscript."[59]

But Mary Emerson's ambitions extended beyond sharing her journals. Soon after she returned to Malden, she proposed a scheme to her new friend. The letter has not survived, but Van Schalkwyck's response makes clear its general aim. Mary had asked her to collaborate on a series of essays, or written debates, with an eye toward eventual publication. She wanted Van Schalkwyck to begin the project with a statement about friendship.

"The pleasant hours I lately passed with you, my dear Miss Emerson," Van Schalkwyck replied, "would furnish me with the most cogent arguments in favour of the advantages of Friendship, had I previously needed them." But she declined the invitation. "I really *feel* my inability to improve, or even greatly amuse, the public. Will you then candidly allow me to be actuated by better motives than false shame, indolence, or stupidity, when I decline entering the lists with an antagonist who does me honor by selecting me for her opposer?"[60]

Mary Emerson let the matter rest for three months. Then she sent another letter. This time she included her own thoughts on friendship—a transparent ploy. "Permit me to say," Van Schalkwyck replied, "you have only changed the name, not the nature of the correspondence you proposed." This time, however, she rose to the bait. Mary's letter had proven too suggestive to ignore, for it argued that friendship had "a natural tendency to weaken and corrupt." Close attachments diminished the most important thing a person possessed: "independence of the mind."[61]

Van Schalkwyck argued just the opposite. "Were we, my dear Miss Emerson, designed for independence? Are we not naturally dependent on each other's aid? . . . Does not our whole structure, moral, intellectual, and physical, demonstrate our mutual dependence?"[62] These sentences were written by a person who had been saved from earthquake, fever, and revolutionary violence, and had enjoyed communal solidarity upon her return as a young widow to the tight-knit community of Concord. Mary Van Schalkwyck respected her friend's determination to live unrestricted by society. But she believed her friend's fierce attachment to personal liberty bordered on selfishness.

Mary wasn't finished. Friendship not only limited one's freedom, she argued. It cooled "the ardour for a purer state, and turn[ed] the tide of our affections from eternal to mortal beauty." Every moment spent in the company of another robbed one of the opportunity to contemplate God, she argued. Schalkwyck again responded: "Do we adore the Creator less fervently because we admire the reflection of His splendor in the soul of His creature? On the contrary, when conversing with a friend on the wisdom and goodness of our common Father, does not 'our heart burn within us,' and do we not feel the ardour of our love increased by being participated?"[63]

Who won this argument—which echoed throughout Mary Emerson's life for years to come—is not important for the moment. The conflict between the freedom for which her father had died and the limitations imposed upon that freedom by others would preoccupy her for the rest of her life. For the present, however, she had accomplished her more immediate goal. The two women were soon composing a series of epistolary essays in the hope of publication.

5.

A new nation requires its own literature. That was the premise behind the *Monthly Anthology and Boston Review*, which began appearing in Boston's bookstalls in November 1803—roughly the same time Thomas Jefferson doubled the size of the United States with the Louisiana Purchase. The *Anthology* was a far more meager production—octavo-sized and just forty-five pages in length. But it was also something new under the sun: an American literary journal.

It was the creation of David Phineas Adams, an overtaxed schoolmaster who longed to enter the ranks of gentlemanly literature. Adams borrowed his nom de plume from the editor of London's *Gentleman's Magazine*, "Sylvanus per Se," and he modeled his new magazine on popular British publications such as *The Spectator* and the *Edinburgh Review*, miscellaneous collections of essays, letters, poetry, and didactic material written in a polished Augustan style. The first issue included an essay on America's commercial strength, a satire on "AMBITION," and a didactic essay on the art of conversation. (Among the recommendations: avoid politics, employ "sentiment.") A treatise on dueling, a pair of biographical sketches, and an article on the Aeolian harp (the latter pirated from the London *Mirror*) appeared side by side with original poetry, book and theater reviews, and squibs of all sorts.

Within a few months, "Sylvanus" had grown weary of belles lettres. Adams announced his decision to return to teaching, suggesting, among other things, just how unremunerative was the literary life in the new nation. But by then, readers in Boston had grown fond of the magazine. They looked forward to its monthly contents for much the same reason they looked forward to their evening meal: it had become a habit. Supporters of the journal prevailed upon the head of Boston's First Church to take up the editorship. William Emerson, now thirty-five, was the father of four. His youngest child, Ralph Waldo, had just turned eleven months old. Since coming to Boston, the energetic minister had been busy, taking part in the founding of the Boston Athenaeum and the Philosophical Society. Recently he had been elected fellow of the American Academy of Arts and Sciences. Most evenings he spent racing from one committee to the next, attending teas and lavish dinners on behalf of a dozen or more charities. He barely found time to scribble his weekly sermons.

Nevertheless, he agreed to take on the *Anthology*. Editing a journal suited his talents for organization and alliance-building. He quickly introduced Boston to an impressive roster of contributors that included John Quincy Adams and Daniel Webster. Under his supervision, the magazine became less literary and far more philosophical. It also lost some of its readers—a fact that concerned William not in the least. His goal was to cultivate a "society of gentlemen," not a mass audience.

Before long, he was publishing a new feature: a series of letters. These were written by two women who, guided by the delicacy of their sex, had assumed pseudonyms. The first letter opened with a plea for tolerance: "Should you be disposed to admit into your elegant publication the correspondence of two obscure females, who have hitherto written merely for their own amusement, and who still seek concealment, you will probably receive several letters from *Constance* and *Cornelia*."[64]

Mary Van Schalkwyck was *Cornelia*. Mary Moody Emerson appropriated the same nom de plume as Judith Sargent Murray: *Constance*. Cornelia wrote the first letter, and it begins in mid-conversation—a technique the two authors borrowed from their favorite epistolary novels. According to Cornelia, a mutual friend had recently died. The loss had prompted her to gaze heavenward and wonder if her departed friend had ascended to "the immediate presence of Deity, which would be at once the perfection of bliss and glory." Did the soul migrate to the stars? "[I]s it irrational to believe congenial spirits assemble in the same planet, and thence pass to more glorious orbs, as they acquire greater purity and perfection?"

Cornelia fell asleep mulling over these questions, but she was startled awake by a thunderstorm—a tempest that made her realize "the folly of indulging mere speculations, the pastime of the imagination, by which the heart is little affected, and of course the life unimproved." Restored to piety, she determined to "seek unceasingly the favour of our Maker" and to abstain from further flights of fancy. The letter's conclusion marveled at the human tendency to "resign ourselves to imagination, and rove with delight in the boundless regions of possibility."[65]

William Emerson applauded the sentiment. In an editorial note inserted at the end of the first letter, he addressed his younger sister: "If *Constance* shall manifest the piety of heart . . . which glow in her friend *Cornelia*, the Editor will be proud of his new correspondents."[66] Mary Emerson ignored the warning. She defended the imagination as a "a province so freely conceded us by the Proprietors of mental ground, that to explore and cultivate it seems our bounden duty." She also thumbed her nose at the logic so prized by William, speaking on behalf of all women: "If, as philosophers tell us, the sublime abodes, where truth unveils her light and demonstrates her eternal counsels, cannot be ascended but by an almost endless chain of reasonings, we must be content to remain in the plains of ignorance. But if we indulge the use of our less logical guide, we can climb the ladder of the pious patriarch in the company of angels."

Mary was asserting her belief that religious insights were unreachable by reason and logic alone. In doing so, she was of course assailing the foundations of Unitarian thought. Imagination was a faculty that proceeded not by "an almost endless chain of reasonings" but by intuitive leaps, flashes of perception, epiphanies, and revelations. More important, this superior form of knowledge was a *feminine* ability. The *we* in her statement referred to women unschooled in philosophy but gifted with insight. If women were considered less rational, Mary turned the idea on its head, insisting that precisely for this reason were they more closely linked to "empyrean heavens." Their experience of the world was deeper, richer, more attuned to God. "By fastening ourselves on the pinions of an excursive fancy," *Constance* concluded, "we quickly get beyond the atmosphere of... terrestrial littlenesses, and, after soaring awhile in tracts of thought, return to the realities of ordinary life, with our social feelings more dignified and lovely than before..."[67]

It was the same argument then being made by a handful of German philosophers and writers in the small university town of Jena. It was the same argument that was just beginning to cross the English Channel and to influence poets we now call Romantic. For Fichte and Schlegel, Novalis and Schiller—as well as for William Blake, Wordsworth, and Coleridge—mathematics, logic, and science may have produced new knowledge about the world. But it was a sterile and one-sided knowledge. It failed to account for the vast, invisible landscape of the feelings, the prickling presentiment that there was something more to existence than could be seen or heard or touched. Human imagination revealed the limitations of this mechanistic thinking. The mind, for these thinkers and poets, possessed a generative, visionary power—a force that was capable, in Coleridge's words, of freeing the individual from an "inanimate cold world."[68]

Cornelia did not reply to her friend's verbal barrage right away. Possibly she regretted publishing her thoughts at all. In an undated letter to William Emerson, she wrote, "Not all my confidence in the candour of Mr. Emerson enables me to transmit the superficial production of a winter's morning without reluctance. It is only in compliance with his sister's request I determine to send, by to-morrow's post, what will be perhaps rejected by the judgment and taste of the Editor of the 'Anthology.'"[69] Not until November 1805 did a new letter arrive. It was written by Mary Emerson and was devoted to a completely new topic. *Constance* praised botany and the study of natural science, both "so useful, and so sublime." The two disciplines helped provide clues to God's inscrutable designs. "Every student of nature... will perceive with rapture, that, in searching into the relations of the humblest shrub, he is enabled... to infer the operation of infinite wisdom in regions, which *must* forever remain unexplored by human knowledge."[‡] Then she switched gears and asked if natural science's "beautiful pillars [might one day] be adorned with inscriptions of female achievements?" Cornelia's response was tepid. She pointed out the differences between the "mere naturalist" and the

‡ She was again anticipating Romantic thought; Wordsworth, for instance, would soon transform Isaac Newton from Enlightenment scientist to Romantic voyager in *The Prelude*, describing his "Mind for ever/Voyaging through the strange seas of Thought, alone."

"christian botanist," arguing that only the religious scholar enjoyed the "chaplet of never fading flowers." (She was referring to faith.)[70]

At this point William Emerson apparently reconsidered the experiment in women's writing. Five months after the publication of Van Schalkwyck's letter, Mary wrote her brother asking him to "insert the letter in the Anthology which I shewed you when in Boston . . . It is a favorite production of your sister's, and she thinks it no smale compliment to your understanding to ask the indulgence of her taste when it is so different from yours." The tone here is unusually solicitous—an indication of how badly Mary wanted to appear in print. She apologized for her poor handwriting, then repeated that she was "desirous to publish the letter."[71]

William granted her wish, but the letter did not appear for nearly six months. A change in the *Anthology*'s editorial policy may have contributed to the delay. The Anthology Society, an all-male club that gathered over dinner, decided to read aloud each submission at their meetings. Early in the correspondence, Mary Van Schalkwyck had expressed her concern that William Emerson "would censure me for presumption should I attempt a public disputation with his sister."[72] Now a committee of men decided whether the two women's correspondence was a waste of editorial space.

Mary Emerson's last published writing as *Constantia* appeared in June 1805. It was a letter addressed more to her brother than to Van Schalkwyck, and it began with another defense of the poetic imagination, which "brighten[s] the horizon of life, like the golden bow of promise, auguring future and varied good." She attacked the decorum of the Anthology Society by comparing it to "Genius," which "possesses indeed the power of evolving and embellishing every sentiment that can exercise the understanding *or engage the heart*." True brilliance operated on principles that transcended logic; it ignored gentlemanly taste.

The results of this fusillade were predictable. William appended a footnote correcting one of Mary's assertions ("Our fair correspondent is unfortunate in this instance"[73]). He refused to publish another word that she wrote.

6.

William Emerson served as the editor of the *Monthly Anthology* for six years. Then, on May 11, 1811, having struggled with symptoms of tuberculosis for more than a decade, he succumbed to a different illness altogether: stomach cancer. Just before his death, Ruth Haskins Emerson, now nearly forty-three, gathered her surviving children and led them, one by one and in order of their age, to their father's cramped sickroom to bid farewell. The couple's two oldest children had died young. Now there was William, aged ten, followed by Ralph Waldo, seven. Then came Edward Bliss, six, Robert Bulkeley, four, and Charles Chauncey, two. Ruth at last approached the deathbed with a newborn in her arms. This was Mary Caroline, who would live for three years.

Ruth had always been the practical member of the Emerson marriage. The daughter of a prominent Boston merchant, thriftiness had been bred in her. When she and William were newlyweds in the rural village of Harvard, it was Ruth who milked the cows and churned the butter, selling the surplus. Once the couple moved to Boston, she took in boarders to help with the inflated cost of city living. For thirteen years, and with almost clockwork regularity, she produced children. While her husband wrote sermons and edited journals, she established a large, boisterous family. Of the two daughters and six sons she gave birth to, five would survive childhood. (There was also at least one miscarriage.)

Even for the wife of a rising minister in Boston's First Church, such families came at enormous personal cost. Before modern obstetrics, women lived in terror that their wombs might yield a dead infant, or that their bodies might not survive another child tearing its way into life. Then there was the unceasing work of childrearing, with its daily care and watchful nights when a child was feverish or wracked with coughs. Nearly half of all infants born in the early nineteenth century never reached the age of five; the mortality rate for mothers was only slightly better. A married woman's body was a crucible: an ordeal of milk and sweat and blood. And after the birth of a child, fresh anxieties began.

Phebe Emerson, Ruth's firstborn, died, from canker and diarrhea, before the age of two. John Clarke, the Emersons' oldest son, was sickly. At five, he was sent to relatives in Maine with the expectation that fresh country air would make him robust. Letters from home described a boy "so hardy as to play without mittens," but when he returned to Boston, he was paler and more feeble than ever. Within a year, he was dead from tuberculosis.[74] "No state of no element on the surface of this miserable earth," wrote his grieving father, ". . . could retain the connexion of this soul & body."[75] And then there was Robert Bulkeley, the couple's next-to-youngest son. Bulkeley, as the child was called, suffered from an unspecified mental ailment that left him developmentally disabled. From an early age, he was boisterous and ungovernable. "This boy will never take care of himself," William presciently declared in 1809, just before the infant turned two. After William's death, Ruth continued to care for the child as long as possible. But by the time he was a young adult, Bulkeley was placed in work farms or, when he became especially unruly, institutionalized. ("Waldo and I went to see Bulkeley yesterday," wrote Charles Chauncey Emerson in 1831, "He is quite violent.")[76]

These concerns were now magnified by William's death. Boston mourned its talented minister with a funeral procession that stretched from Chauncy Place to the burial ground at the King's Chapel. But the pomp concealed a painful fact. William had died intestate and significantly in debt. An assessor's list of household goods revealed that he left behind expensive mahogany furniture, a telescope, and 452 books—the last valued at a third of his estate's entire worth. But his debts totaled $2,548, more than twice his annual salary and well above the value of his assets.[77] The aldermen of Boston's First Church agreed to allow the grieving widow to remain in the parsonage if she would rent a portion of the house to the new minister. Ruth took in other boarders and received, for the next seven years, half of William's income, or $500 a year. But this was not enough to keep her children comfortably fed and clothed, let alone educated to the standard expected by the Emerson family. While alive, William had insisted that his sons "take rank with professional characters and the upper classes in society."[78] He expected each of them, except Bulkeley, to attend Harvard when old enough.

After his death, Ruth found herself nearly destitute. To economize, her boys ate bread and milk twice a day. Sometimes two brothers shared a single coat, alternating days and shivering when they went without. Years later, recalling the privation of his upbringing, Ralph Waldo transformed the misery into an advantage, writing, "What is the hoop that holds [the family] staunch? It is the iron band of poverty, of necessity, of austerity, which, excluding them from the sensual enjoyments which make other boys too early old, has directed their activity into safe and right channels."[79]

This was perhaps overly optimistic. The Emerson brothers certainly grew up close-knit and competitive, but they were weighted down by the burden of their mother and deceased father's expectations. "Let your whole life reflect honour on the *name* you bear," Ruth wrote her oldest son, William, not long after he left for college. (He was fourteen.) "Do not forget how important are the minutes and hours, as well as the weeks and months of your time now."[80] To the sickly Edward, who had contracted tuberculosis from his father, she warned, "I hope you will remember how precious your time is, and neglect no opportunity to acquire knowledge in whatever can dignify or exalt your character and qualify you for future usefulness—here and a happy eternity hereafter."[81] Charles, the youngest, prayed "that I may not degenerate from the purity or fall behind the example of my fathers!"[82]

But in 1811, when her oldest child was still barely ten, Ruth was less concerned with raising future ministers and lawyers than with surviving the harsh Boston winter. She accepted charity from her mother- and stepfather-in-law, Phebe and Ezra Ripley. She scrimped on food and clothes. And in the immediate aftermath of William's death, she asked her sister-in-law, Mary Moody Emerson, to help raise the children.

Mary was thirty-seven. The intervening years had done little to temper her arrowy spirit. As a friend wrote, she was a "person at war with society as to all its decorums; she eats and drinks what others do not, and when they do not...." Combustible and demanding, she entered "into conversation with everybody, and talks on every subject; is sharp as a razor in her satire, and sees you through and through in a moment."[83] Another friend observed that Mary still enjoyed "poetic and spiritual raptures, in comparative seclusion from living intellectual companionship."[84] As always, she crammed her Almanacks with a torrent of thought and experience.

In 1805 she had discovered Wordsworth. Here was a visionary who preferred nature and solitude to the formal concessions of society. Soon she was copying entire poems from the *Lyrical Ballads* into her Almanacks. Wordsworth's slender volume, co-authored with Coleridge and published in 1798, heralded a new movement. Mary would later say she had learned to adore Wordsworth "before every or any body liked him," and she was more or less correct, at least in the United States. Wordsworth's rhapsodies to nature and fondness for outsiders appealed equally to her.[85] "I heard a thousand blended notes / While in a grove I sate reclined" might, for instance, have described any number of summer afternoons Mary Emerson spent alone and immersed in the natural world. And the plaintive account of "The Female Vagrant," who endures poverty, homelessness, and the loss of family, spoke to deeper currents, deeper wounds.[§]

After Wordsworth, she discovered Byron. Then, working her way backwards, Pope, whose satire on authors who write for money, *The Dunciad*, became a favorite. She also reread the Dutch philosopher Baruch Spinoza, who argued that an all-pervading God could never be fully understood by frail human understanding. She pored over the great Scottish skeptic David Hume, with whom she quarreled incessantly in her journal, disagreeing with his claim that God's existence could not be determined from the outward design of the universe, and she devoured a wide range of theological tracts: reams of essays and articles that appeared in religious newspapers and periodicals or that she borrowed from local ministers.

The church was the one of the few public institutions in which a woman could exert her influence. Ineligible to become preachers or deacons, disallowed from voting on clerical matters, women nevertheless represented a powerful social force within church hierarchy. Considered more devout than men, more attuned to the mysterious currents of providence, they were also thought to exert greater moral authority. As a result, they shaped church policy more than is commonly acknowledged and, in so doing, helped shape their communities. It was a group of women, for instance, that led a split from Concord's First Parish church with its claims that the long-established congregation had been weakened by its tepid Unitarianism.

When she wasn't in church, Mary could be found in her preferred place of worship: nature. "In communion with trees," she wrote, "with streams and stars and suns, man finds his own glory inskribed on every flower and sparkling in every beam."[86] Human beings and nature were connected by their mutual dependence on the Creator. Nature was a portent of heaven, a portal into the divine. It

[§] Although Wordsworth's massive *The Prelude* would not be published for another half century, its epic account of the development of an individual consciousness in many ways is the poetic equivalent of the Almanacks.

was the language in which God spoke to those with the sense to perceive it. In 1806, after learning about an impending solar eclipse, Mary Emerson went outside and observed the phenomenon through a pinhole pierced in paper, noting "with what rapt devotion did I view my Maker's hand."[87] Elsewhere she enthused, "Yes, this little speck of nature we live on, then seems but a beautifull minature painting from w'h we w^{d} gladly turn our eyes to the vast Original of beauty, & explore scenes where the elect of all ages & nations inhabit perfect righteousness."[88]

As she grew older, she had become increasingly migratory. On the spur of the moment, she might pack her scanty luggage and travel, by horseback or coach or occasionally a borrowed wagon, to some New England town, often in the hopes of boarding with a tolerant minister who would answer her endless barrage of theological questions. That she could travel so freely was the result of unexpected good fortune. She had inherited money from her grandmother, the other Mary Moody Emerson, enough to purchase a farm near South Waterford, Maine. The land was nearly fifty miles from the coast and was shadowed by Bear Mountain (figure 12). It abutted the 250-acre Bear Pond, which, with pine trees lining the shore, resembled the slightly larger Walden Pond in Concord. It was a rugged place, harsh and remote, where members of the Ripley and Haskin families had preached and traded since 1800. Mary fell in love with the countryside during a visit, and in 1813, with money she received from her grandmother's estate, purchased Elm Vale—her name for the farm that for the next thirty years she would share with her sister Rebecca and her husband, Robert Haskins, who for obscure financial reasons was listed as the farm's owner.

Maine became her spiritual home. Its austere beauty reflected her deepest sensibilities. "I rode far on horseback," she wrote in appreciation of the area's towering peaks and wooded swales. "The mist rose from the waters & mingled with the blue haze of the mountains, and formed that soft atmosphere w'h invelopes the traveler in a new & complete solitude..."[89] A fast-moving brook, not far from the farmhouse, crashed against granite stones, and some days the sound of water was her only companion. The seclusion of Elm Vale—and the income Mary received from leasing it—allowed her to pursue her intellectual interests. It enabled her to construct a comparatively unusual life, that of an independent woman.

Her Almanacks were as usual filled with a wide range of references, from Isaac Newton and the Koran to a compendious church history by Johann Lorenz von Mosheim and Gibbon's *Rise and Fall of the Roman Empire*. One Sabbath morning in 1811, the same year her brother William died, she went to church with a "cold mind. Yet what an internal feast—objects which in other years appeared dismal are now gilt with... bright beams." If the minister failed to kindle her enthusiasm, the warmth of her mind, the fire of her sensations, filled her with ecstatic awakening. Was the excitement, she wondered, caused by "health or divine influence"?[90] This question led to others: were her actions predestined by God, plotted and

Figure 12. Mary Moody Emerson's farm was at the foot of Bear Mountain.

arranged in advance by an all-knowing divinity? Were they the spontaneous acts of her own volition? The question of free will—of special interest to a woman who insisted on her own freedom—became an obsession.

While ablaze with these thoughts, Mary received the summons from her sister-in-law, Ruth Haskins Emerson. Ruth was desperate for someone to help with her children. She could barely keep house and cook meals for the lodgers she had taken in to make ends meet. Her five boys were growing up ragged and wild. Mary resisted at first. She valued her independence too much to leave her farm for the sake of others. She had purposefully avoided the entanglements of domestic life. But eventually she acquiesced. Perhaps she remembered what it was like to lose a father at a young age. There was also her abiding desire for "agency"—her wish to influence a world of thought and action she could only glimpse from the margins. By overseeing the education of her nephews, she could leave a mark on posterity. She could even transmit her insights into nature and spirit to a future generation.

What began as a stopgap measure to help her brother's grieving widow soon developed into something more. For the next twenty years, Mary would serve as a surrogate parent to her five nephews, living with the family for months at a time in Boston and counseling them from afar in Waterford. In 1812, when the war with England put an abrupt halt to business and straitened Ruth's circumstances even more, Mary welcomed Bulkeley and Charles to Maine, where she was staying with family. (The rest of the Emersons moved to Concord to live with relatives.) Expressing her gratitude, Ruth declared, "I do not think [Mary's] place could be supplied [to] these *fatherless children* by any one [else] on earth."[91]

7.

She became fiercely protective of the Emerson boys. Writing to Ruth about Bulkeley and Charles, who were still living with her in Maine, Mary enthused, "And were *our* children to be bro't up in the simplicity & innocence of rural life, how very pleasantly might we descend into a peacefull grave."[92] Her own "orphanship," which she never forgot and which she never entirely forgave the universe for, made her especially sensitive to the raw, gaping emptiness now experienced by her fatherless nephews.

About their future she was never in doubt: "they were born to be educated." It was her firm intention the boys would enter college and follow in the footsteps of six generations of Emerson ministers, thereby redeeming the glory of her father's name.[93] To nudge them, she wrote letters filled with reminders to live in purity and renunciation. "What is man without piety?" she demanded of the volatile Edward. "The most abject and destitute being in the universe."[94] To William she advised "that however lofty the pinicle of fame on which you are mounted,.... if you have not an open ingenuous temper, & humble, pious heart, your memory... will perish [and] your name be mentioned with contempt."[95]

The boys loved her. Writing her years later, William fondly recalled "those bygone days when you devoted your hours & thought so kindly to the boys that have since become men."[96] A letter she wrote to Charles when he was four or five reveals a streak of playful affection:

> My own dear boy, I send you a little cake, as a remembrance of our sweet friendship. And I would have it answer a noble purpose. Let the milk, flour and eggs of which its constituent parts are composed represent the solid virtues of your character, the sugar its sweetness—the flavor of its fruit and the fragrance of its spices be emblematical of the ornaments and graces of your soul. But especially let the white incrustation [the frosting] be a type that the lovely veil of modesty will

> cover ever to your virtues . . . If Mother will permit you to go to school the first letter you write with your own hand shall be rewarded by/MME/Kiss R. Bulkey[97]

She was generous with her nephews, taking them on walks, acquainting them with the names of trees and the infinite shades of the afternoon sky. She encouraged them to read Wordsworth's "Immortality Ode" and *The Excursion*, both of which were "sublime" in her opinion.[98] In 1814, three years after she began her tutelage, she shared another discovery—the novels and philosophical writings of Anne Louise Germaine de Staël-Holstein (*neé* Necker), better known as Madame de Staël (plate 2).

De Staël was the flamboyant, larger-than-life French writer who in 1810 coined the term "Romanticism." Mary first learned of her in the pages of her brother's *Monthly Anthology*, which in 1808 had reviewed her novel *Corinne*, praising its "incidents . . . striking and novel."[99] The novel centers around a heroine whose special talents are her riveting conversation and ability to improvise verse on any topic. Corinne is variously described as a sybil and a prophet, a woman whose boundless spirit becomes most poetic when soaring amid the empyrean. Yet she is also shut out from the world of action by the oppressive culture in which she resides. That culture happens to be Italian, and de Staël's novel was read by many for its vivid depictions of Italian art, literature, and politics.

Mary raced through the book, with its witty and passionate heroine, and then she moved on to de Staël's most influential work, an intellectual survey of German literature and philosophy entitled *On Germany*. If *Corinne* included descriptions of paintings and love sonnets from the Renaissance period, de Staël's other work focused on the exciting new literary and philosophical culture centered around the college town of Jena. *On Germany* presented a worldview strikingly similar to Mary's. De Staël argued that religion was less a matter of convention and orthodoxy than a "feeling of the infinite," an influx of emotion felt by sensitive people that was both "positive and creative."[100] Tracing these ideas to the philosophy of Kant, who argued that our perception of the world is guided by categories of thought inherent in every person, as well as to the literature of Goethe, de Staël closed her work with a tribute to the power of feeling and enthusiasm.

If Mary easily convinced her nephews to read Wordsworth and de Staël, she was less successful in her efforts to push them into the ministry. William, the oldest, would be the first to abdicate his duty. Serious and dark-haired, sober and responsible, William physically resembled his father and grandfather. Upon graduating from Harvard in 1818, he decided to study theology in Germany, where the famous biblical scholar, Johann Gottfried Eichhorn, taught at the university in Göttingen. Eichhorn, who knew de Staël, was at the cutting edge of a new academic discipline that interpreted the Bible through literary and historical analysis. By scrutinizing the language of the Old Testament and reconstructing its historical context, he had determined that scripture was not divinely inspired but produced by many authors at different periods. This approach, both thrilling and disorienting to those who encountered it for the first time, eventually undermined William's belief in the Bible. Midway through his studies, he paid a visit to his aunt's latest literary idol, Johann Wolfgang von Goethe. The great author, recovering from a near fatal heart ailment, listened patiently to William describe his wavering faith. Then he advised the young American to keep his doubts to himself and to preach anyway.

William ignored this advice. On his way back to the United States, aboard a packet ship from Liverpool to New York, a tempest nearly sunk the vessel. Writing to Mary, William described how "The winds blew so fearfully, and the waves made sometimes such a mocking sport of our ship, that I was more than once compelled to sit down in the cabin, and tranquilly to make up what I deemed my last accounts with the world."[101] What he didn't tell her was that the storm had forced him to make a decision. The gale still whistling in his ears, he renounced the ministry and decided to pursue law instead. As Ralph Waldo later recalled, "in that storm, he felt that he could not go to the bottom in peace with the intention in his heart of following the advice that Goethe had given him."[102]

Edward and Charles proved even greater disappointments. Both nephews were brilliant orators and writers. Both were first in their respective classes at Harvard. Edward, just six when his father had died, was the more mercurial. He chafed at Mary's intrusions and efforts at guidance, and their relationship was one of perpetually hurt feelings. ("I have often wished the few last days spent with you had been otherwise," Mary wrote to him after one particularly fraught encounter.)[103] When she encouraged the thirteen-year-old to "rise with yet untasted ardor to the study, the knowledge and practice of his heavenly Father's will," Edward replied with a starchiness he reserved for no other member of the family. "You hope I shall be a Minister," he told Mary, "but I have some doubts about my ever arriving at that exalted station."[104]

Charles's renunciation hurt even more. He had long been Mary's favorite. Shortly after his father's death, the two-year-old boy had been sent to live with her in Maine, where he remained for more than a year. An attachment formed between child and aunt, both of whom had been sent from home at an early age to live with relatives. As he grew older, Charles shared with Mary thoughts and feelings he shared with no one else. He confided his fears of failure, his vocational doubts, his agonizing spiritual uncertainties.

He was by far the most academically talented Emerson, having won the Boylston prize in elocution during his first year at Harvard. But like many gifted young people, he was haunted by private insecurities. When he wrote Mary to ask about a career choice, she replied in an entirely predictable, if rather disingenuous, manner: "You kindly speake of my wishes & opinion about your profession of theology," she said in 1827. "I advise a man to place himself as a sort of mediator between God and his fellows—take an office so essential to the welfare of his

Country & the salvation of immortal souls." While that office might not be in the pulpit, Mary left no doubts about her own preference. "With views like these it is difficult to find an excuse for any benevolent man of mind who *dont* preach."[105] Charles ultimately joined William and Edward in law, and Mary, heartbroken, responded with grim fatalism, writing in the autumn of 1832, "I hold myself unworthy to paint your destiny. God himself guide you far from the curse of ambitious & selfish accommodations." By then, she could afford to be resigned. For although Charles opened a law office in Boston and entered the Court of Common Pleas, her expectations for a ministerial Emerson had been satisfied in other quarters.

In many ways, Ralph Waldo Emerson was the least likely candidate for this exalted position. As a boy and adolescent, he had been dreamy and whimsical, more interested in poetry than theology or philosophy. When Edward developed symptoms of mental illness as a clerk in the office of Daniel Webster, Waldo (as he insisted on calling himself) declared himself too "silly" to ever become depressed. Yet it was this slender, inward boy with the faraway blue eyes—not the more promising Emerson boys—who embarked on the study of theology in 1824, entering Harvard's Divinity School a year later. By 1829, he was ordained at Boston's prestigious Second Church, becoming its head pastor at the age of twenty-seven (figure 13).

By then, Mary was in her fifties. She had devoted countless hours to encouraging Waldo, exchanging dozens of letters about poetry and ambition and the spiritual life, even writing imaginary dialogues between Plato and her deceased father in which the pair of spirits sagely considered Waldo's future success. She

Figure 13. Waldo Emerson, around the time he was ordained.

cajoled him, fortified him, argued with him, and inspired him to greater efforts. When he struggled with vocational doubts or with poor health—he too had symptoms of tuberculosis—she soothed and counseled him. In the process, she took on a new role—not that so much of muse as of hero.

8.

There were other friends and preoccupations, of course. For all the care Mary expended on her nephews, she also managed to maintain a wide range of relationships with exceptional women scattered throughout New England. Mary Wilder Van Schalkwyck was no longer among this group. She had remarried—to the lawyer and congressman, Daniel Appleton White, from Salem—and died soon after giving birth to her second daughter, in 1811. But other women took her place in Mary's high regard, including Sarah Alden Bradford, a friend she had met in Concord not long after the death of her brother William.

Bradford, who eventually married Mary's half-brother Samuel Ripley, could trace her ancestry back to Plymouth's first governor, the Pilgrim historian William Bradford. She had grown up in a house full of books and a tolerant father who, when asked if she might study Latin, replied, "Yes, study Latin if you want to. You may study anything you please."[106] Bradford took this advice to heart. Besides Latin, Greek, French, Italian, and German, she taught herself botany, astronomy, and chemistry. From her scientific pursuits, she developed the habit of viewing life from an empirical perspective, and this outlook served as a foil to Mary's more intuitive and otherworldly disposition. Describing "the great obstacles to my reception of your views of religion," Bradford wrote her in 1813, there was her "dread of enthusiasm, of the mind's becoming enslaved to a system perhaps erroneous and forever against the light of truth."[107]

Despite their differences, the two women created a learned society between them. "Ever you read Dante?" Mary queried in 1814. "Why is it that his infernal regions are so much more interesting than his celestial?"[108] They gathered in the parlor of the old parsonage, talking as the room grew dim and the old familiar furniture gleamed in the warm light of the fireplace. Sarah Bradford, who was eighteen years Mary's junior, felt awed by her restless, overbearing companion at first. But she quickly gained her footing, taking delight in contrasting science with Mary's Romantic nature: "Why can't you be disinterested enough," she taunted, "after you have exhaled the fragrance of autumnal wild flowers to press some of them for me . . . ?"[109] Even after Bradford married Mary's half-brother and began to raise children of her own, the conversation continued, with Sarah confessing that she worried she had "lost the power to interest you; [that] you have given me over to Domestic inanity, and while you are catching inspiration from a cloud, inhaling it in a breeze; while the rustling of falling leaves, or the sighing of the winter's wind may make you forget you are still embodied in a mortal case, I may perhaps fret or trifle away some 30 or 50 years more...."[110]

Another new friend was Ann Sargent Brewer. Back in 1808, Mary's brother William had been approached by a wealthy parishioner named Daniel Sargent, who confessed he was the father of an illegitimate child. The girl's mother had recently died, and the product of their illicit union was now approaching fourteen years of age. William offered to relocate the teenage girl in the home of his Ripley relations in Waterford, Maine. This would save Sargent's reputation and, at the same time, spare the girl social humiliation in Boston. Samuel Ripley, the man who would soon marry Sarah Bradford, was enlisted to drive the horse-drawn sleigh that carried the frightened girl.

Once in Maine, Ann Brewer quickly became Mary's protégé, a "poet bro't up in pure mountain air."[111] At the older woman's instigation, Brewer greedily read de Staël's writings and Wordsworth's poetry. Mary confided to her the difficulties sustaining a life of the mind. "As to society & literature—the rapture of a few days & hours are no compensation for the evils which polite life induces." To one who had felt the divine spirit emanating from the stars—who had tramped in the shadow of Waterford's mountains with an exultant soul—the monotony of daily life was a curse. "However we theorise contemptuously of earth," she complained, "it gets dominion & the grandure of the soul lies beneath rubbish."[112]

Still, she was happy to tell Brewer that while in Boston to visit her nephews she had found time for "Orators, publications & my attendance on conferences in Mr Channings Vestry."[113] This last was a reference to the Unitarian minister, William Ellery Channing, who was fast becoming famous for his eloquent rejection of Calvinism. Channing denounced the inherited image of a punitive God, insisting the deity was wise and benevolent, a tolerant father, not a tyrannical sovereign. Recently he had proposed a small vestry hall for "the young ladies" of his congregation, where they might gather and discuss scripture and philanthropic projects. It was among this group that Mary Emerson now found herself when she visited Boston.

She was creating an informal salon of her own. Much like her beloved de Staël, whose weekly soirees in Coppet, Switzerland had been a gathering place for European intellectuals and American revolutionaries a decade earlier, Mary gathered a circle of talented intellectual women who shared her taste for thought and reading despite their lack of formal education. If Mary clung to her solitude, her flights of imagination, she also longed for intellectual communion. She needed people with whom to share her ideas. More important, she realized that thought became more volatile, more interesting, when discussed with others. As she had learned during her early experiments with Mary Van Schalkwyck, thinking was a collaborative affair.

In subsequent years, Mary's circle would expand to include Elizabeth Hoar, the fiancée of Charles Chauncy Emerson (figure 14). She would also attract a talented

Figure 14. Elizabeth Sherman Hoar

young woman from nearby Salem named Elizabeth Peabody. But during the 1810s and early 1820s, her friendships were mainly comprised of Sarah Alden Bradford and Ann Brewer, both of whom gladly followed Mary as she explored new philosophy from Germany and English poetry. Mary also enlisted these friends to help educate her Emerson nephews. Brewer took up the daunting challenge of teaching Bulkeley, who spent much of his time in Maine running boisterously through meadows and woods. The youngest nephew, Charles, learned more from Bradford; he once described her as "the female Hero of Science." Bradford's gift for teaching is apparent in a letter she wrote to Waldo, along with a copy of her translation of Virgil's Fifth Bucolic. "My dear friend," she said, "You love to trifle in rhyme a little now and then, why will you not continue this versification of the 5 bucolic. You will answer two ends... improve in your latin as well as indulge your taste for poetry."

Waldo, eleven at the time, responded to the challenge with a translation that began with an endearing scrap of doggerel:

Your favor I receiv'd of late
But I know that I cannot like you translate
But yet my humble efforts I will make
Not in the Greek 'tis verse I undertake.[114]

He would later complain how little he had learned as a student at Harvard. His professors had been hidebound, insipid, their ideas fusty. Far more stimulating was his eccentric Aunt Mary, who had written "prophetic and apocalyptic" prayers for him to read each morning during family devotions and who had bequeathed him with a fresh, joyous way of seeing the world. He did not mention Bradford and Brewer in these reminiscences, but their contributions were a part of the education provided by Aunt Mary. Without her tutelage, his entire schooling "would have been a loss. She was as great an element in my life as Greece or Rome."[115]

In 1817, when he entered Harvard, Mary and Waldo began to exchange letters—a written conversation—that would prove especially meaningful to the young man. "Indeed," Mary told him, "*we* can only commune by pen."[116] For the next ten years or so she produced some of her most inspired writing in letters she sent to Waldo, also sharing with him huge extracts from her Almanacks. Waldo delighted in "the wild freedom of MME's genius . . . the fire of her piety, her zeal for learning, her brilliant expression."[117] He answered her correspondence with imitations of her prophetic voice, and together they engaged in a seemingly endless, free-flowing conversation that included discussions of free will (still a favorite topic of Mary's), the healing capacity of nature, and the qualities of true poetry.

She had learned from her oldest nephew, William, not to insist too forcefully upon the ministry. From an early age, Waldo had imagined himself a poet. As an adolescent, he pestered his brothers' more "prosaical temper[s]" with rhymed couplets and snippets of doggerel.[118] Mary therefore urged Waldo to consider himself a writer instead of a man of the cloth. "How is thy soul?" she asked him in 1821, his final year at Harvard. "Not that of which Paul speaks—but thy poetic?"[119] Elsewhere she referred to him as a "Magician Maker," comparing his talents to those of Prospero in Shakespeare's *The Tempest* and boldly predicting that his name would "go down, and tell on his Country's page a line which time will not blot."[120] She shamelessly flattered him. "Son of——of——poetry——of genius," she exclaimed, "ah were it so—and I destined to stand in near consanguinity to this magical possession."[121]

These strategies failed to conceal her larger goal. Mary never quit believing it was her duty to install at least one of her nephews into the religious calling of her deceased father and brother. "Go on, my dear Waldo, and exert every nerve to gain the favor of God," she wrote him earlier, when he was just nine. Five years later, after he had entered college (fourteen was the standard age of entrance), she pressed him to acquire "those virtues and graces which do not pretend to dazzel, but which shed a pure and steady light, over the interests of humanity and religion."[122] Cautiously, cagily, she was preparing him for ordination.

Sometimes she worried she was sacrificing too much of herself in this time-consuming relationship. She offered Waldo her best ideas. She imparted her choicest moods, her transporting inspiration. Wasn't she at risk of losing a "portion of one's soul—that all of existence"?[123] Ultimately, she considered the time well spent. By nurturing Waldo's intelligence and sensibility, she was shaping the world through a refracted form of publication. "Think of a De Stael treasuring up sentiments & ideas for a son," she mused in her Almanacks, imagining her favorite author in a similar situation, "abandoning her own publick existence that he might be 'decked with unfading honors!' "[**124] Mary had abandoned dreams of a "publick existence" long ago, when her brother had quit publishing her contributions to the *Monthly Anthology*. But by instructing Waldo, she was able to contribute, however indirectly, to her "Country's page a line which time will not blot."

Waldo sometimes scoffed at Mary's power to influence him. To William, who was in Maine, he noted, "If I were Aunt Mary, I should tell you how auspicious an omen it was to your future happiness that you had commenced the year 1818 in the 'delightful task—&c,' in the mind-expanding air, & piety-inspiring regions of Kennebunkport..."[125] But his gentle mockery concealed a deep respect. Elsewhere he wrote of his admiration for her "Genius always new, subtle, frolicsome, musical, unpredictable." Her mind was like a Gothic castle, many-chambered, improvisatory in its design: "What liberal, joyful architecture, liberal & manifold as the vegetation from the earth's bosom, or the creations of frost work in the window! Nothing can excel the freedom & felicity of her letters... this absence of all reference to style or standard: it is the march of the mountain winds, the waving of flowers, or the flight of birds."[126]

Aunt and nephew shared a private language. Telling her of an evening spent gazing at the stars, Waldo described the heaven's "solemn and silent revolution," relating his sense that it contained "something honourable... something lofty something sublime."[127] He was speaking in her voice. In 1818, when Waldo was fifteen, Mary encouraged him to write poetry that would guide the reader along "the path to the attainment of moral perfection." She summoned his "vagrant flower clad Muse" and hoped his inspiration might "preene her wings."[128] She was referring to Queen Mab—the ruler of fairies who in *Romeo and Juliet* is said to "deliver the fancies of sleeping men." When Waldo started keeping a journal of his own, he echoed her language once more: "I do hereby nominate & appoint 'Imagination' the generalissimo & chief marshall of all the luckless ragamuffin Ideas which may be collected & unprisoned hereafter in these pages." Then he echoed his aunt. "O ye witches assist me!...

** She was paraphrasing Horace.

Pardon me Fairy Land! Riche region of fancy & gnomery, elvery, sylphery, & Queen Mab!"[129]

It is no exaggeration to say that the young Waldo paid more attention to Mary's writing than to any other author. He would one day call her "the best writer... in Massachusetts, not even excepting Dr. Channing or Daniel Webster."[130] Inspired by her energetic style, he copied so many passages from her letters and conversation that they eventually filled four notebooks totaling nearly nine hundred manuscript pages. The transcriptions were a form of apprenticeship: a way of internalizing her voice, appropriating her style. Would he have copied so much of her writing if Mary had been a man? Would he have copied them if the Almanacks had been written for publication? It is hard to say. "M.M.E.'s style is that of letters," he once observed, "an immense advantage—admits of all the force of colloquial domestic words, & breaks, & parenthesis, & petulance—has the luck & inspirations of that,—has humor, affection, & a range from the rapture of prayer down to the details of farm & barn...."[††131]

Yet her influence stretched well beyond aesthetics. Mary also shaped Waldo's attitude toward nature. In 1822, when out of college for a year, he embarked on a walking tour of New England. Returning, he confessed an unresponsiveness to the natural beauty of the mountains. "I thought I understood a little of that *intoxication*, which you have spoken of," he wrote to Mary; "but it was a soft animal luxury, the combined result of the beauty which fed the eye; the exhilarating Paradise *air*, which fanned & dilated the sense; the novel melody, which warbled from the trees." Nature offered sensuous pleasures, he admitted, but its charm "passed away rapidly"; not once "was I in any mood to take [up] my pen..."[132]

Mary replied as if personally wounded. Nature was not a luxury, she scolded, but a *necessity*. It was the fountain, the source of poetic vision. More important, it provided contact with the divine. "You do not 'ask' but impel me to speake of that Muse—so loved—so wild—so imaginative so dear to me," she scrawled in six furious and indomitable pages, explaining how nature nourished her soul because it was God's creation.[133] Such thoughts were a staple of the Almanack: "the stars glowed," she exclaimed, "with what rapt devotion did I view my Makers hand."[134] Now she directed her nephew to abandon his cloistered study for contact with the living natural world. "I had rather my young favorite w[d] wander wild among the flowers & briars of nature—would scale the 'tempel where the Genius of the Universe resides...'"[135]

[††] Just how much his own style was indebted to her is apparent in "The Poet," published decades later in his *Essays: Second Series*. There he declared, "Small and mean things serve as well as great symbols. The meaner the type by which a law is expressed, the more pungent it is, and the more lasting in the memories of men..." And in "The American Scholar," delivered in 1837, he made a similar point: "The meal in the firkin; the milk in the pan... show me the ultimate reason... and the world lies no longer a dull miscellany and lumber-room, but has form and order."

She exhorted him to strike beyond conventional thought. "[S]ome of the best intellects have been infidels,"[136] she wrote, urging him to topple all "bounds which circumscribe the imajanation."[137] She also challenged him to cultivate solitude, where "minds become oblivious to care & find in the uniform & constant miracle of nature, revelation alt[a]r & priest."[138] In a particularly convoluted passage, she described the future she pictured for Waldo—one that combined solitude, poetic inspiration, and service to Christianity:

> Solitude w'h to people, not talented to deviate from the beaten track (w'h is the safe guard of mediocrity) without offending, is to learning & talents the only sure labyrinth (tho' sometimes gloomy) to form the eagle wings w'h will bear one farther than suns and stars. Byron & Wordsworth have there best and only intensely burnished their pens. Would to Providence your unfoldings might be there—.... Could a mind return to its first fortunate seclusion, when it opened with its own peculiar coulers & spread them out on its own rhymy palette, with its added stock, and spread them beneathe the cross, what a mercy to the age.[139]

This passage, written in the summer of 1824, is full of key words and ideas that would assume importance for the burgeoning transcendentalist movement. They include an insistence on inspiration, a faith in the individual's innermost feelings, and an elevation of the poet to the status of visionary prophet and priest. Mary had been cultivating these ideas for the past twenty years when she wrote them. If in Waldo she found a receptive ear, she also worried that he might one day stray from these values. She feared he was "one whose destiny tends to lead him to sensation rather than sentiment," and entreated him to heed "The images, the sweet immortal images [that] are within us—born there, our native right." She linked her own rebellion against Enlightenment materialism with her father's heroic resistance to the British monarchy. "We are not slaves to sense any more than to political usurpers."[140]

In the spring of 1824, Waldo announced his intentions to pursue the ministry. Mary, privately elated, allowed herself at last to return to her own reveries. "The imajanation was given... to scale the skies," she wrote in her Almanack, expressing profound gratitude that she could "hold high converse in walks of boundless thought."[141] The enthusiasm she had always felt when gazing at the stars was to her "the best idea we have of Heaven," an opportunity to "individuate myself with [God's] presence...—oh how rich."[142] The night sky, as always, filled her with rapture: "My glasses downstairs," she scribbled one evening in Maine, "yet these stars shining thro' these naked trees on a misty atmosphere is so like Heaven bearing comfort on poor man that I can't go to bed."[143]

Mary's Almanacks throughout the 1820s—the decade in which she turned fifty and Waldo entered divinity school—are filled with praise to a "nameless excitement of existence." They chronicle her ambitious program of reading, with extracts copied from Bacon, Newton, Plato, Shakespeare, Montaigne, the Scottish Common Sense philosophers, and many others. Waldo's letters, which continued after he entered advanced study, elicited her deepest beliefs. "How ridiculous to represent enthusiasm as a disease," she wrote in her Almanacks, as if resuming the argument with her deceased brother. Enthusiasm was that "light of the soul—that spark of glory which will continue to burn thro' eternity..."[144]

Her writing engaged with various intellectual currents of the era while remaining focused on the private exultations of the soul. "Oh how gratefull am I for solitude & independence," she wrote, ".... Oh prison of prisons to the soul is that condition of asking leave to breathe."[145] She praised God for the gift of consciousness, for the way thought quickened and animated the visible world: "Mankind may be frozen & subdued like the snake by discipline, but thaw it &——!"[146] Daniel Bliss Ripley, a half-brother, referred to Mary around this time as "the etherial incorporeal supernatural immortal soul"—a moniker that jokingly summed up the otherworldly character of a woman who fused Puritan piety and Romantic enthusiasm, creating her own manner of experiencing and thinking in the world.[147]

As Waldo embarked on his theological training, he looked to Mary for inspiration. He sought her help especially when it came to his preaching. As he put it in his journal, "The religion of my Aunt is the purest & most sublime of any I can conceive... It is independent of forms & ceremonies & its ethereal nature gives a glow of soul to her whole life."[148] Waldo worried he had not lived enough to say anything of value in the pulpit. He asked her for ideas: "Can you not suggest the secret oracles which such a commission needs... ?" As his ordination drew nearer, he made an audacious request: "[I]f my gross body outlive you, will [you] bequeath me the legacy of all your recorded thought[?]"[149] What he wanted was the Almanacks. And although he did not come out and say it, he also wanted permission to borrow from them in his sermons.

Mary took some time before answering. She occasionally sent portions of her journals to friends—she believed they provided the best picture of her inner life. But there had never been any possibility that the Almanacks would reach an audience beyond the one she selected. Now Waldo wanted to mine them for the benefit of his congregation, to appropriate her inspired thoughts for his own sermons. How was she to consider such a proposition? Should she be flattered or annoyed? Finally, she acquiesced. She sent him portions of the Almanacks, asking that he keep them no longer than necessary. Waldo hungrily transcribed passages into his journal, delighting in the pleasures of his aunt's writing. And he kept her gift for nearly a year. Then he made an even more importunate request: "I grow more avaricious of this kind of property like other misers with age, and like expecting heirs would be glad to put my fingers into the chest of 'old almanacks' before they are a legacy."[150] Mary again complied, and the transmission of manuscripts continued for several more years. But in 1830, she finally lost her patience.

"I send you an Almanack!" she exclaimed after Waldo made another request. "... I will not until you return the others. They are my *home*—the only image of having existed."[151]

Mary was in her mid-fifties when she wrote this. In a state of permanent exile, she had constructed a refuge of paper and ink. She had built a home, with faith and diligence, in the pages of her Almanacks, creating a native place that was far more hospitable than the houses of relatives, where she still was sometimes called to serve as nursemaid and housekeeper. The Almanacks were the only property that mattered to her, the testament of a life spent in thought and spirit.

Waldo had already pilfered countless pages from this prized document, modeling his prose on hers: "To forget for a season the world & its concerns," he wrote in a phrase almost directly lifted from Mary, "& to separate the soul for sublime contemplation till it has lost the sense of circumstances & is decking itself in plumage drawn out from the gay wardrobe of Fancy is a recreation & a rapture of which few men avail themselves."[152] (This was written in 1820, when Waldo was seventeen.) Mary's journals helped him with the arduous but necessary task faced by all young writers: that of discovering a voice. By mimicking his aunt's singular style—and the attitude that had produced that style in the first place—he was learning to write.

We do not have an adequate term for this generative process of imitation. Appropriation, theft, influence, homage—the words fail to convey just how much Waldo internalized Mary's enigmatic expression, her habits of consciousness, her mode of being. Perhaps it is more accurate to say that aunt and nephew were engaged in an intimate form of co-authorship, a shared response to the world made possible by the language they forged together.[153] But it must also be acknowledged that Mary sometimes felt robbed of her personhood in the process.

Waldo's descriptions of nature increasingly sounded her exultant tone: the "bloom of summer fields" is "the pavilion God built in the beginning for the residence of man."[154] And his defense of enthusiasm could have been lifted directly from the Almanacks: "Is it not true that modern philosophy has got to be very conversant with feelings?" he asked. "Bare reason, cold as a cucumber, was all that was tolerated aforetime, till men grew disgusted at the skeleton & have now given him inward into the hands of his sister, blushing shining changing Sentiment."[155] Just how much he owed Mary is apparent in a letter he wrote to her on August 1, 1826, as a divinity student of twenty-three:

> There are, I take it, in each man's history insignificant passages which he feels to be to him not insignificant; little coincidences in little things, which touch all the springs of wonder, and startle the sleeper conscience in the deepest cell of his repose; the Mind standing forth in alarm with all her faculties, suspicious of a

> Presence which it behoves her deeply to respect—touched not more with awe than with curiosity, if perhaps some secret revelation is not about to be vouchsafed.[156]

The statement is drenched in Wordsworth, particularly in its intimation of a sublime presence. It also anticipates sentiments Waldo would make famous in works such as *Nature* and *Essays: First Series*, where daily life suddenly gives way to insights that have the capacity to overturn our sense of reality. But buried in the letter is an acknowledgment of his debt to Mary. If the feminine pronoun was often used to depict the soul and the imagination, his application of it to "Mind" suggests how much his aunt had come to stand for him as thought itself.

Two months after writing the letter, Waldo delivered his probationary sermon to the Middlesex County association of ministers. Mary sat upright and eager in the congregation. For years she would cherish "that day in Waltham." To have witnessed Waldo climbing the pulpit, clad in his black ministerial robes, and to have listened to his rich baritone read the scripture was to have realized a dream: "the attainment," she admitted, "of so many desired objects of... hearing the minister among my Nephews." To Sarah Bradford Ripley she expressed her pleasure "in the serious simple dignified *manner* of Waldo in pulpit—of his *thoughts*—style &c...."[157] She failed to mention just how much of herself she had given to make it happen.

9.

She read, as always, ravenously. Throughout the late 1820s her Almanacks—part commonplace books, part reading journals, part reflective essays—refer to Cicero, Milton, Dante, Plato, and Aristotle. They chronicle her reading of the ninth-century Irish Neoplatonist theologian John Scotus, the eighteenth-century natural religionist William Wollaston, and a full complement of German philosophers, including Kant and Fichte. She was interested in hailstorms and earthquakes and volcanoes, interested in angels and the hermits of ancient Christianity. Reading well into the middle of the night, she absorbed accounts of exploration, her mind traveling across the Atlantic to tramp through tropical forests and meet indigenous peoples. "We love to wander over seas with Columbus," she wrote, "sympathize in all his rare & great qualities." Much as she admired him, though, she was sorry, for the sake of the original inhabitants, that he had discovered the West Indies. "Alas that their peacefull natures were ever discovered, or their gold added to the pride of Spain."[158]

She especially loved histories of the Revolutionary War, reliving its battles in vivid detail. "My God how glorious is the story of our war. It thrills it absorbs. I see the streets of my native Town. I hear the fire, I see the smoke—God of battles protect the injured." Imagining the Battle of Concord invariably turned her thoughts inward. "I see my father—I forget him—my infancy, begun how grandly, how sunken now..." Her father's enlistment and early death had resulted in "protracted sufferings w'h quench the light even of such a noble struggle—w'h doom the helpless orphan to find liberty & all that makes life valuable sunk in the beloved grave."[159]

The memory of her brother similarly rose before her. "Today 16 years have come & gone since I closed with this hand the eyes of one who was the first object of my enthusiastic love & admiration." William's death had released him "from the cares of a profession in w'h the views of his theology *I thought* defective." Her disagreements with him over religion meant that at first "I could not grieve for him." But she had made up for this failure by caring for his family during their "struggles with poverty." She now celebrated "the zeal and fidelity with which the elder sons have performed the duties of sons & brothers that their characters have been formed to high praise."[160]

As always, she craved solitude as well as society. "I have found no one to sympathise with," she complained, "tho' I sympathise in general benevolence from the President to the cat." Was there any human being, she wondered, "able to excuse my defects & to confer society"?[161] At the same time, social contact irritated her, interrupting her thoughts. "A day all alone, without venturing down, lest fervor should be interrupted," she wrote, "and then weak enough to send for some of the visitors. Oh pride how dost thou curdle the blood at the highest times when forced into contact." Snappish and defensive, she blamed her painful interactions with others on her "bile." One June day, at four in the morning, she awoke to the sound of creatures with whom she *could* get along: "Here are my cotemporaries Monsieur Fly so merry—Don Spider as busy—& I've slept, amid the gay beauty of sun & trees & air."[162]

Her primary focus was theology—its labyrinthine corners and esoterica, to be sure, but primarily its mysteries. Did prayer play a role in altering the world? If so, by what mechanisms were those alterations effected? She challenged the Calvinist's emphasis on salvation by grace and questioned the premise behind the trinity. She waged endless battles against philosophical materialists, pecking away at "the wild & atheistical account of Diderot & his predecessor Lucretius," drawn to their skepticism like a crow to a blackberry, if only to disgorge it in triumph.

She devoted countless pages analyzing the "fine invisible vehicle" of the soul. Was it possible to discern "an immortal substance in the midst of the five material sensorium"?[163] She argued with pantheistical writers, suggesting they "imagined they saw God in everything when it was the idol of their own beauty & rectitude they worshiped."[164] And she continued to question the existence of free will. Had God set his creatures on earth to act completely on their own, wholly without intervention? Or was he deeply involved in every decision they made? Could humans ever be truly free? She herself was unable to decide. Ultimately the best she could do was settle on the idea that whether the "Deity has cast his creatures from him to take their own way—or is intimately connected with their phisical & moral actions, there is unspeakable danger in doing a doubtful action."[165]

A grim ecstasy always accompanied her thoughts on death: "I sing Te Deum over my pale face & sunk eyes," she rhapsodized, "& would more heartily, if the worm were at the door w'h would crawl in & crawl out."[166] This passage was written in 1827, around the same time she began to wear a white merino shroud and to arrange her bedclothes in the shape of a coffin. Both gestures served as memento mori. "Aye yes," she said, "I feel as tho' I could coil down in my coffin conscious if at ease, & lie in thought till ages had run on & the great year of redemption had circled."[167] Another time, she prophesied, "Oh in woe-worn hoary age to lose one's self in this glorious Being, like the drop in the ocean."[168]

She counseled to "let alone anxiety to know which system of xian faith was best."[169] And in 1828, she confessed that she was "Weary of reading praying hoping searching the nature of things. Ask nothing but a calm peace if I can't have the better rest of grave."[170] On another occasion, having immersed herself in German philosophy for a week or so, she offered this advice: "Well well be quiet old heart—time was when thou beatest thy head about these things—when the hour was tedious unless something learnt—now the days—the seasons grow round thee—and thou feelest the bark of age, like the fabled tree, closing up thy aspirations."[171]

More often, though, she was enthusiastic, even joyous, in her speculations. If she sometimes asked, "for what do we exist—its end?" she just as often had an answer: "To enjoy the contemplation of the ineffable Beauty! This is end w'h satisfys the largest desires & strikes the soul with ever new delight." To truly live meant that "take all & all[,] there is now"—a glorious, ever-unfolding moment of creation, infinitely interesting. The mind's eye lit the world with its ever-devouring flame. Or, as she put it in the Almanacks, referring to Shakespeare's *The Tempest*, "As the light like Prospero's wand raises images of beauty & splendor so does the strange power within us, and gloom & disappointment themselves weave out a sweet landscape."[172] Theology strengthened her mind. Poetry nourished her soul. "[T]o poetry we owe the charms of the glow-worm's lamp—science, as it too often does, has robbed the meadow of much beauty by detailing the history of the little harlots, who shine to capture the lover." Indeed, as she put it one October day, "no faculty perhaps leads to the invisible world so readily as imajanation."[173]

10.

One summer night in 1826, Mary awoke from a dream so vivid and disturbing that she immediately got out of bed to commit it to paper. The dream took place in

Concord's Old Hill Burying Ground, the Puritan-era cemetery with its weather-worn tombstones dating almost as far back as 1636, the year of the town's establishment. Mary was standing amid the graves, accompanied by her four nephews. But a stranger had joined them, a "highly interesting woman" who, in the vague manner of dreams, Mary knew to be the wife of one of her nephew's without quite knowing which one. The Emerson family was somber, respectful. They had gathered before the memorial stone of Mary's father with the inscription she had helped write:

ENTHUSIASTIC ELOQUENT

AFFECTIONATE AND PIOUS

Then the silence was broken. The strange woman spoke up, saying the "quiet office of priest in an Army" did not seem to her to warrant such a monument.

In the dream, it was William, the oldest, who replied. He defended "the character of [his] Ancestor," claiming the Reverend William Emerson had in fact risked his life by enlisting as chaplain in the Continental Army. He had ministered to the souls of frightened young soldiers, comforting men on the cusp of death and serving his country with honor. At this point, Mary awoke with a jolt of indignation. At least *one* of her nephews had defended her father's memory.[174]

The dream proved strangely prescient. On Christmas Day, 1827, while serving as supply preacher in Concord, New Hampshire, Waldo met the sixteen-year-old Ellen Tucker (figure 15). She was spirited and artistic and came from a large, loving, prosperous family. Ellen wrote poetry and adored animals of all kinds. (She owned several white mice, a squirrel, a canary, a lamb, and a spaniel named Byron.) She was also witty and sociable: just the sort of companion a shy and self-conscious young minister hoped to find.

Waldo proposed to her in 1828. A year later, on September 20, 1829, the newlyweds moved to Boston, where the young minister had accepted a position as associate pastor at the Second Church. Just as in Mary's dream, the strange young woman entered the Emerson circle, threatening it. Waldo would never again be so close to his aunt.

Ellen Tucker Emerson was vivacious and rich. She was also dying of tuberculosis. The disease, which had already killed her brother two years earlier and which afflicted her mother and sister, was called consumption: it devoured its victim in much the same way a fire consumes wood. Tuberculosis was one of the most determinative social forces in New England during the first half of the nineteenth century, killing roughly a quarter of the population. A few months before they were married, Ellen began coughing blood. Over the next year and a half, she grew alarmingly thin, her cheeks scarlet with the "hectic" flush that was another characteristic of the disease. While the young couple understood the seriousness

Figure 15. Ellen Tucker Emerson, Waldo's first wife.

of her condition, they embraced their roles as doomed lovers and committed themselves to living fully in the brief time allotted to them. "Few, let them love ever so ardently and purely, have the happiness to lie down in the earth together," Ellen wrote Waldo during their courtship. ". . . . Let us love thus, oh my good Waldo."[175]

Mary reacted to the alliance with cold asperity. "I hope you dont paint nor talk french," she wrote Ellen. "Hope you'll be a unique. And *love* Poetry—that musick of the soul."[176] (She was gratified in this last wish.) But her real concern was with losing Waldo. For more than a decade, her nephew had served as her most penetrating correspondent. He had been her student and collaborator, a companion in thought and spirit. Now, just as he had attained the position for which she had helped train him, he was drifting away. Mary refused to attend the wedding. Soon she was writing Waldo to complain about his silence: "Your Eve and Eden . . . spoil philosophy."[177]

Her attitude changed when she met Ellen in person. This was in March 1830, when Ellen's illness forced her to travel to the milder climate of Philadelphia. The two women met in Wethersfield, Connecticut (Mary was in the middle of one of her sojourns) and hit it off immediately. "I like her better than I dreamt," Mary soon told Edward Emerson, "but not near so handsome—genius and loveliness are enough."[178] In a rhymed journal account of this trip, Ellen described her version of the meeting, humorously recounting Mary's disappointment in her appearance:

Waldo to Weathersfield did ride,
And to my joy I soon espied
Him homeward bound—& by his side
Aunt Mary's eyes her niece did scan
Compared it with her previous plan,
The building was not half so fine
Nor did the painted windows shine...
But hard enough to like she tries
To faults determined closed her eyes
And wouldn't mind them—[179]

Within weeks, the two women were corresponding. "The man that God has blest you with is devoted to the highest & most urgent office," Mary reminded Ellen. ".... Be yourself a ministering angel to him and society."[180]

Ellen, in turn, offered regular reports of Waldo's sermons. She described his homilies and discussed her favorite poets. She shamelessly flattered the older woman. "I look back on your visits to us delightedly," she told Mary, "and strange to tell if I felt an eagerness to see you once I feel a tenfold desire to know you more."[181] To Edward Emerson, the brother-in-law who was beginning to show signs of tuberculosis himself, Ellen admitted that "Aunt Mary... seems not of the earthly nor altogether of the heavenly—to be wondered at and in some sort admired."[182]

Even with the trip south, however, Ellen's health continued to deteriorate. "How is Ellen?" Mary anxiously wrote Charles on January 6, 1831. "Do let me know our Synosure is better surely."[183] Charles's reply was not encouraging. "Ellen is still with us—tho' her spirit seems winged for its flight."[184] By February, it was obvious she would not recover. Torpid with opiates, flushed with fever, she asked Waldo to read from the Bible. The two lovers held hands for hours at a time. The last letter the young woman wrote was to Mary: short, laced with dark humor and foreboding—"My Mother has raised blood, a drop of vermeil should be the family coat of arms." Then she signed off for good: "Goodnight dear Aunt Mary..."[185]

On the morning of February 8, 1831, Ellen died. Waldo dragged himself to his desk and wrote his aunt. He was exhausted, heartbroken—and yet strangely relieved. "Dear Aunt, My angel is gone to heaven this morning & I am alone in the world & strangely happy. Her lungs shall no more be torn nor her heart scalded by her blood nor her whole life suffer from the warfare between the force & delicacy of her soul & the weakness of her frame."[186] He continued to write his weekly sermons, delivering them each Sunday in a kind of trance. But the central moment of each day was the hour when he trudged to his wife's tomb in the Boston suburb of Roxbury (she had been buried beside her father) and stood before it, feeling empty and helpless and alone. In the evenings, he tried to cauterize his grief by writing poetry:

> In yonder ground thy limbs are laid
> Under the snow
> And earth has no spot so dear above
> As that below[187]

Numb, "unstrung [and] debilitated by grief," he was haunted by her final hours, when the blood had seemed to boil in her throat. "I have again heard her breathing," he noted in his journal, "seen her dying."[188]

The previous year, Mary and Waldo sought to bury their anxieties over Ellen's health by discussing philosophy. Both had discovered the works of Samuel Taylor Coleridge, Wordsworth's erstwhile friend, who had collaborated with the poet three decades earlier on the groundbreaking *Lyrical Ballads*. Coleridge was a philosopher, a theologian, a raconteur, and a lecturer. He was also one of the principal conduits by which the English-speaking world learned of German philosophy. Now Mary and Waldo shared their discovery with each other, philosophizing as their beloved Ellen wasted away.

Aunt and nephew were struck by Coleridge's use of two words borrowed from the German philosopher Immanuel Kant: *understanding* and *reason*. In English, these words are nearly synonyms. Coleridge injected them with new, opposed meanings. *Understanding* referred to thoughts derived from the senses—logical conclusions originating from our daily interaction with the world. There are any number of things we can know through the understanding: the heft of a stone, the effects of gravity, the smell of spring garlic. *Reason* was something else entirely. Lodged in the soul, distinct from commonplace thought, it was nothing less than an influx of vision. Reason made it possible to experience the delights of the imagination, the abrupt inrushing perception of God's goodness—the very sorts of experiences Mary considered the most important.

What she found so exhilarating in Coleridge's work was its relevance to morality. If the Creator had endowed each person with reason, then everyone possessed the capacity for determining right from wrong. "Nothing that god has made is more intelligible than the emotions," she wrote in February 1830, shortly after finishing Coleridge's *Aids to Reflection*. The emotions, conveying the inherent rightness or wrongness of a thing, was "to use Cole.'s phrase reason..."[189] The importance of this statement cannot be overstated. It marks the first time anyone in the Emerson circle used the term *reason*—a phrase that would soon acquire central importance within the transcendentalist movement.

The concept of reason appealed to Mary's nephew, as well. Ellen's death had left him indifferent to the ministry. "And here come on the formal duties which are to be formally discharged," he wrote two months after her passing, "and in our sluggish minds no sentiment rises to quicken them."[190] But Coleridge's description of reason and understanding enabled him to realize that his current state of apathy was not permanent. Reason, dormant perhaps, lay within him, untouched by external events. It provided direct revelation of God and helped explain those intermittent moments when divine power seemed to course through the individual soul.

By the summer of 1831, Waldo was describing the "distrust of reason" as "suicidal." He objected to "this doctrine that 'tis pious to believe on others' words[,] impious to trust entirely to yourself." In July, he declared his new conviction: "To reflect is to receive truth immediately from God without any medium. That is living faith . . . A trust in yourself is the height not of pride but of piety, an unwillingness to learn of any but God himself."[191]

That summer, Mary was traveling throughout New England. Even from a distance, she detected troubling signs of heresy in her grieving nephew. She had worried that Waldo was straying from orthodoxy before Ellen's death, demanding after one of his sermons, "where is the miracle power of the Savior? The athority of the Founder? The wonders He performed?"[192] Her anxiety stemmed from several sources. Although she was a fearless thinker herself, she thought her nephew's growing emphasis on the self drew everything—nature and people alike—into its centrifugal force. More concerning was the possibility that Waldo's radical speculations might lead him away from the ministry. Of what use was religion if the individual's inner resources answered for all? "Do you want '*principles*' beyond what [Christ's] ministry teaches?" she pointedly asked him. "Then penetrate like the Newtons of nat. phi. far higher than the common traveler." Go ahead, she said: explore. But remember that every branch of knowledge ultimately derived from "the origin of the light of revelation w'h is shed so—so—like every day things . . ."[193]

Her efforts were to no avail. A year after Ellen's death, Waldo confided his doubts to Mary about whether he could continue preaching. Her response was explosive. "And is it possible," she sputtered, "that one nurtured by the happiest institutions whose rich seeds have been bedewed by them—should be parrisidical [parricidal]!"[194] To throw away the career for which he had trained his entire life was to kill his father and grandfather all over again. "You most beloved of ministers," she railed, "who seemed formed by face manner & pen to copy & illustrate the noblest of all institutions, are you at war with that angelic office? What a problem your existence[.]"[195] To Charles she wrote even more dispiritedly; Waldo was "lost in the halo of his own imagination," she declared, ". . . . It is time he should leave me."[196]

Two months later, in April 1832, Waldo stood before the parishioners of his church and announced that "the theological *scheme of Redemption*" seemed to him "absolutely incredible." This was a forewarning of his decision, three months later, to resign the ministry entirely. "I cannot go habitually to an institution," he wrote in his journal, "which they esteem holiest with indifference & dislike."[197]

Mary responded to the news with heartbreak. She also blamed herself. "I have done wrong to speake," she told him. "I was dazzled by your presence—degraded by the love of your office & situation." She respected his decision: "My solitude opens far distant views—& would see you climbing the hieghts of salvation thro' the lonely roads of what appears to you truth & duty."[198]

After that, their letters ceased. On Christmas Day, 1832, Waldo boarded the brig *Jasper* and sailed for Europe. From Rome he managed a brief note to her, quoting Byron and describing the city as an embodiment of her values, a place where "the spiritual affinities transcend the limits of space."[199] He spent several weeks in Paris studying the botanical cabinets at the Jardin des Plantes and then, in England, met two of the authors who had sustained Mary through years of private meditation and searching: Wordsworth and Coleridge. But he wrote her no more.

From her farm, Mary clutched at any scrap of news of him. To Charles she admitted, "it is far sader than translation of a soul by death of the body to lose Waldo as I have lost him."[200] Despite their falling-out, he remained firmly fixed in her thoughts. "Tell him . . . that I dont see a star in the nightly Heavens with out often thinking he is standing on deck & reading their fates."[201] This melancholy statement concealed as much as it expressed. Waldo had just turned thirty—nearly the same age as Mary when she had stepped from the meetinghouse in Malden to gaze at the stars and dance to "the musick of my own imajanation." Yet he was unbound by the limitations of gender and could travel to Europe, could lose himself in "the halo of his imagination," could even walk unchaperoned along a country road in the Lake District, conversing with the very man whose verse had helped illuminate her life so many years before. If she fretted that Waldo's thinking had grown "confused and dark—a mixture of heathen greatness," she also admired the scope of his intellect, the infidel pride of his convictions.[202] Picturing him aboard a ship, gazing up at the stars, she saw herself—and realized just how dissimilar were the possibilities each had been afforded by society.

He did not return to New England until October 1833. One year later, he decided to settle in Concord—living in the parsonage where Mary had been born nearly sixty years earlier. By then, he had begun to write a series of lectures for the lyceum system that was just beginning to spread across the region. He preached on occasion, filling in as a supply minister when vacancies arose in nearby villages. But mainly he worked on the manuscript he had first conceived in the dismal months following Ellen's death. It was a book that synthesized the thought he had learned from Mary and then reformulated in the wake of his life's central tragedy. Sitting in the soot-stained study on the second floor of the parsonage, writing at a table placed between two tall, mullioned windows, he could peer through the wavy glass at the meadow where the first shots of the American Revolution had been fired and at the gnarled, mossy apple orchard where his Aunt Mary had played for a brief halcyon period before her father had died. "Henceforth," he declared, "I design not to utter any speech, poem or book that is not entirely and peculiarly my own work."[203] This vow did not preclude him from using ideas and language he had learned from Mary.

As it happened, she was in Concord, too, lodging at a boarding house secured for her by friends. Although still disappointed by Waldo's resignation from the ministry, she had gradually accommodated herself to his determination to leave it. In the process, the two had become less estranged. Unable to stay away from her wayward protégé, she had packed her bags and returned to her native town where, in a setting rich with personal and national history, she debated theology and philosophy with him, jousting, cajoling, endlessly disputing. Often their arguments were made purely for the sake of arguing. "Here is M.M.E.," Waldo wrote in his journal in July 1835, "always fighting in conversation against the very principles which have governed & govern her."[204]

Yet these quarrelsome dialogues prompted fresh insights for Waldo. "In talking... with M.M.E.," he wrote, "I was ready to say that a severest truth would forbid me to say that ever I had made a sacrifice." He was speaking of Ellen's death, of the unfathomable tranquility that had settled over him in the months that followed. Much as he had loved his wife, "when she was taken from me, the air was still sweet, the sun was not taken down from my firmament, & however sore was that particular loss, I still felt that it was particular, that the Universe remained to us both, that the Universe abode in its light & in its power to replenish the heart with hope."[205] This would become an article of his new faith—a faith in nature as a repository of spiritual truth, a place of healing and perception. Personal tragedies did not prevent the universe from conducing toward the good. Mary had helped prompt this insight, which he recast later the same day in a passage that eventually made its way into *Nature*: "In the woods,... I feel that nothing can befall me in life,—no disgrace, no calamity, (leaving me my eyes,) which nature cannot repair."[206]

The process of conversation and collaboration continued. Each day Mary and Waldo interrogated one another, probing each other's beliefs, arguing, synthesizing, grudgingly ceding ground. Then they said goodbye and embarked on the laborious exercise of putting sentences down on paper—Mary in her Almanacks, Waldo in his manuscript. He might as well have been speaking on her behalf when he announced in his journal, "I will no longer confer, differ, refer, defer, prefer, or suffer... I embrace absolute life."[207]

11.

In the autumn of 1836, when Mary Moody Emerson was sixty-two, a slim green volume entitled *Nature* was anonymously published in Boston. Only five hundred copies were printed, but those five hundred copies proved enormously influential—a bright green thread running through American thought and literature. Even today, it is difficult to imagine our cultural inheritance without Waldo Emerson's first book. The poetry of Whitman and Dickinson, the pungent descriptions in Thoreau's *Walden*, even Henry James's *The Portrait of a Lady*—all are unthinkable without the activating example of *Nature*. Adam Mickiewicz, Friedrich Nietzsche, Aaron Copeland, Ralph Ellison, and many, many others take Waldo's first book as their condition of possibility.

Nature's underlying premise is that old forms of thought and feeling are no longer adequate to the present moment. Waldo believed his era demanded the primacy of personal vision, a "poetry and philosophy of insight and not tradition, a religion by revelation to us..." Making this possible is the spark of divinity inside each person—the godlike glimmer of Coleridgean reason. The book's final chapter contains one of the most radical descriptions of the transformative possibility of individual vision in all American literature: "Every spirit builds itself a house; and beyond its house a world; and beyond its world, a heaven... Build, therefore, your own world."[208]

Soon after the book was published, Waldo sent his aunt an inscribed copy:

Miss M. M. Emerson
from her affectionate nephew/R. W. E.

By now, Mary Emerson had returned to Maine. She had recently cut her yellow hair to fit in a misshapen mob cap of her own design. (She wished for "a bonnet that would not conform.")

There were other eccentricities. Once, while boarding at a New England village, she made off with a stranger's horse, riding side saddle and cloaked in a scarlet dimity shawl she had also taken without asking. And she was increasingly plagued with afflictions. Her penetrating blue eyes bothered her; she had contracted a painful skin inflammation, erysipelas, which hurt her face and blurred her vision. But she still read everything she could, including the memoirs of a missionary to Burma, a commentary on Newtonian physics and, as if returning to an old friend, Coleridge. Intermixed with all this were heaps of theology and poetry.

When Waldo's package arrived, she opened the slender book and turned to its introduction. The opening sentences must have felt like an affront. "Our age is retrospective," Waldo began. "It builds the sepulchres of the fathers."[209] The image, of course, came from her father's monument in the Concord burying ground—the one she had dreamed about a few years earlier. It was bad enough that Waldo had abandoned his ancestral profession, but now, like the mysterious woman in her dream, he belittled the memory of her revered father.

But she read on. Waldo's sentences sparkled, and she could not help, now and then, feeling proud. She marked his book with her crabbed penciling. The seventh chapter, titled "Idealism," included her nephew's statement that "we learn that man has access to the entire mind of the Creator."[210] Mary flagged this sentence. "Have the seraphim?" she asked dryly. Waldo's view of human capacity, she thought, was too optimistic; it failed to account for human flaws. While the divinity certainly provided His creatures with wondrous faculties, it was too much to say that they had access to "the *entire* mind of the Creator."

She was more approving of another sentence in the same chapter: "The best, the happiest moments of life, are these delicious awakenings of the higher powers, and the reverential withdrawing of nature before its God."[211] Mary marked this with an emphatic exclamation point. She was even more enthusiastic about his chapter on "Language." Here Waldo argued that words were "signs of natural facts," that natural facts were symbols of larger spiritual facts. Taken together, "nature is the symbol of spirit."[212] To a woman who had so often marched through frosty meadows or retired into the woods to enjoy God's handiwork, Waldo's formulation was a confirmation, and at the end of the chapter, she summed up her feelings: "A chap. as full of beauty as of true philosophy."[213]

Sometimes it must have seemed as though she were reading a book from her own mind. *Nature* is permeated with her enthusiasm, her otherworldliness, her diction. Her prickly on-again, off-again relationship to society forms its very texture. "To go into solitude," Waldo wrote in the book's opening chapter, "a man needs to retire as much from his chamber as from society." But for the masculine pronoun, the sentiment could have been lifted directly from the Almanacks. A bit later, Waldo again transformed one of Mary's central experiences into masculine terms: "But if a man would be alone, let him look at the stars . . . in the heavenly bodies [is] the perpetual presence of the sublime."[214]

It is true that Waldo borrowed from other sources. The chapter on "Idealism" is a rehearsal of Kantian and Coleridgean philosophy. Other pages are shaped by Plato, Wordsworth, and Swedenborg. An important, if unacknowledged, source is his brother Charles, Mary's youngest nephew, who had died of tuberculosis on May 9, 1836, a few months before Waldo completed the book. Yet Mary's contribution to *Nature* is of another magnitude altogether. For years, Waldo had borrowed her language, imagery, and sentiments—always without attribution.[215] Her personality and expressions had turned up in numerous sermons and lectures. But in *Nature* he assimilated her spirit, metabolized the side-angles of her vision, spoke in the discordant clangor of her speech. Her presence in Concord while he worked on the book left an indelible mark, and *Nature*'s patent love of landscape, as well as its pursuit of visionary rapture, is Mary's as much as it is Waldo's—arguably even more. Her presence is so tightly interwoven with the book's aphoristic sentences as to create much of its defining texture.

Nowhere is the congruence between aunt and nephew more apparent than in *Nature*'s most famous passage. One evening in January 1836, while walking through the slush of Concord's streets, Waldo felt suddenly, unaccountably elated. His consciousness seemed to dilate, to expand, to spill out of him and into the night sky, and then gradually to return. "Crossing a bare common," he wrote, "in snow puddles, at twilight, under a clouded sky, without having in my thoughts any occurrence of special good fortune, I have enjoyed a perfect exhilaration. I am glad to the brink of fear... Standing on the bare ground,—my head bathed by the blithe air, and uplifted into infinite space,—all mean egotism vanishes. I become a transparent eye-ball; I am nothing; I see all; the currents of the Universal Being circulate through me; I am part or particle of God... In the tranquil landscape, and especially in the distant line of the horizon, man beholds somewhat as beautiful as his own nature."[216]

The experience echoes a letter Mary had written to him fifteen years earlier, when Waldo was a fresh-scrubbed, dreamy-eyed student just entering Harvard. Mary, still full of hopes for each of her nephews, was in a triumphant mood. "The spirits of inspiration are abroad tonight," she declared. "We love nature—to individuate ourselves in our wildest moods; to partake of her extension and glow with our color and fly on her winds..."[217]

But the "perfect exhilaration" described in Waldo's transparent eyeball passage even more closely reproduces Mary's experience of 1804, when she had stepped outside of the Malden meetinghouse to peer at the stars in rapture. Admittedly, aunt and nephew's imagery are different. Waldo becomes an organ of vision through which universal power flows. Mary dances "to the musick of my own imajanation," embodied in a way that was wholly alien to her nephew. But the underlying experience is the same. Alone beneath the winter skies, giddy with a sense of freedom, of unplumbed depths and possibilities, aunt and nephew, each thirty-one years old at the time of their mutual experiences, had exalted. Each had dared express that exaltation in writing.

None of this prevented Mary from feeling apprehensive. If Waldo had borrowed many of her ideas for his book, he also pushed them in directions she considered too extreme. In an Almanack entry of 1827, for example, Mary marveled at the mysterious movements of the compass needle. "Why do I feel such delight that nature keeps secrets?... more proofs to me of the Author of nature being the Author of reve[lation]. And they excite curiosity w'h never can be sated here."[218] Waldo had read this passage, and in *Nature* he made a similar claim: "Nature never wears a mean appearance. Neither does the wisest man extort, and lose his curiosity by finding out all her perfection."[219]

The difference between the two statements is important. If Mary traces a connection between nature's mystery and God's inscrutable presence, Waldo announces the human capacity to discover "all [nature's] perfection." Despite her imaginative flights, Mary never abandoned her sense that humans were flawed and broken creatures. The Almanacks are filled with abject portraits of her own failures, including her tendency to be judgmental and unkind, to be governed by "bile," drawn too much to the prideful promptings of self. While her theological speculations questioned nearly every aspect of formal Christianity, she never relinquished her belief that humans desperately needed Christ for their redemption. This belief was the result of her experiences as a minister's daughter, an "orphan," a woman.

Waldo, on the other hand, burst with newfound confidence that every person was perfectible, potentially divine. "I see the spectacle of morning from the hill-top over against my house," he wrote in his third chapter on "Genius," "... with emotions which an angel might share."[220] Mary believed quite literally in angels. She believed in the elevation of the soul upon death. Waldo, on the other hand, presumed to say that people were *already* angelic. Heaven was on earth. Beside this offending sentence, she penciled a stern and censorious question mark, almost tearing the paper with the motion. She would have to have a word with her nephew.

12.

Soon after she finished reading *Nature*, she wrote a letter. It was not addressed to Waldo, but to Lydia Jackson Emerson: a woman from Plymouth whom Waldo had married on September 14, 1835. "Some of it is invaluable to the lover of nature," Mary conceded about her nephew's book. "Yet the solitary admirer of the Author's youngest pen little thought that when his plumes were grown he would like some other classical bird set fire his gentle nest."[221] Waldo had abandoned his faith, had rebuked his upbringing. Mary feared he had destroyed the legacy of his ancestors.

To Ann Sargent Gage, her friend in Maine who had recently married, she offered an even more astringent assessment of the book: "tho' poetic," she wrote, "'tis obscure & does the Author no justice."[222] She admitted that she found her nephew's writing beautiful. Its imagery stirred her imagination. But as she put it to her oldest nephew William, she both admired and was annoyed by its tendency "to wonder into strange 'universes' and find idealised people and alas, 'new laws.'"[223]

It was precisely the "new laws" portrayed in *Nature* that soon excited readers. Waldo's book heralded the beginning of a period of staggering creative fertility in American culture. It initiated an epoch of exuberant national expression and social activism that was driven by a desire for transcendence. Within months of the book's publication, Waldo's new house on the Cambridge Turnpike would be populated by dreamers and revolutionaries eager to discuss all sorts of daring concepts. As one visitor wrote at the time, "I find social life in a precious state of fermentation. New ideas are flying, high and low."[224]

This "newness," as it was often called, soon acquired another name. "You ask me what *is* transcendentalism," the novelist Lydia Maria Child wrote several years after Waldo's book was published, "and what do transcendentalists believe? It is a question difficult, nay, impossible, to answer; for the minds so classified are incongruous individuals, without any creed."[225] The transcendentalist movement would always be difficult to categorize, impossible to sum up in just a few words. In part this was because it contained an eclectic mix of theology, philosophy, and literature. It borrowed from German philosophy, English romanticism, and the sacred texts of eastern religion—works many of which were first read and then shared by Mary Moody Emerson.

But transcendentalism was also difficult to categorize because its members were indeed "incongruous individuals"—a loose confederation of men and women who valued independent thought above all else. Nathaniel Hawthorne, who moved to Concord in 1842, described the transcendentalists he encountered there and in Boston as a "variety of queer, strangely dressed, oddly behaved mortals, most of whom took upon themselves to be important agents in the world's destiny..."[226] If any common principle bound them together, according to the transcendentalist minister James Freeman Clarke, it was their mutual dissatisfaction "with the present state of religion, philosophy, and literature." This dissatisfaction expressed itself in a shared "desire for more of LIFE, soul, originality in these great departments of thought."[227]

The same attributes of course applied to Mary Emerson. She had arrived at similar positions three decades earlier. Now, from her refuge in Maine, she followed the developments involving her nephew with sardonic curiosity. About Waldo's writings she observed, "they gather the mists & coruscations of light from Germany and transcendentalism" and then mixed "in the whirl of antagonist principles & views & theories w'h alarm some friends to virtue & encourage others." While she found herself in disagreement with some of his circle's ideas, she allowed herself to hope that "this new school may be a wheel within a wheel moving under the Great Mover to give some apprehension of the relation to Himself that the philosophical could not otherwise so highly attain."[228]

There would be rocky times ahead. In 1837, the year he delivered his famous address on "The American Scholar," Mary quarreled with Waldo about his "high, airy speculations," storming out of his house and promising never to enter it again. (Neither aunt nor nephew revealed precisely what the argument was about, and Mary eventually relented, although she never spent another night in his house.) Brooding in private, Waldo acknowledged his debt to her. "She must always occupy a saint's place in my household," he admitted, "and I have had no hour of poetry or philosophy since I knew these things, in which she does not enter as a genius."[229] Long ago, he had learned to accept and forgive her compulsion to wound the very people she cared most about, knowing she suffered pangs of guilt as soon as she lashed out. "She tramples on the common humanities all day," he observed, "& they rise as ghosts & torment her at night."[230]

These observations appeared in a notebook labeled Tnamurya—an anagram of "Aunt Mary"—into which he copied yet more extracts from Mary's letters and Almanacks. Waldo still considered her the finest writer in Massachusetts. He still valued her penetrating observations of nature and human nature. And in 1836, he began introducing her to members of his growing circle, including an exceptional woman who fulfilled her dream of an educated woman author. Mary first heard of this person from a mutual friend. The woman's "wit, her insight into characters, such that she seems to read them aloud to you as if they were printed books, her wide range of thought & cultivation, the rapidity with which she appropriates all knowledge, joined with the habits of severe & exact mental discipline, (so *very* rare in women.) .... All these things keep me filled with pleased admiration & (true to the nature of genius) constantly inspire me with new life new hope in my own powers, new desires to fulfil the possible in myself."[231]

The woman was Margaret Fuller. Twenty-six years of age, Fuller possessed one thing Mary Emerson deeply envied: a classical education. She had been taught by her father to read at age four. By the time she was six, she was learning Latin. From there, her academic progress grew by leaps and bounds, and when Mary first learned of her, she was already considered the best-read woman in New England.

In 1836, Fuller became a part of Waldo's transcendentalist circle. From then on, a part of each summer she spent in Concord. It was immediately following one of these visits, in September 1839, that she came up with the idea of gathering a group of women to discuss a wide range of learned topics, including "the great questions. What were we born to do? How shall we do it? which so few ever propose to themselves 'till their best years are gone by."[232] Two years later, in 1841, Mary Moody Emerson wrote her nephew Ralph Waldo Emerson to thank him for a gift "borrowed not begged." She was referring to a copy of the transcriptions of Fuller's "Conversations." These had been copied out by the fiancée of Charles Chauncey Emerson, another Concord resident named Elizabeth Hoar.

Mary was sixty-six when she received the Conversations. She still lived in Waterford, Maine. If she was increasingly solitary, she was also, as always, curious about the latest ideas circulating in Boston. She devoured the transcriptions Waldo sent and, as if to give him a taste of his own medicine, hung onto them for a year before writing him to say thanks. She admitted, somewhat surprisingly, that she would have preferred to "hear *practical* questions discussed among these *young* ladies" rather than the philosophical topics that predominated. She was curious to know how the women involved proposed to achieve agency in the world. And she concluded on a characteristic note, managing to praise and damn at the same time, conveying a lifetime of longing and disappointment in one succinct sentence. "The Fuller 'conversations,'" she told Waldo, "are *beautifull* (tho' they are open to ridicule)."[233]

2

Elizabeth Palmer Peabody at 13 West Street

1.

Soon after her nephew Waldo abandoned the pulpit in 1832, Mary Emerson received a letter from an unusually ambitious young schoolteacher in Boston. The teacher was not yet thirty, but she had already written a series of history books, a grammar manual, and an unpublished six-part treatise on the Hebrew scriptures. Mary Emerson immediately recognized "a gifted mind." She applauded the young woman's determination in "Becoming an Autheress" and briefly considered whether her talented correspondent might make a suitable match for the recently widowed Waldo.[1]

The writer of the letter was named Elizabeth Palmer Peabody. She lived in a four-story boardinghouse on the edge of Beacon Hill with her sister, Mary Tyler Peabody. (A third sister, Sophia, was then living with their parents in nearby

Salem.) The two oldest Peabody sisters lived in genteel poverty. Each owned a single dress, and in the evenings they carefully rinsed their white embroidered collars to preserve some semblance of tidiness. Mary Peabody was frequently referred to as the most beautiful Peabody sister. She was also somewhat more conventional. She worried about money. At night, she dreamed of silver coins discovered by the side of the road, enough to pay off the Peabody family's debts.

Elizabeth was consumed by other matters. She lay "extended full length on the floor," Mary told a friend, "... studying astronomy at the top of her voice and ever and anon calling my attention to some beautiful explanation of the constellations."[2] When she was not in the classroom or studying the heavens, Elizabeth wrote flattering, gushing letters to her idol, the poet William Wordsworth. She also brushed up on ancient history, or explored the new pseudo-science of phrenology, or practiced her Greek. On Sunday afternoons, she attended tea parties at the home of Boston's leading Unitarian minister, William Ellery Channing, where she dominated the conversation with a breathless torrent of talk.

She was a prodigy. Before the age of twenty-five, she had acquired a reading knowledge of at least ten languages and was said to speak every day in Greek, Latin, Hebrew, and Sanskrit.[3] In 1830, when she was twenty-six, she published an anonymous translation of the French jurist and philosopher Joseph de Gerando's *Self-Education: Or the Means and Art of Moral Progress*. The book reads like a mission statement for the emerging transcendentalist philosophy in America. "The fundamental truth," de Gerando proclaimed, "which solves all the problems that agitate the youthful heart, and trouble the growing reason ... is this:—*the life of man is in reality but one continued education, the end of which is, to make himself perfect.*"[4]

Elizabeth Peabody decided to write Mary Emerson because she had heard the older woman was a fount of new and exciting ideas. She had also heard of Mary's legendary disregard for dress. All her life Elizabeth had been told to mind her appearance, reminded that women were supposed to be lovely, silent figures in the romantic landscape of the male imagination. Mary Emerson's disdain for these strictures—her uncompromising intellectuality, her eccentric attire—were especially appealing to a young woman whose hair was perpetually unkempt and whose mother admonished her well into adulthood about her disheveled clothing. She admired Mary Emerson's utter indifference to convention, her freedom to "compete with life like a girl of fifteen who knows herself sovereign and can afford to play with *All*."[5]

According to Mary, Elizabeth's first letter was crammed with "the natural complainings of genius and disappointed aspirations—w'h in this exile state attend talents & virtue as the most beautiful body has it's shadow."[6] Mary sympathized with its sender. In a characteristically impulsive move, she decided to travel to Boston to pay her new acquaintance a visit. This was in December, the same month Waldo was preparing to leave for Europe. Perhaps Mary hoped to say farewell to her heretical nephew. At any rate, she failed to tell Elizabeth she was coming, arriving one morning unannounced at her boardinghouse in Beacon Hill.

Elizabeth liked nothing better than to talk. She conversed freely and easily—to anyone and everyone—never pausing to edit her thoughts. "I wish I had the blessed faculty of not speaking until I am aware of what I am going to say," she declared, "but when I am among people and a subject arises in which I have interest, the impetuosity of my feeling seeks expression in words and I endeavor to say everything in a breath, beginning at the end, or dash into the middle."[7] Conversation, for Elizabeth, was the source of thought. Speaking with a responsive friend fledged new ideas, it lifted her spirits by bringing her into contact with others. Once, when she was eleven, she found herself cast into an inexplicable depression. She rallied, though, after "four days continual conversation" with a local minister.[8]

Mary Emerson had come to Boston, Elizabeth later recalled, "to see me, and wanted to know what I thought and felt about God[,] the theme of all her thoughts." Normally, Elizabeth would have had plenty to say on the subject. But as it turned out, that day she had to teach in the private academy she ran with her sister. There was no time for conversation with her unannounced guest. To keep her occupied, she gave Mary "a journal of thoughts I fitfully kept."[9]

Sharing journals was a common activity in the first half of the nineteenth century, especially among women. Mary had distributed her Almanacks to various friends, believing it offered them a picture of her restless mind. Commonplace books—journals filled with the extracts of one's reading—were likewise circulated among friends. (The Almanacks also served this function: "This holiday of the soul I begin the 1st vol. of Cousin," Mary wrote, "get scraps & write them down, as the buzzing fly sips from the rich floweret.")[10] Exchanging journals and other manuscripts expanded the reach of women's writing, widened its audience. But it also implied a certain level of trust. By handing over her journal, Elizabeth was sharing some of her most private writing, in the process launching an intimate conversation with a near stranger.

Scattered among the untidy, ink-splotched pages of Elizabeth's journal, Mary Emerson found an essay the young woman had written seven years earlier, in 1826, during a particularly tumultuous period of her life. The essay no longer exists, but Elizabeth's summary of it does. Her description provides a glimpse into some of her wide-ranging interests. It was, she said, a "very free paraphrase of the Gospel of St. John," translated from the original Greek and concerned with the verses that start: *In the beginning was the Word, and the Word was with God, and the Word was God.*

Elizabeth wanted to know exactly what was meant by "Word"—or Logos, as it was in the original Greek. The question still preoccupies biblical scholars. As an adolescent Elizabeth had studied the work of a sixteenth-century theologian, Nathaniel Lardner, entitled *A Letter Written … Concerning the Question, Whether the* LOGOS *supplied the Place of an human Soul in the Person of* JESUS CHRIST.

In that book Lardner argued that Logos was the embodiment of God's wisdom and had been received only once in human history—by Jesus. Elizabeth disagreed. She "translated the word Logos into 'moral truth-speaking,'" meaning any speech act that flowed from the intuition of God's goodness.[11] Her interpretation differed from Lardner in a crucial way: divine intuition was available to *all* people, not just Jesus. Elizabeth believed God had instilled in everyone the capacity to experience the truth of divine inspiration.

While Elizabeth taught schoolchildren, Mary Emerson read her essay. She was transfixed. Elizabeth's writing contained insights much like the ones at which she had arrived at Elm Vale in Maine. It was reminiscent of the rapturous passages she scrawled in her Almanacks. (In 1826, the same year as Elizabeth's essay, she had exulted in her intuitive sense of God: "Great Author of existence.... too grand to realise...if it must pass the ordeal of analysis.")[12] Elizabeth's writing even bore a family resemblance to the argument Mary had made years ago in the pages of her brother's *Monthly Review*—that the imagination was a form of divine knowledge available to women at least as much as to men.

Yet if its ideas were familiar, Elizabeth's essay was radically different in presentation. Mary's Almanacks were passionate and improvisatory—organic, in Coleridge's terms. Elizabeth's essay was marked by sturdy reasoning and a deep, systematic learning. It could have been written by a talented Harvard graduate or a theologian at the Divinity School. This impressed Mary, who frequently regretted the haphazard nature of her learning. In fact, she was so taken with her new friend's essay that she did the only thing she could think to do: she sent it to her nephew Waldo.

2.

To understand the complicated bundle of energy that was Elizabeth Peabody, you first have to know something about her mother. Eliza Palmer Peabody, as she was called, believed the world would be better off with women in charge (figure 17). She also believed if this was not immediately practicable, the work might at least commence in the newly formed United States.

As a girl, Eliza had been solemn, precocious, passionate about reading. She liked to sprawl out on the polished mahogany floor of her grandfather's study and recite from his enormous folio of Shakespeare's plays.[13] "I have known her frequently," said one family member, "when standing at the wheel—set down on the stairs—take out her pen—and write an ode."[14] Several of these odes were published in the *Haverhill Federal Journal*, a newspaper produced thirty-five miles north of Boston. This was in the last year of the eighteenth century, some four or five years before her oldest daughter Elizabeth was born. The poems appeared under the pseudonym "Belinda," and if a common theme runs through them, it is

Figure 17. Sketch of Eliza Palmer Peabody by Sophia Peabody Hawthorne.

outrage at the destiny of women. In one long poem entitled "The True Woman," for instance, Eliza defended her sex against the mischaracterizations that appeared so frequently in epistolary novels and instructive essays written by men:

> This all their writings speak
> That women, to be *lovely*, must be *weak!*[15]

Eliza Palmer was certainly no weakling. She was decided in her opinions, fearless in stating them. Her children—three daughters and three sons—later attested to her "peculiar fortitude and self dependence," a "strength & firmness united with delicacy which never failed her."[16] According to her youngest daughter, Sophia, no other woman she knew possessed "such a noble pride."[17]

Like Mary Moody Emerson, a near contemporary, she had been the child of revolutionaries. In 1773, her father smudged his face with paint and dumped chests of tea into Boston Harbor. And her grandfather, Joseph Palmer, became a Revolutionary War general. He fought in the Battle of Lexington, six miles from Concord, and later led a failed attack on British forces in Newport, Rhode Island. But his greatest glory occurred before the war, when he made a fortune manufacturing glass and salt and expensive tapered candles from the oil of sperm whales. Joseph Palmer's estate in Quincy, Massachusetts was designed to resemble a country house in England, with turrets and slate shingles and winding pathways through an emerald, well-kept lawn. Among the treasures at "Friendship Hall," as he called the place, was an orchard, "a fruit garden, a nursery of trees, a large poultry yard," and an especially fine library over which hung a varnished portrait of the estate's owner, executed by the foremost American artist of the era, John Singleton Copley.[18]

Revolution proved ruinous to the Palmer family. Joseph's "property poured out like water during the first years of the war," according to a relative.[19] By the time Eliza was sixteen, the family was so destitute that she was forced to enter one of the very few professions then open to studious young women—teaching (plate 3). In many ways, it was the perfect occupation for her. Educators shape the future, and Eliza Palmer firmly believed the future needed shaping. In a series of private academies, or "dame schools," she taught grammar and spelling and history to girls and young women. She especially delighted in stories from classical Greece and Rome, as well as historical accounts from the Old Testament. But the lesson she worked hardest to impress upon her pupils was that women were intended to play a vital role in the creation of the young republic. As her oldest daughter later said, the "idea of the paramount importance of woman to American civilization was with her a governing principle, and she wished to impart it to other women."[20]

While teaching in New Hampshire she met another young educator named Nathaniel Peabody. Nathaniel was the oldest son of an illiterate farmer from nearby Hillsborough County, in the southern part of the state. He was short and stooped—the world would always seem a burden to him—but he excelled in Latin.

In the single most audacious undertaking of his life, he abandoned the rock-strewn soil of his father's farm and traveled fifty-six miles north, where he attended Dartmouth College and where his fellow students thought he possessed "something original in his genius."[21] His greatest triumph occurred when he was elected to Phi Beta Kappa.

Eliza was smitten. "I beheld you as I should one of the planets in the canopy of heaven," she wrote Nathaniel in February 1800, shortly after their first meeting. A few weeks later she declared "the decided preference my heart instantly felt for you." In reply to one of his letters, she confessed her deeply held conviction that "the fate of our Country is in some degree dependant, on the education of its females—a subject upon which I am almost enthusiastic."[22] To reinforce her point, she sent him one of her published poems, a blistering ode in iambic pentameter that proclaimed the boundless scope of female talent and belittled the notion that a woman's sole domain was her heart:

> Oft is my soul with indignation fir'd
> At sentiments by half the world admir'd.
> Has not each writer, and each poet strove
> To prove, that all our end and aim, is love?[23]

Nathaniel did not immediately respond to this letter. Perhaps he was busy with classes at Dartmouth. Perhaps he harbored second thoughts about a woman with such decided, even vociferous, opinions. Perhaps he sensed just how ill-prepared he was to care for a wife and a burgeoning family. At any rate, Eliza immediately fired another salvo: "In writing again so soon," she admitted, "I may perhaps overleap the bounds, custom has prescribed for our sex." She assured him she *was* capable of lofty, enduring love: "To endeavour to pursuade the generality of mankind, that a woman, can feel the ennobling passion of love in all its purity, without its weakness," she wrote, "... would be to out Quixote Cervantes. Yet I am confident that a rightly educated woman is capable of so much greatness of mind. Are you of my opinion, my friend?"[24]

This time, Nathaniel answered. His letter has been lost—Nathaniel's letters seldom seemed worth preserving—but he must have responded in the affirmative, for soon Eliza was setting a date for their wedding. She made all the arrangements herself, reassuring her timid lover that she was "content to begin *life* in plain economical manner." Despite her grandfather's former affluence, she found no "happiness in possessing much wealth" nor "in having a finer house than their neighbours." The only thing she required was to be "employed in the humbler but respectable circle of domestic duties, with those I love around me."[25]

The wedding took place on November 2, 1802, in the village of Billerica, Massachusetts, where Nathaniel had apprenticed himself to a physician named Dr. Pemberton. During the first year or so of marriage, he accompanied the aging doctor in a wagon, clattering up and down High Street and sometimes along the nearby cranberry bogs, learning to treat malignant fevers and the flux, to ease the symptoms of dropsy and croup. He set bones. He bled and blistered patients. He mixed plasters and poultices. To those afflicted with whooping cough, he administered the preferred medicine of the time: arsenic.

While he would never be a successful doctor, the training he received in Billerica proved invaluable, because Eliza soon discovered she was pregnant. Over the years, she would give birth to seven children, six of whom survived and all of whom were delivered by Nathaniel. The growing Peabody family would spend its early years in a series of rented houses. After Billerica, they moved to nearby Cambridgeport, where Nathaniel attended classes on human anatomy and *materia medica* at Harvard. (Timothy and Sarah Margarett Fuller soon began their married life in the same Boston suburb; their oldest daughter, Margaret, was born there in 1810.) Then, in 1806, Nathaniel opened a medical practice in Lynn, about fifteen miles away. When this proved unprofitable, he uprooted the family and relocated yet again, this time farther north, in the old seaport town of Salem.

To make ends meet, Eliza returned to teaching. She opened an academy for young girls on the ground floor of their rented home, providing board for an extra charge and cooking the meals herself when she could neither find nor afford a servant. She was capitalizing on a new trend in American education. Academies for young women had begun to sprout up all over the country, their formation encouraged by the idea that students would one day instruct their own sons and daughters in the production of rational citizens. (This was the same argument Eliza had been making since she was a teenager.) While some of the new institutions focused more on embroidery and etiquette than mathematics, they nevertheless created new possibilities for female education. Eliza soon found that by teaching she could earn an income far more reliable and often larger than Nathaniel's.

But running a school wasn't easy. The first decade of the Peabody's marriage proved particularly difficult. Eliza was either pregnant or nursing much of the time. The sobs of children filled her ears, and she was often busy washing clothes, dishes, dirty faces. Then there was spelling and grammar to correct. At some point, amid the chaos of domestic life, she managed to write her own history textbook, believing there was nothing of the sort suitable for young girls.

A cough she had first developed while teaching in New Hampshire grew steadily worse. She treated it—almost certainly at Nathaniel's suggestion—with opium, a drug that was legal at the time and easily obtainable. The narcotic produced fierce headaches, making it difficult for Eliza to concentrate. Over time the drug contributed to her darkening spirits. Family and friends observed her despair. Nat, the Peabody's oldest son, believed his father never fully appreciated "the length, breadth and depth" of his mother's character, adding that every one of the "family misfortunes were keenly felt by her."[26] A friend described Eliza's smile as "like the shining...of an angel's face from behind a mask where brave struggles with heavy sorrows had left imprints of mortality."[27] To her oldest daughter she would one day acknowledge her feelings of powerlessness: "I long for means and power,...but I wear peticoats and can never be Governor...nor alderman Judge or jury, senator or representative."[28]

To console herself, she practiced Christian resignation. "I may as well be quiet," she added, "content with intreating the Father of all mercies."[29] And she directed her considerable ambitions toward her oldest daughter, her namesake, Elizabeth Palmer Peabody.

3.

She came into the world crying and red-faced in a rented house in Billerica, Massachusetts on May 16, 1804—"nursed," in her mother's words, "while my heart was at rest, and my hopes *all* of happiness."[30] From the beginning, the infant girl was attended with love and care. The young mother believed she saw the glimmerings of genius in her firstborn, and she determined to summon it forth. Elizabeth Peabody once remarked that "any other mother I have ever known would have been a calamity," and toward the end of her life, Eliza returned the compliment.[31] Addressing her oldest daughter with exquisite tenderness, she called her, "My own Elizabeth, my first, my treasured one."[32]

Before the infant could walk, her mother set about educating her. Eliza read to the child from the Bible and Spenser's *Fairie Queene*. She read articles in old copies of *The Spectator* and the *Edinburgh Review*. She told the little girl that the blood of Puritans and revolutionaries pulsed through her veins, that she was fortunate to live in a boundless country of unparalleled promise. God, she said, had provided women with "the same immortal mind" as men.[33] Above all she taught her that learning to think was the best gift a parent could bestow upon a child.

Years later, Elizabeth recalled the unconventional education she had received from her mother. She had scarcely learned to read when Eliza began passing along the didactic novels of Maria Edgeworth, "who broke the way of authorship for women." Eliza also assigned her daughter an essay arguing that "the higher interests of society must be cared for by women; that is, literature, art, and all the virtues and graces that make society progressive spiritually, morally, and intellectually."[34] She stocked her daughter's "mind with images of kind, heroic, and thoroughly high-principled people," most of whom just happened to be women: Madame Dacier, the seventeenth-century French scholar and translator of the *Iliad* and *Odyssey*; Mary Somerville, the Scottish science writer; the English social reformer Elizabeth Montagu; and Madame de Staël.[35]

Eliza also encouraged her daughter to seek knowledge wherever she could. The girl was barely five when she made the acquaintance of Nathaniel Bowditch, a self-taught scientist living in Salem, who would one day become the first professor of mathematics at Harvard. (London's Royal Society made Bowditch an honorary member in 1818.) Elizabeth walked to his three-story clapboard house and discussed geography with the thirty-two-year-old polymath. Bowditch even allowed her to peer through his portable brass telescope one evening, explaining that the bright constellations wheeling overhead followed a perfect mathematical order. Thus began a pattern of Elizabeth forming intellectual attachments to men who had attended college and pursued careers beyond her reach.

Several times a week, she entered her father's study to learn Latin from Nathaniel's battered copy of *Lily's Latin Grammar*. She was a sponge, absorbing grammatical declensions and the stern accounts of Thucydides as easily as she absorbed novels about women beset by temptation and vice. By age twelve, she was so intellectually advanced that her mother asked her to instruct her two younger sisters. Mary, born in 1806, was to become Elizabeth's closest companion for the next eighty years. Sophia, born three years later, was regarded as the family's artistic genius. The three sisters were born in such rapid succession that their mother, Eliza, thought they were eternally linked "in heart, in opinions and in talents."[36]

They were inseparable as children—so close that when Eliza spoke of the family's Puritan *ancestors*, Elizabeth heard the words *Ann Sisters*. She conjured a mental picture of women in white robes, all named Ann, kneeling "down in the snow under the trees of the forest" to thank God for their safe passage across the Atlantic. As Elizabeth recalled, "my mother took pains to tell me[,] . . . they built a schoolhouse where all the children were to be taught to read the Bible."[37]

There were also three brothers—Nathaniel, Wellington, and George, each of whom displayed their father's singular lack "of get-along-ity," as Elizabeth called it. She spent far less time instructing the boys, who had access to formal education, introducing her sisters to "History and Literature, beginning with the English, but extending backwards, to the history and translated literature of Greece and Roman."[38] In a manner they must have found imperious, she monitored Mary and Sophia's moral development, insisting "that life was a serious thing—& that character was of little importance unless the groundwork & foundation was seriousness." (She was barely in her teens when she wrote this.)

Elizabeth also directed their extracurricular reading. She encouraged her sisters to study the eighteenth-century nature poet William Cowper (the same poet cherished by Mary Moody Emerson) as well as the works of Madame de Staël, especially her best-known novel, *Corinne* (also cherished by Mary Moody Emerson). Elizabeth considered *Corinne* valuable less for its exquisite depictions of Italy than for its positive image of womanhood. The book's eponymous heroine, a gifted conversationalist, was able to connect in her speeches "all that is natural, fanciful, just, sublime, powerful and sweet, [and] to vary the mental banquet every instant." The book proved beyond dispute the same lesson Elizabeth's mother had instilled in her, that "mind has no sex."[39]

At fifteen, Elizabeth was better educated than most young men. Her immersive reading in theology, begun at age twelve, was as rigorous as the curriculum at Harvard's Divinity School. Her fluency in languages surpassed that of many teachers. She had cut a large swath through ancient Greek and Roman literature, had devoured Shakespeare and Milton and much of the eighteenth-century canon of English writers. She was also something of an expert in American history, a discipline then in its earliest stages. In almost every respect, she exemplified her mother's belief that women needed only a well-rounded education to contribute meaningfully to American society.

The only problem was that intellectual women were not particularly valued or respected. A woman who preferred intellectual work to the duties assigned her sphere was deemed "unfeminine," "manly." "No sensible woman will suffer her intellectual pursuits to clash with her domestic duties," wrote a critic in 1840. Another asserted that "the greater the intellectual force, the greater and more fatal the errors in which women fall...."[40] Both of these statements were made by women, and it was in much the same spirit that Eliza wrote her oldest daughter when she was fifteen and away visiting relatives in Boston.

"You have arrived at the most interesting, most perilous age, a young woman can reach," Eliza began. Then she warned her daughter to resist the temptation of displaying her education. "Minds cast in a superior mould will command your sympathy and affection," Eliza wrote, "and the low and groveling you will feel anxious to raise and improve." It was important to resist both impulses. "Maintain your own opinion with the modesty of youth. Begin, even now, more carefully to guard yourself that in conversation you need not wound the pride or sensibility of others."[41]

Eliza was forty-one when she wrote this letter. She was also pregnant with her seventh child. A sense of foreboding clutched her heart—she was convinced she would not survive another delivery. Her letter was therefore a deathbed warning: a plea for her oldest child to avoid making the same mistakes she had made. She had come to the dismal conclusion that if the world was controlled by men, women were better off concealing their intelligence.

By some accounts, Elizabeth was back home in time to help her father deliver Eliza's last child, a baby girl. (The mother's fears were misplaced; it was the infant who died, shortly after its birth.) If so, the experience must have underscored the lesson she took from her mother's letter. For fifteen years, Elizabeth had watched her mother's intellectual life threatened and all but destroyed by marriage and family life. She had witnessed the shriveling of her mother's autonomy, the burial of her soul and the toll exacted by nearly continuous pregnancies. She decided therefore not to conceal her learning, as Eliza had counseled. Instead, she would renounce marriage.

4.

Aside from a silhouette that depicts a ruffled sleeve, a book in her outstretched hand, and a bonnet that obscures all but her reading glasses, no image of the young Elizabeth Peabody exists. Verbal descriptions abound, however. Elizabeth's childhood friend, Anna Q. T. Parsons, described "a slight, lovely young girl of seventeen or eighteen, with an abundance of fair hair, her face all aglow."[42] A male acquaintance from Salem's boys' academy remembered her lustrous intelligence and changeable features. She was "fair and bright-cheeked, with brown hair neatly pasted on her forehead," the young man recalled, adding "how good and pure and gentle, and even beautiful, she looked, with the soul shining all through her and the light pouring all over her face and figure as she moved."[43]

She loved to talk. Her journals capture some of the urgent, impulsive quality of her speech, though none of its angular New England accent. At the same time, as a young person she often felt as though no one was listening. "As I grew older," she recalled, "I felt my mind grow more solitary. Living voice did not come in contact with it, and when I spoke, nobody seemed to know what I meant." To "relieve… [the] oppressive feelings" of loneliness, she enrolled in dancing school, but learning the cotillon did nothing to allay her isolation. She felt buffeted by "unregulated feeling."[44]

Part of the problem was her education. She had been taught by her mother to a standard well beyond that of most young women. She had also been instructed to value her intelligence. "[T]he idea that women were less capable of the highest education in literature and science…," she once recalled, "truly never entered my mind."[45] Yet with very few exceptions, society provided almost no outlets for a woman with her training. And to complicate matters, as she watched her friends enter courtship and marriage, she made an uncomfortable discovery: she was not entirely immune to romantic longing. "I can get food for my mind in books—in observation of life—in my own reflections," she said, "but food for my heart must come direct from others—& *my heart* always craved more than my mind."[46]

In 1822—the year she turned eighteen—Elizabeth moved to Boston (figure 18). Eliza wanted her to open a school in the city to help earn enough "money to educate at College my brothers."[47] She had already spent several years teaching in her mother's private academy, where she assumed more and more responsibilities as her mother grew increasingly frail. There she developed a pedagogical style of her own that relied less on rote learning than on discussion with her students. Early that spring, she traveled twenty-five miles south to the city, where she roomed in the house of relatives in Beacon Hill. Her fifth-floor chamber overlooked slate roofs and dusty elms and the cobbled Boston streets that seemed to twist and turn for no apparent reason. In the distance, the city's harbor glimmered in the sun, its wharves a thicket of masts and riggings and sails.

Figure 18. Boston in 1825.

Elizabeth arrived in Boston just as the city was becoming a major cultural center. During the 1820s, new museums and art galleries opened on an almost monthly basis. The *North American Review*, founded by members of William Emerson's Anthology Club, had become the preeminent literary journal in the nation, and the Athenaeum, an independent library and reading room also founded by members of the Anthology Club, had recently moved to a spacious mansion on Pearl Street. Soon it would add a lecture hall and gallery. Much of this activity was funded by families who had made their fortunes from shipping, textiles, and manufacturing. They dreamed of transforming the provincial city founded by the Puritans into an artistic and cultural hub that would rival the capitals of Europe.

Elizabeth immediately fell in love with the place. She felt at home amid the hurried tramp of pedestrians, the rattle of carriages, the discordant music of human activity. In this urban setting, she also discovered a new talent: making friends. Within weeks, she had joined a group of young women who attended lectures given by George Ticknor, the newly appointed Harvard professor of French and Spanish languages and literatures. She was invited to tour Harvard's library—a memorable occasion for a bookish young woman.

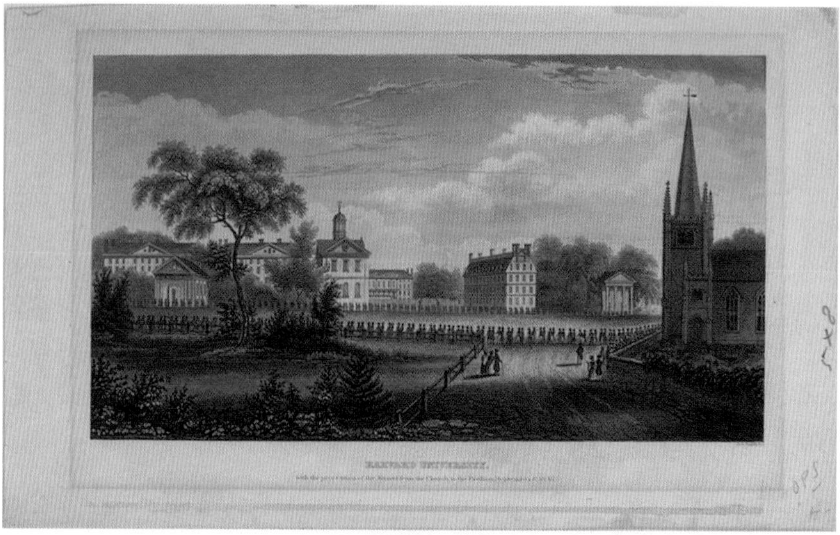

Figure 19. Harvard in 1835.

In Cambridge, a drowsy suburban town dominated by Harvard's campus, academic families provided "a constant stimulus of improvement" (figure 19). They also offered Elizabeth fierce intellectual competition. She soon learned that "even if you do know today more than some others, they may sit up all night and put you down tomorrow." To her delight, this competitiveness was limited not only to male scholars—women, too, strove to acquire learning. As she delightedly told a friend, none of them cared a thing about "dress and visiting."[48]

In late spring, she undertook private Greek lessons with a recent Harvard graduate whose name was Waldo Emerson. He was a year older than Elizabeth, and in several months would make his inauspicious debut as an author by publishing "Thoughts on the Religion of the Middle Ages" in the *Christian Disciple and Theological Review*. It was difficult to tell who was the more reticent—Waldo or Elizabeth. They sat "opposite each other at the study table," she remembered, "not lifting our eyes from our books—I reciting the poems of the 'Graeca Majora,' and he commenting and elucidating in the most instructive manner." When the lessons concluded, the young man refused payment, explaining he could take no money from someone who knew as much Greek as he did.[49]

In Cambridge, Elizabeth also met Washington Allston, at the time the most famous painter in America (figure 20). Allston was Southern-born, Harvard educated. He had lived in Europe for nearly two decades. He had first studied painting in Italy, then settled in England, where he commenced a lifelong friendship with the poet Samuel Taylor Coleridge. In 1818, following the death of his wife, he returned to Cambridge, producing a series of bold landscapes with glowering

Figure 20. Washington Allston.

cloudbanks and other atmospheric effects that heralded something new in painting. These works focused less on objective depictions of nature than on the artist's emotional response to the landscape—more on *reason* than *understanding*, in the language of his friend Coleridge. They were among the earliest examples of what would come to be known as American Romantic painting.

Allston was a brilliant talker. Many years later, Elizabeth recorded their "immortal conversations" in a book, chronicling the exuberant flow of Allston's speech, which "had the beauty of a work of art, though it was always the unaffected and spontaneous outflow of a nature in which no faculty had been left to grow rank, but all were cultivated harmoniously and faithfully."[50] Allston in turn recognized Elizabeth's remarkable talk, the way she spoke breathlessly, hurriedly, jumping from idea to idea in associative leaps and bounds. Before long, others took notice of her conversational ability; one admirer recalled the "rare and exquisite grace of her expression," while another likened Elizabeth's insatiable talk to a natural force, something akin to "the rapids above Lake Eerie, and the opening of the Gulf of the St. Lawrence."[51]

Despite making new friends, Elizabeth had difficulty attracting students to her Beacon Hill academy. The market was glutted with educational institutions, and despite her hard work, she barely supported herself, let alone managed to pay for her brothers' college tuition. After a year in Boston, she took a teaching position in Maine, where she soon found herself "walking—riding—drawing—reading—studying—teaching—all delightful employments" in the home of a wealthy landowner who had hired her to tutor his children.[52] But she remained homesick for Boston. She missed its busy streets, its museums, and lectures and "feasts of reason"—the term she used to describe suppers where conversation aspired to an artform. In 1825, when she was twenty-one, she moved back to the city, this time bringing her sister Mary. The two opened the first of several schools together in the nearby suburb of Brookline.

The move was shadowed by sorrow, however. Nearly four years earlier, when she was seventeen and still living in Salem, Elizabeth had met a pensive divinity student named Isaac Lyman Buckminster. Lyman was the youngest son of an illustrious ministerial family. His older brother, Joseph Stevens Buckminster, had been a member of William Emerson's Anthology Club, a brilliant scholar whose translations of the German "higher criticism" had inspired a generation of Unitarian ministers. Joseph reached the peak of his meteoric career when he delivered Harvard's annual Phi Beta Kappa oration in 1810. The following year he gave the funeral oration for William Emerson. (Mary Moody Emerson sat in attendance.) But in 1812, soon after his twenty-eighth birthday, he died from an epileptic seizure.

Lyman, not nearly as talented as his older brother, more closely resembled his father, the Reverend Joseph Buckminster, Sr., who was a popular minister but prone to extreme mood swings. Every few years, the senior Buckminster plunged into black depressions that left him disabled. Lyman, too, was subject to fits of melancholy, especially concerning his prospects as a minister. But in 1822, at age twenty-five, having just graduated from Harvard's Divinity School, he took the momentous step of proposing to Elizabeth Peabody.

She declined, having already made up her mind never to marry. Yet she must have been tempted. "I *know* what the feeling of *love* is," she later confessed, "for I have been sought and all but *won*."[53] Her refusal produced tension in the Peabody family, her brother Nat bitterly reminding her that "perhaps if you had been married when you had the opportunity, the fortunes of... our family would have been different[,] perhaps prosperous, and I believe it was as much your duty to have been married when you could, as to have toiled for your own and other's subsistence by your personal labors in a single state, unless indeed you preferred a single state."[54]

The point, of course, was that Elizabeth *did* prefer a single state. A marriage proposal from the scion of an intellectual family of ministers was certainly flattering, but she had no desire to repeat the mistakes of her mother—to sacrifice the life she imagined for herself to the endless cares of childrearing. Soon after Lyman's proposal, she moved to Boston, thriving within the city's intellectual community, involved in a new project to write textbooks and translations for her students. She now dreamed of one day writing a work of enduring value, a novel, much like her hero Madame de Staël.

Lyman Buckminster continued to hover in the background. In late 1822 he and Elizabeth attended, separately, a dinner party in Cambridge, the jilted lover appearing "very melancholy."[55] The next morning a group of young people, including Elizabeth and Lyman, walked to Boston to hear the Reverend William Ellery Channing preach. Then, she left Boston for Maine, where the complete absence of his name in her correspondence suggests that she considered the matter closed.

During her absence, Lyman grew increasingly despondent. Plagued by thoughts of persecution, he was convinced that "his friends and the publick expected from him the exhibition of talents and devotion equal to those of his brother." According to his older sister, he had become "deranged."[56] Compounding this black mood was his difficulty securing a ministerial position. With few prospects in Boston, he traveled to nearby Norton, Massachusetts, a rural enclave south of the city, where he assisted the Reverend Pitt Clarke at the First Congregational Church. He had been there only a short time when, one winter morning in January 1825, he stepped outside of Clarke's white clapboard house, trudged into the bare woods that bordered the rear of the property, and placed a pistol in his mouth. His body was found later that day.

When exactly Elizabeth learned of the tragedy is unclear. She returned from Maine in May 1825, four months after Lyman's death, to open the new school in Brookline with her sister Mary. Her correspondence, normally so voluble and frank, is silent on the topic. But nine years later she finally admitted the "horrid feelings" that had washed over her at the time, admitting that it still pained her to recall how "poor L.B. found his way in such a horrid way out of the world." Although she tried to console herself with the knowledge that he "was not sound-minded nor well-principled," she was plagued by a sense of guilt. Lyman's death continued to press "like a dead weight on my heart."[57]

5.

Autumn, 1825. From out of the gloom came a voice. Elizabeth had recently begun to attend the Federal Street Church to hear the celebrated Unitarian minister, William Ellery Channing, whose preaching somehow managed to calm her (figure 21). The church was tall and angular and painted white. Channing was

Figure 21. William Ellery Channing.

short and angular and eloquent. His congregation adored his rich baritone and bold ideas, and Elizabeth, a new convert, walked six miles each Sunday, from Brookline to Boston, to hear him instruct his flock.

She had first met Channing as a child. Her mother had taken her to see the young preacher at the North Church, in Salem, where he was temporarily filling the pulpit. ("I must go, and take Elizabeth," Eliza declared, "because it takes genius to reach children.")[58] Six years later, in 1817, Elizabeth heard Channing deliver another sermon in Boston. Afterward, she was invited to join a conversation circle for the women of the Federal Street Church, the same "Vestry group" Mary Moody Emerson attend several years later (figure 22). The women were supposed to discuss the story of Jesus's baptism, but Channing was the only one who said a word. The others were awestruck by their minister. Elizabeth followed their example, saying nothing, but when the meeting was over, she stayed behind for a private conversation with Channing. As he later described it, "a child ran into my arms and poured out her whole heart in utter confidence of my sympathy!"[59]

Channing was famous for provoking such reactions. At forty-four, he was an unprepossessing figure, standing exactly five feet high and weighing one hundred

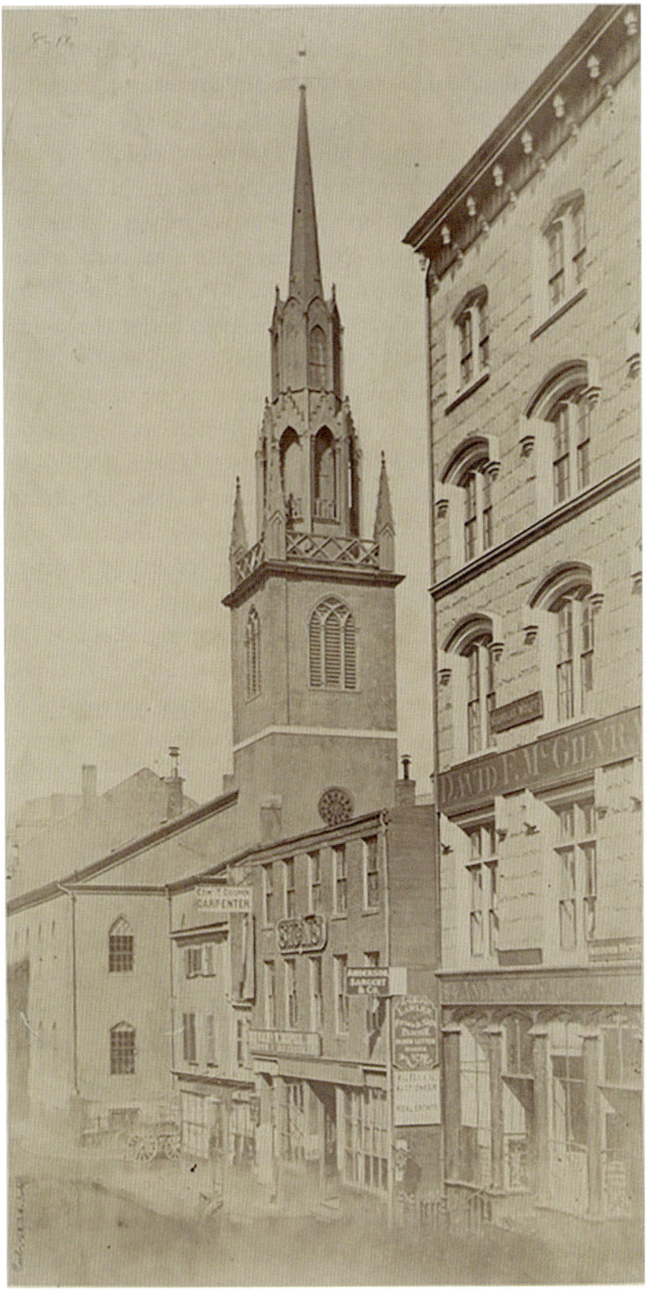

Figure 22. The Federal Street church.

pounds. He was sick with tuberculosis. His portrait, painted by his brother-in-law Washington Allston, reveals a delicate, childlike face dominated by huge blue eyes that shine forth like candle flames. It was precisely this winsome countenance that encouraged confessions and confidences among his parishioners.

In 1825, still distraught over the death of Lyman Buckminster, Elizabeth found herself inexorably drawn to Channing's preaching. She arrived at the Federal Street Church each Sunday, early enough to study the way he stepped up to the pulpit, "with rapid, nervous motions," and "then slowly lifting his large, remarkable eyes with an expression of 'seeing something,' began to read the devotional hymn."[60] When he finished preaching, she walked the six miles back to her rented room in Brookline and wrote down as much of his sermon as she could remember.

On this Sunday morning in October, she had traveled through a "cold damp smoky fog" to hear Channing—only to learn he would not be preaching. She sat through the service, disappointed, then joined friends for a ride through Boston, returning to the church in time for the afternoon service. But Channing didn't preach this time, either. With a friend she walked through the dense, milky fog that still covered Boston Common. Their conversation rose and fell, disembodied in the haze. Then, save for the light tapping of footsteps, all was silent. A deep, sonorous voice sounded, and Channing materialized from the fog. "His voice so unexpectedly coming upon me," Elizabeth recalled nearly sixty years later, "fluttered me to my very hearts core... [its] thrilling tones vibrated in my ear and soul."[61] Channing invited the two young women to continue their discussion at his home on Mt. Vernon Street, where he lived with his wife Ruth and their children.

That afternoon, it was mainly Elizabeth and Channing who talked. They discussed the tendency of education to prepare young people for worldly gain instead of true religious feeling. They spoke of the spiritual wholesomeness of primitive peoples. They touched on "the mercenary calculations in the relations of marriage & parentage." (Elizabeth may have been thinking of Lyman Buckminster.) Time passed with dreamy quickness. At some point, she declared her hope that one day "our new young country" might provide a "shared equality for all."[62] She was not speaking about slavery, an issue she would take little notice of until the 1850s. She was speaking of women.

It was the beginning of an intense, enriching friendship. "Dr. Channing was a prevailing influence in all my intellectual and religious experience," Elizabeth later wrote. "[H]e seemed to me a fixed centre, around which was much revolution of thought in Massachusetts."[63] Soon after their October meeting, she began attending his weekly discussion groups. Then the two took to walking together each Saturday, wandering Boston's cobbled streets and discussing theology like a pair of divinity students. Channing's daughter Mary enrolled in the Peabody sisters' school, and within a year, Elizabeth had practically become a member of the household. She visited the minister's family nearly every evening, and soon took upon herself the task of transcribing his chicken-scratch handwriting into legible transcripts. Channing, in return, read aloud from his favorite poets.

He had already served as pastor at the Federal Street Church for a quarter of a century, a time during which he had emerged as the undisputed leader of Unitarian theology. On May 5, 1819, preaching in Baltimore at the ordination of Jared Sparks, he fiercely rejected the Calvinist notion of a punitive God, insisting that a wise and benevolent deity would never create innately sinful humans. He then introduced a still more revolutionary insight: that "God is infinitely good, kind, benevolent... not to a few, but to all... [to] every individual, as well as to the general system."[64]

Elizabeth had arrived at a similar conclusion herself, back when she was thirteen and, in a burst of self-improvement, had read the gospels thirty times and annotated each verse.[65] One day, around this time, she marched into the family parlor and announced her opinion that Jesus was not God himself, but human, and that it was the duty of all believers to achieve the insights he had expressed so memorably in the New Testament.[66] But it wasn't Channing's liberal theology only that appealed to her. It was also his experiences. In 1823, he had traveled to Europe for his health, where he met his favorite poet, William Wordsworth.* He also met the poet-turned-journalist Robert Southey, with whom he discussed the sermons of Lyman Buckminster's brother, Joseph. Most important for his thinking, however, was his acquaintance with Coleridge (figure 23).

In 1823, Coleridge was ravaged by opium and alcohol abuse. He was alienated from family and friends. His greatest accomplishments were well in the past, including the publication of his poetry and his dense critical masterpiece, the *Biographia Literaria*. A decade earlier, he had singlehandedly revived interest in *Hamlet* with his mesmerizing—and largely improvised—lectures on Shakespeare. Now, in the mid-1820s, he occupied himself with a series of knotty theological essays that would not be published until after his death.

What intrigued Channing most about Coleridge was his distinction between *reason* and *understanding*—the same terms that were soon to captivate Mary Emerson and her nephew Waldo. Channing was arguably the first American to recognize the importance of Coleridge's terminology, and he embraced the concepts because they confirmed his own experience that intellect alone was inadequate for perceiving God. He had come to believe that every person possessed "*insights of principle* which are deeper than all phenomena," and that a loving God had created immense, if still largely untapped, capacities in people that would one day enable them to join their Maker in perfection.[67] The process of aspiring to this divine state he called "self-culture."

* Nearly two decades later, Wordsworth still remembered Channing's statement that Christianity "put no checks upon the activity of the human mind, and [does] not compel it to tread always blindly in a beaten path."

Figure 23. Samuel Taylor Coleridge.

For Channing, any person who "does what he can to unfold all his powers and capacities, especially his nobler ones, so as to become a well proportioned, vigorous, excellent, happy being, practices self-culture."[68] But this pursuit entailed certain risks. It potentially led to an exclusive focus on personal development, a strident individualism that dissolved communal bonds. Channing called this "egotheism."

In addressing these issues, Channing was not just working out a problem of theology. He was grappling with the emphasis on the self that increasingly served as a bedrock of American culture. The American Revolution had insisted upon "the rights of man" (however exclusive those rights turned out to be). The transition to political self-determination had been accompanied by a cult of the individual—what the French political scientist Alexis de Tocqueville termed for the first time, in *Democracy in America*, "individualism," or the desire by individuals to be self-ruled. Channing worried that the national preoccupation with independence was eroding older community standards. To counter this trend, he insisted that "our life is woven into a social web," encouraging his parishioners to redirect their attention to God and society. In "Self-Culture," the essay which most clearly articulated these thoughts (and which later influenced Waldo Emerson and Margaret Fuller, among others), he argued that the true aim of self-culture was "to enthrone the sense of duty within us."[69]

Elizabeth Peabody's friendship with Channing coincided with his working out of these ideas. She also learned from him about Coleridge and was soon reading everything she could find by the poet. Mary Peabody, still sharing an apartment with her older sister and mildly exasperated with her abstractions, reported that Elizabeth "has been living this winter upon Coleridge, Wordsworth, and Dr. Channing, and is more than usually sublimated as you may infer from these facts."[70] Just how seriously Elizabeth absorbed Coleridgean thought can be seen in the way she employed his ideas in her classroom. "At this time," she recalled, "I was particularly interested to learn and state for myself, for my own and my pupils' mental discipline, Coleridge's distinction of the reason and understanding, the relations of intuition and reflection in the discovery and for the demonstration of truth."[71]

But Elizabeth was drawn to Channing for other reasons, too. In the aftermath of Lyman Buckminster's death, she had become acutely introspective. "I have been sitting at the window," she wrote, "... retracing the progress of my character from the neutrality of infancy to its present state of decided chequer mark." As she looked back, she saw that "love of knowledge was one of the presiding spirits—I felt knowledge was power, & my sense of weakness made me covet power & knowledge too." The pursuit of knowledge and power had left her feeling estranged, however, infecting her with "the pestilence of egotism."[72] She craved friendship. She longed for consideration—even love. "And thus I fluctuate," she wrote, never certain "which is my real state of mind."[73]

Channing's example helped her navigate the crisis. His concept of self-culture gave her a way of thinking through the conflicting demands between her own nature and that of others. It enabled her to modulate desire and duty. His use of Coleridge's term *reason* assured her that the disorienting gusts of feeling she sometimes experienced might provide clues to the moral universe. Thus, at twenty-two years of age, she began to formulate her own philosophy of personhood.

This philosophy was a mixture of Channing and Coleridge, but its conclusions were uniquely her own. If each person had access to *reason*, she argued, then knowledge must be shared at some basic, deep level. The best way to plumb the depths of the self, Elizabeth thought somewhat paradoxically, was through interactions with others. The name she gave this idea was *self love*. "What I have called self love here is a consciousness of the infinite nature of the soul," she wrote in her journal. She was attempting to define an "emotion of infinity produced by the better part of ourselves" and only fully realized in communion with others. As with Channing's notion of self-culture, there were dangers associated with Elizabeth's concept; when *self love* interfered "with the right of others, it is obvious we are transferring the emotion of infinity to the baser part of ourselves." Similarly, "when love of others interferes with our own good, we are not loving the infinite soul of our neighbor."[74] Self love, then, was "balance preserved." It taught that "what is good for us individually is good for all."[75]

6.

Elizabeth would later describe 1826 as "the first year of my intellectual life properly speaking."[76] In the space of twelve months, she wrote the essay on the Gospel of St. John that later impressed Mary Moody Emerson, as well as a series of essays on the "Spirit of the Hebrew Scriptures," some 40,000 words of dense theological reasoning. And she sent her first letter to her favorite poet, William Wordsworth, initiating a correspondence that would last, off and on, for nearly two decades.

In the first letter she called him "*Mr. Wordsworth*, who can define all the mysteries of the heart, whose eye can penetrate natural expression and find meaning wherever there is any to be found." She described herself as "an American girl of twenty two" (she was actually twenty-one), and made a bold announcement. To Wordsworth alone she revealed "what is in my heart, with fervour and simplicity."[77] What was in her heart, it turned out, was anger. She told the poet of her upbringing, burdened by parental expectations. "When very young, & during the whole period of youth, I was dissatisfied with the manner in which the old communicated with the young—...especially...the system pursued in schools." She was speaking, of course, about her mother Eliza. "[T]he education I received was wanting in power to connect together the heart and the intellect."

Her mother had expected nothing less than brilliance from her and had set about creating a genius to prove that women were equal to men. For Elizabeth, the results had been disorienting. "I often felt a want of reality in everything around me," she confided to Wordsworth, "and experienced a thrill of terror inexpressible at the sense of loneliness amid the universe." She hoped he would take inspiration from her personal history and write "a volume for *children*." As an educator, she believed a collection of Romantic verse would instill in young readers the confidence to follow their own impulses. It would enable them to worry less about satisfying the expectations of others. "No one knows that I have written," she hastily concluded. "I fear it is taking too great a liberty and dare not ask advice."[78]

Wordsworth, who was then fifty-five and had recently published *Yarrow Revisited*, politely declined the invitation. "[I]f I am to serve the very young by my writings," he replied, "it must be by benefitting at the same time, those who are old enough to be their parents."[79] But to Elizabeth, his response was encouraging. She had been acknowledged by the foremost Romantic poet of the era, deemed worthy of a response. With newfound confidence in her own value, she began a project she had dreamed of since the age of thirteen: translating the entire Bible into contemporary language. She started with the Gospel of St. John.

The gospel begins with an origin story: *In the beginning was the Word, and the Word was with God, and the Word was God.* As we have already seen, Elizabeth translated "the word Logos into 'moral truth-speaking.'" She was influenced here by something like Coleridge's *reason*—the idea that all people were endowed with the capacity to discern higher truths, "first by the things of Nature, then by the processes of conscious life and reason, etc." To some extent she was also responding to Channing's belief that "the universe in which we live, was plainly meant by God to stir [us]."[80] Finally, she was indebted to Wordsworth, who in "Lines Composed a Few Miles above Tintern Abbey" proclaimed nature as the "guardian of my heart and soul/Of all my moral being."

But by reinterpreting the gospel of St. John to mean that *all* people were capable of divine inspiration, Elizabeth was suggesting something new, something even revolutionary. Her translation was an important harbinger of transcendentalism—an early rumbling of the intellectual earthquake that would soon shake the cultural landscape, first in New England and then throughout the rest of the nation. Written a decade before Waldo Emerson's *Nature*, Elizabeth's reformulation of scripture argued that humans were born with the innate capacity to seek meaning for themselves, *within* themselves. A person's inner promptings—not scripture—was a perfectly adequate guide for this quest. In Elizabeth's account, God gave permission to all people to think and act for themselves, to develop their minds and souls as they saw fit. Freeing worshippers from the dogma of the Bible, her translation was a breathtaking expansion of the Protestant Reformation.

When she had finished the work, she showed it to Channing, recalling much later "how I was startled with mingled terror & delight when he said to me in words I can never forget, 'These manuscripts are very interesting. They are full of original thought.'" But Channing's praise was qualified. "You must remember," he told her, "that if God has given you a deeper insight into this higher subject than others have, you are to devote your powers to the service of your fellow creatures, and not use them to make yourself distinguished."[81]

It was her mother's message all over again. Channing may have been trying to protect Elizabeth from doctrinal controversy. He undoubtedly perceived that Elizabeth's "loose translation" contained a radical, even heretical, assertion: that moral intuition was just as effective as the teachings of the church. But he was also responding to Elizabeth as a woman. Channing admired her intellect and conceded her genius in matters of theology. Over the coming years he would embrace the incipient women's movement as a natural outgrowth of "self-culture." But he also was the product of a time and place that believed women should manage their ambitions and channel their egos into submission and obedience.

In a letter to "Mrs. N-," written around this time, Channing observed, "It has been taught, you know, that you [women] are distinguished by quickness and delicacy, rather than by profoundness of thought: that you reach truth by a kind of intuition rather than reasoning; that human nature and life are a woman's appropriate studies and experience, and society her best school, and that she is to do good chiefly by the culture of the affections and the taste, by spreading love, order, refinement, etc." Channing seems genuinely not to know how to interpret these platitudes. Did they reflect essential differences between men and women? Were they cultural stereotypes that reinforced the status quo? "Are these heresies which the stronger party are passing off as orthodoxy," he asked; "or are they true, and ought they to influence education?"[82]

Almost a generation later, the *Christian Inquirer*, another Unitarian periodical, framed the question even more pointedly with reference to Elizabeth's situation. "What shall then the woman of genius do; what can she do, and be woman still?" Intellectual women, suggested the anonymous author, were anomalies, freaks of nature. "She finds herself in possession of riches for which she never sighed nor prayed... and what shall she do with it [*sic*]? Was it given to her to be a curse, to settle on her soul, as the mildew and the blight of Egypt, to separate her from her kind merely to unsex her, with her woman's inspirations and sensibilities ten thousand times refined by it?"[83]

Channing worried that Elizabeth's intellectual bent might further estrange her from society. Her desire to write risked making her unfit for the role assigned to all women of "doing good chiefly by the culture of the affections and the taste, by spreading love, order, refinement, etc." Elizabeth did not entirely disagree with him—or at least not openly. But his praise of her writing, as well as the response she had received from Wordsworth, encouraged her to continue down the path she had set upon. "I feel that I grow in independence," she told a friend around this time, adding that "when by the progress of [my] individual mind a real legitimate independence was acquired," she had determined "to enjoy it."[84]

She therefore began to explore the ideas about self and society that were aswirl inside her. These thoughts had been brought to the surface by Channing. They had been given fresh emphasis by her introduction to Coleridge and correspondence with Wordsworth. But Elizabeth felt she had something new to contribute. Her message, grounded in her experience as a woman, appeared in her most ambitious effort of 1826, a long philosophical series on "The Spirit of the Hebrew Scriptures."

To the extent these obscure essays are read at all today, they are usually dismissed as turgid or unsystematic. Elizabeth's efforts to parse the book of Genesis demands much from readers, especially those ungrounded in theology. But they are not much different in style from the dense, closely reasoned arguments that regularly appeared in the religious press of the time. Nineteenth-century readers would have understood the essays' organization; following an interpretation, Elizabeth provided applications to contemporary life—precisely the same format used in countless New England sermons. The series, in other words, were sermonic pieces she might have delivered to a congregation had she been allowed to become a preacher.

The first essay is devoted to the creation story. Elizabeth's argument, still somewhat radical for its time, was that Eve's Fall did not imply inherent sinfulness. God had endowed Adam and Eve with the "perpetually recurring idea of infinity, which makes us look with a sense of superiority on whatever is transitory. . . ."[85] The first couple, blessed with spiritual insight, could not be faulted for wanting to achieve the same knowledge as God. Much like Judith Sargent Murray, who had made a similar argument decades earlier in "On the Equality of the Sexes," in Elizabeth's telling Eve's transgression was no transgression at all. Tasting the forbidden fruit was merely striving for a better understanding of creation. In addition, the parable proved "the moral equality of man and woman," since Eve was the *first* to act on her desire for divinity. This equality, Elizabeth declared, was "a great truth . . . so calmly and simply stated in that early age, when even in this it was hardly admitted."[86]

The next essay in the series, on temptation, continued the theme. Elizabeth argued that the story of Eden was a parable of education, of self-culture. It illustrated the importance of resisting worldliness in favor of heavenly knowledge. By acting on her own free will, Eve exemplified the human desire to find meaning. The loss of innocence therefore was not a tragedy, but rather "a new aspect to the social state, . . . the moral and physical dependence of man on man."[87] The Fall forced people to enter the social world, which an all-knowing God had always intended so that people might eventually learn to care for one another.

Elizabeth's third essay asserted that Abel's murder was "a crime against the social principle, whose operations are . . . connected with the operations of the religious principle." Despite her message, she could not resist transforming Cain into something of a Byronic antihero, a misunderstood outlaw who was merely rebelling against the restrictions of the material world. "It seems as if the heart had felt that man could *do* nothing which would not mock him, when done, by its finiteness," she wrote, "and so it desired to destroy something,—or itself,—as a symbol of the immeasurableness of the impulse from within."[88]

Elizabeth's first three essays on the Hebrew scriptures represent an important moment in American intellectual history. They not only reinterpret the Old Testament but also offer something altogether different: a fusion of Unitarian theology and Romantic ideology. Like Shelley's Prometheus, Elizabeth's Eve and Cain recognize the divine spark within themselves and rebel against the limitations of their earthly existence. They risk everything, including God's displeasure, to discover their own godlike nature. At the same time, they illustrate an idea that had become increasingly important for her: what she called the *social principle.* Human connection, she insisted, was "the very principle of our nature . . . that principle which is capable of being God within us."[89] Having survived a lonely adolescence as well as the raw wound of Lyman Buckminster's suicide, having endured the persistent belittling directed toward any woman of intellect, she had at last found shelter in her friendship with Channing and his circle. A renewed sense of sociality made her hopeful for the future.

Of the six essays that Elizabeth wrote on "The Spirit of Hebrew Scripture," only three have survived. Just twenty-two when she wrote them, she would have to wait until she was thirty before those three saw the light of day. In 1834, they were published in the *Christian Examiner*, the most prestigious Unitarian review in the United States. Precisely how they made their way into the hands of the *Examiner*'s editor, Andrews Norton, is uncertain. Norton had championed Unitarian doctrine alongside Channing during the first two decades of the century and had long served as Harvard's first Dexter Professor of Sacred Literature, a position that earned him the sobriquet of the "Unitarian pope." Stiff and aloof, his students liked to joke that upon entering heaven he would look around, nose curled, and announce, "It was a *very* miscellaneous crowd."[90]

In 1834, when Elizabeth's essays were published, Norton had grown increasingly alarmed by what shortly came to be known as transcendentalism. He was especially troubled by the movement's emphases on intuition, the priority of the self, and the inadequacy of religious institutions. These were the topics Elizabeth directly confronted in her essays on the Hebrew scripture, which makes it somewhat puzzling that Norton accepted them in the first place. What is more certain is that after publishing the first three, he had had enough. Just as William Emerson had preempted his sister Mary's groundbreaking essays on the imagination, Norton now quit publishing Elizabeth's essays on Hebrew scripture.

Norton "cut off untimely my little series," Elizabeth recalled, "opposed to a series on any one subject." This sounds like prevarication on Norton's part. Why accept three essays if he was opposed to a series? Given his increasing resistance to the "new thought," as transcendentalism was sometimes called, it seems more likely he ended Elizabeth's contributions because he realized their dangerous implications. Misogyny played a role, too. Elizabeth later admitted that Norton did not "condescend" to read the remaining three essays "because, as he said, I must needs be incompetent to the subject from want of learning."[91]

Had Norton published the fourth essay, however, history would have been made. In this essay, Elizabeth invented a label for the new ideas she had discovered with the help of Channing and Coleridge. "[T]he word *transcendentalism* I never had seen except in Coleridge's friend," she recalled. (She was referring to the poet's short-lived periodical, *The Friend*, published in 1809–10.) In 1826, as she reinterpreted the first verses of the Bible, she borrowed Coleridge's term to describe her ideas about Eve. The word *transcendentalism* appeared in her fourth essay—for the first time in American literary and intellectual history.†

Later she realized just how remarkable the work had been. How surprising and unexpected, she thought, that "there in the bosom of Unitarianism, an unlearned girl, with only the help of those principles of philosophizing she gathered from the perusal of Coleridge's friend & relying simply on her own poetical apprehensions," had anticipated and even named the most important intellectual movement of her era.[92]

7.

Between the time she wrote the essays on Hebrew scripture and the time they were eventually published—between 1826 and 1834—Elizabeth continued to operate her private school with her sister Mary. She initiated correspondence with Mary Moody Emerson and kept writing to Wordsworth, telling him that "Everything in the forms of society & almost in the forms of thought is in a state of flux."[93] She became even more of a fixture in the Channing household. At the minister's request, she now led a conversation group with "older young ladies" from the Federal Street Church. On Saturday mornings, before hosting these conversations, she and Channing walked along the cobbled streets of Boston, discussing the topics she had in mind for the women of the church. Soon she realized that in "every instance, the subject of composition I chose for my class on Saturday proved to be the subject of Dr. Channing's sermon the next day."[94]

In 1830, Channing encouraged her to translate a treatise written by French educational theorist De Gerando. (This was the book that Waldo Emerson read with interest some two years later.) She also published *First Steps in the Study of History: Being Part First of a Key to History*, a student manual meant "to give the pupil's mind a sort of mental independence, a freedom from the peculiar influence of authors."[95] And she started a new venture that would eventually have major consequences for both the transcendentalist and feminist movements. This was her "historical conferences."

† Margaret Fuller would use the term in July 1833 in a letter to her friend James Freeman Clarke, telling him that Frederic Henry Hedge said he "was better qualified to translate transcendentalism than he had supposed."

Twice a week, beginning at ten in the morning and continuing until late in the afternoon, a group of young women gathered to discuss ancient Greek and German texts under Elizabeth's tutelage. At first, the impulse for this project was money. Hoping to help her improvident family, she charged $10 per person for her informal classes. But the experiment was important for other reasons. To begin with, it was an early effort to provide women with the kind of education they were so often deprived of—in classical Greek and Latin literature. As Elizabeth told a friend, "We employed six days in reading various beautiful things about Socrates—including some manuscript translations I have of Plato."[96]

Just as important, the gatherings were an early example of what soon became the primary expressive form of transcendentalism: conversation. More than any other mode—more than the essay or the lecture, for example, both of which were fixed by generic conventions—conversation embodied the transcendentalist ideals of spontaneity, inspiration, and intuition. Bronson Alcott, a chief theorist of the practice, described talk as "an abandonment to ideas, a surrender to persons.... circular and radiant of the underlying unity." Waldo Emerson called conversation a "lively exercise, in which subjects are played with like a ball, which in turn comes back to the hand of the thrower."[97] Evanescent, unrehearsed, reciprocal—conversation was the product of minds casting off the sparks of thought, fueled by mutual exchange and improvisation. As Madame de Staël said in her book on Germany, talk "animates the spirits, like music among some people, and strong liquors among others."[98] It was also the primary way of dispersing transcendentalist ideas throughout New England in the 1830s and 1840s.

Many conversation circles consisted solely of women who were otherwise shut out from other venues of public exchange. ("Debate is masculine," Bronson Alcott said, "conversation is feminine.") In parlors and dining rooms—the New England equivalent of salons and coteries—women gathered to discuss their reading, the latest literary reviews, or the sermons they had recently heard. They discussed history and science using the textbooks handed down by brothers and husbands. They practiced pronunciation in foreign languages, and described art exhibitions and musical concerts that they had attended. Even women who could not attend conversation groups for one reason or the other were able to participate, however indirectly, by receiving reports from others.

The qualities that made conversation so attractive to the transcendentalists—its spontaneity and ephemerality—pose serious problems for the historian. Unless transcribed or reported, conversations leave few traces. All that remains of Elizabeth's "historical conferences" are her recollections, which tell us that twenty women—six married, fourteen unmarried—paid her to lead them in their discussion. After encountering some "beautiful things about Socrates," she introduced them to "Herder on the Spirit of Hebrew Poetry—which is an exquisite book."[99] Everything else about these important discussions has been lost to history.

Figure 24. Amos Bronson Alcott.

Talk also organized the next major project in which Elizabeth was involved. This was her work at the Temple School, an experimental academy created by Bronson Alcott, a former itinerant salesman who had turned teacher (figure 24). Elizabeth was introduced to Alcott in 1828 by William Ellery Channing, who was intrigued by the schoolteacher's ideas about spiritual education. Alcott's account of the meeting is unflattering. He believed that Elizabeth "may aim perhaps at being 'original,'" but that she "fail[ed] in her attempt, by becoming offensively assertive. On the whole there is, we think too much of the *man*, and too little of the *woman*, in her familiarity and freedom, her affected indifference of manner."[100]

Elizabeth was not put off by this sort of chauvinism, especially if new ideas were involved. And Alcott was a repository of new ideas. Like Elizabeth's father, Nathaniel Peabody, he had grown up on a hardscrabble farm, which he had left for good when he was eighteen. Traveling throughout the South, Alcott sold pins, needles, combs, scissors, buttons, clocks, and other housewares produced in New England. He resembled Nathaniel Peabody in another way—he had no head for business. By the time he was in his early twenties, he was $600 in debt. It was at this point he decided to become a schoolmaster.

It says something about the quality of education in the 1820s that a rural school district in Connecticut would hire someone entirely unqualified for the position. Alcott had no formal education. His learning came entirely from his voracious and idiosyncratic reading, much of it done during idle moments in the libraries of Southern plantations when he had been a Yankee peddler. He was hopeless at mathematics. His knowledge of history was spotty. He possessed no languages whatsoever.

But these deficiencies, strangely enough, made him an effective teacher. Alcott was never really interested in whether his students mastered a particular topic or discipline. Preparing them for educational standards or for a future occupation seemed to him in fact utterly beside the point. He was much more interested in his scholars' ability to think for themselves, to reason independently, to learn truth from inward reflection. Alcott understood the mission of teaching as the production of *individuals*.

At some point in his reading, he had stumbled upon a translated work by Johann Heinrich Pestalozzi, the Swiss educational theorist. Pestalozzi believed genuine education entailed the cultivation of a student's personality and character. He opposed rote memorization and other mechanical approaches to learning that were then accepted features of the classroom. Alcott adopted Pestalozzi's principles wholesale, transforming his Connecticut schoolhouse into an educational laboratory. He decorated his classroom with flowers and pinecones and encouraged his students to play outside several times a day. He introduced music and art into the curriculum. He built individual desks for each student, acknowledging their unique body type, and he separated these desks so that the students no longer sat hunched together on a single bench.

Ultimately, these methods proved too unorthodox for the parents of Cheshire, Connecticut. They voted, after several probationary years, to remove him from his position. Alcott then moved to Boston in search of a more enlightened field for his endeavors. A year after meeting Elizabeth Peabody, she appears again in his journal, this time in a completely different light. Now she possesses "a mind of superiour order. In its range of thought, in the philosophical discrimination, and originality of its character, I have seldom, if ever, found a female mind to equal it."[101] The reason for Alcott's change in attitude was not entirely disinterested; between their first and second meetings, Elizabeth had favorably reviewed his fledgling school in the *American Journal of Education.*

That school lasted little more than a year. Alcott then left Boston to teach in Philadelphia, where his ideas once again proved controversial. (One student later described him as "the most eccentric man who ever took on himself to train and form the youthful mind.")[102] After five years there, he returned to Boston—around the same time Elizabeth's essays on Hebrew scripture were appearing in the *Christian Examiner*. He was accompanied by his wife, Abba, and two daughters (the second-born, Louisa, would grow up to become the bestselling author of *Little Women*). Alcott presented his young family to William Ellery Channing, and the minister quickly became the schoolmaster's chief patron. The acquaintance with Elizabeth was soon renewed.

Elizabeth now thought Alcott "a man destined, it appears to me, to make an era in society, and *I believe he will.*" She was particularly impressed by the amount he had read in five years spent in Philadelphia.[‡] He had absorbed much of German Romanticism, especially Schiller, Goethe, and Herder, and had also read Coleridge's *Aids to Reflection*, published for the first time in America five years earlier by James Marsh.[§] This edition of Coleridge quickly became a foundational text of transcendentalism. Waldo Emerson read it with enthusiasm, as did the Unitarian minister Frederick Henry Hedge, who referred to the book's "transcendental philosophy" in 1833, thus getting credit for naming the "new thought" instead of Elizabeth, who had used the term half a dozen years earlier.

Coleridge reaffirmed notions Alcott had been steadily groping toward, especially the idea that all people, created by a benevolent God, had innate access to moral knowledge. Like Elizabeth, he would apply Coleridge's *reason* to education, reorienting the classroom to become less about the mastery of subjects than the process of inward discovery. Within a week of returning to Boston, Alcott visited Elizabeth at her boardinghouse, bringing with him a stack of journals and letters written by his Philadelphia students. These chronicled their spiritual growth. Elizabeth, struck by the compositions, thought they were original, reflective, free from pretense. She "told him I wanted him to make an effort for a school here," even volunteering to "inquire about the children in town." The same day she recruited four children for the new venture and agreed to "be his assistant, that is, I would teach two hours and a half for a year at his school, for such compensation as he could afford to pay."[103]

Alcott's new school was located on Tremont Street (figure 25). It was called the Temple School because it occupied the upper floor of the newly constructed Masonic Temple. The spacious classroom was lit by arched Gothic windows at one end. Four plaster busts—of Plato, Socrates, Shakespeare, and Sir Walter Scott—stood in the corners, and an oil painting of William Ellery Channing hung on one wall. The most prominent work of art, however, was an enormous bas-relief of Christ, positioned directly over Alcott's chair. The symbolism was no accident: Alcott arranged his students like disciples, seating them in a semicircle around him. The mornings were devoted to Socratic dialogue, with the instructor asking his

‡ As for Elizabeth, she had studied Pestalozzi in the intervening years, publishing, in 1830, her *First Lessons in Grammar on the Plan of Pestalozzi*. (Interestingly, the title page attributes the work to Nathaniel Peabody, a sign that Elizabeth was not yet willing to affix her own name to public authorship.)

§ The president of the University of Vermont, Marsh had published a translation of Herder's "Spirit of Hebrew Poetry" in 1826, the same year Elizabeth wrote her "Spirit of Hebrew Scriptures."

Figure 25. The Masonic Temple.

students questions about the importance of the spiritual world, or whether conscience was seated in the head or the heart, or if justice was a sense or a convention.

Sometimes these conversations yielded comic exchanges. When Alcott announced that a child who possessed a single thought was worth "more than a person who had earned five thousand dollars," an older student objected: "[He] thought five thousand dollars was better than a thought." Alcott replied that thoughts were the wealth of heaven. Another boy said he would "rather have five thousand dollars than all the thoughts he had had this last hour."[104]

These and other incidents appeared in the journal Elizabeth began keeping shortly after assuming her duties at the Temple School. Although she had promised to work for only two and a half hours a day, she quickly found herself staying late in the afternoons to read with more advanced students. She also began transcribing Alcott's conversations with the children. "Miss P—is now present every day," Alcott recorded in his diary in December 1834, four months after the school had opened, "and keeps a Journal of the *operations* and *Spirit* of the *Instruction*...."[105]

Elizabeth's motivations for transcribing the daily conversations were, as always, partly financial. Her piecemeal work as editor, translator, and tutor barely produced enough income to survive, let alone help her struggling family. Writing a book about Alcott's new approach to education might contribute to her purse. At the same time, she believed the new "school is not understood, even by those most interested in it."[106] Her *Record of a School: Exemplifying the General Principles of Self Culture*, published in July 1835, was meant to change that (figure 26).

RECORD OF A SCHOOL:

EXEMPLIFYING

THE GENERAL PRINCIPLES

OF

SPIRITUAL CULTURE.

He that receiveth a little child in my name, receiveth me.—*Jesus Christ.*

BOSTON:

PUBLISHED BY JAMES MUNROE AND COMPANY.

NEW YORK:

LEAVITT, LORD AND CO. 180, BROADWAY.

PHILADELPHIA:

HENRY PERKINS.

1835.

Figure 26. Title page.

The book created something of a furor in Boston. Adopted by the fledgling transcendentalists as one of the first public statements of their idealist philosophy, it spurred debate—and sometimes outrage—among more conservative Bostonians. Much of the anger was directed toward Alcott's teaching, which to many readers didn't resemble teaching at all. More threatening were the premises behind his pedagogy. If a child was endowed from birth with a moral and spiritual sense, what role did parental influence play? Alcott's school threatened to undermine the very structure of the New England family.

In hindsight, Elizabeth's *Record of a School* is more than a chronicle of the daily operations of the Temple School. It is also a veiled account of her growing distress at Alcott's methods. In the first part of the *Record*, she portrayed Alcott as a visionary educator whose methods were likely to transform American society. Gradually, though, she started to doubt his approach. She suspected that Alcott was primarily interested in directing students to answers he had already determined. One conversation she recorded had Alcott supposedly paraphrasing his pupils by saying "instinct and affection, *and reason*, are the feelings of the soul."[107] But no student had in fact said that Coleridgean reason was a product of the soul. Alcott had deftly inserted his own opinion.

Elizabeth reported other troubling aspects. "It will be seen," she wrote, "... that Mr. Alcott is very autocratic."[108] Alcott demanded total silence in the classroom. He paused for as long as five minutes if a child interrupted him. Even worse was his propensity for corporal punishment. "[T]*he hurting of the body*," as he termed it, was sometimes necessary "to bring you back to the law of the spirit."[109] (He was mindful to administer whippings in another room, away from the children.) One day, when two boys persisted in ignoring him, Alcott called them to the front of the classroom and gave them a ferule. Holding out his hand, he told the boys to beat *him*. When the two boys begged not to, Alcott remained "determined that they should not escape the pain and the shame of themselves administering the stroke upon him, except by being themselves blameless." A tense stillness fell upon the classroom. Alcott led the two offenders out, "but it was not without tears, which they had never shed when punished themselves."[110]

At least one other visitor to the Temple School found Alcott's behavior troubling. In the winter of 1834, Elizabeth invited the English writer Harriet Martineau to attend one of the classes. Martineau, a year and a half older than Elizabeth, had grown up in a Unitarian household in Norwich, England, and had been educated in the same rigorous curriculum as her four brothers. At age twenty-one, she had written her first article, "On Female Education," where she protested the inequity of training women to do nothing but stay at home. (Her argument was indebted to Wollstonecraft.) Before long, she was publishing a steady stream of novels and works of political philosophy.

Profoundly hard of hearing, Martineau was a keen observer of human foibles. In 1834 she traveled to the United States to gather material for a book that would compare the nation's lofty democratic rhetoric to its actual social arrangements. (One chapter was bluntly entitled "The Political Nonexistence of Woman.") Elizabeth, with her talent for befriending intellectuals, proved to be an important conduit for Martineau. She eventually introduced the Englishwoman to Waldo Emerson and Margaret Fuller. Now she invited her to visit the Temple School.

Martineau appeared one morning, ear trumpet in hand, bristling with energy. According to Elizabeth, she wrote her books as quickly as possible, in a maelstrom of composition, bothering neither to correct nor to revise them. As soon as she finished one, she would "pick up her manuscript, send it to the publisher, take out new books & new paper & immediately commence another."[111] Not surprising, at the Temple School she made quick work of Alcott. "The master presupposes his little pupils possessed of all truth, in philosophy and morals" she sniffed; "and that his business is to bring it out into expression; to help the outward life to conform to the inner light; and, especially, to learn of these enlightened babes, with all humility." Because Alcott signaled the answers he was looking for in advance, Martineau thought he provided "them every inducement to falsehood and hypocrisy."[112]

Martineau's critique would not appear in print for two and a half years. Long before that, Elizabeth had arrived at a similar view. In 1835, she wrote to Mary Peabody: "Mr. Alcott's teaching is superlative, but he seems to me to require *too much* in the way of self control. It is unnatural."[113] Alcott's emphasis on introspection, moreover, led to morbid self-consciousness in the children. And he manipulated his students. When he led a young girl to conclude that mercy was preferable to justice, Elizabeth delivered a withering indictment: "N.B. I generally agree with the views that Mr. Alcott brings out from his pupils; but in this instance I disagreed; and I am inclined to think that he unconsciously led them into his own views... I think the opposing of mercy and justice, is false philosophy, and false religion."[114]

In the *Record*'s afterward, Elizabeth advanced her own radical ideas about education. Since every person was the product of divine spirit, "the practical philosophy of *know thyself*" was all-important. The ancient Greeks had "analyzed the theory of obedience to the will of gods, and found that man had within him a power of questioning the right of even that power." This prompted her to make a bold pronouncement: "all other souls are potentially what Jesus was actually."[115]

Elizabeth wrote this in the summer of 1835—a summer that vibrated with momentous changes. In England, Caroline Herschel and Mary Somerville would become the first women elected to the Royal Astronomical Society. Elsewhere, a young naturalist named Charles Darwin had just arrived on the Galapagos Islands, setting off a string of events that would eventually transform the way people looked at themselves and the natural world. Elizabeth's statement at the end of *Records of a School* was earthshaking, too, if somewhat more modest. She called into question the very premises of organized religion, suggesting that spiritual intuition was a better guide than religious doctrine. And her concluding statement—that all people were potentially Christ-like—was a premonitory rumble of the nascent transcendentalist movement.

8.

Record of a School was published under Elizabeth's name in July 1835. Initial reviews were encouraging.** "We are in love with this little volume," wrote a critic for the *Eastern Magazine*. Others hailed Elizabeth's work as "strikingly original" and "one of the most interesting books of the year." Buoyed by the response, Elizabeth sent a copy to Wordsworth, thanking him "for all you have sung of *women* (in the name of my sex)."[116] She also sent copies to the French biographer of Madame de Staël and to Maria Edgeworth, the novelist and children's writer in England. Closer to home, she sent a copy to her old Greek instructor, Waldo Emerson, who promptly wrote to thank her for "the pleasure & hope the Rec. of a School has given me." Waldo declared it "the only book of facts I ever read that was as engaging as one of Miss Edgeworth's fictions."[117]

For the first time in her adult life, Elizabeth was approaching something like financial security. She had fronted the *Record*'s book's printing costs—at the time a common practice—and in return would receive most of its profits. (Where exactly she got the money to print the book is unknown.) The book sold better than expected in its first weeks, and although conservative Bostonians grumbled about its unorthodoxies, Elizabeth was so encouraged by the book's reception that she began preparing a second edition for the coming year. Increasingly, she thought of herself as a female author—the fulfillment of a childhood dream—and was soon making fresh plans to "ply the pen for bread and butter."[118]

Then everything collapsed. In October, the warehouse where the book was stored burned to the ground. (Remaining copies of Elizabeth's translations of de Gerando were also destroyed.) Hoping to avoid complete ruin, she hastily prepared a second edition, this time adding a sixteen-thousand word "Explanatory Preface" meant to address criticism that the Temple School children learned from no textbooks and studied no recognized academic subjects. Here she carefully detailed the instruction in Latin, mathematics, and grammar she provided the children. She also buttressed the sometimes confusing theoretical framework for Alcott's instruction, writing, "I am told that I must ascribe this to my own want of perspicacity,—especially in the last chapter, in which I undertook to sum up the general principles of Spiritual Culture, deduced from a view of the soul, that some persons say is unintelligible."[119] Elizabeth now stressed that Alcott's requirement

** The book was published by James Munroe, of Boston. At Elizabeth's recommendation, Emerson would soon publish *Nature*, "The American Scholar," and "The Divinity School Address" with Munroe.

that students examine their own spirit was preparation for the systematic study of the material world—for chemistry, geography, history.

To the complaint that Alcott's focus on self-analysis produced unwonted egotism in his students, Elizabeth countered, "The objection seems to me, to have arisen from taking the word *self* in a too limited signification. The spirit within, is what is meant by *self*, considered as an object of philosophical investigation."[120] Yet a note of caution intruded. "It is true," she acknowledged, "that one person ... may sometimes give cast to the whole inquiry, through the influence of his own idiosyncrasies and favorite doctrines."[121] About Alcott she now admitted, "I am not myself prepared to say, that I entirely trust his associations."[122]

There were other misgivings. Her book's destruction by fire had threatened her livelihood. So, too, did Alcott's burning ambition. Spurred by the *Record*'s success among avant-garde readers, he had decided to produce a new book from the Temple School experience. It would resemble the *Record*, composed of Elizabeth's transcriptions of conversations between teacher and students. But it would take on new topics—specifically, the life of Christ as perceived by children. "I have often been taught by what very small children have said," Alcott explained. "All wisdom is not in grown-up people."[123]

Alcott now began revising Elizabeth's transcriptions to illustrate this belief. Worse, he introduced taboo subjects into the classroom. A discussion about the Virgin Mary led to the subject of birth; Alcott viewed it as an emblem of spiritual growth, but when he asked the children where babies came from, one little boy replied that "the body is made out of the naughtiness of other people."[124] Elizabeth removed this sentence, knowing the outrage it would prompt. But Alcott restored it in a footnote. When Elizabeth tried removing another passage involving circumcision ("Was there any spiritual meaning in it?" Alcott asked the children), she was again overruled.

To protect herself from the anticipated outcry, Elizabeth wrote a "Recorder's Preface," insisting that the children's views were not necessarily those of Alcott's. "[S]till less are they to be regarded as any intimation of the recorder's; who, though occasionally an interlocutor, was, in general, a passive instrument, and especially when she felt that she differed from Mr. Alcott, on the subject at hand, as was sometimes the case."[125] After an altercation with Abba Alcott, who "predicted to me 'eternal' damnation" for criticizing her husband, Elizabeth resigned from the Temple School and moved back to the family home in Salem.[126]

This was on August 1, 1836. A week later, Elizabeth wrote Alcott to express her continued reservations about his book. "[Y]ou as a man can say anything; but I am a woman, and have feelings that I dare not distrust, however little I can *understand them* or give an account of them." She begged him to omit her remarks on any controversial topic and "to put a preface of your own before mine, and express in it, in so many words, that on you rests all responsibility of introducing subjects, and that your Recorder did not entirely sympathize or agree with you with respect to the course taken..."[127]

When Alcott's *Conversations with Children on the Gospels* was published at the end of the year, it was almost universally assailed. One newspaper declared it filled with "filthy and godless jargon." Another described the book as "one third absurd, one third blasphemous, and one third obscene."[128] Alcott was described as "an ignorant and presuming charlatan," "either insane or half-witted." Even more considered reviews expressed grave reservations: "The essence of the system," wrote the editor of the *Boston Daily Advertiser*, "appears to be, to select the most solemn of all subjects—the fundamental truths of religion as recorded in the gospels of our Saviour,—and...to invite the pupils to express, without discrimination or reserve, all their crude and undigested thoughts upon it."[129] Not surprisingly, the book sold poorly. Famously—or infamously—a Boston lawyer eventually bought the remaining 750 copies to use as toilet paper.

Alcott's school would struggle on a while longer. Elizabeth's younger sister, Sophia, briefly took over the role of assistant teacher, much to Elizabeth's chagrin. She was followed, also briefly, by Margaret Fuller. Neither woman was paid. Early in 1839, when a Black family asked Alcott to admit their daughter, he obliged, prompting the parents of his white students to issue an ultimatum. To his credit, Alcott refused to expel the new student. The school closed soon after, ending his career as a teacher.

Elizabeth would not teach again for decades. Back in Salem, she began editing a new magazine, *The Family School*, enlisting her mother and sisters as contributors and even convincing Washington Allston to supply a poem. She still hoped to earn a living by her pen. An encouraging review of *Record of a School* had appeared in *The Knickerbocker* magazine, written by the novelist Catherine Maria Sedgwick. It complained that Elizabeth's comments were sometimes "too deeply *spiritual* in their character," but still said the book's author deserved "all praise for the method she has adopted" and that she was "evidently a woman of genius."[130] If it had destroyed her teaching career, the Temple School nonetheless enabled Elizabeth to burnish her growing reputation as a writer and editor. But *The Family School* folded after just two issues. Elizabeth remained undaunted. "Enthusiasm is a delightful delirium," she wrote in her journal, unconsciously echoing the sentiments of Mary Moody Emerson three decades earlier.[131] Besides, she had found another genius to encourage.

9.

Almost the moment she resigned from the Temple School, Elizabeth received an invitation from the former Lydia Jackson, of Plymouth, who had recently married Waldo Emerson. "Mr E...feels the kindest interest in your success and

Drawn by J. W. Barber—Engraved by J. Downes, Worcester.

CENTRAL PART OF CONCORD, MASS.

The above is a northern view in the central part of Concord village. Part of the Court-House is seen on the left. Burying-ground Hill (a post of observation to the British officers in the invasion of 1775) is seen a short distance beyond. The Unitarian Church and Middlesex Hotel are seen on the right.

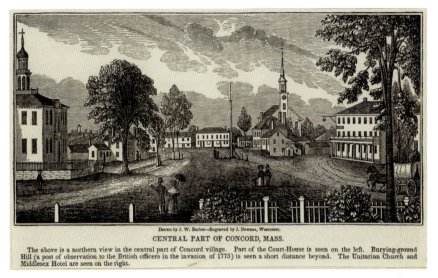

Figure 27. Concord town square.

happiness," Lydia wrote, "and hopes you will soon be able to arrange some plan that will be altogether—eligible." In the meantime, the Emersons wished to extend an invitation "to visit us before you decide upon any new arrangement"[132] (figure 27).

Elizabeth had known Waldo for some time. Not only had she once studied Greek with him years ago, she had visited his home in Chardon Street, Boston, soon after Mary Moody Emerson paid her visit in 1832. There she had found the young widower "quite absorbed in Goethe and Carlyle; but he immediately turned his attention to Saint John's grand peroration, and we discussed every phrase of it. It was one of those conversations which 'make the soul,' to use a favorite expression of his aunt Mary's."[133] More recently, she had accompanied Harriet Martineau on a visit to Concord, serving as an intermediary between the tough-minded English writer and the former minister.[††]

Waldo was not yet the leading spokesperson of the transcendentalist movement, but there was something calm, rarefied, good-humored—something almost magical—about the home he and Lydia had recently set up. Elizabeth marveled at the graciousness with which the couple hosted Martineau. She basked in the atmosphere of thought and culture they created. By the time she paid a longer visit in November, Waldo had become a minor celebrity.

[††] Martineau, who accompanied Emerson to one of his lectures to the women mill workers in Lowell, was more impressed by the audience than by Emerson, reporting how "they thus sat listening to their lecturer, all wakeful and interested, and well-dressed and lady-like."

His book, *Nature*, had been published in September 1836. It capped off a year of important works in American thought, including Elizabeth's *Record of a School*, George Ripley's *Discourses on the Philosophy of Religion* and Orestes Brownson's *New Views of Christianity, Society, and the Church*. Together these works heralded what would increasingly come to be known as the "new thought." In his *Discourses*, Ripley (who happened to be Waldo's cousin) argued that humans were "emanations" of God and therefore able to achieve religious insight through their intuitive faculties. Brownson called for "a new synthesis of spirit and matter" to remedy the ills of traditional Christianity. Both declared the importance of inspiration over logic.

Waldo's book was somewhat different. Like Ripley's and Brownson's works, it was indebted to the crucial terms of *understanding* and *reason* set forth by Coleridge. But *Nature* wed these ideas to poetic images. As Brownson himself said, the book was "aesthetical rather than philosophical."[134] Abstruse in many places, more suggestive than persuasive, the slim green book evoked a series of rapturous descriptions of the natural world, including the famous "transparent eye-ball" passage. In Waldo's hands, transcendentalism became not only a philosophy but a *style*—a mode of expression that emphasized the elevated and ideal. One Concord matron, describing her son's letters, said they were "all written . . . in a beautiful spirit (as the Transcendentalists say)."[135] She was being facetious, but she was also noticing an important fact. Under the influence of Waldo Emerson, aspiring transcendentalists would begin to speak in breathy raptures about the *beautiful* and *ethereal*.

When Elizabeth arrived in Concord in November, she found the Emerson household emotionally charged. Waldo's younger brother, Charles Emerson, had died of tuberculosis in the spring, and the household remained in mourning. Elizabeth Hoar, who had been engaged to Charles, now joined the family as a de facto sister. A gifted conversationalist as well as a talented Greek scholar, Hoar was a fierce advocate of reform and the abolition of slavery. Ruth Haskins Emerson, the family matriarch, also lived with Waldo. Ruth had outlived four of her seven children (a fifth, Bulkeley, was now in a mental institution), and when Elizabeth mentioned her burgeoning friendship with Mary Moody Emerson, the older woman struggled to maintain her composure. Mary, she said, had taken Charles's death particularly hard. "She loved him like a parent."[136] In her journal Elizabeth wrote, "There is something inexpressibly touching in her calmness so tender and trembling."[137]

Intermingled with grief, however, was the joyful presence of new life. Less than a month earlier, the Emersons' first child, Waldo, had been born. Elizabeth noted that the new father "was very much taken up with the baby, whom he looked at and tended a great deal."[138] As for his wife, Elizabeth had previously met the former Lydia Jackson, of Plymouth, shortly before her marriage to Waldo. At the time she thought her "neither beautiful, nor elegant, and very frail, as if her mind wore out her body." But once the two women sat down to visit, they "had a beautiful talk about a variety of intellectual and spiritual things." Elizabeth concluded that the betrothed woman possessed one of "the rare characteristics of genius—inexhaustible originality."[139] Now, with Lydia recuperating from childbirth, Elizabeth helped out around the house, even sleeping in the same bed as Lydia to assist in the night if required.

It was Waldo who most interested her, though. Soon after her arrival in Concord, she and her former Greek instructor launched into a conversation about French philosophy, Orestes Brownson's new book, and the foibles of Bronson Alcott, whom Emerson called "the only man of one idea that he ever liked."[140] When Elizabeth generously suggested that Alcott's single idea was a *deep* one, Waldo countered by calling him "a man of genius with very few talents."[141] He then told an unflattering anecdote about Alcott, who had written a birthday ode to himself to be delivered by his students. Sympathizing with Elizabeth's ordeals with the egotistical schoolteacher, Waldo addressed Alcott's sense of entitlement, observing that he "'had never felt the humiliation of being deeply in debt; that he felt the public owed him a living.'"[142]

Later that evening, conversation turned to Waldo's recently deceased brothers, Edward and Charles. Staring into the flickering light of the fireplace, Waldo told Elizabeth that he missed Charles' facility with Greek. Then he asked her why more young women did not study the language. Elizabeth answered that women who wished to learn it "required leisure and a competence." Waldo evidently missed her point. If money was the issue, he said, merely to "enter into its spirit and see with its eyes would be riches" enough. Did he really not see how domestic chores and responsibilities constrained so many women, including his own wife? His response, at any rate, was anything but helpful: "Poverty is the belt that girds in the powers, and hurls them up to action."[143]

The next day, Elizabeth and Waldo walked through the woods surrounding Concord. The trees, lit from above by a brilliant November sky, reminded Waldo of "painted Gothic windows." They trudged through fallen leaves on their way to Walden Pond, where the clarity of the water was ruffled now and then by wavelets. Elizabeth said the scenery reminded her of Wordsworth's poetry, eliciting an unexpectedly defensive response from Waldo. He claimed that "he owed no debts" in *Nature*, "except to Charles."[144] Then he admitted he had lifted a handful of sentences from Charles's commonplace book he considered too exquisite to remain in obscurity. The rest of the book, he repeated, was his and his alone. The intellectual and stylistic debts he owed to his Aunt Mary, as well as the love of nature she had instilled in him, were left unmentioned.

On the walk back home, the two of them spoke of Margaret Fuller, who had visited Concord just four months earlier, arriving with a letter of introduction from Elizabeth. Waldo admired Fuller's passion for European literature, especially that of her hero, Goethe. But he thought her weak in philosophy. The "moral did not lead to the intellectual in her," he added, apparently meaning her ideas did not proceed from a deeper, spiritual, source.[145] He nevertheless appreciated Fuller's biting wit and her responsiveness to all things aesthetic, which he thought suited her for European society. He had tried to convince her "it was best for her to go to Europe."[146]

It was during this conversation that Waldo reported a startling comment Fuller had made: "all the marriages she knew were a mutual degradation." In her journal, Elizabeth let the statement stand without comment. She may have wondered whether it referred to anything in Waldo's own marriage, but she kept it to herself. Nor did she excavate any memories of Lyman Buckminster, which still rose from time to time, unexpected and always painful. The next sentence in Elizabeth's journal suggests rather that she took the comment as a broader critique of the institution of marriage: Waldo "thought her satires usually founded on truth, but not always kind."[147]

The marriage Elizabeth was now most interested in was of two minds—hers and Waldo's. It was clear from the moment she arrived in Concord that each understood and admired the other. Waldo was impressed by Elizabeth's depth and breadth of learning, her ability to systematize ideas in a manner he sorely lacked. Soon he wrote that she possessed a "wonderful literary head, with extraordinary rapidity of association, and a methodising faculty which enabled her to weave surprising theories very fast & very finely." He also appreciated how she conversed with an "ease & scope & authority of a learned professor or high literary celebrity in her talk."[148]

For Elizabeth, the trip to Concord was even more transformative. Although she would always prefer the bustle and hum of Boston, she admired the beautiful life Waldo and Lydia had created in their rural seclusion. It made her feel as though she were "in the center of things, on ideal ground, around which all actualities revolve."[149] To Waldo's insistence on the importance of the self, she responded with joy. Having spent the past ten years trying to make her living as a female intellectual despite the jeers of society, she found Waldo's philosophy liberating. He "makes me feel free," Elizabeth wrote in her journal that November; "he feels my infinite capacity just as I do."[150] Soon she was telling a friend that her core value was now the "unfolding & cultivating [of] the human being."[151] To her youngest sister, Sophia, she wrote, "I feel as I never felt before that to be true to one's self is the first thing—that to sacrifice the perfect culture of my mind to social duties is not the thing—that what we call disinterestedness of action is often disobedience to one's *daimon*." Increasingly she understood "that one's inward instinct is one's best guide..." and that "it is better to be called selfish and old-maidish than to lose one's own soul."[152]

In August, after resigning her position at Alcott's Temple School and returning to her parents' home in Salem, Elizabeth had despaired. "Never was ever a *Woman* creature made so little calculated to live out woman's only true abiding place (home) as I."[153] Like Mary Emerson, she felt unhoused and rootless. As a woman drawn to the life of the mind, she was a permanent exile. She did not question whether most women *belonged* in the home—not yet, at any rate—but she felt herself painfully ill-equipped for such a life. Waldo encouraged her to think less of social expectations, more about her own requirements. He even led her to renounce "the social principle" she had proclaimed in her series on Hebrew scripture. "I begin to grow independent," she wrote after departing from Concord. "Wherever I can be myself and *act* if not speak my soul, is my home. Mr. Emerson says *our home* is not this home or town, or even a particular body. It is the *unity of our character*. I am not only coming to the *place* home, but to the *being* home."[154]

10.

Her visit to Concord was so rejuvenating that she briefly toyed with the idea of forming a school or private class in the village. (The plan was scuttled by Elizabeth Hoar, who explained that every literary woman in Concord was already attending school; it's possible she was concerned about Elizabeth's reputation in the wake of the Alcott scandal.) When Lydia invited her to return the following September, she quickly agreed, arriving soon after Waldo delivered his famous Phi Beta Kappa address at Harvard on "The American Scholar." "I feel burdened with the fulness of life," she wrote on her first day back in Concord. "Thoughts crowd upon each other—I cannot get my mind into a simple state."[155]

Two weeks earlier, Waldo had invited her to attend a meeting of the so-called "Transcendental Club," in nearby Newtown. These informal gatherings had begun a year earlier and were the brainchild of Frederic Henry Hedge, a Unitarian minister in Bangor, Maine who was also the most learned German scholar in the country. (He was a particularly close friend of Margaret Fuller's.) On September 8, 1836—one day before *Nature* appeared in print—Hedge and his fellow Unitarian ministers George Putnam and George Ripley, along with Waldo, agreed to form a club to discuss a wide range of topics. Hedge would later say that "There was no club in the strict sense . . . only occasional meetings of like-minded men and women." James Freeman Clarke, whose house in Newton hosted the first meeting, wryly explained that the gatherings were called "the 'club of the like-minded,'" because "no two [participants] . . . thought alike."[156]

The club eventually grew to include the most prominent thinkers in the transcendentalist movement, including Bronson Alcott, Margaret Fuller, William Ellery Channing, Orestes Brownson, and Henry David Thoreau. Topics were eclectic; when Alcott hosted the group, the conversation was devoted to "American Genius—the causes which hinder its growth, and give us no first rate productions." Other discussions included the "essence of Religion as distinct from morality" and "the character and genius of Goethe."[157]

Waldo, never a joiner, was skeptical of the whole enterprise. The previous November he had told Elizabeth, "People do not perceive revelations from their Genius, except when alone—never in company."[158] Yet he attended at least twenty sessions of the club, often bringing new members. The day after he delivered "The American Scholar" address, he and Lydia hosted a meeting at their home, welcoming Margaret Fuller, Elizabeth Hoar, and Sarah Alden Ripley—the first time the Transcendental Club admitted women.[‡‡] The following week, in Newton, Elizabeth attended her first meeting, accompanied by the sister of James Freeman Clarke, Sarah, who was an aspiring painter. The gathering was a "congregation of the bright youths from all parts," as Elizabeth put it, who engaged in "talk about the progress of society, and the mode of presenting Christ to the minds of people so as to make it most effective."[§§159]

Now, back at the Emerson household, Elizabeth found Lydia a bundle of nerves, having spent much of the summer hosting a steady stream of visitors and organizing an "all-day" party after Waldo's Phi Beta Kappa address. While her husband spoke to an audience about the need to escape "from under [society's] iron lids," Lydia fretted over the details of housekeeping, determined to "peep in at every nook—and order every thing to know its place"—all while tending her ten-month-old son. To Elizabeth, she poured out "the theosophy of her marriage and of marriage in general"—a "theosophy" predicated on the idea "that each individual should consider himself as but a part of a great whole."[160] In sharp contrast to her husband, Lydia believed God had placed people *in relation* to each other, linking them together in a web of mutual respect and reverence.

Elizabeth was sympathetic to this idea, especially as it pertained to marriage. Much later, she would write, "It is *because* I believe marriage is a sacrament, and nothing *less*, that I am dying as an old Maid. I have had too much respect for marriage to make a conventional one in my own case."[161] She also found herself drawn to Waldo's individualism. Staying in the guest room across the hallway from his study, she waited until her friend finished writing each morning before engaging him in long conversations about Goethe, Wordsworth, and the young child who continued to mesmerize his doting father. "Mr Emerson was holding his beautiful boy in his arms just now," she recorded in her journal, "and I asked him if he expected before hand to see as much beauty grace and intelligence. He said 'No! This is all new to me! It is a beautiful provision that to every man is provided this little angel. This is a part of his own life a man never sees.'" The boy

[‡‡] Ripley, the wife of a Waltham minister, was the brilliant autodidact and friend of Mary Moody Emerson.

[§§] Elizabeth ranked the gathering as follows: "Mr Emerson, Henry Hedge, Mr. Alcott, J[ohn]. S[ullivan]. Dwight seemed in a higher sphere than the rest. Next below were George Ripley and Mr Stetson & James Clarke. I do not know where to place Mr [Convers] Francis whom I like very much and who can comprehend a vast deal more than he can or does do..."

then began to clap his hands and gurgle. "'Much you care for being father's diagram,'" Waldo announced. "'So you but enjoy yourself.'"[162]

Elizabeth was even more taken with Waldo's example as an author—as someone whose entire life was devoted to the expression of beautiful thoughts. Reading his lectures in manuscript, she noted how they "surprise, astonish, satisfy delight me. They prove Mr E to be a far greater man than I thought him." She conceded that he was neither logical nor systematic in his thinking, that he lacked method and organization. But this was only because he was so "many-sided, all-sided… He is not only the most live man I know, but the completest." In this estimate she cast off her earliest mentor, admitting, "Yes, I yield up my Dr. Channing as second…And then I feel as if none could know how beautiful this mortal life can be made, unless they witness [Waldo's] daily walk and conversations… It is by this clear communion with the universal mind that he daily fights off the incursions of the narrow, the peculiar, the little, the low…"[163]

In praising him, Elizabeth was adopting Waldo's increasingly radical vision of the individual. She was abandoning Channing's insistence that "our life is woven into a social web" and adopting Waldo's philosophy of the autonomous self.[164] She knew this version of independence was largely a fiction—that Lydia's supervision of the kitchen, for instance, made Waldo's daily walks possible, and that no single person could exist without the mutual support of others. But to someone who was burdened by family obligations and forever anxious about her status as a single woman, Waldo's call "to stand aloof, and suffer no man and no custom, no mode of thinking to intrude upon us and bereave us of our infinitude" was intoxicating.[165]

His example inspired a new ambition in her: to become a poet. One morning, on a ride to nearby Lexington, Elizabeth read aloud Goethe's "Ganymed." The poem is a reinterpretation of the Greek myth in which a beautiful youth is seduced by Zeus. (The poem was one of Goethe's most popular; Schubert set it to music.) Immediately after finishing, Elizabeth recited four verses of her own, which she had written in reply. "Mr. Emerson listened quite graciously but asked me where I wrote it," she noted in her journal. Elizabeth told him. Then Waldo "criticized my talking about the nightingale & lark, because he said, I 'never heard either.'"

It was a fair point. But Elizabeth was not quite ready to give up these fixtures of European poetry. She told him she *wished* America had larks. Waldo replied that "nature everywhere had enough forms and sounds to symbolize all our thoughts." He encouraged her to continue writing poetry, even if she felt uninspired, telling her she might be surprised at how good it was when she read it later.[166] "If the universal mind is the centre of Philosophy," she wrote during her stay in Concord, "yet I will maintain that the wonderful depth of personality is the centre of poetry. May I not then find myself a poet…?"

By learning to rely on her own impressions, by trusting herself, as Waldo urged her to, Elizabeth hoped to become like another one of her heroes,

William Wordsworth. In her journal she now critiqued Waldo's poetry, saying, "Mr. Emerson fails to sing because he is not enough of an egotist," adding that because he "has never cultivated an ear for music," he was deficient in versification. "Mr. Emerson might sing like [Goethe] if he would allow himself to do so," she concluded. "His wife was right when she said his heart was like the song of the locust to some individuals, which is pitched above their own ear, by reason of its fineness and loftiness."[167]

At the conclusion of her visit, Elizabeth summed up her second stay in Concord: "What a holiday has every day been... Waldo Emerson seems to have given me the freedom again of my own reason." Her friend's insistence on the sufficiency of the self enabled her to forget the opinions of others, to "think & rejoice that I feel less egotistical than when I could only look upon myself with dislike." Waldo had taught her the paradoxical truth that greater trust in herself resulted in less painful self-consciousness. "Now I can realize that self has no beauty but what is made by the intense light that shines upon it... It was misery that made me egotistical. Happiness will deliver me from myself."[168]

She carried these ideas back to Boston and Salem, back to a life split between family responsibilities and efforts to pursue the life of a writer and intellectual. In the spring of 1838, Elizabeth's brother George was slowly dying of spinal meningitis at home. Soon she found herself enlisted to help another brother, Nat, start a school of his own, in West Newton, ten miles from Boston—a short-lived experiment that quickly alienated her from her resentful brother. Perhaps it was these challenges that put an end to her poetic aspirations—there is no mention of them again in her journal. Instead, when she returned for another stay at the Emerson household, this time in August of 1838, she was focused on an entirely different project: editing Waldo's lectures for publication.

Again, she felt a load lift from her shoulders in his presence. "There is this peculiarity," she wrote, "that he makes me feel free... He is the only friend I have no anxiety to please... he will not withdraw the light of his mind & the general warmth of his kindness from my earthly path because I make mistakes, occasionally offend his taste, or jar with his opinions." Best of all, "He feels my infinite capacity just as I do myself."[169]

The atmosphere of the Emerson home had undergone a subtle transformation since the year before. On July 15, Waldo, had delivered an address to the graduating class of Harvard's Divinity School. There he announced, "In this refulgent summer it has been a luxury to draw the breath of life." Contained in this seemingly innocuous phrase was Waldo's belief that nature mirrored the divine spirit—"the breath of life"—which could be known through intuition but never "received at second hand." In preparation for the address, he had pored over old letters from his Aunt Mary, channeling her prophetic voice. Now he preached that Christ had understood the importance of direct experience of God, but that the religion formed in his name had forgotten this fundamental truth, instead becoming a repository of empty forms and orthodoxies. Like Aunt Mary, Waldo wanted to revive religion, to insist upon its soul-ravishing capacities. He challenged the graduating class of divinity students to become "Yourself a newborn bard of the Holy Ghost," and to "acquaint men at first hand with Deity."[170]

Elizabeth, who attended the address, later described it as "the apocalypse of our Transcendental era in Boston."[171] She was electrified by her friend's fiery language, his soaring, defiant rhetoric. But the fuse she had helped light with her *Record of a School* now exploded into controversy as the new transcendentalist philosophy was decried as heretical. For Elizabeth, the address was a revelation, a "lecture on Holiness," but for the Unitarian community at Harvard, it was nothing less than blasphemy.[172] According to one member of the Transcendental Club, the address had given "dire offense to the rulers of Cambridge."[173]

Most offended was Andrews Norton, the man who had summarily ended Elizabeth's series on Hebrew scripture six years earlier. Writing in the *Boston Daily Advertiser*, he now labeled Waldo's speech an "incoherent... insult to religion." The transcendentalists, he continued, were guilty of "great ignorance and incapacity for reasoning." (Ironically, most of those he accused had studied with Norton at Harvard.) Behind the polemic was a serious theological concern. Waldo's lecture rejected "all belief in Christianity as revelation," insisting instead that divinity infused the very air we breathe. Norton vehemently disagreed. "There can be no intuition," he denounced, "no direct perception of the truth of Christianity."[174] The Bible provided the only reliable access to faith.

Elizabeth arrived at the Emerson home just as the fallout from the "Divinity School Address" was reaching a fever pitch. She was impressed by Waldo's outward calm. He "seems not to be saddened," she observed, "but deepened rendered more earnestly serious by this late opposition."[175] The time they spent together involved discussion of his other lectures and sermons. Having abandoned poetry, Elizabeth now wanted to publish her friend's orations. "There is one thing that I wish," she had earlier written him, "and that is—that you would leave me *in your will*—all your sermons—to keep for two years giving me leave to make extracts according to my judgment & *print them*."[176] This was the same request Waldo had made years earlier when he asked Mary Emerson for her Almanacks. But Elizabeth didn't want the manuscripts for inspiration, or at least not primarily. She wanted to write the life of her friend. "But what a heavenly dream would be such a biography of Waldo. How I should like to have the writing of it. I should do it only by arranging extracts from his journals, letters, lectures, sermons, in chronological or logical order, with no commentary."[177]

More pressing were plans for his lectures. Waldo asked her to help organize the confusion of his papers.[178] Elizabeth quickly discovered a problem that was also a feature of Waldo's writing. The "lectures create in the hearers a constant series of surprises. They involve intense attention. But they can not be understood fully at the time, nor remembered at once. This is very provoking, and it gratifies spleen and soothes vanity to rail or to laugh at them as unintelligible in their nature and of not much value." The source of the confusion, she realized, was that Waldo wrote each sentence separately, "in different states of sentiment and linked them together into one discourse to be read by some other state of mind."[179] If he was enacting his call to heed the spirit with this procedure, he was also alienating many potential readers.

The most immediate chore was publishing his address to Harvard's Divinity School. After he conferred with her about the text, she noted how "careful and assiduous [he was] in correcting the proofs of his sermon," revising in such a way as to eliminate "every shadow of petulance that could be detected."[180] One day, while she and Lydia were doing needlework, he came in to ask about other revisions. He read aloud a passage calling Christ "the friend of man"; Elizabeth suggested he capitalize the "F." "He seemed to reflect a few moments, and then deliberately replied, 'No; directly I put that capital "F" my readers go to sleep!'" When Elizabeth encouraged him to include a paragraph explaining some of the disputed parts of the address, he ultimately decided to leave it out: "I must abide by what I delivered, whatever was its lack of full expression."[181]

Elizabeth was again struck by the congruence of Waldo's thoughts with her own. The controversy surrounding the Divinity School Address drove home the perils of expressing the "new thought" in public. But the speech also convinced her of the validity of her own ideas. As she explained to a friend, "As to his doctrine, it was my creed *before* I knew it was his." She was referring to the translation of the Gospel of John she had shown Mary Moody Emerson five years earlier. "It is pretty plain therefore that this heresy does not belong to his mind alone, and it is not strange, is it, that I am interested deeply in his having a chance to promulgate views so dear to my own soul, being the theory of its life and resurrected from my long previous miseries of mind."[182]

It was during a walk through the cemetery at Sleepy Hollow that Waldo addressed Elizabeth's situation with her improvident family. "[W]e had not learned yet how to live," he said, "so that what was best for ourselves, should be combined with our duty to others." He then stated his belief that duty made it impossible "to stay or go where & when we willed according to what we felt the inward oracle said." He paused and looked at Elizabeth. "You... have been and are in a difficult position & if overpowered by your relations to others should not perhaps blame yourself."[183]

Elizabeth was touched. She was also surprised. It had never occurred to her that Waldo might notice the strain she was under to support her family, "since I never have talked of my personal relations to him—even those of Mr Alcott." Had Lydia, always more alert to the pain of others, spoken to him? Or had his own recent experiences as the target of anti-transcendentalist anger sensitized him to the feelings of others? Either way, she left Concord feeling consoled and cared about.

"Give me the friend who divines my needs," she wrote in her journal. "This is the true heart."[184]

11.

A month later, she found herself alone in a room with a madman. Jones Very, age twenty-five, was the illicit son of a Salem sea captain and a woman notorious for her atheism. (The two were cousins; they never married.) Tall and angular, with a bony face and a towering forehead, Very was a study in black. His hair was black, his eyes were black, and he dressed entirely in black. He even carried a black walking stick.

From an early age, he had been a brilliant scholar. This enabled him to attend Harvard despite his mother's poverty and scandalous reputation. (His father had died at sea when he was ten.) After graduating in 1836, he became a Greek tutor at his alma mater. Elizabeth met him one year later, on December 27, 1837, when she attended his talk on epic poetry at the Salem Lyceum. She sat on the front row with her father and was so struck by Very's insights that she convinced Nathaniel Peabody to invite the young man to their home on Charter Street. That evening they discussed "all the current subjects of the day, which were mainly transcendental topics." Nearly a decade younger than Elizabeth, Very was gifted and eccentric and painfully shy—"he grasped my outstretched hand like a drowning man a straw," she recalled. More than anything he wanted to write poetry.[185]

She discovered his ideas were similar to her own. A year earlier, Very had read Waldo's *Nature* and, like so many others of his age and predisposition, was struck as if by revelation. He identified with passages that described the indwelling God within each person. (His copy of *Nature* was thoroughly marked up, covered with check marks and underscorings and marginalia.) Learning of his admiration for Waldo, Elizabeth wrote her Concord friend and encouraged him to invite Very to speak at the lyceum there.

Four months later, in April 1838, Very walked twenty miles from Salem to Concord to lecture on Shakespeare and dine at the Emerson house. There he explained his theory that Shakespeare was "a man who had looked through all human knowledge yet without being sure of the divine knowledge which complements it in order to give the mind peace.... This was his difference from Christ."[186] Waldo wrote Elizabeth the next day, thanking her for her "sagacity that detects such wise men as Mr. Very, from whose conversation and lecture I had a true high satisfaction." Lydia, too, was impressed. She described the shy scholar as "high-souled—pure—loving—and lovely a being... Mr. E. loves him as well as I do."[187] Before Very departed, Waldo invited him to a meeting of the Transcendental Club. Soon he was praising the young poet to his aunt Mary, telling her, "There is a young man at Cambridge named Jones Very who I think would interest you & will presently finish & probably publish an Essay on S.[hakespeare] and from a point of view quite novel & religious."[188]

Neither Elizabeth nor Waldo realized that Very was undergoing a mental crisis. On a railroad trip from Boston to Lowell in 1837, he had been seized with terror at the train's speed. Telling himself that he had survived "movements far more worthy of alarm yet with perfect safety," it suddenly occurred to him that God had been watching over him his entire life, and that he was destined one day to achieve perfect union with the deity. Suddenly euphoric, he realized he was "borne along by a divine engine" and endowed by divinity with "man's powers and gifts."[189] By 1838, and without the Harvard authorities' knowledge, he spent less time instructing his students and more time preaching to them. He also started an informal Sunday school where, according to one of his students, there "were assembled twenty Freshmen, who read two verses each of John, 1st Chapter, which Mr. V. then explained to us." (His interest in John was possibly spurred by conversations with Elizabeth.) Soon after visiting the Emersons, he attended a meeting of the Transcendental Club and there spoke of his mystic experiences, impressing Waldo with his "expression of devout sentiment" that contained "all the air & effect of genius."[190]

Waldo had Very in mind as he labored over his address for the graduates of Harvard Divinity School. Acutely sensitive to language, he compared Unitarianism's exhausted vocabulary to Very's fresh, poetic descriptions of spiritual experience. When the young man described his struggles to discover God, his words were stripped of cant, vivid with firsthand perceptions. His example lay behind Waldo's call for the divinity students to become "newborn bards of the Holy Ghost."[191]

That summer, Very wrote a series of sonnets. By the time Harvard classes resumed, his religious preoccupations had intensified. He now told his students that "he was a man of heaven, and superior to all the world around him."[192] Then, on the evening of September 13, 1838, Very informed a professor at Harvard that he was "moved entirely by the Spirit within me to declare to all that the coming of Christ was at hand." When the professor objected, Very said "he had fully given up his own will, and now only did the will of the Father." The next day in class, he told his students to "flee to the mountains, for the end of all things is at hand."[193]

Two days later, Josiah Quincy, the president of the college, relieved Very of his position. The young man then returned to Salem and visited the Peabody house. "One morning I answered a ring at the door and Mr. Very walked in," Elizabeth recalled. "He looked much flushed and his eyes very brilliant and unwinking. It struck me at once that there was something unnatural—and dangerous in his air—As soon as we were within the parlor door he laid his hand on my head—and said 'I come to baptize you with the Holy Ghost and the fire'—and then he prayed. I cannot remember his words but they were thrilling—and as I stood under his hand, I trembled to the centre."[194]

She was terrified. “I felt he was beside himself and I was alone in the lower story of the house,” she later wrote. Her only hope was to remain calm, to treat him as quietly as possible. After several moments of silence, Very asked her if she felt any change. She said no, and he replied, “‘But you will.... I am the Second Coming—Give me a Bible.’”[195] After poring over it a while, he left.

Elizabeth soon learned that she wasn’t the only person Very visited that day. He turned up at the homes of three Salem ministers, including the Baptist clergyman, Lucus Bolles, who physically threw him out, as well as Charles Upham, the minister of the Unitarian First Church, who, according to Elizabeth, “at the time was a good deal excited against the transcendentalists.” Upham immediately suspected Waldo Emerson as the source of Very’s derangement. He “called Mr. Emerson an Atheist—and declar[ed] that it was wrong to listen to him—and told Mr. Very that he should see that he be sent to the Insane Asylum.”[196]

That evening, Very returned to the Peabody house. He was calmer this time, telling Elizabeth he had “misunderstood the Holy Ghost—the time is not yet for the baptism of fire.” Then he pulled out “a monstrous folio sheet of paper” and presented it to Elizabeth. Scrawled neatly in four double columns were the sonnets he had composed the previous summer. The “Spirit had enabled” him to write the poems, he told her, then left. The next day, Elizabeth found out the troubled man had agreed to enter McLean’s Asylum, in Somerville, where he would remain for a month.[197]

Writing to Waldo, Elizabeth expressed her hope that Very “was sick of a brain fever—which would prove his insanity but a temporary delirium.” But a week after his hospitalization, Very was as delusional as ever. The madness, Elizabeth now told Waldo, was thought to be from “water on the brain” and “was probably produced by intense application.”[198] Despite this explanation, she was left with a series of troubling questions. Had Very’s delusions been prompted by Waldo’s philosophy? Had he taken too literally the message of “The Divinity School Address,” which emphasized the primacy of the spirit within? Had it been Very’s desire to live “wholly from within” that ultimately unhinged him?

Elizabeth hinted at these concerns in her letter to Waldo. “*These impulses* from above I think are never sound minded,” she wrote. “.... I wonder whether some thing might not be written by a believer in the doctrine of Spirituality—which would show the difference between trusting the Soul & giving one’s mind to these *individual illuminations*.”[199] She was groping here for a terminology that would distinguish between genuine glimmers of insight from the godhead and those “*individual illuminations*” caused by illness or overwork. Falling back on Coleridge’s vocabulary, she continued: “What frightful shallowness of thought in the community—that sees no difference between the evidence of the most manifest insanity & the Ideas of Reason.”[200]

But how to tell the difference? Waldo did not consider Very insane. It was society, he told Elizabeth, that was mad. Soon after being released from McLean’s

Asylum, Very again visited Concord, this time for five days in October. His behavior was eccentric—at times bizarre and aggressive—yet Waldo claimed to be "very happy in his visit as soon as I came to understand his vocabulary" and described the young man as "profoundly sane." Very had merely rejected traditional religion in his quest for an inner and deeply personal vision.[201]

Elizabeth disagreed. She sided with William Ellery Channing, who had met Very around this time and said, "He has not lost his *Reason*. He has only lost his *Senses*."[202] She and Channing believed something was organically wrong with Very, and that this defect was not to be confused with inspiration. As she reported to Waldo, most people in Salem thought the deranged poet's behavior was "nothing but *transcendentalism*—which shows how very entirely they do *not* apprehend *the ground* of a *real belief* in *Inspiration*."[203] But Elizabeth insisted on the importance of distinguishing insanity from transcendentalist philosophy—to do otherwise was to invite attacks on the "new thought."

There was also something deeply personal in Elizabeth's response to the episode. Unlike Waldo, she had witnessed Very at the height of his mania. She had trembled as he stepped forward to place his hand on her head, touching her without permission, baptizing her in the name of a deity he claimed to feel surging through his body. She had been frightened—too frightened to call out for help. It had taken all her self-control to remain calm before "this poor crazy youth" whose "beautiful light had gone down in darkness."[204] Standing before him, frozen in fear, she had felt terribly alone, vulnerable in a manner inconceivable to Waldo.

The incident changed her. It altered her course. Although it would take some time for Elizabeth to recognize it, her encounter with Very brought into sharp relief her growing distrust of Waldo's philosophy of the self. She did not publicly discuss the topic until much later, in 1858, when she published an essay entitled "Egotheism, the Atheism of Today." In that work she discussed the problem of focusing too exclusively on one's inner responses. People who fixated on their inward life tended to "deify their own conceptions," Elizabeth wrote; "that is, they say that their conception of God is all that men can ever know of God." The result was not only personal disappointment—"for man proves but a melancholy God"—but detachment from the social world.[205]

Behind this idea was more than just her experience with Very, however. The trajectory of her life during the 1830s was another factor. When she wrote "Egotheism," she was thinking of her experiences with Bronson Alcott, Jones Very, even Waldo Emerson. Each of these men, charismatic in their various ways, had followed inner visions with uncompromising fervor. Yet the cost of pursuing that vision had been the absence of communion—of community—with others. While Waldo was neither as narrow nor as dogmatic as the other two, Elizabeth believed all three fell into the same error. They refused to acknowledge fully that "there is, beyond our conception, inconceivable Power, Wisdom, and Love," an "immanence of whose substantial being within us our best conception is but a transient form."[206] To ignore the self's limitations—its frailties and failings, its blindness as well as its insight—was to risk insanity, disgrace, or censure. The risk was heightened immeasurably if one was an unmarried woman on the cusp of middle age.

At the same time, Elizabeth was not alone in these ideas. Her desire to balance the imperatives of the self with those of society resembled the thinking of her first mentor, William Ellery Channing. It had much in common with the reformist concerns of Orestes Brownson, Theodore Parker, and others. These men were preoccupied with the inequality imposed by growing industrialization; as Brownson suggested, too many were suffering and made unhappy by "all our social arrangements," which could not "be cured without a radical change in those arrangements."[207] Elizabeth contributed to this discussion in an essay she wrote for *The Dial* in October 1841, entitled "A Glimpse of Christ's Idea of Society." "The Problem of the present age," she wrote, "is human society, not as a rubric of abstract science, but as . . . an actual reconciliation of outward organization with the life of the individual souls who associate . . ."[208] How to create a community that allowed the individual full and free expression was the problem that now began to occupy her.

In many ways, she had returned full circle—struggling yet again with the old conflict between independence and the longing for collaborative companionship. She still was in the process of inventing what it meant to be an intellectual woman, still navigating the treacherous waters of gender expectations in antebellum America. Three years under the sway of Waldo Emerson's radical individualism had led her at last to recognize its limits—especially when applied to a woman without the financial security of marriage. And this recognition, so necessary to her development, was marked by yet another dislocation. This time, she and the entire Peabody family left Salem and settled in the city where Elizabeth had set out so many years ago—Boston.

12.

"About 1840 I came to Boston and opened the business of importing and publishing foreign books," she later recalled, "a thing not then attempted by anyone"[209] (plate 4). Exactly how long she had been considering the enterprise is unclear. The decision came in the wake of the Very affair, just as she was beginning to withdraw from the excesses of Waldo's brand of transcendental individualism. Yet there were less philosophical reasons for opening a bookshop, too. As she confided to friends, she was increasingly exhausted from years of teaching and writing to support her family—worn out from "*fifteen years* of this intense worry, this feeling that I could not possibly perform *actually* what I was *potentially* capable of in slightly different circumstances . . ." She now admitted that for much of the 1830s she had been "in a state of considerably exquisite *irritability* and sometimes *felt* pretty near the insane hospital, yet I believe I have never lost my *benevolence.*"[210] What she had once complained of to her sister Mary was still true—that "my own peculiar intellectual life has been *sacrificed—consciously sacrificed*—my whole life."[211]

The bookstore was meant to ease, if not entirely resolve, these difficulties. Elizabeth had managed to convince a wealthy backer—whose identity is unknown—to lend her enough money to purchase the books that her transcendentalist friends longed to read: German and French journals, works of philosophy, all the major English quarterlies. Before opening her shop, curious readers in the United States had to ask friends traveling overseas to bring back new works. Now there would be a reliable source for such material. "E. P. PEABODY, having a foreign agent on whom she can entirely depend," announced an advertising broadside, "is prepared to receive orders on England, and the Continent, for Books, Periodicals, Newspapers, Stationary, and Artists' materials; the latter selected at places where the articles are known to be genuine, and have been approved by the best artists. *Orders* will be answered by Cunard's Line of Steamers, *within* six weeks of the date *generally.*"[212]

To help their eldest daughter, the Peabody family left Salem and occupied the second floor of the bookshop. Nathaniel, now retired, sold homeopathic medicines to customers. Mary, in a second-floor room, taught a girls' school in the mornings and tutored in the afternoons. She also followed her older sister's example by writing textbooks in the evening. Sophia, now nearly thirty, used her room as an artist's studio, selling art supplies downstairs to bolster the family income. Eliza helped wherever she could, sometimes running the bookstore when Elizabeth was out, sometimes helping Mary with her students. Elizabeth had finally merged her family responsibilities with her intellectual interests.

The new home was in a Federal-style townhouse on West Street, half a block away from the Common where Elizabeth had met William Ellery Channing nearly fifteen years earlier. Around the corner was Boston's "publisher's row," on Washington Street. By the summer of 1840, the downstairs parlor, which housed the bookstore, contained "a foreign library of new French and German books," more than a thousand volumes, "on shelves in brown-paper covers," as well as the latest journals.[213] According to Elizabeth, there "were to be *no worthless* books… and nothing of any kind of a secondary quality."[214]

Her timing was impeccable. The ferment of new ideas that characterized so much of the 1830s had finally culminated in a definable movement. Although its members were sometimes ridiculed by an older generation, sometimes proclaimed heretical by those who thought their philosophy undermined religion, a growing cohort of thinkers and writers were bound together by their desire for a moral revolution, a transformation of human nature they hoped would change society. In opening her bookstore, Elizabeth had created the first gathering place for the transcendentalists—for men and women, she soon wrote, "who have dared to say to one another... Why not begin to move the mountains of custom and convention?"[215]

Nathaniel Hawthorne called the shop at 13 West Street "Miss Peabody's caravansary," and George Bradford, a German teacher who frequented it, called the place the "Transcendentalist Exchange." "Many persons of high culture," he recalled, "or of distinction in the sphere of religion, philosophy, philanthropy, or literature, were often here, and likely to meet others, like themselves, interested in the questions then agitating the community, or to talk on the calmer topics of literature and philosophy."[216] So popular was the shop that Elizabeth soon opened a circulating library where, for five dollars a year, customers could borrow the latest journals and books.

Next, she purchased her own printing press and began publishing a steady stream of works. Her first publication was an antislavery tract entitled "Emancipation," by William Ellery Channing, printed in 1840. That same year she also issued some of Hawthorne's children's stories in a limited edition. Then she agreed to print the new transcendentalist journal, *The Dial*, edited by Margaret Fuller, after its original publishers declared bankruptcy. Amid this activity, the Transcendental Club met in Elizabeth's shop to discuss art, religion, and philosophy. Informational meetings about an experiment in communal living at Brook Farm were also held. Abolitionists such as Maria Weston Chapman and Lydia Maria Child, both of whom lived nearby, regularly visited the store and spoke of the need for the immediate emancipation of enslaved people in the South. On Wednesday nights, Elizabeth's shop held an open house for free thinkers and liberal Unitarians, and earlier in the day Margaret Fuller conducted her famous "Conversations."

The idea for the Conversations had occurred to Fuller in the fall of 1839. She had written her friend (and co-founder of Brook Farm), Sophia Ripley, about the plan: "The advantages of a weekly meeting, for conversation, might be great enough to repay the trouble of attendance, if they consisted only in supplying a point of union to well-educated and thinking women..."[217] Fuller's idea owed much to the "historical conferences" Elizabeth had hosted a decade earlier. In fact, its subject matter—classical history and mythology—was the same Elizabeth had lectured on. Both events were aimed at women otherwise excluded from formal education and with few outlets to discuss history, philosophy, and the arts.

The Conversations took place over four years. During that time, at least seventy women attended. Most of these were drawn from Fuller and Elizabeth's overlapping circles of friends and family. They included Elizabeth Bliss Bancroft, the future travel writer and wife of the historian George Bancroft; Caroline Sturgis and Ellen Hooper, sisters and transcendentalist poets; Mary Channing, daughter of William Ellery Channing; Lydia Emerson; Elizabeth Hoar; Sophia Ripley; Elizabeth's sisters, Mary and Sophia Peabody; and Lydia Maria Child.

Progressive socialites and young women fresh out of the female academies also attended.

During the first meeting, Fuller famously announced her intentions to discuss "the great questions" confronting all women: "What were we born to do? How shall we do it?" These were the same questions Elizabeth had been asking since childhood, the same questions she continued to grapple with even now as she approached her forties. But here, in the unconventional home she had created for herself and her family, they were being asked anew. As Fuller put it, some of the best-educated women in New England were now encouraged to "state their doubts and difficulties with hope of gaining aid from the experience and aspirations of others."[218]

For nearly twenty years, Elizabeth had been a crucial figure in the intellectual excitement that led to these historic Conversations. Now, each Wednesday around noon, she sat among the circle of twenty or so women and listened as friends and acquaintances discussed the very issues that had long preoccupied her. She joined in—she could not help joining in—but she also performed another important role. As she had once done for Channing and Alcott, she now took copious notes on the proceedings. Her transcriptions remain among the only records we have of the meetings, the most detailed accounts of what was said and by whom.

The young feminist Caroline Dall, who attended the Conversations and took notes of her own, wrote in 1841 that "E. P. P. lent me her Journal, and her reports of Margaret's talks.... she is so familiar with the subject and the talkers, that she follows the train of thought of each, but perhaps not always successfully."[219] Soon Elizabeth's records were circulated and copied by other women, especially those who lived too far away to attend or who missed them on account of illness. Eventually they were distributed throughout New England to an informal network of readers, reaching as far away as Mary Moody Emerson's farm in Maine. When she finished reading them, Mary passed them on to her niece Hannah Haskins, reporting that although she longed for more "*practical* questions discussed among these *young* ladies," she was nevertheless grateful for "the pictures of beauty & elegance...—for they inspire Hannah whose rays of genius have been... awakned."[220]

The most powerful effect of the Conversations, though, was on those who attended them. One participant later recalled, "In these gatherings the blind received their sight and the dumb spoke." Another described the "gifts and graces" of the group, extolling the "Platonic dialogue" that lacked all "pretension or pedantry."[221] A third woman enthusiastically reported, "I know not where to look for so much character, culture, and so much love of truth and beauty, in any other circle of women and girls."[222] Sitting scrunched together on the mismatched chairs Elizabeth had borrowed, the assembled women spoke to one another in ways they scarcely ever spoke to anyone else. They discussed art, beauty, history, religion. They analyzed the meaning of Greek mythology and shared their enthusiasm for contemporary poetry. And they returned, time and again, to a question of fundamental importance to each of them: what women might achieve if left to their own devices.

Elizabeth's "Book Room" almost immediately became the hub of transcendentalism. The "Transcendental Exchange"—*not* Concord—became the white-hot center of new ideas in America. Presiding over it all was Elizabeth herself. If she was sometimes "desultory, dreamy," as one visitor wrote, she was also "insatiable in her love for knowledge and for helping others to it."[223] In her cramped parlor smelling of ink and paper, she had created a home that satisfied her mind and fulfilled the obligations of her family. She sat at its heart, pen in hand, capturing the rapid exchange of thought that swirled about the bookshop, content at having finally created a shelter for the various, sometimes warring, dimensions of her personality. In the process, she had created the conditions for the Bright Circle of women who would shape the contours of transcendentalism and help build American feminism.

3

Sophia Peabody in Cuba

1.

One of the most effervescent women to attend the Conversations at 13 West Street was Elizabeth Peabody's youngest sister, Sophia Amelia Peabody. Sophia (her name was pronounced So-*fie*-a) stood just under five feet tall. Her personal motto was "A free & aspiring mind is the only reality worth seeking; for such a mind will find what it seeks—even Freedom & Excellence Infinite."[1] She was cheerful, vivacious, demanding—and she was the opposite in nearly every way of her older sister Elizabeth, who once remarked of her, "I never knew any human creature, who had such sovereign power over everybody—grown and child—that came into her sweet and gracious presence."[2]

Sophia was considered the most artistic of the Ann Sisters. By the time Margaret Fuller began hosting the Conversations in 1839, she had studied with some of the nation's preeminent artists, including Elizabeth's friend, Washington Allston.

She was among a handful of women in the United States to make a living as a painter. Her canvases were reproductions of European landscapes, usually from Italy, although her feathery trees and sublime, snow-crusted mountains also anticipated the Hudson River School. These copies were lucrative, prized by middle-class Bostonians who had few opportunities to see the originals. But Allston, who was sometimes called the "American Titian," so respected her talent that he advised her to quit copying other painters and to copy nature instead.

Sophia was also a talented writer. Her son Julian once remarked that she "had an unusual gift of expression, in writing as well as in conversation," and it is true that her prose is almost always more imaginative and verbally engaging than her sister Elizabeth's.[3] As a young woman she dashed off occasional poems and essays, but her most remarkable prose survives in the 1600 letters written to her family and friends. The very best of these letters takes the form of an epistolary journal she composed during an eighteen-month visit to Cuba for her health while still in her twenties. The *Cuba Journal*, as it came to be known, brims with wit and energy. Many pages are filled with vivid, euphoric descriptions of tropical vegetation and local customs. And the work possesses that ingredient necessary for all good writing: a *voice*. Part travelogue, part memoir, part *bildungsroman*, the journal is the portrait of an artist awakening into a life of the senses—a world rich with color and fragrance and textures that were largely unknown in frosty New England. Like Mary Emerson's Almanacks, it also one of the earliest works of transcendentalist nature writing we have, anticipating Waldo Emerson's *Nature* by two years and Henry David Thoreau's *Walden* by more than a decade.

In 1840, the year Elizabeth opened her bookshop, Sophia lived with the Peabody family above the business. She soon began attending Fuller's meetings, drawn to the talk of the women, especially when it concerned the topic of art. But she was even more charmed by Margaret Fuller, who seemed to her an example of fearless and uncompromising vision. By the time the second series of Conversations began later that year, Sophia had become one of the group's most committed participants. She composed an essay on music, which she read aloud to the gathered women. On another occasion, she assembled a small collection of her paintings and drawings and exhibited them for the entire group. And she wrote a worshipful sonnet to Fuller entitled "To a Priestess of the Temple Not Made with Hands" (the temple was the group of women who congregated at 13 West Street). The poem concluded with the following tribute to Fuller's talk:

> My Priestess! thou hast risen through thought supreme
> To central insight of eternal Law;
> Thy golden-cadenced intuitions seem
> From that new heaven which John of Patmos saw—
>   Behold! I reverent stand before thy shrine
>   In recognition of thy words divine.[4]

The image is of Fuller towering—almost levitating—above the rest of the women, a modern-day prophet revealing a new society in which women played a more active role. In truth, the revelations that arose during the Conversations did not come from Fuller alone, but were almost always collaborative, the shared product of minds abuzz with thought. And word of those ideas was spreading. By early 1841, news of the meetings had reached much of cultured New England, where they were alternately praised and ridiculed. The Reverend William Ellery Channing alerted Elizabeth that "misunderstandings and ugly things" were being said about the talks, and a young Julia Ward Howe wrote her sisters to let them know she was attending "to-morrow (don't be shocked!) a conversation at Miss Fuller's."[5] One woman in Concord archly noted, "I am urged on every side to go to Miss Fuller's 'Conversations,' but do not feel much interested in them. I do not believe they will amount to much good, because the members are not all *genuine* people."[6]

Still, many forward-thinking New Englanders believed Fuller's gatherings were exciting—a harbinger of things to come. When Waldo Emerson eventually attended a talk (Fuller invited men for one ill-fated series), he came away thinking that he had witnessed some of "the most entertaining conversation in America."[7] And the artist and transcendentalist Sarah Freeman Clarke, James's sister, felt the Conversations forever altered the way she perceived the world. She attributed their popularity to Fuller herself, who had "unusual truth-speaking power. Encountering her glance, something like an electric shock was felt. Her eye pierced your disguises."[8]

Although Sophia Peabody did not talk during the Conversations as much as her sister Elizabeth—almost *no one* talked as much as Elizabeth—she brought to the gatherings a profound sensitivity to beauty. To the gathered women she described her trips to the Athenaeum to copy a sculpture of Orpheus by Thomas Crawford (a mildly scandalous subject, since the figure was almost completely nude). She asked Fuller to recite sonnets about Greek art. And she absorbed the ideas of Fuller and the other participants about the role of women in the nineteenth century. In fact, the question that preoccupied her most was whether a woman could form an equitable and fulfilling relationship with a man.

Like her oldest sister, Sophia had from a young age determined never to marry. To be an artist required time and freedom. It required solitude. Besides, she was terrified by the hazards of childbirth—a fear no doubt intensified by girlhood memories of her mother's final pregnancy. Once, when a close friend married, Sophia dreamed of a sky filled with clouds in the shape of coffins. The message was clear: marriage was a form of death, both an end to possibility and a mortal risk to body and soul. "I never intend to have a husband," she wrote her mother, and then underscored her conviction that marriage was a form of possession: "Rather I should say I never intend any one should have me for a wife."[9]

Yet by the time she joined Fuller's Conversations, she was secretly engaged to a moody, reclusive, stunningly beautiful man named Nathaniel Hawthorne, at the time a little-known writer who lived with his mother. In accepting him as her future husband, she had rejected the example of her sister Elizabeth. She had also disappointed her mother, Eliza, who was determined to keep Sophia in the Peabody household for as long as possible. She had accepted Nathaniel (her father's name, as well), perfectly aware of the dangers of marrying a man incapable of supporting his family.[10] But she was determined that her marriage would be different. She would prove to the world that a union between a man and woman could be a creative partnership, a collaboration of equals, that it could produce a life as satisfying and exquisitely formed as a work of art.

2.

By the time she was born, on September 21, 1809, the Peabody family had settled in Salem, a seaport town notable for its Gallows Hill, where dozens of women, accused of flying on broomsticks and sickening cows through black magic, had been hung as witches in 1692 (figure 29). The streets of Salem were lined with elegant Federal homes built by silk merchants and ship captains with an eye to

Figure 29. Salem, ca. 1810.

displaying their prosperity. Beneath their hipped and gabled roofs were spiral staircases, mahogany paneling, brocade divans, and crystal from Calcutta, all imported before Thomas Jefferson's disastrous Embargo Act of 1807 curtailed much of the city's sea trade. When Nathaniel Peabody moved his family to the first of several nondescript clapboard houses and opened a medical practice, it was already too late to capitalize on the town's wealthy patients. Salem's dwindling prospects, painfully evident in the ships that lay tilted and rotting along the waterfront, quickly forced him to abandon medicine altogether. He took up dentistry instead, fashioning wooden dentures in a little workshop attached to the house and proselytizing about the novel benefits of brushing one's teeth. In 1824, he wrote a modest treatise entitled *The Art of Preserving Teeth*, which recommended, among other things, "a tincture of myrrh" for gums that "are tender and spungy"[11] (figure 30).

Sophia, born in Salem, was a worrisome child: "high-strung, quick-witted, and quick-tempered," according to her son. As a child, her most notable characteristic was an inclination toward "playful mischief."[12] But her headstrong personality was accompanied by a sense of beauty that bordered on the voluptuous. One of her earliest memories was of stepping outside to admire the "bright sunshine, as it flooded the grass and shrubbery." Intoxicated by "the clear, fresh appearance of every object," she felt as though the entire world had been "washed and then arrayed in gold."[13] When she was eleven, she wrote to Elizabeth, who was then teaching in Maine, a rhapsodic description of a sunset that already reveals her painterly eye: "Light purple clouds high above the horizon tinged with gold and a large black cloud above that is ringed with white."[14]

Two of Sophia's earliest friends were the daughters of Mary Moody Emerson's onetime friend and collaborator, Mary Van Schalkwyck. After the death of her French planter husband, Van Schalkwyck had returned to Concord and eventually married a second time—to the distinguished judge and Massachusetts state senator, Daniel Appleton White—bearing two daughters before dying at the age of thirty-five. Mary and Eliza White became acquainted with Sophia when their widower father moved to Salem, and with Sophia they shared secrets and opinions, including their thoughts on the attributes of men and the "spiritualizing" influence of the moon. To them she in turn confessed a tendency to lose herself in ecstasies of sensation: "I always seem to myself to be blended with anything that excites my admiration," she told Mary White, "& I am lost in what I gaze upon."[15]

She was just three when the family moved to a brick rowhouse on the corner of Union and Essex streets. Directly behind the new home was a large wooden structure known as the Manning House, inhabited by a family thought peculiarly "unsocial in their temperament"—a reclusive mother, her son, and two daughters. These were the widow and orphans of Captain John Hathorne, "the sternest man who ever walked a deck," a sea captain who had died of yellow fever off the northeast coast of South America in 1808, one year before Sophia was born.[16]

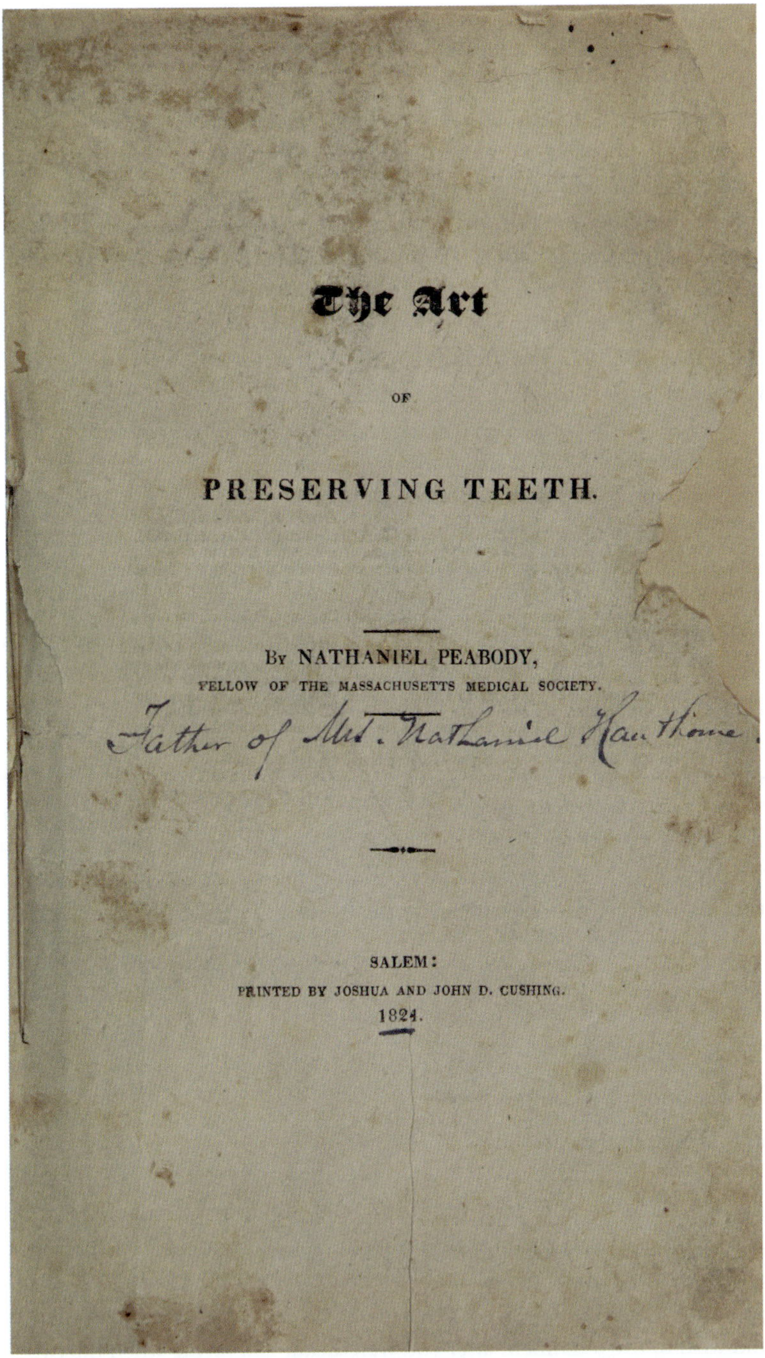

Figure 30. Nathaniel Peabody's treatise on dentistry.

The boy, Nathaniel, would later call the Manning house "Castle Dismal," a reference to its cloistered, funereal atmosphere. The Peabody girls "used to play with the Hawthorne children," according to Elizabeth, although they were less interested in the "broad-shouldered little boy, with clustering locks" than in his older daughter, known as Ebe, a thin, raven-haired presence whose regal intensity prompted the Peabody sisters to regard her as "a brilliant young girl."[17]

Around this time, and with her mother Eliza's approval, Elizabeth assumed the task of educating Sophia. The girl was just four when Elizabeth directed her away from the "dreadful doctrines" of Calvinism, introducing her to the more benevolent teachings of Unitarianism. Soon she guided Sophia's early reading. "*I hope from my inmost heart*," she told the child, "...that the studies in which you are now engaged will be pursued with unremitted industry." When Sophia was eleven, Elizabeth instructed her to use "the *leisure* you at present enjoy for obtaining a classical education," for "if it is best for minds of boys—it is best also for the minds of *girls*."[18] Greek, Latin, and Hebrew were necessary elements of Sophia's education, Elizabeth thought, since, as their mother believed, "mind has no sex."

Elizabeth instructed her young protégé to continue the "cultivation of your intellect, your taste, and your heart, by literature & science, by the fine arts, and by those habits of pious meditation, charitable judgement, benevolent feeling and severe self examination which taken together constitute religion."[19] And she proposed an ambitious reading list that included important masterworks from the previous generation: William Paley's *Natural Theology* (1802) and *Evidences of Christianity* (1794); William Enfield's *History of Philosophy* (1791); and Joseph Priestley's *History of the Corruptions of Christianity* (1782). A year later, when Sophia was twelve, Elizabeth assigned half a dozen theological tracts and treatises before advising her to "read the [New] Testament thro' in relation to each of these documents *separately*."[20] Elizabeth eventually even devised a study schedule for her younger sister:

Monday and Thursday: French
Tuesday, Friday, and Wednesday morning: Latin
Saturday morning: composition
Saturday afternoon: drawing.[21]

Sophia was a diligent pupil, eager to please. But resentment simmered just below the surface of her relationship with Elizabeth. She did not like to be told what to do, and from a young age she felt ambivalent about her oldest sister's disregard for conventional femininity. "I have often told you I believe that I never felt as if I could wish to live a moment after you were dead," she wrote when the two were adults, then added: "—I have thought of this so much that I have dreamed of your death a hundred times with every particular circumstance."[22] She loved Elizabeth and felt grateful for the education she had received. But it was only by imagining her absence that she felt entirely free.

She kept a commonplace book filled with extracts of contemporary verse. These pages suggest another source of tension between the two sisters, revealing a mind drawn less to history and philosophy—Elizabeth's primary interests—than to poetry and art. Written in an immaculate hand, Sophia's extracts featured some of Elizabeth's favorite poets, including Wordsworth and Coleridge, but also included were the more voluptuous verses of Keats, who claimed that with any great artist "the sense of Beauty overcomes every other consideration, or rather obliterates all consideration."[23] She admired as well the risqué Byron, a poet Elizabeth vigorously denounced for his immorality. Sophia's commonplace book is also filled with poetry by Americans: Longfellow, James Gates Percival, and William Cullen Bryant, whose descriptions of nature especially pleased her.

At some point, she copied into her book the work of a Danish dramatist named Adam Oehlenschläger, a close friend of Goethe, Fichte, and Germaine de Stäel. Oehlenschläger introduced Romanticism to Denmark with a work called *Correggio, a Tragedy*. Although it is now forgotten, the drama, published in 1811, offered one of the first Romantic depictions of the tragic artist. The play describes the Renaissance painter Correggio as an artist buffeted by operatic gusts of feeling, an artist whose work reflects, as one critic put it, the "struggle of genius with adverse circumstances, its hopes, its dreams, its disappointments, its consolations, its antagonism to whatever is ignoble and mercenary..."[24] Sophia copied the entire five-act play into her commonplace book.

Elizabeth never entirely approved of her sister's aestheticism. She criticized Sophia's prose style as too ornamental and complained that her writing was marred by the "peculiar manner of expression which... arises from your adopting the French idiom into our language—that you first began to do for fun... & which I must confess strikes me as *slang*."[25] Yet she was pleased with her sister's diligent efforts to learn a classical curriculum. Sophia, in turn, was grateful to have had such an exceptional preceptress. "All I hope for is that I should succeed as well as *you* did," she wrote Elizabeth when she was fourteen, describing an ambitious course of study that included six days a week of French (taught by a M. Louvosier), Italian, ancient literature, and arithmetic.[26]

Elizabeth kept the girl apprised of the new ideas she encountered in Boston, so that by the time she was twenty, Sophia could exclaim, "How immeasurable and exquisite are the analogies between Nature and man!... The butterfly, child of the sun, bursts from its self-wrought tomb,... and flutters away its day—its all of heaven, touched by the finger of light with sunset hues—like the resurrection of man in all but duration of bliss."[27] The sentiment could have come directly from a sermon by the Reverend William Ellery Channing—or, more likely, from Elizabeth's rendering of a sermon in the letters she sent home to Salem.

At the same time, Sophia expressed the idea of human transformation in a resplendent language Elizabeth was incapable of producing herself.

Throughout her life, Sophia espoused the view that the world was presided over by a benevolent spirit who managed the ultimate progress of the universe. This belief was filtered through an aesthetic sensibility, causing her to suppose that natural beauty led to the perception of God. To gaze upon a bank of wildflowers or to study the sculpture of a young faun by Praxiteles, Sophia believed, was to glimpse the creative power of the deity as it was translated by nature or human creativity.

Elizabeth disagreed. In 1835, after receiving a letter filled with Sophia's rapturous descriptions, she starchily proclaimed, "Sentiments about beauty do not constitute religion."[28] Sophia felt neither chided nor rebuked. She respected her sister's learning, her curiosity, and her openness to new ideas. But she thought that Elizabeth was blind to an entire category of human experience. As she expressed it, "Beauty is the subtle, invisible bond that connects the outward with the inward. Sever this association . . . and man is shorn of glory."[29]

3.

By the time her youngest daughter was born, Eliza Peabody was tired and thin and thoroughly discouraged by life. Her husband's talent for failure had not abated, and the family would soon rely on Elizabeth's entrepreneurial efforts, as well as Mary's salary as a teacher, to stay afloat. Eliza was entering "the most agonized period of my life," as she later called it, a period of overwork and "stupyfying" headaches treated with opium.[30] Perhaps this was why she treated Sophia so differently than her two older daughters. "I firmly resisted all coercion in your bringing up," she told her years later. "When you shreiked, I soothed & comforted till your affectionate heart melted and to save me from suffering, you made an effort to subdue the rebellious spirit within."[31] Instead of encouraging her youngest daughter to venture into the world, as she had with Elizabeth and Mary, Eliza determined to protect her from disappointment, to shelter her from feeling thwarted or defeated.

She excused Sophia from chores. She excused her from church attendance. She even excused her from helping in the classroom. She cossetted and spoiled. While Elizabeth and Mary left home as teenagers to help support the family, Sophia remained behind, coddled by her mother and adored by her three younger brothers. In 1819, the year Eliza's last child, Charlotte Peabody, was born (she lived only a few weeks), Mary Peabody returned to Salem and found "a tall girl sitting in the doorway, dressed in mourning calico"—a girl "so altered that I did not know her." It was Sophia, aged ten, "weary & worn . . . an embodied headache."[32]

Sophia had been a robust and active infant, but her "teething was difficult," wrote her son, "and, by way of relieving her, she was incontinently dosed with drugs, from the harmful effects of which she never recovered, and which subjected her, among other things, to acute nervous headache."[33] Nathaniel Peabody was merely following standard medical practice by administering teething powder laced with mercurous chloride, also known as calomel, to his daughter. The powder, which was sold in the United States until the middle of the twentieth century, was believed to calm cranky children and rid their digestive systems of parasites. Opium was often an ingredient.

"Heroic medicine"—an aggressive regimen of bloodletting, purgatives, and powerful drugs—remained a popular form of treatment until later in the century. Administering large doses of calomel was thought to shock the body into healthfulness. Unfortunately, mercury is highly toxic. Even small doses cause excessive salivation and a grotesque swelling of the face and tongue. The element's long-term effects, when consumed, are even more insidious. The writer Louisa May Alcott received large doses of calomel as a young nurse during the Civil War, and for the next twenty years, her health steadily deteriorated, her hair and teeth falling out, a sharp pain radiating down her back and arms, and her throat blistered and raw for months at a time.

Sophia first began to experience severe headaches around the time the infant Charlotte died—almost a decade after being treated with calomel by her father. At times, the throbbing in her temples was so severe that the clanking of silverware from downstairs proved an "excruciating torture."[34] She writhed at the noise "the carriage made, growling over the pavements," and took to her sick bed amid the "clishmaclavering among the cows."[35] In letters to friends and relatives, she called her affliction the "demon in my head," and described her headaches as "cork-screws, borers, pincers, daggers, squibs and bombs."[36] The pain was accompanied by other symptoms: fever, delirium, "terrific visions." Mary reported that sleep seldom seemed to refresh Sophia. She often woke "in a state of wild chaos."[37] On several occasions, the headaches were so bad she could barely walk; at other times, her headaches produced a euphoric, almost manic, state. "[W]hat a singular elation of mind [the pain] brings with it," she wrote during one of these occasions. "I could study Hebrew or hieroglyphics, or solve the abstrusest problems better now than ever if my eyes would keep steady and would see."[38]

Her symptoms were made worse by a battery of dubious treatments. From a young age, Sophia was given the same drug Eliza relied on—opium. By the time she was twenty she had become dependent on it. Elizabeth later recalled that for an entire year, Sophia "was living on hyoscyamus"—a concoction of black henbane, another narcotic, that produced a twilight sleep and caused rapid pulse, headache, and delirium.[39] The treatments seemed to blur the boundaries between self and world, and in 1829, Sophia recounted to a friend how she had taken "too much" ether, which produced a "comical as well as disagreeable effect. I felt as if there was a raging conflagration within me, and then just as the water looks when you throw a stone into it and the circles widen ad infinitum around it. My senses were these circles, and I became more and more confused as they were farther removed from the centre until I was obliged to yeild up wholly to the diffusion."[40]

Other treatments included arsenic, as well as leeches, which Sophia whimsically described as those "incomparable, lovely, gentle, delicate, considerate, generous, fine, disinterested, excellent, dear, elegant, knowing, graceful, active, lively, animated, beautiful *leeches*."[41] When the Peabody family moved to Boston, a succession of physicians "tried their hands at curing her," according to Elizabeth, "and she went through courses of their poisons, each one bringing her to death's door, and leaving her less able to cope with the pain they did not reach."[42]

One doctor was Walter Channing, the younger brother of Elizabeth's mentor, William Ellery Channing. He had a drooping moustache and long, flowing hair, which meant he cut a romantic figure in the hidebound world of Boston medicine. (In his youth, he had planned to become an artist, and despite his busy rounds as a doctor he managed to write essays on *Hamlet* and *King Lear* (figure 31).) His treatment of Sophia was unconventional. He prescribed shower baths, carriage

Figure 31. Dr. Walter Channing.

rides, and trips to the seashore. He also recommended rest cures in South America or Cuba—an impossibly expensive proposition for the struggling Peabody family. When Sophia described the severity of her headaches, Channing soothed her. He said "that how ever long, and severe the hours of pain may be, the mind may still remain true to itself." He added that despite her suffering, the "disease [had] made no conquest." Then he contradicted this prognosis; Sophia was without any "disease but *the habit of being sick*."[43]

Eliza felt uneasy about Channing. She encouraged her daughter to consider herself an invalid: "It must be expected that every year of physical suffering will render her nervous system more sensitive." She fretted that her daughter was infatuated with the physician, confiding to Mary Peabody that Sophia "so loves Dr. C., that if he prescribed decapitation I believe she would feel uneasy not to submit."[44] Her insistence on Sophia's poor health was also a strategy meant to prevent her from leaving home. Under Eliza's management, meals were brought upstairs to the invalid. Nathaniel and the Peabody boys walked on tiptoes and spoke in hushed voices. In 1828, having moved to Boston for a brief spell, the Peabodys solicited the governor of Massachusetts to refrain from firing cannons during the Fourth of July. The governor refused, but in deference to the request, he directed the fusillade to be aimed away from the Common and toward the river.[45]

Illness can become a part of one's identity. It can serve as a shield and an escape. Sophia's invalidism certainly protected her from having to prove herself as exceptional as her older sisters. At the same time, she portrayed her suffering as an illustration of moral purity, of Christlike resignation. "To night I feel like the embodied spirit of pain," she wrote, "as if my veins were finer than a cambric needle and that through them a deluge of fiery metal was struggling to wend." (She was eighteen when she wrote this.) But bodily torment could be a source of joy—it illustrated "GOD's inexpressible love" by instructing her in the art of renunciation. As she explained on another occasion, "I do believe that Sickness and Pain are some of the highest ministers of GOD's inexpressible love."[46]

Eliza encouraged this perspective. "Perhaps no one better than myself can appreciate the benefit past years of pain have been to you," she told Sophia. "They have formed for you a character at once lovely and elevated, correcting, subduing, eradicating self-sufficiency, pride, obstinacy." What Eliza did not say was that these "years of pain" also kept Sophia home and dependent. "We live for our dear invalids," she murmured, "our happiness is to devote time and talents to their comfort."[47]

Sickness had other benefits. It freed Sophia from the work of her sisters. When Elizabeth asked her to assist in her Maine classroom, the girl gently refused, claiming headache. In 1838, when Elizabeth tried to coax her again, this time with their brother's school in West Newton, the answer was the same. "Do not suggest any plans to me dear, for mercy's sake," she replied. "You can have no idea how it wearies me.... I do not want anything expected of me."[48]

But if illness afforded certain freedoms, it stripped away others. When Sophia was thirteen, she announced her desire to read Edward Gibbon's six-volume *History of the Rise and Fall of the Roman Empire.* Eliza overruled the idea; Sophia "had had enough history for one her age."[49] As she grew older, she longed to escape the sickroom, to escape her mother's anxious, claustrophobic supervision. In 1825—and only with the rare interposition of her father—she was allowed to travel by chaise to New Hampshire. Three years later, she visited her Aunt Mary Palmer, Eliza's younger sister, in Brattleboro, Vermont. There she climbed nearby mountains and rode horseback with her cousins. Miraculously, her headaches vanished, prompting Eliza to respond with panicked letters urging her immediate return. She argued that her daughter didn't have enough clothes for an extended visit. Then she noted that Sophia's continued presence was inconvenient to her hostess. Next, she employed guilt: "you have not health enough to make yourself useful in the family or the school, and if you had it would be your duty to be home studying & assisting the boys." She swerved to flattery—"I must acknowledge, that the kind & cheering tone of your voice and your mirth inspiring laugh . . . would be cordial to me." Then she made a final, imperious demand: "The high state you are in is not exactly the thing for your head. Come home now, and live awhile upon the past."[50]

Sophia was not yet twenty. She had no desire to live upon the past. That her symptoms vanished the minute she left home suggests that mercury poisoning wasn't the only toxic ingredient in her system. Something about the Peabody family dynamic—with its exceptional young women who defied gender roles, as well as its disappointed mother who clung to her youngest and a largely absent father—affected Sophia's health. It made her sick.

Two years after the trip to Vermont, in the summer of 1830, she embarked upon an even more audacious experiment. She left home to live alone in nearby Dedham, Massachusetts. The trip was apparently prompted by a health crisis, for she explained in her journal that she hoped the "voluntary rustification" would ease her symptoms.[51] But the departure from home was also an assertion of independence, a shedding of her reliance on Eliza.

Dedham is a quintessential New England town, with a small green overlooked by a white church. A decade or so later, the settlers of Brook Farm, including Nathaniel Hawthorne, would launch their utopian community just three miles away. Settling into a boardinghouse on the outskirts of town, Sophia rejoiced in her newfound freedom, celebrating the chance to immerse herself "in the holy country, alone with the trees & birds, my first retreat into solitude." Like Mary Moody Emerson before her—or like Henry David Thoreau a decade and a half later—she found herself deeply stirred by long, private walks through pastures, pine groves, and the chain of stony hills southeast of town. One day, while reading de Gerando's treatise on education in French (Elizabeth had not yet translated it), she felt a strange sensation. "I looked from the illuminated page to the wide heavens & spreading earth—& felt something ~~within me~~ which answered to [Jean Paul] Richter's sentiment, *Man has a universe within him, as well as without.*"[52] She probably learned of Richter from Thomas Carlyle's recent essay in *Blackwood's Magazine.* But the melding of inner and outer worlds Sophia described would soon become a hallmark of transcendentalist thought.

Her Dedham journal repeatedly describes such ecstatic experiences. Horseback riding is "an exhilaration I never dreamed of elsewhere—even I!" The moon passing through a scrim of clouds at the same moment a breeze ruffles her hair is a "celestial anodyne." One night, awakened by a thunderstorm, she suddenly thought, "God is here." Feeling "wrought up to the highest pitch of excitement, & my pulses beating madly," she knew herself to be "in the arms of Infinite love."[53] Like the time she had inhaled too much ether, she now found herself enlarged and diffused, her spirit pouring out into nature. She strolled the nearby woods, pencil and sketchbook in hand. The weather had started to cool. The leaves were turning russet and orange, and the atmosphere shimmered with life. "I held my breath to hear the breathing of the spirit around me," she wrote, convinced of nature's restorative properties: "Oh I know I shall be better than I have been for years in this solitude."[54]

While Sophia exalted, Eliza suffered. "[I]t is *forgotten* that I have a heart to feel and a mind to enjoy," she wrote, reminding Sophia of her "sensitive nature,… shattered nerves,…precarious health."[55] The trips to Vermont and Dedham would set a pattern between them. Calling her mother "the tenderest and loveliest mother in the world," Sophia nevertheless sought reprieves from her cloistered existence.[56] The trip to Dedham also revealed something else: not only did her mother exacerbate Sophia's illness—her art did, as well.

4.

Like theology or literature, law, or medicine, painting historically was a man's domain. Genteel ladies learned to draw and paint flowers or baskets of apples in watercolor. But as Samuel Johnson declared at the end of the eighteenth century, the "[p]ublic practice of any art and staring in men's faces is very indelicate in a female."[57] Oil painting especially was considered a masculine pursuit, a brawny grappling with a difficult medium. To top it off, artistic ambition was unladylike.

These attitudes were beginning to change in the nineteenth century. "What a variety of mechanic arts may be executed by the fair sex…when they possess a reflecting mind and genius?" asked the American painter Charles Willson Peale in his autobiography from the 1820s.[58] Peale was an uncle to four nieces—Anna, Harriet, Sarah, and Margaretta—each of whom painted still lifes and trompe l'oeil arrangements of hymnals and flutes. Occasionally they ventured an oil portrait of political figures. (Their father, James Peale, and their cousin, Rembrandt Peale,

Figure 32. Sarah Goodridge.

remain best remembered for their portraits of George Washington and Thomas Jefferson, respectively.)

Other women in the United States were beginning to make a name for themselves as artists. The Connecticut-born Ann Hall, whose airy, sentimental portraits helped spur a renaissance in miniature painting, had been instructed as a young woman by Samuel King, the painting master of Gilbert Stuart. At the peak of her fame, she made $500 per portrait—more than ten thousand dollars in today's money. The Goodridge sisters, Sarah and Eliza, also miniaturists, painted as many as three portraits a week (figure 32). (Sarah's audacious portrait of her own breasts, a delicate miniature entitled *Beauty Revisited*, was given as a present to one of her more famous subjects and possible lover, Daniel Webster.)

Sophia Peabody had been interested in drawing from an early age. When she was fifteen, she studied painting with an aunt. Her room smelled of pigments and oils and spirits, its corners crammed with rolls of canvas that she stretched and tacked onto wooden frames herself. It was Elizabeth who furnished Sophia with her first formal art lessons. She enlisted an "eccentric German drawing-master" named Francis Graeter, who had taught art in her Boston school (and would later instruct pupils at Bronson Alcott's Temple School). Elizabeth was convinced

Graeter possessed "the spirit of Art more completely than any instructor who has ever taught in this country." She may have been right; the young artist eventually instructed Henry Wadsworth Longfellow and his wife Fanny, along with other notable Bostonians. At the same time, he produced a series of exquisitely tinted lithographs for the *Atlas of Plates Illustrating the Geology of the State of Maine Accompanying the First Report on the Geology of that State*, written by Charles Jackson, the brother of the future Lydia Emerson.[59]

Graeter's talent extended beyond painting. The same year he instructed Sophia, in 1829, he published a novel entitled *Mary's Journey: A German Tale*. The book's titular heroine, a fugitive from revolutionary Europe, flees from the sexual predation of a cabal of decadent aristocrats. But the novel is really about her development as a landscape painter. Nature's "elementary spirits," Grater wrote, are "conjured up by the charms of her inspired mind, her art."[60] Equally appealing was the book's message that art could enable one to transcend all earthly difficulties: "If we cannot *break* our chains, the next best thing we can do, is to *play* with them."[61]

Graeter was eventually replaced by a morose young painter from Philadelphia named Thomas Doughty, later associated with the Hudson River School. Doughty was brooding and melancholy. He had a shaggy beard and thatch of wild, uncombed hair. He was the first American artist to paint landscapes exclusively (figure 33). Never particularly sociable, he instructed Sophia by example rather than by words, setting up his easel in an adjoining dayroom and painting for one

Figure 33. Thomas Doughty, *View of West Point* (1827).

hour while Sophia observed from her couch. Once he left, she placed her work next to his and copied what he had done. During the first lesson, her "whole organization underwent an agitation at the sight of him . . . It seemed as though he embodied art in some way, so that I was in its immediate presence and I felt consequently awestruck."[62]

Within weeks, she was producing credible reproductions of Doughty's landscapes (panoramic mountains, luminous clouds, brilliant sheets of water). But his method of instruction was intimidating; Sophia could barely "keep my eyes upon his creating finger, though he *was* raising rocks and flinging out branches of trees in a masterly manner."[63] She "had never felt so much about anything before" as she now felt about painting. Loading a brush with oils, lifting it to the canvas, building up layers of paint: all caused her to "tremble . . . from head to foot."[64] When she closed her eyes at night, she saw splashes of color, shadows and light.

Soon she was taking instruction from yet another painter, Chester Harding (figure 34). He was an imposing figure, six feet three inches in height, with a large, blunt countenance and hooded, staring eyes. Harding had marched as a drummer during the War of 1812. Then he worked as an itinerant carpenter, a chair-maker,

Figure 34. Chester Harding, ca. 1825.

an innkeeper, and finally a sign painter. Trying to produce a portrait of his wife on a scrap of wood, his life changed. "The moment I saw the likeness," he recalled, "I became frantic with delight: it was like the discovery of a new sense; I could think of nothing else."[65]

He had already spent time in Kentucky and St. Louis refining his talent, then traveling to England, where he painted portraits for members of royalty, including the Duke of Sussex (twice). *Blackwood's Magazine* called him "a fair specimen of the American character.... ignorant of drawing" but nevertheless able to produce likenesses "of extraordinary plainness, power, and sobriety."[66] When he returned to the United States, Harding briefly roomed in the same boarding house as Elizabeth and Mary Peabody, where the older sister told him about Sophia's lessons with Doughty. "Mr Harding wanted to see my picture," Sophia wrote in her journal in July 1830, "and politely praised it—and offered to teach me to paint heads—said I should copy his portrait of Allston which he would not suffer any body else in Boston to do." Sophia admired the portrait immensely, which captured "the attitude of a receiver of supernatural communion with something up and beyond—the eye looking through things temporal with the piercing fire (Promethean) of inspiration."[67] But she demurred from copying Allston's portrait, instead taking on a small painting of Harding's five-year-old daughter, Margaret, which she eventually gave to Mary Peabody for her classroom.

That summer, Harding painted the earliest and best-known portrait of Sophia. Posed against a somber backdrop, the twenty-one-year-old gazes with coy directness at the viewer. Her eyes are bright, her smile reminiscent of the Mona Lisa's. (Sophia never cared for Harding's version of her mouth; she retouched it several times in the coming years.) Her fingers are buried in the sateen billows of her dress since Harding remained abysmal at painting hands. If the young woman in the portrait is not conventionally pretty (as her older sister Mary was said to be by practically everyone), she is nonetheless arresting. Forthright, unflinching, she appears endowed with a rich inner life.

Toward the end of 1831, Elizabeth borrowed a landscape painted by Washington Allston and gave it to Sophia to hang in her room. Sophia stared at it, studied it, memorized each block of color, each tree and cloud. Then, in early January, she began to paint. The process gripped her. Painting was "a perfect rapture," an "enjoyment—almost intoxicating," she wrote. It was "altogether too intense for my physicals."[68] Working to recreate Allston's painting caused her to imagine other works. "What do you think I have actually begun to do?" she asked Elizabeth in a letter. "Nothing less than create and do you wonder that I lay awake all last night after sketching my first picture. I actually thought my head would have made its final explosion. When once I began to excurse, I could not stop. Three distinct landscapes came forth in full array besides that which I had arranged before I went to bed and it seemed that I should fly to be up and doing. I have determined not to force creative power but wait til it has mastered me and now I feel as if the time has come and such freedom and revelry does it bring!"[69]

Like her adored Romantic poets and painters, Sophia believed art was the product of inspiration. The true artist was but a vessel to be filled with divine vision. Sometimes this could lead to disappointment. Attempting to write a poem, she noted, "I have been wrapt in a cloud of poetry to night; but my Muse could not discharge it[self] of all the electric fluid of inspiration which it contained, as did Franklin's kite the thunder cloud."[70] Still, when the activity was lit by inspiration, nothing was more exciting. Her "whole mind, soul, heart & body [was] awake & busy" when she painted. The process was like "drawing up buckets of life with hard labour from the well of the mind."[71] Sometimes she even entered a kind of trance, surrendering herself to higher forces, "bodying forth the poet's dream—*Creation!*"[72]

In May of 1832, Allston visited Sophia to examine her copy of his landscape. "He took down my poor picture," she wrote Eliza, "& looked very attentively & long at it—I stood behind him, trembling like a sinner—Mary whispered 'Tell him you painted it in perfect ignorance' & like a parrot I said 'Mr. Allston I painted it in perfect ignorance'—He turned & replied 'But you have not painted it ignorantly—it does you great credit. I am very much surprised at it, for it is superior to what I expected, altho' I have heard it much spoken of.'"[73] Then he told her to paint from nature, not other artists. Her apprenticeship was over.

5.

From 1829 to 1832, Sophia developed rapidly as an artist. She made extensive notes "on the Uses of Colour," carefully delineating the use of contrasting and complimentary colors. These notes also set forth various artistic principles: "In Landscapes seen abounding with hues allied to green a red object, properly painted according to such hues in light shade or distance, conduces wonderfully to the life, beauty, harmony & connection of the colouring."[74] The journals chronicle her growing artistic maturity, as well as her worsening headaches.

One explanation for this is the painting itself. Some ingredients used to mix colors and varnish were nearly as noxious as calomel. For instance, lead white was hazardous, especially if ground or scraped from a palette or canvas, when it released its airborne particles. Symptoms from lead poisoning develop slowly. They include insomnia, delirium, hallucinations, abdominal pain, and weakness in the extremities. But the most common symptom is headache. Julius Caesar Ibetson's *An Accidence, or Gamut, of Oil Painting*, published in 1828, describes how lead white was made by mixing the lead with "a large proportion of spirits of turpentine," another poisonous substance that caused headaches, dizziness, even vomiting.[75] For Sophia, who described her fondness for the smell of turpentine and oil paints, her poor health was likely exacerbated by painting in a small upstairs bedroom, her "dear little chamber & studio in one," where bottles of turpentine for cleaning paintbrushes and preparing varnish sat open for hours on end.[76]

Less tangible forces also contributed. If Elizabeth taught her that "mind has no sex," Sophia nevertheless found this maxim confounded by her experience. Young women were not expected to pursue art with the singlemindedness of the male "genius." To achieve the highest level of skill required academic training and figure classes in which models posed nude—all of which was forbidden to women. So was the appearance of ambition. (This is why the essayist Judith Sargent Murray's hope one day to "descend with celebrity to posterity" was so scandalous.)

Once, when Sophia visited a friend, her hostess asked her not to paint or draw: "I always feel somehow, as if it was giving up, or losing something, when anyone is so all absorbed in any pursuit." Sophia's friend went on to complain that artists seemed selfish and unladylike, "living for their art, & not humanity."[77] Such statements were the norm. During a trip to Boston, Sophia attended a conversation that included her sister's mentor, William Ellery Channing, who mentioned a book "he had been reading about some women who would be painters—& that it was said they were generally wanting in strength, or as Fuseli said, 'There was no fist in it.'" Channing turned to Sophia, hoping for a rebuttal, but she was too embarrassed to answer. "I tried to respond to his kind notice of little me," she recalled; "but I found no thought could find expression."[78]

Her family's response to her painting was mixed. Eliza encouraged Sophia's art, believing it would tie her to the household. Elizabeth urged her to paint to earn an income. At the same time, her mother counseled ladylike modesty, while Elizabeth's unconventional independence inspired fearful hesitation. Sophia's own belief that an artist relied upon divine inspiration meant she could never produce work on demand. And the knowledge that she was permanently barred from traditional training was made all too clear when Washington Allston suggested that she find her way to Italy and devote several years to copying statues in charcoal, graphite, and crayon.

Painting, in other words, was a source of anxiety. Fired with enthusiasm when she first daubed burnt sienna or mustardy yellow ochre on a canvas, she quickly felt the weight of competing expectations, most arising from her family. In November 1832, she wrote Mary that she had begun to "*create*" an original work, describing a visionary experience in which "Landscape after landscape came past like Shakespeare's line of kings. Distant mountains—verdant vallies—winding rivers—graceful waterfalls—golden skies—Oh what a troop—I really feared for my senses." But the next day, she collapsed, her head "whirling like a top."[79]

Her journals now became a daily chronicle of the toll of creative effort. During one restless night she "understood the majesty—the beauty—the sublimity with startling clearness. Visions of landscapes and scenes such as never rose upon other mental eyes—ideal beauty—marble starting into curved lines of grace."[80] But ecstatic passages like these were often followed by descriptions of nightmares—one in which she was shot in the stomach by an unknown assailant—and agonizing headaches.

Those nightmares intensified in 1833, when Elizabeth hit upon another scheme to earn money for the Peabody family. She had just completed a "reading party" for women interested in learning Greek history and mythology, the success of which inspired a plan to publish a large, expensive volume of "Greek Theology and Mythology," with Sophia providing lithographic illustrations. The project was ambitious: "The whole cost will be 4770 dollars," Elizabeth wrote "—for paper… letterpress & printing." But the potential rewards persuaded her to embark on the venture. Soon she was firing off a barrage of instructions to Sophia. The illustrations were to copy the neoclassical style of John Flaxman, then in vogue for the spare line drawings he copied from Grecian urns. The first part of the book would "consist of questions of Senecas Theogony & Mythology—together with the heroic legends—& I wish to have every thing illustrated by a drawing either of a statue or a gem—or a cameo." She told Sophia she would herself "make tracings at the Athenaeum of every thing that is there which will suit my purposes (on thin paper)… and would like to know if you think you could copy from such models."[81]

Sophia jumped at the chance to illustrate her sister's book. Addressing Elizabeth as "my dearest Betty," "dear Biddy," "my Lizzie," she soon declared that drawing "the figure, drapery, and face[s]" of Venus and Hesiod had become her "great work." Images kept "welling up from the everlasting fount" of inspiration, and the task of bringing "these divine creations into the common light for all to see gives me a blessed feeling of serene pleasure."[82]

The art of lithography was still in its infancy, having been invented in 1796 by a German actor who needed an inexpensive way to reproduce theatrical posters. The process was tricky. An artist drew on a polished slab of limestone with oil-based crayon, then used a strong acid to etch away the surrounding blank areas. Ink was applied, and damp paper pressed onto the stone, leaving an image that was the reverse of the original drawing. The form required the artist to work quickly, backwards, and without correction.

Sophia had assumed Elizabeth would hire someone to transfer her images onto the stone. Her sister had other plans. "I can have any thing copied on stone & beautifully too by my sister Sophia," she told a friend.[83] Letters between the two grew tense. Elizabeth wrote that her budget included "baggage waggoning for 100 stones—each weighing I fancy nearly an hundred pounds."[84] Sophia, who had never worked in lithography, fretted: "I should not like to put a line upon the stone which was not perfect."[85] Because her hand trembled, she began tracing her work onto tissue paper laid atop crushed ochre, then transferring the image, using a fine steel point, onto the limestone—a laborious process that left her increasingly weak and nerve-wracked.

At first, she put on a brave front for Elizabeth. But her head had "taken to whirling," and her eyes blurred whenever she tried to draw.[86] She reassured Elizabeth that her ailments were "not on account of this"—meaning the book project—but by August she was bedridden.[87] Contributing to the strain was her anxiety that hundreds of readers would see her drawings. Public display always left Sophia feeling vulnerable, much as it did Emily Dickinson three decades later, when in "Publication—is the Auction/Of the Mind of Man," she expressed the commonly held notion that for a woman to display her work in public was a form of prostitution:

> Thought belong to Him who gave it—
> Then—to Him Who bear
> It's Corporeal illustration—sell
> The Royal Air—

For Sophia, the anxiety about public exposure manifested in nightmares. One dream involved her stepping into the dim family parlor and discovering Elizabeth lying stiff and pale in a coffin. The dream was part wish fulfilment. It was also fear that her failure might be the death of her sister's hopes. She woke in tears.

It was at this moment that a fortuitous incident occurred. Three years earlier, when Sophia was living in Dedham, she had received a letter from a family friend named Dorcas Hiller Cleveland, whose husband was a customs officer in Cuba. Sophia had written to ask about living in their Havana home. In response, she received a nightmarish depiction of the city: "Your olfactories are continually offended even to sickness," wrote Cleveland,

> with the hot steaming effusion from jerk beef half spoiled salt fish & dried fish pan fried or rather burned lard garlic, old tobacco mingled with the filth of streets never dry, & the slimy mud of which, is daily increased by the slop & trash of houses, & the whole kept constantly impregnated by the natural solution of urisalts from horses, mules & dogs innumerable & also by the blacks & white male population which contribute, by copious streams from the side of every door & every post & corner, to keep up the rank odours of the city.[88]

Men and animals pissed anywhere and everywhere.

Cleveland acknowledged this was "a disgusting subject—yet it is much worse to realize than to imagine; I will only add as a proof that I do not exaggerate, that—the stone of the houses is rotted away in holes every where by the continual repetition of this unhealthful & offensive custom." Moreover, the noises of the city were almost as bad as its smell. There was a perpetual cacophony "from multitudes of negroes, wholly unrestrained in their manner—together with the waggons,—& volantes & mules, & every hour the ding, dong, of the convent bells & the firing of cannon I assure you we have to approach quite near each other to converse understandingly & not infrequently suspend what we are saying till the clattering is past."[89]

Now, in the summer of 1833, and despite these dire warnings, Mrs. Cleveland contacted Elizabeth with a proposition. A physician in the countryside outside Havana needed a governess to teach his fifteen-year-old daughter and two small sons. Perhaps one of the talented Peabody sisters might be interested? Elizabeth immediately formed a plan: Mary would take the position as governess, accompanied by Sophia, who would convalesce in Cuba's healthful climate.

At first, Sophia resisted. "[D]o not send me to the Havanas among strangers," she wrote. "I do not want to lay my head under the pomegranates & citron trees—& do not know how I ever bore the idea of leaving my kith & kin."[90] It was Mary—always the more reasonable and diplomatic sister—who convinced Sophia of the idea's soundness: "There is nothing in this plan, surely, that is wild or visionary—it seems to unite everything desirable, and I feel as if it might do you a real lasting good."[91]

Preparations for the trip would take several months. Friends were enlisted to escort the sisters on the ship from Boston to Havana. Then, on the starlit morning of December 4, 1833—several weeks before Waldo Emerson set out on his grand tour of Europe after the death of his wife Ellen—Sophia and Mary Peabody rose early and inspected their trunks a final time before setting off from Boston Harbor for the most momentous journey of their lives.

6.

The brig *Newcastle* met crashing waves and icy gales after leaving port. At times the sea was so rough that Mary and Sophia were lashed to hogsheads of beef to keep from being washed overboard. Then, just as quickly, the storm passed. The waters calmed. Within days, the weather grew deliciously warm and resolved into a vision of blues: endless sea and endless sky. Sophia befriended the captain, who lent her his spyglass to peer at the horizon, and a mile or so from Cuba she caught sight of a palm tree through the collapsible brass tube.

She made another acquaintance on the passage. James Rice Burroughs was a courtly Bostonian in his forties. He owned a sugar plantation in Cuba. Despite chronic seasickness, Burroughs stood next to Sophia at the ship's rails, "devotedly attentive," woozily pointing out flying fishes, "a large majestic tropical bird," and a pod of porpoises, which the captain tried, unsuccessfully, to harpoon.[92] On one romantic evening, Burroughs accompanied Sophia on deck to watch the moonlight silver the quiet expanse of water. As soon as they reached Havana, where the Peabody sisters were to rest up before traveling to their ultimate destination, he accompanied them around the city in a *volante*, a special two-wheeled carriage popular in Cuba (figure 35). The trio toured the Espada Cemetery, with its

Figure 35. A Cuban volante.

towering crypts, and the botanical gardens, as well as the just-completed Paseo, built to resemble a Parisian boulevard.

Havana, as Mrs. Cleveland had warned them, was considerably louder than Boston or sleepy little Salem (plate 6). A deluge of noise assaulted them from morning to night, including the relentless drumming at dawn to awaken the soldiers, the chanting of African stevedores hauling sugar and coffee into the ships, the ceaseless cries of fruit vendors, and the church bells that tolled throughout the day—"Tinkle, tinkle, bang, bang, squeak, squeak," Sophia wrote. Then there was the continuous hammering and clanking, and "the scream of macaws & parrots and all the unmusical birds that make a grand noise." To make matters worse, a noisy Catalan family lived on the floor below the Clevelands. Their perpetual shouting was enough, Sophia said, "to create a slow fever."[93]

Mary and Sophia soon traveled to a coffee plantation forty-five miles west of Havana. The trip required two days of jarring travel over narrow, boggy roads. In the distance were red-tiled haciendas scattered among endless rows of palm trees. Even farther away, the jagged, plum-colored San Salvador mountains loomed and towered. The sisters were accompanied by Burroughs, who by now was something of a fixture, and a driver named Carlos, their employer's servant, who made sure the party stopped to refresh themselves every few hours with *naranjadas*, a local orange drink. Around sunset of the second day, Mary and Sophia arrived at La Recompensa, the estate where they would spend the next eighteen months.

The hacienda, with its cool tile floors and large plastered rooms, was owned by Dr. Robert Morrell, a prominent local physician and enslaver with a thick French accent. He had a lucrative sideline hosting New Englanders with chronic illnesses. A previous guest and an acquaintance of the Peabody family, Abiel Abbott, had written a book about his stay in Cuba, describing his host as "exceedingly well informed, and judicious, and possess[ing] colloquial powers."[94] Absent from Abbott's account was the story of Morrell's childhood in Haiti, where his family fled Toussaint Louverture's revolution against slavery before settling in Cuba. They lived in the fertile San Marco region, which produced much of the island's corn, indigo, tobacco, and sugar.

Morrell's wife, Laurette de Tousard Morrell, was also from the Caribbean, the daughter of a French artillerist who traveled to America with Lafayette and lost an arm fighting in the Revolutionary War. (The Chevalier Louis de Tousard later convinced his friend George Washington to open West Point.) Sophia admired her dark complexion and thick black hair, always adorned with tropical flowers, as well as her sociability. Señora Morrell "treats Mary and I with the greatest confidence," Sophia reported, "as if she had always known us."[95]

The Morrells had three children—Luisa, Eduardo, and Carlito—and the entire family spoke a different language at each meal: French, Spanish, or English. In the evenings, they gathered around an ebony grand piano and took turns playing waltzes and minuets. Almost immediately, Sophia's health improved, as Mary noted in a letter to their mother soon after arriving. "[W]hen I tell you that Sophia rode 45 miles three days ago, over roads which pass all description for horrors, and that she slept soundly all that night, and was not wakened even by the great bell that hangs near the house, got up to breakfast, and has been better ever since, except being very tired and achy, you will allow that I was right in my expectations that she would be cured by this same trip to Cuba."[96]

Sophia soon wrote her own letter home, the first in a series of descriptive accounts that eventually came to be known as the "Cuba Journal." In its entirety, the journal contained fifty-six letters and numbered more than 900 pages. Most of the correspondence was addressed to Eliza, but it soon gained a wider readership, thanks to Elizabeth who, tireless as ever, copied and distributed them to at least twenty-five friends. (As always, she was eager to promote her artistic sister's latest production.) Among those who eventually read or heard portions of Sophia's letters were Bronson and Abba Alcott, Waldo and Lydia Emerson, and the Channing family. Elizabeth even hosted reading parties, some of which lasted as long as seven hours, festive gatherings in which the guests took turns reading

Sophia's letters out loud. Elizabeth tactfully omitted her sister's "offensive enthusiasms" whenever she read.[97]

There was good reason for all this interest. Throughout the nineteenth century, a steady wave of books about Cuba appeared in the United States. Besides the one by Abiel Abbott, there were prominent books by Richard H. Dana, the author of *Two Years Before the Mast*, and Julia Ward Howe, who attended Margaret Fuller's Conversations and later achieved fame by writing "The Battle Hymn of the Republic." A year after Sophia and Mary left the island, a scurrilous anti-Catholic novel was published in the United States called *Rosamond: or, A Narrative of the Captivity and Sufferings of an American Female Under the Popish Priests, in the Island of Cuba, with a Full Disclosure of Their Manners and Customs, Written by Herself*. The novel, which told of a young widow seduced by a wicked priest, claimed to reveal "the general depravity of a whole country."[98]

These works suggest some of the reasons Cuba exerted a powerful pull on nineteenth-century imaginations. The island nation was exotic, lush: Spanish and therefore Catholic. It sat astride important shipping lanes, making it the object, according to former president John Quincy Adams, "of transcendental importance to the political and commercial interests of our Union."[99] Most important, it was a hub in the larger empire of slavery, a capitol in the international economy built on labor stolen from enslaved Africans. The coffee enjoyed by New Englanders and the sugar with which they sweetened it were the result of the blood and toil of *bosales*: men and women captured on the coast of Africa and shipped by the Middle Passage to replace those who had died in the brutal conditions of Cuba's plantations. The island was a flashpoint and symbol for pro- and antislavery activists alike (figure 36).

Sophia's Cuba Journal rarely addressed these topics. She considered art and politics incompatible and showed little interest in the island's economy and history.* To some extent, she was defining herself in opposition to Elizabeth, who would have immersed herself in these very aspects of Cuba. She also sensed that even to consider the island's brutal slave regime was to threaten her health. Her journal, concerned primarily with aesthetic descriptions, is almost entirely a record of intrinsic experiences—a chronicle of morning rides, subtropical flora, temperate climate, and the joyful emotions these things summoned within her.

She had been in Cuba less than a month when she learned she had created a minor scandal back home. Elizabeth had learned of James Rice Burroughs's attentions. The news was soon confirmed by Mary, who added that Burroughs still addressed letters to Sophia at La Recompensa. Sophia admitted that the

* By contrast, another traveler from this time wrote, "There were more idle people in Havana than I ever saw in one place of the same size; there seem to be hundreds of respectably dressed persons who have nothing else to do than smoke cigars and play dominoes and billiards."

Figure 36. A sugar plantation in Cuba.

businessman had given her gifts and even asked her to marry him while they were aboard the *Newcastle*. She refused, promising to keep the matter quiet. But apparently Burroughs did not. According to Mrs. Cleveland, who had become an informant for Elizabeth, the older man was boasting of his love affair and even reading portions of Sophia's letters to friends in Havana.

Elizabeth immediately fired off a series of missives to Mary. She accused her sister of neglect: "[Y]ou ought to have insisted on seeing & knowing the whole—I should have done so—or have quarrelled outright—even at the expense of being called a highhanded tyrant,—for the relation of a sister . . . I should have told her that if she intended to have secrets—she had better go straight home."[100] Mary defended herself, explaining that Sophia had behaved without her knowledge. And she added, with cutting reference to her older sister's garrulousness, that Elizabeth would "lose [her] reputation in a week in such a country."[101] In the end, Sophia agreed to return Burroughs's letters. When she asked him to return hers, he instead sent them to Elizabeth, who read them before tossing them into the fire.

None of this appears in the Cuba Journal. Nor is it clear how much Eliza Peabody knew about her youngest daughter's flirtation with Burroughs. Sophia *did* write things that were intended to alarm her mother, however. "What think

Figure 37. The waltz.

you, dearest Mother, I did this evening?" she wrote. "You will never imagine in the world. I *waltzed* and though I was very dizzy the first time, I whirled round without discomfort before I gave up."[102] The waltz had arrived in England in 1813 from Viennese dancehalls and long carried a whiff of impropriety in New England. It was a couples' dance—not a traditional group dance—which meant that men clasped their partner's waist, sometimes so tightly that the dancers' cheeks touched. In 1825, no less an authority than the *Oxford English Dictionary* considered the dance "riotous and indecent." An etiquette book translated from the French and published in Boston in 1833 explained that "The waltz is a dance of quite too loose a character, and the unmarried ladies should refrain from it in public and in private"[103] (figure 37).

Eliza reacted as expected. She warned Sophia, "Your mind is too active for your body, and when your throbbing temples tell you, you must be quiet, pray leave every exciting object, and if possible, be idle in mind and spirit." There followed an even more urgent note: "It frightens me to see your excitement," she wrote. "Subdue it, my precious one."[104]

"My dearest Mother," replied Sophia. "You can not think how often I dream of you, delightful dreams too. You always appear to me with a most happy countenance, full of hope and satisfaction, and *I* am always well."[105] The implication was clear: Eliza's unhappiness, and the neediness it produced, had impaired Sophia's health. In another letter, Sophia rejected her mother's beloved New England, declaring, "I always felt in a perfectly unnatural state of existence in the north."[106] Then she added that when an acquaintance from Boston visited La Recompensa, "he had no words to express his amazement at my change of appearance. He even went so far as to say he should not have known me for the same person!"[107] Being away from home—away from her mother's anxious attention—had done her more good than endless rounds of treatment in Boston.

Eliza shifted tactics. She now agonized over the unscrupulous attentions of men. Much like the society matrons in Jane Austen's *Pride and Prejudice* who believed that "to be fond of dancing was a certain step towards falling in love," she counseled her daughter to avoid such gatherings and to "live uncorrupted by the heartless flatteries and caresses of such of the Lordly sex, as look on such loveliness only with a wish to contaminate it."[108] She was not referring to James Rice Burroughs, however. By now, Eliza was worried about another young man who was a persistent presence in Sophia's letters.

Fernando de Zayas was the handsome son of a local politician and a member of Cuba's sugar nobility. He looked, according to Sophia, "like a very Apollo," and had "more an air of nobility about him than either of [his] other brothers." It was Fernando who had convinced Sophia to waltz. And it was Fernando, an accomplished pianist, who sat down one evening and "played the most beautiful Waltz I ever heard with exquisite taste & expression & then 'his own compositions.'"[109] Sophia was immediately drawn to him. Nearly every letter she sent home featured some mention of their horseback rides together, their games of chess, their visits to neighboring plantations. Like the dashing hero of a novel, Fernando was described in abundant detail, with Sophia devoting considerable time to depicting his dark eyes, his bashful mannerisms, his halting efforts at learning English. On several occasions, she tried to capture him by sketching a profile, once managing to portray his beguiling expression—only to ruin it with an errant stroke of her pencil.

Fernando served as an informal tour guide and cultural attaché, introducing Sophia to nearby attractions as well as to the enslaved people at La Recompensa. Her letters now contained descriptions of Isabella, the Morrell's laundress; Old Tomas, the keeper of turkeys; Pope Urbano, who took care of the horses; and several domestics, including Juana, Feliciana, and Francisco. Not long after her arrival, Fernando took her to watch an evening dance among the enslaved community. There was conga drumming and a large circle of participants. Sophia watched a man and woman enter the ring and go "thro' their strange evolutions in w'h the object seems to be to move every joint in their body."[110] Likely she was describing a precursor to the rumba, a dance form that originated among slave communities in Cuba and was considered by Europeans to be scandalously primitive and sensual. By comparison, the waltz looked tame.

Figure 38. Cuban sugar refinery.

Fernando also took Sophia and Mary to a nearby sugar plantation, where they toured the works and sampled the freshly boiled loaves of sugar, which tasted like honey (figure 38). Here it was impossible for Sophia to ignore the cruel reality of slave labor. "The fires are fed by the cane after the juice is expressed from it," she explained, "and as [the canes are] very light stuff, it keeps the poor negroes forever feeding the flames day and night without a moment's cessation." Compared to La Recompensa, the sugar plantation was poorly managed; the enslaved workers were "badly treated and have no holiday from one end of the year to another."[111] What she failed to mention—what she may not have even known—was that the island's sugar manufacturers had long ago determined that it was cheaper to work enslaved laborers to death and replace them with new *bosales* than to treat them humanely.

The tour of the sugar refinery produced complex feelings. Describing a laborer, Sophia at first resorted to racist stereotype: "One with his fierce eye and brow, and brawny black and blue limbs looked like the very spirit of evil." But her impression quickly changed when the man helped her sample a bit of molten sugar so she would not burn herself. His "promptitude... wrung my heart a great deal more than if he had flung the burning fluid in my face." Increasingly she tried to square her prejudices with her sense of guilt. "He looked like the untamable *obliged* to *appear* tame," she observed, then quickly changed her mind: "if, by scalding me he could have given vent to some of his pent up agony, I could have borne it with more equanimity, than I bore that little act of courtesy, which proved that he had a soul not yet incapable of gentle movement."[112] A fantasy of punishment—of retribution for tasting the sweetness of luxury at the expense of others—animated her account.

But it was the natural world that inspired her most vivid descriptions. "And now we were riding by a dark impenetrable wood & over it was a new moon like a silver bow," Sophia rhapsodized, "clouds of deep saffron upon the intense blue had caught & retained the glory of the sun's farewell. In a few moments we were in another stately gothic gallery of bamboos . . . where two gorgeous peacocks were squalling like orphans, clothed in eternal mourning by the brilliant lime green hedge."[113] Her descriptions were prompted by the resumption of an old passion: riding. She had begun the sport in Dedham, but in Cuba she rode as often as possible, frequently rising before dawn to explore the six-by-six-mile plantation on a horse named Guajamon.

The lush surroundings delighted her artist's eye. She savored the contrast between green vegetation and bright red earth, the middle ground fringed with "many flowers of brilliant hue, which I never saw before."[114] After a lifetime of chill New England winters, Sophia found Cuba's balmy climate appealing, the atmosphere like a fine merino shawl, soft and warm, wrapped about her shoulders. One morning in early January, she wrote Eliza that she was sitting beside a rose-tree in bloom, the temperature seventy-eight degrees and the landscape "a bright gorgeous dream."[115] She ate a sun-warmed guava ("had there been an Adam near, I am sure I would have said, 'take thou & eat likewise'"); oranges, a rarity back home, were plentiful, cultivated in fine emerald groves near the hacienda.[116] But it was the scenery that she responded to the most. Washington Allston, her former painting instructor, had recommended she "take views . . . of all the peculiar effects of atmosphere—clouds—trees &c—as a stock for future use."[117] Sophia dutifully sketched exotic plants, mountain ranges, cloudscapes, and the residents at La Recompensa.

But although a special room in the Morrill home had been set aside for her studio, she almost never picked up her brushes. Away from her mother and Elizabeth, did she no longer feel the compulsion to excel as an artist? Or had she begun to associate her poor health with painting? Whatever the reason, she now created word paintings for her mother, deploying language as if it was a study in color. After one pre-dawn ride, she described "two short allées of palms . . . along which is planted a thick hedge of roses in full bloom, a laguna or small lake is between, surrounded also with this rose hedge, and like wise with the lime trees trimmed & pruned so as to resemble a diadem of brilliant green."[118] Another landscape "terminates in a very beautiful wood & behind it rise up the golden mountains of San Salvador, one or two leagues distant, on both sides [of which] are groves of palms."[119] "The green of the trees is greener than any green I ever saw before," she exclaimed, describing "a beautiful rainbow on a dark spreading cloud of dun blue."[120]

In one of the best-known passages in the Cuba Journal, Sophia described her discovery of the night-blooming cereus, a cactus whose flower blossomed like a candle in the night. She first noticed the glossy blooms during one of her sunset rides and hurried back to La Recompensa to enlist Mary to help collect them. "When she put the gathered flowers into my hand, such was the extraordinary beauty & splendor, & so sweet & strong the perfume that I could not help shouting to the extent of my capability—If I had not given vent to the superabundant swelling of my heart in this way—I do believe I should have suffocated."[121] It was a moment of Keatsian rapture: the perfection of the flower's beauty counterpoised by its tragic impermanence, and both blended in a powerful aesthetic experience. "Nothing more could be asked of a flower—I wished for no more excepting that it were *immortal—deathless*, unsusceptible of change for that any thing so glorious should die seemed a prodigality of *waste* of surpassing beauty."[122]

Besides its flowers, Sophia became a connoisseur of the island's garish sunsets. European landscape painting had long concerned itself with the smoldering colors of dusk and dawn, but the subject achieved new importance during the Romantic era. The works of Caspar David Friedrich and J. M. W. Turner inspired the Hudson River School painters as early as the 1820s, when Thomas Cole invested the sunrise with a distinctly American interpretation. (Morning light spreading across the nation's wilderness represented the dawning of democracy.) Sophia's descriptions resemble ekphrastic versions of these famous paintings. "The clouds looked like giants dipped in liquid jasper," she wrote in March 1834, "and amethyst and gold towering up in magnificence in a striking contrast with the calm repose of the rest the sky." On June 2, she wrote: "The sun was so low that the light was no longer pale yellow but a rich orange gold. & with this superb light was the whole earth illuminated.... gigantic & splendid clouds were just catching the dolphin hues of the dying day."[123] In yet another account, she wrote:

> The sunset was in the last degree splendid. Just before the sun was a dark blue sharp angled cloud like a huge rock of lapis lazuli;—on one side, from a broad base—a purple & rose coloured mass floated up like a soft dream.... On the other side an immense arch of the most brilliant saffron & gold from the blue sweep of the mountains was thrown over nearly to meet that proud, retreating form, & making a vast circuit—But what words can paint the space they enclosed![124]

Over time, the Cuba Journal became less concerned with pure description. Sophia's letters turned toward more speculative matters as she absorbed the work of German philosophers Elizabeth encouraged her to read while in Cuba. Sophia was particularly interested in the effect the island's natural beauty had on the imagination. "Nature wakes all your poetry of mind & heart," she declared six months into her visit.[125] Like Elizabeth, she increasingly believed that God was perceived—*felt*—through an intuitive process. (Elizabeth had called this instinctive experience "moral truth-speaking" in her translation of the Gospel of John.) But Sophia also resembled Mary Moody Emerson, whose raptures were invariably sparked by the sensory experience of nature. Gazing at the moon in Cuba, Sophia wrote, "There is no need of logic to convince the harkening spirit that there is a GOD—intuition is the unerring truth—for it is knowledge communicated by the still voice—& in that is the majesty of the Lord made manifest as clearly to the consciousness as this moon to the eye."[126]

When towering thunderheads rolled in from the ocean, Sophia discerned "the hand of the creative Power." God was an artist. He created boundless vistas for his creatures because "the perception of the beautiful is . . . a reminiscence of infinite perfection." To witness natural splendor was to experience the "mortal struggle between the perishable & the everlasting"—the same tension she had perceived in the flowering cereus.[127] It was also to discover one's inner depths: the private infinity Elizabeth had labeled *self love*. "While under the young Palms I lifted up my eyes in uncontrollable worship of the Omnipresent Divinity of which I seemed to be especially conscious at just that moment."[128] Fusing Cuba's fecund landscape with the perception of God's presence, Sophia wrote, "it is pure, single Nature, alone in her power & loveliness, that touches subdues and exalts the soul,—We do not remember the godlike here—but we think of GOD here."[129]

These ideas are remarkably similar to the ones that appeared two years later in Waldo Emerson's *Nature*, the book usually considered the most important founding text of the transcendentalist movement. "Within these plantations of God," Waldo wrote, "a decorum and sanctity reign, a perennial festival is dressed, and the guest sees not how he should tire of them in a thousand years."[130] The phrasing here is more pungent, more *original* (in the Romantic sense of that term) than Sophia's. But it was also the expression of a professional writer who aimed to reach a wide audience. Sophia's letters were intended for a small family circle.

As it turned out, even Waldo Emerson had read some of those private letters. In August 1834, Sophia was alarmed to learn that her writing was being shared beyond the family circle. Elizabeth had read the journal aloud and circulated the letters among interested friends. "I am aghast to find what publicity my journal has had," Sophia told her mother.[131] She complained directly to Elizabeth, telling her she felt "as if the nation were feeling my pulse." She especially resented the fact that her sister had not even bothered to ask permission to share her writing. "There are a great many little bursts & enthusiasms & opinions & notions in [the journal] which I do not relish having exposed to such congregations."[132]

Elizabeth ignored the complaint. "I doubt ever such a picture of the tropics was put on paper," she replied. It would be "wicked of us," she said, "to hoard it."[133] Sophia's next letter was scathing: "If I were stuck up bodily upon a pole & carried about the streets I could not feel more *exposed*," she replied.[134] Elizabeth ignored this complaint, too. "I have been looking over your letters, and thinking that some extracts might be made from them which it would do very well to publish." She offered to serve as an agent with the *American Monthly*, "where you may get a dollar a page," and suggested that Sophia "go on & make extracts—descriptive of the climate &c—for every number." Anticipating that the Morrell family would not want publicity, Elizabeth advised her to obscure their identity. "But leave out nothing about the *slaves* as they give life to the picture by their various individualities & will never know that you mentioned them!"[135]

It was Sophia's turn to pay no attention. She continued writing to her mother, describing her morning rides and the tropical sunsets, but she made no extracts for publication. Her descriptions of the Christmas season at La Recompensa are among the most vivid in the entire journal, filled with cotillions and banquets and an endless round of visits to nearby haciendas. "All this disipation has not been bad for my *head*," she assured her mother, who nevertheless worried that Fernando de Zayas might cause the "lovely daughters of America" to "yield [their] pure affections to the polluted wretch, who deserves the name of libertine and seducer." Eliza beseeched Sophia to "be *sober-minded*," to resist the pull of her high spirits; remember "that the delicate tenement in which your soul dwells, must still be tenderly used."[136]

And then Sophia's letters stopped. From late January to March 1835, the Cuba Journal is a blank. Perhaps Eliza's letters—panicked, overwrought—account for the gap. Sophia admitted she had reached "a dead halt" in her "journalizing," but she offered no reason for it. Or maybe she did. In the same letter, dated March 11, she announced, "Every day we have seen Fernando & Manuel nearly—*always* Pepillo." She had been too engaged with the de Zayas brothers—especially Fernando, who had "grown lovelier & more interesting" during their "more than three months daily intercourse"—to write home.[137]

A month later, Sophia and Mary were preoccupied with preparations for the return home. They had spent a year and a half in Cuba; with Sophia's health restored, it was time to leave. A note of distress now crept into her letters home. About Fernando, she worried that "I might not see him anymore forever." And on April 24, the date of the last entry in the journal, she observed, "When we are so short a time together in this world—what a loss are the reserve and coldness in intercourse. It is a dead blank in the eye of the soul I think."

She was speaking of New England—its stiff formalities, its chilly suppression of feelings. But she was also speaking of Fernando. She mourned their imminent separation. They had been "united & then torn asunder—forever."[138] The sentence, certain to alarm Eliza, echoed the language of the marriage ceremony.

Toward the end of April, Sophia and Mary made their way to Havana. They stayed with Caroline and Pepe Fernandez, friends of the Morrells, until their ship was ready to depart. The Fernandez family owned a fine painting of the Magdalene by the seventeenth-century baroque Spanish master, Bartolomé Esteban Murillo. Blackened with smoke, soot, and years of neglect, the subject of the painting was nearly indecipherable. "Don Pepe acquainted us with its history & lamented it obscuration, & this led me to dip my finger in some aromatic oil upon the toilette table, & touch a corner of the picture. A gorgeous crimson tint was revealed at once." As she rubbed more oil on the painting, it seemed to come alive: "The golden glory of the floating hair, the majesty of contrition in the upraised brow & lustrous eyes, which actually seemed to start from the canvass & move in urgent prayer, the deep flush of the cheek, the parted lips—so sadly sweet—the 'white wonder' of her folded hands & the splendor of her robes."[139] Sophia sat all afternoon in front of the painting, absorbing its shape and gemlike colors.

She had always been prone to moments of "perfect exhilaration"—moments when the boundaries of self and outer world fused, blurred, then dissolved. "I could not endure my own delight," she had once written after gazing at the sunshine on the lawn, "from mere inability to look alone upon such loveliness." But Cuba had intensified this tendency, enriched it. Away from the Peabody home, away from the rivalries and disappointments and expectations that characterized her family's dynamics, she had encountered moments of aesthetic exhilaration with greater frequency. She had grown confident in the perfect adequacy of beauty and pleasure, in the setting aside of intellection in favor of gorgeous, ecstatic vision. From now on, Sophia's conception of nature would be one of delighted bliss, a timeless dissolution she believed put her in direct contact with God. As much as her renewed health, this was the gift she received from Cuba.

7.

The two Peabody sisters arrived in Boston on May 17, 1835. Their first night was spent in the cramped bedroom Elizabeth was currently occupying in the Alcott house. Ink-stained and excitable, their oldest sister, as always, was full of projects. Just then finishing up the lengthy afterward to the *Record of a School*, which would be published in two months, she had also recently published her three essays on the "Spirit of the Hebrew Scriptures" in the *Christian Examiner*. Four months earlier, she had escorted Harriet Martineau to Concord, where she reconnected with her old Greek instructor, Waldo Emerson. And now she was full of the transcendentalist ideas that were beginning to surface in Boston and its environs.

"I am not quite clear about the transcendentalists yet," Mary Peabody wrote a friend two weeks later, still trying to make sense of Elizabeth's enthusiasms, "and if you know I wish you would give me an intimation about it."[140] Resentment lurked just below the surface of these comments. Before leaving for Cuba, Mary had fallen in love with a widowed lawyer and legislator named Horace Mann, who lived in the same Beacon Hill boardinghouse as she and Elizabeth. Leaving Boston for Cuba entailed an enormous romantic sacrifice on her part—one made worse by letters from Elizabeth that described intimate conversations with Mann and, on one occasion, placing her head on his shoulder and asking him to attend one of William Ellery Channing's sermons. Elizabeth insisted she had never "felt *more* than friendship for him," but her letters to Mary reported the time she spent with him, rankling the normally placid Mary.[141]

Mary returned to Mann. Sophia, back in Salem, fell into depression. Her parents' house felt cloistered and claustrophobic, her life paltry. Without the stirring presence of Fernando and the thrilling thunderstorms and blazing heat of La Recompensa, her illness soon returned. As she told Mary, she felt an "enduring & nightmare-y weight upon my mind since I came home."[142] To Elizabeth, she described herself as a "poor, miserable, maimed—nerve-twisted, trembling, wearied concern." Even worse, it was "vain for me to set up for being any better."[143] Almost overnight, she was afflicted with lameness; even walking was difficult.

It didn't help matters that the Peabodys had recently moved to a different house in Salem, at 53 Charter Street, "in the most ruinous condition, antique and ugly"[144] (figure 39). Three stories high and otherwise featureless, the home sat next to the village's Old Burying Point, with the cemetery, as Sophia reported to Mary, "close under the parlor windows—(Ugh!)." The ground floor looked directly onto a plot of moss-eaten headstones, many of them tilted or completely fallen over, and Sophia's room, facing north, offered "a wide sweep of the place of the dead."[145] She

Figure 39. The Peabody house on Charter Street, Salem.

found herself staring morosely upon the final resting place of Puritan divines and Revolutionary-era women who had died in childbirth. If Cuba had awakened her senses, she now felt like a tropical flower, wilting in the frigid atmosphere of New England.

As she said to Elizabeth, she was in a "Babel of confusion." Suddenly her Cuba memories were painful. She now repudiated the entire experience, claiming that she had never wanted to socialize as much as she had, that each conversation with Fernando or the Morrell family had caused her head to throb. Nor had she appreciated the splendors of the tropics: "I have no doubt I should have lived too much in the senses if I had ever been able to find any peace or pleasure in them," she continued to Elizabeth. She felt "an illimitable—inexhaustible, ever new springing gratitude to GOD for His gracious tenderness for my immortal being, in so arranging my condition as to leave me no resting place of joy or repose but the inner world."[146]

Nothing in the Cuba Journal suggests that any of this is even remotely true. As if realizing that the happiest time of her life was over, Sophia was trying to insulate herself against despair. She struggled to add color to her drab existence by painting—an activity she had all but forsaken in the Caribbean. Converting a room on the ground floor into a studio, she set up her easel, placed plaster casts of Hercules and Apollo upon the mantel, and commenced to work. A list of her paintings, detailed in the back of a journal she kept for 1836, lists nine completed canvases for the next year. Along with a handful of painted baskets and fire screens that she sold to families in Boston and Salem, Sophia earned at least $300 for her art—more than Elizabeth received from her various projects.

Among her most ambitious works was a copy of Washington Allston's *Lorenzo and Jessica*, a smallish cabinet picture the artist completed in 1832. Allston's canvas portrayed two lovers, one Jewish, one Gentile, from Shakespeare's *The Merchant of Venice*. In the drama, the pair have eloped to a villa outside Venice—far away from the betrayals and sadistic violence that otherwise mark the tragedy. Allston, with exquisite erudition, had applied the techniques of Venetian painters to create his two lovers. Layering one pigment atop another, then coating it with shimmering lacquer, he created the illusion of jewel-like depth.[147]

The painting was meant to capture the moment when Lorenzo addresses his lover:

> Sit, Jessica: look how the floor of heaven
> Is thick inlaid with patines of bright gold;
> There's not the smallest orb which thou behold'st
> But in his motion like an angel sings,
> Still quiring to the young-eyed cherubins;
> Such harmony is in immortal souls

Prompted by her recent experiences with Fernando, the subject of two lovers from widely differing cultures powerfully resonated with Sophia. The subplot involving Lorenzo and Jessica provides a peaceful interlude in a play primarily concerned with bloody revenge—a glimmer of hope in an otherwise bleak drama. Sophia's painting, which she eventually sold for the respectable price of $100, remained faithful to Allston's painting in every respect but one: Instead of calling the painting *Lorenzo and Jessica*, she inverted the names, thereby placing her heroine in the foreground.

Another ambitious work from this period was Sophia's long-expected original composition. In the summer of 1835, she complained to Elizabeth that "I have never produced anything"; now, she hoped to "shadow my images forth . . . . I find I have greater facility in painting than formerly—I mean I have gone on even without practicing."[148] The new work was titled *Flight into Egypt*, a conventional subject from art history. (Tintoretto, Caravaggio, and Rembrandt, among many others, had created versions of Mary and Joseph spiriting the infant messiah away to escape King Herod's murderous edict.) Sophia minimized traditional religious iconography, replacing it with a romantic landscape. Mary and Joseph are partially obscured by the limbs of trees and shrubbery, barely visible. Rustic figures and animals are scattered in the composition; they, too, are miniscule in the vast landscape. Sophia was signaling a shift from scripture to nature, a hallmark of Romanticism.

Unfortunately, these bouts of creativity created splitting headaches—a pattern that repeated itself so often that Elizabeth suggested Sophia give up painting. It was Elizabeth who also recommended a new treatment. In 1832, she had become fascinated with the science of phrenology, which claimed to decipher character from the bumps on the skull. Four years later, she was drawn to the work of Franz Anton Mesmer, a German physician who in 1814 had published his theory of "animal magnetism." According to Mesmer, the body was governed by an invisible, magnetic fluid—something like electricity. People became sick when this fluid was obstructed; they were cured when the magnetic circuit was restored. Mesmer's technique was to sit face-to-face with his patients, his knees touching theirs, and to put his subject into a somnambulistic trance. A session could last for hours. It was successfully concluded when a patient achieved a "crisis," usually involving convulsions or a loss of consciousness.

There was something vaguely illicit about mesmerism. Treatment involved a complete loss of control for the patient, a surrender of the body's mysterious energy to another. And because the patient was usually a woman and the mesmerist a man, the procedure carried more than a whiff of sexual abandon.[149] In June 1836, Elizabeth heard a lecture by Charles Poyen, a young French mesmerist who introduced the theory of animal magnetism to America. (Poyen published his *Report on the Magnetical Experiments* in 1836; the

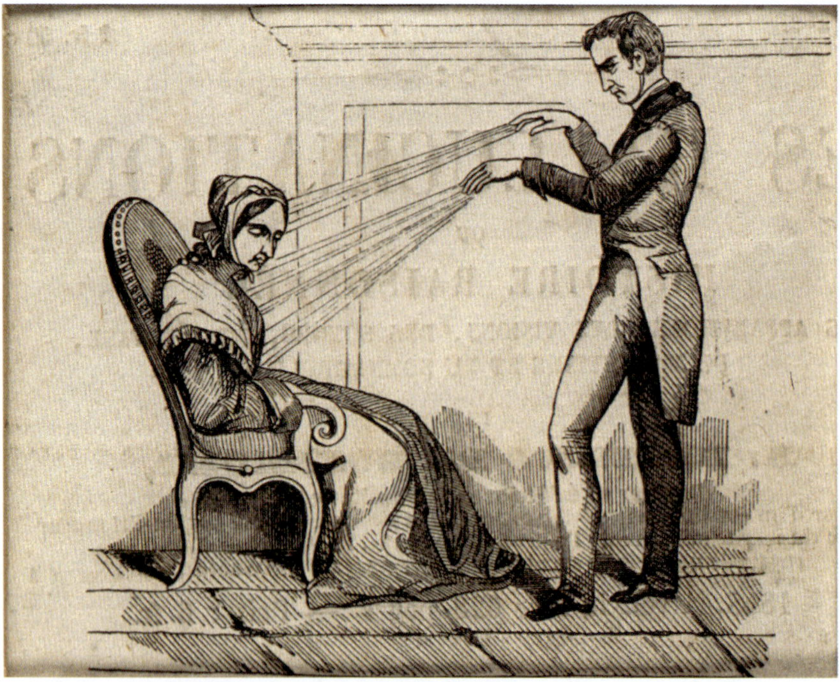

Figure 40. Mesmerism.

following year, he published *Progress of Animal Magnetism in New England.*)† Speaking with him after the lecture, Elizabeth reported to Mary, "He said I was a highly magnetized body—he thought I might magnetise if I could concentrate my power in a strong act of the will—& I do not know but I shall try to cure Sophia"[150] (figure 40).

As it turned out, Elizabeth did nothing of the sort. She instead enlisted her father's dental assistant, Joseph Emerson Fiske, who was one of Poyen's first American converts. For the next four years, Fiske labored to relieve Sophia of her chronic headaches. Several sessions occurred under the tutelage of Poyen himself, who visited Salem in September 1837. During each treatment, Fiske ran his fingertips along Sophia's head and temples. He gently brushed her eyebrows with his thumbs. Keeping his hands an inch or so from her body, he passed them along her shoulders and arms. Throughout the treatment, Fiske and Sophia's knees touched; their eyes peered directly into one another's. Mesmerism and waltzing, it turned out, were not so dissimilar.

† Poyen had inherited sugar plantations in Martinique and Guadeloupe, the same island where Mary Van Schalkwyck had departed with her husband a generation earlier. The proceeds of slave labor allowed him to travel throughout New England, proselytizing the benefits of a new treatment that required the subjugation of the will.

Sophia experienced some relief from these measures. (So would Margaret Fuller, who was treated by a mesmerist for backaches.) Although Fiske was never able to induce a trance, the sessions apparently soothed Sophia's pain, although they did not cure her entirely. By late 1837, she was again bedridden with headaches. She quit painting downstairs, took meals in her upstairs bedroom. Sarah Clarke, an artist friend, reported at this time that Sophia was "more susceptible and requiring more careful nursing and seclusion than ever."[151] That was why she did not come downstairs one cold, blustery night in November when three visitors arrived and pulled at the doorbell. They were two sisters, Ebe and Louisa Hawthorne, each wearing a hood and cloak. Between them stood their tall, reclusive brother. His name was Nathaniel.

8.

When or where Elizabeth first met Nathaniel Hawthorne is anyone's guess. Sarah Clarke later thought the two were introduced at the home of the Honorable Daniel Appleton White, the widower of Mary Moody Emerson's friend in Concord, Mary Van Schalkwyck. (Their daughter, Mary Wilder White, had recently married Nathaniel's bosom friend, Caleb Foote, the editor of the *Salem Gazette*.) But the two might have happened upon one another in any number of Salem drawing rooms, especially given the size of the town and Elizabeth's penchant for knowing everyone of interest (figure 41).

For a while now she had been in search of an author who had written several short stories published anonymously in *The Token*, an illustrated gift book that appeared annually. "My Kinsman, Major Molineaux" and "The Minister's Veil" were unlike any work being published in New England at the time—not just dark and Gothic-tinged, but their prose exquisitely wrought, each word freighted with deliberate ambiguity. At some point, Elizabeth learned that the author's name was Hawthorne. She assumed it must be Ebe Hawthorne, the little girl who had once carried herself as though she were guarding a fortress when Elizabeth was a child. She gathered her reticule and trooped over to the Herbert Street house where the Hawthornes still lived. Only then was she told by Louisa, the other sister, that "it was not Elizabeth but Nathaniel who was the author."[152]

Nathaniel soon presented Elizabeth with a copy of *Twice-Told Tales*, which had been published earlier that year. Elizabeth in turn invited him to call at the Peabody house. He arrived with the stately Ebe and the gregarious Louisa on either arm, but neither Elizabeth nor Mary Peabody could take their eyes off *him*. Nathaniel Hawthorne was so beautiful that people stopped whatever they were doing when he passed. Ebe recalled that as a youth he was "the finest boy many strangers observed whom they had ever seen," and Henry Wadsworth Longfellow, who attended college with him twenty years earlier,

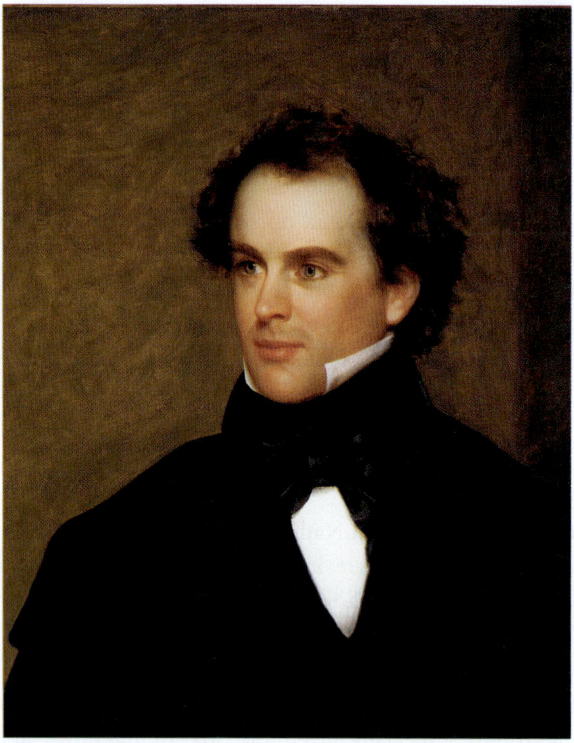

Figure 41. Nathaniel Hawthorne, 1840.

thought him "a strange owl . . . but very pleasant to behold."[153] In an era that exalted outcast Romantic heroes, he exuded a silent charisma. This was largely the product of shyness; until the age of thirty he lived in his mother's house at 12 Herbert Street, occupying an attic room and seldom leaving the premises (or so he said) before dusk. He avoided people on the street, avoided making eye contact. During what would soon become his long, secret engagement to Sophia, he kept her love letters tucked inside his breast pocket, like one of the characters he eventually became famous for: a recluse harboring a private mystery.

Elizabeth and Mary swooned over Nathaniel's long hair, the deep staring intensity of his eyes. "He has a temple of a head (not a tower)," Mary soon wrote, "and an eye full of sparkle, glisten, & intelligence."[154] Elizabeth recalled, years later, the way he stood in the Peabody parlor "in all the splendor of his young beauty." After presenting the Hawthorne siblings with a copy of the *Iliad*, Elizabeth hurried upstairs to Sophia's sickroom, exclaiming, "O Sophia, you must get up and dress and come down! Mr. Hawthorne and his sisters are come, and you never saw anything so splendid—he is handsomer than Lord Byron."[155]

Sophia did not budge. "I think it would be rather ridiculous to get up," she said. "If he has come once he will come again."[156] According to family legend—a legend nurtured by Elizabeth, who told it after its main participants were no longer alive to contradict her—sometime during the spring of 1838, Nathaniel paid one of his visits to Charter Street and Sophia at last came down from her room. She instantly found herself drawn to him—as if *he* were a mesmerist whose attraction could not be resisted. Elizabeth said that when Sophia entered the room, Nathaniel "rose and looked at her intently." The conversation proceeded stiffly; "she would frequently interpose a remark, in her low, sweet voice. Every time she did so, he would look at her again, with the same piercing, indrawing gaze." From the very beginning, "his presence... exercised so strong a magnetic attraction upon her, that instinctively, and in self-defense as it were, she drew back and repelled him."[157]

The truth about their courtship was more complicated. For one thing, Nathaniel was entangled in a romantic attachment with another Salem beauty, Mary Silsbee. For another, Elizabeth was herself deeply infatuated with him. Still reeling from the Temple School scandal and her encounter with Jones Very, Elizabeth received Nathaniel's courtly attention as a balm. Whether he reciprocated Elizabeth's feelings has been the matter of much speculation. Certainly, he appreciated her enthusiasm for his writing, and was grateful to Elizabeth for introducing him to her circle of friends, which included publishing contacts in Boston. But he kept his feelings to himself. Before long, local gossip linked the two. One Salem lawyer reported that "N. Hawthorne and Miss E. P. Peabody or some of the Sisters are betrothed—so the world may be blessed with transcendental literary production."[158‡]

It was during one of Nathaniel's earliest visits that Elizabeth lent him the *Cuba Journal*. Possibly she hoped to expose Sophia's invalidism and therefore her unsuitability for marriage. If so, the plan backfired. Five months earlier Nathaniel had written Longfellow to complain about his "great difficulty" as an author, "in the lack of materials; for I have seen so little of the world, that I have nothing but thin air to concoct my stories of, and it is not easy to give a life-like semblance to such shadowy stuff."[159] Now he kept Sophia's journals, riveted by their frank depiction of a young woman's thoughts. At least eleven passages made their way into his journal.

Sophia was equally fascinated with him. When Elizabeth went to West Newton to help her brother Nat open a school, Sophia hid behind her door upstairs whenever the handsome author visited. "I opened my door and tried to hear what he said," she recalled. Unable to resist temptation, she at last stepped down the stairs to catch a glimpse of his handsome face, with its "celestial expression...

‡ Nathaniel had fun with the gossip; in April 1838, he wrote a friend, "I have heard recently the interesting intelligence that I am engaged to two ladies in the city" (MM 362).

What a beautiful smile he has."[160] Before long, she was hurrying to answer the door whenever the doorbell rang. She led him to the parlor and answered his questions about Cuba. When Nathaniel, who called her the "Queen of Journalisers," told her that he wanted to use her experiences in a story, she wrote Elizabeth, "To be the means of any way of calling forth one of his divine creations is no small happiness, is it?"[161]

The tentative courtship continued. When Nathaniel took a secret trip to western Massachusetts and upstate New York, he took the Cuba Journals with him. His own notebooks show the gradual absorption of their tone and material into a corner of his imagination. In one entry, for instance, he describes a richly hued sunset that illuminates a cluster of young women who are "warm and voluptuous—not languidly voluptuous, but with a mild fire. The whole scenery and personages acquire, methinks, a passionate character." He now imagined a setting in which the "trees and the grass have now the brightest green…in short the splendor of a more gorgeous climate than ours might be brought into the picture."[162] The early mention of "warm and voluptuous" women associated with the surrounding wilderness, drawn from Sophia's depiction of Cuba, suggests the heroines whom he would later create, including Hester Prynne in *The Scarlet Letter* and Zenobia in *The Blithedale Romance.*

It was also during his secret trip that Hawthorne wrote "Edward Randolph's Painting," a tale inspired by Sophia's account of the smudged Murillo she had illuminated with aromatic oil. Earlier, in April, Sophia had written Elizabeth, "He said he had imagined a story of which the principal incident is my cleaning that picture of the Ferndandez'—which he shall write down very soon!"[163] The story describes an old oil portrait "so dark with age, damp, and smoke, that not a touch of the painter's art could be discerned."[§164] The obscure work turns out to be a portrait of Edward Randolph, the stern colonial administrator who betrayed the Puritans. Once the painting is cleaned, it reveals a face tormented by guilt and shame.

"Edward Randolph's Painting" introduces one of Nathaniel's first fully developed female characters. In previous stories, his women tended to be flat cut-outs: symbols rather than complex human beings. There is much of the symbolic in Alice Vane (her name points to the futility of revealing the true subject of her painting). But the "childlike" painter, who seems to be "a stranger from another clime" and for whom "the rude atmosphere of New England had cramped her hand, and dimmed the glowing colors of her fancy," is clearly modeled on Sophia. "[C]lad entirely in white, a pale, ethereal creature," Alice is both frail and

§ Nathaniel's future friend, Herman Melville, likely had this description in mind when he described the chiaroscuro painting at the Spouter Inn in *Moby-Dick.*

redemptive, a figure of authorial wish-fulfilment, one finally incapable of thwarting the darker forces around her.[165]

If Sophia served as a muse for Nathaniel's story, she was eager to reverse roles. Soon she took one of his stories for artistic inspiration. Late in the fall of 1838, she began an illustration for a story from his *Twice-Told Tales*, "The Gentle Boy," a fable of Puritan cruelty and intolerance that Elizabeth particularly liked. Sophia's line drawing is in the style of Flaxman: spare and eloquent as a string of geese against a gray November sky (figure 42). It represents the Puritan child, Ilbrahim, orphaned because his father has been put to death for being a Quaker. The illustration became widely known throughout Salem, and a local arts patron, Susan Burley, decided to fund a special edition of *The Gentle Boy: A Thrice-Told Tale*. Nathaniel crafted a preface for the new volume, speaking with joy that the story had "wrought an influence upon another mind, and has thus given to imaginative life a creation of deep and pure beauty." The book began with a dedication:

Figure 42. Sophia Peabody's illustration of "The Gentle Boy.

To Miss Sophia A. Peabody

THIS LITTLE TALE,

TO WHICH HER KINDRED ART HAS GIVEN VALUE

IS RESPECTFULLY INSCRIBED

BY THE AUTHOR[166]

Reviews for the book were uniformly positive—particularly its illustration. Park Benjamin, writing in *The New-Yorker*, praised Sophia's "most exquisite genius." Her old mentor, Washington Allston, admired her "simple severe lines" and allowed himself to hope that the artist would illustrate more of "Mr. Hawthorne's exquisite fancies."[167]

But by the time *The Gentle Boy* appeared in January, Sophia and Nathaniel were involved in another collaboration. They were engaged to be married. The decision had been reached when both were in Boston. Nathaniel had accepted the job of Weigher and Gauger of the city's Custom House, a position that Elizabeth had helped him find. Sophia was staying with friends to study sculpture with Shobal Clevenger, a former stonemason who had been commissioned by the Boston Athenæum to create a bust of Allston.

For two magical months that winter, Sophia and Nathaniel saw each other as often as possible. (He "wants to come every day," she informed Elizabeth, who remained in Salem, but "etiquette alone prevents him.")[168] Separated from their respective families, free to do as they liked, they experienced the special aloneness of young lovers, strolling through the Common at dusk, the city streets remote and muffled as snow drifted down. But there were obstacles to overcome. First and foremost was Elizabeth's lingering infatuation with Nathaniel. In November 1838, Sophia had written her to say Nathaniel was but "a thousand brothers in one," dissimulating her true feelings for the man Elizabeth considered *her* discovery.[169] Not until June the next year—six months after their secret engagement—did she reveal to Elizabeth her true feelings for Nathaniel. Elizabeth's response was characteristically magnanimous. She assured Sophia she never wanted to marry. This was of course the same thing that Sophia had told Elizabeth. Now Sophia confessed that "I have often doubted whether you considered your destiny the proper one"—she was referring to Elizabeth's unmarried state—and now felt "thankful to have you say that you think it is."[170]

Another obstacle was Nathaniel's family. He insisted that the engagement remain a secret to his mother and two sisters. Ebe Hawthorne later speculated that her brother had kept silent because he had worried that news of the engagement might prove fatal to their mother. Equally plausible is Nathaniel's almost pathological reticence which, according to Mary Peabody, caused him to suffer "inexpressibly in the presence of his fellow-mortals." Regardless, he refused to make the engagement public. "The world might, as yet, misjudge us," Nathaniel wrote Sophia shortly after she announced the engagement to Elizabeth; "and therefore we will not speak to the world."[171]

9.

The engagement, which lasted three and a half years, is chronicled in the cache of love letters sent by Nathaniel to Sophia while he worked in the Boston Custom House and then moved to the utopian community at Brook Farm. No courtship letters from Sophia survive. Nathaniel destroyed them in 1858—another act of control and concealment. Still, the one-sided correspondence provides a peek into their relationship. The letters are among the most passionate and revealing things Nathaniel ever wrote, ardent and demanding—most of all, love-struck. They reveal the persistent anxiety Nathaniel felt about his ability to support a wife. Just as often, they entail visions of an expansive future together. Throughout the letters, he conjures up Sophia in a variety of guises—*dis*guises—that have less to do with the real person than with his own emotional requirements.

In the first letter, from March 1839, he initiated a pair of contrasting terms that continued throughout the entire correspondence: "my Dove" and "naughty Sophie." With both terms, Nathaniel was employing familiar stereotypes of women—stereotypes that emphasized their moral purity as well as the shameful physical desire their beauty provoked. In July, he began making plans: "When we live together in our own home, belovedest," Nathaniel wrote, "we will paint pictures together—that is, our minds and hearts shall unite to form the conception, to which your hand shall give material existence. I have often felt as if I could be a painter, only I am sure that I could never handle a brush;—now my Dove will show me the images of my inward eye, beautified and etherealized by the mixture of her own spirit."[172] In another letter, he imagined a cottage "where we could be always together…And you should draw, and paint, and sculpture, and make music, and poetry, too, and your husband would admire and criticize."[173]

The vision of a shared artistic home must have been appealing to Sophia, given the chaotic atmosphere of the Peabody house. But there were too many distractions beyond the insular walls of their romance. Elizabeth, as always, was trying to make ends meet through various schemes. One was to encourage Nathaniel to write a series of children's books, which she proposed to publish. Another was to open a bookshop in Boston. Having spent the past several years under the influence of Waldo Emerson and extolling the "inward life," she was now determined to "*do something*" practical in the world.[174] If she could scrape together money enough to lease a building and acquire an inventory of foreign books, she might be able to move the entire family to Boston.

There were also Margaret Fuller's Conversations. Mary Peabody apparently hosted the first of these in her rented apartment, before the family had moved to Boston. From the beginning, Sophia was an enthusiastic member. In her commonplace book, she wrote a poetic description of the gatherings: "Persons meeting, like minded, excite thoughts in each other. Soon they feel the common thought rising to an equal height in each. It swells it arches over, united—they are united—a temple is there whose arches reverberate with a grand harmony."[175] The passage contains the germ of the poem she wrote about Fuller's Conversations, and it conveys some of the excitement of the gatherings in their earliest form.

During the first Conversation, Fuller challenged the women to consider what they were born to do. It was a question "which so few ever propose to themselves 'till their best years are gone by." At the time, Sophia believed she knew what she was born to do. However ambivalent she remained about painting, she still considered herself an artist. When Nathaniel expressed his desire, "sometime or other, [to] behold a creation of your own" on his bare apartment walls, she immediately plunged into work, producing a pair of stunning paintings.[176] Both depicted the Italian countryside around Lake Como, with alpine mountains and red-tiled *cittadinas*, a subject familiar to her from engravings she had copied years earlier. But in the painting called *Isola*, she made a tiny addition, a couple crossing a bridge: Sophia, in bridal veil, and Nathaniel, holding a dove, the symbol he used in his letters to describe the spiritual, unearthly qualities of his bride-to-be (plate 7).

At Sophia's request, Nathaniel placed dark curtains over the paintings to protect the wet canvases from the soot of his fireplace. Even after the varnish had dried, however, he left the curtains in their place, a private reference to his story "Edward Randolph's Portrait," in which remnants of an old curtain cling to the frame of the blackened, obscure painting. He informed Sophia that he placed the "curtains before them every morning," away from the prying eyes of the woman who tidied his room, "and they remain covered till after I have kindled my fire in the afternoon."[177]

Sophia also began working in a new medium: clay. One of her first projects involved Waldo Emerson, whom she had come to know and admire through Elizabeth. When Waldo had traveled to Salem to lecture four years earlier, in 1836, she had written with enthusiasm of the "gleam in his *diffused* smile; the musical thunder of his voice; his repose, so full of the essence of life; his simplicity—just think of all these, and of my privilege in seeing and hearing him." She believed that his "oceanic calm" would enable her to "paint Cuban skies better than even my recollections could have made me."[178] For his part, Waldo, much impressed by Sophia's version of Allston's *Jessica and Lorenzo*, had written to his second wife, Lydia, "I rejoiced in the genius of the young lady very much."[179]

Figure 43. Sophia Peabody's bas relief of Charles Chauncy Emerson.

At some point, Sophia had also become acquainted with Elizabeth Hoar, the fiancée of Charles Chauncey Emerson, who had died of tuberculosis. Now she began modeling a bas-relief of the deceased man from memory. The medallion was completed in the spring of 1840, and when casts were made, she sent one to Waldo, who soon ordered five more. He wrote to Fuller: "Sophia Peabody's medallion is a likeness: a fine head; & in the circumstances of its execution, wonderful. She never saw Charles E. but once & had only for her guide a pencil sketch taken by herself at the that time, but *not like*, & a profile-shadow taken at Plymouth"[180] (figure 43).

Nathaniel was also impressed, writing, "Thou art a miracle thyself, and workest miracles." But an anxious, controlling tone now entered his letters. He worried about the toll Sophia's art took on her health. "I by no means undervalue thy works," he wrote in April 1840, "though I cannot estimate all thou hast ever done at the price of a single throb of anguish to thy belovedest head." While he believed she was capable of "do[ing] great works," he worried about the crippling headaches that followed the completion of her medallion. "I would rather that thy art should be annihilated, than that thou shouldst always pay this price for its exercise."[181]

In June, Waldo invited Sophia to Concord to discuss the bas-relief with Elizabeth Hoar. "We all count it a beautiful possession," he wrote; "the gift of a Muse, and not less valuable that it was so unexpected."[182] In Concord, Sophia finally discussed her art with one of her intellectual heroes. Waldo commended her "beauty making eye, which transfigures the landscape," and she basked in the attention of Lydia Emerson, a woman who had married a literary figure in her thirties.[183] Lydia was soft-spoken yet acerbic, a striking woman who held her own against the extended Emerson family. Writing to Nathaniel, Sophia described Concord's scenery and pleasant company, prompting him to reply, "Belovedest,.... if thou findest thyself comfortable at Concord—and if the Emersonians love thee and admire thee as they ought—do not thou too stubbornly refuse to stay a week longer than the term first assigned."[184] Two weeks later, he was so enthused about her descriptions of the village that he wrote, "Would that we could build our cottage this very now, this very summer, amid the scenes which thou describes."[185] And when he learned that Sophia had revealed her engagement to the Emerson household, he rejoiced, happy that "thy friends have faith that thy husband is worthy of thee."[186]

By the time Sophia returned to Salem, the Peabodys had begun to pack their belongings for the move to Boston. Elizabeth had secured the modest brick rowhouse at 13 West Street for her proposed bookshop, and the family soon took possession of their new home at the end of July. Dinner time was punctuated by the clopping of horses from the livery across the street. Elizabeth ordered a long counter to be installed in the front room, and her time was now spent loading shelves with German, English, and Italian books.[187] At the suggestion of Washington Allston, she stocked her shop with fine arts supplies, enlisting Sophia to sell them when she was not too busy painting or sculpting in the second-floor room that doubled as her studio. Mary moved her day school for young girls to the second floor, and Nathaniel Peabody, otherwise unemployed, opened an apothecary downstairs, where he sold homeopathic drugs.

Thirteen West Street opened for business in early August and almost overnight became a hub for Boston's avant-garde thinkers. Elizabeth's knack for knowing the latest trends in thought and culture meant the bookshop was the most influential intellectual gathering place in the city. Poets, philosophers, social reformers, as well as the merely curious, crowded into the cramped front room to discuss the latest offerings from across the Atlantic as well as the new ideas percolating throughout New England. In September, Elizabeth became the first and only woman to host the Transcendental Club.** And in October, Waldo Emerson and the historian George Bancroft contributed books for another venture associated with the shop: Elizabeth's small, select circulating library.

One of the most ambitious social schemes discussed was led by an intense, bespectacled man named George Ripley, who was dissatisfied with practically everything in contemporary society. A Unitarian minister who had become disenchanted with the church, he believed it valued dogma and orthodoxy over heartfelt religion. He was even more distressed by the social divisions caused by rapid industrialization. Writing to Waldo, he described his plans for a utopian community to be called the "Brook Farm Institute of Agriculture and Education."

** The topic for the final meeting was a debate whether the church was capable of reformation or "vicious in its foundations."

The project would explore new ways of cooperative living and "insure a more natural union between intellectual and manual labor." It would "prepare a society of liberal, intelligent and cultivated persons, whose relations with each other would permit a more wholesome and simple life than can be led amidst the pressures of our competitive institutions."[188]

In October 1840, Ripley tried to convince Waldo to join the venture—to no avail. But another writer, Nathaniel Hawthorne, was surprisingly interested in the scheme. In November, he wrote Sophia to ask if a mutual friend "will not come and settle with us in Mr. Ripley's Utopia."[189] It was his first written acknowledgement that he had decided to join the Brook Farm experiment. Unlike Waldo and the circle of transcendental enthusiasts at 13 West Street, Nathaniel was by nature a skeptic. He did not believe in the perfectibility of human beings, nor did he consider it likely that they could ameliorate social ills. He certainly was not one to join any organization. Yet he was desperate to leave the Custom House, to bid farewell to its conniving politicians, its tedium—and to settle down with Sophia. Perhaps he was enticed by Ripley's dream of "industry without drudgery, and true equality without its vulgarity."[190] More likely he was persuaded by Sophia's cheerful optimism, and their shared vision of a rural home in which to write and paint.

While Nathaniel extricated himself from the Custom House, Sophia attended Fuller's second series of Conversations. Many of the same participants gathered as the year before. In addition to Sophia and Elizabeth, there was the novelist and abolitionist Lydia Maria Child; the transcendentalist poet Caroline Sturgis; Sarah Clarke; Mary Channing, the daughter of the Unitarian minister; Sophia Ripley, unhappily married to George Ripley; and Elizabeth Davis Bancroft, whose husband, the historian George Bancroft, had secured Nathaniel's job at the Custom House in the first place. From Concord, Lydia Emerson and Elizabeth Hoar took the morning stagecoach to attend.

The second series of conversations were, if anything, more electrifying than the first. Caroline Healey, a young woman of seventeen, recalled that Fuller was "lively and sarcastic in general conversation," her laughter infectious, "childlike."[191] Standing before the assembled women, she spoke freely, spontaneously, the flow of her ideas rapid, associative, and often brilliant. There was something majestic about her presence, something grand about her deft handling of ideas.

The talk flowed so quickly that it was difficult to transcribe. At one point, Elizabeth admitted the inadequacy of her efforts to capture the quicksilver conversation, her scratching pen woefully behind the torrent of speech. Even so, from these imperfect records it is apparent that ideas poured forth from each woman's deepest core, like subterranean fountains revealing subjective truths. For Sarah Clarke, Fuller's talk was "the most powerful stimulus, intellectual and moral. It was like the sun shining upon plants and causing buds to open into flowers. This was her gift, and she could no more help exercising it than the sun can help shining. This gift, acting with a powerful understanding and a generous imagination, you can perceive would make an educational force of great power."[192]

By all accounts, something magic happened during the Conversations. Fuller herself felt transformed by the gatherings. She no longer examined the world objectively, she said, but trusted her innermost perceptions more than ever, drawn to "the law with which she identified herself."[193] And she credited this change to her interaction with the women. As she spoke, the entire group, "with glistening eyes, seemed melted into one love." During that first meeting, Fuller said, one woman "sat beside me, all glowing; and the moment I had finished, she began to speak."[194] The exchange was intimate, exhilarating.

That woman may have been Sophia. We know that she had become enamored of Fuller by this point, that she admired her lofty conversation and her ability to pierce to the very core of any topic. And she evidently expressed her opinions, feeling greater more confidence to speak among the gathering of women than she had years before at William Ellery Channing's circle. But Elizabeth Peabody never mentions her in her transcriptions. Her focus, too, was largely on Fuller. "It is sometimes said," she wrote, "that women never are so lovely and enchanting in the company of their own sex, merely, but it requires the other to draw them out." Elizabeth thought the opposite was true. "Certain it is that Margaret never appears, when I see her, either so brilliant and deep in thought, or so desirous to please, or so modest, or so heart-touching, as in this very party."[195]

To Sophia's delight, the topic for the second series of Conversations was art. Poetry and painting "were one compensation for the necessary prose of life," Fuller announced. They were expressions "of the sublime and beautiful, whether in measured words or in the fine arts."[196] This conception of aesthetic transcendence matched Sophia's ideas precisely. Art was not simply a reflection of the outer world, Fuller declared, a mirror held up to nature. It summoned beautiful and sublime experiences within each person. Three of the Conversations were devoted to sculpture (Fuller's favorite art), with another two or three devoted to painting. It was likely during this sequence that Sophia exhibited her own art to the members of the Conversations, enacting Fuller's statement that art symbolized a deeper need to enact "the poetry of life," which was the daily rediscovery of the beauty of existence.[197]

Interestingly, the essay she chose to write for Fuller was on music—a work that no longer survives. Nor do we have for certain her reply to Fuller's request that the women write "articles upon the intellectual differences between men & women." At the next session, Fuller read a few of these essays, including one that addressed the "fineness & delicacy of organization" that was typical of women. (The word *organization* was a catch-all term for physical and mental attributes.) The unnamed essayist—Sophia possibly wrote it, given her longstanding awareness of her own "delicacy"—went on to explain that woman's greater sensitivity meant they experienced a "greater openness to impressions."[198]

Fuller thought this constituted no "essential difference"—both sexes possessed a sensitivity to impressions to greater or lesser degrees. The poet Ellen Hooper then asked whether "the difference of organization was not essential—if it did not begin in the mind."[199] She thought men and women experienced the world differently as a result of their physical differences. Fuller countered that the essay's author had identified no quality that did not belong to the minds of both women *and* men, prompting Hooper to ask if there was *any* quality that belonged solely to one of the sexes.

Fuller paused a moment. Then she said she thought not "& therefore she wished to see if the others fully admitted this, because if all admitted it, it would follow of course that we should hear no more of repressing or subduing faculties because they were not fit for women to cultivate." Any talent stirring within a woman—whether it was to paint a historical allegory or to study law—should be cultivated accordingly. There was no excuse "on the ground that we had not the intellectual powers for it; that it was not for women to do, *on an intellectual ground*."[200]

At last Fuller read her own essay, which was calculated to provoke outrage. "Man had more genius," she declared, "woman more taste—Man more determination of purpose—woman more delicacy of rejection—Man more versatility—woman more power of adaptation." As soon as she finished reading, she was challenged. Several unnamed participants provided examples of women who had revealed determination and genius. Fuller did not waver. "Is not man's intellect the fire caught from heaven," she asked, "woman's the flower called forth from earth by the ray?"[201]

It is possible that she actually believed this. She was still trying to understand why so few women had left their mark on history and art, still working out her theory of gender and its role in shaping the possibilities of one's existence. But she was also being provocative. She wanted to push the women to consider why they had been shut out of the worlds of art and thought. She wanted Sophia, for instance, to consider why her head ached when she was most bold in her artistic creations. She wanted all the women to imagine a world in which they were allowed to speak their minds and follow their interests, without hindrance, without being ostracized. If the Conversations revealed anything, it was that they were capable of such activity if they would only venture forth.

10.

Around this time, Nathaniel's letters to Sophia became more urgent and possessive. Those posts he sent on Wednesdays—the day of Fuller's Conversations—were especially defensive. One Wednesday morning in early January 1841, for instance, he asked, "what wilt thou do to-day, persecuted little Dove, when thy abiding-place will be a Babel of talkers? Would that Miss Margaret Fuller might lose her tongue!—or my Dove her ears, and so be left wholly to her husband's golden silence!" He portrayed their relationship as the exact opposite of the Conversations: silent, holy, requiring no vulgar words. "Dearest wife, I truly think that we could dispense with audible speech, and yet never feel the want of an interpreter between our spirits."[202]

He now portrayed Fuller in a negative light. When he moved to Brook Farm, he learned that Fuller had left a cow there to be cared for. (Fuller was interested in the community but unwilling to give up her privacy to join.) Nathaniel's letters were soon full of this "transcendental heifer," which he described as "very fractious, I believe, and apt to kick over the milk pail. Thou knowest best, whether, in these traits of character, she resembles her mistress."[203] On another Wednesday, he reported, "Belovedest, Miss Fuller's cow hooks the other cows, and has made herself ruler of the herd, and behaves in a very tyrannical manner."[204] Later that week he wrote a thinly disguised fantasy of wish-fulfillment: "Belovedest, the herd have rebelled against the usurpation of Miss Fuller's cow; and whenever they are turned out of the barn, she is compelled to take refuge under our protection. So much did she impede thy husband's labors, by keeping close to him, that he found it necessary to give her two or three gentle pats with a shovel.... She is not an amiable cow; but she has a very intelligent face, and seems to be of a reflective cast of character."[205]

There is humor in all this, of course. But there is also something wary, even hostile. Nathaniel was referring to Fuller as much as her cow. She was fractious, intelligent, prone to interfering with his labors. At the same time, he was communicating his ideal of womanhood to Sophia. "I doubt not that she will soon perceive the expediency of being on good terms with the rest of the sisterhood," he wrote.[206] (Not coincidentally, talk of the cow ends when Fuller's second series of Conversations concluded.) Contributing to Nathaniel's chronicle of the cow was his anxiety over Sophia's artistic career, which was progressing more rapidly than his own. Recently she had begun casting profile medallions, like the one of Charles Chauncy Emerson, for wealthy Bostonians. And that summer she was commissioned by Samuel Gridley Howe, founder of the Perkins Institute for the Blind, to create a full-sized bust of Laura Bridgman, a remarkable twelve-year-old deaf and blind girl who was the first person to be educated by manual alphabet, decades before Helen Keller. Bridgman was already a national celebrity. According to the publicity-minded Howe, she was the second-most famous woman of her time after Queen Victoria. In 1842, Charles Dickens paid her a visit during his travels through America, eventually devoting ten pages to the disabled prodigy in his *American Notes*. He was struck above all by her face, "radiant with intelligence and pleasure. Her hair, braided by her own hands, was bound about a head, whose intellectual capacity and development were beautifully expressed in its graceful outline, and its broad open brow."[207] Sophia's sculpture captures these qualities, revealing a composed and graceful girl, eyes shielded by the green ribbon worn by all the blind students at the Perkins Institute.

Nathaniel expressed concern about the commission. "Dearest, do not thou wear thyself out with working upon that bust," he wrote in late September.[208] By this point, he had lost much of his enthusiasm for Brook Farm, with its endless cleaning of stables and plowing of fields—labor he now considered more tedious than that of the Custom House. He had begun paying $4 a week for room and board instead of working on the farm, and suddenly felt "free from ... bondage—free to think of his Dove—free to enjoy nature—free to think and feel!" Upset that he had been "unable to set seriously about literary occupation" at Brook Farm, he worried that Sophia felt obliged to sculpt Bridgman to help fund their life together. He warned Sophia against creating art solely for profit—what he called "this intrusion of an outward necessity into labors of the imagination and intellect."[209] And he added that if producing the sculpture "cause so much as a single head-ache, I shall wish Laura Bridgman were at Jericho."[210]

As it turned out, the sculpture *did* cause a headache—a sick, juddering pain in the temples that sent Sophia to her sickbed as soon as the bust was completed. Once again, she resorted to mesmerism to ease her symptoms, this time consulting an old friend, Cornelia Hall Park, who had recently become interested in the treatment. Connie Park was two years younger than Sophia. In 1834, her husband had abandoned her to seek his fortune in California, and she had moved into rented rooms in Boston, where she hosted intellectual soirees, attended lectures, and was a member of Fuller's conversation group. Park eventually moved to Brook Farm herself—although Nathaniel had already departed by that point.

When Sophia reported her mesmeric sessions to him, she received the most brittle and imperious reply in their courtship. "[M]y spirit is moved to talk to thee to-day about these magnetic miracles," he began, "and to beseech thee to take no part in them. I am unwilling that a power should be exercised on thee, of which we know neither the origin nor consequences, and the phenomena of which seem rather calculated to bewilder us, than to teach us any truths about the present or future state of being." Then he took a censorious tone: "If I possessed such a power over thee, I should not dare to exercise it; nor can I consent to its being exercised by another. Supposing that this power arises from the transfusion of one spirit into another, it seems to me the sacredness of an individual is violated by it; there would be an intrusion into thy holy of holies—and the intruder not be thy husband!"[211]

Much has been made about the sexual panic evident in these statements. Nathaniel's letter is only slightly less jarring when we recall that mesmerism was in fact associated with illicit carnality. But his outrage also has something to do with Park's independence, her financial autonomy. Like Sophia, she was earning a living through unconventional methods—something Nathaniel was himself struggling to do. And the mesmeric sessions reminded him of just how much his own personality had become interfused with Sophia's—how dependent he had become on her. His response was to make demands, to assert the privileges of male prerogative.

A conflict was imminent. Nathaniel asked Sophia to give up her art when it made her sick. At the same time, he wanted her to renounce the only treatment that seemed to offer relief. Sophia, on the other hand, wanted to make art. She also wanted to become a wife. If she sometimes imagined both goals to be possible, she just as often felt them to be incompatible. Added to this was her longstanding ambivalence toward independent women—her deep-seated discomfort at the social ridicule aimed at her sister Elizabeth—and her fear of not living up to her mother and sister's high standards of excellence.

In the end, rather than conflict there was acquiescence. Sophia underwent a subtle shift in emphasis, a reorientation of values. She now began to consider her future life with Nathaniel a work of art. "My prince of the world is in himself an ideal I shall never exhaust," she confided to Elizabeth Hoar. "His nature is a scroll of magic which I unroll & unroll & find no end, & it is illuminated with a various beauty, which keeps me in a saving wonder as the Hours dance on."[212]

11.

The wedding took place on July 9, 1842, in the bookshop on West Street. Sophia was attended by her mother and two sisters, as well as by Connie Park, the mesmerist, and the artist Sarah Clarke, whose brother, James Freeman Clarke, officiated. (Nathaniel Peabody was such a vaporous presence that Sophia later could not remember whether he had congratulated her after the service.) When she descended from the second floor and appeared before her husband-to-be, she was in a white dress, her hair adorned with waxy white pond lilies that she didn't remove until after the two-hour carriage ride through wilting heat and a sudden summer downpour on the road to Concord, where they had rented the old parsonage on Monument Road. This was the same home where Mary Moody Emerson had been born and where Waldo had written *Nature*. It was now a musty old house with leaning stone gateposts, a tree-lined lane, and, on the front door, a ponderous iron knocker shaped like the head of an Egyptian sphinx. In the front yard was a garden bursting with peas, corn, squash, and other vegetables: a wedding present by a twenty-five-year-old villager named Henry David Thoreau. Vases were scattered throughout the house and filled with flowers, a gift from Elizabeth Hoar, who had written a poem for Sophia prophesying the moment of their arrival:

These and more July shall ope
Their blossoms wait for thee,
And what in June was only hope
Shall bright fulfillment be.[213]

It had always been Sophia's idea to live in Concord. To Mary Wilder White Foote—the daughter of Mary Emerson's old friend—she described her vision of married life in the rural retreat:

He [will have] a study & I a studio, one over the other, & while he is in the hands of his Muse in the morning, I shall be subject of mine—In our several vocations we shall joyfully exert our faculties during the first hours—Then in after noon we shall meet to interchange the thoughts that have visited us from the Unknown deep—Oh just think of the felicity of hearing him & also of telling him all that I have discovered & showing him my inscriptions with pencil & sculpting tool.[214]

From the very first day, bride and groom believed they had discovered paradise. "It is a perfect Eden around us," Sophia declared on July 10, writing her mother. "We are Adam and Eve."[215] Like the original parents, the two of them bestowed names upon everything they encountered. Nathaniel rechristened the parsonage the *Old Manse* and he called Sophia his *lily* and his *Angel*. She in turn called him *my lord* and *Apollo* (the same term she had once bestowed on Fernando de Zayas). They referred to their sexual relations as *ethereal dainties*—as *blissful interviews*—and they commemorated their life in a shared notebook with green marbled covers that chronicles a mutually besotted honeymoon:

he is the liveliest being who ever breathed life, Sophia wrote.

she is a beloved woman, Nathaniel replied.

I care very little what guise the heavens wear, Sophia wrote, *whether it be sunny or shadowy abroad, so complete & sufficient is my inward happiness.*

she is sunshine, he countered, *and delicate Spring and delightful Summer, in her own person.*[216]

An erotic energy crackles throughout the shared journal. It opens with Sophia's account of the pair entering the nearby woods (they had apparently just quarreled) and sitting "down upon the carpet of dried pine leaves. Then I clasped him in my arms in the lovely shade, & we laid down a few moments on the bosom of dear mother Earth. Oh how sweet it was!"[217] In the future, Sophia would be condemned by critics as a literary prude incapable of sharing her husband's earthy language or fully understanding his greatness as an author. (The reason for the rebuke is that she excised portions of her husband's journals when they were published.) But her entries in the shared notebook are full of a frank and newfound pleasure in her body: "Before our marriage I knew nothing of its capacities & the truly married alone can know what a wondrous instrument it is for the purposes of the heart."[218] One day, when Margaret Fuller startled the couple in a passionate embrace during a visit to Concord, the embarrassed lovers parted and quickly invited the interloper to tea.[219]

The days settled into routine. Sophia arose before her husband while it was still dark. After a serving woman filled a tiny copper tub in the kitchen with well water, she sat shivering in it, convinced of the homeopathic benefits of bathing in ice water to prevent colds. Nathaniel rose and took his customary walk to the Concord River, passing through the purplish gloom of the apple orchard planted seventy years earlier by Mary Moody Emerson's father. When he reached the river, he stripped off his clothes, waded into water "as soft as milk, and always warmer than the air," and swam back and forth, roughly fifty yards each way.[220]

While Nathaniel wrote, Sophia learned to cook from Miss Leslie's *Directions for Complete Cookery*, and she paid a young farmer, George Prescott, to bring three pints of milk each day. She also remodeled the soot-covered study on the second floor, where Ezra Ripley had written more than three thousand sermons and Waldo Emerson had composed *Nature*. Sophia painted the woodwork and hung gold-trimmed wallpaper. She replaced the prints of Puritan divines with a reproduction of Raphael's Madonna and with the paintings that she had given Nathaniel of Lake Como.

The second-floor window made the outside lawn shimmer and wobble as though it were underwater. Through the undulating glass, Sophia gazed upon the Concord River. She loved its "blue eyes," opening "here and there" among the trees. She loved its jeweled radiance against "the long, quiet lawn—the woods nearby—the innumerable riches of earth & sky."[221] One day, while returning from a visit to the Alcotts on the other side of town, she allowed herself to be rowed back home. "It was utterly still," she wrote, ".... And the clouds of fleecy whiteness floated through the blue ether down far below us—as if we were sailing in mid-air between two firmaments & all the emerald garniture of earth were poised by the power of counter-forces around us." This was transcendentalist talk: the same sort of nature imagery Thoreau would use almost a decade later in *Walden*. "The yellow water of the river turned all the plants that grow in its bed into pure gold," Sophia continued. "... God paints better than man can imitate."[222]

If her husband was considerably less impressed—"This river of ours is the most sluggish stream that I ever was acquainted with," he groused—Sophia began subtly to change her husband's perspective toward nature, eliciting latent attitudes he had buried with his habitual skepticism. The day after his grumbling complaint about the river, he climbed a hill near the Old Manse and gazed down upon the water, struck now "that I had done [the

Plate 1. The Great Awakening.

Plate 2. Madame de Staël.

Plate 3. A "dame school."

Plate 4. Boston in the 1840s.

Plate 5. Sophia Peabody, aged 21.

Plate 6. Havana in the 1830s.

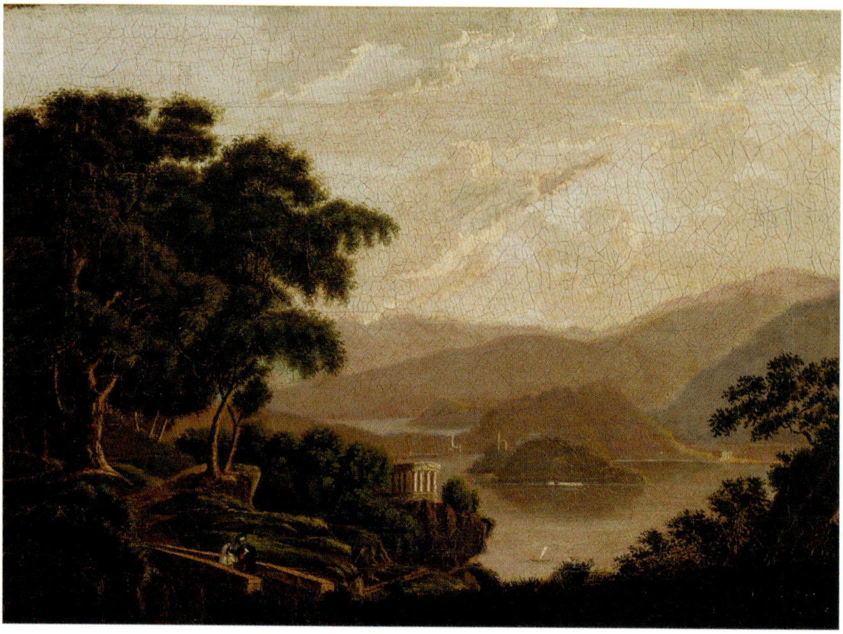

Plate 7. Sophia Peabody, *Isola San Giovanni*, 1839–40.

Plate 8. Twin inkstand at Emerson house.

Plate 9. Lydia Jackson Emerson with Edward.

Plate 10. Margaret Fuller.

Plate 11. Harriet Martineau.

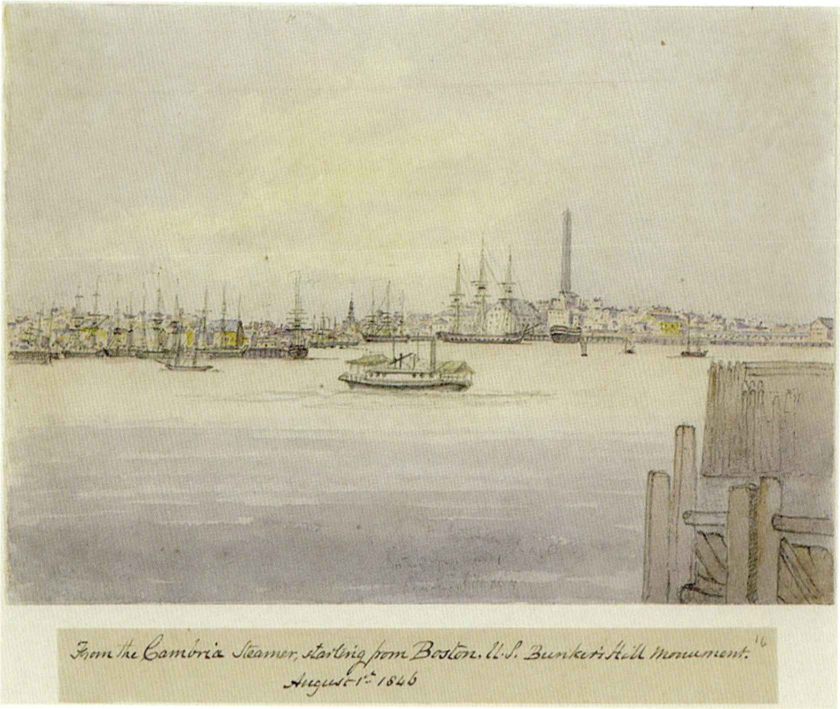

Plate 12. A view from the ship Fuller took to Europe.

river] some injustice." From above, the shimmering waterway struck him as "one of the loveliest features in a scene of great rural beauty," and he began to adopt Sophia's language of optimism: "At a distance, it looked like a strip of sky set into the earth, which it so etherealized and idealized that it seemed akin to the upper regions." If the river "can give such an adequate reflection of Heaven," he continued, "it cannot be so gross and impure as I described it yesterday. Or, if so, it shall be a symbol to me, that even a human breast which may appear least spiritual in some aspects, may still have the capability of reflecting an infinite Heaven in its depths, and therefore of enjoying it."[223]

Like a drop of ink clouding a glass of water, Nathaniel's views also came to alter Sophia's own. In the spring of 1838, having made her first visit to Concord, she had written to Elizabeth that Waldo Emerson was "the greatest man—the most complete man—that ever lived."[224] But soon after her marriage she revised her opinion, telling her mother that "Waldo Emerson knows not much of love—He has never said anything to show he does... [and] has never yet known what union meant with any soul."[225] When Eliza warned her daughter not to adopt her husband's perspective automatically, she received a heated response. "Do not fear that I shall be too subject to my Adam," Sophia wrote, "my crown of Perfection. He loves power as little as any mortal I ever knew; and it is never a question of private will between us, but of absolute right."[226] In another letter she added, "Our love is so wide & deep & equal, that there could not be much difference of opinion between us upon any moral point."[227] Now she admitted that Waldo "as well as Mr. Hawthorne is *great*, but Mr. Emerson is not so whole sided as Mr. Hawthorne."[228]

One trouble with Eden was that it was continually interrupted. Sophia's friends George and Susan Hillard visited soon after the marriage. Waldo often dropped by the Manse, as did Elizabeth Hoar, and Thoreau, whom Nathaniel particularly liked ("his ugliness is of an honest and agreeable fashion," he commented), as well as a feckless young poet named Ellery Channing, who had recently married Margaret Fuller's sister, Ellen, and who hoped to board with the Hawthornes.[229] (The proposal was quashed in a polite, yet firm, letter to Fuller.)

The Alcotts had recently moved to Concord, too, and they became a part of Sophia and Nathaniel's expanding social circle. If Nathaniel complained of those who "intruded into the hallowed shade of our avenue," he nevertheless was friendly enough with Concord's writers by winter to take part in an extraordinary scene.[230] Sophia recorded the event, describing the thick ice on the Concord River, and Waldo and Thoreau's invitation to join them in an ice-skating party behind the Manse. "Henry Thoreau is an experienced skater," Sophia wrote to Mary Foote, "and was figuring dithyrambic dances and Bacchic leaps on the ice—very remarkable, but very ugly, methought. Next him followed Mr. Hawthorne, who, wrapped in his cloak, moved like a self-impelled Greek statue, stately and grave. Mr. Emerson closed the line, evidently too weary to hold himself erect, pitching head-foremost, half lying on the air." When the skating was finished, Waldo followed Sophia into the house and complimented her husband, saying he was "a tiger, a bear, a lion—in short, a satyr, and there was no tiring him out; and he might be the death of a man like himself. And then," Sophia continued, "turning upon me that kindling smile for which he is so memorable, he added, 'Mr. Hawthorne is such an Ajax, who can cope with him!'"[231]

It was on the same frozen patch of the Concord River that sorrow first entered their lives. Shortly after the skating party, Sophia realized she was pregnant. In February, the newlyweds went for a walk to the river. The day was raw, the cold scraping their cheeks. Nathaniel put on skates and sped across the ice, circling Sophia in great loping strides while she gingerly scuffed the frozen river with her boots. Then she slipped, prompting a miscarriage. From her recovery bed, Sophia sought to minimize the event. To her mother she insisted, "I have only to regain my former plumpness to be as I was before," admitting she felt "more active & light & freer" than she had when pregnant.[232] Ambivalent about the enormous changes a child would make to her life, she told Mary White that her spirits had remained untouched while her "own little Hawthorne flower... [had] passed unfolded again into the Paradise of God."[233] She instructed the maid to straighten her husband's study so that it would be difficult for him "to believe that anything at all had happened to us."[234]

While still recovering, she told Nathaniel that "men's accidents are God's purposes"—a sentiment he promptly entered into his journal. Later that year, using Sophia's diamond engagement ring for the purpose, the two of them etched the message into the wavy old windowpane of the study. This began a new domestic ritual. Two months later, they inscribed the following:

> Nathl Hawthorne
> This is his study
> 1843
> Inscribed by my
> Husband at sunset
> April 3rd 1843
> In the gold light. SAH

On the first anniversary of their marriage, Nathaniel wrote a love letter to Sophia. "We were never so happy as now—never such wide capacity for happiness, yet overflowing with all that the day and every moment brings us. Methinks this birthday of our married life is like a cape, which we have now doubled, and find a more infinite ocean of love stretching out before us."[235] Sophia's response was more straightforward: "This is the anniversary of our wedding day, my dearest lover. It is the loveliest weather & the moon is full. What a sweet return of that happy hour."[236]

By then, she was pregnant again. Miserable with morning sickness, she refused to complain, describing her condition as "the very poetry of discomfort, for I rejoice at every smallest proof that I am as ladies wish to be who love their lords."[237] News of the pregnancy prompted Eliza to suggest she take up her painting again "during this interesting period," not only to help pass the time but to "put some dollars in your purse to meet the . . . expenses consequent on your state."[238] Sophia liked the idea. Although she had set up a studio when they first moved to Concord, she had done little in it. Now she began working on the first canvas of her married life: a painting inspired by a print she had borrowed from Waldo Emerson. It was one of those "pale brown monochromes of the most remarkable finish and beauty of draftsmanship," a reproduction of a scene from John Keats's *Endymion: A Poetic Romance*, published a quarter century earlier, in 1818, the year before he produced his great odes.[239]

Keats's poem famously opens with a line that described Sophia's outlook on life: "A thing of beauty is a joy forever." The work recounts a love affair between the moon goddess and an earth-borne shepherd named Endymion. In selecting the poem and print for a subject, Sophia was ahead of her time. Some five years later, Holman Hunt and Dante Gabriel Rossetti each produced works based on Keats's poetry, convinced that "no one had ever painted before any subject from this still little-known poet."[240] Their paintings heralded the beginning of the Pre-Raphaelites.

Sophia was drawn to the circumstances and theme of *Endymion*, which she considered an allegory of her marriage. Endymion, in Greek myth, was a shepherd. In Keats's poem, he falls in love with Cynthia, the moon goddess, and embarks on a long journey through the underworld in search of her. Both Endymion's lonely quest and Cynthia's dual identity as earthly beauty and immortal divinity appealed to Sophia. She always believed her marriage to Nathaniel had redeemed his years of solitude, ending his long quest for genuine love.

But creating a "thing of beauty" turned out to be more difficult than she had anticipated. The cloudy winter weather thwarted her efforts to work on the painting. When conditions were poor, she visited Lydia Emerson, who was pregnant with her fourth and final child. Sometimes she stopped to see the ethereal Ellen Channing, formerly Fuller, who was also pregnant. In the evenings, Nathaniel read aloud to her from Shakespeare, finishing *Hamlet* on December 6, then moving on to the comedies. His own creative work, Sophia told herself, was "perfectly inimitable and inimitably perfect as usual . . . To read anything of his after all other reading is like lifting one's head out of the bogs & quagmires of earth into the clear empyrean."[241]

Her painting continued to go nowhere. "I painted from 10 till after one," she wrote, "or rather sat during that time before Endymion, brush & palette & mahl stick in hands..." She was restless, tired. The child inside her felt "heavy," a presence that weighed her down. Her moods oscillated, and when she found it impossible to paint, she decorated the house, placing a "lovely half statue of Ceres" on the secretary, "& opposite, on the other, is Margaret [Fuller]'s browned vase."[242] When Nathaniel accidentally brushed against the statue and sent it crashing to the floor, she broke down. "I was amazed," she wrote in her journal, "but seemed very quiet at first. Then I began to feel nervous & shocked & as if I must have a thunder gust of tears to relieve myself. I found it would not do, however, for this immediately [line obliterated] & I made a great effort to stop. But I could have done nothing without the tenderest & best husband in the world, who held me in his arms & soothed & calmed me with his divine caresses & seraph-tones." A few days later, she still felt "desolate & nervous & as if I wanted to sit down & weep a river." Unable to remain alone, she went upstairs to the study and "spoiled my dear husband's vein for writing & that was hard for me to bear & I was more nervous still."[243]

These mood swings were likely the result of pregnancy. But they were also connected to her painting in some crucial way. Art had often proven as challenging as it was exhilarating to Sophia. If it promised the satisfactions of creation, it was also freighted with extremely high expectations, which dated back to Elizabeth's introduction of her to Washington Allston. The imminent arrival of a child now forced her to confront the course she had charted for her life. If painting was difficult now, would it not be all but impossible when she became a mother? Did she really wish to be "as ladies wish to be who love their lords"—that is, maternal? Was the dream of her youth—the coffin-shaped clouds floating over a friend's wedding—a prediction of her own artistic ambitions? Or were the dreams she frequently had of Elizabeth, laid out in a casket and covered in cerements, a message that her older sister's achievements as a single woman weren't worth the sacrifice of love and security?

Her journal during this time frequently refers to the one inviolable rule of her marriage: Nathaniel was not to be disturbed when he was upstairs writing. During their three years in Concord, he would complete an astonishing seventeen stories: most of the material for *Mosses from an Old Manse*. Sophia, on the other hand, painted very little. She found herself absorbed elsewhere, in learning to cook, in protecting her husband from social callers, in striving to transform married life into an aesthetic object. Little wonder that the destruction of Ceres—goddess of fertility and motherhood—so unsettled her.

Only rarely did she admit to the difficulties of her new life. Once she conceded that Nathaniel "is so seldom satisfied with any thing—weather, things or people, that I am always glad to find him pleased." Another time she revealed that he could hardly bear to "have a cracked or broken dish on the table" (such imperfections grated upon *his* aesthetic sense) and that he hated "to be touched more than any one I ever knew."[244] To her sister Mary, who had by now married Horace Mann and returned from a honeymoon in Europe, she repeated one of Nathaniel's convictions—a belief that was nothing less than blasphemy to the aspiring Peabody women: "He cannot bear to have a woman come out of the shade, far less his wife, & never has forgiven himself for dedicating his Gentle Boy to me."[245]

This last remark was made shortly after she completed *Endymion.* Nathaniel considered it her best work. Rather than encouraging her to sell it or exhibit it, however, he convinced her to keep the painting, believing it too personal to hang in someone else's parlor. It took Sophia longer to warm to the work. Only after she had varnished it and found a suitable frame was she able to express her belief that it had "come out of my soul . . . a record of these happy, hopeful days!" She considered the painting a clue to the life she had made in the Old Manse. "The divine dreaming shining in Endymion's face, is it not my dream & my reality too?" she asked her mother. "His body entranced in sleep, his soul bathed in light—every curve flowing in consummate beauty—in some way, it is my life."[246]

It was the last painting she ever completed.

12.

She would scratch a final message into the wavy glass window of the old parsonage before leaving Concord. The Hawthorne family—there was a daughter now, named Una, after Nathaniel's favorite character in *The Fairie Queene*—departed in the summer of 1845. Samuel Ripley, Mary Moody Emerson's step-brother, had inherited the home from his father, the Reverend Ezra Ripley, and decided now to occupy it. (His decision was prompted in part by the fact that the Hawthornes were woefully behind in rent.) By then, Nathaniel had almost completed his second collection of short fiction, *Mosses from an Old Manse,* which came out the following year and for which he was paid $75—considerably less than Sophia would have earned by selling *Endymion.* Most contemporaneous critics thought Nathaniel's new work better than *Twice-Told Tales,* but one insightful critic, Edgar Allan Poe, discerned the influence of transcendentalist Concord on the stories and advised the author to "mend his pen, get a bottle of visible ink, come out from the Old Manse, cut Mr. Alcott, hang (if possible) the editor of 'The Dial' [this was a dig at Margaret Fuller], and throw out the window to the pigs all his odd numbers of the *North American Review.*"[247]

In 1845, another book came out that generated far more critical reaction. This was Margaret Fuller's *Woman in the Nineteenth Century,* a passionate argument for the equal treatment of women. The ideas in it had originated in her Conversations at 13 West Street. They had been honed and refined by the women who gathered in Elizabeth Peabody's cramped parlor. Sophia and Nathaniel are present in its pages. After visiting the newlyweds for the first time in 1842, Fuller had proclaimed theirs "a holy and equal marriage."[248] In a letter to Sophia, she admitted that she could not "think of love merely in the heart, or even in the common destiny of two souls, but also as necessarily comprehending intellectual friendship, too." Fuller then made a prediction, telling Sophia she believed "the happiest lot imaginable . . . lies before you."[249]

In *Woman*, Fuller described four sorts of marriages. They ranged from those of mere convenience to the very highest, which she compared to "a pilgrimage to a common shrine." In this ideal form, husbands and wives engaged in "intellectual communion, for how sad it would be . . . to have a companion to whom you could not communicate thoughts and aspirations as they sprang to life."[250] She had the Hawthornes in mind when she wrote this passage.

Woman in the Nineteenth Century created an uproar, even among the forward-thinking townspeople of Concord. One village woman wrote, "It is very entertaining—but I do not think there was any particular call for such a book just now—I don't know much about the *world*—but Concord women are by no means slaves—they have without doubt impressive powers." Another woman told her daughter, "I have been reading Miss Fuller's new book 'Woman in the nineteenth century'—It does not appear to me that it is a book that is required at all—or one that is calculated to do much good.—I think with a few exceptions, women in this country have all their rights—but I am not a fair judge as I am a novice & unacquainted with the abuses of society."[251]

Sophia, rather surprisingly, had reached a similar conclusion. In 1845, just three years after writing her sonnet praising Fuller, she told her mother: "I suspect a wife only can know how to speak with sufficient respect of man,—I think Margaret speaks of many things that should not be spoken of."[252] Perhaps she was referring to Fuller's lengthy discussion of prostitution—one of the most scandalous portions of *Woman in the Nineteenth Century*. But Sophia's comments also indicated a larger shift in her views. She no longer considered herself a maverick artist. She now thought of herself as a wife and mother. When friends and family urged her to send her children to school so she could resume her career, she replied, "Poetry, painting—for the present must go by the board—& what is more, shall go—I said in my heart—but not aloud. I shall paint better & write sweeter poetry by & by than I should now." Her children, she added, "are the best pictures I ever painted, the finest poetry I could write, better poetry than I ever can write."[253]

For Sophia, the thrill of creation had often been accompanied by excruciating headaches. Perhaps this is why she gave up her art so easily. While Nathaniel remained upstairs, scribbling away, she nursed her child, bathed her, fed her, taught her new words. Yet she must have sometimes regretted sacrificing her artistic ambitions to perform these tasks. After all, she had seen her mother worn from childrearing, dejected and dispirited from too many responsibilities. And she had felt the thrill of creation. She had experienced rapturous moments during her painting when all sense of self disappeared, when to live was to surrender to something higher, something even sacred.

A few months after the publication of *Woman in the Nineteenth Century*, the Hawthornes celebrated their third wedding anniversary in Concord. "The three years we have spent here will always be to me a blessed memory," Sophia told her mother, "because here all my dreams became realities, twice better than even the dreams."[254] At the start of the year, she had scratched another message in a window at the Old Manse, again using her wedding ring to leave a mark on posterity, a poetic statement that remains visible to this day:

> Una Hawthorne
> stood on this window
> sill January 22d 1845
> while the trees were all
> glass chandeliers—a goodly
> show which she liked
> much tho' only ten
> months old.

4
Lydia Jackson Emerson's Marriage of Heaven and Hell

1.

Lydia Jackson Emerson was a late riser. She detested the morning sun, which gave her a headache. She also thought it revived symptoms from the scarlet fever she had suffered fifteen years earlier. She enjoyed reading late into the night, a habit she had picked up as a young woman after learning that Napoleon required only four hours of sleep. At night, she marched through stacks of books. In the morning, when the rest of the household was rising, she recovered from the excitement her reading had caused.

But early in November 1839, when she was thirty-six years old, she began to rouse herself before dawn on Wednesdays. Shivering in the dark, she bathed in a tub of ice-cold water, then dressed, had a sip of something to drink, and boarded the seven o'clock stage for Boston—a jarring, jerking trip through mud and snow and sometimes a staunch Nor'easter that pierced the carriage windows and froze the breath of the horses. At first, it followed the same road where British redcoats had retreated some sixty-five years earlier. Later it joined the turnpike into Boston. The trip took roughly two and a half hours, but if a tree had fallen across its rutted path, or if a puddle sprang up after a rain, the journey took considerably longer. It would be like this until 1845, when the Fitchburg railroad came to Concord.

In Boston, the carriage ride was a voyage through odors: horse dung, coal smoke, the acrid smell of the forge, urine and sweat—sometimes the tang of salt marsh and sea, too, with the gust of oysters at low tide, which reminded Lydia of her childhood in Plymouth. The narrow, cobbled streets vibrated with iron-rimmed wheels and shod horses. The air between the bluff brick rowhouses was disturbed by the cries of hawkers and drovers, the piping yells of boys herding cattle, the shrieks of children playing.

Lydia's destination was a respite from all this—a refuge from the tiresome and trite, from noise and mundanity and tedium. When Lydia stepped from the carriage at 13 West Street, she stood before the ungainly brick rowhouse a moment before entering the front door. The front parlor resembled no other front parlor in America. It was lined from floor to shoulder-height with books, some still wrapped in twine, some littering the floor and the sofa along the wall.

In the parlor was a group of women. They were shedding winter cloaks, untying bonnets, peering at the titles of all those books. The room was filled with laughter and gossip and news from various towns near Boston. Lydia saw the familiar figure of Elizabeth Peabody, presiding over introductions, pointing out new books, her spectacles sliding down the bridge of her nose as she talked. And there was her sister, Sophia, whose hair was a scarlet cockade and whose laughter now and then rang out like the chiming of a crystal wineglass. The Peabody sister's mother, Eliza, now in her sixties, peered occasionally from the stairs and smiled at the gathered women.

They were waiting for Margaret Fuller. Lydia Emerson had known Fuller for three years now. She and her husband had been introduced to her by Elizabeth Peabody, who confessed a "strong but unjustifiable prejudice against Fuller."[1] To her credit, Elizabeth thought the Emersons might find her interesting, nevertheless, and she was right: both Emersons had been immediately charmed. "Miss Fuller is with us now," Lydia wrote Elizabeth, "and you will be glad to hear we find real satisfaction—Miss F. Mr E. & myself—in our intercourse with each other. We like her—she likes us—I speak in this way—because . . . the tendencies of all three being strong & decided—[we] possibly not such as could harmonize."[2]

Each summer after that, or sometimes in early fall, Lydia looked forward to the younger woman's visit to their Concord home. Fuller was clearly a creature of the city, an urbane woman who loved Boston, but she found the Emerson household a welcome break during the sweltering weather. Lydia enjoyed her company, and the two women often stayed up late talking. (They both adored German literature.) It was during one of these visits, with its endless talk of books and reform and the coming new age, that Fuller first considered hosting a series of conversations for women. The first was held on November 6, 1839, an occasion during which Fuller outlined her plans in greater detail. She might have had Lydia in mind when she announced that the Conversations would provide "a point of union to well-educated and thinking women," lasting two hours and covering a range of topics.

Twenty-five women attended the first meeting. Most were widely read. They were familiar with Dante, Shakespeare, and Goethe. Many spoke a second language. Some botanized or painted or wrote verse. But they all felt as if they had been shut out of the great conversation that constitutes history and art and philosophy. Their opinion counted for little. Fuller wanted them to ask why this was so. She wanted them to interrogate their condition, to ask if it could be improved.

It was to engage in these discussions that Lydia Emerson overcame her aversion to the morning and traveled to Boston each Wednesday—for she loved to talk. "Conversations seem to be Mother's natural field," recalled her son Edward. "I regularly hear when there has been one either that 'It was a failure because Mrs. E wasn't there,' or 'Oh yes they talked a good deal about cats and rats and sealing-wax and whether pigs had wings, but at last Mrs. Emerson spoke, and then all the fools went silent.'"[3] She could be combative, acerbic, even a bit jesuitical. Whenever Lydia told her children not to bicker, they repeated the formula they had learned from her: "We aren't bickering, we are conversing on various subjects."[4]

The various subjects Lydia liked best were politics, religion, and the latest novels. She was deeply concerned about the sufferings of the less fortunate, making her an early and outspoken advocate of abolition and women's and animal rights. And her feelings about religion ran the range from orthodoxy to borderline blasphemy. Her oldest daughter, Ellen Tucker Emerson, remembered her fondness for dispute, especially the spirited quarrels she engaged in with her husband's Aunt Mary Moody Emerson. Lydia enjoyed disagreeing with complacent ministers and other authority figures. She even carried on a lifelong dispute with the local butcher, convinced he was cheating her.

But the gatherings at 13 West Street were among the few occasions Lydia could participate in uninterrupted intellectual work. Peabody's parlor was now a hub of artistic and philosophical exchange for women, the center of "a most gifted and extraordinary circle," as one of Fuller's participants called it.[5] The early feminist reformer Elizabeth Cady Stanton, evoking Mary Wollstonecraft, called the Conversations "a vindication of woman's right to think," and Fuller herself spoke for many of the women, including Lydia, when she said she believed the talks provided something even more basic: "real society, which I have not before looked for out of the pale of intimacy. We have time, patience, mutual reverence and fearlessness eno' to get at one another's thoughts."[6]

From the outset, the Conversations engaged in what today would be called sexual politics. While discussing the Greek idea of genius, for instance, one woman asked if genius was "banished... from the domestic hearth." Another "said she did not want to believe it—& enlarged upon the action of Genius in the domestic circle."[7] When Fuller pushed the women to determine "what was the distinction of feminine & masculine when applied to character and mind," one woman replied that she "thought women were instinctive—they had spontaneously what men have by study & induction." A different woman observed that instinctiveness was "said to be the distinction of poets among men. Another said that this would confirm Coleridge's remark that every man of great poetical genius had something feminine in his face."[8]

All of the women gathered in Elizabeth Peabody's parlor agreed that men had been afforded opportunities for self-development that the women had not. Women were burdened by the eternal round of domestic responsibilities, making it all but impossible to paint a masterpiece or write an epic poem when kitchen pots needed scouring and infants required tending. This led them to explore whether there was something inherently unfair about marriage. It led to conversations in which they imagined marriages where power and property were equally distributed, where husband and wife were linked in a common goal.

Lydia Emerson listened to all of this with the greatest of interest. Sometimes she wished Fuller would touch on the issue of slavery and New England's complicity in the institution. And she was not entirely certain that Fuller understood the profound satisfactions of motherhood, having never experienced it. (In this way, she agreed with Sophia Peabody Hawthorne.) But the topic of marriage captured her undivided attention. It caused her to sit still and listen intently. For marriage was a subject about which she was decidedly ambivalent.

2.

Four years earlier, when Waldo Emerson traveled to Plymouth to declare his intention to marry her, he had found himself in the parlor of a stately old mansion with a woman who refused to open her eyes. Lydia Jackson was determined not to look at him while he spoke. She would keep her eyes closed when she talked, too. There were some very definite items she had to address—a history to impart, conditions to impose—and she did not want to be distracted by Waldo Emerson's forcible gaze.

Their courtship had been irregular from the start. To begin with, they barely knew each other. Lydia had first seen the young minister in Boston, while visiting her older sister, Lucy Jackson Brown. On that memorable Sunday, she had wandered into the Twelfth Congregational Church on Chambers Street, where a substitute minister was preaching. He was tall and lank and had the longest neck she had ever seen, but as he stepped up to the pulpit, his slight frame seemed to shelter a serene passion, a frigid flame. He surveyed the congregation and noticed the tall, grave woman who sat less than ten feet away. Her face was radiant, her large gray eyes luminous.

According to their oldest daughter, after the sermon Lydia "found herself leaning eagerly forward, and as she looked back on the whole dear & beautiful service and noticed that now she felt tired of her position she made up her mind that she must have taken it when the minister said his first words and had been too much absorbed to move from beginning to end." A strange feeling swept over her. Unbidden words arose: "That man is certainly my predestined husband."[9]

She was given to such premonitions. From youth on, she had looked for signs and portents, omens and auguries. She supposed they were clues from the universe, traces of intention left half hidden by a wise Providence. To Lydia, intuition comprised a form of knowledge every bit as significant as the studies pursued by her younger brother, Dr. Charles T. Jackson, a scientist and inventor who seemed to take peculiar delight in exploding the phials and test tubes in his home laboratory. All her life, Lydia would follow the occult sciences of mesmerism and phrenology. She dabbled in astrology. In middle age, she eagerly followed the accounts of three sisters from New York who claimed to communicate with the dead through ghostly rapping on a small walnut table in their parlor. (It turned out they had been cracking the knuckles of their big toes.) And until her death at the age of ninety she would remain fascinated by the claims of spiritualism, which promised to relay messages from the shadowy regions of the afterlife.

Yet her strongest presentiments involved Waldo Emerson. Two years after she saw him preach, he visited her hometown, Plymouth, Massachusetts. This was in 1834. Waldo had been invited to deliver two sermons by a local German teacher named George Partridge Bradford, who happened to be the younger brother of Mary Moody Emerson's close friend Sarah Bradford. (He also happened to be Lydia's German instructor.) Waldo's sermons were delivered in the newly built First Parish Church, located one block from Cape Cod Bay. For his text, he took a verse from Psalms 139: "I am fearfully and wonderfully made."

Waldo had undergone tremendous changes in the two years since Lydia Jackson had last seen him. A grieving widower, he had abandoned his position at Boston's Second Church and traveled to Europe on a journey of self-discovery. There he had met Wordsworth, Coleridge, and the popularizer of German philosophy, Thomas Carlyle. He had then returned to his ancestral home, the parsonage in Concord, where Sophia and Nathaniel Hawthorne would live seven years later. In its low-ceilinged parlor, with the grandfather clock ticking in the corner and the spring sunshine pouring through the mullioned windows, he debated religion and philosophy with Aunt Mary Moody Emerson. Their disputes enabled Waldo to shape and hone the ideas for the book he was writing, a treatise on the sufficiency—the supremacy—of the solitary self. It was the sort of compensatory philosophy that a young man who had recently lost his beloved wife might construct.

Lydia may have already known some of this when Waldo stood before the congregation and declared human consciousness a miracle. Each person was endowed with godlike gifts, he announced; the capacity to think, to perceive the world's splendor, was a story every bit as astonishing as the raising of Lazarus or the parable of the loaves and fishes. Each individual's "existence in the world was more amazing than any other fact."[10] When the service was over, one of Lydia's friends approached her and asked how she liked hearing her own ideas preached in public: "What Mr Emerson said was just what you always say."[11] And when Waldo preached the following week, his words "so lifted [her] to higher thoughts," as her daughter later put it, that she hurried out of church afterward to avoid speaking. She did not want anyone to disturb the spell of his rich, baritone voice.[12]

They met soon afterward. Waldo's sermons were so popular in Plymouth that Bradford invited him back to give a lecture, which Lydia attended. At a gathering after, the two were introduced. Waldo wrote a fairy-tale account of the event in his journal, his prose shifting from the past to the present tense at the moment that they first became aware of one another:

> It happened once that a youth and a maid beheld each other in a public assembly for the first time. The youth gazed with great delight upon the beautiful face until he caught the maiden's eyes. She presently became aware of his attention, and something like correspondence immediately takes place. The maid depressed her eyes that the man might gaze upon her face. Then the man looked away, that the maiden might gratify her curiosity. Presently their eyes met in a full, searching, front, not to be mistaken glance. It is wonderful how much it made them acquainted.[13]

This was in the spring of 1834. The next January, Lydia experienced another premonitory vision. It was a sudden, subsuming glimpse of the future. She saw herself on the wide staircase of her family home, attired in a brilliant white bridal gown. Waldo stood beside her, holding her arm. He escorted her down the stairs. The image upset her; she had not been thinking of him—she did not wish to think of him. Recently she had told her brother that she planned to establish herself "in the character I have always intended formally to assume in due time—that of an Old Maid."[14]

But a few weeks later, the vision returned. Now she saw only Waldo's face. It was "very beautiful, close to her[,] gazing at her, just for a moment."[15] Again she felt distressed. To compound matters, the next day she received a letter from him. "I am rejoiced in my Reason as well as in my Understanding," he wrote her, "by finding an earnest and noble mind whose presence quickens in mine all that is good and shames and repels me from my own weaknesses. Can I resist the impulse to beseech you to love me?"

It was a marriage proposal.

Later she told her daughter that doubts immediately sprang up in her mind. "How could he condescend to her?" she wondered. "And then how little he knew her!"[16] In the past year, they had exchanged hardly a dozen words. How could he love her? She sat down and composed a response. Then she threw it away. She started again. This time she invited him to come to Plymouth. They would discuss the subject in person.

When Waldo appeared several days later, he was led into the parlor, where Lydia sat upright with her eyes closed. In this manner, she delivered the message she had been unable to send by letter. She said she had never taken care of a home. "[S]he should not be a skillful mistress of a house and that it would be a load of care and labour from which she shrank and a giving up of an existence she thoroughly enjoyed and to which she had become exactly fitted." She liked her life in Plymouth. She was fond of her friends, absorbed in the community. She had leisure to read and think and do as she pleased. She wanted him to know that she could not give up these things "unless he was sure he loved her and needed her enough to justify her in doing it..."[17]

Waldo later referred to this episode as "that catechism with the closed eyes." But he apparently answered her questions as honestly as he could, because at some point Lydia opened her eyes. Suddenly anxious she had been talking too much, she asked him if all her palaver was uninteresting. "Uninteresting!" Waldo exclaimed. "It is heaven." And at that moment, wrote their daughter, "his eyes seemed to her to be like two blue flames."[18]

3.

Lydia's father could have stepped out of an eighteenth-century novel. Charles Jackson stood six feet tall. He wore white silk stockings and a fine blue coat with brass buttons. He was a man of fixed and solid habits, a man who refused to speak while he chewed his food, refused to mix milk and molasses in his cornmeal pudding, refused to taste cheese of any sort. He was also a captain of industry. Charles Jackson owned a large counting house at the end of Plymouth's wharf. In partnership with his brother, he kept a small fleet of ships that imported and exported goods from Ceylon and the Bahamas and Dieppe. Lydia considered him "the most dignified person she ever saw," and as a girl she would loiter along the noisy waterfront just to admire the beautifully carved figureheads of his ships.[19] When she entered his warehouse, she was given chocolate or dates or some other delicacy from distant lands. From this man she inherited her height, her oaken majesty, and her flair for the dramatic. One of her most cherished childhood memories was of him as he prepared for church. While her mother plaited his long hair and tied it with a black ribbon,

A VIEW OF PLYMOUTH,
From the beach east of the Harbor – the oldest town in New England and landing place of the Pilgrim Fathers

Figure 45. Plymouth, Massachusetts.

Charles Jackson held open a hymnal so the two of them could sing together (figure 45).

Lucy Cotton Jackson was two years older than her husband. She was from an old Plymouth family—ministerial rather than commercial. Her great-great-grandfather was the revered Puritan divine, John Cotton, whose son would become Plymouth's fourth minister and who was remembered decades later for visiting every single household in town and inquiring into the condition of each person's soul. Lucy's grandfather was the nephew of Cotton Mather, and a well-known missionary to Native Americans in the early eighteenth century. Her own father, John Cotton, had preached in nearby Halifax for two decades before poor health forced him to resign and return to Plymouth, where he became the town's registrar of deeds and treasurer. He was locally famous for his excellent library of Greek and Latin.

If Lydia's mother was permitted access to that library—if she was knowledgeable in the classical languages—there is no mention of it. There is little mention of her anywhere in the record. According to Lydia, she possessed "a very timid and shrinking nature."[20] Soon after her wedding, on February 26, 1794, she began to produce children—a total of eight in all. She and Charles endured an appalling amount of child mortality, however. Only three children, two sisters and a brother, survived into adulthood.

Lydia, the youngest daughter and the seventh child overall, remembered her mother as eternally occupied with domestic chores: spinning wool, baking custards, frying doughnuts. She also remembered her beautiful singing voice, as well as a handful of tunes she sang to her children. And there was this recollection: once, when Lucy Jackson caught Lydia staring into the mirror, she suddenly recited a poem she remembered from her own girlhood.

> While at the mirror, lovely maid
> You trifle time away
> Reflect how soon your bloom will fade
> And transient charms decay.*

There is one other detail about Lucy Cotton Jackson worth mentioning. This descendant of Puritan ministers never formally joined the church. She attended meetings; she recited prayers and sang hymns. But she refused to undergo the process of membership. Lydia thought her refusal was on account of her shyness; "the person who was to join the church had to stand up in the aisle and 'give their relation' [of conversion], and if the church-members were satisfied that she had the proper sense of sin and of pardon... she was admitted."[21] But there may have been another reason, too. Lucy Jackson may have opposed the subtle coercion of witnessing. She may have felt it violated her experience of religion. She may even have been in rebellion against the empty forms of the church. Certainly, her youngest daughter, Lydia, never submitted to public opinion in matters of faith. She detested the hypocrisy that too often accompanied formal religion, and she resented, on behalf of her mother, "that such sinners as she knew the church members to be should think of being able to judge whether a saint might come to the Lord's table."[22]

In 1813, when Lydia was ten, her father inherited the Winslow House, a stately Georgian mansion built by a British loyalist who had fled to Nova Scotia during the Revolutionary War. For the rest of her life, Lydia considered its corkscrew newel posts and fireplaces tiled in Delft the height of refinement. Nearby was the North Street academy, where she and her older sister Lucy were educated by a morose disciplinarian known as Miss Patty, who sat before the class with a stick so long she could strike any ill-behaved child without leaving her seat. Lydia remembered that she and the other girls "sewed most of the time. The mistress basted their seams & hems, till they were old enough to do it themselves, inspected all their work and had bad sewing picked out." One other memory from these

* The poem had appeared in the British periodical, *The Universal Magazine of Knowledge and Pleasure*, in 1788.

academy years stayed with her. This concerned the catechism from *The New-England Primer*, which opened with the dour reminder that original sin was the dispensation of all people. "She, and all Plymouth," wrote her daughter Ellen, "called a doll a dawl, and when she said after her mistress 'in Adam's fall, we sinned all' she wondered what sort of dawl was a sinny dawl."[23]

Other teachers were employed by Charles Jackson to teach his daughters watercolor and dancing. There was a French dancing master to instruct Lydia in the finer points of the quadrille and the cotillon, a discipline that entailed standing for an hour each day in a *tourne hanche*, a wooden contraption that splayed the feet outward to achieve what is known in ballet as turnout. For two decades, Lydia dedicated herself to this torturous practice, sometimes reading her lessons while standing in the stocks. She attributed her graceful carriage to the routine.

A year or so after the family moved into the Winslow House, Charles Jackson bought his daughters matching beaver bonnets and merino dresses and sent them to a boarding school some thirty-five miles north, in Dorchester. The female academy was operated by a cousin of the essayist Judith Sargent Murray, the same woman who had inspired Mary Moody Emerson a quarter-century earlier to write under the name *Constantia*. The school was one of Murray's projects to educate young women. In 1804, she had purchased a house and a quarter-acre of land on the village's Meeting House Hill, asking her cousin to contrive the curriculum, which was both ambitious and conventional: "Reading, Writing, English Grammar, Arithmetic, Plain Sewing, Embroidery, Tambour, French Language, Painting, and Geography, including the use of Globes."[24] For an extra charge, students learned needlework, painting on velvet and ivory, and music on the pianoforte (figure 46).

Away from home for the first time, Lydia wrote plaintive letters to her mother. "The summer dear mamma passes very rapidly, but I hope by *me*, not without improvement. I am too well aware of the present advantages offered me, and that I have come here expressly to avail myself of them, to be idle, or careless."[25] To her father she assumed a playful and less dutiful tone: "Why do you not write to me dear Papa? What is the cause of your silence?... Tell me dear Father the reason of the excessive high price of provisions when the earth has produced so bountifully? Everything is extravagantly dear, yet everything abounds, you are my Oracle dear parent, so you must expect me to question you on every, to me, inexplicable subject."[26] She was ten years old.

Lydia and her older sister Lucy stayed in Dorchester for exactly one year. When they returned, still wearing their beaver bonnets and merino dresses, it was because their mother had developed an ominous cough. Two hundred years earlier, the English physician Thomas Sydenham had suggested horseback riding for the treatment of tuberculosis. Motion, according to his theory, relieved the disease's symptoms. Lucy Cotton Jackson followed this time-honored prescription, setting out each morning from Winslow House on the family horse before

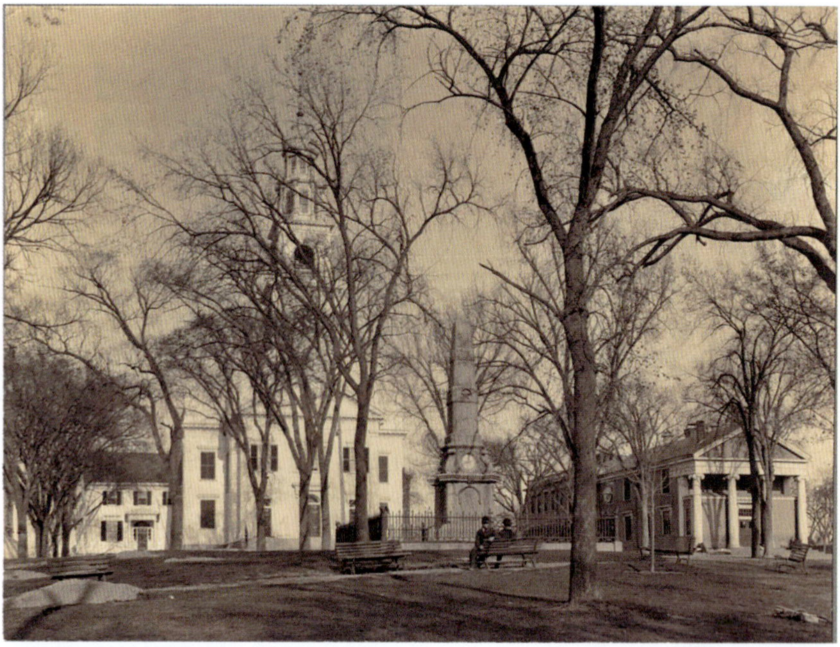

Figure 46. Meeting House Hill, Dorchester.

the wind began blowing in from the sea (a sea-breeze was considered especially harmful to consumptives). But before long, she was bedridden. Lydia remembered her ever after as "sick and sad."[27]

Despite her mother's illness, the girl was happy to have returned to Plymouth. In the summer months, neighbors sat on doorsteps or within their large front windows and greeted one another until nearly midnight. In the winter, there were dances, which were "always [an] utter delight" to her.[28] A fiddler or sometimes a string quartet would occupy a corner, and when the music started, young men sprang into the air, "changing their feet" three times before landing. Lydia soon stepped onto the dance floor and performed intricate steps with names like the "ladies' chain" and the moulinette.[29]

Among her closest childhood friends were Mary Howland Russell, Sarah Kendall, and Elizabeth Davis—the last of whom would attend Margaret Fuller's Conversations and eventually marry the historian, George Bancroft. This quartet of friends "read with zeal every book that came within their reach," exchanging volumes and discussing their favorite authors. Lydia was partial to *Don Quixote*. Once, while reading in bed, Cervantes's comic picaresque made her laugh so hard "she had to roll to work off her infinite amusement. She felt that the bed wasn't wide enough, jumped down, and continued to read lying on the floor."[30]

In the summer of 1818, when Lydia was sixteen, Charles Jackson was struck by a sudden illness while in Boston. He sent for his oldest daughter Lucy to care for him, and from his sickbed explained to her the tangle of securities and mortgages and hidden accounts that made up his business. (He had, among other things, smuggled goods during the War of 1812.) Upon one thing he insisted: no one was to open the top drawer of his bureau except his lawyer.

Lucy paid no attention. She was nineteen, disinclined to business, overwhelmed with the care of a father who even in mortal illness could be intimidating. Charles Jackson soon died on a stuffy day in August. He was followed, two months later, by his wife. Aunts and uncles from both sides of the family gathered at the Winslow House during the grieving Lucy Cotton Jackson's final illness, with Lydia keeping vigil at her mother's bedside. She was present when the dying woman opened her eyes and calmly remarked, "I can't tell you with what power and sweetness passages of scripture keep coming into my mind."[31] Just before dawn, Lydia fell asleep. When she awoke, she was an orphan.

The loss of both parents marked the beginning of a new epoch. The three surviving Jackson children each inherited fourteen thousand dollars—a substantial sum, but considerably less than expected. As Lydia's daughter later explained, "Whether it was at once or by degrees that the suspicions of fraud arose I don't know, neither am I sure that it was ever made quite certain that there had been any. But the day they heard of [Charles Jackson's] death in Boston, his partner's son came over and demanded the key to the upper drawer of the bureau in the parlor where [he] kept his papers. It was given to him and he sat right down to it and was busy there all day long... [A] sudden memory for the first time came to Aunt Lucy of her father's talk to her."[32] For the rest of their lives, the Jackson children were convinced they had been swindled of their fortune.

Soon the orphaned sisters were sent by guardians to another boarding school, this one in Jamaica Plain. The "Seminary for Females" was operated by a formidable matron named Elizabeth Mc'Keige, who had lived in France for five years. She taught in French exclusively, levying a two-cent fine for every English word used in class.[33] (Several years later, Margaret Fuller's parents considered sending her to this academy, believing its teacher "*well bred* in all polite forms of etiquette in social life.")[34†] Lydia returned to Plymouth in 1819, when she was seventeen, to board with an aunt and uncle and to pursue her studies in solitude.

† Life at Mc'Keige's is detailed in one of the school's advertising brochures:

> The hours for rising, from May to December, are at half past five; and from December to May, at half past six. In summer, the bell rings for prayers at half past six, and in winter at half past seven; all the Pupils are expected to attend, with their hair, teeth, and nails, in exact order; having made their beds, and regulated their clothes. The Young Ladies enter class at eight, and pursue their studies until one; during which period, at eleven o'clock, twenty minutes are allowed for recreation. After dinner, the Pupils retire to their chambers to dress for the afternoon. At three, they enter the class again, and prepare their duties for the

Eventually she returned to the Winslow House, now owned by another relative, where for the next decade or so she inhabited a room overlooking the sea. "Mother's Plymouth life was exactly to her taste," wrote her daughter. "She loved perfection and exquisite order and with her small space of one room to care for and her command of her own time she was able to have it."[35] A full century before Virginia Woolf declared that "A woman must have money and a room of her own" to become a writer, Lydia was in possession of both.[36] She had "solitude & liberty to study, and at the same time she lived fully in the town life, and had the happiest intimacies with her own set."[37]

Her circle of friends now included nine young women, all of whom were "very earnest for intellectual culture." They met in each other's houses, sipped tea, and discussed their reading. They even produced a newspaper, entitled *The Wisdom of the Nine.* (Unfortunately, not a single copy has survived.) "No mortal ever loved society better," Lydia's daughter said of her mother, speaking of this time. "She was as quick and keen as she could be and had a skill in repartee."[38] Her closest friend remained Elizabeth Davis, an ebullient young woman who was her equal in conversation and intellect. Lydia's daughter recounts a curious story about Davis, who once said, "'Lydia, I lay awake all last night, thinking we are twin souls.'" Ellen Tucker Emerson wrote, "I knew very well what that meant when Mother told me of it. 'And did you lie awake thinking of her sometimes?' I asked. 'No. I loved her very much, but I don't think I ever lay awake thinking of her.'"[39] Was Lydia's daughter suggesting Davis felt same-sex attraction toward her mother? Or was she merely uncomfortable at such extravagant declarations of affection? She quickly moved on to other topics.

In 1821, Lydia woke up one morning feeling achy and flushed. A fever developed, and then a rash spread across her body. The diagnosis was scarlet fever—the same disease that later destroyed the sight and hearing of Laura Bridgman, whose bust Sophia Peabody would sculpt. Lydia was nineteen: older than usual for the onset of the disease. Without treatment (and there was no treatment), the bacteria could migrate to a patient's lungs and kidneys. It could also cause rheumatic fever. In Lydia's case, it left her a semi-invalid for the rest of her life. According to her daughter, "her head was hot ever after, and she never was so well in other ways."[40]

ensuing day, until five; after that hour, they amuse themselves with reading, music, or walking, until half past eight; when the bell rings for prayers, and they retire, in silence and good order, to rest; no conversation or noise will be allowed afterwards. In half an hour a person will attend, to take the lights. It is also a regulation of the Seminary, that a young lady cannot receive or write letters, without the inspection of Mrs. Mc'Keige, or receive visitors until the afternoon; as such interruptions during the morning, would be detrimental to improvement.

To counter the aftereffects of the disease, she dosed herself with calomel—the same mercury compound that likely triggered Sophia Peabody's headaches—and restricted her diet. (Her friends referred to her as "the living skeleton.")[41] On the other hand, she may have relieved some of the effects of ill-health and mercury poisoning with a lifelong insistence on fresh air, loose clothing, and hydropathy, a regimen that meant, as her daughter said, she invariably "used a cold bath and slept with open windows and never wore corsets but buttoned her skirts onto a waist."[42]

As troublesome as her frail body was her spiritual health. Lydia had been reared in the stern tradition of Calvinism; she long remembered the gruesome illustrations of God's wrath in her hymnal, which had terrified her as a girl "when every lightning seemed the beginning of conflagration, & every noise in the street the crack of doom."[43] Death and damnation, she liked to say, had been bred in her bones, and their horrors returned whenever she felt cast down or vulnerable. As an adolescent, she began to feel the gnawing of spiritual hunger. The need for religion—for a system of belief that would allay the uncertainties of existence—grew powerful. There were periods of doubt, even tearfulness. Increasingly she was consumed by "questions which she remembered collectively always as 'What is truth?'"[44]

When she was twenty-three, she visited an aunt in Woods Hole, where she underwent a profound religious experience. By now, she considered herself a Unitarian, having rejected the doctrine of original sin. But suddenly she was seized by an intuition—an ineffable *feeling*—that Unitarianism, with its insistence on logic and reason, failed to explain. Lydia experienced the overwhelming sensation that her dead mother was "very near." She felt reborn. As her daughter later explained, "It seemed to her that she entered into a new state in those weeks, and that dimly all her future was shown to her and she was mercifully prepared for all that was to come . . . I heard her several times in my life speak of it in the words 'Christ was shown to me.'"[45]

In 1833, a different sort of perturbation shook the Jackson family. The husband of Lydia's sister, Charles Brown, belonged to a trade firm at Boston's Long Wharf and convinced members of the family to let him invest their money. He either lost or squandered it. The guilty man then abandoned his family—there were two small children—promising to return when he could pay back his debt. Lucy and her son and daughter took up residence in the Winslow House, but the circumstances brought "shame and sorrow" to the family, as well as "the sense of its utter irremediableness, the feeling that the children were now not only without a Father and probably without means to be educated but that they could never hold up their heads."[46] From this time on, Lydia became the protector of her older sister.

Throughout her twenties, she attended lectures on chemistry and traveled to Boston to take riding lessons. (Another student was Waldo Emerson's first wife, who was learning to ride in the hope it would help combat her tuberculosis.)

Mostly, she read novels by Maria Edgeworth and Sir Walter Scott, and sermons by Joseph Stevens Buckminster (the older brother of Elizabeth Peabody's ill-fated suitor). She rejoiced when the *North American* magazine attacked James Fenimore Cooper, whose writings she enjoyed but nevertheless thought "deserve more censure than praise."[47] She even tackled the weighty *Institutes of Natural Philosophy*, a scientific work by the English Unitarian William Enfield, telling a friend that "if it is fit to use at Cambridge"—meaning Harvard—"it will answer for me."[48]

In 1833, she began to study German with an exuberant young scholar named George Partridge Bradford—the same man who eventually introduced her to Waldo Emerson. Interest in German thought and culture, fueled in large part by de Staël's *On Germany*, was then approaching its zenith among New England intellectuals. To read German literature was to be on the vanguard of cultural life. Lydia's faith in intuitive experience prepared her for encounters with the poetry of Herder and Schiller as well as with Goethe's formative novel, *Wilheim Meister*, which, according to her daughter, she never tired of reciting: "Mother was carried away with it."[49]

Without quite knowing it, she had become a transcendentalist—not the same kind of transcendentalist as Elizabeth Palmer Peabody, who was drawn to the movement by religious and philosophical convictions she had worked out for herself. Rather, Lydia found herself drawn to the "new thought" the way most people find themselves gradually embracing a set of new beliefs: tentatively, haphazardly, feeling her way toward a cluster of ideas, an emotional atmosphere that seemed to accord with her experience and disposition. Her premonitions and interest in omens had revealed to her the importance of things unseen. The religious culture in which she was brought up prepared her to focus on spiritual matters. And her vast reading indicated a tendency toward reflection and inwardness. By the time she was thirty, she had established a life that perfectly suited her.

4.

She had only to close her eyes to remember when love had altered the trajectory of that life. "The tremendous manner in which she loved Father," wrote her daughter, "was always... astonishing to me."[50] After their betrothal, Waldo sent letters from Concord twice a week, and the arrival of mail now became an occasion of terrific agitation. Twice weekly Lydia retreated to her room and waited for the return of the boy she had sent to the post office. Then, pulse hammering as it had when she had suffered from scarlet fever, she closed the door and carefully opened the letter. It was "utterly impossible for Mother to open it in the presence of another person," her daughter wrote, "it must always be with locked doors, and she must read it many times, get used to it, and recover from the excitement" before she could share it with anyone else. "[T]his lasted some ten years after she was married."[51]

The two of them suddenly realized how little they knew of each other. "My Mother rejoices very much," Waldo wrote Lydia, "& asks me all manner of questions about you, many of which I cannot answer. I dont know whether you sing, or read French, or Latin, or where you have lived, & much more. So you see there is nothing for it but that you should come here & on the Battle-Ground stand the fire of her catechism."[52] Waldo's frolicsome sentences raised a thorny question: Where would they live?

Lydia preferred Plymouth, of course. But in the same letter, Waldo wrote, "Under this morning's severe but beautiful light, I thought dear friend that hardly should I get away from Concord. I must win you to love it." He explained that a poet required daily contact with "sunset, a forest, a snow storm, a certain river-view.... Now Concord is only one of a hundred towns in which I could find these necessary objects but Plymouth I fear is not one. Plymouth is streets; I live in the wild champaign."[53] Lydia resisted these blandishments. She loved Plymouth's bustling, friendly streets. She loved its sense of community and its proximity to the sea. In the early months of their courtship, according to her daughter, she hoped Waldo "would consent to come to Plymouth to live, but he said he thought she must follow him to Concord where there weren't so many eyes. 'In Plymouth you can't even take a walk without it being known to the whole community.'"[54]

Then there was the matter of her name. The familiar story is that Waldo disliked the New England pronunciation of her married name, which inserted an "r" between two vowel sounds. (*Lydiar* Emerson grated on his poetic ear.) Within weeks he had rechristened her as *Lidian*, the name he would use for the rest of his life. But to name something or someone is to claim possession, to assert sovereignty. Consciously or not, Waldo was trying to claim her, to place his imprimatur on her, to change Lydia Jackson of Plymouth to Lidian Emerson of Concord. He was severing her from her previous life, from her family and childhood home. Again she resisted. She signed letters to her Plymouth acquaintances as "Lydia." And she got some measure of revenge by forever calling him "Mr. Emerson"—a name he detested.

All of this prompted serious misgivings on Lydia's part. She later alluded to her doubts about her marriage when she described a friend's engagement as "for the first few months as bitter as mine."[55] But despite the conflict over names and where to live, 1835 was also a year of joyous expectation. Lydia told friends "that to be married was the greatest earthly bliss," and she waited impatiently for her wedding day.[56] To her sister Lucy, always her greatest confidante, she said, "I look at all through which I have been conducted[,] at the mercies which have been granted to me *so unworthy*—in deep gratitude—in calm amazement."[57]

In May, she visited the Boston home of her girlhood friend, Elizabeth Davis Bliss (soon to be Bancroft). Now widowed and the mother of two small boys, Elizabeth had for the past few years been drawn to the new ideas circulating around Elizabeth Palmer Peabody and her network of friends. She had enrolled her sons in Bronson Alcott's Temple School and she attended William Ellery Channing's Federal Street Church. Like Peabody, she had begun to consider Waldo Emerson the movement's de facto leader. When she had first heard of Lydia's engagement to him, she "walked the room unable to . . . do anything but keep saying, 'My Lydia! My dear Lydia!'"[58] To celebrate the upcoming wedding, she hosted a dinner party as well as several informal gatherings, introducing Lydia to her cousins, Ellen and Caroline Sturgis, both of whom would become transcendentalist poets, as well as Elizabeth Peabody, who described the meeting to her sister Mary in a long, gossipy letter to Cuba.

Lydia appeared "*very refined*," wrote Elizabeth Peabody, "but neither beautiful or elegant—and very frail—as if her mind wore out her body." Peabody thought she "was *unaffected* but *peculiar*"—both terms were meant here as compliments—and suffused with a calm self-possession she could only envy. "She sat down by me—and we had a beautiful talk about a variety of most intellectual and spiritual things—And I should think she had a rare characteristic of genius—inexhaustible originality."[59] Before the meeting, Peabody had worried the stranger from Plymouth might prove incompatible for Waldo. "I have no doubts now."[60]

Another person Lydia met was Sarah Clarke, a longtime friend of Sophia Peabody's. Clarke, writing to her brother James Freeman Clarke, considered Lydia "almost equal to Mr. Emerson, though very different; quite equal, if I knew how to rank them; as remarkable among women as he is among men. She is a singular looking person, and to my thinking, very handsome. Her eyes are somewhat like lamps, and the expression of her face is that of a beaming soul, shining through. Then, while she talks, she thinks and you see it. Her movements are free and graceful; she is a soaring transcendentalist; she is full of sensibility, yet as independent in her mind as—who shall I say? Margaret Fuller."[61]

It was Clarke who recorded an exchange between the new woman and Elizabeth Peabody that reveals the acerbic, unflappable quality of Lydia's conversation. Talk had "wended, with alternate merriment and seriousness" until it reached the solemn topic of Unitarianism. "I respect Unitarianism," Lydia declared, "for without it we should never have had Transcendentalism. That was a foothold."

"It was terra firma," said Peabody, ever loyal to her mentor William Ellery Channing.

"And nothing else," Lydia replied, "cold and hard, with scarceful a firmament above it."[62]

The trip to Boston was a resounding success. Lydia had held her own against a crowd of curious, skeptical transcendentalist women and men who privately suspected Waldo Emerson would never find a suitable match. She had shown her mettle, her knife's-edge intelligence, and had charmed the fold of earnest and rarefied thinkers who made up the incipient movement. Less successful was her next visit—to Concord. "How soon will you decide to come?" Waldo impatiently asked.[63] The trip was scheduled for spring. Before it could occur, however, Lydia received an unexpected visitor. Mary Moody Emerson, small and imperious, adorned in her rumpled mob cap, appeared one day at the Winslow House and announced, "You know, dear... we think you are among us, but not of us."[64]

Mary proceeded to make herself disagreeable. She told Lydia's sister Lucy, who oversaw dinner, that she considered eating fish a tremendous luxury. Lucy had planned a traditional New England dinner of roast beef, but she now hurriedly changed the menu, only to learn at the supper table that Mary never ate fish. The old woman announced, disingenuously, that she had assumed people who lived on the coast ate fish exclusively and was only trying to set her host's mind at ease.

Then there was the incident with the local minister. The Reverend Kendall paid a visit to Winslow House when he learned it housed the sister of the late and esteemed William Emerson. Kendall, Lydia, and Mary sat in the parlor for a little while, politely talking. Then the older woman stood and left the room without a word. From a door behind the minister, she beckoned to Lydia. "Come, my dear," she said when Lydia excused herself, "leave him, and come take a walk with me!"[65] Baffled—enraged—by this inexplicable conduct, Lydia returned to the minister and resumed their conversation.

After Waldo came to Plymouth to pick up his aunt, another incident threatened the entire engagement. As Mary later admitted to Lydia, "I spent the whole time we were riding to Concord in trying to make Waldo give you up, and ran you down in every way I could. I cannot bear to lose my nephews and I did the same when Charles was engaged to Elizabeth [Hoar]."[66] Swayed by his aunt, Waldo directed a stern letter to Lydia. He accused her of the "sentiment... of valuing herself too highly and imagining that she was able to judge others."[67] This prompted a heated response. Lydia defended herself against Mary's baseless charges and Waldo, at last realizing his mistake, apologized. "I could cut myself up into bits for plaguing you so!" As Lydia explained the episode to her sister, "it was only from Aunt M's talk he perceived I had said what he complained of." The elderly woman now, however, "far from speaking to my disadvantage—... calls me—'*her other half* there in Plymouth!'"[68]

She encountered somewhat less interference in Concord. The extended Emerson family was living in the old parsonage built by Waldo's grandfather and now inhabited by his step-grandfather, Ezra Ripley. Lydia met Elizabeth Hoar, the fiancé of Waldo's talented younger brother Charles. "Aunt Lizzie," as the young woman came to be known in the family, was the daughter of a local judge. Ten years younger than Lydia, she was celebrated in Concord for her seriousness, her beauty, and her talent in classical languages. She loved the rustic village, claiming the "yellow grass and mortar" of Boston was "enough to drive away any poetic ideas, that may have inhabited my brain when I breathed Concord air."[69] Lydia immediately believed she and Hoar were "born sisters," the younger woman speaking so often "as from my own heart."[70] She was equally drawn to Ruth Haskins Emerson, Waldo's mother, who was "beyond praise," and whose presence seemed to moderate Mary Emerson, for "in Aunt Mary," Lydia now observed, "I have found a congenial soul—one who understands and says she likes with all her heart everything I tell her."[71]

Still, the visit to Concord was inauspicious. Charles Emerson, writing to his oldest brother William about the newcomer, said, "The lady is a sort of Sybil for wisdom—. She is not beautiful anywise that I know, so you look at the outside alone. Mother is pleased, & everybody."[72] This equivocal judgment was apparently shared in the family, for Lydia's oldest daughter, who grew up hearing stories about the courtship, claimed her father "was disappointed in the effect she had on his family." Waldo admired "her air of lofty abstraction, like Dante," but he believed she had been too aloof while visiting the Emersons. "Naturally they didn't want him to marry, and their will was not toward her."[73]

Lydia must have sensed this. After the trip to Concord, "the unutterable joy of her engagement had somehow undergone a change." She now balked at the prospect of marriage, but Waldo remained "absolutely firm." Tucked into this account by their daughter is a private drama—a crisis, even. Lydia, no longer certain about the marriage, seems to have considered ending the engagement. Waldo somehow managed to convince her otherwise. "It was decided that they should live in Concord," Ellen Emerson continues. "Mother told him Aunt Lucy and the children were dependent on her. He said they should still have the use of all her income and Aunt Lucy should come to Concord and live with them."[74]

Still doubtful, Lydia consulted her Bible. She opened a page at random and landed on the following passage: "Sit still, my daughter, till thou see how the matter will fall."[75] Gradually, things improved. The letters between them that spring and summer are filled with references to Goethe, poetry, and the German concept of a "world soul." Lydia asked for details about the Emerson family, pressing Waldo to explain the peculiar reverence afforded Aunt Mary. "[T]hough we flout her, & contradict her, & compassionate her whims," he answered, "we all stand in awe of her penetration, her indignant eloquent conscience, her poetic & commanding Reason."[76] By June, he was quoting Lydia in his journal: "Society suffocates, as Lidian said, and irritates."[77]

That summer, Lydia wrote Elizabeth Peabody to describe her developing thoughts about marriage. "[T]he conjugal union," she said, "is strengthened and perfected and made productive of mutual goal by the very dissimilarity of the natures thus joined by the order of Providence." A perfect marriage, she believed, entailed radically divergent natures. Each person compensated for and corrected the faults of the other. This was a "clear and beautiful" truth that reflected a "Divine Order." It ensured "mutual improvement . . . only when the differing spirits thus joined co-operate with Providence—conform to Divine Order . . . harmony and mutual improvement is the result."[78]

Her ideas were informed by a recent enthusiasm: Emmanuel Swedenborg (figure 47). Waldo had been introduced to the Swedish mystic by Aunt Mary

Figure 47. Emmanuel Swedenborg.

many years earlier. Mary had learned of his writings through de Staël. But Lydia had discovered him recently, and her fascination with his writings seems to have renewed the family's interest during her engagement. "Do you know," Lydia's brother wrote her, "that the disciples of Swedenborg consider you & Mr Emerson among their number?"[79]

Swedenborg, an eighteenth-century engineer-turned-mystic and the author of numerous obscure tracts, was then enjoying something of a vogue among New England's avant-garde. His thought is Neoplatonic, which is to say that he believed the human body was merely an envelope for the eternal soul. Like Lydia, he had been prone to visions. In one, Jesus came to him while he sat in a tavern and described the future redemption of human society. In another, he was led by angels up a staircase to heaven, where he was shown a village filled with frolicking couples blissfully married for eternity.

To be associated with Swedenborgian ideas in America in 1835 was to be on the outer fringes of religious thought. (Eliza and Nathaniel Peabody, as well as their oldest daughter Elizabeth, had read and discussed Swedenborg—none of them subscribed to his views.) Elizabeth soon wrote Lydia to ask if the rumors of her Swedenborgianism were true. She replied:

> in all kindred speculations, I catch one ray of light, . . . but in the writings of Swedenborg and his followers—and yet more, in the sayings of Christ and his apostles I seem to have traced the light to its source, the rill to its fountain.—Not that I am a Swedenborgian—or expect to become one—yet repeated experience of this kind, affords, to me at least, a strong presumption in favour of what the N[ew] J[erusalem] Church Christians assert of their faith.[80]

Two of Swedenborg's ideas especially appealed to Lydia. The first was his conviction that modern society was hindered by its obsession with the *self*. Swedenborg called this obsession the *proprium*, and he considered it "nothing but falsity and evil."[81] The other idea concerned marriage. In 1768, Swedenborg had written *Wisdom's Delight in Marriage ("Conjugial") Love*, published in Latin and written, like the Bible, in chapters and verses. The book was his most extensive treatment of marriage and love. (A typical aphorism: "there is spiritual heat and there is spiritual cold; and spiritual heat is love, and spiritual cold is deprivation of love.") To Swedenborg, husband and wife were divine symbols.[‡] Man represented truth, woman goodness. Marriage on earth corresponded to a loftier "spiritual marriage." Earthly marriage was merely a preparation for "spiritual nuptials," a heavenly union of truth and goodness lasting for all eternity.[82]

[‡] Swedenborg's belief that physical facts corresponded to spiritual facts would become a key precept in Waldo's transcendentalist philosophy.

In her letter to Elizabeth Peabody, Lydia expanded on her personal "theosophy"—a word she also borrowed from Swedenborg. God had created people with unique strengths and weaknesses. "[E]ach individual should consider himself as part of a great whole." The *great whole* was humankind. People living and working together were of primary importance—not the individual. Within this framework, the family was a microcosm. "Each Family circle is perhaps, or was intended to be, a harmonious whole," Lydia wrote, "each member having his own part to perform in it that the harmony may be perfect. It is a consoling thought, that God has ordained that our very defects & infirmities should be the means not only of improving each other's virtue, but of uniting us more strongly in affection." Lydia's "theosophy," in other words, valued relationships over personal interests, interdependence over autonomy. "Our individual being... is not complete in itself—was not created with chief reference to itself."

This was the opposite view of her husband-to-be. Waldo, then at the height of his philosophy of individualism, thought Americans were living "in the age of the first person singular." The self was *the* all-important unit of value and worth. To Lydia, this difference of opinion only advanced her main point; she and Waldo were to be "united for the purpose of correcting each other's defects and supplying each other's deficiencies."[83]

The wedding was scheduled for September 14, two days after Waldo delivered an oration at Concord's bicentennial celebration. In the meantime, he searched for a place for them to settle, deciding at first on a farmhouse located a mile or so outside of town. The purchase fell through, and after several panicky and despairing letters to Plymouth, he hit upon the idea of buying the Coolidge house, just off the Cambridge turnpike. It was a large rectangular home, near the town center, its broad front yard barren of any plants or trees to give it interest. Waldo soon described his plans to "crowd so many books & papers, &, if possible, wise friends into it that it shall have as much wit as it can carry."[84]

A day or so before the wedding, Lydia met a Jackson cousin who predicted, "How happy you will be! How you will love to hear his step when he comes home! How you will love to see him come in at the door!"[85] A somewhat different notion of marriage was suggested by the wedding gift she received from Elizabeth Bliss. It was a twin inkstand, containing two silver-topped inkpots and a space for two pens (plate 8). Beautifully engraved in silver, the object was symbolic of the union that Bliss and her transcendentalist friends considered ideal between man and woman. The inkstand was meant to suggest a collaborative marriage, a meeting of two minds, a shared life. Bride and groom would be joint authors, allies, collaborators. Together they would write their future.

5.

"A man needs a wife to be silly unto," wrote Waldo in his journal.[86] Sometimes, in the evening, he would stand at the foot of the stairs and bellow out, "The dinner waits, O Queen!" Lydia replied in a grand, operatic tone: "One moment, O King, and I will come."[87] They invented pet names for one another. He called her "Queenie" and "Asia," his "Lidian Queen"; she called him, always with mock formality, "Mr. Emerson." One morning, waking in a particularly good mood, he began to declaim a spontaneous poem:

> How beautiful in the morning is the human race
> Getting up to breakfast—

Lydia, picking up the strain, continued without missing a beat:

> Head foremost tumbling
> Out of bed grumbling
> They wash their face and neck first.[88]

Their style was bantering, playful. To Elizabeth Peabody, Lydia wryly noted that "management of the concerns of this present life [are] not [Waldo's] forte you know."[89] He forever feigned amazement at her tendency to stay in bed until noon. Once, after he had arranged for a driver to pick her up from a train station, she asked how the man would recognize her. "I can tell him to look for a tall, thin lady," Waldo answered, "dressed in black, with a white face and her eyes fixed on the distant future."[90] Mixed with this faraway look was an unexpected "gift to curse & swear." All their married life, Waldo admired the way she could "every now & then in spite of all manners & christianity rip out on Saints, reformers, & Divine Providence with the most edifying zeal."[91]

A few days after the wedding, Lydia wrote her sister from Concord. "All is bright & peaceful here—all are pleasant & kind and I feel at home and as among familiar friends." If anything worried her, it was that she was *too* happy. It made her superstitious. "[D]isappointment in some form probably awaits us—and let it come—if our God will. It is a medicine salutary as bitter."[92]

From the beginning, the Coolidge house bustled. Waldo's mother, Ruth Haskins Emerson, soon became a permanent resident. Plans were made for Charles Emerson and his fiancée, Elizabeth Hoar, to join the household once they married. Aunt Mary also put in frequent appearances, dominating conversation through the lamb and apple dumplings, then departing as quickly as she had arrived, rooming elsewhere in town. There was also the orphaned son of one of Waldo's college friends—a boy named Hillman Sampson—who lived in the house. (Waldo paid the boy's expenses to attend Alcott's Temple School.) Three servants resided with the family, too, bringing the total number of occupants to a minimum of ten at any given time.

Another Emerson also took up residence in the new house: the deceased Ellen Tucker Emerson. Waldo's first wife was present in the empty mint-green rocking chair that sat in the dining room. Her large eyes peered from the portrait hanging in the parlor. Sometime during their first year of marriage, Lydia asked Waldo about the ghostly woman, and he recorded the ensuing conversation in his journal. "Last night a remembering & remembering talk with Lidian. I went back to the first smile of Ellen on the door stone at Concord. I went back to all that delicious relation to feel as ever how many shades, how much reproach."[93] Why did Waldo rebuke himself? The answer is unclear. But Lydia had opened a door into his past he did not wish to close. "Your Father gave me all her letters to read," Lydia later told her daughter. "She was a holy creature, truly religious." And one night, Lydia dreamed she was strolling in heaven with Waldo when they encountered the young woman. Without thinking, Lydia quietly withdrew, allowing her husband to spend eternity with his first wife. When she reported the dream to Waldo, he replied, "None but the noble dream such dreams."[94]

Within the crowded Emerson household, a routine soon developed. "We have prayers in the morning a little before 7," Lydia reported to her sister, "breakfast at 7—then I hold a consultation with Nancy [the cook] about dinner and can go to my work reading or writing without further care. We dine exactly at one—Mr E & myself then set about writing letters if there are any to write or finish—." After a nap, she walked with Waldo or Aunt Mary as far as Walden Pond. "We drink tea at six—half an hour before which Mr E. issues forth from his sanctum to sit the blind-man's-holiday with me. In the evening he brings down his work and I take mine and after talking a bit we 'make a mum' and keep it till 9 o'clock when we call the girls and have prayers—Then we talk a while, or I read to my blind man."[95]

Often these peaceful evenings were disrupted by guests. In January, Harriet Martineau visited, accompanied by Elizabeth Peabody, who had appointed herself unofficial emissary for the British writer. Lydia had a lengthy conversation with Martineau. Into the writer's brass ear trumpet she poured forth her thoughts on women and abolition. Then Charles Emerson moved into a small room upstairs, filling the house with his ebullient talk. Like Lydia, he had a special fondness for dancing, and would come downstairs in a camlet cloak to caper around the dining table. After Waldo published *Nature*, a year after their marriage, the house became even more crowded. Bronson Alcott, busy with his Temple School in Boston, increasingly found time to stop by. Elizabeth Peabody and Margaret Fuller became regular summer guests. The constant influx of people created so much stir and commotion that Nancy the cook threatened to paint a sign for the front gate that would read "This House is not a Hotel."[96]

"[D]isappointment in some form probably awaits us," Lydia had written to her sister upon arriving in Concord, and the words proved prophetic. On May 9, 1836, Charles Emerson died from tuberculosis. The Emerson family was devastated. "My husband.... feels and must ever feel that his loss is not to be expressed nor measured," Lydia wrote Elizabeth Peabody. "He cannot *see* that it is not absolute loss—that God can make it in *reality* gain."[97] Charles's death brought Lydia and Elizabeth Hoar closer. The two women now became the first to hear Waldo read drafts of his lectures at night. When Lydia became pregnant, Hoar learned the news first. In June, writing to Aunt Mary, the grieving woman reported that Waldo still mourned Charles. "The year however may bring him a new source of pleasure & hope," she added, referring to Lydia's pregnancy, "which may give an interest to life."[98]

Although she experienced acute morning sickness, Lydia still mustered the strength to spar with Mary. "Father & Grandma trembled when Mother answered back and enjoyed the combat," recalled her daughter; "and were astonished and most thankful to find that it was pure pleasure to Aunt Mary to find a foeman worthy of her steel."[99] The two women possessed wits like "diamond cut[ting] diamond," the older woman growing "more and more violent, and Mother undismayed and laughing at her shafts."[100] Despite their disagreements, they shared sympathy and social commitments. Both women were deeply opposed to slavery. Mary Emerson joined the cause in 1835, when an agent for the county's Anti-Slavery League visited her and met

> an elderly lady—say sixty—unmarried I think. Her name is Mary Emerson and she... has been very much prejudiced... against Abolitionists.... I answered all Miss Emerson's questions as well as I could, & do believe I removed some of her prejudices. She seems to be a good hearted woman, easily excited, inclined too hastily to take up wrong opinions, but willing to abandon them as soon as the error is clearly pointed out to her.[101]

Lydia needed no such convincing. She subscribed to *The Liberator*, the premier antislavery newspaper of the time, and in 1837 attended lectures at the Concord meetinghouse by the Grimké sisters, Angelina and Sarah, who had been raised on a plantation in South Carolina and now traveled throughout the country speaking on the horrors of slavery (figures 48 and 49). The year before, Sarah Grimké had written a pamphlet entitled *Appeal to the Christian Women of the South*, where she explained to her readers that women exerted untapped influence on national events. "I know you do not make the laws, but I also know that you are the wives and mothers, the sisters and daughters of those who do; and if you really suppose you can do nothing to overthrow slavery, you are greatly mistaken."[102]

Lydia invited the Grimké sisters to tea after their lecture. Both proved to be so inspiring, she told Lucy, that "it was a pleasure to entertain such angel

Figure 48. Angelina Emily Grimké.

strangers—pure & benevolent spirits are they. I think I shall not turn away my attention from the abolition cause till I have found whether there is not something for me personally to do and bear to forward it."[103] The next month, she joined sixty other women to create the Concord Female Anti-Slavery Society, an organization that remained active until the end of the Civil War and that included, besides Mary Moody Emerson, the sisters of Henry David Thoreau: Helen and Sophia.

But her enthusiasm for abolition created tension from an unexpected quarter. "Lidian grieves aloud about the wretched negro in the horrors of the middle passage," Waldo wrote shortly after the visit by the Grimké sisters; "and they are bad enough. But to such as she, these crucifixions do not come. They come to the obtuse & barbarous to whom they are not horrid but only a little worse than old sufferings. They exchange a cannibal war for a stinking hold. They have gratifications which would be none to Lidian."[104§]

§ The idea eventually made its way into an essay, "The Tragic," published in 1844, in which Waldo noted: "A tender American girl doubts of Divine Providence whilst she reads the horrors of 'the middle passage,' and they are bad enough...."

Figure 49. Sarah Moore Grimké.

The passage, surely one of the ugliest in all of Waldo's journals, grew from his philosophy of the individual. Waldo refused to acknowledge the misery of the enslaved—as if to do so was to threaten his own sovereignty, to puncture his hard-won equanimity. His most strident public expression of this notion would appear—notoriously—in "Self-Reliance," where he argued, "If an angry bigot assumes this bountiful cause of Abolition, and comes to me with his latest news from Barbadoes, why should I not say to him, 'Go love thy infant; love thy wood-chopper: be good-natured and modest: have that grace; and never varnish your hard, uncharitable ambition with this incredible tenderness for black folk a thousand miles off. Thy love afar is spite at home.'"[105]

This position could scarcely have been more different than Lydia's. She insisted that "Our individual being... is not complete in itself—was not created with chief reference to itself," and encouraged her husband to imaginatively enter into the conditions of the enslaved. A few days later, he revised his initial assessment: "The fury with which the slaveholder & the slavetrader defend every inch of their plunder, of their bloody deck, & howling Auction," he wrote, lamenting "... The loathsome details of the kidnapping; of the middle passage; six hundred living bodies sit for thirty days betwixt death & life in a posture of stone & when brought on deck for air cast themselves into the sea."[106]

More than once Lydia's example worked as a corrective to his more extreme ideas. She suggested how inadequate were calls for self-reliance when enslaved people leaped into the ocean in a desperate bid for freedom. And her presence in his life confuted him in other ways. "In company with a lady," he acknowledged, "it sometimes seems a bitterness and unnecessary wound to insist, as I incline to, on the self-sufficiency of man."[107] On yet another occasion, when Elizabeth Hoar confessed her ongoing despair over Charles's death, Waldo apparently remained mute. In his journal, he justified his coldness: "It seems to me as if what we mainly need, is the power of recurring to the sublime at pleasure. And this we possess." But written in pencil, in Lydia's hand, was an addendum: "I'll tell you what to do. Try to make Humanity lovely unto itself."[108]

In their first years of marriage, her influence was particularly obvious in yet another controversy then roiling the nation. In April 1838, Lydia wrote Lucy about the issue. "Doing good you know is all out of fashion, but there happens just now to occur a case so urgent that one must lay aside for awhile all new-fangled notions."[109] She meant the federal government's enforcement of its sham treaty with a splinter group of Cherokee leaders after years of resistance. Although Waldo privately confessed his unwillingness to speak on the subject (to do so was "like dead cats around one's neck"), he nevertheless agreed to Lydia's request and spoke to a protest meeting in Concord.[110] He followed this up with a letter to President Van Buren condemning "so vast an outrage upon the Cherokee Nation."[111] The letter was published in newspapers across the country, making Waldo one of the first non-Native public intellectuals to speak out on the topic.

Decades later, Lydia was still proud of Waldo for his stance. "Your father is not combative," she told her daughter, "*with exceptions!*—Yet he exercised great moral combativeness in writing to the Pres. of the U.S. in defense of the Cherokee Indians. It was against the grain he did it... But no one else raised a voice—and he did to his everlasting honour & glory."[112] What she failed to mention was that it was *she* who had convinced him to speak out in the first place. Enacting Sarah Grimké's call for wives to influence their husbands, she convinced him to address the protest meeting organized by Concord's Female Antislavery Society. She also urged him to write the letter to Van Buren. In similar fashion, she asked her sister to encourage Plymouth's women to bring up the matter with those "gentlemen most likely to care that something be done."[113] The strategy worked: a petition opposing the Cherokee removal, signed by Plymouth's prominent men, was soon addressed to Congress.

Despite these victories, the marriage had its rough patches. The responsibilities of a large household were particularly overwhelming for Lydia. They recalled a couplet written by her friend, Ellen Sturgis Hooper: "I slept, and dreamed that life was Beauty;/I woke and found that life was Duty."[114] Lydia's daughter remembered the painstaking attention her mother devoted to domestic tasks. "It was her nature to take them with a curiously exaggerated view of their importance and to expend on them an amazing amount of indignation and shame."[115] On one occasion she dreamed she had died and was lying in her coffin in the parlor; suddenly she sat up and scolded the servants, who had neglected to clean the house properly.

These domestic pressures only increased after Waldo vaulted into national prominence. On the last day of August 1837, he delivered his address on "The American Scholar," which was soon published in newspapers across the country. Lydia attended the talk and considered it a "noble doctrine."[116] But she was tasked with hosting a celebratory dinner that evening in Concord. As she facetiously reported to Elizabeth Peabody, she was "to be honoured with the opportunity of ministering to the earthly comfort of the whole transcendental coterie."[117] The invitation list included not only members of the Transcendental Club but also Margaret Fuller, Sarah Ripley, and Elizabeth Hoar—the first time women were allowed to attend the Club's meetings. Yet Lydia missed much of the conversation. When her sister Lucy accused her of being a "Martha"—the traditional name for a dutiful housekeeper derived from the gospel story of Martha and Mary—Lydia responded more conventionally than in her sarcastic letter to Elizabeth Peabody. "Oh no, when I turn my attention from high discourse to Martha-like care of wine & custards—I am happy in knowing how much blessed satisfaction others are receiving."[118]

Despite these protestations, others noticed a transformation in Lydia—from formidable intellect to domestic drudge. Marriage entailed a cost to her autonomy, her happiness. It smothered her personality—something Margaret Fuller seems to have noticed in a cruel statement she made to a friend. Lydia was in "every-way calculated to make Mr. Emerson happy," Fuller admitted, but she could not understand why "men who marry a second time usually select a wife of character and manners utterly unlike their first." Fuller compared Waldo's second marriage to that of "a gentleman in N York [who] married . . . a gentle, fanciful, golden-haired blue-eyed maid. . . . She died at the age of 19 . . . and here he is engaged to a woman . . . as ugly, as ungraceful, and as simply devoted to duty as possible."[119] The implication was clear: Lydia was neither a poet nor a beauty nor an intellectual companion. She was dutiful—and little more.

But did Lydia feel this way? Did she consider herself diminished by marriage? Much of the life she shared with Waldo, like all married life, was concealed and confidential. It included pet names, private references, a personal brand of wit, erotic passion. "O could I live upon memory alone might I select the *blessed* hours and moments of the Past," she wrote him in one fervent letter, alluding in part to unspoken private moments.[120] Even her sister expressed embarrassment at the sexual current that passed between them whenever they looked at each other.

Lydia was proud of her husband's success, a fact made clear in numerous letters, and she was equally proud of her ability to influence him. If she struggled to balance household chores with the cultured life that she had known before marriage, it is not quite accurate to view her as a passive domestic prisoner, overshadowed by a charismatic husband, as Fuller and others sometimes suggested. Writing to her sister, she confessed "how very happy I am—blest above all mortals—I should tremble at such perfect happiness… that it should continue as long as we do not forfeit it by great unfaithfulness."[121] The cost of marriage, heavy though it was, did not entirely preclude happiness.

Waldo was the beneficiary of an arrangement whereby his wife sacrificed a portion of her freedom to oversee his comfort and well-being. One night, roughly a year and a half into their marriage, he stepped outside and stood in the snowy front yard, gazing at the field of stars. Then he returned to his study. "My gentle wife has an angel's heart," he wrote, "& for my boy, his grief is more beautiful than other people's joy."[122] He was speaking of the single greatest fact of his shared life with Lydia, an event that bound them more closely than words or friends or ideas or passion. It was the birth of a son.

6.

Everyone who saw the infant Waldo Emerson described him as angelic. His hair was straw-colored, his eyes the same serene blue as his father's. The ancient Reverend Ezra Ripley, tottering down Monument Road in his silk knee breeches and old-fashioned buckle shoes, came to visit soon after the birth and placed the infant face down in his lap. Then he lifted the child's undershirt. Alarmed, Waldo and Lydia asked if anything was wrong. Ripley pulled down the shirt and announced he had been told "the child of this couple would probably have wings." He wanted to see for himself[123] (figure 50).

The pregnancy had been arduous. Lydia, worn and dyspeptic much of the time, spent weeks in bed. Waldo grew so alarmed by her condition he called Concord's leading physician, saying, "It does not seem just that the Mother should have so much pain and suffering and the Father none." The physician replied with stunning obtuseness. "She is repaid," he said. "She has the pleasures of lactation."[124]

But Lydia's suffering was not only physical. Bitter memories attended the pregnancy. "When a baby was born or a person died in Plymouth," her oldest daughter explained, "it was the custom for the children all to go in to see the baby or the corpse; the first was amusing[,] the latter was considered impressive. It would keep the children in mind that they must prepare for death."[125] Birth and death were therefore permanently associated in Lydia's mind, a connection

Figure 50. Waldo Emerson, age. 5.

reinforced by the premature death of five siblings. (Her favorite brother, John, died when she was just seven.) In her twenties, Lydia had attended the lying-in of an aunt, who was ill with tuberculosis. Asked to hold the newborn child while the mother was cared for, Lydia took the swaddled child and sat by the fire. The infant died in her lap. The next morning the mother died, too.**

One of the more painful episodes of the Emersons' early married life occurred during this time. Lydia prepared for the child's arrival by draping the couple's bed in white dimity curtains. Waldo asked her to take them down. Such displays were too showy, he argued. Lydia submitted to his wishes, only to be scolded by Elizabeth Hoar, who told her she should not regard Waldo "as an oracle for my department."[126] Hoar had her own reasons for being upset. Waldo had decided to name the child after himself rather than Charles. When Elizabeth Peabody arrived a few weeks after the birth, she found the household still tense. "Lidian sympathizes with Elizabeth," wrote Peabody, "& regrets she did not know how Elizabeth felt early enough to have prevented her husband's decision."[127]

The arrival of the child altered the dynamics of the household. Waldo had completed his first book, *Nature*, during Lydia's pregnancy, and the work is full of references to the impending new life: "The lover of nature," he wrote, "is he . . . who has retained the spirit of infancy even into manhood." The stars

** In *Little Women*, the same thing happens to Beth March, who contracts scarlet fever from an infant who dies in her lap. It seems quite possible that Louisa May Alcott, who grew up as a neighbor of the Emersons, heard and repurposed Lydia's story.

awakened in an adult "the simplicity of his childhood," the sun shone "into the eye and the heart of the child."[128] Lydia, too, subscribed to this Romantic, Wordsworthian conception of childhood, believing her baby closer to God because unspoiled as yet by society. "Every day a child presents a new aspect," she told her husband, "... as the face of the sky is different every hour, so that we never get tired."[129] She begrudged leaving the infant for even a second, painfully aware that he grew "so fast that each look is new & each is never to be repeated."[130]

Her correspondence brims with descriptions of the child. To a relative she wrote, "In the morning, while I am in the room next to Waldo's nursery, dressing myself—I hear a sweet little voice talking—and I think somebody is there with Baby—he seems so sociable. But when I open the door and peep in there sits little Waldo all alone in his crib—telling stories to himself." She tried to reproduce his childish babble in letters (he called himself "Misser Baldo") and described his fascination with a nest of swallows just outside the nursery window. To her niece she depicted him crawling "like a young turtle—with his little headie sticking straight up in the air. But he often goes with a velocity more like that of a spider..."[131] The child had taken to borrowing his father's walking stick, she told her nephew, to "ride on a horse."[132]

An entry in Waldo's journal reveals just how smitten Lydia was with her first child. Entering his study one afternoon, she

> found the towerlet that Wallie had built half an hour before, of two spools, a card, an awl-case, & a flourbox top—each perpendicularly balanced on the other, & could scarce believe that her boy had built the pyramid, & then fell into such a fit of affection that she lay down by the structure & kissed it down, & declared she could possibly stay no longer with papa, but must go off to the nursery to see with eyes the lovely creature, & so departed.[133]

She adored the child: his cooing smiles, his first steps—even the way he suffered "just like a little angel" when he was sick. "If he should flap his little wings & fly straight up to heaven, he would not find there anything purer than himself."[134] To Elizabeth Peabody she boasted, "Having no other baby to compare him with we [cannot] of course say what he is comparatively—but we think that he is *positively* all that we can wish."[135]

Sometimes she sought to minimize her attachment to the child. As if to safeguard herself against possible tragedy, she told Lucy, "Every one that visits us falls in love with him, but I do not myself think him so very uncommon. He is a fine child but there are hundreds of fine children in the world."[136] She braced herself against the fear he would die. Speaking of her sister's children, she told Lucy, in an oddly detached tone, "I do not know that I love Waldo any better than I did Frank or Sophia. I loved them with *all* my heart. [But] I think I should feel more if Waldo were to die than if one of yours had died."[137]

7.

The child had been born into a clamorous, eventful household. "All sorts of visitors with new ideas began to come to the house," Lydia's daughter wrote, "the men who thought money was the root of all evil, the vegetarians, the sons of nature who did not believe in razors nor in tailors, the philosophers and all sorts of come-outers."[138] Lydia later remembered of this time, "Poor Grandma [Ruth Haskins Emerson] and I were never half through eating our meat before the whole company of Grahamites, having bolted their potatoes and squash and beans, were sitting looking hungrily at the pudding, which to them was the main dinner."[139] Elizabeth Hoar referred to the company as "Waldo's Menagerie." "Oh!" she exclaimed, "when I looked in the parlour one day and saw him sitting in that circle,—it gave me a feeling of horror—men with long beards, men with bare feet."[140]

Other guests were more welcome. Elizabeth Peabody was a regular visitor. So were Bronson Alcott and Margaret Fuller. Another frequent caller joined the Emerson household in the winter of 1837. Lydia learned of a young man who had walked to Boston—some twenty miles—to hear her husband speak. She invited him for dinner. Henry David Thoreau had already come to the family's attention earlier that year, when Lydia's sister was boarding with the Thoreau family. One April morning she found a bouquet of violets tossed through her bedroom window, the fragrant flowers tied with string and wrapped in paper upon which was written one of Thoreau's earliest poems, entitled "Sic Vita" (or "Such is Life"). It begins:

> I am a parcel of vain strivings tied
> By a chance bond together,
> Dangling this way and that, their links
> Were made so loose and wide,
> Methinks,
> For milder weather.[141]

Lucy promptly took the poem to her brother-in-law, who admired its wit and audacity. Before long Lydia reported that Waldo viewed the young man "with great interest & thinks him uncommon in mind & character."[142][††]

[††] According to a governess in the Emerson household, Thoreau in later years "loved... Mrs. Brown and was as a son to her. She depended on him [and] would say, 'Run over to Mr. Emerson's and see if H is there. Get him to come over and see if anything can be done about my stove's smoking.' He would look at the damper or latch and mend and fit. While at work at these jobs, he would prolong the conversation. It seemed a favour to him to ask him to do something." Sometimes he amused her by solo dancing (Walter Harding, *The Days of Henry David Thoreau: A Biography* [Princeton: Princeton University Press, 1994], p. 105).

Another houseguest was the poet Jones Very. In April 1838, Elizabeth Peabody sent the Harvard tutor to Concord. Lydia believed he was "high-souled pure-loving and lovely." To Lucy, she described him as "a specter spirit if possible than G. P. B. [George Bradford] whom he most reminds me of. Mr. E. loves him as well as I do. We had no acquaintance with him till yesterday... But I feel richer that I have seen him, and hope now never to lose sight of him through all my being."[143] Very returned to Concord later that year, after he had been fired from Harvard and briefly committed to McLean's Asylum for the Insane. His messianic delusions, still evident, perturbed Lydia not in the least. She marveled at the young man, "restored to a state of childlike simplicity. How he sat there with a piece of gingerbread in each hand so innocent and unconscious."[144] A few months later, during another visit from the poet, she told Peabody she had caught glimpses of heaven "in listening (as I could steal leisure) to *Very's* holy words."[145]

It was Peabody who had first urged the Emersons to invite Margaret Fuller to Concord. A diminutive woman with reddish-brown hair, Fuller immediately admired Waldo, she slowly warmed up to Lydia, and she adored their child, telling a friend that the boy "was beautiful to me, a perfect May morning, after regular, grown up winter people."[146] In subsequent years, after she had become a frequent guest, she enlisted little Waldo to carry notes across the hall to his father, calling the boy her "Living Word."[147]

Another child entered the Emerson household in 1839. This was Ellen Tucker Emerson, born on February 4 (figure 51). Lydia and Waldo, "both rejoicing at the fulfillment of our strongest earthly wish," were parents once more.[148] Again the mother suffered during pregnancy—so much so that she asked Ruth Haskins Emerson to take over housekeeping chores. But in other ways the second birth was different. Lydia ignored her husband's objections and draped the couple's bed with her elegant dimity bed curtains. And this time it was *she* who named the child, even though her choice was calculated to please her husband.[149] "Lidian," he wrote in his journal, "who magnanimously makes my gods her gods, calls the babe Ellen. I can hardly ask for more for thee, my babe, than that name implies. Be that vision, and remain with us, and after us."[150]

Not everyone took such a charitable view. One neighbor, Jane Prichard, wrote that "Mrs Emerson has a Daughter, which she has named Ellen for his first wife, quite a piece of heroism as I view it...."[151] Prichard considered Lydia's action ostentatious: a histrionic performance of self-sacrifice and humility. But Lydia's decision can be seen in another light, as well. By naming the child after Waldo's first wife, she was paying homage to the precursor she had supplanted and replacing his Ellen with her own.

Soon after their second child's birth, Waldo started an essay on "Love." The work, which appeared in his *Essays: First Series*, was a summation of his feelings for his second wife. He extolled the "private and tender relation of one to one,

Figure 51. Ellen Emerson.

which is the enchantment of human life," and he claimed that romantic love, "like a certain divine rage and enthusiasm, [which] seizes on man[,] . . . unites him to his race, pledges him to the domestic and civic relations, carries him with new sympathy into nature, . . . establishes marriage, and gives permanence to human society."[152] Love formed attachments, he wrote; it revealed the importance of "social instincts," it delighted in "perfect equality."[153]

The essay was his version of Lydia's "theosophy of marriage." It expressed her belief that a necessary and reinforcing bond existed between people, especially lovers. Elsewhere in "Love" he made his debt to her even more explicit: "In the particular society of his mate [a lover] attains a clearer sight of any spot, any taint, which her beauty has contracted from this world, and is able to point it out, and . . . with mutual joy they are now able, without offence, to indicate blemishes and hindrances in each other, and give to each all help and comfort in curing the same."[154]

This lesser-known essay comes soon after the more famous "Self-Reliance," both of which appeared in Waldo's first collection. It can therefore be understood as part of an ongoing dialogue between individualism and interdependence, solitude and community—a conversation that now characterized the dialogic nature of his writing and his married life. As he put it in a letter to Thomas Carlyle, "My wife Lidian...keeps my philosophy from Antinomianism."[155] Without her, he was lawless, lost.

8.

"For five years Mother said she and Father were getting more & more married all the time," wrote Ellen Emerson. "[T]hey were as happy as it was possible to be."[156] Then something happened. Cracks began to emerge in the marriage. Mary Moody Emerson sensed as much from a distance, intuiting that the marriage had entered a period of strain. "[Waldo] is not happy as formerly I suspect," she wrote Elizabeth Hoar in 1841.[157]

The institution of marriage had suddenly become a topic of heated debate among the nation's reformers. Numerous utopian communities were springing up around the country in the hopes of improving relations between men and women. The Shakers practiced celibacy to this end. The community in Oneida, New York practiced free love, a term they invented. Lydia and Waldo were both interested in the new theories of the French socialist and marriage reformer Charles Fourier. The first English-language book to introduce these ideas was called *Social Destiny of Man*, and it was written by Albert Brisbane, son of a wealthy New York landowner who had spent much of his twenties roaming throughout Europe. He saved his controversial attack on marriage for the end.

Brisbane had been converted to Fourierism after reading the philosopher's magnum opus, *Treatise on Domestic and Agricultural Association* (1821). Fourier argued that cooperation—not competition—was the key not only to greater productivity but also to personal happiness, and he proposed creating *phalanxes*, or small communities, in which every member performed the task to which they were best suited. (Among his other proposals was a minimum wage for people unable to work and an increased wage structure for the least desirable jobs.) Fourier's plans for a socialist utopia attracted the interest of many Americans in the wake of the disastrous financial crisis in 1837. The newspaper editor Horace Greeley became a convert. Elizabeth Peabody even wrote an article inspired by Brisbane's book, entitled "A Glimpse of Christ's Idea for Society," published in 1841 in the *Dial*. During the 1840s, at least three hundred intentional communities, many borrowing Fourier's principles, were founded.

But Fourier's concerns extended well beyond the problems of industrialization and work. He was also interested in the relations between the sexes. "The extension of the privileges of women is the basic principle of all social progress," he wrote in 1808.[158] (Fourier originated the word *feminism*.) For many women, childrearing and domestic chores resembled a form of enslavement rather than a path to liberation. To remedy this, Fourier conceived of a "New Amorous World" that would replace marriage. In his system, men and women would be given latitude to satisfy their sexual proclivities. For some this might mean "vestalic" virginity, while for others it could take the form of opposite- or same-sex promiscuity.[‡‡]

It was Fourier's discussion of sex and marriage, predictably, that caused the greatest sensation. Brisbane suppressed many of these ideas in his *Social Destiny of Man*. What he retained went into a final chapter with the provocative title, "Passional Attraction." (According to Brisbane, an adjectival form of the word *passion* was needed to match *emotional* and *physical*.) The world was filled with an astonishing range of sexual attraction, Brisbane wrote. God must have created so many permutations with a final plan in mind. It was therefore the "duty of man... to search for the Divine code in the study of Attraction."[159]

All this had some salience in the Emerson household at the start of the 1840s. It was around this time that Margaret Fuller introduced two of her young protégés to Waldo and Lydia. The first was Anna Hazard Barker, the daughter of a ship-owning merchant considered one of the most beautiful women in New England (figure 52). While traveling in Europe, Barker had had her features sculpted by the American artist Hiram Powers, who believed they represented the spiritual essence of womanhood. (Powers was a Swedenborgian.) Barker was accompanied to Concord by a young poet named Caroline Sturgis, who had been briefly involved with Ellery Channing, the erratic nephew of the Reverend William Ellery Channing (figure 53). Years later, a young Henry James, struck by her presence at a dinner party, described her as a lovely member "of that young band of the ardent and uplifted."[160] Twenty-two, bold and free-spirited, she was a full-fledged follower of Waldo's philosophy, as the opening lines of her best-known poem make clear:

> Greatly to Be
>   Is enough for me
>   Is enough for thee.

Barker and Sturgis paid a visit to Concord in the summer of 1840, and Waldo found himself immediately infatuated with both. "Anna's miracle," he noted, "next to the *amount* of her life, seems to be the intimacy of her approach to us."[161] Even stronger were his feelings for Sturgis, whom he called his Muse and with whom he embarked on a quasi-erotic epistolary exchange that would last for years. In 1841,

‡‡ In his *New World of Love*, which remained unpublished until 1967, Fourier outlined ritualized orgies and ceremonies in which "high priestesses" were selected to match men and women according to their sexual "affinities." He even imagined a system by which the most attractive men and women periodically serviced the least attractive.

Figure 52. Anna Hazard Barker Ward.

Figure 53. Caroline Sturgis Tappan.

while Lydia was in Staten Island visiting in-laws, Sturgis visited Concord again. This time she and Waldo took long walks through the nearby woods and spent evenings together stargazing. Later that year, when Waldo complained of receiving no letters from her, she replied with unabashed affection: "Dear Waldo, It is not because I have not loved you every day that I have not written to you for so long a time.... I like to think the same beautiful days shine over you, that you walk in the woods with glittering trees all around you, & that your heart is filled with beauty."[162]

What Lydia thought of all this is not clear. Her comments about Sturgis and Barker are invariably charitable. And she had long ago learned to contend with the crush of female attention that attended her husband. Yet if she read his journals, as she had done in the early years of their marriage, what she found in them could not have been very pleasing. "The husband loses the wife in the cares of the household," Waldo wrote. "Later he cannot rejoice with her in the babe for by becoming a mother she ceases yet more to be a wife."[163] He was referring to the termination of sexual relations that continued while an infant was nursed—a practice considered healthful to the baby as it prevented lust from entering the mother's milk. His protests were repeated in a poem written sometime in the early 1840s:

> Whither went the lovely hoyden?
> Disappeared in blessed wife;
> Servant to a wooden cradle,
> Living in a baby's life.[164]

In his most pointed expressions of unhappiness, Waldo wrote, "Swedenborg exaggerates the circumstance of marriage.... one to one, married and chained through the eternity of ages is frightful beyond the binding of dead and living together."[165] Bitterest of all was a statement that seemed directly aimed at Lydia: "I marry you for better, not for worse."[166]

Lydia never described her own marital sorrows, but they were noticed by others. According to Ellen Emerson, beginning in 1841 and continuing "for the next thirty years sadness was the ground-colour of her life..."[167] Ellen thought some of her mother's malaise was the result of spiritual disappointment: "In 1841, Mother waked to a sense that she had been losing—had lost—that blessed nearness to God in which she had lived so long, and she never regained it. Her religion was still the foundation of her life, but its fulness was gone."[168] Even this loss was attributed to Waldo—it was around this time that he gave up family prayers and quit going to church. Lydia, who had long believed that the two of them shared similar religious beliefs now realized, according to her daughter, "that he was not a Christian in her sense of the word, and it was a most bitter discovery."[169] Without the "blessed nearness to God," Lydia suddenly felt alone, an isolated self.

Her sadness had other sources, too. "For a great many years she had only had Father's [friends,] whom she had got in the habit of regarding from the housekeeper point of view, as people for whom everything must be done very beautifully, and much trouble taken, so that her work must be set aside, but who would probably not regard her as anything but the housekeeper."[170] Waldo's friends, busy expressing fine sentiments and dreaming up outlandish schemes, were often thoughtless and callous, treating Lydia as though she was hired help. "Every injustice, every slight, every wrong to her that anyone was guilty of lived before her mind and caused her permanently the same resentment that she felt at the first moment."[171]

Edith Emerson, the couple's youngest daughter, later took exception to her sister's account of things. "I think the picture of Mother's sorrow is too dark & decided," she said. "No doubt she felt so in her dark hours & when fatigue—or dyspepsia or some wound to her oversensitive spirit oppressed her. But she was of too hopeful and healthy a mind naturally to be always sad."[172] Perhaps there is truth here. But the fact remains: in 1841, Lydia "seemed so feeble that Aunt Lizzy thought she ought to make a journey."[173] (During this trip, Waldo stayed behind with Sturgis.) When she returned, her mood remained much the same. Frail from scarlet fever, suffering from headaches and what may have been postpartum depression, she began to spend increasing amounts of time in her room, often in bed.

The only written clue she left about her unhappiness is a document composed in pencil on a single sheet of paper. It is a manifesto of sorts, a personal credo, a work of humor, as well as a cry of pain. The piece is often referred to as Lydia's "Transcendental Bible." A better name for it might be her "Marriage of Heaven and Hell."

9.

Lydia's "Transcendental Bible" is the most trenchant critique of transcendentalism written by someone within the movement. The work is a scathing attack on the tendency of its devotees to advance the self—or *selfishness*, as she saw it—above all other considerations. For her, the emphasis on the individual was little more than an excuse for bad behavior, a license to pursue one's impulses without regard for how they affected others. Transcendentalists supposedly looked inward and tried to discern the laws of their being. In so doing, they often seemed to consider the rest of the world beneath their concern. This is what Waldo meant when he wrote, "Queenie says, 'Save me from magnificent souls. I like a small common sized one.'"[174]

Lydia's work is written in the style of Proverbs—simultaneously a parody of transcendentalism's prophetic style and an homage to Swedenborg. It is also a prediction of William Blake's satire, "The Marriage of Heaven and Hell" written in 1790 but unavailable to American readers for years to come. Blake's work was a polemic against Swedenborg. It is obscure and often impenetrable. But the portion most people remember are the "Proverbs of Hell," written in a faux biblical style (Blake was ridiculing Swedenborg, who had used this technique in *Wisdom's*

Delight in Marriage ["Conjugial"] Love). An example: "The lust of the goat is the bounty of God," or, famously, "The road of excess leads to the palace of wisdom."

Lydia had not—could not have—read "The Marriage of Heaven and Hell." But in 1842, the Emerson household was introduced to Blake's verse by Elizabeth Peabody, who sent them an inscribed copy of *The Songs of Innocence and Experience*, with an introduction by J. J. Garth Wilkinson, a well-known Swedenborgian who interpreted Blake's verse through the lens of the master.[§§] According to Wilkinson, Blake subscribed to the Romantic belief that "the visionary form of thought was higher than the rational one."[175] Blake's insistence on personal vision sometimes led him into what Wilkinson termed "Ego-theism," or the worship of the self. (William Ellery Channing and Elizabeth Peabody may have taken their use of this term from Wilkinson.) Yet there were times when Blake's poetry rose above such petty concerns, when he "transcended Self and escaped from the isolation which Self involves; and, as it then ever is, his expanding affections embraced universal Man, and, without violating, beautified and hallowed, even his individual peculiarities."[176]

This is much the same point that Lydia made throughout her "Transcendental Bible." Each proverb is designed to reveal the hypocrisy and mean-spiritedness lying just below the surface of the movement, as in the following cluster:

> Loathe and shun the sick. They are in bad taste, and may untune us for writing the poem floating through our mind.
>
> Scorn the infirm of character and omit no opportunity of insulting and exposing them. They ought not to be infirm and should be punished by contempt and avoidance.
>
> Despise the unintellectual, and make them feel that you do by not noticing their remark and question lest they presume to intrude into your conversation.
>
> It is mean and weak to seek for sympathy; it is mean and weak to give it. Great souls are self-sustained and stand ever erect, saying only to the prostrate sufferer 'Get up, and stop your complaining.' Never wish to be loved. Who are you to expect that? Besides, the great never value being loved.
>
> If any seek to believe that their sorrows are sent or sent in love, do your best to dispel the silly egotistical delusion…
>
> Let us all aspire after this Perfection! So be it.
>
> Abstract of New Bible[177]

Throughout her document, Lydia had identified a key weakness of transcendentalism. Often when readers first encounter its revelatory writing—Waldo's *Nature*,

[§§] Henry James, Sr., perhaps the best-known Swedenborgian in America, named one of his sons Garth Wilkinson James.

for instance—they are struck by a sense of liberation. All traditions are suddenly held up to scrutiny. Social conventions are discarded, religious orthodoxy abandoned. The individual, endowed with godlike judgment, is encouraged to make a clean break with the past, to reimagine a new heaven on earth. But this leaves out a crucial fact: human life is *collective*. People need each other. (Waldo needed Lydia to ensure the household remained quiet when he wrote each morning.) In any society, some of us will require more help than others—some will elicit more compassion, more generosity, more care. And in this view of things, sympathy should not be considered a weakness, but the requirement of a flourishing society.

Lydia had long been convinced that human flourishing depended upon ties to others. The lesson had been instilled by her tightknit group of Plymouth friends. It was further reinforced by her involvement in Concord's abolitionist society, strengthened by the examples of Elizabeth Hoar and Elizabeth Peabody, both of whom had helped her during difficult pregnancies, as well as by Ruth Haskins Emerson, who had taken over the household while she convalesced. Granted, these activities were expected of women, who were relied on to tend children and care for the elderly and the dying. But it was precisely because she had lived through such experiences that Lydia valued the care from others so much.

In the "Transcendental Bible," she reacted against the erstwhile visitors and terminal houseguests, the talkers and faddists and dreamy hangers-on, all of whom sat in her Concord dining room and spoke of freedom and individualism while they waited for her to serve a second helping of pudding. If her belief in social interconnectedness made her politically progressive—well in advance of her husband on such issues as abolition and women's suffrage and animal rights—it also made her somewhat more conventional in her religion. Increasingly she fell back on the Calvinism of her childhood, believing—much like Mary Moody Emerson—that Christ's death and resurrection implied a flawed and broken human nature in need of salvation, atonement, and grace.

Ellen Emerson grew up hearing about Lydia's manifesto, which Waldo referred to as "The Queen's Bible." But it was not until she was much older that she discovered it among the family papers. One evening she brought it into her father's study and read it aloud to both parents. "Father laughed all the way through and said 'Yes, it was a good squib of your Mammy's.' Mother at once fell into the strain of it and made a few remarks on those views and those times."[178]

Ellen's recollection suggests that the "Transcendental Bible" was meant as entertainment, that its intent was primarily satirical. But that glosses over the disappointment that had prompted it in the first place—disappointment Lydia felt about her marriage, her circumstances, even the premises upon which her husband had constructed his intellectual life. The "Bible" is in many ways a direct response to Waldo's essay on "The Transcendentalist," where he declares that "the height, the deity of man is to be self-sustained, to need no gift, no foreign force.

Society is good when it does not violate me..."[179] Lydia's work is an expression of disappointment, outrage, anger.

At the root of her complaint was the recognition that the transcendentalist turn from others—whether by refusing to participate in a political cause or by building a cabin by the shores of Walden Pond—was a man's prerogative. It was also corrosive to society. Ultimately, if the "Transcendental Bible" was a heartfelt testament to Lydia's unhappiness in the 1840s it was further darkened by the sort of trouble she had once anticipated from the earliest days of her marriage. For it was written around the time of the single greatest tragedy to visit the Emerson household.[180]

10.

John Thoreau, Henry's older brother, was stropping his razor one morning in January 1842 when he accidentally cut his hand. The razor carried the tetanus bacillus. It germinated rapidly in the wound, spreading its neurotoxin throughout his body and sickening the young man. His death—on January 11, 1842—was excruciating.

John was considered the more promising of the two Thoreau brothers. He was bright and outgoing, a born leader. It was his idea, for instance, to have a daguerreotype taken of young Waldo Emerson, now approaching age five, when the first traveling photographer to visit Concord appeared one October day. The boy in the sepia photograph is somber, serious, his hair parted down the middle, a ruff tucked beneath his chin. He must have been impatient—it took as long as five minutes to complete a daguerreotype.

After John's death, Henry Thoreau, who had been living with the Emersons in exchange for work around the house, left to be with his family. At first, he showed little signs of grief. As he explained to Lydia, after John said farewell to the family, he turned to Henry and said, "now sit down and talk to me of nature and Poetry. I shall be a good listener for it is difficult for me to interrupt you."[181] Several days after John's funeral service, however, Henry also began to show signs of lockjaw. He grew feverish, convulsive; his jaws clenched. The family gathered around his bed and prayed. Gradually the symptoms abated—they had been a sympathetic reaction to John's suffering.

But Henry's recovery coincided with another calamity. On January 24, little Waldo developed a fever. Three days later, he was delirious, calling for his mother. The illness was scarlet fever—the same disease Lydia had contracted at the age of nineteen. Dr. Bartlett was summoned, and when the anxious mother asked him how long it would be before her son recovered, the doctor replied, "I had hoped to be spared this." Only then did she realize the boy would die.[182]

Six months earlier, she had given birth to a second daughter. (The girl still had no name; eventually she would be called Edith.) On the evening the boy died, the grieving mother held the tiny unnamed infant in her lap while Waldo and his mother sat in the room consoling her. Throughout their conversation, Lydia "kept stretching 'way over to look at something behind [Edith's] little head, and smiling most rightly at it." There was nothing there. But according to Ellen Emerson, her mother hoped that "the angel Waldo [was] smiling to his innocent little sister...."[183] The three adults sat up late into the night. They recalled incidents in little Waldo's brief life, his blue eyes, and now were especially grateful for the daguerreotype that had been taken three months earlier. Once the grieving father and mother-in-law left the room—Ellen, who also had scarlatina, was to sleep with her mother—Lydia collapsed. "[G]rief, desolating grief came over me like a flood," she wrote Lucy, "and I feared that the charm of earthly life was forever destroyed."

> I lived over my life with the child and recalled all his sweet and lovely traits or rather they came to me unsought—and remembered them with sorrow—the memory of his love made grief more bitter—and I wondered I could ever [have] thought there could be any sweetness in the memory of the beautiful being of a lost loved one. His innocence, his wisdom, his generosity, his love for his mother I wished I could forget them all. But now I think of them with deep joy[.] I was not worthy to be his mother—except my love for him made me worthy. My care of Ellen kept me awake nearly all the night—and in it I seemed to have lived through two lives—one with Waldo and another—my future earthly life—without him and in the morning it seemed strange that the event was recent and his little form still in the house.[184]

The women in the Emerson circle reacted to the news with shock and empathy. Mary Moody Emerson wrote her nephew to ask, "How is poor dear Lidian." The death of the boy was the "saddest of many sad news my old ears have received.... I more than grieve—could any ills of mine have saved him—without personal attachment I did value him as an extraordinary being & wanted to hear of his soul warmed & expanded into this very old stale world."[185] Margaret Fuller wrote a friend to say, "I am deeply sad at the loss of little Waldo, from whom I hoped more than from almost any living being. I cannot yet reconcile myself to the thought that the sun shines upon the grave of the beautiful blue-eyed boy, and I shall see him no more... why he, why just he, who 'bore within him the golden future,' must be torn away?"[186] And to Elizabeth Peabody, Fuller added, "I loved him more than any child I ever knew, as he was of nature more fair and noble."[187]

Peabody was anxious not to intrude on the bereft parents. She could not help remembering a visit to Concord three and a half years earlier, when the child had been playing on the floor. Waldo and Elizabeth were discussing the recently deceased Charles Chauncy Emerson, "& taking him in his arms [the father] lifted him, saying every now & then in a playful tone, 'Waldo! Why do people die? Will you die, Waldo—say no Papa, I will not die—nothing is farther from my thoughts than dying."[188] Now she wrote to Elizabeth Hoar, beginning her letter with lines from her favorite poet, Wordsworth:

> A simple child
> That lightly draws its breath
> And feels its life in every limb
> What should it know of death?

She turned her thoughts to the grief-stricken mother: "I have thought of writing to Lidian—But this too has seemed superfluous—I wish I were where I could receive the overflowing of her exceeding faith & sweetness—she enjoys *this life* so much less than others—that I can think *death* is not to her what it is to her *husband* even—Waldo exists for her [now]—does he not—almost as much for enjoyment as when he was in her daily vision."[189]

Elizabeth's description was more hopeful than accurate. Lydia, devastated by her son's death, would grow even sadder when her husband left, barely two weeks after the tragedy, for Providence, Rhode Island, where he was to deliver a series of lectures.*** From a distance, he worried about Lydia. "Have the clouds yet broken, & let in the sunlight?" he wrote. "Alas! Alas! that one of your sorrows, that our one sorrow can never in this world depart from us!" If there was any comfort, he added, it was that "Ellen and Edith shall love you well, and fill all your time, and the remembrances of the Angel shall draw you to sublime thoughts."[190]

But for the next year, Lydia was debilitated by grief. When Margaret Fuller arrived in September on her annual visit, she found "all things looked sad," the house still overshadowed by heartache and sorrow. When Fuller met Nathaniel Hawthorne during one of her walks—he and Sophia had moved into the Old Manse a few months earlier—he expressed surprise at having recently "met Lidian out at noon day; it seemed scarce credible you could meet such a person by the light of day."[191] Sophia also worried about the grieving woman. On the last day of August, she walked to the Emerson house to pay a call. "Poor Mrs. Emerson," she told her mother, was "very ill with ague accompanied with fever. She took tons of calomel and now walks abroad but is exceptionally feeble and paler than snow."[192]

In addition to her fever, Lydia was suffering the effects of dental surgery, which she treated with opium. "She does look very ghostly now," Fuller wrote in her journal,

> as she glides about in her black dress, and long black veil.... The other eveg I was out with her about nine o'clock; it was a night of moon struggling with

*** The family was apparently in some financial difficulties at this time; Lydia wrote to Waldo that Elizabeth Hoar "& Mamma [Ruth Haskins Emerson] are always more anxious about your pecuniary straits than is your wife." *LLJE*, p. 108.

> clouds. She asked me to go to the churchyard, and glided before me through the long wet grass, and knelt and leaned her forehead on the tomb. The moon then burst forth, and cast its light on her as she prayed. It seemed like the ghost of a mother's joys, and I have never felt that she possessed the reality. I feel that her child is far more to her in imagination than he ever was in reality.[193]

These comments are uncharitable. But they do suggest the extent to which Lydia's sorrow was the predominant feature of the Emerson house. Fuller had refrained from visiting the grieving woman's room, "simply because I was engaged all the time and kept expecting to see her down stairs. When I *did* go in, she burst into tears, at sight of me, but laid the blame on her nerves, having taken opium &c." Now embarrassed, the younger woman was uncertain whether to stay or leave. Lydia then said something that "made me suppose she thought W. passed the evenings in talking to me, & a painful feeling flashed across me, such as I have not had, all has seemed so perfectly understood between us."[194] Fuller replied that she spent her evenings with Thoreau and Ellery Channing while Waldo remained in his study to write.

Another evening, during dinner, Lydia said to Fuller, "I have not been out, will you be my guide for a little walk this afternoon." Fuller replied, "I am engaged to walk with Mr E but—(I was going to say, I will walk with you first,) when L. burst into tears. The family were all present, they looked at their plates. Waldo looked on the ground, but soft & serene as ever." Fuller assured Lydia she would walk with her, but the distraught woman burst out: "'No! . . . I do not want you to make any sacrifice, but I do feel perfectly desolate, and forlorn, and I thought if I once got out, the fresh air would do me good, and that with you, I should have courage, but go with Mr. E. I will not go.'"[195]

In the end, the two women took their walk and, according to Fuller, they "talk [ed] so fully that I felt reassured." But Fuller, who seems not to have fully grasped Lydia's despair at losing her child, believed she "will always have these pains, because she has always a lurking hope that Waldo's character will alter, and that he will be capable of an intimate union; now I feel convinced that it will never be more perfect between them two. I do not believe it will be less: for he is sorely troubled by the imperfections in the tie . . . . And where he loved her first, he loves her always."[196]

Much has been made of Fuller's account, which seems to offer proof of a faltering marriage. But this version of events should be read with some skepticism. Fuller invariably wanted Waldo's undivided attention. She longed for a friendship with him he was unable to provide. And Lydia, still grieving, was also experiencing the side effects of mercury and opium. What Fuller interpreted as Lydia's jealousy was just as likely the inconsolable mother wanting her feelings acknowledged: *If you can stay up late and speak with my husband, why not with me?* Certainly, the letters Lydia and Waldo exchanged after their child's death paint a different picture than Fuller's. The correspondence is marked by deep affection as well as by the recurring wound of their shared tragedy.

"My turn of expression is so happy," she wrote him in January 1843 (a year after the boy's death), "that I think you must believe the time of my breaking forth into verse is at hand." She had lost none of her satirical edge, as was evident in her description of a gathering of reformers.

> We had a meeting of the wise men and their admirers on Sunday evening... as you may suppose, all the wild schemes were talked over again, and the poor human race are to be allowed in future, if they would walk in innocence, to walk in no clothing but white linen spun by their own hands. No more hats or shoes—and I fear on reconsideration of the decision we must give up even linen and dress as did the sinless inhabitants of Eden—for how can we spin without a sin-made wheel—how can we raise flax without guilt-stained—iron to dig the ground?[197]

Waldo's letters were tender and solicitous. In February 1842, acutely aware that he had left her at a time of unbearable sorrow, he begged, "Write to me quickly that you are all well." Repeated requests were made for news about Ellen and Edith—"poor little girls whose crown of glory is taken from them"—and when Lydia's letters were not forthcoming (their correspondence often crossed or was delayed during his peregrinations), he wondered, miserably, if her silence was meant "to punish my philosophy?"[198] Far from jealous or despairing, her replies were full of affection, frequently boasting, as parents will, of their children. She could not remember ever having seen "such intelligent looks... from *any* baby [Edith's] age."[199] Ellen, her little helpmeet, was wise beyond her years, solemn and considerate.

Both referred to their shared loss. "It is true that the Boy is gone," Waldo wrote, "the far shining stone that made home glitter to me when I was farthest absent—for you & I are passing, and he was to remain; and with him I feel that my house has lost how much magnetism!"[200] A year after the boy's death, Lydia, who was visiting friends in Boston, wrote, "I was thinking of Waldo my Husband and of Waldo in Heaven. The sacred anniversary of my (virtual) marriage and the sickness and death of my first-born—brought realities near to me and the pangs of bereaved affection were lost in hope and trust."[201] Despair punctuated their lives. One day in 1843, Lydia went into Waldo's study and wrote the following in his journal: "Dear husband. I wish I had never been born. I do not see how God can compensate me for the sorrow of existence."[202] What prompted this lament is unknown, but her continuing struggle with melancholy is clear in another journal entry written soon after, this one in Waldo's hand: "Queenie's epitaph[:] 'Do not wake me.'"[203]

Waldo dealt with the loss as he dealt with nearly everything—by writing. One of his best poems, a long work called "Threnody," emerged from this period:

> The hyacinthine boy, for whom
> Morn well might break and April bloom,
> The gracious boy, who did adorn
> The world whereinto he was born,
> And by his countenance repay
> The favor of the loving Day,—
> Has disappeared from the Day's eye...[204]

The loss of his son also animated Waldo's greatest essay, "Experience," a work that can be read as an update on his shared life with Lydia. "Where do we find ourselves?" the essay begins. The answer is an image drawn from Swedenborg as well as from Lydia's marriage vision. "We wake and find ourselves on a stair; there are stairs below us, which we seem to have ascended; there are stairs above us, many a one, which go upward and out of sight." Once a prophet of the self's endless possibilities, Waldo now chronicled a lethargic, dreamlike state of existence in language similar to that which Hawthorne and Fuller had used to describe Lydia the summer after her son's death: "Ghostlike we glide through nature, and should not know our place again."[205]

Waldo's theme in "Experience" is the difficulty of living completely. As if finally glimpsing his wife's long-running predicament—the problem of how to live a rich and fulfilling life within the confines of marriage—he laments how seldom we manage to pierce the depths of existence, how frequently our life feels just beyond our reach: "In the death of my son, now more than two years ago, I seem to have lost a beautiful estate,—no more. I cannot get it nearer to me,... I grieve that grief can teach me nothing, nor carry me one step into real nature."[206] For Waldo, the numbness that accompanies profound loss can only be relieved by a return to the self: "in the solitude to which every man is always returning, he has a sanity and revelations, which in his passage into new worlds, he will carry with him."[207]

Lydia's response was altogether different. Becoming a mother had provided her with consolation and purpose. Now she opened herself fully to her loss, allowing grief to wash over her, to rain down, its presence thick and immediate. In letters to Waldo, she described the experience as honestly as she could. In February 1843, she told him of Ellen, who was "a year in advance of Waldo in reading." The reference to the departed child suddenly prompted a new agony: "Torn is my heart as I write that cherished name. The wound of separation is as fresh as it was a year ago. At least it seems so to me. I am bruised in heart—and cannot be healed by Time. Only a new spiritual experience can bring balm to that wound... Flowers grow over the grave—yet it is a grave no less. I know there is healing but it has not yet come to me. I trust it will—though probably not in this life."[208] Two years later, Lydia wrote him of a strangely comforting dream: "I went into the tomb and opened Waldo's coffin—which I had a strong yearning to do. There lay the darling innocent on his side—he moved and rubbed his face on the pillow—rubbed his eyes & looked sweetly at me. I took him from his narrow bed and carried him home . . . I tell you this dream because it is on me like a spell and has been all day."[209]

Grief brought them together. It bound them to one another. There were no more slighting references about marriage in Waldo's journal. His letters henceforth address a "dear Wife,"[210] and are filled with praise for her replies, "so generous & so true to what is best in my wife. Such thoughts so deep & pure, enrich the reader & the writer, and the world is better for them."[211] He wrote to assure her "that I am the same aspiring all-loving person whom you have known so long,"[212] and he wanted her to understand how "Very refreshing it is to me to know that I have a good home, & so much truth & honor therein . . ."[213]

For her part, Lydia continued to endure bouts of grief and poor health from which there was seemingly no cure, only the daily heroics of carrying on. She oversaw the education of her children—there were three now, with a boy, Edward Waldo, born in 1844—and directed Henry Thoreau in various tasks about the house. One day she received a letter from Waldo, who was writing from a small lecture hall in New York. "I see not how it will hold people enough to answer any of my profane & worldly purposes which you & I at this moment have so much at heart." As for "sacred purposes," however, it was more than ample: "why we know that a room which will hold two persons holds audience enough: is not that thy doctrine, O unambitious wife?"[214] Quietly, tenderly, he was suggesting how much he owed to her thought and example, to her belief that influencing one person for the better was sufficient. Lydia's response came in the letter that recounted her "thinking of Waldo my Husband and of Waldo in Heaven." She had finally managed to call him by his first name (plate 9).

11.

Toward the end of January 1843, Lydia rose early and traveled to Boston. The ostensible purpose of her trip was to visit her brother and sister-in-law, Charles and Susan Jackson. But she had another motive as well. "I went on *Wednesday* and it was partly because I hoped to be able to get to the conversation of 'the wise men' that I chose that day." This group, apparently a mixture of male and female transcendentalists, had gathered to discuss, among other things, Bronson Alcott's plans to create a "new Eden" at Fruitlands, an agrarian utopia much like Brook Farm. (The short-lived experiment proved a disaster.) Lydia considered some of the conversation ludicrous and self-serving, but she was nourished nonetheless by the gathering of friends.

> When I found myself seated in the midst of the company of disciples I was very happy, and even said to myself This is like Heaven. And why was I so happy? Not at what I heard for it was [what] I had heard much—though that was good. It was because I saw so many angels at once, and remembered there were more, elsewhere. There sat Caroline Sturgis—looking like an incarnation—such was it to me as she sent me bright and loving glances from afar. Then there was Sarah Clarke—the sight of whom as Wordsworth says of the sound of some heavenly person's voice—almost makes me "wish to go aside and weep"—and Margaret Fuller was there too.

She also attended one of Fuller's Conversations, neither jealous nor tearful in her presence, but instead gratified by the younger woman's "reverence" for her husband. Again, there was a feeling of warm sociability. "Every body who loves my husband likes to meet my husband's wife—and it is dear to me to be recognized as belonging, in any sense, to him." She was reminded of a story: A traveler, weary from walking, sat beneath a tree, completely unaware of its association with the Virgin Mary. At length the man "meekly assured the reverent passers-by that he was not wholly worthy of such consideration but actually a man like themselves." Lydia felt just like that man, she told Waldo—although "I believe I never mistook the object of reverence for I was aware of my position."[215] As usual, she was modest about her own abilities to influence "the object of reverence."

In 1844, Mary Moody Emerson wrote from Maine: "I have often thought of your stronge reliance in affliction on a *particular* providence." She was referring to Lydia's belief that suffering was sent by a caring God.[216] Mary, now in her seventies, thought her bereaved niece a "dear favored Child of Providence,"[217] and she "repent[ed] of my faults at Plymouth" a decade earlier, when she had attempted to sabotage her nephew's marriage.[218] Now, in a steady stream of letters, the two women discussed a wide range of ancient and contemporary authors, including Plotinus, de Staël, Jean Paul Richter, and Ralph Cudworth. Lydia was particularly interested in John Ruskin's *Modern Painters*, a five-volume work that defended the moody, dramatic landscapes of J. M. W. Turner. She also pored over Robert Chambers' *Vestiges of the Natural History of Creation*, one of the earliest works to posit a theory of evolution. Her interest in the latest intellectual developments is evident in a letter she wrote her son Edward some years later:

> What I have this eveg. been thinking of is, That it seems to me two of our modern Infidel Philosophies... nullify each other—Certain Rationalists (or whatever they are called), believing that the universe is a machine set a-going ages since, and then left to itself to grind on at its own stupid will... say, that nature is reckless of the Individual but careful to preserve the Type [and] The Darwinians

> whose Philosophy seems to me [to] say on the contrary that there *are* no fixed types—but that one type is perpetually shading—blending, into another, so that all creatures beast bird and fish, came from one germ or monad.[219]

In 1848, Aunt Mary wrote Lydia to express her pleasure that Waldo had moved "beyond the mists & rainbow visions of transcendental philosophy (however it has truths of nature) and once more mingle[s] with the woes & cares of *practical* life"—a development she attributed in large part to Lydia.[220] Two years later, she wrote about a recently married young friend. "If ever a happy girl is to be pitied it is the first year of leaving a good home & mother. After that the yoke becomes easier and bye & bye after a few years dragged out in mutual efforts for the pocket prosperity they become necessary to each other."[221] Fearing she had gone too far in lambasting marriage, Mary quickly fired off another note to Lydia, asking her to excuse the "raving letter" about the "dark side of matrimony."[222]

This prompted a response: "You ask if I think what you said about marriage in general true," Lydia began. "It is I am sure both true and false—that is it is most true of marriage without love—and I suppose the majority of marriages are so. Some have married the wrong person, though they could have loved the right one—and not many, I half believe, are capable of love." But there were exceptions. Marriages existed like those described by Swedenborg, who had written that "True marriage love is known only to the few who are near to God."[223] To Mary she explained, "A true husband is incomparably more than father mother & early home to the true wife's heart. A true marriage is a 'perfect freedom'[,] there is no *yoke* there. But the yoke of an unfit marriage may I should say be more galling and degrading than that of the Negro Slave. Unless her children bind her, a true woman should quietly slip her neck out of the snare."[224]

Lydia had sacrificed portions of herself when she married Waldo. She had surrendered her home, her name, to some extent even her health—all in order to become his wife. And while it was true that she had been painfully disappointed by his "heresies," which clashed with her own religious beliefs, she clearly thought she had found a "true husband... incomparably more than father mother & home." Despite its difficulties—*because* of its difficulties—their marriage now seemed to her "a perfect freedom."

She remained a sharp-eyed critic of herself and of Waldo. Writing in 1866 to Edward, she confessed, "Your father is called a great philosopher and your mother styles herself a Christian—but such instances of content and equanimity one may look for in vain."[225] She also refused to gloss over her own feelings of disappointment, expressing to her husband her painful sense of loss and unworthiness. "God be merciful to me—dwindled to nothing. Nothing in myself, and forsaked of God, because I have forsaken Him. Oh! what shall become of me. I dared to marry you, simply because I believed that my Creator and Redeemer, who had as I believed destined me for union with you, would enable me to be to you—."[226] The rest of this letter is missing.

As she grew older, she spent more and more time in bed, strategically avoiding housework and surrounding herself with stacks of medical texts with which to diagnose herself. She survived, her husband said, "on poppy and oatmeal." Sometimes she wished for greater agency—for the ability to influence national events. Discussing with her oldest daughter the plight of Native Americans in California, who were warring with federal troops after years of abuse, she admitted, "Now I wish I could speak for these Modocs in every paper in the land—I don't do it for a good reason—chief of which is, that I am nobody & editors would not publish any thing I wrote. Another, that I don't know well enough how to write English not to make myself ridiculous—and if I published in my language how would Papa like that? I have done enough in that line already."[227] Yet this observation, so characteristically modest, ignores the subtle and pervasive influence she exercised over her husband.

She was not Aunt Mary: she did not provide Waldo with a vocabulary—a way of *seeing* the world. But she offered him something else: a conscience. Lydia's insistence on the rights of the most oppressed served as constant friction to his individualism. Her phrases and thoughts are sprinkled throughout his writing. "Mr. Emerson wouldn't be the man he is if it wasn't for Mrs. Emerson," a mutual friend said. "People have no idea how much he owes his wife."[228] She proudly told her children how much Waldo relied on her judgment: "Father has come to my room several times today laterly to talk over his Dartmouth Oration—with which I was well pleased."[229]

At the end of his essay on "Experience," Waldo arrived at a reason for hope: "Never mind the ridicule, never mind the defeat: up again, old heart—it seems to say—, there is victory yet for all justice...."[230] This conclusion, more chastened than in previous works, was to some extent the product of his shared grief with Lydia. It was the product of their shared humanity, experienced primarily in the loss of their child. And it was a restatement of her conviction that a "kind and wise guide leads us tenderly—even by the hand—in all our paths—however dark and devious they may at first appear."[231]

In a letter to Edward written in the 1870s, she wrote to complain of her husband's being called to Chicago. Then she interrupted herself: "Up heart—and bear it."[232] Was she quoting Waldo's essay? Or had he borrowed one of *her* characteristic sayings with which to conclude his essay? It is impossible to say. The two of them had grown together, their personalities intertwining, permeating each other.

This was the experience she tried to convey to Aunt Mary. In a "true marriage," she said, each party became the other's home, their history. Attachments did not impinge on the self—rather, they extended it, pushing it into new realms. The sacrifice of the individual was nothing compared to the splicing together of two souls—even if one of the souls was sometimes as remote and insular as Waldo's. The task of each partner was to bring out the best in the other. While it was true that Lydia's "theosophy" was not fulfilled every day, it happened often enough for her to believe her husband was, as she told Aunt Mary, "incomparably more than father mother & early home to the true wife's heart."

It was in the same letter to Mary, written in 1850, that she turned to another topic: "I feel personally bereaved in the loss of Margaret Fuller. She did me the honour and it was truly an honour to care for me somewhat." For months now, Lydia had been looking forward to Fuller's return from Italy. She had not seen the magnetic young woman since she had left New England to become a journalist, first in New York and then in Europe. From there, rumors had grown of a mysterious husband and a young son. "But I am very glad for her. How should I be other than glad now that the first shock and dread has passed? How happy to be taken with Husband and child—to know no pang of separation to be, after a short struggle with the waters, 'alive forever more.'"[233]

5
The Tempests of Margaret Fuller

1.

Always there were nightmares. As a child, she dreamed she was drowning in an ocean of blood, its crimson rising over the buttons of her shoes, up her plain black dress, sloshing thickly, menacing. When she tried to pull herself from the sticky fluid, when she clutched at the gnarled roots and limbs of the trees on shore, they too bled, leaving her hands slick and red. The blood continued to rise, slowly reaching her neck, approaching her mouth, much like the ocean in Emily Dickinson's "I started Early—Took my Dog," where the tide

> Went past my simple Shoe—
> And past my Apron—and my Belt
> And past my Boddice—too—

And there were other dreams: the recurring one of her mother's death (she woke in tears each time), or the singular one of her father's ruination. There was the mystifying dream, set in a large, empty mansion, where she and her friends cavorted like mad witches, causing "the walls to ring again with bursts of wild laughter."[1] There were nightmares that featured pitch-black caves, horrible dreams in which rocks cut her bare feet, when spiders ran across her face. From these she woke up crying, gasping, inexpressibly sad. Less often she dreamed she had entered a "heavenly state," a realm where she was neither alive nor dead but in an "intimate communion" with the divine.[2]

Once she dreamed that she lived in a castle surrounded by snow. Another time she dreamed she was aboard a plunging, pitching ship, imprisoned in the hold, "the waves all dashing round, and knowing that the crew had resolved to throw me in."[3] And a few days after she turned thirty, that age of anxious stock-taking, when the derisive term "spinster" was applied to unmarried women, she dreamed she was dying. She was again on a seashore, this time sitting among the castellated rocks with her friend Waldo Emerson, his cool genial face in the sun, the two of them engaged in conversation. She was serenely aware that she was passing from this worldly life into some "transparent spiritual feeling... as if separated from the body and yet with memory enough of its angelic mood." The ocean's waves crashed around her, an eternal, foaming roar. "We talked on every subject, and instead of that perpetual wall which is always grieving me now, the talk led on and on...."[4]

2.

Talk was her salvation, her métier. It was the medium in which she felt most alive. Everyone who knew Margaret Fuller said the same thing about her talk: it was splendid. One friend described her conversation as "finished and true as the most deliberate rhetoric of the pen." The dazzling flow of her speech was an effortless freshet, always polished yet somehow managing to evince "an air of spontaneity which made it seem the grace of the moment,—the result of some organic provision that made finished sentences as natural to her as blundering and hesitation are to most of us."[5] Waldo Emerson said that "in discourse, she was quick, conscious of power, in perfect tune with her company, and would pause and turn the stream with grace and adroitness."[6] Another friend, the Unitarian minister James Freeman Clarke (the same man who married Sophia and Nathaniel Hawthorne), said that Fuller's conversation was "Full of thoughts and full of words; capable of poetic improvisation... capable of clear, complete, philosophic statement, but for the strong tendency to life which melted down evermore in its lava-current the solid blocks of thought..." Fuller's conversation was unlike anything Clarke had ever heard before; it made "our common life rich, significant and fair ... [giving] to the hour a beauty and brilliancy which shall make it eminent long after, amid drear years of level routine!"[7]

Her fame as a conversationalist grew exponentially in the winter of 1839, when she began hosting weekly gatherings of women in Mary Peabody's rented rooms. These soon moved to Elizabeth Peabody's bookshop in Boston, where twenty-five women paid the princely sum of $25 to attend thirteen sessions. While each was expected to contribute to the discussion, some were at first perfectly willing to sit and listen as Fuller produced her remarkable flow of talk. Julia Ward (later Howe) considered Fuller's very presence at these meetings "Glowing," her speech imbued with "power" and her thought "so brilliant ... so heart-touching."[8]

Another participant believed Fuller possessed "power undisputed in making people talk freely." When she spoke, she inspired her listeners with a respect for their "secret interior capability ... All her friends will unite in the testimony, that ... they have never seen one who, like her, by the conversation of an hour or two, could not merely entertain and inform, but make an epoch in one's life. We all dated back to this or that conversation with Margaret, in which we took a complete survey of great subjects, came to some clear view of a difficult question, saw our way open before us to a higher plane of life, and were led to some definite resolution or purpose which has had a bearing on all our subsequent career."[9]

Fuller was proud of this ability. "Conversation is my natural element," she boasted. "I need to be called out, and never think alone, without imagining some companion."[10] For her, letter-writing "does not refresh like conversation."[11] The presence of another person, the frisson of two minds developing thought together, occasioned her finest ideas. In the solidarity of discussion, her companion seemed to her as if "Born under the same star, and bound with us in a common destiny ... There is no separation; the same thought is given at the same moment to both,—indeed, it is born of the meeting, and would not otherwise have been called into existence at all."[12]

She was also ambivalent about her talent for conversation. To speak so fluently, she worried, "bespeaks a second-rate mind."[13] Conversation was ephemeral, evanescent—nothing at all like the solid masterpieces of literature she had studied since childhood. "I seem to be only a poor improvisatrice," she lamented, referring to the tragic heroine Corinne in De Staël's novel.[14]

In *Woman in the Nineteenth Century*, Fuller set out to translate her conversation into writing. The book, published in 1845, ranks as the first major work of feminism by an America author. It remains a landmark in the history of women's studies. From start to finish, it rustles with the spoken word: with dialogues, speeches by various personae, with the associative back and forth of conversation. *Woman in the Nineteenth Century* is as close as we can get to hearing Margaret Fuller's voice, her inimitable speech.

She began writing it when she was thirty-three, at a time of life when most of her friends were married and had become pillars of respectability. Margaret Fuller was none of these things. Her heart was just as ambitious as her intellect, eager for conquests and partners. But she had been supremely unfortunate in love and had come to agree with her literary idol Goethe "that women who love and marry feel no need to write. But how can a woman of genius love and marry?"[15]

Fuller wanted to be a genius *and* she wanted to be loved. She wanted to write, to cultivate her intellect, to feel passion, to be a mother. "I love the stern Titanic parts, I love the crag, even the Drachenfels of life," she wrote (she was referring to the steep mountain on which Goethe's *Faust* is set), "I love the roaring sea that crashes against the crag—I love its sounding cataract."[16] Thomas Carlyle, who met her toward the end of her life, wrote of Fuller's insatiable hunger for experience: "Such a predetermination to *eat* this big universe as her oyster or her egg, and to be absolute empress of all height and glory in it that her heart could conceive, I have not before seen in any human soul."[17]

That women *should* have the opportunity to experience as much as possible is precisely the argument she made in *Woman in the Nineteenth Century*. When the book appeared, Lydia Maria Child, a member of Fuller's conversation group, described it as "a contralto voice in literature: deep, rich, and strong...." She admired Fuller's courage in questioning the inequity of marriage and admitted that "I should not have dared to have written some things in it, although it would have been safer for me, being married. But they need to have been said and she is brave to do it."[18] Child was responding to the kind of criticism levied by the one-time transcendentalist Orestes Brownson, who declared, "Miss Fuller thinks it is man who has crowded woman to one side, and refused her full scope for self-development; and although the sphere in which she moves may really be that most appropriate to her, yet man has no right to confine her to it, and forbid her to take another if she prefer it...All very plausible. But God, and not man, has assigned her the appropriate sphere."[19] As news of the book spread, it roused the curiosity of Mary Moody Emerson, who called its author "The Fuller." From Maine, she wrote her nephew Waldo, asking, "Have you Fuller's 'Woman.' I am longing to see it, & Brownson's review of it. I want something exciting...."[20]

By the time the book was published, however, Fuller had left the scene of its conception. She had given up her Conversations, given up Boston altogether, abandoned New England's parochial concerns and the limitations that transcendental personhood posed for a woman. A chronic reinventor of herself, a believer in the German concept of *bildung*, she had other lives to live, other persons to become. She had already been an artist, an intellectual, a friend, and a mystic—now she wanted to be an activist, to help in the great work of improving society. Drawn to "the tangible and real," as her friend James Freeman Clarke put it, she left her native region for good, relocating first to New York, and then, in the fulfillment of a lifelong dream, to Europe, where she became some of the things she had always aspired to be.[21] She also took up a new occupation, this time as a newspaper journalist.

3.

In 1822, the young and ardently gifted Elizabeth Palmer Peabody started hearing rumors of "a wonderful child at Dr Park's school."[22] Peabody had recently left home to teach in Boston. She knew that "Dr. Park" was John Park, a former naval surgeon and newspaperman who had spent several years in the British West Indies before returning to his native country and opening what he called a Lyceum for the Education of Young Ladies. The school was in Park's home, at 5 Mount Vernon Street, surrounded by cow pastures and a view of the Common. According to one of his friends, the academy was among the earliest efforts to "offer young ladies the means of pursuing more diversified and elevated studies than had hitherto been embraced in their literary education."[23]

The "wonderful child" Peabody heard about was a girl from nearby Cambridgeport. She was energetic and assertive, and fleeringly sarcastic. Peabody was told this prodigy could discuss "pure mathematics with her father, at 12 years."[24] She also excelled at languages and literature, reading French and Spanish and Latin better than any other student in Boston, even those much older than her.

Elizabeth always had a soft spot for intellectual girls. She knew from experience that all sorts of trials awaited them. If they displayed their intelligence, they were mocked. If they hid their learning, they were miserable. She soon learned the girl's name, which was Margaret, and found out that she had been educated, much like herself, by an ambitious parent. In Fuller's case, the parent was a prickly, vain father who nurtured one unusual idea: that a woman, properly instructed, was every bit as capable of intellectual growth as a man.

Timothy Fuller worshipped the mind. He valued reason, logic, clear expression. In the only surviving likeness of him—a portrait painted in his twenties by an unknown artist—he appears guarded, haughty, hawk-like, the expression in his eyes almost insolent. He was born in Chilmark, Massachusetts, one hundred miles south of Boston, the son of an unyielding minister who had served as a delegate to the Constitutional Convention and who had refused to ratify that document because it accepted slavery into the nation. A streak of principled obstinacy ran throughout the Fuller family. Like his father, Timothy attended Harvard. Also like his father, he led a student rebellion against the institution's tyrannical regulations. (He opposed the requirement to say prayers before meals; in opposing these prayers, he was also rebelling against his father.) Possessing an Enlightenment faith in the capacities of all human beings, he believed Harvard's students could decide for themselves when to pray.

Sometime in his youth, Timothy ran across Mary Wollstonecraft's *Vindication of the Rights of Woman*, which set off a seismic revolution inside him that gradually rippled through the lives of those he was closest to (figure 55). (Given his future actions, it seems likely he read Wollstonecraft's earlier book *Thoughts on the Education of Daughters.*) Wollstonecraft's reputation in America was mixed, to

Figure 55. Mary Wollstonecraft.

put it mildly. Thanks to the posthumous biography written by her husband William Godwin, she was known more for her illegitimate children than for her ideas. In New England, she inhabited a reputational purgatory reserved for sexual outlaws, not unlike the one Nathaniel Hawthorne portrayed for Hester Prynne in *The Scarlet Letter.*

But Timothy wasn't particularly concerned about Wollstonecraft's character—or, at least, not enough to prevent him from reading her. He approved wholeheartedly of her claim that "truth must be common to all, or it will be inefficacious with respect to its influence on general practice." He also condemned the prevailing opinion, as Wollstonecraft put it, that "the whole tendency of female education ought to be directed to one point to render them pleasing." He thought she was entirely correct that the "FRIVOLOUS accomplishments" taught at most female academies led only to a "trifling turn to the conduct of women in most circumstances."[25]

When he was thirty, Timothy married Sarah Margarett Crane, ten years his junior, a strapping country girl from nearby Canton who stood a foot taller than her fiancé and who possessed ideas of her own about female education. "The *first* wish of my heart is to make you happy," she once told her husband, "and the second to cultivate my mind."[26] Sarah Crane Fuller cultivated her mind as best she could, considering the little formal schooling she had received. She read the works of Germaine de Staël, increasingly an intellectual rite of passage for young women of the era, and she probably perused Wollstonecraft. Unlike her husband, she loved novels, particularly English novels, although she permitted herself (like Lydia Emerson) to dip into the bestsellers of James Fenimore Cooper. "I am *predisposed* to think favorably of *American* geniuses," she told her husband, "and I should mark the 'Pilot' [Cooper's fourth book] among the first *American novels.*" She even tackled, with somewhat less enthusiasm, David Hume's massive, polemical six-volume *History of Great Britain.*[27]

The couple was happy. Margaret Fuller would later write that her father's "love for my mother was the green spot on which he stood apart from the commonplaces of bread-winning, bread-bestowing existence."[28] Timothy's fiery ambition, his obstinacy, his bantam-like jockeying for influence and power—all were perfectly tempered by Sarah Margarett's calm support, which is to say they each conformed to their era's expectations for male and female behavior. Surviving letters between them are intimate, caring, and often passionately romantic. Like Sophia and Nathaniel Hawthorne a few decades later, they enjoyed reading Shakespeare aloud in the evenings. This is probably how their oldest child first heard *The Tempest*, which for the rest of her life she felt a special affinity, considering Shakespeare's last play a "beautiful work" and relishing the sonorous drama of a wizardly father who conjured storms and shipwrecks and who educated his beloved daughter, Miranda.[29]

Sarah Margaret Fuller (she dropped her first name at age nine) was born on May 23, 1810, a year after her parents' marriage. At the time, the family lived in an austere three-story house on 71 Cherry Street, in Cambridgeport, Massachusetts. Its rooms were spacious, but they were also damp and odorous—the structure stood on marshy ground near a soap factory that smelled of potash and animal fat. Timothy had selected the property believing it would prove a solid investment. A decade earlier, the West Boston Bridge had been completed, halving the distance between Harvard Square and downtown Boston, where he had set up his legal practice in Boston in 1804. Despite its boggy location, the suburban village was on the cusp of becoming fashionable at the time Margaret Fuller was growing up. The painter Washington Allston (who instructed Sophia Peabody) lived in Cambridgeport. His studio, filled with Romantic landscapes and portraits of the Boston gentry, was located on nearby Magazine Street (figure 56). Within a mile or so of the Fuller house was Harvard, with sheep grazing on the lawns and undergraduates skylarking between classes. Its bookish culture appealed to both Timothy and Sarah.

It was on Cherry Street that Timothy set about educating his oldest child. Inspired by the writings of Wollstonecraft, he was also prompted by another, less exalted, motive: vanity. Timothy wanted nothing less than an exceptional child, a genius. "To excel in all things should be your constant aim," he told the young

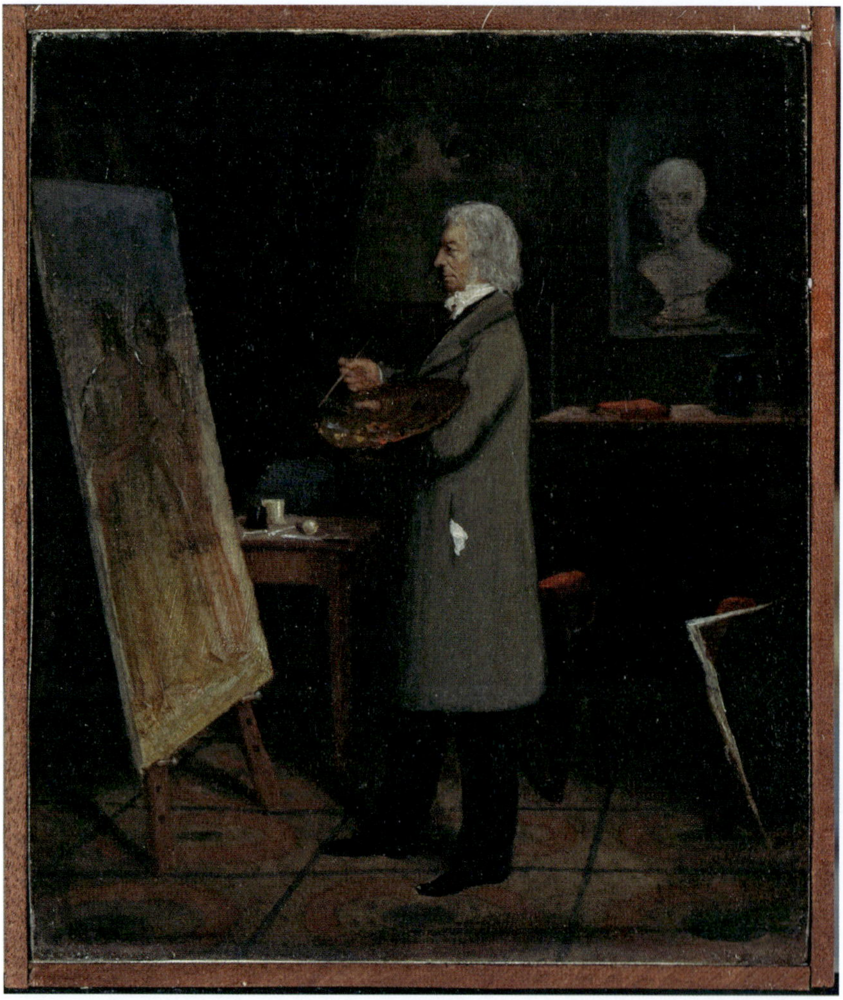

Figure 56. Washington Allston in Cambridgeport.

girl: "mediocrity is obscurity."[30] With this principle in mind, he taught her to read when she was four. At six he introduced her to Latin. Eventually he supplemented these studies with mathematics, natural philosophy, history, and grammar.

Fuller's education has long been the focus of biographers, mainly because she described it in such fraught terms. Her father had "hoped to make me the heir of all he knew," she said, but her training took an enormous toll. Fuller believed her instruction had started too early. Even worse, her father's expectation had been crippling. Timothy's ambitious program put her "at once under discipline of considerable severity," with "more than ordinarily high standards presented to me."[31] Adding to the stress was Timothy's cold reserve, his withholding of approval. From a very young age, Fuller learned that her father's affection was conditioned on her success. In a letter of 1814, for instance, when the girl was not yet four, he asked his wife to send "My love to the little Sarah Margaret. I love her *if* she is a good girl and learns to read."[32]

All her life, Fuller believed her father had nourished her mind and starved her heart. She blamed her night terrors on his demands, which had created in her "a premature development of the brain" that "made me a 'youthful prodigy' by day, and by night a victim of spectral illusions, nightmares, and somnambulism, which at the time prevented the harmonious development of my bodily powers and checked my growth, while, later, they induced continual headache, weakness and nervous affections, of all kinds."[33]

It did not help that her education coincided with her father's political career. In 1813, Timothy was elected to the Massachusetts House of Representatives. Soon he entered the state senate. Then, in 1817, when Margaret was seven, her father became a U.S. Congressman, and for the next eight years spent half his time in Washington, where he gained a reputation as an accomplished speaker and a staunch foe of slavery.

Fuller understandably felt abandoned. Thirty years later she still recalled "how deep the anguish, how deeper still the want, with which I walked alone in hours of childish passion, and called for a Father, often saying the Word a hundred times till it was stifled by sobs."[34] Like Shakespeare's Miranda, she felt stranded on an island controlled by her father, an island that sometimes seemed like a brave new world but seldom like home. As she eventually came to realize, there was *no* place to feel at home for a precocious, well-educated young woman.

"Home!" she exclaimed years later to one of her closest friends, Caroline Sturgis. "O Cary, my extreme weakness has made me feel so homeless, so forlorn!"[35] She was speaking of a recent illness, but the image comes up time and again in her correspondence. To another friend she announced, "I am more and more dissatisfied with this world, and *cannot* find a home in it... Heaven knows I have striven to make my mind its own place."[36] Other times she put the matter like this: Timothy had taught her to think like a man but done nothing to educate her womanly feelings. While she was grateful to have received an education, she considered herself a freak, a hybrid, Caliban-like creation—born, as she phrased it, with a woman's heart and a man's mind.

4.

On November 5, 1839, a ferocious storm struck much of the northeast. Gale-force winds bellowed; torrents flooded Boston's cobbled streets. According to the city's

Courier, ships harbored at Long Wharf broke from their moorings, hulls smashed, rudders splintered. One vessel, the *Madawaska*, "had her foremast nearly chafed off, rigging fore and aft carried away, larboard-bow and quarter stove..." Not far away, on the sandy curve of Nantasket Beach, a brig was flung like a scrap of flotsam against the rocks. The two-masted ship swiftly went to pieces in the storm, its timbers washing ashore. Search crews found no bodies among the wreckage. "All hands," reported the newspaper, "undoubtedly perished."[37]

The next morning, Margaret Fuller's began her first series of Conversations. By the time the meeting started, the storm clouds had cleared off and sunlight spilled through the windows of Mary Peabody's rented room on Chauncey Place.* Mary had recently moved here, near the city's First Church, where William Emerson had preached a generation earlier. In the afternoons, she taught a dozen or so children in her own small school, emulating her mother and older sister. This morning, the children's chairs were arranged in a circle.

For many who attended that day, what happened next would prove transformative. Fuller's conversations reshaped their perceptions, altered their understanding of their place in the world. The talk expanded their sense of who they could be. Most agreed that Fuller could be demanding, even caustic. Shortly after the first Conversation, Sarah Freeman Clarke described a woman who insisted "upon her sex's privilege to judge of things by her feelings, and to care not for the intellectual view of the matter. 'I am made so,' says she, 'and I cannot help it.'" Fuller gazed coldly upon her, then said, "'Yes,... but who are *you*? Were you an accomplished human being, were you all that a human being is capable of becoming, you might perhaps have a right to say, 'I *like* it therefore it is good'—but, if you are not all that, your judgment must be partial and unjust if it is guided by your feelings alone.'"[38]

Fuller pressed the women to think hard. She asked them to consider whether they were truly happy with their lives. If they were not, she wanted them to imagine better ones. But her provocations weren't the only things that made the Conversations so memorable. When she first proposed them, she had "been told that several persons are desirous to join, if only they need not talk." She rejected this proviso out of hand: "I do not wish any one to join who does not intend, *if possible*, to take an active part. No one will be forced, but those who do not talk will not derive the same advantages with those who openly state their impressions and consent to learn by blundering as is the destiny of Man here below."[39] The environment she created for her participants was a crucial element of the Conversation's success.

Sitting in Mary Peabody's rented room—or later, standing on the hearthrug in Elizabeth Peabody's bookshop—Fuller managed to establish an atmosphere of

* "Clouds in the morning but it cleared," Charles Francis Adams wrote in his diary that day. "The night was a very stormy one and the morning opened... unpromisingly..."

warmth and communion. One woman described the mutual sympathy in this way: "As I sat there, my heart overflowed with joy at the sight of the bright circle...."[40] Fuller dressed up for the meetings, as though the exchange of ideas was an event worthy of celebration. "Margaret," one participant wrote, "beautifully dressed,... presided with more dignity and grace than I had thought possible."[41] Another reported, "Margaret used to come to the conversations very well dressed, and, altogether, looked sumptuously. She began with an exordium, in which she gave her leading views; and those exordiums were excellent, from the elevation of the tone, the ease and flow of discourse, and from the tact for which they were kept aloof from any excess, and from the gracefulness with which they were brought down, at last, to a possible level for others to follow."[42]

The Conversations were ostensibly devoted to academic subjects: Greek mythology, history, the fine arts. But they invariably found their way to topics of interest to contemporary women. During the first session, Fuller began with female education. The training of past generations had been scanty, she said, yet "healthy." Women in the past had been trained for nothing beyond their "sphere." They had not learned Latin—a language used in professions from which they were excluded—which meant that if they remained ignorant, they were unburdened by longings that could never be fulfilled under society's current arrangement.

Fuller contrasted that training with "what was called the improved education of the present day." The education of many women in the circle "had been enlarged but not filled up faithfully—& consequently superficialness, unhealthiness, & pedantry had been introduced."[43] She was speaking to some extent about the education she had received not only from her father but from her formal training after Timothy moved to Washington. At age ten, she been sent to the Cambridge Port Private Grammar School, located near her family's home (figure 57). (Fuller's mother by this time was preoccupied with a houseful of young children.) The coeducational academy specialized in the preparation of local boys for admission to Harvard. Among them was the future physician and author Oliver Wendell Holmes, who remembered Fuller as haughty and stand-offish, "with the reputation of being 'smart.' To her schoolmates she bestowed an air of stately distance, as if she had other thoughts than theirs and was not of them. She was a great student and a great reader of what she used to call 'náw-véls.'"[44]

Indeed, reading was by this time a central fact of Fuller's girlhood. Literature structured the maelstrom of her inner life, soothed the pressures of her father's expectations. During her tenure at the Private Grammar School, she plowed through piles of contemporary novels, including the works of two favorite novelists, Jane Austen and Charles Brockden Brown. She also mastered many classic works of Italian and Spanish literature and began to read French. (Within a few years, she had discovered Madame de Staël and the great French philosopher Jean-Jacques Rousseau, whose novels of doomed love and whose unvarnished

Figure 57. Cambridge Port Private Grammar School.

Confessions would serve as a model of frank truth-telling.) In poetry, her tastes ran toward the Romantic: Wordsworth, Coleridge, Shelley, Byron.

In 1822, when she was twelve, her father decided it was time to advance her education. He sent her to Dr. Park's school in Boston, where Elizabeth Peabody learned of the prodigy. Although Park "had never had a pupil with half her attainments at her age," Fuller was miserable. She was teased mercilessly, as one friend later recalled, especially for her "nearsightedness, awkward manners, extravagant tendencies of thought, and... pedantic style of talk." This friend blamed Fuller's unpopularity on her having been "overtasked by her father, who wished to train her like a boy." Routinely "exposed to petty persecutions," she was made "a butt for ridicule" among her classmates.[45]

A year and a half later, Timothy summoned her back home to the Private Grammar School in Cambridgeport, telling her "to be a little reserved... & by no means display your attainments too soon, lest you should excite observation and incur dislike."[46] This was almost the same advice Elizabeth Peabody had received from her mother at a comparable age. Concerned about his daughter's marriageability, upset by her unpopularity, Timothy decided to send her to a more conventional finishing school—Susan Prescott's Young Ladies' Seminary, in nearby Groton—where he hoped she would learn "modest & unassuming deportment." "[Y]ou have a fair opportunity to *begin the world anew*," he counseled, "to avoid mistakes & faults, which have deprived you of *some esteem*, among your present acquaintances."[47]

But Fuller's time at Prescott's Academy was even worse. She was again ostracized. In a short story called "Mariana," she later chronicled this unhappy period, describing a young girl humiliated by her classmates for wearing too much rouge. Mortified by the ridicule, Mariana seeks revenge by sowing jealousy among her classmates. When she is confronted by the older girls, she throws herself to the floor and strikes her head on the hearth. The gentle attention of a teacher heals her sorrow and resolves the tale: "Do not think that one great fault can mar a whole life," the teacher tells her. In a moment of expiation, Mariana realizes that by seeking vengeance she had betrayed her better self.[48]

"Mariana" is fiction, a stylized drama. Yet its narrative energy arises from some unspecified, yet clearly painful, event that befell Fuller at Prescott's school. Five years later, she wrote the headmistress and referred obliquely to "those sad experiences." Then she added, "Can I ever forget that to your treatment in that crisis of youth I owe the true life,—the love of Truth and Honor?"[49]

When Fuller mentioned education to her conversation group, she was alluding to all these experiences. She contrasted "that practical good sense & mother wisdom & wit which grew up with our grandmothers" with "the evils of unhealthiness of mind—pedantry—superficialness" that marked contemporary female education.[50] And she asked the assembled women to consider *why* that education was so unsatisfactory before offering her own answer. "Men are called on from a very early period to *reproduce* all that they learn," she declared. "First their college exercises—their political duties—the exercises of professional study—the very first action of life in any direction—calls upon them for *reproduction* of what they have learnt."[51]

Women, on the other hand, were educated for little. Nearly everything they learned in school was useless for their preordained destiny as wives and mothers. There were no occasions to work on mathematical theorems, to study the constellations, to read Latin while also raising children. "This is what is most neglected in the education of women," Fuller said, "they learn without any attempt to reproduce [that knowledge]."[52]

5.

Sometimes she was certain there had been a mistake. She was really a princess, a queen-in-waiting, born in Europe, awaiting royal office. For reasons mysterious and unknown, she had been left in the care of Margarett and Timothy, who would one day explain everything and rightfully restore her to the throne. This impression, which dated from earliest childhood, was confirmed by her father, who watched the young girl parade across the lawn and said, *Incedit regina*, "there moves a queen." In subsequent years her friends described her regal bearing, her imperial demeanor, "like the queen of some parliament of love," a monarch possessed of "a haughty assurance,—queen-like."[53] And years later, when she wrote to a man she had fallen in love with in New York, she referred to herself in the third person, saying "that if Margaret dared to express herself more frankly than another, it is because she has been in her way a queen and received her guests as also of royal blood."[54]

But a queen requires a court. Not long after she returned from Prescott's Academy, Fuller began assembling hers. "Some seasons later," recalled her friend William Henry Channing (nephew of the Unitarian minister), "I call to mind seeing . . . a girl, plain in appearance, but of dashing air, who was invariably the centre of a listening group, and kept their merry interest alive by sparkles of wit and incessant small-talk."[55] James Freeman Clarke, another friend from this period, had a similar impression: "She was the centre of a group very different from each other, and whose only affinity consisted in their all being polarized by the strong attraction of her mind,—all drawn toward herself."[56] Elizabeth Hoar, who became acquainted with Fuller later, described the young woman to Mary Moody Emerson: "She knows so many beautiful people that her friends are like a diamond chain about her neck, and she surrounds herself with an atmosphere of beautiful associates."[57]

Shunned in school, Fuller had decided to make herself popular—to become a brilliant, irresistible, demanding friend. Clarke recalled some of the conditions she imposed upon those in her circle: "all, in order to be Margaret's friends, must be capable of seeking something,—capable of some aspiration for the better."[58] Freeman's sister, Sarah, was initially intimidated by Fuller, but gradually she realized the young woman possessed an "immense capacity for social intercourse" and that though "she spoke rudely searching words, and told startling truths, though she broke down your little shams and defenses, you felt exhilarated by the compliment of being found out, and even that she had cared to find you out. I think this is what attracted or bound us to her."[59]

Fuller was sixteen when she added a bold and fearless young woman to her group of friends. Lydia Maria Francis (later known as Lydia Maria Child) was already considered one of America's leading women writers (figure 58). Just eight years older than Fuller, she had written several best-selling historical novels and founded a children's magazine, for which she contributed the bulk of material. In later years, she would produce the *Mother's Book* and *American Frugal Housewife*, both concerned with women's education, and, in 1833, her antislavery polemic, *An Appeal in Favor of that Class of Americans Called Africans.* Fuller instantly spotted a kindred soul. Like her, Francis had been educated by a male family member, in this case her older brother, the Unitarian minister and future transcendentalist Convers Francis, who had encouraged her to take up the pen when she was still a teenager. She also admired her new friend's conversational talents, calling her talk "charming,—she brings all her powers to bear upon it; her style is varied, and she has a very pleasant and spirited way of thinking."[60] Francis was an important—and

Figure 58. Lydia Maria (Francis) Child.

still comparatively rare—model of a woman who used her mind and talents as an author to create a career for herself.[61]

A few years later, Fuller became acquainted with another such woman. This was Harriet Martineau, then on her extended tour of America to research her book about democratic culture (plate 11). It is not clear when the two were introduced by Elizabeth Peabody, but their rapport was immediate. In a rush of feeling, Fuller confided her life story to Martineau. "She told me what danger she had been in," recalled the older woman,

> from the training her father had given her, and the encouragement to pedantry and rudeness which she derived from the circumstances of her youth. She told me that she was at nineteen the most intolerable girl that ever took a seat in a drawing room. Her admirable candour, the philosophical way in which she took herself in hand, her genuine heart, her practical insight, and, no doubt, the natural influence of her attachment to myself, endeared her to me, while her powers, and her confidence in the use of them, led me to expect great things from her.[62]

Fuller was equally captivated. "I sigh for an intellectual guide," she wrote in her journal soon after meeting Martineau. ".... I had hoped some friend would do—what none has ever done yet, comprehend me wholly, mentally and morally, and enable me to better comprehend myself. I have had some hopes that Miss Martineau might be this friend, but I cannot yet tell. She has what I want, vigorous reasoning powers, invention, clear views of her objects, and she has trained to the best means of execution."[63†]

Fuller longed for women friends who understood her. She also sought out young men who could read Latin and discuss literature with her. Even before she met Martineau, she had established herself with the brilliant Harvard graduating class of 1829, a group that included Oliver Wendell Holmes, James Freeman Clarke, Frederic Henry Hedge, William Henry Channing, and the eccentric mathematician Benjamin Peirce. Among these talented scholars, Fuller quickly developed a reputation for her fearless intelligence. The future senator Charles Sumner, a year younger than the rest, remembered his first impressions of her: "I was much frightened, for everybody talked of her genius . . . I nearly sank through the floor, as I found myself sitting by her trying some small talk. My fear increased when she began to catechize me on my reading. I told her I had been reading Hoole's translation of the Ariosto; she told me I was quite wrong—Rose's was the best. I retired full of awe at a young lady who not only read books in the original, but knew all about every translation."[64]

At age eighteen, Fuller was already beginning to cement her reputation as the best-read woman in America. She devoured the German Romantic authors who would influence her thinking for the next two decades. Having taught herself to read the language, she spent hours studying Schiller, Winckelmann, the Schlegel

† Martineau was apparently the first person to mention Fuller to Waldo and Lydia Emerson. During her visit to Concord, Waldo wrote, "she returned again and again to the topic of Margaret's excelling genius and conversation, and enjoined it on me to seek her acquaintance: which I willingly promised."

brothers, and Novalis. But it was Goethe, above all, who became her polestar. Goethe's emphasis on youthful self-discovery and his insistence that mature adults accept their responsibilities to society, as well as his sparkling cosmopolitan attitude toward culture and politics—all these things appealed to her sensibilities. "I am enchanted while I read," she told Clarke of her marathon encounters with Goethe. "He comprehends every book, it seems as if I had lost my personal identity."[65] On another occasion, using language similar to that she had used in describing Martineau, Fuller explained why the author meant so much to her: "How often have I thought, if I could see Goethe, and tell him my state of mind, he would support and guide me! He would be able to understand; he would show me how to rule circumstances, instead of being ruled by them...."[66]

Clarke described Fuller's bold, grasping mind at this time: "I felt how she traced ideas through minds & works, how questions rose before her, how she carried the initiative idea everywhere. In other words how comprehensive & understanding is her intellect."[67] Her immersion in German literature encouraged introspection, self-knowledge; increasingly she tried to emulate Goethe whom, she wrote, "loved to study the secret principles of the individual mind and to study the inward workings of love and grief rather than criticize or dramatize the words or acts which were their outward results."[68]

Love and grief: the two emotions preoccupied her, propelled her. Much as she enjoyed the exchange of ideas and the clash of conversation, she also desired what Wordsworth, one of her favorite poets, called the "lively gushing thought-employing spirit-stirring passion of love."[69] She craved a consuming, passionate romance—an obliterating ardor of the kind she had so far only read about. For a brief period, she thought she found it. His name was George Davis, and he was a slender young law student with a famously sharp tongue. Fuller, nineteen, fell completely in love with him.

Davis was neither as brilliant nor as talented as some of his Harvard classmates, although one later remarked on "the air of refinement which marked his face and general aspect." Fuller was drawn to his gift for talk, which was "quick, alert, fruitful in allusions, copious in illustrations." Some years later, when William Makepeace Thackeray toured the country, he declared Davis the "best conversationalist he met in America."[70] Until the end of her life, Fuller believed that she and Davis had been able to "communicate more closely with one another than either could with the herd."[71]

In January 1830, Davis wrote Fuller to ask about her religious beliefs—a question that traditionally signaled growing interest in a prospective partner. She replied with shocking candor: "I have decided not to form settled opinions at present. Loving or feeble natures need a positive religion, a visible refuge, a protection, as much in the passionate season of youth as in those stages nearer to the grave. But mine is not such."[72] Davis's response has not survived, but it must have been disapproving, if not disappointed, because it prompted the following response from Fuller: "I do not *dis*believe or even *carelessly set aside* Revelation; I merely remain in ignorance of the Christian Revelation because I do not feel it suited to me at present."[73]

When the school year ended, Davis moved to western Massachusetts to practice law. He and Fuller maintained their correspondence for several months, but eventually he ended the relationship. (Within a year, he had married someone else.) Fuller's reaction was despondent: "You are the only person who can appreciate my true self," she told him, before magnanimously wishing he might "be happy and untroubled by me. My heart does not wish this, but my reason does."[74]

According to James Freeman Clarke, after the breakup Fuller spoke "in words of tragical pathos, of her own needs and longings,—her demands on life,—the struggle of mind, and of heart."[75] Once again, she felt homeless, unmoored. "There comes a consciousness," she told Clarke, "that I have no real hold on life,—no real, permanent connection with any soul. I seem a wandering Intelligence, driven from spot to spot, that I may learn all secrets, and fulfil a circle of knowledge. This thought envelopes me as a cold atmosphere."[76] She sank into depression. "At moments," she said, "the music of the universe, which daily I upheld by hearing, seems to stop. I fall like a bird when the sun is eclipsed, not looking for such darkness. The sense of my individual law—the lamp of life—flickers."[77] In her journal, she confessed her continued yearning for Davis. "I feel dreadfully lonely. I would not go alone, but there is no person whose companionship would be endurable to me—except one—and reason forbids me even to wish for that person's society—reason alas! pride too—In a profound but not a cold reserve I must shroud my heart, if I would escape the most deadly wounds." Soon her dark mood was accompanied by headaches, some quite severe. She spent more and more time in bed, craving nothing so much as "sleep.... I would now lie down in the middle of the day and sleep for hours."[78]

A change came on Thanksgiving Day in 1830. To please her father, she attended church services, although the experience only further demoralized her. Sitting in the family pew, she suffered "a feeling of disunion with the hearers and dissent from the preacher." She was smothered by "a mood of most childish, child-like sadness, I felt within myself great power, and generosity, and tenderness; but it seemed to me as if they were all unrecognized, and as if it was impossible that they should be used in life." Troubled by the thought, she stood and abruptly left the church. Through nearby fields and woods she walked, agitated, her surroundings a blur. This continued for at least two hours. Then she stopped by a stream, drawn to the sound of trickling water as it poured into a dark pool. "I did not think; all was dark and cold, and still. Suddenly the sun shone out with that transparent sweetness, like the last smile of a dying lover, which it will use when it has been unkind all a cold autumn day." Something about the sunlight caused her to recall a moment in her childhood when she had stopped "on the stairs" and posed a series of questions to herself: "[H]ow came I here? How is it that I seem to be this Margaret Fuller? What does it mean? What shall I do about it?"

The same questions plagued her now; they would follow her into the future. With only minor modifications, they were the questions she posed to the women in her Conversations, the questions she would seek to answer in their presence, once and for all. But now, at age twenty, she felt only the painful restrictions of her life, a cruel destiny she had not chosen, leaving her to feel rejected and misunderstood. "I saw how long it must be before the soul can learn to act under these limitations of time and space, and human nature; but I saw, also, that it MUST do it,—that it must make all this false true,—and sow new and immortal plants in the garden of God, before it could return again."

And then another insight came over her: "I saw there was no self; that selfishness was all folly, and the result of circumstances; that it was only because I thought self real that I suffered; that I had only to live in the idea of the ALL, and all was mine. This truth came to me, and I received it unhesitatingly; so that I was for that hour taken up into God. In that true ray most of the relations of earth seemed mere films, phenomena."[79]

The experience is reminiscent of Waldo Emerson's famous Transparent Eyeball passage. "[T]he currents of the Universal Being circulate through me," he wrote; "I am part or particle of God." Fuller's vision, though, was prompted by unhappiness. It was the release of pressure long pent up. Yet it also offered her a path out of isolation and despair, so that when the sun emerged from the clouds, she felt a larger force, a transcendent power that seemed to render her own concerns insignificant and to place the mystery of her unhappy self within a larger, grander scheme.

The only problem with such revelatory experiences is that they are temporary. Reality eventually reasserts itself, quenching the remembered afterglow of vision and transcendence. It would take time—several years—before Fuller finally escaped the pain of Davis' rejection. Part of that process involved writing a short story about the affair, a thinly disguised roman à clef that recounted her early love in starkly moralistic terms. The story, "Lost and Won," was published in the *New England Galaxy*, in August 1835, making it one of Fuller's earliest published pieces of writing. The character modeled on Davis is ultimately rejected, condemned to a life of bachelorhood, while the woman he abandons finds a true and lasting love. The piece was carefully plotted and written—polished enough to appear in a periodical that referred to itself as "a weekly epitome of news, literature, and the arts." But if Fuller was proud of the story's publication, she quickly regretted writing it.

James Freeman Clarke, who had long encouraged her to become an author, was also proud of her fledgling effort. He purchased copies of the *Galaxy* and distributed them to a handful of mutual friends, including, inexplicably, George Davis and his wife Harriet. When Fuller learned of this, she panicked; the thought of him reading the story mortified her. Her reaction led to a serious illness. "For myself," she recalled in her journal, "I thought I should surely die; but I was calm and looked to God without fear."[80] Her fever lasted nine days. So ill was she that Timothy Fuller, concerned for his daughter's life, visited her sick room. "My father habitually so sparing in tokens of affection was led by his anxiety to express what he felt towards me, in stronger terms than he had ever used in the whole course of his life," she wrote. "He thought I might not recover, and one morning coming into my room, after a few moments of conversation he said: 'My dear, I have been thinking of you in the night, and I cannot remember that you have any faults. You have defects of course, as all mortals have, but I do not know that you have a single fault.'"

At these words, Fuller began to cry. Touched by her father's kindness, "so strange from him, who had scarce ever in my presence praised me and who, as I knew, abstained from praise as hurtful to his children," something inside her fell apart.[81] Then came relief. Grateful for his unexpected blessing, she began to recover. The obsession with Davis finally eased. Before she had fully recuperated, however, her father grew sick. The illness was cholera, contracted while standing in contaminated water on his farm. Within three days, he was dead.

6.

In 1839, transcendentalism needed a platform. Waldo Emerson's scandalous "Divinity School Address," delivered a year earlier, meant that Harvard officially no longer welcomed the "new thought." Members of the Transcendental Club—which now included Fuller as one of its few females—found it increasingly difficult to publish their work in the *North American Review* or the *Christian Examiner*, conservative venues that had closed ranks in the wake of Waldo's address. In October, at one of the club's meetings, the group hit upon the idea of producing their own periodical. Bronson Alcott suggested a name—*The Dial*—which turned out to be his most enduring contribution to the venture. The question of who would serve as editor arose next. Frederic Henry Hedge, Theodore Parker, and Waldo Emerson each declined the office. On October 20, 1839—two and a half weeks before she began her first series of Conversations for women—Fuller accepted the position.

Much had changed in her life by this point. Before her father's death, she had dreamed of escaping the rural enclave of Groton, Massachusetts, where Timothy had moved the family in 1833. She imagined launching her literary career in Europe, traveling to the Lake District, home of her favorite poetry, and then onward to Germany to visit the Drachenfels, its crumbling Gothic ruins memorialized by Byron and Goethe. At last she would return, a queen-in-exile, to the rich and storied culture that had nourished her throughout childhood and adolescence, her "head full of Hamlet and Rousseau, and the ballads of chivalry."[82]

But Timothy's death spelled the end to these dreams. He had died intestate, his farm heavily mortgaged and his other real estate investments, according to Fuller, "not fortunate." Moreover, she was expected to assume full responsibility for the support of her family—a burden made especially urgent as her mother succumbed to poor health and grief. At age twenty-five, Fuller found herself, much like Elizabeth Peabody, the nominal head of a large and improvident family. "Grant, oh Father, that neither the joys nor sorrows of this past year shall have visited my heart in vain!" she exclaimed in her journal. "Make me wise and strong for the performance of immediate duties."[83] For the next decade or so, her life would be circumscribed by these responsibilities.

The death of those we love does not end their hold upon us. Timothy's exacting personality remained a haunting presence throughout Fuller's life. "To night is the anniversary of my father's death," she wrote nine years after his abrupt passing, "just about this time he left us and my hand closed his eyes. Never has that hand since been employed in so holy work..."[84] Without Timothy's stern encouragement, she plunged into doubts about her abilities. "What can I do with my pen," she wrote in 1836, a year after he had died, "I know not. At present I feel no confidence or hope. The expectations so many have been led to cherish by my conversational power, I am disposed to deem ill-founded."[85] She was plagued by headaches, blinding migraines that left her bedridden in curtain-shrouded darkness. Even worse, she felt deprived of the one person who, however gruffly, affirmed her value. Nearly a decade after her father's death, Fuller portrayed herself "as a child never finding repose on the bosom of love," an orphan seeking love "childishly perhaps, God knows all about it."[86]

She was gradually becoming aware of the disadvantages of her sex. If Fuller was now the putative head of the family, a stingy and irrational uncle had legal oversight of her father's embattled estate. Her letters from this period are riddled with negotiations with this arbitrary man, who seems as a matter of principle to have distrusted women to make sound decisions. "I have often had reason to regret being of the softer sex," Fuller told a friend, "and never more than now. If I were the eldest son, I could be guardian to my brothers and sister, administer the estate, and really become the head of my family."[87]

In October 1836, at age twenty-six, she struck out for Boston to earn a living by teaching languages to young women. Soon she replaced Elizabeth Peabody at Bronson Alcott's Temple School, where she took up her predecessor's chores of transcribing the headmaster's conversations and teaching those subjects for which he was unqualified. Then she moved to a considerably more lucrative position at the Greene Street School in Providence, Rhode Island, supervising sixty girls who possessed "well-disposed hearts" but minds that were "absolutely torpid."[88]

It was during her time at the Temple School that she was first invited to visit the Emersons in Concord. Lydia, pregnant with the couple's first child, welcomed the visitor as a timely diversion. "We like her," she quickly reported to Elizabeth Peabody, "she likes us." The two women spent time getting to know each other in Lydia's flower garden and in the downstairs parlor, trading lines in German from *Wilhelm Meister*—both women's favorite novel. Sometime during this visit, Elizabeth Hoar wrote Mary Moody Emerson to describe the stimulating new guest.

> Her wit, her insight into characters, such that she seems to read them aloud to you as if they were printed books, her wide range of thought & cultivation, the rapidity with which she appropriates all knowledge, joined with the habits of severe & exact mental discipline, (so *very* rare in women.).... All these things keep me filled with pleased admiration & (true to the nature of genius) constantly inspire me with new life new hope in my own powers, new desires to fulfil the possible in myself.[89]

Around Waldo, Fuller was a different person altogether. She could be shamelessly ingratiating, then, in a whirling reversal, hugely self-respecting. Waldo found her emotional turbulence tiresome and overbearing. "We shall never get far," he thought the day she arrived. Her conversation, a dizzying torrent, taxed him. As if to compensate for her uneasiness, she displayed "an overweening sense of power, and slight esteem for others." But soon Waldo discovered what everyone else did: that her flamboyant cleverness was a defense, a protective carapace shielding a sensitive, vulnerable soul. She was "too intent on establishing a good footing between us to omit any art of winning," Waldo later wrote. Part of her charm was to challenge "frankness with frankness, and [she] did not conceal the good opinion of me she brought with her, nor her wish to please... it was impossible to hold against such urgent assault."[90] By the second day, he was won over.

If Waldo soon became one of Fuller's most important friends, he would also be her most frustrating. She was drawn to him in part because he reminded her of her father. Aloof, emotionally guarded, a connoisseur of the intellect, he differed from Timothy in that he was more poet than logician. But he was every bit as emotionally chilly as her stern parent, and while Fuller basked in his enigmatic smile, she quickly discovered that it was impossible to plumb his depths, to really *know* him. Nevertheless, she was drawn to the charisma of success that surrounded him—for although he was just then putting the final touches on *Nature*, New England's cognoscenti already considered the former minister a leader at the vanguard of American culture. In the next few years, as he became a national figure, Fuller fell increasingly under the sway of his influence, "intoxicated with your mind," as she once told him.[91] Soon she began to speak in the peculiar dialect of transcendentalism: high-minded, rapturous, breathily ineffable. When she told a friend that "the attainment of a divine nature was the faith that reconciled her to this human nature as the pedestal of that divine nature," she was speaking in that obscure and lofty vernacular.[92]

At the same time, she never assigned as much importance to spiritual ideals and abstractions as Waldo and the other transcendentalists. She was more earthbound, more realistic, more responsive to immediate physical beauty. And she was keenly aware that her circumstances were vastly different from Waldo's. He lived independently, thanks in no small part to the interest from his first wife's estate and the constant ministrations of Lydia. This meant he could pursue a life of the mind with few disturbances. Fuller had no such luxuries. Her greatest aspirations were thwarted by the tedium of want and responsibilities, and she once confessed to Lydia, "I have done and suffered much without obtaining my object,... and I cannot be joyful."[93]

By 1839, when she began her first Conversations, her family had advanced little in the way of financial security. Fuller tried remedying the situation with a series of projects she hoped would remove her from the necessity of teaching. She completed a translation of Johann Peter Eckermann's *Conversations with Goethe*, which was published that spring. She also contemplated writing a biography of the great German author. And she agreed to edit *The Dial*. The salary was paltry: three hundred dollars a year. But combined with other ventures, it promised financial relief and a chance to contribute meaningfully to the broader culture. From the outset, Fuller took seriously the periodical's mission of presenting groundbreaking work. "[Y]ou prophecied a new literature," she wrote to Frederick Henry Hedge shortly after taking on the editorial position, "it will dawn on 1840."[94] Under her leadership, *The Dial* became an avant-garde publication committed to new, experimental voices, the first "little magazine" in the country. Nothing quite like it had existed before. Nothing like it would exist again for another eighty years.

Under Fuller's direction, the journal was a forum of conversation. Chatty and rarefied, wide-ranging and parochial, *The Dial* was a symposium for young people seeking new forms of expression. In the first issue, which appeared in July 1840, poetry appeared by Christopher Cranch, the deceased Charles Emerson, and Fuller's closest friend Caroline Sturgis. There were also essays by Waldo, Theodore Parker, Henry David Thoreau, and Fuller herself. A notice of an exhibition of Washington Allston's paintings appeared, as did a survey of music in Boston. Most notorious was Bronson Alcott's hazy, mystifying utterances, titled "Orphic Sayings," which Fuller accepted against her better judgment as a personal favor to Waldo.

Her own contribution, "A Short Essay on Critics," was the journal's first piece. In it, she argued that while criticism was not creative, it was nevertheless vital: a necessary element in the relationship between artist and audience. "The maker is divine," she wrote; "the critic sees this divine, but brings it down to humanity by the analytic process." She was describing her own predilections when she defined the critic's job as sifting through the vast, murmurous conversation of culture and making sense of it for others. The essay also served as a mission statement for *The Dial* itself. As Fuller put it, too many contemporary periodicals strove for "uniformity of tone, so that from the title of a journal you can infer the tenor of all its chapters. But nature is ever various, ever new, and so should be her daughters, art and literature."[95] In two years as editor, she would make the publication various and new, publishing work by many of the authors we now consider classic transcendentalists. She accepted writing by Thoreau, holding him to extremely high standards and making him a better author through her editorial remarks. She published essays by Elizabeth Palmer Peabody, Orestes A. Brownson, and her most prolific author, Waldo Emerson. In addition to Sturgis's poetry, she published that of Sturgis's sister Ellen Hooper, as well as verse by a twenty-one-year-old James Russell Lowell. Fiction appeared less often, but she accepted stories by another close friend, William Henry Channing. In 1841, she began to include more socially oriented work, such as Waldo's "Man the Reformer," Theodore Parker's "Thoughts on Labor" and, most remarkably, Sophia Ripley's essay on "Woman," which grew directly out of Fuller's Conversations.

Altogether, in two years Fuller edited eight issues of *The Dial*, publishing 193 works (thirty-two of them her own) totaling well over a thousand pages. She was never entirely happy with the effort. The journal was "far from the eaglet motion I wanted," she confessed to Waldo after the first issue appeared, tacitly acknowledging the ridicule that accompanied the venture.[96] One Whiggish newspaper said that "duck tracks in the mud convey more intelligible meaning," while the *Cincinnati Review* called the journal "wild raving, mixed with German metaphysics and coarse infidelity." A Yale professor snidely asked, "Who reads *The Dial* for any purpose than to laugh at its baby poetry or at the solemn fooleries of its mystic prose?"[97] Alcott's contributions drew special ire. Parodies quickly appeared in newspapers—one was titled "Gastric Sayings"—and a Boston critic likened his rambling work to "a train of fifteen railroad cars with one passenger"[98] (figure 59).

To make matters worse, Fuller was never paid the three hundred dollars per annum she was promised. In fact, the journal barely made enough money to pay for its printing. After two years of tireless labor and still in need of a steady income, she resigned her editorial position. *The Dial* would continue for two more years, with Waldo taking over its management until its printers went bankrupt, and then Elizabeth Peabody stepping in to publish the final issues. But by then, Fuller had moved on to other ways to make a living, other venues for cultivating her intellectual growth. Far more profitable—financially, intellectually, personally—was another project she launched in 1839: her Conversations.

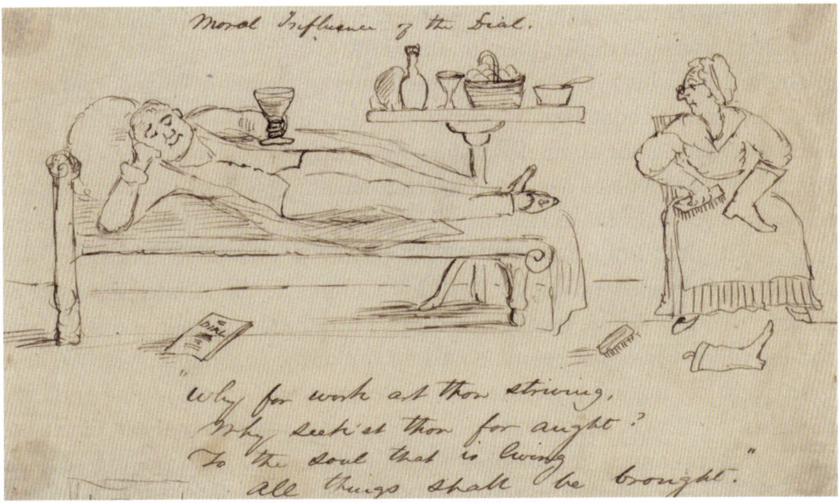

Figure 59. Christopher Cranch's cartoon about *The Dial.*

7.

The talks were her lecture hall, her lyceum circuit, her platform and public forum. They brought out the best in her—not just her capacious learning, not just her sharp critical judgment, but her empathy, her voluble warmth. "M[y] class is singularly prosperous," she announced soon after the first conversation. "I was so fortunate as to rouse at once the tone of simple earnestness, which can scarcely, when once awakened, cease to vibrate. All seem in a glow and quite as receptive as I wish. They question and examine . . . and thoughts (not opinions) have been trumps every time."[99]

The testimony that survives agrees with this description. Something electric happened whenever the twenty-five women gathered in Elizabeth Peabody's bookshop. The atmosphere felt charged, vibrant with possibility. Fuller started each session with a brief lecture, but the ball of conversation was bounced from person to person, often with surprising results. Ideas the women had only vaguely considered in solitude suddenly gushed forth, as if from an underground spring, dazzling them in the light of day.

For Fuller, the Conversations were physically taxing. After each session, she suffered piercing headaches—most likely migraines—that left her enervated for days. Sometimes she found it difficult to read and impossible to write in their aftermath. But they provided her with a forum in which to try out her thoughts, a venue for friendship and mutual support. The day after the first meeting, Fuller attempted to describe the tangle of feelings she was still experiencing: "But I want far more, I want habitual intercourse, cheer, inspiration, tenderness, I want these for myself, I want to impart them to others."[100]

She bristled whenever she became the center of attention. "I could not make those ladies talk about Beauty," she complained to Waldo in November 1839, upset that many of the assembled women were perfectly content to sit and listen to her.[101] But she redoubled her efforts to create an atmosphere of collaboration, and was evidently successful, as she told a friend: "So even devoutly thoughtful seems their spirit, that, from the very first I took my proper place, and never had the feeling I dreaded, of display, of a paid Corinne…All are intelligent; five or six have talent."[102] Before long, she discovered that the Conversations offered "real society, which I have not before looked for out of the pale of intimacy. We have time, patience, mutual reverence and fearlessness eno' to get at one another's thoughts."[103] It was the intellectual digging—the steadfast pursuit of elusive ideas—that prompted the pioneer feminist Elizabeth Cady Stanton to later describe the gatherings as "in reality a vindication of woman's right to think."[104]

Fuller first outlined her plan for the talks in a letter to Sophia Ripley, wife of the disaffected Unitarian minister, George Ripley. (The Ripleys soon created the utopian community of Brook Farm, where Fuller kept a cow and Nathaniel Hawthorne gloomily mucked the barn when not complaining to Sophia Peabody.) She first wanted to "pass in review the departments of thought and knowledge and endeavor to place them in due relation to our minds." The goal was to acquaint the women with the basic fields of study and to arrange these fields in logical order. The aim was high Romantic: to produce a unified understanding of the sprawling work of human culture. Her second object was to "systematize thought and give a precision in which our sex are so deficient, chiefly, I think because they have so few inducements to test and classify what they receive."

The first two goals were methodological. The third was more aspirational. Fuller wanted the women in her conversation group to "ascertain what pursuits are best suited to us in our time and state of society." If they could identify these pursuits, they would be better equipped to determine "how we may make best use of our means for building up the life of thought upon the life of action."[105] This was Fuller's lifelong goal, her embrace of Germanic *bildung*: the development of mind and personality toward something better, if not perfection itself. It was her hope that each woman who participated in the Conversations would cultivate an independent intellectual life and embark on a journey of personal liberation.

After first discussing the deficiencies of female education, "Miss F suggested Grecian mythology as the subject of the first conversations." So begins the transcription of the Conversations made by Elizabeth Palmer Peabody and later copied by Elizabeth Hoar. (It was Hoar's copy that eventually made its way to Mary Moody Emerson's farm in Maine.) Nearly a decade earlier, Peabody had offered her own series of "historical conferences" for young women. The topic then had been on the history of ancient Greece and Rome. Fuller's focus was on art and literature; she chose Greek mythology because it was "quite separated from all exciting local subjects" and was "serious without being solemn, & without excluding every mode of intellectual action[,] it is playful as well as deep" and, most important, because it was "associated with all our ideas of the Arts."[106]

At first, the topic made some women uncomfortable. Many knew next to nothing about mythology. Eliza Morton Quincy, the wife of Harvard's president, registered horror at a group of "*Christians* enjoying *Heathen Greeks*." But Fuller pressed on. She said it was shallow to "look upon the expression of a great nation's intellect as a series of idle fancies."[107] Anticipating the use of mythology later employed by Freud and others, she insisted that classical myths were symbolic truths of human personality. Apollo represented genius, for instance; Mercury stood in for the executive powers.

Almost immediately the Conversations swerved into more urgent subjects—especially having to do with the condition of womanhood. In the story of Minerva and Vulcan, for instance, the Roman goddess of wisdom posed questions with which Fuller continued to wrestle. "Minerva was Execution—Practical Ability," she told the women. "She springs armed from the head of Intelligent Creative Power."[108] But did that mean Minerva was, in the parlance of the time, "mannish"? Was female intellect somehow different in ancient Greece than in nineteenth-century America? Did the goddess possess elements of masculinity *and* femininity? If so, was it possible to determine which elements belonged where? Or were the terms *masculine* and *feminine* inadequate in the first place?

Lydia Maria Child, the friend of Fuller's youth, was now thirty-seven, married, and compelled by financial straits to write a sequel to her earlier success, *A Family Nurse; or Companion to the Frugal Housewife.* (She likely had Fuller in mind when she wrote that "dropsy in the head" was "often produced by unnaturally forcing the intellect of children, from the unpardonable vanity of having them appear as prodigies.")[109] She tried to answer Fuller's questions with another: Was it possible that Minerva's wisdom was a "union of the affections & understanding"—in other words, that the goddess combined characteristics thought to belong to male *and* female?[110]

Before Child's question could be explored, the conversation abruptly shifted again. One woman suggested that Minerva's wisdom could not exist without her perception of beauty. "Miss Fuller said we never should get along till we had defined Beauty & [she] proposed that each should define it." Caroline Sturgis spoke up. Beauty, to her, was "the *attractive* power." Another participant thought beauty was "*the Infinite apprehended* under *the fewest conditions possible*." Anna Shaw, daughter of Fuller's friends Frank and Sarah Shaw, agreed. She said beauty was "the *Infinite revealed in the finite*." Sophia Ripley, waiting her turn, suddenly burst out with a new idea: beauty was the "*aspect of the all*."

The exchange took another turn. What differentiated beauty from the sublime? Several women thought the sublime more intense, more emotionally demanding.

Fuller said it was her hope to rise above the sublime; she longed to transcend its physical sources. She wanted to ascend, she said, through sheer spiritual willpower into a higher sphere. This prompted Ellen Sturgis Hooper, the poet, to say she most definitely did *not* want to rise above the sublime—"nor could she conceive of ever being in a state when there would not be an infinite above us—to excite emotions of the sublime which she seemed to conceive to be the meaning of reverence."[111]

As the winter days grew shorter, the Conversations grew in scope, spreading out in all directions. Ancient mythology became a pretext for more contemporary topics, with many sessions devoted to what we would now call sexual politics. During the third session, Fuller said the Greek idea of "Genius," as represented by Apollo, encompassed the love of various women as well as "forever rising above." This upset Lucy Goddard, a young abolitionist friend of Lydia Emerson's, who declared that "it disturbed her that Genius was so inconstant in its loves." Fuller reminded her she was using the Greek gods as *symbols*; Apollo's inconstancy represented the truth that genius was attracted to beauty "in all its manifestations & forever pursued it & was always unfortunate."[112]

But this statement raised other concerns. One woman asked if the restless, questing nature of genius meant that it was "banished...from the domestic hearth." Elizabeth Bancroft, Lydia Emerson's childhood friend from Plymouth, spoke up, saying she refused to believe that men alone possessed creative talent. She offered several examples of "the action of Genius in the domestic circle" (these examples unfortunately were not recorded), and the talk centered now upon the question of whether a wife and mother could possess genius and artistic power.[113]

Peabody's transcripts make clear that Fuller was a spellbinding storyteller. In the fifth Conversation, she mesmerized her audience with a long narrative account of Cupid and Psyche, spinning a story of jealousy and eros first chronicled in Apuleius's *Metamorphosis.* As Fuller told it, Psyche was the victim of jealousy. Banished by Venus, who resented her beauty, she was visited each night by Cupid, who arrived in darkness and made love to her. There was only one condition to their happiness: Psyche could never look upon her lover or know his identity. When she broke these rules and gazed at Cupid, she was banished to the underworld and told not to look inside a box—another rule she disobeyed. Eventually she was found and rescued by Cupid, who gave her the drink of immortality so she might enter into a marriage of equality with him.

Fuller told the story "with a grace & beauty that was of itself an exquisite delight." As soon as she finished, someone asked her to explain the symbolic meaning of the box. "Miss F. said it was a wile of Venus. She knew Psyche would open the box—for Psyche was always *human*—stimulated by what was forbidden." Someone then asked why it was "wrong in Psyche to wish to see & know her husband? Do we not wish to understand our happiness[?]"[114] The account of Psyche and Cupid prompted them to consider questions about knowledge considered appropriate for female minds. Were they all modern-day Psyches, exploring topics once considered forbidden? Was their desire to learn a crime against society? Or did Psyche symbolize every human soul, rising from innocence to experience, with its ultimate goal an immortal love?

For her own part, Fuller was interested in two aspects of Psyche. The first was the young mortal's abiding hunger for knowledge: her inability to resist the temptation of learning more. Fuller thought this was inspiring. She agreed with Keats, who in "Ode to Psyche" proclaimed the young woman the "loveliest vision far/Of all Olympus' faded hierarchy," a being capable of inspiring "branched thoughts, new grown with pleasant pain." The other part of the fable that interested her was the immortal love between Cupid and Psyche. During the first series of Conversations, Fuller was in love again, and this time it was more hopeless than ever.

8.

Samuel Gray Ward was beautiful. So was Anna Hazard Barker. Ward was Harvard educated, well-heeled, from a wealthy family. His father was the American agent for a prominent London banking firm. Barker's father had lost one fortune and moved his family in 1834 from New York to New Orleans, where he proceeded to make an even larger sum of money. Anna frequently traveled north to visit relatives in Cambridge or Newport or New York when the southern summers became unbearable.

Margaret Fuller loved them both.

She had met Ward in the summer of 1835. Mutual friends—Professor John Farrar, of Harvard, and his famously cultivated wife Eliza—had invited the two young people, along with "several other delightful persons," on a sightseeing excursion up the Hudson River.[115] Fuller was instantly drawn to the young man, seven years her junior, who resembled a Greek god. Amid thundering torrents and waterfalls, on hikes along the fringes of blackberry brakes, she learned that Ward was an aesthete and an aspiring artist—he liked to draw and, occasionally, to paint. He hoped, one day, to leave his mark on the art world.

She had known Barker even longer. It was Barker who had been coaxed into posing for the Swedenborgian sculptor Hiram Powers while traveling in Europe, and it was she who would impress Waldo Emerson with her vitality and lovely features. According to William Henry Channing, Fuller lived vicariously through Barker's beauty, seeking "by genial sympathy thus to live in another's experience." At the same time, she longed, "as it were, to transfuse with her force [Barker's] nymph-like form, and to fill her to glowing with her own lyric fire."[116]

Barker did not accompany Fuller and Ward on the Hudson River trip. But all three were invited to the Farrars' next excursion, an eighteen-month tour of

Europe. Harriet Martineau was enlisted to accompany the party across the Atlantic—she was finally leaving the country she had come to report on—and Fuller began preparing to pursue research in Europe for a new project: a biography of Goethe. But the trip was scheduled for 1835, and Timothy Fuller's death put an end to his daughter's plans.

Her friendship with Ward continued by mail. On those occasions when they saw each other, Fuller grew increasingly enamored with him. Her attachment to Barker is murkier, more complicated. She was powerfully attracted to the younger woman, a fact made evident in several journal entries. Yet what that attraction entailed is difficult to pin down. She referred to the "divinest love" she felt for Barker and spoke of "the same love we shall feel when we are angels." She dedicated poems to her "beloved" Anna, whom she described as "my heart's sister and my fancy's love." To James Freeman Clarke she asked, "Have I ever told you how much I love her?. . . . If I write a novel I shall take Anna for my heroine."[117] For his part, Clarke believed Fuller was smitten with Barker because the young woman idolized *her*. Knowing how much his friend craved affection, he observed "how happy it must make you to be loved by her so much."[118]

But in a journal entry written several years after the peak of their relationship, Fuller spoke of her friend in more suggestive terms. The occasion for the entry was an engraving of Madame Rècamier, the famous Parisian literary *salonnière* who was a close friend of Madame de Staël (figure 60). "I have so often thought over the intimacy between her & Mme de Stael," Fuller wrote after studying the engraving. "It is so true that a woman may be in love with a woman, and a man with a man. It is so pleasant to be sure of it because undoubtedly it is the same love we shall feel when we are angels when we ascend to the only fit place for the Mignons, where

Sie fragen nicht nach Mann und Weib."

Mignon was the androgynous young woman in Goethe's *Wilhelm Meister.* The tag, also from Goethe, can be translated as follows: *it is not a question of man or woman.*

Love between women, Fuller continued, "is regulated by the same law as that love of persons of different sexes, only it is purely intellectual and spiritual, unprofaned by any mixture of lower instincts, undisturbed by any need of consulting temporal interests, its law is the desire of the spirit to realize a whole which makes it seek in another being what it finds not in itself." The passage in some ways echoes Lydia Emerson's "theosophy" of marriage. But it quickly leads Fuller to recall examples from history of same-sex love, beginning with Socrates and Alcibiades and concluding with herself. "I loved Anna for a time with as much passion as I was then strong enough to feel—Her face was always gleaming before me, her voice was always echoing in my ear, all poetic thoughts clustered round

Figure 60. Madame Récamier.

the dear image. This love was a key which unlocked for me many a treasure which I still possess."

And according to Fuller, Barker felt the same toward her. "She loved me, for I well remember her suffering when she first would feel my faults and knew one part of the exquisite veil rent away, how she wished to stay apart and weep the whole day. Then again that night when she leaned on me and her eyes were such a deep violet blue, so like night, as they never were before, and we both felt such a strange mystic thrill, and knew what we had never known before."

The journal entry concludes with a tantalizing, if elliptical, reflection: "I thought of all this as I looked at Me Recamier and had one thought beside which has often come into my mind, but I will not write it down; it is so singular that I have often thought I would never express it in any way; I am sure no human being but myself would understand it."[119] Fuller's unspoken thought cannot be recovered, of course. But if her love for Barker was truly "unprofaned by any mixture of lower instincts," it is also clear that her attachment went well beyond the conventional language of friendship.

In the fall of 1839, at the same time she was formulating her plans for the Conversations, Fuller was passionately attracted to Ward and Barker. But that October, she was shocked to learn they were in love with each other. The two had grown close during the European tour Fuller had missed. Now, four years later, they announced their engagement to be married.

The news was devastating. "Black Friday it has been," Fuller scrawled in her journal, "and my heart is well nigh wearied out. Shall I never be able to act and live with persons of views as high as my own?"[120] She tried to swallow her pride and to write Ward, assuring him that "though I might grieve that you should put me from you in your highest hours and find yourself unable to meet me on the very ground where you had taught me most to expect, I would not complain or feel that the past had in any way bound either of us as to the present."[121] But she was distraught and shaken. To her first love, George T. Davis, she now wrote a despairing letter, confessing the whole affair and adding that "the lasting evil" from the ordeal "was to learn to distrust my own heart and lose all faith in my power of knowing others."[122]

As she had after Davis jilted her, Fuller now experienced a crisis of the soul. "I have alluded to the fact," Waldo Emerson would later write, "that, in the summer of 1840, Margaret underwent some change in the tone and the direction of her thoughts, to which she attributed a high importance." According to him, this transformation "combined great happiness and pain for her affections."[123] Her emotions oscillated from one extreme to the next, and she soon began to experience something like religious mania, a state she described as one of "infinite loveliness," where everything was "radiant with faith, and love, and life."[124]

All this made her friends uncomfortable. William Henry Channing compared her to "a Bacchante, prompt for wild excitement," captive to "delirious mirth."[125] Waldo wrote that she "remained for some time in a sort of ecstatic solitude. There was a certain restlessness and fever, which I did not like should deceive a soul which was capable of greatness."[126] Rapt, euphoric, giddy—the heartbroken Fuller seemed, at least to her friends, on the edge of collapse.

She described the experience as a return home. "When we meet you will find me at home," she informed Caroline Sturgis. "Into that home cold winds may blow, keen lightnings dart their bolts, but I cannot be driven from it more."[127] To Waldo, she exclaimed, "But oh, I am now full of such sweet certainty, never never more can it be utterly shaken. All things have I given up to the central power, myself, you also; yet I cannot forbear adding, dear friend, I am now so at home."[128]

In a journal from the period, she observed, "I grow more and more what they call a mystic. Nothing interests me except listening for the *secret harmonies of nature*."[129] Employing the water imagery so often accompanying her descriptions of intense experience, she told Sturgis, "Rivers of life, seas surge between me and you."[130] Her language became increasingly exalted, increasingly obscure. In another letter to Sturgis, she wrote, "Of the mighty changes in my spiritual life I do not wish to speak, yet surely you cannot be ignorant of them.... All has been revealed, all foreshown yet I know it not. Experiment has given place to certainty, pride to obedience, thought to love, and truth is lost in beauty."[131] To Waldo, she boldly declared there would "come a purer mode of being even in the world of Form."[132]

This period of strained, exalted mood coincided with the pressures of editing *The Dial* and writing many of its articles. Compounding the stress were her preparations for the weekly Conversations. To William Henry Channing, she now described the physical toll her labors were taking and declared that she was "little more than an aspiration, which the ages will reward, by empowering me to incessant acts of vigorous beauty."[133] But the most draining circumstance of all was her relations with Waldo Emerson, which had begun to fray.

For some time, she had encouraged him to enter more deeply into their friendship. She had dared and cajoled him to share his deepest feelings with her. He resisted. Waldo had a wife and children, an extended family to look after. But he was also temperamentally unfit for the kind of intimacies Fuller craved. In his journal, he grumbled whenever she shared her disappointments: "On comes a gay dame of manners & tone so fine & haughty that all defer to her as to a countess, & she seems the dictator of society. Sit down by her, & talk of her own life in earnest, & she is some stricken soul with care & sorrow at her vitals."[134]

Annoyed by his reserve, Fuller lashed out, telling him she preferred to hear him lecture than to speak with him in person. "[T]he best of you is there," she accused him. Instead of taking offense, he reluctantly agreed. "Most of the persons whom I see in my own house I see across a gulf," he admitted. "I cannot go to them nor they come to me."[135] Shy, diffident, absorbed in his thoughts, he recognized and regretted his limitations. But he also accepted them.

Fuller could not. In the fall of 1840, after an especially frustrating visit to Concord, she told him: "How often have I said, this light will never understand my fire; this clear eye will never discern the law [with] which I am filling my circle; this simple force will never interpret my need of manifold being." His frosty reserve irked her, dredging up memories of her distant father. "[W]hen my soul, in its childish agony of prayer, stretched out its arms to you as a father," she told him, "did you not see what was meant by this crying for the moon...."[136] Similar complaints were lodged in the privacy of her journal. "Mr E. scarce knows the instincts, and uses them rather for rejection than reception where he uses at all." After four years of courting his favor, she had finally realized that in "friendship with R.W.E., I cannot hope to feel that I am his or he mine. He has nothing peculiar, nothing sacred for his friend. He is not to his friend a climate, an atmosphere...."[137] This critique, however accurate, reveals the extraordinarily high demands Fuller placed on her friendships. She wanted nothing less than a bond that was all-encompassing, exclusive.

Her disappointment reached a fever pitch in the middle of September 1840. Fuller and Waldo paid a visit to the newly engaged Anna Barker. On the way back home, in the privacy of their stagecoach, Fuller exploded. The substance of her accusations can be inferred from letters Waldo later wrote to Caroline Sturgis. Evidently, she condemned him for his "inhospitality of soul," his tendency to pontificate and muse rather than engage in heartfelt communication.[138] Waldo again took these charges seriously. As when Lydia confronted him with the horrors of slavery, he used Fuller's accusations as an opportunity for self-examination. "She & C[aroline Sturgis] would gladly be my friends," he wrote, rehashing the argument in his journal, "yet our intercourse is not friendship, but literary gossip. I count & weigh but do not love." He wished that this was not the case. Nothing in fact would "be so grateful to me as to melt once for all these icy barriers."[139] But he could not change the natural bent of his personality. To try was to betray the self, to betray his *philosophy* of the self.

Meanwhile, Fuller despaired. "Can no soul know me wholly," she asked, "shall I never know the deep delight of gratitude to any but the All-Knowing?"[140] She longed for a friend who understood and accepted her complex needs. And she believed she was uniquely able to understand and accept Waldo. "There is enough of me, could I but reveal it. Enough of woman to sympathize with all his feelings, enough of man to appreciate all thoughts. I could be a perfect friend, and it would make me a nobler person."[141]

She needed other people to grow. Experience had taught her that sharing thoughts and emotions enabled friends to enrich one another. She valued the solitude in which thoughts matured, but the prospect of a lifetime of seclusion felt to her like a prison. Part of this had to do with her tragic view of life. "We are, we shall be in this life mutilated beings," she once told Caroline Sturgis. To another friend, she confessed, "...I have lived to know that the secret of all things is pain and that Nature travaileth most painfully with her noblest product."[142]

Waldo refused to countenance either notion. Convinced that the self only grew in solitude, that it found itself best when others were absent, he also embraced a vision of perfection that disregarded life's heartrending events. Part of this was his response to personal losses, especially the death of his first wife, Ellen Tucker Emerson. But it was a credo he could not afford to relinquish. The flurry of letters he exchanged with Fuller in the fall of 1840—letters that oscillate between accusation, hurt feelings and tender rapprochement—ultimately founder on these different outlooks.

The argument in the stagecoach occurred a week before Sam Ward and Anna Barker's marriage. Fuller's period of spiritual exaltation would last almost another year. It ended one moonlit night in August 1841, while she visited Caroline Sturgis in Newport, Rhode Island. There Fuller had one of her more vivid dreams. She was in a liminal, twilight space, hovering between death and a "heavenly state" that put her in "intimate communion far more full" than any she had ever before experienced. Instead of feeling soothed, however, she was frightened. She no longer felt in control. "It made me shudder," she recalled, "for I seemed no more mine own. And yet it seemed some heavenly state that once let go might ne'er again return." A spirit appeared and offered her a cup filled with potion. To herself she thought: "O let this cup pass from me, yet not so[.] Wait but a moment I will drink it all and then come death."[143]

She awoke to the sound of the surf crashing against the cliffs below. Then she rose, wrapped herself in a shawl, and sat by the window, staying until dawn, watching the progress of the moon. She felt shriven, renewed. "[S]ome crisis in my life," she realized, "took place."[144] Years earlier, when she had wandered out of the church on Thanksgiving Day and found herself by a pool of water, she had realized "there was no self; that selfishness was all folly, . . . that I had only to live in the idea of the ALL, and all was mine." This time, there was no ALL to acquire—the self, *her* self, now felt truly obliterated.

Since her father's death, she had felt intensely divided. There was the need to earn a living for her family, the desire to leave a permanent mark on the world of literature. At the same time, she aspired toward a perfection of the self, including perfect friendship and love. These competing needs collided within her, raised her to an exalted pitch, then dashed her life like waves onto rock. Her requirements for friendship with Waldo, her attachments to Sam Ward and Anna Barker—these had been the demands of an insatiable ego. When those demands receded at last, they left her spent, exhausted.

Later, she considered the entire experience a form of madness. "Now that my mind is so calm and sweet," she told Elizabeth Hoar, "there seems to be no fire in me to resist or consume, and I can neither bear nor do what I could while much more sick, but am very weak. No doubt this finds its parallel in what we know of the great bodily strength of the insane."[145] And years later, while living abroad, she wrote Waldo to recall those "glorious hours, [when] angels certainly visited me." She was surprised that the feverish period had not transfigured her completely. "There must have been too much of earth,—too much taint of weakness and folly, so that baptism did not suffice."[146]

As it turned out, the moonlit baptism led to more earthly concerns. After the vigil in Newport, her life began to shift its orientation. From now on, she turned outward, not just to other people but to the larger events and circumstances that shaped them. She was beginning to move beyond transcendentalism.

9.

None of the women wanted the Conversations to end. When the first thirteen-week session was over, Fuller and the class determined to extend the series into spring. This time the discussions would be devoted to the "fine arts" (these were the talks that interested Sophia Peabody so much). Fuller announced she would "drop the Mythology, and begin again by dividing the universe into Poesy, Philosophy, Prose."[147] Here she was following Coleridge's definition of Poesy as a range of fine arts, including music, poetry, painting, sculpture, and theater.

Again, the discussions veered into topics concerning the participants' identity as women. If a meeting started with a discussion of music, it quickly shifted into questions about the rarity of women virtuosi. Why were there no women composers? Was there some fundamental—some *essential*—difference between men and women that made men ostensibly better at creating melody? It was during this second series of talks that Fuller asked "what... the distinction of feminine & masculine [was] when applied to character and mind"? She seems to have taken for granted that there *was* such a distinction. How else could one explain the radical differences in their respective destinies, the parceling out of "spheres," wherein one sex, from time immemorial, had been assigned private domestic work while the other sallied forth to earn money and acclaim and to make decisions of vital importance to the world?

What exactly had determined this seemingly immutable order of things? Was there some dark conspiracy against women, some plot to keep them from leaving the confines of domesticity? Was it a benign, if misguided and increasingly outmoded, scheme to protect a woman's natural modesty from public exposure? (Did women *have* natural modesty?) Were women—and this was the uneasy thought running just below the surface of the talks—poorly suited to create artistic masterpieces? For wasn't it true that young women were routinely taught piano and watercolors and still failed to produce worthwhile music or pictures? Even Sophia Peabody, who participated in these talks and whose copies of Italian landscapes were as finished as their originals, was hesitant about embarking on

Figure 61. Ellen Sturgis Hooper.

original work of her own. Why was it that so few young women had managed to leave the confines of these "polite" pursuits and to venture into more daring artistic expression?

Ellen Hooper was the first to answer (figure 61). She "thought women were instinctive—they had spontaneously what men have by study & induction." Others agreed. But they felt that this instinctiveness should be no reason for discrimination. After all, as one woman noted, possessing intuition and instinct was "said to be the distinction of poets among men."[148] But this brought the discussion back to the beginning. Why had women so far failed to achieve much in the annals of creativity?

Fuller was suddenly struck with a new thought. She recalled Child's statement from earlier that Minerva possessed qualities that were both masculine *and* feminine. If men and women each possessed instinctiveness, perhaps the difference lay in the combinations typical of each. Maybe, Fuller ventured, "the man & the woman had each every faculty & element of mind—but that they were combined in different proportions[,] that this was proved by the praise implied in the expression 'a courageous woman—a thoughtful woman—a reasonable woman. & on the other hand by the praise which we bestowed on men who to courage—intellect &c. added tenderness &c. &c."[149] Perhaps their peculiar mixture of faculties, Fuller posited, favored men when it came to the creation of art.

This comment stirred a barrage of comments. Someone asked whether a woman could embody the same characteristics as Napoleon. Yes, was the reply: Queen Elizabeth and Catherine the Great were examples. Was it possible, then, for "a man [to be] as Corinne" (De Staël's sibylline prophet)? Surely it was. Many of these ideas would eventually find their way into the pages of Fuller's *Woman in the Nineteenth Century*, as would the topics discussed in the following week, when one woman asked whether *any* quality existed that was specific to one sex? After thinking a moment, Fuller said no. This was a dramatic shift in her earlier position. A week before she had insisted that men and women were different in their capabilities. Now she believed each sex possessed every element of the other—"& therefore she wished to see if the others fully admitted this, because if all admitted it, it would follow of course that we should hear no more of repressing or subduing faculties because they were not fit for women to cultivate."[150]

A boisterous conversation ensued. The women asked why they had rollicked so buoyantly through life as girls, only to be brought down to earth as young women, shackled to conceptions of duty and destiny, wifehood and motherhood? Why had becoming an adult so often entailed the end, not the beginning, of possibilities? Why was so much ridicule directed toward intellectual women? And what was the point of educating women if they were forced to give up that education as soon as they were married?

Fuller asked each woman to write an essay about the differences between men and women. Only one of these was transcribed in full—that of a young woman named Sally Jackson Gardner, a friend of the Peabody sisters who lived in rural Newton. Each Wednesday, Gardner made the ten-mile journey to attend the Conversations. Unlike many of the other women, she was not particularly enthusiastic about the "new thought" of transcendentalism. She had once written Mary Peabody a scalding letter that expressed her surprise "at the unqualified approbation you say you have bestowed on Mr. Emerson. He is the sage and the enchanter of a few, but all our ministers are opposed to him, and the grave, sensible people who never hear him, think it necessary to their own character for staidness, &c, to pass him by on the other side."[151]

Yet Gardner took on Fuller's assignment with gusto. She not only tried to identify the differences between men and women but also used the exercise to answer Fuller's original questions from the previous autumn: "what were we born to do and how shall we do it?" "I recognise between man & woman," she began, "a necessary difference of position, of which results are accidental or arbitrary." Men and women occupied different positions because of their respective physical characteristics: men had greater strength, women could bear children.

Yet if these differences were a fact of life, their *results* were by no means natural or immutable. In fact, throughout "the world's history there are women who have set aside the accidents of position, & left their mark on the ages." These women proved "that reflection & the power of concentration in men exist in women, and only require a more earnest culture." Here Gardner was inching toward a critique of women's longstanding social conditioning. "Still *might* makes *right* & other remnants of barbarism linger amongst us," she admitted. She dreamed of another version of history, another possibility, one in which physical differences played no role in the way men and women were treated. "Let men & women be gentle & firm," she wrote; "brave & tender, instinctive but confirming their instincts by reason... let reflection preserve women from folly... forbid the apathy & self-indulgence which their physical condition induces, & bind on them the necessity of use, cultivate, elevate all that self-consciousness reveals to them, let them listen to their heart's dictates not fearing that they will lead them astray & we shall no longer hear of masculine women or effeminate men."[152]

Once prejudice ceased to exist, Gardner concluded, women would assume larger roles in world history. "How do we know that in the possible future," she asked, "woman's intellect may not manifest itself in forms as beautiful as poetry & art, permanent as empires, all emanating from her home—created out of it, from her relations as daughter, sister, wife, & mother?"[153] Not quite able to imagine circumstances in which a woman might step away from the bonds of domesticity, she nevertheless acknowledged that Fuller, Elizabeth Peabody, and other women in the Conversations were striving to create precisely such a life. Her essay hinted at a "possible future" of greater autonomy and respect for women.

You can almost picture the women in Elizabeth's bookshop discussing Gardner's essay. Some leaned forward to speak. Others silently mulled over the essay's implications. At some point, Fuller told them she believed it was the duty of every human to strive after perfection. "The young soul true to itself, desired—*demanded* in its unfoldings the *Universe*—it wanted to reform society—to know every thing—to beautify every thing & to have a perfect friend." If this was not always possible, there was no reason for despair. The courageous soul, she said, "accepted the limitation &... trusted that it *may* be what it is not..."[154] Others joined in at this point, asking questions, raising objections. The talk moved from topic to topic, circled back on itself, set out in unexpected directions. On and on the women continued, pulling threads of conversation from the tapestry of their lives, pursuing thoughts wherever they led, encouraging, challenging, inspiring one another.

10.

The year 1842 was one of endings. In the spring, Fuller gave up the editorship of *The Dial*. Tired and overworked, she continued to suffer from headaches that had begun after her father's death. Adding insult to injury, she had yet to be paid. (The magazine, groundbreaking in so many ways, never turned a profit.) As with her stint at Alcott's Temple School, she had unwillingly volunteered her time and talent. When the original publishers of the journal went bankrupt, she and Waldo cast about for new ones. From January 1842 until July 1843, *The Dial* would be published by Elizabeth Peabody.

Other endings were sharper, more painful. That summer, Fuller visited Concord, where she found Lydia and Waldo still in deep mourning for their son. She, too, felt the sting of the boy's death. "I have loved one little boy so long and so well," she told an acquaintance, "that I have some idea of what the second life may be."[155] She had enjoyed carrying the little boy around the lawn, pointing out birds and flowers. The grief pervading the household was as thick and impenetrable as fog on the Concord River.

Then, toward the end of the year, and in a mood of profound melancholy, she wrote a letter to her old flame, George T. Davis, now an established lawyer and the owner of a small-town newspaper. Davis was married, the father of several children and, like her own father, a state legislator. "I have thought of you many times," Fuller wrote, "since we parted on that dreary night in that dreary street." The end of their relationship had set into motion a cycle of moods that now seemed the rhythmic pulse of her life. At first, there was black, despairing depression, followed by spiritual rapture. These were followed by an uneasy calm. The pattern had repeated itself with the marriage of Sam and Anna Ward.

Now, in a fragile, tentative mood, she asked Davis for a favor. The next time he was in Boston, she hoped he would bring his "children as you promised and show me. I love to know these new lives in which my friends bloom again." Then she made a surprising admission: "the darkest hue in my own lot is that I have neither children, nor yet am the parent of beautiful works by which the thought of my life might be represented to another generation."[156]

It would be several years before she became a mother, but her first "beautiful work," the child of her mind, appeared the following spring, in 1843. That was when Fuller began a long essay called "The Great Lawsuit. Man *versus* Men; Woman *versus* Women," which marks an important breakthrough in the history of American feminism. If the unwieldy title gestures toward her father's profession, there is nothing legalistic about the piece. Demanding and erudite, the work is more conversation than lawyer's brief. Fuller's writing, densely allusive, fearlessly improvisatory, is like the flight of a bird, alighting from topic to topic—precisely the sort of sustained, restless riffing her discussion group had grown accustomed to. As she would later explain, the title referred to "the fact that, while it is the destiny of Man, in the course of the ages, to ascertain and fulfill the law of his being…, the action of prejudices and passions which attend…the growth of the individual, is continually obstructing the holy work that is to make the earth a part of heaven." Lest her readers misunderstand her use of the masculine pronoun, she added: "By Man I mean both man and woman; these are the two halves of one thought."[157]

This idea had emerged from the Conversations held in Elizabeth Peabody's bookshop. The same could be said for much of the essay. When Fuller claimed that "Shelley, who, like all men of genius, shared the feminine development," she was repeating an insight from the Conversations.[158] An even more important

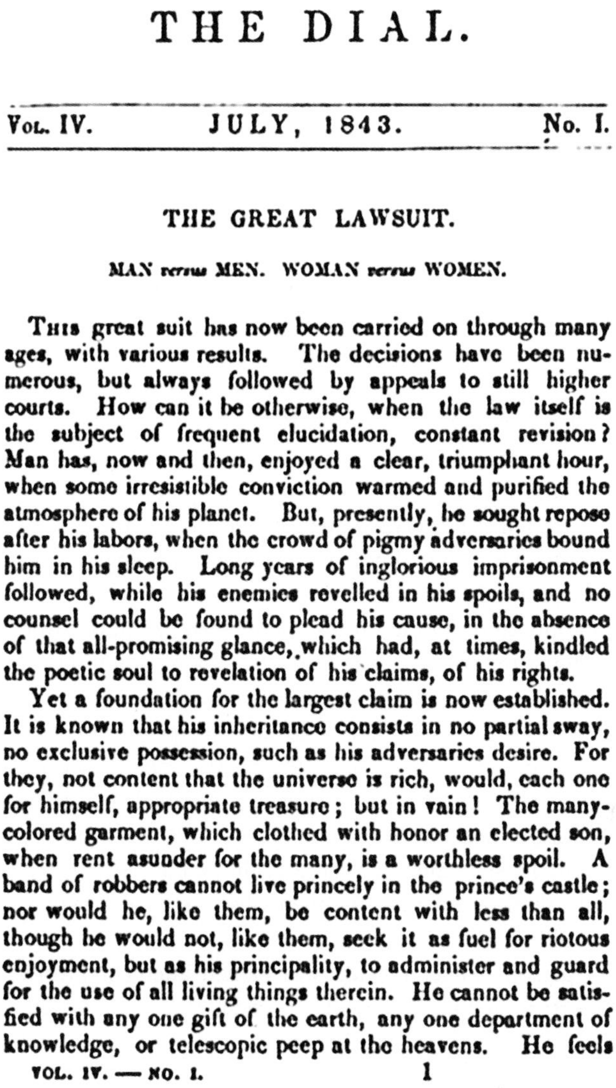

THE DIAL.

Vol. IV. JULY, 1843. No. I.

THE GREAT LAWSUIT.

MAN *versus* MEN. WOMAN *versus* WOMEN.

This great suit has now been carried on through many ages, with various results. The decisions have been numerous, but always followed by appeals to still higher courts. How can it be otherwise, when the law itself is the subject of frequent elucidation, constant revision? Man has, now and then, enjoyed a clear, triumphant hour, when some irresistible conviction warmed and purified the atmosphere of his planet. But, presently, he sought repose after his labors, when the crowd of pigmy adversaries bound him in his sleep. Long years of inglorious imprisonment followed, while his enemies revelled in his spoils, and no counsel could be found to plead his cause, in the absence of that all-promising glance, which had, at times, kindled the poetic soul to revelation of his claims, of his rights.

Yet a foundation for the largest claim is now established. It is known that his inheritance consists in no partial sway, no exclusive possession, such as his adversaries desire. For they, not content that the universe is rich, would, each one for himself, appropriate treasure; but in vain! The many-colored garment, which clothed with honor an elected son, when rent asunder for the many, is a worthless spoil. A band of robbers cannot live princely in the prince's castle; nor would he, like them, be content with less than all, though he would not, like them, seek it as fuel for riotous enjoyment, but as his principality, to administer and guard for the use of all living things therein. He cannot be satisfied with any one gift of the earth, any one department of knowledge, or telescopic peep at the heavens. He feels

VOL. IV. — NO. I. 1

Figure 62. The Great Lawsuit.

aspect of the essay stemmed from Child's idea that men and women shared the same characteristics. "Male and female represent the two sides of the great radical dualism," Fuller wrote in "The Great Lawsuit." Masculinity and femininity were "perpetually passing into one another. Fluid hardens to solid, solid rushes to fluid. There is no wholly masculine man, no purely feminine woman"[159] (figure 62).

Fuller's central focus was on the obstacles that prevented female happiness and fulfillment. As she stated early in the essay, "What woman needs is not as a woman to act or rule, but as a nature to grow, as an intellect to discern, as a soul to live freely and unimpeded, to unfold such powers as were given her when we left our common home."[160] Domestic space was both a metaphor and a contested realm throughout the essay. Fuller complained that the "current opinion" of home that influenced most women's lives was the "belief that she must marry, if it be only to find a protector, and a home of her own."[161] She was thinking of Lydia Emerson here, and possibly the newly married Sophia Peabody, both of whom sacrificed much of their own lives to marriage.

This arrangement, Fuller declared, was utilitarian, unpoetic. "The man furnishes the house, the woman regulates it."[162] The problem with domesticity was that it deprived women of their right to grow and develop. Now Fuller imagined a "higher grade of marriage," one in which "home sympathies, and household wisdom" enabled each partner to "know how to assist one another to carry their burdens along the dusty way."[163]

Throughout the essay, Fuller presented her opinions in the voices of two personae. The first was Minerva, a central character in the first Conversations. Minerva partook "of the Masculine" qualities of intellect: logic and rationalism. In "The Great Lawsuit," Fuller was less interested in Minerva's intellect than in placing her in opposition to the Muses, those Greek goddesses who inspired the creation of literature, science, and the arts. A long tradition already existed whereby women served as muses for male artists. Passive, beautiful handmaids to creation, they inspired the composer to song, the painter to portraiture. Fuller wanted to upset this dynamic. Unlike the Muse, whose "especial genius" was "electrical in movement, intuitive in function, spiritual in tendency," Minerva excelled in "classification, or recreation" (she meant creative activity).[164] Fuller believed that she herself embodied these qualities, but her larger point was that women should think and create for themselves—should imagine their role as producers of culture.

The other persona Fuller created was named after her favorite heroine in Shakespeare. Assuming the guise of Miranda, the shipwrecked daughter of Prospero in *The Tempest*, Fuller now drew on her complex relationship with Timothy Fuller. In "The Great Lawsuit," Miranda "was the eldest child, and came to [her father] at an age when he needed a companion." Fuller does not allude to her father's rigid expectations; rather, she says that Miranda's father "addressed her not as a plaything, but a living mind." Her head "was to him the temple of immortal intellect. He respected his child, however, too much to be an indulgent parent." Given her unusual upbringing, Miranda "was early led to feel herself a child of the spirit," a young woman whose inner confidence, cultivated by her father, had left her "securely anchored" in life.

"And yet we must admit that I have been fortunate," Miranda admitted, "and this should not be." The assured independence she received from her father was considered a flaw in most women—a situation Miranda blamed on male prejudice. "[E]arly I perceived that men never, in any extreme of despair, wished to be women," Miranda says. "Where they admired any woman they were inclined to speak of her as above her sex... It is well known that of every strong woman they say she has a masculine mind."[165]

The voice of Miranda—confident, judicious, wise—enabled Fuller to explore social structures that were oppressive to women. Here she began to shift her argument away from the transcendentalist focus on self-culture and more toward a critique of social ills that subjugated women. She compared the plight of women to that of enslaved people, saying, "If the negro be a soul, if the woman be a soul, apparelled in flesh, to one Master only are they accountable." If her emphasis remained on the need for inner development, in "The Great Lawsuit" she increasingly found external impediments to that development. "It is not surprising that it should be the Anti-Slavery party that pleads for women," she observed, "when we consider merely that she does not hold property on equal terms with men; so that, if a husband dies without a will, the wife, instead of stepping at once into his place as head of the family, inherits only a part of his fortune, as if she were a child, or ward only, not an equal partner."[166] She condemned her society's belief that intellect was allotted to women "in a much lower degree," and railed against traditions that limited a daughter's education because it wanted them "to have a sphere and a home," or that understood marriage as an arrangement of property, a *possession* of another. And she countered these misguided assumptions with a vision of the future that released untapped potential: "We would have every path laid open to woman as freely as to man. Were this done, and a slight temporary fermentation allowed to subside, we believe that the Divine would ascend into nature to a height unknown in the history of past ages, and nature, thus instructed, would regulate the spheres not only so as to avoid collision, but to bring forth ravishing harmony."[167]

Fuller had long felt trapped between two competing impulses. One was the desire to express herself freely, to speak to an audience as an artist and critic. The other was a longing for love and home. If one had been spurred by her father's ambition, the other was a social ideal she could never entirely resist. While writing "The Great Lawsuit," she discovered that it was not her fault she had so far been unable to accomplish either goal. She no longer needed to blame herself. The problem was outside, broader than the individual. It would require a dramatic reorientation.

11.

"What do you think of the speech which Queen Margaret has made from the throne? It seems to me that if she were married truly, she would no longer be puzzled about the rights of woman." These words were written by a woman who had once worshipfully attended Fuller's Conversations and had even praised her in a poem. Sophia Peabody Hawthorne had been married to Nathaniel Hawthorne for a year now. Her opinion of Fuller had obviously changed. She was writing to her mother, Eliza Peabody, now sixty-five, who in her youth had written poems celebrating the abilities of women in the new republic.

Sophia declared that Fuller's essay on women's rights was the result of inexperience. Marriage was "the revelation of woman's true destiny and place, which never can be *imagined* by those who do not experience the relation. In perfect, high union there is no question of supremacy. Souls are equal in love and intelligent communion, and all things take their proper places as inevitably as the stars their orbits." Sophia admitted that many marriages were deeply flawed—the product of lesser emotions, baser motivations. "Had there never been false and profane marriages, there would not only be no commotion about woman's rights, but it would be Heaven here at once."

She was basically making the same argument as Fuller in "The Great Lawsuit." Equitable marriages—marriages founded upon "love and intelligent communion"—entailed no subservience. A woman sacrificed neither her freedom nor her will in such a relationship. Fuller had simply argued that such marriages were rare—and that most women would be better off remaining celibate than entering an unfulfilling union. Even if Sophia agreed in principle, her comments signaled a new conservatism in her thinking. That conservatism is best seen as a compensatory rationalization for the way her life had gone, an enthusiastic embrace of that which she had once considered a constraint.

"Even before I was married," she continued, "I could never feel the slightest interest in this movement. It then seemed to me that each woman could make her own sphere quietly, and also it was always a shock to me to have women mount the rostrum. Home, I think, is the great arena for women, and there, I am sure, she can wield a power which no king or conqueror can cope with." Sophia was revising her own personal history here. She had, after all, once announced her intention never to marry. But her comments illustrate the difficulties that continued to plague her as an artist. Having internalized standards of female modesty, she felt acute discomfort entering the predominantly male realm of painting.

Her mother's response to "The Great Lawsuit" was more nuanced. "Seems to me I could have written on the very same subjects," she replied, "and set forth as strongly what rights yet belonged to woman which were not granted her, and yet have used language less offensive to delicacy, and put it in clearer view the only source (vital religion) from which her true position in society can be estimated." Eliza was much in agreement with "The Great Lawsuit." Her complaint was about Fuller's tone, which she found unladylike. And her own experiences as wife and mother had tempered any expectations she had for the rapid improvement of women's lot. "I believe that woman must wait till the lion shall lie down with the lamb," she told Sophia, "before she can hope to be the friend and companion of man. He has the physical power, as well as the conventional, to treat her like a plaything or a slave, and will exercise that power till his own soul is elevated. . . ." Like Fuller, Eliza believed the problem of women's rights could only be addressed when both sexes reached their full potential as divinely created humans.

She was more charitable toward Fuller's work than her youngest daughter. Yet she found much to criticize in the style of Fuller's book. "How is it that one who talks so admirably should write so obscurely? The book has great faults, . . . yet it is full of noble thoughts and high aspirations. I wish it may do good, but I believe little that is high and ennobling can have other foundation than genuine Christianity."[168]

Other readers had difficulty with Fuller's style, as well, including the great English prose stylist, George Eliot. Fuller's mind, she wrote, at least as it appeared in her essay, was precisely "like some regions of her own American continent, where you are constantly stepping from the sunny 'clearings' into the mysterious twilight of the tangled forest." The author's sentences shifted with no warning from "forcible reasoning" to "dreamy vagueness." But Eliot, a woman who obscured her identity behind a pseudonym and lived with a married man who could not obtain a divorce, was sympathetic to the cross-currents of prejudice that made it difficult to even *speak* of women's rights. "On one side we hear that woman's position can never be improved until women themselves are better," Eliot observed, "and, on the other, that women can never become better until their position is improved—until the laws are made more just, and a wider field opened to feminine activity."[169] Fuller's difficult style was an effort to navigate these countervailing attitudes, to show that women *were* capable of improvement even as they imagined a society where such efforts were unnecessary.

Not everyone saw it that way. Some bristled at the high-culture training presupposed by Fuller's essay, including the anonymous author of an 1853 serialized novel entitled *Stray Leaves from a Seamstress's Journal*. Lucy Vernon, the working-class heroine who embodies a proto-feminist ideal of the independent woman, says of Fuller: "She is the child of genius, and as such must be an idealist; a veil is between her and the rude, practical, every-day working world." Vernon wishes Fuller could only "come into our attics, our cheerless, comfortless homes, where there is nothing beautiful"—*then* she would see "how difficult, how almost impossible is self development where there is only the means of keeping soul and body together."[170]

Many in Fuller's circle saw past these difficulties, recognizing the importance of the essay. In 1859, one of Fuller's youngest acolytes, Caroline Healey Dall, claimed "The Great Lawsuit" had "stated with transcendent force the argument which formed the basis of the first 'Woman's Rights Convention' in 1848."[171] Dall was referring to the Seneca Falls Convention, organized by Elizabeth Cady Stanton and widely considered the founding event of the woman's rights movement. That gathering, and the movement that resulted, had its roots, Dall insisted, in Fuller's visionary manifesto.

In Concord, Waldo Emerson wrote to express his appreciation. Back when she was writing the essay, he had informed her that Sam and Anna Ward had a new baby. "Though no son," he added, "yet a sacred event." Fuller snapped back: "Why is not the advent of a daughter as 'sacred' a fact as that of a son. I do believe, O Waldo, most unteachable of men, that you are at heart a sinner on this point."[172] Now the sinner had repented—sort of. Speaking of "The Great Lawsuit," he said, "I think the piece very proper & noble, and itself quite an important fact in the history of Woman; good for its wit, excellent for its character." He especially appreciated the essay's potential to change minds: "It will teach us to revise our habits of thinking on this head."[173]

Other male friends agreed. Theodore Parker considered Fuller's essay "the best piece that has seen the light in the Dial," and Thoreau was equally complimentary: "Miss F's is a noble piece," he wrote Lydia and Waldo, "rich extempore writing, talking with pen in hand."[174] But it was another appreciative reader, this time a woman, who soon altered the course of Fuller's life. Mary Greeley was an arresting, round-faced young suffragette with enormous dark eyes. Greeley had for a while attended the Conversations, making the trip from her home in New York to Boston. Before her marriage, she had been a schoolteacher in North Carolina. An advocate for numerous reform movements—she followed a strict Grahamite diet, refused to wear clothing made from animals, and was a ferocious abolitionist—she ardently wished to improve the world. In later years, when she was constantly pregnant and grief-stricken by the death of her children, she became obsessed with spiritualism, convinced that her youngest surviving son was a medium with direct access to spirits from the afterlife (figure 63).

Her husband, Horace Greeley, also wanted to change the world, but he wanted to do it with words. Nine years earlier, Greeley had founded a daily newspaper, the *New-York Tribune*, promising his readers a "new morning Journal of Politics, Literature, and General Intelligence." The newspaper quickly became the leading vehicle for progressive thought, promoting Fourierism, abolitionism, vegetarianism. It introduced the writings of Waldo Emerson and Henry David Thoreau to an audience beyond the parochial borders of New England.

Although unhappily married, Mary and Horace Greeley agreed on many things, including the significance of "The Great Lawsuit." Mary had long ago convinced her husband of Fuller's brilliance. Now she impressed upon him the issue of *The Dial* containing her essay on women's rights. "[T]here is but one woman in America who could have written it," Horace Greeley said soon after reading the work.[175] He was determined to hire her for his newspaper.

Figure 63. The Greeley family at home.

12.

Not long after Fuller agreed to become the first woman literary editor for a major newspaper, her nightmares returned. "Visions come to haunt me," she wrote in her journal on October 14, 1844.[176] The dream in which her mother died returned. Another one, vivid and harrowing, involved her friend Caroline Sturgis, who was drowning. Fuller stood on the shore, feet planted in the earth, unable to move, to take a step, completely powerless as Caroline sunk into the water. "Three times," Emily Dickinson would write, "'tis said, a sinking man/Comes up to face the skies,"

> And then declines forever
> To that abhorred abode[177]

The dreams were prompted by change and uncertainty. After completing "The Great Lawsuit," Fuller's life seemed to accelerate and expand, as though a pent-up body of water had suddenly burst its dam. Soon after finishing the essay, she traveled with James and Sarah Clarke to what was then considered the far west: Illinois, Michigan, and Wisconsin. Along the way she visited Niagara Falls—a longstanding dream—and hiked the bluffs overlooking Lake Michigan. She visited frontier settlements, rejoicing that the women "do not suffer as our Eastern women do; they have, for the most part, been brought up to work in the open air and have better constitutions . . . ."[178] More dispiriting was Chicago, a town that seemed wholly given up to the spirit of materialism and a "merely instinctive existence."[179]

Fuller was particularly drawn to the native peoples she encountered, painfully aware that white culture's westward expansion had impoverished their lives. To her brother Richard, she wrote, "It is only five years since the poor Indians have been dispossessed of this region of sumptuous loveliness, such as can hardly be paralleled in the world. No wonder they poured out their blood freely before they would go."[180] Sometimes she employed the shopworn trope of the "vanishing Indian," but more often she labored to understand the lives and customs of the indigenous peoples. She visited a Chippewa burying ground, canoed with natives around Mackinac Island, even tended a child stricken with smallpox. She was deeply moved by her encounters, especially with those involving women, toward whom she had initially felt repulsion before gaining an appreciation of their "ladylike precision." If she admired the hardy settler women, she was equally taken with the manners of the Indians.

These experiences would soon be published in her first original book, *Summer on the Lakes*, a hybrid work of travel narrative, ethnographic study, interpolated stories, and occasional philosophical musings (figure 64). To research the work, she sought permission to use Harvard's library—becoming the first woman to gain admission to the college's collection of books. Thomas Wentworth Higginson, who eventually became Fuller's biographer (and the man who helped bring Emily

Figure 64. Sarah Clarke Freeman's illustration from *Summer on the Lakes*.

Dickinson's poetry to light), was a student at Harvard then, and he later recalled Fuller sitting in the library's reading room, "day after day, under the covert gaze of the undergraduates who had never before looked upon a woman reading within those sacred precincts."[181]

The proofs for *Summer* were finished on her thirty-fourth birthday: May 23, 1844. Several months later, she paid her last visit to Concord, this time varying her routine and spending time with the Hawthornes as well as the Emersons. In the creaking old parsonage where Mary Moody Emerson had lived until age three, Fuller rose early and walked along the Concord River. "[I]t was so pleasant to be in the old house with its avenue of whispering trees," she wrote. "The orchard sloping down to the river's bank is delightful, and two hills are near which command the best prospects."[182]

New life was everywhere. "It is at present the world of infants," she wrote a friend, referring to the transcendental baby boom occurring in the village.[183] Hawthorne had recently become the parents of Una. Fuller's sister, Ellen, who lived just outside Concord with her erratic poet-husband Ellery Channing, had given birth to a daughter, Greta, who was named in honor of her increasingly well-known aunt and who had been born on Fuller's birthday.

Always fond of infants, she now found herself surrounded by them, their faces sweet-smelling, animated, miraculous. But their presence posed interesting questions. "How entirely dissimilar that baby-boy I saw yesterday in every act and attitude from Una and Greta," Fuller wrote in her journal, referring to Edward Emerson. "And yet where lies this difference betwixt male and female? I cannot trace it... How all but infinite the mystery by which sex is stamped in the germ." The distinctions between men and women continued to preoccupy her, now more than ever as she began to revise "The Great Lawsuit" while in Concord. Mulling over her interactions with the infants of her friends, she was struck by the mysterious, ineffable differences she observed between male and female babies. (She seems not to have considered that the infants' behavior may have been conditioned by the way they were treated by their parents.) "By what modification of thought is this caused?" she asked herself. "Impossible to trace; here am I the child of masculine energy & Eugene [her brother] of feminine loveliness, & so in many other families."[184]

The question was still in her mind that October, when she became interested in the female penitentiary in Ossining, New York. By this time, Fuller had made up her mind to accept Horace Greeley's offer to work at the *Tribune*. Early in the month, she stopped at his home on the remote east side of Manhattan to cement the deal, then traveled sixty miles north along the Hudson River to work on expanding "The Great Lawsuit" into a book. Nearby was Mount Pleasant, the women's portion of Sing Sing Prison, where one of Fuller's friends, Georgianna Bruce, had recently taken a position as an assistant to the warden.

With the instincts of a born reporter, Fuller began interrogating this new source of information. "You say few of these women have any feelings about chastity," she wrote Bruce. "Do you know how they regard that part of the sex, who are reputed chaste? Do they see any reality in it; or look on it merely as a circumstance of condition, like the possession of fine clothes?"[185] These were not prurient questions. In "The Great Lawsuit," Fuller had alluded to the familiar notion that men were naturally more lustful than women and therefore less in control of their moral and physical selves. The overwhelming number of prostitutes in cities such as Boston, New York, and Philadelphia were the tangible result of this belief. Now she wanted to explore the human toll that accompanied this double standard. Bruce dutifully questioned one of her prisoners, who replied that "everybody in the world knew that promiscuity was wicked," but "if no one knew, you did not seem a bit different from anybody else. In fact, you did not stop to think of yourself at all."[186]

Late in October, Fuller visited the women in Mt. Pleasant prison and spoke to them about their experiences. (About the trip, her journal for Sunday, October 27 simply says: "I need not rememorate: it is all inscribed on my brain, a theme for long instruction.") These interactions would inform the second half of *Woman in the Nineteenth Century*, the book that emerged from Fuller's essay in *The Dial*. In it, she extended her analysis of the double standard that allowed men to seek sexual gratification from women who could be imprisoned for the act. She now saw that what was often considered a necessary evil—an unfortunate accident of biology—was in fact a societal evil, deliberately unfair and hypocritical. Speaking on behalf of the women at Mount Pleasant, she raged at men who were "incapable of pure marriage; incapable of pure parentage; incapable of worship; oh wretched men, your sin is its own punishment!"[187]

Fuller made another substantial addition to her essay. For a dozen or more pages, she described celibacy as a form of resistance to the unfair sexual economy which resulted in prostitution. She may have had in mind Mary Moody Emerson and Elizabeth Palmer Peabody, women who had made conscious decisions to remain outside the marriage market. "In this regard of self-dependence," she wrote, "and a greater simplicity and fulness of being, we must hail as a preliminary the increase of the class contemptuously designated an old maid."[188] Marriage might be "the natural means of forming a sphere, of taking root on the earth," Fuller continued, echoing Waldo's essay on "Love," but she admired those women who had found alternative ways to contribute to society, women like Aunt Mary, who served as "spiritual parents" for their nephews and nieces.

A final addition to the original essay was its rousing conclusion. "I think women need," Fuller proclaimed, "especially at this juncture, a much greater range of occupation than they have, to rouse their latent powers." Only when society's arbitrary barriers were torn down once and for all would the world see what women were truly capable of. And for those who still insisted that certain spheres of activity were unfit for women, she had a message: "[I]f you ask me what offices they fill; I reply—any. I do not care what case you put; let them be sea-captains, if you will. I do not doubt there are women well fitted for such an office, and, if so, I should be glad to see them in it...."[189]

Concluding in this triumphant tone, she finished the book in November 1844. As she explained to her friend William Henry Channing, at last she felt as though she had accomplished something worthy of her early promise. The last day of writing remained a fever dream: "After taking a long walk early on one of the most noble exhilarating sort of mornings I sat down to write and did not put the last stroke till near nine in the evening. Then I felt a delightful glow as if I had put a good deal of my true life in it, as if, suppose I went away now, the measure of my foot-print would be left on earth."[190]

She had little time to revel in her accomplishment, however. By the time she finished *Woman in the Nineteenth Century*, Fuller was preparing to move to New York. In November she said farewell to New England—her birthplace, her training ground, her point of reference—for good. But for brief visits home, she would never return. By happenstance, the last person who saw her in Boston was Eliza Peabody. White-haired, careworn, the woman who had raised three remarkable daughters broke into a broad smile when she saw Fuller, "nodding adieux," as Fuller later told her brother, "to the 'darling,' as she addressed me."[191]

13.

During the eighteen months that she lived and worked in New York, Fuller published two books and wrote an astonishing number of essays—roughly two hundred and fifty—for Horace Greeley's *Tribune*. Her achievement as the first woman newspaper reporter cannot be overstated. Years earlier, Mary Moody Emerson had longed to write for her brother's *Monthly Anthology*; Elizabeth Peabody had gotten closer to this ideal, publishing occasional essays on religion and education, as well as translations of French books and history primers. But it was Fuller who at last achieved a career as a working writer. She served as the newspaper's cultural and literary critic, writing on topics that ranged from New York's social ills to the latest books from home and abroad.

The city's frenetic artistic culture appealed to her. During her first year at the newspaper, she lived with Horace and Mary Greeley in their secluded home on Turtle Bay. But she was invariably drawn to Manhattan's teeming streets, its crush of humanity, the crowded thoroughfare of Broadway running like an artery down the island, its sidewalks filled with art galleries, concert halls, and popular amusements such as P. T. Barnum's Museum. Fuller immersed herself in the theater of New York street life, becoming an astute observer of public behavior. She visited art exhibits, attended concerts of Beethoven or Italian opera, and regularly appeared at literary soirees. She also launched an ambitious tour of what she called "the Institutions here of a remedial and benevolent kind."[192]

Increasingly she felt destined for greatness. Every age produced "*a few* in whose lot the meaning of the age is concentrated," she confided to a friend. "I feel that I am one of those persons in my age and sex. I feel *chosen among women.* I have deep mystic feelings in myself and intimations from elsewhere."[193] Adding to her confidence was not just her new role at the *Tribune* but five years of Conversations and the publication of "The Great Lawsuit" and *Woman in the Nineteenth Century.*

New England was not the only thing she left behind. She also abandoned transcendentalism. She would stay in contact with Waldo Emerson—her first newspaper review was of his writings—and other friends associated with the movement. But she now questioned the core tenets animating these thinkers, more and more considering them parochial and quaint. Observations of the devastated Native peoples in Wisconsin as well as interviews with the women at Sing Sing called into question her transcendentalist belief in progressive history. Her longstanding inclination toward a tragic view of life flourished as New York's gritty street life forced her to replace idealism with more pragmatic concerns.

Beside the review of Waldo's *Essays: Second Series*, she wrote pieces on Child's *Letters from New-York*, Poe's *Tales* and *The Raven and other Poems*, Frederick Douglass's autobiography, Hawthorne's *Mosses from an Old Manse*, the poetry of Shelley and Browning, George Sand's *Consuelo*, and countless lesser-known works. Her social criticism included a long essay on the "Asylum for Discharged Female Convicts," descriptions of visits to almshouses and mental asylums, a consideration of the Irish immigrants flooding the city, and polemics on slavery and abolition. She reviewed the singer Jinny Lind, the violinist Ole Bull; she discussed learning languages and the U.S. Exploration Expedition; she wrote observational essays about Thanksgiving and New Year's Day.

In "The Wrongs of American Women. The Duty of American Women," Fuller observed, "Much has been written about Woman's keeping within her sphere, which is defined as the domestic sphere." But this overlooked a crucial fact—"that a vast proportion of the sex, if not the better half, do not, cannot have this domestic sphere." Parents and guardians died, husbands proved poor breadwinners. Many women had to enter the workforce. Moreover, women were endowed with searching minds, with restless spirits that quickly outstripped the enclosing walls of domesticity. Fuller imagined a time when women might serve as physicians and ministers, but in the present moment she encouraged them to consider teaching, "the aim of all education [being] to rouse the mind to action, show it the means of discipline and of information..."[194]

In Manhattan she quickly found herself surrounded by a less ethereal group of writers than her New England coterie. Known as the Young Americans, these writers looked askance at the wispy pronouncements of transcendentalism, instead devoting their energies to the building of a national literature. She also discovered the literary salon of Anne Lynch, situated at 116 Waverly Place, a more worldly substitute for Elizabeth Peabody's bookshop. Lynch, a schoolteacher and sculptor whose social world had blossomed when she befriended the actress Fanny Kemble, hosted weekly gatherings of writers and other artists. Guests included Horace Greeley, Herman Melville, Evert Duycinck, and a pale, genteel Southerner named Edgar Allan Poe, who first read "The Raven" at one of Lynch's weekly gatherings and who was counted on to write the best Valentine verses during February.

Poe could be cutting when it came to Fuller. He once declared that humanity was divided between men, women, and Margaret Fuller. But he also respected her talent, and he left for posterity one of the most vibrant portraits of her ever written. It appeared in his series of articles entitled "The Literati of New York," which ran throughout 1846 in *Godey's Magazine and Lady's Book.* "She is of medium height," Poe wrote,

> nothing remarkable about the figure; a profusion of lustrous light hair; eyes a bluish gray, full of fire; capacious forehead; the mouth when in repose indicates profound sensibility, capacity for affection, for love—when moved by a light smile, it becomes even beautiful in the intensity of this expression; but the upper lip, as if impelled by the action of a sneer. Imagine now, a person of this description looking at you at one moment earnestly in the face, at the next seeming to look only with her own spirit or at the wall; moving nervously every now and then in her chair; speaking in a high key, but musically, deliberately, (not hurriedly or loudly,) with a delicious distinctness of enunciation.[195] (See figure 65.)

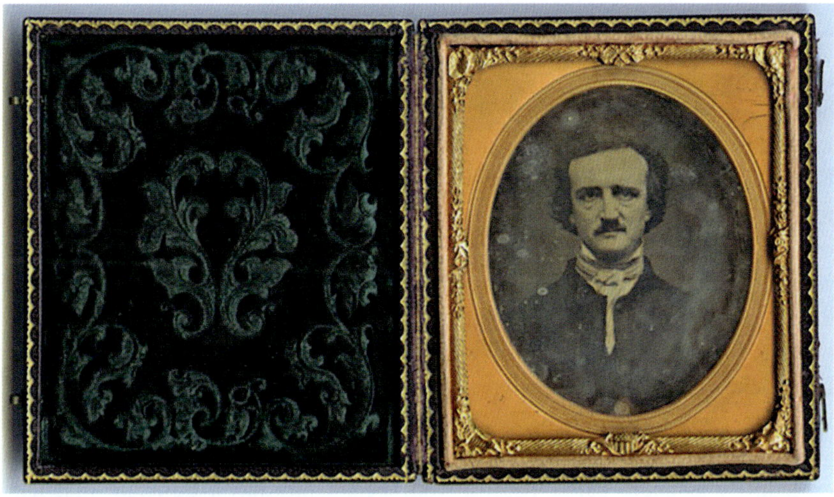

Figure 65. Edgar Allan Poe.

Poe's depiction suggests just how quickly Fuller had conquered New York. In its recognition of her "capacity for affection, for love," the portrait also alludes to another fact of her Manhattan life: her love affair with a German-Jewish banker she met at Anne Lynch's salon during a New Year's party. James Nathan had dark hair, a thick, hedgy beard, and brown, soulful eyes. He harbored aspirations to become a writer. He was a member of Manhattan's swelling immigrant population, having arrived from Hamburg as a teenager and, like some character in the novels soon to be published by Horatio Alger, risen from the rag trade to a respectable position on Wall Street. Fuller and Nathan shared a fondness for German literature and music, especially Goethe. But something besides his cultured reading and native German attracted her—he made her feel, she told him, "at home on earth."[196]

In the coming months, the two saw each other almost every day. They attended concerts, strolled down Broadway, met at evening sessions of the mesmerist Theodore Leger, who in the following year would write his popular book, *Animal Magnetism, or Psychodunamy.* (Leger treated Fuller for spinal pain.) Nathan sometimes visited Fuller at the Greeleys' house, even leaving his guitar and dog there when he traveled on business. When they weren't together, they exchanged dozens of letters, and while Fuller later destroyed Nathan's correspondence, he kept her letters. In them, she called him her "beloved," "mein liebst"; their love, she wrote, could never "be violated and may grow into what it will." Much as she had with George Davis and Sam Ward, she fell quickly, impetuously, headlong in love. This time she gladly sacrificed her autonomy. "I am with you as never with anyone," she told him. "I like to be quite still and have you the actor and the voice."[197] Another time, she wrote, "I hear you with awe assert the power over me and feel it to be true."[198]

But within a few months, Fuller discovered that Nathan was involved with an "English maiden" whom he had conveniently neglected to mention. Fuller confronted him about the woman, who was almost certainly his mistress, and was told he was merely rehabilitating a "fallen" acquaintance. (He evidently had read Fuller's writings in defense of such women.) "Could the heart of woman," wrote Fuller, desperately needing to believe Nathan's explanation, "refuse its sympathy to this earnestness in behalf of the injured woman?"[199]

Then, a week later, in April 1845, Nathan made a sexual overture to Fuller. She was deeply shaken. "Yesterday was, perhaps, a sadder day than I have had in all my life," she wrote him, feeling as though "some ill demon... had exposed [me] to what was to every worldly and womanly feeling so insulting. Neither could I reconcile myself to your having such thoughts, and just when you had induced me to trust you so absolutely."

She tried to sort out her feelings: "When you approached me so nearly, I was exceedingly agitated, partly because your personality has a powerful magnetic effect on me, partly because I had always attached importance to such an act, and it was asked of me so as to make me conscious, and suddenly, partly because this seemed the moment to express all I had felt for you, but I could not."[200]

She did not end the relationship. The two continued their correspondence and attended events in the city. When Nathan suddenly announced that he would return to Europe that summer, Fuller made plans to follow him. Two new friends, Marcus and Rebecca Spring, had asked her to accompany them on an extended tour of the Continent the following year. (Her expenses would be paid in exchange for tutoring their twelve-year-old son.) In the spring of 1846, she therefore made arrangements with Greeley to report on her travels for the *Tribune*, making her the first foreign correspondent in America. For as long as she could remember, she had longed to see Europe, having imagined England, France, and Germany through the works of her favorite authors. Visiting those places would be a homecoming of sorts—a return of the queen to her rightful throne. During the year that she remained in New York, she sent letter after letter to Nathan, who remained largely unresponsive, writing one letter for every six or seven of hers. Finally, she coaxed from him a tentative agreement to meet in London in September 1846.

As the date for departure approached, she wrote a heartfelt "Farewell to New York" for her *Tribune* readers. She thanked them for their enthusiasm and warm acceptance. "[T]wenty months have presented me with a richer and more varied exercise for thought and life," she told them, "than twenty years could in any other part of these United States."[201] Her time in the city had brought her face to face with people from every stratum of society, from celebrities to prostitutes, and artists, criminals, and the insane. She had become involved in a literary culture with markedly different goals and methods than the ones in which she had come of age. And she had spoken on behalf of women, of immigrants from Ireland, and of enslaved people. Her horizons had broadened appreciably.

Another thing about her time in New York: she had learned to write more clearly. At the *Tribune*, her language became more direct, more forceful and vivid. Gone were the Teutonic mannerisms and twisted syntax of her earlier work. While by no means telegraphic (that invention was just beginning to transform American language), her writing achieved a new clarity and freshness. This evolution would continue when she moved to Italy and began to speak almost exclusively in its language. In Rome, her prose became even more pared down, more rhythmic, stripped of adjectives and conventionalities. It became modern.

Fuller left New York on August 1, 1846, aboard the *Cambria*—a new Cunard ship equipped with twin thousand-horsepower engines. The year before, the ship had made the fastest westbound voyage across the Atlantic. Four months before Fuller's departure, it had grounded off the coast of Cape Cod, victim of a storm, but had been successfully towed away and repaired. Fuller, accompanied by Marcus and Rebecca Spring and their son Eddie, felt the massive shudder as the ship's wooden paddles began churning the water. It was time to embrace the dream of Europe.

14.

The *Cambria* arrived in Liverpool in mid-August (plate 12). Fuller and the Spring family stayed briefly in the coal-smudged city, then left immediately for Scotland—a common itinerary for nineteenth-century travelers from America. The small group visited literary landmarks made famous by Robert Burns and Sir Walter Scott, then traveled northwest from Glasgow, some thirty miles toward the Highlands, at last reaching the crumpled mountain of Ben Lomond. In Liverpool, Fuller had written a London bookseller who knew James Nathan. "Is Mr Nathan now in London?" she asked. "If he is there, perhaps he will come here as I am told he can in 24 hours by mail from London and go 'The short tour' with us, thus giving me a good opportunity to see him... If he cannot come, I hope he will not fail to wait for me in London."[202]

The very same day, she received a letter from Nathan. He told her he could not meet her—in London or anywhere else. He was engaged to another woman. Fuller destroyed the letter in a rage, then wrote him an accusatory, incendiary note. His reply: he had never promised a deeper relationship.

In the meantime, as she traveled through Scotland, her mood grew volatile and reckless. On a cold day with driving rain, the party traveled from Glasgow to Loch Katrine and Ben Lomond. Fuller insisted on riding atop the carriage, in the process getting thoroughly soaked. Then she hiked up the mountain by herself, deliberately getting lost as mist-shrouded night descended on the crag.

She may have had in mind the popular, forlorn eighteenth-century love ballad, "On the Banks of Bonnie Loch Lomond," as she set off:

> By yon bonnie banks and by yon bonnie braes,
> Where the sun shines bright on Loch Lomond,
> Where me and my true love were ever wont to gae,
> On the bonnie, bonnie banks o' Loch Lomond.

Regardless, she trudged up the hill without food or warm clothing, much as she had stumbled out of a New England church years earlier and walked to exhaustion in the wake of George Davis's jilting. To her brother Richard, she later transformed the incident into an adventure, telling him, "On the lofty Ben Lomond, I got lost, and passed the night out on a heathery Scotch mountain, alone, and only keeping my life, by exertions to ward off the effects of the cold and wet, to which I should have feared my bodily strength and mental patience alike unequal, *if* I had not tried." Missing from the account is the impulse that drove her to a desperate night in the mountain. "I was rather ill for a few days after it," she continued, "and the Springs suffered much from anxiety and excitement, for they were up and had a crowd of shepherds out searching the mountain all night..."[203]

The rest of the trip was less dramatic. Fuller, armed with letters of introduction from Waldo and other friends, met Thomas De Quincey, the onetime friend of Wordsworth and the author of *Confessions of an Opium-Eater*, who was now a doddering wreck lost in a tangle of memories. Sometime that fall she arrived in the Lake District and met the great poet himself, no longer an "Apollo flaming with youthful glory... but instead a reverend old man."[204] Wordsworth, then in his mid-seventies, spoke glowingly of his sister Dorothy, now senile and an invalid. He showed Fuller a portrait of the woman who had inspired some of his finest poetry and recited lines from the journal she had kept decades earlier.

In London, she found herself received "with a warmth that surprised me; it is chiefly to *Woman in the 19th* &c that I am indebted for this."[205] An English edition of the book had appeared concurrently with her arrival, and Fuller found many people in the metropolis talking favorably of the work. She reconnected with Harriet Martineau and met the bombastic Thomas Carlyle, Waldo's old friend, who had grown increasingly conservative and retrograde over the years. "The worst of hearing Carlyle," she reported to Waldo, "is that you cannot interrupt him."[206] The Scotsman spoke without cessation about poetry, reform, and the state of contemporary French literature. She left the dinner party exhausted and wishing to contradict Carlyle on a hundred critical points, but also feeling as though she had entered the pinnacle of Britain's literary culture.

To Caroline Sturgis she affirmed a poignant milestone: "I find how true for me was the lure that always drew me towards Europe. It was no false instinct that said I might find here an atmosphere needed to develop me in ways *I* need. Had I only come ten years earlier; now my life must ever be a failure, so much strength has been wasted on obstructions which only came because I was not in the soil most fitted to my nature."[207]

Of all the celebrated people she met, the one who made the biggest impression on her was Giuseppe Mazzini, who had lived in London for more than a decade, exiled from his native Italy after fomenting revolutionary ideas. He was, somewhat improbably, a friend of Carlyle's, and like Fuller, he was an intellectual who had written criticism and contributed to newspapers. His primary interest, however, was politics—specifically the unification of Italy's disparate city-states into a modern republic. After serving a prison term in Savona for his radical activities, Mazzini continued to lead various revolutionary movements from London as the nominal head of a group of Italian nationals that numbered sixty thousand. Writing to Caroline Sturgis, Fuller described him as "the most beauteous person I have seen.... He is one in whom holiness has purified, but nowhere dwarfed the man."[208]

The language here echoes that which she had used a decade earlier to describe another intellectual leader, Waldo Emerson. But the differences between the two men were immense. While Waldo was content to spend his time constructing beautiful thoughts in his study, Mazzini was dedicated to putting his ideas into action. His life was guided by a mission that was as practical as it was ideal. Mazzini was also committed to the cause of women's liberation. The equality of men and women, he argued in *The Duties of Man* and *Thoughts on Democracy*, was necessary for a truly democratic society. This belief echoed Fuller's claim in *Woman in the Nineteenth Century* that the Declaration of Independence foretold the extension of full rights to women. From Mazzini, then, Fuller would get her first—but certainly not her last—taste of the revolutionary spirit just beginning to sweep throughout Europe.

In November, the small group of Americans crossed the English Channel and entered Paris, where Fuller promptly discovered, much to her chagrin, that her French was inadequate for conversation. She hired an instructor, who came every day to help her improve. Writing to Waldo, she expressed her feverish impatience to experience as much as she could in the brief months allotted to the city. "French people I find slippery," she added, "as they do not know exactly what to make of me, the rather as I have not the command of their language. *I* see *them*, their brilliancy, grace, and variety, the thousand slight refinements of their speech, and manner, but cannot meet them in their way."[209] For the first time in her life, she found herself unable to command a situation with conversation.

Nevertheless, she managed to observe and meet some of the foremost artists in the French capital. One was the actress Elisabeth Félix, better known as Rachel, who at twenty-five was already considered the greatest tragedian of her time. Fuller attended the opera or theater every night, watching Rachel perform in *Phedre* and the lesser-known *L'Ombre de Moliére*, a one-act comedy in which the playwright defended himself to Pluto in the underworld. On Valentine's Day, she was invited to a private piano concert by Frédéric Chopin, then considered one of the foremost composers of the era. Chopin suffered from tuberculosis. His long, turbulent affair with Aurore Dupin, better known as George Sand, was approaching its stormy conclusion. (Fuller gossiped to Elizabeth Hoar that the novelist and musician lived "on the footing of combined means, independent friendship!")[210] Yet he had lost none of his virtuosity, and his pianoforte produced waves of melancholic sound that perfectly captured the spirit of Romanticism.

Sand interested Fuller even more (figure 66). From her twenties onward, she had read the Frenchwoman's novels, and in *Woman in the Nineteenth Century* had written approvingly about the most successful female writer of the era. Knowing that at a young age Sand had entered into an unhappy marriage from which there was no escape, she had tacitly condoned her extramarital affairs in her book. At the same time, she expressed discomfort that the wildly

Figure 66. George Sand.

unconventional novelist—notorious for her cigar smoking and men's attire—was too often made an example of what happened when women entered the public sphere.[‡]

As luck would have it, Sand had left her chateau in Nohant to negotiate with her publisher in Paris when Fuller was in the city. Fuller arrived at the author's residence only to be told she was not expected. As she tried to explain herself in broken French, "Madame Sand opened the door, and stood looking at me an instant. Our eyes met. I never shall forget her look at that moment." What transfixed Fuller's attention was "the expression of *goodness*, nobleness, and power that pervaded the whole,—the truly human heart and nature that shone in the eyes." Sand led the visitor to her study, where Fuller announced, "Il me fait de bien de vous voir." *It does me good to see you.*

[‡] For her time and place, Fuller was remarkably broadminded about sexual relations outside marriage. When her sister's husband, Ellery Channing, dashed off to be with a former flame, Fuller declared that he should be free to do so, apparently believing that it was wrong to thwart such impulses.

At last, it seemed, she had found a soul mate. "I heartily enjoyed the sense of so rich, so prolific, so ardent a genius," she wrote to Elizabeth Hoar. "I liked the woman in her, too, very much; I never liked a woman better.... For the rest, she holds her place in the literary and social world of France like a man, and seems full of energy and courage in it. I suppose she has suffered much, but she has also enjoyed and done much."[211] In Sand, whose brown, sympathetic eyes seemed to convey immense depths of experience and suffering, Fuller saw herself: a woman whose "masculine" traits had brought unspeakable anguish but also great joy: a grand life.[§]

Yet another person in Paris left a lasting impression on Fuller. This was Adam Mickiewicz, the Polish poet and exile, a Byronic figure with long, flowing hair and a moody countenance (figure 67). Mickiewicz had been friends with Pushkin and Goethe and was an important dramatist, if better known for his verse. Like Mazzini, he had spent much of his life among dissident exiles, in this case those who hoped to liberate Poland from Prussia. When Fuller learned that he was interested in transcendentalism, she sent him a copy of Emerson's recently published poems. He soon paid her a visit, and she "found in him the man I had long wished to see, with the intellect and passions in due proportion for a full and healthy being, with a soul constantly aspiring."[212]

It is not clear how much time she spent with Mickiewicz. Rebecca Spring, who continued to chaperone her in France, believed she was in love. "You ask me if I love M.," Fuller wrote her from Rome in April. "I answer he affected me like music or the richest landscape, my heart beat with joy that he at once felt beauty in me also."[213] But if Mickiewicz stirred her heart, he also insinuated there was something missing from her otherwise rich emotional life. In a letter he sent the following year, he sketched her personality as he might have done for one of the characters in his plays: "Her *base* is the old world; her *sphere of action* is the new world; her *peace* is in the world to come." All of this had prepared Fuller for a unique world-historical role: "Your mission is to contribute to the deliverance of the Polish, French, and American women." Still, Markiewicz told her he believed there was something preventing Fuller from fulfilling her complete destiny as a woman—her chastity.[214]

When she received this bit of scurrilously sexist advice, Fuller was living in Italy, where, she had once written, "the great poets wove into their lives an ideal love which answered to the highest wants. It included those of the intellect and the affections, for it was a love of spirit for spirit." After six event-filled months in the United Kingdom and France, Fuller had finally entered the country she had romanticized above all others. In the process, she had moved not only beyond New England but also beyond America, traversing boundaries at a breathtaking

§ In Concord, Elizabeth Hoar passed along Fuller's account of Sand to Waldo, who wrote a message of sympathy: "It was high time, dear friend, that you should run out of the coop of our bigoted societies full of fire damp & azote and find some members of your own expansive fellowship."

Figure 67. Adam Mickiewicz.

rate. She had met celebrated authors and artists and had discovered a world of political revolutionaries, whose goals of remaking Europe into a less feudal and more democratic entity she was beginning to adopt.

Throughout it all, she felt as though she were making up for lost time. Her previous life had been a dream: foggy and unreal. Finally, she was where she belonged. "Italy fulfills my hopes," she told her friend William Henry Channing; "it could not do more, it has been the dream of my life."[215] She loved the country, loved the language, its goldenrod-warmth as it rolled on her tongue, the way it prompted her hands to alight like birds, here, there, never settling, as she spoke.

At the conclusion of *Woman in the Nineteenth Century*, Fuller had surveyed her life from an elevation that stripped away illusion. "I stand in the sunny noon of life. Objects no longer glitter in the dews of morning, neither are yet softened by the shadow of evening.... Yet enough is left, even by experience, to point distinctly to the glories of that destiny; faint, but not to be mistaken streaks of the future day. I can say with the bard,

'Though many have suffered shipwreck, still beat noble hearts.'"[216]

Those words would prove prophetic. In the spring of 1847, Fuller arrived in Italy by way of an English steamer. Among its passengers was the young American publisher George Palmer Putnam, who had helped publish a volume of her *Tribune* reviews in 1846. (Putnam, it turns out, was a cousin of Elizabeth and Sophia Peabody.) According to him, somewhere in the Ligurian Sea the steamer was involved in a head-on collision with a French ship. "[S]uch a shock in the dead of night," Putnam later wrote, "knocking us out of our berths, was not fitted to soothe an anxious spirit."

Rushing to the deck to see if the steamer was sinking, he found the damage minimal and then raced to the women's cabin to reassure his wife. "The door was opened by Miss Fuller in her night-dress," he remembered. "Instead of hysterical fright, as I expected, my hurried report... was met by Miss Fuller by the remark that seemed to me superhuman in its quiet calmness: 'Oh, we—had not—made up our minds, that it was—worth while—to be at all—alarmed!'"

Putnam was deeply impressed. There was something dauntless and brave, something even reckless, about Fuller when she was in extremis. He marveled: "Verily woman—American woman, at least—is wonderful for her cool philosophy and strong nerved stoicism in great danger!"[217]

Epilogue

Circles

1.

The freighter was called the *Elizabeth*: a 530-ton sailing vessel captained by a New England mariner with the sibilant name of Seth Libby Hasty. Sailing ships were not as safe as steamers, but they were considerably cheaper, and in the case of Margaret Fuller and her tiny family, they were the only transportation she could afford. In addition to its human cargo, the *Elizabeth* was loaded with scented soap, silks, almonds, and 150 tons of creamy white Carrara marble quarried from Tuscany. Robert Browning, then a resident of Florence with his wife and fellow poet Elizabeth Barrett Browning, escorted Fuller to the Livorno wharf. When he saw how low the ship sat in the water, heeling and wallowing from so much marble, he advised her not to board.

But Fuller desperately wanted to return to America. She was convinced that only in her native country would her history of the Roman revolution be published. (Thomas Carlyle, acting on her behalf, had already tried to interest English publishers, telling one that Fuller was "*considerably* a higher-minded and cleverer woman than any of the Lady Lions yet on your Books"—but to no avail.) And besides, she was homesick. While she had come to disdain the narrow provinciality of New England and had distanced herself from the ethereal sentiments of transcendentalism, she missed her increasingly frail mother and her sister Ellen Fuller Channing, whose marriage to the poet Ellery Channing was disintegrating. She also yearned for her many, many friends. Scattered along the Eastern seaboard, these people had once been bound together by Fuller's marvelous talk. Now she wanted to introduce them to the more recent people in her life.

For she was a wife and mother—a fact she had managed to keep secret until quite recently. There are several explanations for her silence. Elizabeth Peabody believed it was to spare her husband's brother, who as a chamberlain for the pope would have suffered from the scandal of a Protestant in the family. Others believed Fuller had had a child out of wedlock, or that she had never legally married. As Elizabeth Barrett Browning put it to a friend, "The American authoress Miss Fuller . . . has taken us by surprise . . . retiring from the Roman field with a husband & child above a year old!—Nobody had even suspected a word of this underplot,

& her American friends stood in mute astonishment before this apparition of them here."[1]

In the spring of 1847, having traveled for six months through England, Scotland, and France, Fuller had parted ways, in Rome, with her chaperones, Marcus and Rebecca Spring. "I was by my nature destined to walk by inner light alone," she explained to them. "It has led, will lead me sometimes on a narrow plank across deep chasms." She did not mean that she was in any danger of falling—only that if such a danger arose, she wanted to face it alone, authentically and with courage. "I wish to be free and absolutely true to my nature, and if I cannot live so I do not wish to live."[2]

Rebecca Spring believed Fuller had fallen in love with Adam Mickiewicz. When she confronted her, she received an indirect response. "I have never sought love as a passion," Fuller wrote; "it has always come to me as an angel bearing some good tidings." Then she launched into an evasive account of her romantic history: "I do not know if I have loved at all in the sense of oneness, but I have loved enough to feel the joys of presence, the pangs of absence, the sweetness of hope, and the chill of disappointment. More than once my heart has bled, and my health has suffered from these things but mentally I have always found myself the gainer, always younger and more noble."[3]

The letter was dated April 10, 1847. A week earlier, during a torchlit visit to St. Peter's Basilica, Fuller had met a young man named Giovanni Angelo Ossoli, who was twenty-six years old, thin as a knife, and the cultivator of an enormous drooping moustache too large for his face (figure 68). Ossoli had dolorous eyes and a military bearing. He was an Italian aristocrat, though in his case the title carried neither money nor privilege. He was the least likely of Fuller's lovers—in part because he spoke no English, having received a spotty education from an old priest who had taken an interest in the boy after his mother died. He was "ignorant of great ideas," as Fuller put it, "ignorant of books."[4] Her friends would later exaggerate Ossoli's limitations, claiming (falsely) that he was illiterate, barely verbal. But he certainly lacked Fuller's intellectual prowess.

Perhaps it was for this very reason that she loved him. In *Woman in the Nineteenth Century*, she had described the "highest grade of marriage union" as involving an "intellectual union," a shared spiritual pilgrimage toward a higher ideal. In Ossoli she discovered something else entirely: a man she did not need to impress, a man who returned her affection simply, courteously, without conditions: a man aglow with warmth and generosity. To Fuller he was devoted, tender, loving—all the things she had craved since childhood and lacked in her previous romantic involvements. It didn't hurt that they were deeply and physically attracted to one another.*

* Speaking to Ossoli about their child, Fuller wrote (in Italian), "When you come I will embrace you as I embrace him and I will do you well."

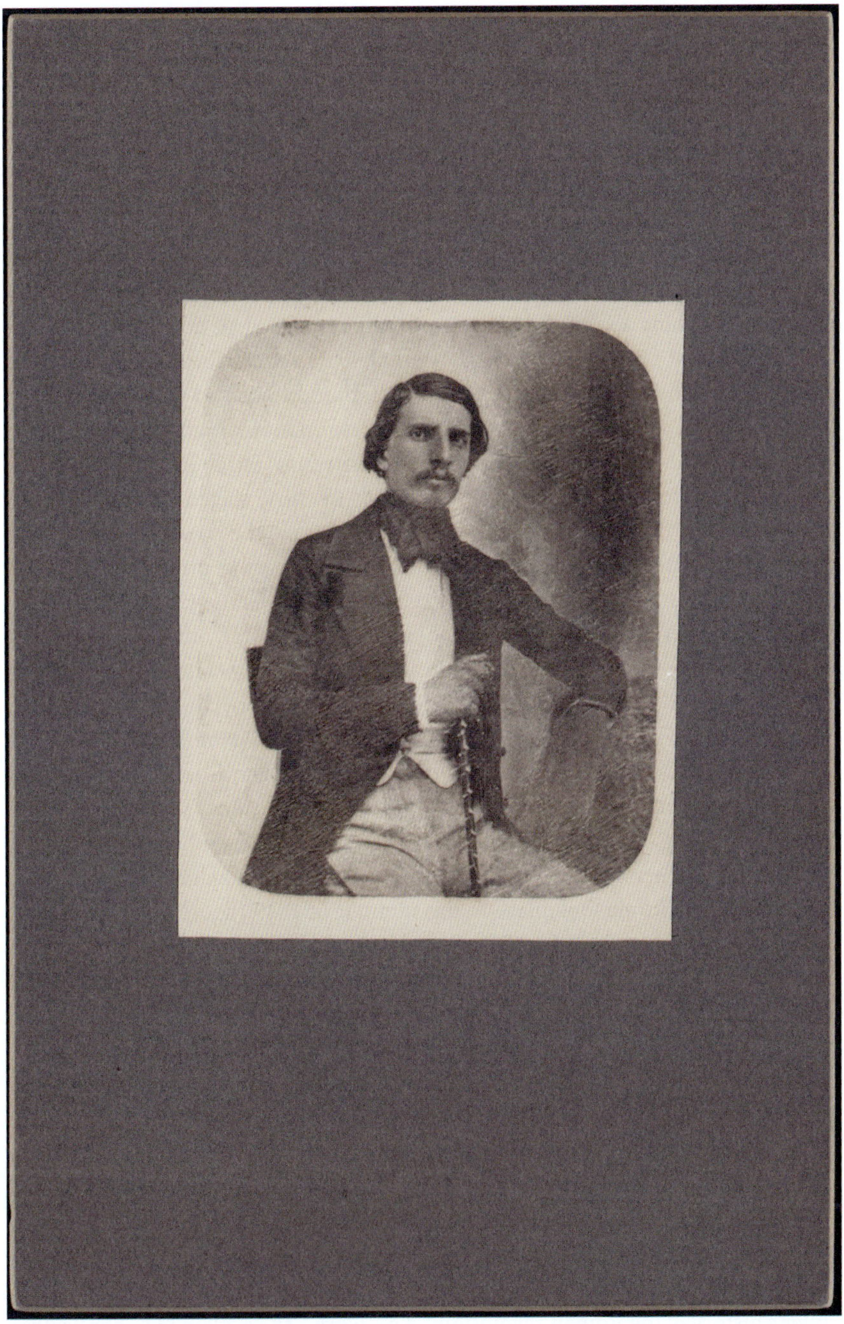

Figure 68. Giovanni Angelo Ossoli.

Although Fuller kept the relationship a secret, glimpses of her new the life with Ossoli peep through the letters she sent friends that summer. "[I]mperfect as love is," she wrote Waldo, "I want human beings to love, as I suffocate without."[5] After she became pregnant, she told him that "Children, with all their faults, seem to me the best thing we have."[6] What she did *not* announce was the news that on September 5, 1848—almost two years exactly from that dreary night she spent alone on Ben Lomond—she had given birth to a boy.

It was as if everything up to this point in her life had been a prelude—the spoken introduction of a play before the action begins. Life in Boston and New York, with its many accomplishments and achievements, had been but a preparation for the great events, internal and external, that suddenly befell Fuller. For her relationship with Ossoli and subsequent motherhood coincided with revolution in Italy. The year 1848 was one of revolt and transformation around great swaths of the world. In the United States, Lucretia Mott and Elizabeth Cady Stanton, inspired by Fuller's *Woman in the Nineteenth Century*, staged the Seneca Falls convention to protest "such disgraceful laws as give man the power to chastise and imprison his wife, to take the wages which she earns, the property which she inherits, and, in case of separation, the children of her love." In France and Germany, mass uprisings protested monarchy. And in Italy, the spirit of revolt took the form of a war for independence. The disparate city-states comprising the nation now rebelled in the hopes of creating a new republic. The revolution began in Rome, where Fuller was living, and then spread north. To the *Tribune*, as well as in private letters home, Fuller reported on these events, her prose assuming a new urgency, a bracing clarity. "Art is not important to me now," she told William Henry Channing, explaining that the struggle for independence outside her window fulfilled her spirit in ways she could never have imagined.[7]

The battle for Rome took place in the summer of 1849 (figure 69). "What shall I write of Rome in these sad but glorious days?" she asked her *Tribune* readers in June. "Plain facts are the best; for my feelings I could not find fit words."[8] While Ossoli fought with the revolutionaries at the Castel St. Angelo, Fuller watched the combat from her balcony through a spyglass. She visited the Roman hospitals, nursed wounded soldiers, changed bandages, brought food and water, and sometimes walked with the convalescents through the beautiful gardens of the apostolic palace of the Pope, now transformed into a clinic. To Waldo, she wrote that although she had encountered just "how terrible gunshot-wounds and wound fever are,—yet I have taken pleasure, and great pleasure, in being with the men; there is scarcely one who is not moved by a noble spirit."[9]

The siege of Rome, which occurred that summer, brought a temporary halt to Fuller's history of the Roman revolution. "This work," she explained to her brother Richard, "if I can accomplish it will be a worthy chapter in the history of the world."[10] To Caroline Sturgis (now married to William Aspinwall Tappan, the son of a prominent abolitionist), she claimed to have written "at least two volumes."

Figure 69. The battle of Rome.

Elizabeth Barrett Browning believed the history would have been Fuller's greatest work, if for no other reason than because for the first time in her life she had had enough "time & labour" to do justice to her subject.[11]

Yet the story of the Roman revolution was ultimately tragic, not triumphant. By June 20, Rome's walls had been breached by French troops, who had arrived in the city expecting to be hailed as liberators but were instead fired upon by the Roman garrison. A siege of the city soon commenced, and within weeks the ancient city fell. Fuller's London friend, Giuseppe Mazzini, who had returned from exile to form a new government, fled the country by the middle of July. "Private hopes of mine," Fuller wrote her brother Richard, "are fallen with the hopes of Italy."[12]

The defeat of Roman forces prompted Fuller to consider leaving the country she loved so much. "I have lived in a much more full and true way than was possible in our country," she told a friend in the United States, "and each day has been rich in joys and pains, actions and sufferings, to say nothing of themes of observation."[13] Only after the Italian republic was overthrown and revolution ended did she begin to disclose the life she had kept hidden for the past two years. She sent letters home that acknowledged her new status as wife and mother, careful to present her husband in a truthful light. "I have united my destiny with that of an obscure young man," she wrote, "younger than myself; a person of no intellectual culture, and, in whom, in short, you will see no reason for my choosing…"[14] At the same time, she was proud of Ossoli, explaining to Sam and Anna Ward why this seemingly unpromising man meant so much to her. "To me the simplicity, the reality, the great tenderness and refinements of his character make a domestic place in this world."[15] To Elizabeth Hoar, she wrote: "Never blame him for ills I may have to undergo; all that he could he has done for me, all that he had he has given. When we look on the sweet face of our child, we think if we can keep him, we shall have courage for whatever we may have to do or endure."[16] To her friend William Henry Channing, she confided, "My love for Ossoli is most pure and tender, nor has any one, except little children or mother, ever loved me as genuinely as he does."[17] And to an unknown correspondent she defiantly announced, "I have, however, no regrets; we acted as seemed best at the time."[18]

About her baby—Angelino, called Nino by his parents—she could speak only in rhapsodic terms. "What a difference it makes to come home to a child; how it fills up all the gaps of life, just in the way that is most consoling, most refreshing. I used to feel sad at that time; the day had not been nobly spent, I had not done my duty to myself and others; then I felt so lonely, now I never feel lonely, for even if my little boy dies, our souls will remain eternally united."[19] Earlier, she had chastised Waldo for belittling the birth of Anna and Sam Ward's daughter. Now she told her sister, "As was Eve, at first, I suppose every mother is delighted by the birth of a man-child."[20]

She resolved to treat her child differently than she had been treated by her father, refusing to set expectations for his development or intellect. "I do not believe mine will be a brilliant child," she told her Italian friend Costanza Arconati Visconti. "Indeed, I see nothing particular about him, yet he is to me a source of ineffable joys far purer, deeper than anything I ever felt before, like what Nature had sometimes given, but more intimate, more sweet."[21] Thinking of other children she had loved and lost—little Waldo Emerson and Pickie Greeley, the son of her employer who had died while she was abroad—she steeled herself, as every parent must, for the prospect of tragedy, saying about Nino, "I must look upon him as a treasure only lent."[22]

As the return to America began to take shape, she was filled with premonitions. "I dread the voyage exceedingly," she wrote her sister Ellen, months before departing, "so long an one would be very terrible to my poor head."[23] Her fears increased as the trip approached. "I am absurdly fearful and various omens have combined to give me a dark feeling," she told Costanza Visconti. "It seems to me that my future upon earth will soon close…I have a vague expectation of some crisis—I know not what." Filled with apprehension, she nevertheless persisted in her plans, reasoning, "Perhaps we shall live to laugh at these, but in case of mishap, I should perish with my husband and child perhaps to be transferred to some happier state; and my dear mother, whom I so long to see, would soon follow, and embrace me more peaceably elsewhere."[24]

The *Elizabeth* left Livorno on May 19, 1850, four days before Fuller's fortieth birthday. There were just six passengers aboard, including a young Italian woman, Celeste Paolini, whom Fuller had hired at the last moment to help care for Nino. Another passenger was Horace Sumner, brother of the future U.S. Senator Charles Sumner and a new friend of the Ossolis.

Within days of the ship's departure, its captain, Seth Hasty, contracted smallpox. A quarantine was imposed for several weeks in Gibraltar, where Fuller and the captain's wife, Catharine Hasty, nursed the sick man. Before long, Angelino began to exhibit telltale symptoms of the disease. But while the child recovered, Hasty grew worse, then perished, and the ship was taken over by an inexperienced first mate named Henry P. Bangs, who captained the ship out of Gibraltar on June 8.

Crossing the Atlantic in a sailing vessel took at least two months and entailed enormous hardships. Before leaving, Fuller had made a laundry-list of concerns, including that "the cabin being on deck will be terribly exposed in case of gale; that I cannot be secure of having good water to drink, far less to wash clothing, and therefore must buy an immense stock of baby-linen; that I cannot go without providing for us poultry, a goat for milk, oranges and lemons, soda hardbread, and a medicine chest."[25] Fortunately, the weather was peaceful and calm for the most part, with balmy nights lit by an enormous, clear moon. By the middle of July, the ship had passed Bermuda, and the passengers were told that soon they could begin preparing for arrival. On July 18, Bangs reported—mistakenly—that he thought he had seen a pilot boat from New York headed their way.

The next evening, the inexperienced captain calculated that the *Elizabeth* was just off the coast of New Jersey. He angled the ship north toward Manhattan. Again, he was mistaken. The ship was in fact sixty miles farther north than he had reckoned. As powerful southern winds began to gather, it soon became apparent the vessel was headed for the shore of Long Island. Just before four in the morning, it hit a sandbar near the beach at Fire Island. The spar tore a hole in the wooden hull and water began to fill the hold. As the distressed passengers clambered onto the deck, they were hit with towering waves and ferocious gales. Almost instantly, heavy sails and rigging—ropes, tackle, and chains—were torn from the masts. As the sky began to lighten, the terrified passengers waved and shouted to a small crowd of people gathered on the shore—in vain.

Catherine Hasty would later remember Fuller's preternatural calmness during the calamity. When Nino started crying, she wrapped him meticulously in her shawl and sang him to sleep. According to the second mate, she "sat in her white night dress, flat on the deck, with her back to the leewards on the upper or windowed side, & her feet toward the foremast."[26] When the ship began to slide into the ocean, the stranded passengers inched upwards toward the forecastle, pummeled by waves. Ossoli, in broken English, encouraged everyone to pray.

At some point, the second mate volunteered to return to the cabins to retrieve the passengers' valuables. Fuller asked that he find her jewelry and what remained of her money, about seventy dollars, as well as her spectacles, her writing desk, and "what is most valuable to me if I live of any thing"—presumably her manuscript history of the Italian revolution. After what seemed a very long time, he returned with everything she had asked for.

Then, around ten o'clock in the morning, the blocks of marble in the hold crashed into the water. The *Elizabeth* began to break apart. Passengers and crew members now realized their only chance to survive was to swim to the shore. Horace Sumner dove into the water and never came up. Catharine Hasty and several sailors grappled onto wooden planks and paddled to safety.

Fuller and Ossoli decided to wait, hoping the big lifeboat on shore would eventually rescue them. But according to the second mate, "The men [on shore] had not courage to launch the lifeboat... [they] sat for an hour or two on the side of the boat doing nothing but now & then picking up a hat, (part of the cargo) that came ashore."[27] By then it was one in the afternoon. Fuller had been aboard the deck of the disintegrating *Elizabeth* for nine hours. She was soaked to the skin. At last realizing that no boat was coming, she agreed to let a steward take Angelino and swim toward the shore. The two were drowned. Then Ossoli, who had never learned to swim and who had once been warned by a fortune teller to beware of water, was swept into the sea and drowned, as well. Witnesses would later report that until the very end, Fuller "sat with her back to the foremast, with her hands on her knees.... A great wave came and washed her aft." The last words anyone heard her speak were these: "I see nothing but death before me—I shall never reach the shore"[28] (figure 70).

2.

Fuller's death left a hole in the lives of her friends. Their mutual histories were suddenly split in two: before and after the shipwreck. Memories surged forth. Of Fuller's miraculous talk, of her charisma, of her regal presence that demanded, always, its due. Ellen Emerson was eleven years old when she heard her parents discussing the tragedy; she never forgot their reaction. "I remember well what a shock to them was her death, and how constantly every detail they would gather was talked over."[29] Two days after the shipwreck, Waldo sat in his study and addressed the event in his journal, unwilling to speak of his friend in the past tense. "On Friday, 19 July, Margaret dies on the rocks of Fire Island Beach within sight of & within 60 rods of the shore. To the last her country proves inhospitable to her." He added, forlornly, "I have lost in her my audience."[30]

In New York, Horace Greeley dispatched his best reporter, Bayard Taylor, to the site of the shipwreck, treating Fuller's death as a major news story. Waldo sent

THE DEATH OF MARGARET FULLER OSSOLI.

Figure 70. "The Death of Margaret Fuller."

Henry David Thoreau and Ellery Channing (Fuller's troublesome brother-in-law) to Fire Island to recover the bodies of the Ossoli family, or, if not that, some portion of Fuller's sodden manuscript. The two men searched the shore for several days, interviewing witnesses who had watched Fuller sitting on deck, a dim figure amid the baneful waves, apparently calm until the very moment the ship broke apart and collapsed into the sea. Fuller's body and that of her husband were never recovered, but the tiny form of Angelino eventually washed ashore. Thoreau found Fuller's carpet bag and her writing desk, but the manuscript history of the Roman revolution was lost forever.

As the news spread from New York to New England, Fuller's friends experienced a strange amalgam of emotions: shock intermingled with relief. What had once been a warm community now became judgmental and censorious. Well before the *Elizabeth* departed from Livorno, Fuller's return had been a topic of fraught discussion among her American acquaintances. There were rumors of sexual impropriety—the same sort of rumors that had dogged Fuller's precursors, George Sand and Mary Wollstonecraft. Those who knew something of her romantic history considered it likely she had been seduced by an uneducated Italian lover nine years her junior. Her death, therefore, spared her friends the social discomfort they would have faced upon her return.

Caroline Sturgis Tappan, Fuller's best friend, was one of those who thought her drowning a blessing in disguise. When she read of Fuller's last hours, as reported by Thoreau and transcribed by Elizabeth Hoar, she could not help admiring her friend's bravery. While Fuller was in Italy, Caroline had married and had a child of her own. She perfectly understood Fuller's resolve to stay aboard the collapsing ship rather than abandon her child. But she also believed Fuller would have faced an even greater tempest had she survived the storm: "The waves do not seem so difficult to brave as the prejudices she would have encountered if she had arrived here safely."[31] Another friend of Fuller's, Almira Barlow, also breathed a sigh of relief. "The death seems . . . as fit & good conclusion to the life. Her life was romantic & exceptional: So let her death be; it sets the seal on her marriage, avoids all questions of Society, all of employment, poverty, & old age."[32]

Even before leaving Italy, Fuller had encountered similar reactions. "Much as we should love to see you and strange as it may seem," wrote Rebecca Spring, who had returned home from Europe with her husband Marcus, "we, as well as all your friends who have spoken to us about it, believe it will be undesirable for you to return at present."[33] Others put the matter more bluntly. "You say your friends appear to lay extraordinary stress upon your marriage," wrote Sarah Clarke, the artist who had regularly attended Fuller's Conversations. "It is not exactly that but we were placed in a most unpleasant position because the world said injurious things of you which we were not authorized to deny—not one of us could say that we knew of your marriage beforehand, nor could we tell when it occurred or answer any questions about it."[34] William Henry Channing, arguably her closest male friend during the last decade of her life, diplomatically agreed "in thinking that so far as your publishing matters are concerned, the balance of advantages will turn in favor of you remaining abroad."[35]

Waldo Emerson best embodied the conundrum when he spoke with rancor about the hypocrisy surrounding Fuller's return. "The timorous said, What shall we do? how shall she be received, now that she brings a husband & child home?" Yet he was not exempt from the social bigotries of his set, writing to Carlyle that "She died in happy hour for herself. Her health was much exhausted. Her marriage would have taken her away from us all, & there was subsistence yet to be secured, & diminished powers, & old age."[36]

In the end, Fuller's death allowed her friends to revise her life, to reconstruct her legacy to fit their own preferences. Horace Greeley was among the earliest to do so, writing her obituary for the *Tribune* soon after the shipwreck. "America has produced no woman," he stated, "who in mental endowments and acquirements has surpassed Margaret Fuller."[37] Another friend from her transcendentalist days, Christopher Pearse Cranch, a man who had once poked good-humored fun at the *Dial* when Fuller was editor, now wrote an elegy that would be widely circulated in newspapers. Cranch had become reacquainted with Fuller in Italy, the two sharing a love for the country that bordered on the religious. His poem recast her arrival in America as an event devoutly, if somewhat disingenuously, to be wished for. "O still sweet summer days!" he wrote:

O moonlit nights,
After so dear a storm how can ye shine!...
For she is gone from us—....
Gone full of love, life, hope, and high endeavor,
Just when we would have welcomed her the most.[38]

But the most ambitious effort to remake and sanitize Fuller's reputation was the two-volume memoir assembled by Waldo, William Henry Channing, and James Freeman Clarke—three of Fuller's closest male friends. Published in 1852, the two-volume book was compiled in the tradition of the era, a heterogeneous mixture of reminiscence, letters, and hagiographic biography. The book is good at capturing its authors' vivid impressions of Fuller, especially during her early years in New England. Yet it fails to account for the full range of her life and accomplishments, paying scant attention to her work at the *Tribune* and her life abroad.

Because they had known her before her move to New York, the authors of the *Memoir of Margaret Fuller Ossoli* concentrated on her earlier transcendentalist writing. The picture of Fuller was of a brilliant, unsatisfied woman whose talk was unforgettable but whose pen, as Waldo famously put it, "was a nonconductor."[39] Little attention was given to her essays on reform or to her efforts to bring attention to the most vulnerable members of society, including her extensive work with women imprisoned for prostitution. Waldo and his collaborators instead presented a charming, if egotistical, bluestocking, supremely self-confident, committed above all else to the "mountainous ME."[40] Thanks to the recollections of Elizabeth Palmer Peabody and others, the work devoted ample space to the Conversations held at the West Street bookshop, which were rightfully portrayed as important events in the history of transcendentalism.

Not until 1883 would another book-length biography appear, this one by Julia Ward Howe, who as a young woman had briefly attended the Conversations. Howe, an author most famous for "The Battle Hymn of the Republic," was a longtime activist in the woman's suffrage movement, having served as co-director of the American Woman Suffrage Association and, in 1881, becoming president of the Association of American Women. Her biography of Fuller borrowed extensively from the *Memoirs*, but it also attempted to situate Fuller at the birth of a burgeoning women's movement. Howe made this even more explicit in an 1898 speech in which she surveyed the movement throughout the nineteenth century and declared, "The present century has from its beginning been remarkable for a forward stride in the individuality of women."[41] Fuller was at the forefront of this development, an early example of a woman who refused to remain confined by social expectations and who insisted upon the growth of each person regardless of gender. "As a woman who believed in women, her word is still an evangel of hope and inspiration to her sex."[42]

At least for a while, Fuller continued to live on through conversation itself, invoked in countless discussions by those who knew her, conjured up in parlors and at dinner tables, her words and actions shared and passed on. The Conversations had ended in 1844, but she remained a vivid presence in the memories of their participants. After her death, she became a topic of debate and fond recollection, her vibrant afterlife especially evident in the talk and letters written by the women who had once made up her Bright Circle.

3.

On the first day of August 1850, Sophia Peabody Hawthorne wrote an impassioned letter to her mother, Eliza Peabody. Eliza was now in her early seventies, neither as agile nor as filled with hope as she had been in the past, when she had embarked upon the cheering adventure of raising three promising, independent daughters. In two and a half years, she would be dead, her body buried in the Salem Burying Ground, with its leaning tombstones and sunken hillocks. Before long, her husband, Nathaniel Peabody, would meekly follow her to the grave.

Sophia wrote her mother from the other side of Massachusetts. The Hawthorne family—now there were two children, Una and Julian; a third, Rose, would arrive in 1851—were once again in a state of transition. Since leaving the Old Manse in Concord five years earlier, Sophia and Nathaniel had shuttled back and forth between Boston and Salem, enduring frequent separations as well as months of cramped claustrophobia, when the fledgling family shared rooms with Nathaniel's reclusive mother and older sister. In Salem, the author eventually secured a political appointment as surveyor—the salary was "wretchedly small"—in the Custom House.[43] He lost this position when the federal administration changed in 1848, the same year the revolutionary spirit swept through Europe and the Seneca Falls Convention was held. Now the family found itself living someplace it had never imagined—the Berkshires.

The Hawthornes owed their new situation, at least indirectly, to Sam and Anna Ward—the couple Fuller had once considered the most beautiful man and woman in the world. In the late 1840s, the Wards had discovered the sleepy mountain town of Lenox, nestled between the Berkshire mountains and the Housatonic River. Others had preceded them; in the 1820s, the novelist Catherine Sedgewick and the actress Fanny Kemble had each settled here, drawn to the area's natural beauty. But the Wards turned Lenox into a fashionable artist colony. Rich and aesthetically minded, they had been on the lookout for a scenic resort where they could spend their summers. They soon formed the nucleus of a stylish community that included Fuller's close friend, Caroline Sturgis, who had recently married the Boston merchant and banker, William Aspinwall Tappan. In 1849, the same year Caroline gave birth to the couple's first daughter, the Tappans purchased a farm in Lenox. Eventually they built a house Caroline called "Tanglewood"; this home was later donated by their daughter to the Boston Symphony Orchestra.

In 1850, Caroline offered the Hawthornes a cottage known as "The Red House." The name was a misnomer—the place was a drafty converted barn—but the offer could not have come at a better time. Earlier that year Nathaniel had published *The Scarlet Letter*, which would forever transform his critical fortunes as a writer. Praised by the nation's premier journals, the book became an instant classic, its story of a woman cruelly ostracized for bearing an illegitimate child recasting Fuller's situation—or rather the situation imagined by her friends—in a Puritan setting. But critical success provided little in the way of income, and Hawthorne still struggled to support his family of four. The Red House offered a welcome respite.

On Monday, July 29, Caroline Tappan knocked on the front door of The Red House and handed Sophia a newspaper. Her expression, Sophia told her mother, was one of "great sorrow & foreboding." Sophia sat down and read the account of Fuller's drowning—the first she had heard of the tragedy. Soon there were other accounts, as news traveled back and forth from Lenox to Concord, where Elizabeth Hoar, another close friend of Fuller's, acted as a hub of information. Sophia learned that "Mr. Thoreau and Ellery are at Fire Island, & Elizabeth Hoar sent Caroline Ellery's letter to Mr Emerson & Mr Thoreau's report. Neither

Margaret's nor Ossoli's body had been found up to their date—Ellery was drying papers, but not yet had found the book of Italy."

When Fuller had published *Woman in the Nineteenth Century*, Sophia had spoken disparagingly of her former idol, indignant that an unmarried woman had dared criticize matrimony. But now she could not stop thinking of Fuller's small child. "I wish at least Angelino could have been saved," she wrote her mother, then repeated what was rapidly becoming conventional wisdom about the misfortune: "If they were truly bound together as they seemed to be, I am glad they died together—But Margaret is such a loss, with her new & deeper experience of life in all its relations—her rich harvest of observation." Then Sophia burst forth in a torrent of feeling: "Oh was ever anything so tragical, so dreary so unspeakably agonizing as the image of Margaret upon that wreck, alone, sitting with her hands upon her knees & tempestuous waves breaking over her!"[44]

Sophia's sister Mary Peabody Mann had a somewhat different view. Writing from Boston, where the entire town seemed to be talking of Fuller's death, she had spoken with Lydia Maria Child, one of Fuller's early friends and a regular participant in the Conversations. Child had read several of Fuller's letters from Italy and reported that her "way of speaking of her husband was always apologetic, though she spoke of him with affection. She said he was uneducated & not a man of much ability, & she feared her friends here would not think as well of him as her."

Mary also told Sophia that Catherine Hasty, wife of the deceased captain of the *Elizabeth*, was now claiming that Fuller had initially refused Ossoli's offer of marriage, thinking the match unsuitable. Mary, who had once dreamed of finding silver coins with which to pay off the family debts, was always the most practical of the Peabody sisters. She could not understand Fuller's decision to attach herself to someone whose prospects were so bleak and unsuitable. Ossoli "was wholly unfit to be her husband in this country," she reported to Sophia, adding that "altho' it might have answered in Italy... he would have dragged her down" in the United States. Recalling Fuller's "longing to be loved," Mary could only surmise that Ossoli's "affection prevailed over other considerations."[45]

For both Peabody sisters, Fuller's Conversations—first held in Mary's rented rooms and then in their older sister Elizabeth's bookshop—seemed an eternity ago. Once, in passionate, searching talk they had discussed the role of women in a society that denied them a public platform. Now both sisters found themselves consumed with the task of raising children. Letters between them were filled with information about diets for infants and the most compassionate methods for correcting misbehavior. Each woman had sought love and security in marriage, diverging in this way from their oldest sister, who would ultimately look upon Fuller's final years with greater generosity of spirit.

As the shock of the news faded, Sophia, as usual, turned her attention to her moody husband, who complained of the slightest noise made by the children when he was trying to write. "Thou was born to muse & to be silent," she soothed him.[46] If she felt any longing to paint (by now, she had not touched brush to canvas in half a decade), she never mentioned it. Instead, she continued to proclaim that her family—boisterous, precocious, restless, and a bit odd—was her greatest masterpiece. In 1852, that family returned to Concord, the place where Sophia and Nathaniel had spent their happiest years. They moved into a ramshackle house purchased from Bronson Alcott with royalties from Nathaniel's romances. The plan was for him to write in rustic seclusion while Sophia returned to the transcendentalist town she adored. She soon resumed friendships with Lydia Emerson and Elizabeth Hoar, and her journal was now filled with social events instead of descriptions of sunsets. The three Hawthorne children were instructed not by Bronson Alcott, who had retired from teaching, but by his steadier, more sensible daughters. For the first time in ten years, the Hawthornes had a home of their own, a fact Sophia consecrated by hanging her last painting, "Endymion," in her husband's study.

But the act was premature. The following year, the family uprooted itself once more and moved to Liverpool, England, where Nathaniel served as head of the American consulate, a lucrative position that promised to eliminate the family's financial worries once and for all. By now, Sophia's husband was famous. Writing at a breakneck pace, he had completed three novels in as many years, each praised by an admiring press. Following *The Scarlet Letter*, Nathaniel had written *The House of Seven Gables*, then followed these two masterpieces with a barely disguised account of his time at Brook Farm entitled *The Blithedale Romance.* The heroine of this work, Zenobia, in many ways, resembles Margaret Fuller. Unhappy with the limited options of womanhood while also searching for an understanding mate, Zenobia is, as Nathaniel described her, a "high-spirited Woman, bruising herself against the narrow limitations of her sex."[47] Rather than drowning in a shipwreck, however, Zenobia drowns herself in a river when the man she loves chooses another woman.

The appointment to the Liverpool consulate had less to do with literary success than political acumen. Nathaniel had written the campaign biography of his old college friend, Franklin Pierce, who was elected president in 1853. The lucrative position was part of the spoils system of political office. Nathaniel grumbled about the expense of travel and the discomforts of their unsettled life, but the appointment fulfilled a longstanding dream of Sophia's to visit Europe, where she could finally experience many of the world's art treasures in person (figure 71). For the next seven years, the Hawthorne family followed in Fuller's footsteps. They arrived in Liverpool, where they lived for three years while Nathaniel carried out his official duties. Then they took an extended tour through France and Italy. In Rome, Sophia immediately found herself immersed in an artistic community of expatriate painters and sculptors, many of them American women who found it easier to lead unconventional lives abroad. Henrietta Hosmer and Lois Landers, both sculptors, were part of this new world (figures 72 and 73). Henrietta wore

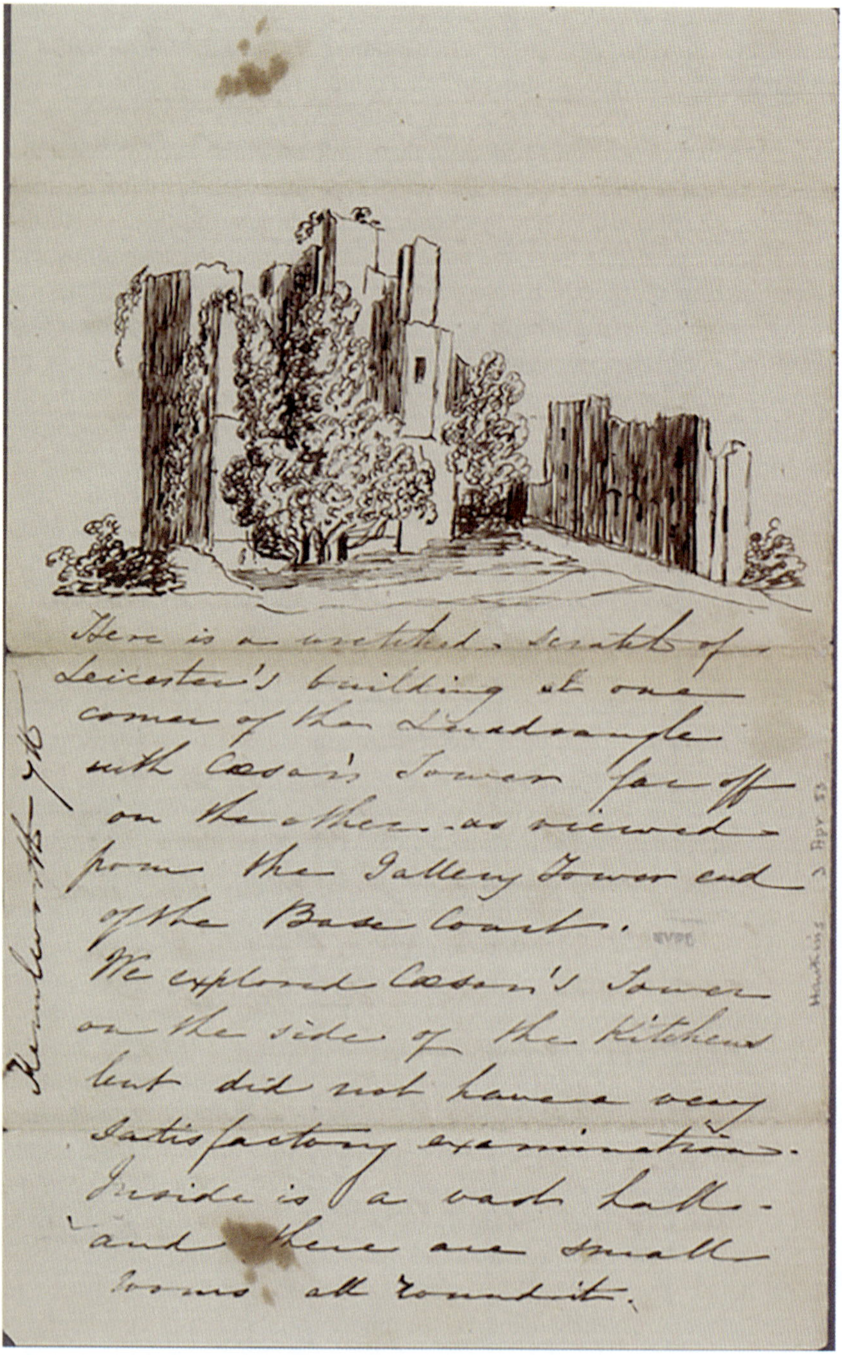

Here is a wretched scratch of Leicester's building at one corner of the Quadrangle with Caesar's Tower far off on the other, as viewed from the Gallery Tower end of the Base Court.
We explored Caesar's Tower on the side of the kitchens but did not have a very satisfactory examination. Inside is a vast hall and there are small rooms all round it.

Figure 71. Sophia Peabody Hawthorne's letter from Europe.

Figure 72. Harriet Goodhue Hosmer.

Figure 73. Louisa Lander.

men's clothing and lived with the lesbian actress Charlotte Cushman; Lois soon became the center of gossip for an alleged extramarital affair. Sophia enjoyed the company of both women, visiting their studios, accompanying them on daily trips to museums and galleries, all three of them debating art and literature during the chilly Roman winter.

Sophia also became acquainted with American expatriate artists Joseph Mozier and William Wetmore Story, both of whom had been close to Fuller during the feverish days of the Italian revolution. She walked the same streets Fuller had when reporting on the battle between French and Italian forces, and she toured St. Peters' Basilica, where Fuller had first met Giovanni Ossoli. Even Fuller's unrequited lovers, Sam and Anna Ward, were now living in Rome, their extended visit coinciding with Anna's recent conversion to Catholicism. Sophia spent evenings with the couple, their talk filled with reminiscences.

But it was the art that most inspired Sophia, who kept a six-hundred-page journal detailing her reactions to the Renaissance paintings and sculptures she encountered. The bulging manuscript book, which rivals the *Cuba Journal* for its depth and freshness of response, is filled with delicate pencil drawings and detailed analyses of the color choices of Fra Angelico and other painters. It was as if her passion for art, latent now for a decade and a half, had returned stronger than ever. "Rome, Rome, *Rome*," she exclaimed to her sister Elizabeth, unwittingly echoing Fuller's shock of recognition at a culture that finally matched her aesthetic imagination: "the eternal-imperial 'Mother of dead empires'—the retreat of the arts & graces—the garden of Nature.... I had all my life long so much desired to see."[48]

In April 1858, Sophia and Nathaniel visited the studio of Mozier, a sculptor Nathaniel judged to be as coarse and earthy as the clay he worked. He nevertheless wrote down Mozier's scandalous gossip about Fuller's secret relationship: "Ossoli himself... was Margaret's servant, or had something to do with the care of her apartments. He was the handsomest man whom Mr. Mozier ever saw, but entirely ignorant even of his own language, scarcely able to read, destitute of all manners; in short, half an idiot, and without any pretensions to be a gentleman." This unflattering account led Nathaniel to wonder what had drawn Fuller to the young Italian. "I do not understand what feeling there could have been, except it was purely sensual; as from him towards her, there could hardly have been even this, for she had not the charm of womanhood." Mozier insisted the two had never married. He also believed Fuller had never actually written a history of the Italian revolution—that her talent had dried up.

Ruminating on this account, disturbed at the portrait of a woman toward whom he had long harbored ambivalent feelings, Hawthorne concluded, "She was a great humbug; of course with much talent, and much moral reality, or else she could not have been so great a humbug... It was such an awful joke, that she should have resolved—in all sincerity, no doubt—to make herself the greatest, wisest, best woman of the age." If Fuller had transformed herself through sheer force of will into a work of art, Hawthorne thought, her life had changed the moment she met a man who returned her love—a situation not unlike the one he was then working out in his last novel, *The Marble Faun*. "On the whole, I do not know but I like her the better for it;—the better, because she proved herself a very woman, after all, and fell as the weakest of her sisters might."[49]

Sophia recorded nothing about the visit with Mozier in her journal. She did, however, speak of Fuller in an uncomplimentary way to the Hawthorne's governess, Ada Shepard, who believed Mozier's gossip "was calculated to lessen the admiration which I have always entertained for [Fuller].... Mrs. Hawthorne knew her intimately, and she, too, tells me painful things about her."[50] Sophia's notes in Rome seem rather to answer the questions raised years before in the Conversations about the comparative scarcity of women artists and writers. Her observations abundantly display the capacity of women to achieve excellence in creative and critical endeavors. Every page of the Italian journal presents penetrating art theory and criticism. And they demonstrate that one woman, at least, was quite capable of beautiful writing.

Nathaniel so admired the work that his publisher, William Ticknor, eventually floated the idea of releasing the journal to the public. Sophia's reply was the same as it had been when Elizabeth suggested she publish the *Cuba Journals*. "Nothing less urgent and terrible than the immediate danger of starvation for my husband and children would induce me to put myself in a magazine or a pair of book covers."[51] Talented, astute, steeped in the writings of Ruskin and other contemporary art critics, Sophia nevertheless refused to appear in public if she could avoid it.

After nearly seven years abroad, the Hawthornes returned to Concord in 1860. There they found the nation transformed beyond recognition. The United States, for decades sharply divided over the question of slavery, would soon enter a protracted and bloody civil war—a development that coincided with the collapse of Nathaniel's ability to write fiction. As the firing on Fort Sumter initiated the four-year conflict, Sophia watched the man she had once called her "Adonis" shrink and age before her eyes. Nathaniel spent his days staring at blank sheets of paper, unable to bring characters to life or plots into motion. Remembering the salubrious effect of her eighteen months in Cuba, Sophia encouraged her husband to travel, certain a change of scenery would soothe him. But the cure was too late; during a trip with his publisher, James T. Fields, he died. The date was May 19, 1864—the Battle of the Wilderness had just concluded.

"The most fortunate event in [Nathaniel's] life was, probably, his marriage with Sophia Peabody."[52] This assessment was made by Nathaniel and Sophia's son, Julian, in his 1884 memoir of both parents, a work rife with late-Victorian ideals of sacrificing womanhood: "She believed in his inspiration; and her office was to promote, so far as in her lay, the favorableness of the conditions under which it should manifest itself."[53] But this office altered dramatically after Nathaniel's death. The problem that had plagued the couple for much of their married life—money—returned with a vengeance after he was buried in Concord's Sleepy Hollow cemetery. Sophia soon learned that her secretive husband had kept much from her, including not only a youthful novel he had never acknowledged but a tangle of debts and loans and careless bookkeeping that now left his surviving family in the surprising position of *owing* money to his publishers. To save herself from penury, Sophia began a task that would occupy the next six years of her life—editing her husband's notebooks for publication, first in *The Atlantic Monthly* and then in book form.

Literary posterity has not been especially kind to her efforts. Even today, Sophia is still depicted as a bowdlerizing prude who wielded the censor's pen upon her husband's more profane and sensuous journal entries. She erased, blotted, even scissored out offensive material from the notebook, eliminating his admission, for instance, that he had consumed "two glasses of hot gin-and-water." Yet by nineteenth century standards for biography, Sophia's editions of Nathaniel's notebooks are remarkably evenhanded. She retained his keen and unforgiving observations of random people he encountered in pubs and taverns, juxtaposing them with his story ideas and his pungent, penetrating character sketches. The picture of Nathaniel that emerged is of a family man and a consummate, if furtively tormented, even obsessive, artist.

Gradually, though, Sophia exhausted the material of her husband's notebooks. At last she was forced to publish her own journals for income. In 1869, still struggling to make ends meet, she moved her family to Dresden, Germany, where the cost of living was lower and where her errant and prodigal son, Julian, could study engineering. (His engineering career lasted two years; after that, he turned to an unremarkable career in writing.) Una and Rose joined her in Dresden. Now the wife of a man who had always felt himself painfully exiled on account of his vocation found herself similarly displaced. In Germany, Sophia completed her *Notes in England and Italy*, a polished version of the journals she had kept a decade earlier when the family was living abroad. A fat, descriptive book, at 546 pages it was considerably longer than anything her husband had published.

In 1850, the year of Margaret Fuller's death, Sophia had written Elizabeth to say, "I think it is designed by GOD that woman should always spiritually wear a veil, & not a coat & hat."[54] This was the precarious position she had arrived at after years of pursuing an artistic career and then marrying an author whose attitudes toward women were stolidly conventional, even reactionary. After her marriage, Sophia repeatedly complained of women who "thrust themselves in to the market place," who dared to walk "unveiled" before the public.[55] Yet with her *Notes in England and Italy*, she violated these very principles, driven by necessity to abandon woman's private sphere. By doing so, she revealed just how flimsy and arbitrary were those strictures, how susceptible to revision. Perhaps it was for this reason she began the book with the following dedication:

TO
ELIZABETH P. PEABODY
THIS VOLUME IS DEDICATED
BY
HER SISTER,
S. H.

For a brief spell, Sophia became a literary celebrity in her own right. *Notes in England and Italy* was widely praised for its "pure taste and enthusiasm." Often as not, however, her prose style, which had been forged decades earlier in the *Cuba Journal*, was attributed to her husband. "It is evident that the spirit of Hawthorne's genius has in some measure enshrouded his wife, and lent a bright lustre to her own thought," announced a newspaper in Syracuse. The *London Saturday Review* made a similar point: "The grace and tenderness of the author of the 'Scarlet Letter' is discernible in its pages."[56]

In the summer of 1870, Sophia moved once last time—to London. For the past twenty years, she had suffered bouts of poor health. Much like her mother, she had developed an incessant, hacking cough, a feeling of weakness in the chest that no homeopathic remedy could relieve. In February 1871, after a brief illness, she died in her rented flat and was buried in the Kensal Green cemetery in northwest London, a sprawling wooded site filled with the graves of actors, artists, and baronets. Una, her oldest daughter, died six years later and was buried next to her mother. A hawthorn tree was planted beside their graves.

Years earlier, when Sophia had traveled to Portugal for her health, she had written to Nathaniel, who remained in Liverpool, "I once thought that no power on earth should ever induce me to live without thee, and especially thought an ocean should never roll between us."[57] She remained buried, an ocean apart, from her husband. Then one day a branch from the moldering hawthorn tree fell and injured hers and Una's headstones. In 2006, the two bodies were exhumed, shipped overseas, and relocated to Concord. A horse-drawn procession took them through the streets of the town where Sophia and Nathaniel had moved after their marriage and where Una had been born. The cortege eventually made its way into Sleepy Hollow Cemetery. There, they were re-interred next to the grave of Nathaniel.

4.

The shipwreck of the *Elizabeth* hit Lydia Emerson especially hard. "I feel personally bereaved by the loss of Margaret Fuller," she wrote Aunt Mary in August 1850. "She did me the honour . . . to care for me somewhat. I had hoped to see much of her in the years to come."[58] Lydia wondered how God could allow such a senseless and malignant fate to so talented a woman. According to her oldest daughter, Fuller's death "seemed so hard to Mother, that it shook her faith. Could a tender Providence have ordered this loss of the whole family just as they were entering the harbour after safely crossing the ocean, longed for by so many friends?"[59]

As she had done before in such times, she retreated to her bedroom room and retrieved her commonplace book, recalling an extract she had once copied from Cowper's hymns:

> we and our affairs
> Are part of a Jehovah's cares.

According to Ellen Emerson, the "circumstance [of the shipwreck] made the hymn speak to her more consolingly, more convincingly. It enabled her to accept the wreck as the intended conclusion of the lives of the Ossolis."[60]

Lydia was forty-eight. Her face was pale as paper, her hair coiled in long thick black ropes about her head, which she covered now with a white veil. She loved thunderstorms and howling winds, because it meant the sun, which always aggravated the residual symptoms of her scarlet fever, briefly was subdued. In the coming years she would continue to endure bouts of unwellness, "little fevers," as she called them, but she also began to enjoy life more on her own terms. For one thing, she was no longer bothered by the rude and careless behavior of transcendentalists who came to sit at her husband's feet. The heyday of the "new thought" was winding down in 1850, and while its high-minded spirit would linger in American culture for decades to come, it was no longer so dominant or disruptive a force. The mood of the nation had changed direction, shifted its quarter. Wispy idealism no longer seemed as compelling in a country defiled by the Fugitive Slave Act and other inequalities.

One month after the sinking of the *Elizabeth*, Waldo received a letter from a suffragist named Paulina Wright Davis, who requested "the sanction of your name and your personal appearance" at the first National Women's Rights Convention in Worcester, Massachusetts. Davis was an activist for women's rights, a fiery speaker with a flair for provocation (figure 74). Four years earlier, in 1846, she had purchased a medical dummy and toured the country teaching women about anatomy—something unheard of at the time. She lobbied for the inclusion of women in medical schools and lectured on the need for reform in the way women dressed. In 1853, she started the prominent feminist journal *The Una*, with its transcendentalist motto, "Out of the great heart of nature seek we truth."

Davis had attended the Conversations in Boston. In the spring of 1850, she had invited Fuller, who was preparing to return to America, to participate in the Women's Right Convention. As she later described it, "many eyes" were turned toward the author of *Woman in the Nineteenth Century* "as the future leader in this movement...To her I, at least, had hoped to confide the leadership of this movement."[61] But Fuller never received the letter. By the time it reached Rome, she was already crossing the Atlantic.

It is not clear whether Waldo discussed the invitation with Lydia. But he ultimately declined to attend the convention, agreeing instead to sign the "Declaration of Principles" that emerged from its proceedings. He did so with some misgivings. As he explained to Davis, while he would gladly vote for the right of every woman to hold property, to run for elected office, and to exercise the right to vote, he did not savor the prospect. "I imagine that a woman whom all men would feel to be the best, would decline such privileges if offered & feel them to be obstacles to her legitimate influence."[62] He believed in the *principle* of equality for women, in other words, but found its expression unladylike. It was not an unusual position for the time. But it was not particularly helpful, either.

Lydia felt no such scruples. She agreed wholeheartedly with the sentiments expressed by the delegates to the National Women's Rights Convention. When her

Figure 74. Paulina Wright Davis.

oldest daughter spoke out against woman's suffrage—Ellen Emerson was by far the most traditional member of the family—she produced an uproar among the other women in her family. "Mother mounts her most belting and snorting war-horse and leaves us all nowhere in less than no time," she reported. "Edith [the Emersons' younger daughter] on a pony of the same breed charges valiantly on her presuming sister and tells her the least those inferior and selfish minds that cannot see the benefit and privilege of voting can do is hold their idle tongues. Father won't speak one word till particularly requested he give his views and as a reward had directed the fury of all his household levelled at him."[63]

If she had become a more conventional Christian than her husband, Lydia was always more radical in politics. Writing to Aunt Mary about a patriotic speech made shortly after the passage of the Fugitive Slave Act in 1850, she said, "How good spirits not yet disembodied [such as] Waldo—could hear it so well, I see not."[64] A few years later, on the Fourth of July, she draped the gates of the house in black cambric to protest the continuation of slavery in a nation that supposedly enshrined liberty in the Declaration of Independence. In 1861, when war broke out, she joyously exclaimed, "This is the beginning of the end of slavery."[65] Two years later, when it was unclear whether Union forces would prevail, she told Ellen, "I have always a realizing and practical sense that this War is wholly directed and controlled by God—being on the part of those who are seeking through it the establishment of *Universal* Freedom—eminently a Holy War—the only Holy War the earth has ever known except the war of the Revolution— . . . ."[66] (figure 75).

Her growing outspokenness coincided with Waldo's decline in health. By the end of the war, in 1865, he had become increasingly forgetful. He struggled for words, wrote less and less in his journals. Each day he woke up convinced he had lost his pocket watch. Ellen Emerson began to accompany him to lectures to make sure he remained on task. Eventually, she took charge of the jumble of papers in his study, putting them in order before he lectured. In the summer of 1872, his dementia took a sudden turn for the worse when he awoke one morning to the smell of smoke. The house was on fire, the second floor ablaze. He awakened Lydia, then ran outside to rouse the neighbors. Next, he did something quite strange. While Concord's citizens raced into the study to rescue his books and papers, he began to hurl other items *into* the fire. He threw keepsakes of his first wife Ellen. Then he tossed items that had belonged to little Waldo. Afterward, according to a neighbor, he wandered "forlornly about in an old muddy coat, & no stockings smiling serenely if any one spoke to him, & looking calmly on the wreck of his home as if it were of no special consequence to him."[67]

In the wake of the disaster, the family moved into the Old Manse (as it was now called, after Nathaniel Hawthorne's book by that title.) The town took up a subscription to restore the Emersons' home, and while the renovations took place, Waldo and Ellen traveled to Europe and then to Egypt, leaving Lydia to remain in Concord to oversee the work. She and her youngest daughter Edith

Figure 75. Lydia Jackson Emerson soon after the Civil War.

picked out wallpaper, bought new rugs and furniture, supervised the construction of oriel windows in her bedroom. Lydia pursued other interests, as well. Although she claimed to be no writer, she contributed anonymous articles to *Our Dumb Animals*, the house organ for the Massachusetts Society for the Prevention of Cruelty to Animals.[†] She also donated time and money to countless charities, attending social events in Concord and Boston. Mainly, though, she read—or asked others to read to her while she worked in her garden or the kitchen. She kept abreast of Darwinian theory, of current theological debates, and of the plight of formerly enslaved people in the South. She continued to read Goethe and other writers in the original German. Unlike her husband, she still devoured novels by the bushel.

When Waldo at last returned to the restored house on the Cambridge turnpike, he had already entered the final decade of a twilit senescence. In 1879, Bronson Alcott opened the Concord School of Philosophy, which offered lectures and

[†] "I have long regretted," wrote Ellen, "that I did not follow this up, learn which they were and secure those numbers in which they appeared, for they did appear."

discussions in the summer. Readings from Henry David Thoreau's unpublished journals were given, as well as lectures on Kant and Fichte and other German idealists who had excited young people half a century earlier. Lydia became especially interested in the new venture. According to Ellen Emerson, her mother, "who had been used all her married life to Father's having 'Conversations' for Mr Alcott, that is his inviting as many friends as he could find to come after tea and hear Mr Alcott talk, invited the philosophers to have conversations in our house." Before long, as many as thirty people crowded into the parlor with the black marble fireplace, some spilling into the hallway and dining room. Waldo, no longer able to participate, sat quietly smiling in his chair. But whenever Lydia joined in the debate, "People rejoiced."[68]

Waldo died in 1882, one month after his seventy-eighth birthday. By then he was largely unintelligible, his eyes dull, his mind all but gone. According to Ellen, during his last hours he kept repeating the same words: "'the beautiful boy.' Mother imagined he was telling her he looked forward in dying to see Waldo again."[69] For a while, Lydia visited her husband's grave in Sleepy Hollow every day. She brought flowers from her garden, arranging them with care. After a while, though, she no longer sensed his presence in the cemetery and stopped going. During this time Ellen believed her mother was "so feeble and wanted him so much, that she would not live long."[70] But she was wrong. Lydia went on living. Gradually she regained an interest in the world around her. In the remaining decade of her life, she was more active than ever.

She visited the women's state prison—as Margaret Fuller had done three decades earlier—where she observed the condition of the inmates. She continued to attend the Concord School of Philosophy, where Waldo now was commemorated each year. She hosted discussions in her home about the condition of Indigenous people in the west, a topic that interested Elizabeth Peabody, as well. She danced well into her eighties. Nothing appealed to her so much, however, as a good argument.

Years earlier, when her son Edward faced a serious case of typhoid fever, she momentarily forgot herself and argued with the doctor over whether the local minister "had spoken as he ought about the sin of our Government."[71] (She was referring to slavery.) Another time, when Bronson Alcott and William Lloyd Garrison quarreled over vegetarianism, Lydia, who agreed in principle with Garrison, got involved. "There was some excitement and some personality on both sides," she explained, "but at last Mr A behaved so beautifully that I from having felt cross at him all eve.g turned round and attacked Mr Garrison in his behalf—for which valour Mr A did me the honour to thank me after the meeting."[72] When a cousin from Plymouth came to visit, the two of them, both in their eighties, argued about religion as they walked down Concord's main street to the butcher.

Never would she feel at home in the village where she had moved upon her marriage. "In her fifty-seven years of life in Concord," wrote Ellen, "she had never taken root there, she was always a sojourner, her home was Plymouth, a never-dying flame of love for Plymouth burned and burst forth in praises of its people, stories of its glorious founding, reminiscences of its peaceful ways, it social life...."[73] In 1885, on her fiftieth wedding anniversary, she and Ellen traveled to her hometown, where they visited the old Winslow House, with its ornate newel posts and tiled fireplaces, and where Lydia relived the day she had been escorted down the broad stairs by Waldo.

Gradually, though, she too lost her memory. For a long time, she could recite German poetry taught her fifty years earlier by George Bradford. Then, almost overnight, those verses disappeared. She began to lose the names of friends and family, then entire areas of her recollection vanished. Nearing ninety, she was smitten with a young man whose name she could not recall. He was a grandson, one of Edith's adult children, who resembled Waldo around the time he had proposed to her.

Unlike the other members of the Bright Circle, Lydia harbored few, if any, ambitions to become a serious writer or artist. Instead, she wanted a life filled with friends and good books and ample time to think. Before her marriage, she had considered herself a transcendentalist. She had been drawn to the movement's idealism, its serious exploration of all that was spiritual, and its desire for social change. But she soon reconsidered her position. She never believed in the perfectibility of human beings, whom she understood as innately flawed, and while she admired Mary Moody Emerson's ferocious independence and barbed opinions, she also understood that the quest for personal freedom at all costs could become disfiguring, even debilitating. It was these insights that made her transcendentalism's most acerbic, if under-recognized, critic.

"In 1891," Ellen wrote, Lydia "began to wish 'to go home,' usually however with 'if I could only go back and find it as it was, with my Father & Mother there.'" Her mind was clouded now, her nights restless. When the rest of the house was asleep, she would suddenly call out to Ellen, referring to her as "Ma."[74] She died in her sleep in 1892. "Mother had said to me several times in earlier years," recalled her daughter, "that she had noticed that those of her friends who greatly feared to die, died in their sleep or unconscious, died without knowing it, and it seemed to her a compassion of God for their timidity. 'Perhaps I may be allowed to go so,' she would say, and so she was."[75]

5.

On December 2, 1851, Mary Moody Emerson accompanied Lydia to the Concord Lyceum where Waldo was lecturing on the recently deceased Margaret Fuller. Apparently the two women quarreled. Later that evening, around midnight, Mary wrote Lydia to apologize for her "oft disagreeable impulses." Then she launched into an excited and syntactically gnarled reappraisal of Fuller: "*What* was the mystery. No *record of her faith in imm*ᵗ [immortality]! Had she been xian! What a spirit! And thro' the future what a bright & burning one who could be so generous *And her truth* Oh what an eternity awaits. And we forget all if with her powers & influence as like the waves wh so soon ceased the feeble agitations w'h interred her remains."[76]

Mary Emerson and Margaret Fuller had met just once, in Newburyport, Massachusetts, a few miles south of the New Hampshire border. The meeting was an unmitigated disaster. Fuller had just completed *Woman in the Nineteenth Century* and was preparing to move to New York. Mary had long admired her from a distance. She had followed Fuller's career, read the transcriptions of the Conversations, and would soon read *Woman in the Nineteenth Century*. She was also aware of Fuller's work editing *The Dial* and the fact that she had been hired to contribute to the *New-York Tribune*. It was as if her own youthful desire to write had at last come to fruition in the younger woman.

But something about Fuller brought out the worst in Mary. She detected a hint—*more* than a hint—of condescension. Fuller acted bored and put-out around the querulous older woman. Mary responded with pedantic obstinacy. As she later described the meeting, Fuller "laid all day & eve. on sofa & catechised me, who told my literal 'traditions' like any old bob[b]in woman."[77]

A generation earlier, Mary had been the primary conduit for many of the Romantic ideas that Fuller now embraced as her own. She had struggled to achieve the life of an independent, free-thinking woman long before Fuller had even been born. That the younger woman now refused to acknowledge her debt to Mary—that she saw instead only a tedious, perverse old lady eager for gossip and disagreement—provoked her to no end. (Fuller would soon tell a friend that Mary "perpetually defaces the high by such strange mingling of the low.... It is certainly not pleasant to hear of God & Miss Gage in a breath.")[78] Apparently Mary erupted at some point in their meeting, her voice swelling with indignation. When the two women said farewell, both were relieved.

But Mary quickly regretted her outburst. She realized she had missed a chance to speak to one of the best-educated women in America—a feeling that stayed with her well after Fuller's death off the coast of Fire Island. "Had I been favored with one sparkle of her fine wit," she said, "one argument for her dissent, from her fine mind, what a treasure to memory."[79]

The same month she heard Waldo's lecture on Fuller, Mary attended another talk at the Concord lyceum. This was by the author and feminist Elizabeth Oakes Smith, one of the first women to appear regularly on the lecture circuit. Smith had been a popular author for a decade, known primarily for her novels as well as for a sentimental poem entitled "The Sinless Child" (figure 76). But in 1850 she began contributing a series of articles to the *New-York Tribune* devoted to "Woman and Her Needs," filling a void in that paper created by Fuller's death. In these pieces

Figure 76. Elizabeth Oakes Smith.

she heralded a new era for women, one that would surpass the present moment when they were still expected to exert their influence within the domestic circle. Increasingly women seemed "disposed to associate as do our compeers of the other sex," Smith wrote, "for the purpose of evolving better views, and of confirming some degree of power... It is folly to meet them with contempt and ridicule, for the period for such weapons is passing away."[80]

On the night Smith spoke at the Concord lyceum, she was "confronted by Aunt Mary Emerson." She recalled a "small, quick-moving woman with eyes sharp and penetrating... [that] not only looked at you but through you." The tiny woman was accompanied by Lydia, who pulled aside the speaker and whispered apologetically that Mary might not stay for the entire lecture: "'[S]he has a way, when not quite pleased with speaker, of getting up and going out, scattering shawl and gloves or hood all along the aisle; you need not mind it.'" But Lydia's warning was unnecessary. As soon as the lecture was over, Mary rushed up to Smith and offered her hand in gratitude.[81]

A year earlier, in 1850, Mary had sold her farm in Waterford, Maine, ending a contentious arrangement with relatives who had been renting the property for decades. She now became a wanderer, a pilgrim, a solitary woman perennially seeking the "home for life" that had eluded her since her exile from her father's parsonage as a small girl.[82] Much of her time was spent in Concord, where she still refused to sleep under her nephew's roof but permitted herself the privilege of pontificating throughout the family dinner. Portions of each year were spent roaming throughout New England, sometimes traveling as far as western Massachusetts, searching, always, for reasonable room and board and a well-stocked library.

She grew, if possible, even more quarrelsome. During a conversation hosted by Bronson Alcott, she sat in a circle that included Henry James Sr. (a new friend of Waldo's) and Henry David Thoreau. James was feeling expansive. Bald, bearded, squinting with nearsightedness, he delivered, in Thoreau's recounting, "*quasi* philanthropic doctrines in a metaphysics dress, but very crude."[83] Mary sat for some time listening to this harangue with "rising wrath," before at last rising from her "chair at the west side of the room, and turning her oddly-garnished head toward the south side, where the offender smilingly sat, she clasped her little wrinkled hands and raised them toward the black band over her left temple (a habit she had when deeply moved), and began to answer to these doctrines of Satan, as she thought them."[84]

She was tinier than ever. A friend of the Emerson children remembered she was "hardly taller than a girl of twelve... dressed in a white woolen 'shroud.'"[85] Another placed her height at 4'8". Yet her eyes remained clear, her mind as curious as ever. In 1851, when she was nearly eighty, she engaged in a long conversation with Thoreau, who afterward wrote that Mary was "the wittiest & most vivacious woman" he had ever met, "a genius" who understood his passion for nature better than anyone else he knew. "It is perhaps her greatest praise and peculiarity that she, more surely than any other woman, gives her companion occasion to utter his best thought."[86]

If she no longer expected to exert her agency and influence upon an otherwise indifferent world, she continued to write. In 1846, she composed "A Meeting of Two Friends after Long Separation by Death," published at first in a local newspaper and eventually picked up by the *Christian Register*. The work is a dialogue—Mary always loved a good conversation—in which two friends, both dead and strolling through heaven, discuss a mutual acquaintance who "did not possess [Truth's] deepest vital power; his missionizing objects were strongest and they discolored facts."[87] (The piece was a veiled reminiscence of her brother William, dead now for thirty-five years.)

And in 1852, she published another piece, this one reduced to a single paragraph by the editors of the *Register* and called "The Woman." This was a belated response to Elizabeth Oakes Smith's lecture and to her newspaper pieces on "Woman and Her Needs." Mary acknowledged there was "much controversy about the rights and duties of both women and men," and she proposed to "teach the true and proper rights and duties of women, and the sacred obligations of men, to treat them with care, respect and tenderness, so that the husband and the wife, in a proper, rational sense, may be considered as *one*, and the benevolent design of the creator be fulfilled who, in His love and wisdom, created man, male and female, for their good comfort and happiness." In many ways, the statement echoed Fuller's portrait of a "holy marriage" in *Woman in the Nineteenth Century*. It also resembled Lydia Emerson's "theosophy of marriage." But it was a contrarian statement by a woman who had not only refused offers of marriage twice but insisted all her life on a fierce independence and had even dared to imagine a path that included neither the support nor the presence of a man. She signed the piece "An Octogenarian."[88]

Although she would never fully reconcile herself to Waldo's apostasy and desertion of the ministry, she did come to accept transcendentalism as the inevitable outcome of the speculation she and her nephew both engaged in years before. One winter's night, when she was in her mid-seventies, she lit her candle and reread "dear Waldo's splendid chapter in Nature which excited me..." This was likely either the chapter on language or beauty, both of which she considered especially fine in their statements on the idiom of nature. She said nothing about her nephew's debt to her own thinking, focusing instead on Waldo's style, which refined and polished her own, even inspiring fresh insights. She looked out her window. "We see these snows & they cover the skeleton trees with the 'beauty' Waldo describes—so I'll not dare—, but may call them winding sheets—sweet emblem of what covers other withered bodies..." Initially refusing to describe a phenomenon already expressed so well by her nephew, she abruptly changed her mind, transforming the snow-clad trees into memento mori.[89]

In 1859, her long pilgrimage came to an end. This was the year she moved to Williamsburgh, in Brooklyn, where she was cared for by a niece, Hannah Haskins Parsons, much as she had once cared for the elderly women in her family. Death, her counsel and constant companion, occupied her thoughts even more than before. To Lydia, she wrote, "When I was journeying once you asked me if I should like to be brought to Concord after death—? I replied that it was a matter of indifference to me where I was buried. Then you said 'Are you *willing* to come?' Now I feel very desirous to do so. I long to see Concord and to lie by my old friends there"[90] (figure 77).

Figure 77. Mary Moody Emerson's death photograph.

On May 1, 1863, three months before her ninetieth birthday, she died. Her body was brought to Sleepy Hollow, where it was buried near her admirer, Thoreau, who had died of tuberculosis the year before, and not far from the spot where Nathaniel Hawthorne, who memorialized her childhood home in a collection of stories, would soon be buried.

In the years before her death, Mary had relinquished her earliest ambitions, confessing, "I am resigned to being nothing, never expect a palm, a laurel, hereafter."[91] But her afterlife proved more durable than she predicted. Waldo promoted her thought and writing, honoring the aunt whose perspective and writing had so deeply influenced him. "I see plainly," he told Elizabeth Palmer Peabody soon after Mary was buried, "that I shall not probably rest until I have copied out some admirable letters & journals of the best days of this devoutest solitariest Muse, & tried whether these writings which I have found so poetic & potent will not speak to others as to me."[92]

The bundles of papers he sifted through had been acquired by his oldest daughter, Ellen. In 1861, Ellen had visited Mary in Brooklyn. The old woman greeted her in her best black dress, eager to relate family history to a receptive audience. She was no longer always lucid, and was sometimes confined to her bed, but to Ellen she recounted in detail the arcane narrative of her family genealogy, a tale of pious and upright ministers stretching back to the founding of New England. She had long considered bequeathing her Almanacks to the wife or daughter of a surviving nephew, once telling Waldo, "I have put into a trunk your richest gifts (letters), with some old Almanacks... The last you may burn or if any of my female freinds wish may have a N[umber]."[93] Now, she determined to bestow the entire manuscript of Almanacks—"piles of journals," as Ellen excitedly described them—upon her grand-niece, who took them with her to the Emerson house in Concord.[94]

Waldo soon set about copying passages from the enormous document into his journal, indexing portions he considered especially important. He noted the last entry his aunt made, in 1858, when she was eighty-four, a passage as vigorous and wide-ranging as ever. It included a plea to the "God of mercy" to "look on thy coloured people. Behold their sufferings." Then it beseeched, "with earnestness," that God effect a speedy end to her life on earth. Finally, she added a caveat: "if I am deluded & not regenerated to love Him with heart & mind that is the spark of reason."[95] This elliptical phrase was an acknowledgement of the transition in thought she had helped summon into existence—the passage from a puritanical Christianity to a Romantic conception of the indwelling *reason*, or intuition. For decades, she had managed to hold both ideas in her mind. Now, in her dotage, she entertained the possibility of delusion.

In 1869, when Waldo was asked by the New England Women's Club to deliver a talk, he decided to speak about his aunt. The Club had been founded a year earlier by Julia Ward Howe, and in many ways, it was an extension of Margaret Fuller's historic Conversations: a weekly gathering devoted to literature, art, and various social causes. Elizabeth Peabody was also among its founding members.

Now Waldo narrated for the assembled women "some of the thoughts and soliloquies of a country girl, poor, solitary...growing from youth to age amid slender opportunities and usually very humble company."[96] He stressed his aunt's self-taught genius and iconoclasm, focusing primarily on her religious zeal and love of nature. The philosophy and theological debates that occupied much of her mental life, as well as her commitment to the cause of abolition, were missing from his account.

In 1872, when the Emerson home caught fire, the Almanacks were among the precious items saved by a small battalion of friends and neighbors who cleared the house of its manuscripts and papers. Louisa May Alcott and her sister May helped sort the singed and water-damaged papers. For decades, they remained in much the same condition. Then, in the twentieth century, the enormous pile of Mary's papers were donated to Harvard University, where they languished, uncatalogued for decades, along with the only known photograph of her—a portrait taken after her death. In it, she wears her mobcap; her face appears youthful, beatific. To this day, Mary's manuscripts, their margins blackened by the flames, smell of smoke from the fire of 1872.

If her Almanacks long remained buried in obscurity, Waldo's lecture, eventually published in the complete works on the centennial of his birth, made her example available to later generations. Virginia Woolf, who invented a talented sister of Shakespeare to reveal the staggering obstacles faced by women writers, discovered Mary when she was in her early twenties and approvingly noted that "she was only self-taught, and her fervour boiled within her, scalding those she loved best." Several decades later, the poet Tillie Olsen placed her in the same category as Dorothy Wordsworth and Alice James, "those female bloodkin of great writers" who possessed "as-great capacities" as their more famous male siblings. And in 1936, the painter N. C. Wyeth painted an imagined portrait of Mary speaking with a young Henry David Thoreau.

To the New England Women's Club, Waldo had declared that his aunt had managed, despite persistent adversity and a temperament that lacked equilibrium, to attain a level of thought and cultivation that still eluded most people. "I confess that when I read these papers I do not feel that religion has made any progress in our community," he said. "Neither do I feel that society and conversation have." Mary's accomplishments had been achieved purely on her own, the product of a lonely, steadfast, and ultimately noble life. "But elevation must always be solitary," Waldo continued, his tone bittersweet. "Plotinus, and Herbert, and Thoreau, and this woman, have no contemporaries..."[97]

6.

In 1846, the same year Margaret Fuller set sail for Europe, Elizabeth Palmer Peabody made a journey of her own. She traveled to Maine, not far from the place she had once taught the children of a prosperous landowner, and there she paid a long-deferred visit to Mary Moody Emerson. For much of the 1840s, the two women—single, intellectual, always in search of a place to call home—had grown closer. Mary, who called Elizabeth "Miss Pea," visited the West Street bookshop whenever she was in Boston. On one memorable occasion, Elizabeth escorted the older woman to a performance of *Hamlet* starring the great English tragedian, Charles Macready. (Elizabeth's brother-in-law, Horace Mann, accompanied them.) Sometime in the middle of the decade, Elizabeth wrote Mary to tell the older woman just how much her example had meant to her over the years. She started, as she often did, by speaking in generalities. She believed "characters which have the most life and joy are those which are not scrupulous. And that the excessive fear of doing wrong which we Unitarian children were all brought up with, strikes a blow at something within us—who is *vital*."

But then she applied this insight to Mary. "You lived before that day, and do not exhibit any of this death-in-life which I complain of, but coquette with life like a girl of fifteen, who knows herself sovereign and can afford to play with *All*." Elizabeth thought Mary had heeded her nephew's command to live according to one's inner convictions better than any woman she knew. "This is subjective transcendentalism I think you must acknowledge," she wrote, "but it is very exciting to see it done. I confess it makes my blood dance and is altogether more *entertaining* than the conscientious nicety of some people."[98]

Throughout much of the 1840s, Elizabeth had been a dervish of activity, publishing issues of *The Dial* and books by Hawthorne on her printing press, writing a series of long, learned letters on religion for the *Christian Register* (these were avidly read by Mary Moody Emerson), and attending countless meetings of reform organizations and the Transcendental Club. She continued to run her bookshop with a bustling, if sometimes diffuse, energy, ordering books at customers' requests, carefully wrapping them in brown paper and inscribing their titles on the spine. The lending library and shop expanded during this time beyond the front parlor; it now included the large drawing room just across the hall.

Mary Emerson's refuge in Maine appealed to Elizabeth, who considered it an American version of Wordsworth's Mount Rydal. "For sixteen years," she wrote, "I have been trying to get to this place of mountains and lakes, and perhaps in my whole life may never see another mountain." But the trip was marred by one of Mary's "storms," as Elizabeth called them. The older woman was jealous when Elizabeth befriended the neighbors. Soon there followed a comic, if unpleasant, incident in which Mary misplaced her spectacles and accused Elizabeth of stealing them. Mary called her guest "meddlesome" and a "busy old maid..." Then she read Elizabeth's correspondence without asking, thereby causing yet another scene.[99]

Elizabeth refused to be shaken by the quarrel. "She is an extraordinary creature," she said of her volatile friend soon after the visit. "I think I never received a greater impression of her genius: the ploughshare of Experience never seems to have broken the wild beauty of her character—which like a wild country of great natural sublimity of feature—retains its untamed rocks & woods & cataracts telling of the creative power of God." Still, there was something sad about the older woman's self-tormenting independence. "It grieves my heart however to realize how entirely impossible it is for her—with all her genius and all the noble views and deep truths before her mind—to be serenely and beautifully *happy.* She has certainly missed the truth of Christianity which gives the power of selfgovernment and takes away the lust of power over others."[100]

Throughout the late 1840s and 1850s, Elizabeth continued to teach her "historical conferences," once the precursor to Margaret Fuller's Conversations. They now lasted six months and included some fifty sessions. One year she instructed a class of women on the French Revolution. Other times she focused on Greek and Roman history. "Our text-books were Herodotus, Thucydides, Zenophon, Livy, and Plutarch," she later recalled.

The quality of these classes was appreciated beyond the walls of the bookshop where they were held. "There were some Harvard students, brothers and friends of my scholars, who came to me *sub rosa*... and asked my advice as to their historical reading, who followed out this course and read the tragedies, and I advised them to read the Greek historians and Livy in the originals." More than ever, she was convinced that for women, history "should take the place that law, medicine, or theology takes in the liberal education of men."[101]

In 1849, she embarked on another venture, this time producing a single issue of a journal she called *Aesthetic Papers.* The periodical was meant to fill the gap left by *The Dial* and other transcendentalist publications, all of which had folded within a year or two of publication. Elizabeth's journal was remarkable for its contents. Drawing on her friendships, she published an essay on "War" by Waldo Emerson; Nathaniel Hawthorne's short story, "Main-street"; and most memorably, Henry David Thoreau's "Resistance to Civil Government," better known as "Civil Disobedience." There were also poems by Ellen Hooper, Thomas Wentworth Higginson, and Mary Emerson's protégé, Ann Sargent Gage. Elizabeth hoped to make a living by editing this ambitious journal, but only one issue of *Aesthetic Papers* was ever published. The journal represented a last gasp for the idealistic transcendentalism of the 1840s; from now on, the movement shifted its priorities to social reforms such as abolitionism and the burgeoning women's rights movement.

There were other changes, other losses. Elizabeth's younger sisters had both married and left the house on 13 West Street. Fuller had crossed the Atlantic and was sending dispatches from Italy. Elizabeth's early mentors, Washington Allston and the Reverend William Ellery Channing, had died. Even her parents, Eliza and Nathaniel Peabody, had decided to move away to West Newton. Elizabeth found herself alone in the "Book Room" and lending library, the ground floor of the rowhouse filled with musty old boxes of *Dials* and *Aesthetic Papers*, stacks of German periodicals, and leftover copies of Hawthorne's *The Gentle Boy*, which Sophia had illustrated a decade earlier and which were now "eaten by mice and other ways damaged."[102] She managed to keep the bookshop open until 1852, when it at last became clear that there was no longer enough business to continue. In February of that year, she closed its doors for good, leaving the building to her brother Nat, who continued to sell homeopathic medicines in the front parlor for several more years. An era in American cultural life had at last ended.

Elizabeth once described herself, rather inaccurately, as "the only practical transcendentalist there is." (Unlike Lydia and Mary Moody Emerson, she was a latecomer to the antislavery cause.) Throughout the 1850s, she strove, often with mixed results, to put her idealism to useful ends, promoting the work of an eccentric Polish linguist, Charles Kraitsir, whose theory of the universal origins of language was irresistible to Elizabeth. She also advanced the ideas of Joseph Bem, also Polish, a soldier who had devised a method of teaching history through huge, color-coded charts. For several years, Elizabeth oversaw the production of these charts, hand coloring many of them herself and distributing them to classrooms throughout New England. In her opinion, the charts illustrated more than mere dates; they revealed the gradual unfolding of providential history, a tale of progress that led inexorably to the discovery of North America and the creation of the first modern democracy. As a practical matter, though, they were too cumbersome to be widely adopted by school districts.

More successful was Elizabeth's advocacy of the kindergarten, an innovation of the German pedagogue Friedrich Froebel, whose innovative schools for very young children were not unlike those once operated by Bronson Alcott (figure 78). They emphasized frequent play, creative activities, and immersion in nature. In 1860, Elizabeth opened the first English-language kindergarten in the United States, on Boston's Pinckney Street (not far from the room where Nathaniel Hawthorne had lived decades earlier while courting Sophia). The kindergarten soon had thirty pupils and required the help of four assistants, including one devoted solely to gymnastics. It operated on the principle that training children to become thoughtful, compassionate adults was best begun at an early age. The rooms Elizabeth rented were filled with the cheerful sounds of children and with examples of their artwork. After a quarter century of writing, editing, and running her bookshop, Elizabeth had returned to teaching, the occupation she had learned from her mother.

By then, Eliza was gone. She and Nathaniel Peabody had left Boston in 1851 on account of her poor health, but the permanent cough she had suffered for years continued to worsen. On January 11, 1853, at age seventy-four, she died. Elizabeth tended her through her final illness, numb, despairing, and ultimately relieved that her mother's "life went out into the free spaces," as she told Sophia, "and here she lies, for I am sitting by her bedside, this first night. Mary has gone home; father has

Figure 78. A nineteenth-century kindergarten.

gone to bed. We are all at peace—peace—peace."[103] Nathaniel died two years later, in 1855.

The loss of her mother left Elizabeth feeling "rather mournfully in freedom to do nothing but business."[104] But now, with her bookshop closed and both parents gone, she found herself in worse financial shape than she had been in for some time. That was when a miracle of sorts occurred. "Last year, some of your friends who love you & who think that you have spent your life & strength in working for others' benefit collected a sum of money." Thus began a letter from Sarah Clarke, the artist and sister of James Freeman Clarke, who told Elizabeth the financial gift was placed into an account guaranteed to yield one hundred dollars a year. Clarke was not at liberty to name who had contributed, "but I can tell you that all of your friends who knew of the plan, and who were able to do so, gladly contributed."[105] For the first time in her life, Elizabeth now had "*leisure* for study—All my life it has seemed to me personally I wanted no other wealth than *leisure*—& now I have got it."[106]

Although she managed to write several essays, her focus remained squarely on the kindergarten movement. In 1867, she traveled to Germany to visit kindergartens and speak with Froebel's widow and acolytes to learn more about his ideas. From this trip came a string of works, including *Kindergarten Culture* (1870), *The*

Kindergarten in Italy (1872), and *Letters to Kindergarteners* (1886). In 1876, Elizabeth founded the *Kindergarten Messenger*, the goal of which was to "describe and explain the moral and intellectual culture that should precede object teaching and book study..."[107] She edited the journal for two years.

Moncure Daniel Conway, a second-generation transcendentalist who knew Elizabeth well, thought her attention to kindergartens a waste of her prodigious talents. "Miss Peabody's devotion to the kindergarten is one of the great literary tragedies," he wrote. "She could be the greatest woman of letters in America. She could spend her last years writing her recollections of literary men and women. She had a larger circle of friends than any other one person, and she should write of 'The Men and Women I have Known.' It would be a literary history of her time, unsurpassed in interest." Instead, remarked Conway, Elizabeth had squandered her energy on the formation of kindergartens throughout the nation. "It is a loss to literature."[108]

But Elizabeth considered the work of training small children more important than literature. She believed it was an application of Unitarian self-culture and transcendentalist self-reliance, a bid for a better future, a contribution to her mother's legacy. She also thought her writing on the kindergarten movement a worthy addition to the intellectual currents of her time.

Ultimately, Conway's criticism was premature—Elizabeth *did* set out to write her "Reminiscences." Although it was never completed, in the process of recalling the memorable incidents of her life, Elizabeth created several memorable portraits of the men and women she had known in the past. Her *Reminiscences of the Rev. William Ellery Channing, D.D.*, recounts the close friendship she enjoyed with her first mentor and collaborator. Her *Last Evening with Washington Allston* captures the sparkling wit of the garrulous painter as he held forth during candlelit evenings of endless talk. After Sophia's death, Elizabeth also expended enormous energy correcting the biographies of her taciturn brother-in-law, Nathaniel Hawthorne, especially those that claimed she had been romantically involved with the writer before her younger sister. And when Mary Moody Emerson died, Elizabeth wrote a fond, frank obituary that captured the woman's rough edges even as it forgave them: "She had a great heart, although she was not tender, like most women; for it was her theory that what was noble and prevailing in human nature was to be brought out by provocation rather than by nursing." Elizabeth fondly recalled that day so long ago when Mary had appeared without warning in Boston, an event that launched a decades-long friendship filled with as many barbs as blessings. She concluded, though, with the observation that Mary had "commanded the homage of her illustrious nephews," and that recognition from such talented young men made it "worth while to have lived amid all the disturbing influence of this 'workaday world,' however much she might enjoy contemplation."[109]

Finally, in 1885, she wrote a lengthy recollection of Margaret Fuller that appeared in the *Boston Daily Transcript*. Thinking back over her first encounter with the eighteen-year-old woman, she said, "I always remember the interview, as if it were a little cluster of diamonds,—she was so courteous, so brilliant, so graceful; every moment dropping such a gem of real thought as is rarely let fall in a casual conversation .... it flowed from a genius on her part, comprehensive of and enjoying all phases of the infinite life variously represented of the individual man."[110] Elizabeth was prompted to write about Fuller by the gossip that continued to surround her memory. "[M]any disagreeable things had been said of the marriage," she acknowledged, "as if it were a matter of pure weakness in Margaret, and the count quite unworthy of the prize he had won." But Peabody offered testimony from those who had known her in Italy and could vouch for the sincerity of the couple's mutual respect. She also discussed the reason Fuller kept the marriage secret, claiming it would have been injurious to Ossoli's brother, a chamberlain of the pope. Then she added, perceptively, that "it was not unpleasant to Margaret's romantic temperament to have this little mystery for a season."

More than anything, though, Elizabeth was sympathetic to the enormous sacrifices Fuller had made to care for her family. After Timothy Fuller's death, she had struggled to provide for them—a position similar to the one Elizabeth herself had long endured. Now she recalled a time when Fuller's younger sister, Ellen, had asked her to persuade Fuller to leave home and travel to Europe. Fuller appeared in "an agony of tears" and demanded to know if Elizabeth thought she should abandon her family to visit France and Italy. "'You would not do it, Miss Peabody; would you? Speak as upon oath; put yourself in my place.'" Elizabeth knew all too well the constraints duty could place upon a talented, oldest daughter. She encouraged Fuller to free herself in the name of self-fulfillment. "[I]f I did feel as you do," Elizabeth continued, "that all the future of my life would be lost, all the past vain, if I did not go—I would go, and trust to make up to them afterwards, especially if my brothers and sisters desired it as much as yours do."[111]

By the time she wrote this, Elizabeth was over eighty (figure 79). She was now something of an institution in Boston, having grown plump ("just as fat and solid and good humored as she can be," according to her sister Mary) and famously absentminded.[112] A story made the rounds of her stepping directly into a tree. When asked if she had seen it, she replied, "Yes, I saw it, but I did not realize it."[113] Another story, recounted by her nephew Julian, described her sitting on a chair of newborn kittens and smothering them as she conversed, wholly unaware of their mewling.

Increasingly, she was regarded by the younger generation with a mixture of respect and bemusement. Edward Emerson, the surviving son of Lydia and Waldo, remembered her with "the gray hair falling down under the bonnet askew, the spectacles slipping down with resulting upturned radiant face, the nondescript garments and general dissolving effect."[114] In 1886, Henry James created a character named Miss Birdseye for his satirical novel, *The Bostonians*, a "frumpy little missionary" who "was the last link in a tradition" and who "when she should be called away the heroic age of New England life—the age of plain living and

Figure 79. Elizabeth Palmer Peabody, cultural institution.

high thinking, of pure ideals and earnest effort, of moral passion and noble experiment—would effectually be closed."[115] James denied his character was based on Elizabeth, but no one was fooled by the disclaimer.

Despite the way she was portrayed by a younger generation, despite her meddlesomeness and abstraction and incessant torrent of talk, Elizabeth was widely admired. Her entire life had been devoted to others, from the training of girls to the publicizing of Native American struggles in the west. And there was her tireless enthusiasm for the mental life, for ideas of all sorts. When Bronson Alcott launched his Concord School of Philosophy, she quickly became a central participant. "I never felt so completely *at home* as I do in this School of Philosophy," she told her sister Mary, with whom she lived off and on for years after the death of Horace Mann in 1859. The spirit of Alcott's school, she continued, "is to listen to & appreciate whatever may be said on the themes whose discussion 'makes the soul.'"[116] Others portrayed her at these lectures more satirically, recalling how she relapsed "at intervals, into apparent slumber, from which she would suddenly arouse herself with a movement that sent flying in various directions her bag, handkerchief, note-book, pencil, and all her various belongings which those of the younger and non-distinguished persons sitting near considered it an honor to scramble about and pick up for her."[117]

In the end, she would outlive nearly all her contemporaries. Waldo died in 1882. Her beloved sister Mary died five years later. Bronson Alcott and his daughter Louisa May were next, both dying in 1888, and Lydia Emerson in 1892. By then, Elizabeth was nearly blind, housebound, increasingly surrounded by the ghosts of her past. Writing to Sam Ward, with whom Margaret Fuller had once been in love, she looked forward to the time when they could speak in "the world to come," when "we shall understand one another without words which at best only *point* to what we want to say."[118]

Despite her extensive friendships and endless involvement in various social causes, she was increasingly alone. Years earlier, Sophia had written a letter to her mother from The Red House in Lenox. "As I sit & look on these mountains, so grand & flowing & the illimitable aerial blue, beyond & over, I seem to realize with peculiar force that bountiful, fathomless, heart of Elizabeth, forever disappointed, but forever believing; sorely rebuffed, yet never bitter; robbed day by day, yet giving again, from endless store; more sweet, more tenderly, more serene, as the hours pass over her, though they may drop gall, instead of flowers upon this unguarded heart."[119] For Sophia, Elizabeth's unmarried state had meant that her life was incomplete, unrequited. Her headlong rush from one idea to another, one cause to another, had left her unguarded, susceptible to ridicule in a way Sophia never allowed for herself. But the younger sister admired Elizabeth's boundless faith, her hard-won optimism, the *courage* with which she had propelled herself into the center of Boston's intellectual life and then made herself a central figure in the transcendentalist movement. She could only marvel at her older sister's resilience, her mountain-like resolve.

Elizabeth died on January 3, 1894, two months shy of her ninetieth birthday. Her life had spanned almost the entire nineteenth century, but as her eulogists made clear, she had never outlived her youthful idealism. "[W]hile most mortals instinctively take care of number one," said Sarah Clarke, who would live two years longer, "she alone totally neglected that important numeral, and spent all her life, all her strength, her marvelous enthusiasm, her generous fiery ardor in the cause of others."[120] When the funeral service was over, her body was transported from Boston to Concord, where she was buried near Waldo Emerson, Henry David Thoreau, Bronson Alcott, Nathaniel Hawthorne, and Mary Moody Emerson—friends of her youth.

7.

A year after Elizabeth Palmer Peabody's death, Caroline Healey Dall stood before the assembled members of the Society for Philosophical Enquiry. The Society had been founded several years earlier by a group of male professors, most of whom were associated with a fledgling institution that came to be known as George Washington University. Their sessions were generally taken up with esoteric questions such as "Whether mind is a substance or a relation" and "the Philosophy of Swedenborg and Emerson, especially as applied to the imagination." During the third meeting, it was agreed that women should be allowed to become members. Dall had been one of the first women invited to give an address. Nearly half a century after Fuller's death, it was no longer uncommon for a woman to speak in public, even if that public was a learned society made up primarily of men.

Dall was seventy-two years old (figure 80). She was a pioneering feminist, having helped found the New England Women's Rights Convention with

Figure 80. Caroline Healey Dall in the 1870s.

Paulina Davis (it may have been Dall's idea to invite Waldo Emerson to the first convention) and co-founding the feminist journal, *The Una*. In later years, she would sermonize in the Unitarian Church—making her one of the first women to perform the ministerial function of which Mary Moody Emerson and Elizabeth Palmer Peabody could only dream.[121] Fifty-three years earlier, at age nineteen, Elizabeth Peabody had invited her to attend Fuller's Conversations in her bookshop at 13 West Street. At that age, Dall embodied a peculiar mixture of brashness and reticence. Also, she was given to what she called "clairvoyance." Her first impression of Elizabeth Peabody was that she would need, "with all my strength, to escape the Maelstromn of her affectionate mistakes."[122] In this she was correct. Elizabeth promptly assumed the role of imperious older sister to Dall, criticizing the younger woman's tendency to offend people by speaking too freely. At one point, Peabody pulled her aside and angrily lectured. "How can you *dare* to speak before a person whom you do not know?" Then Dall added, "as if she were not constantly doing it herself!"[123]

Dall made an even worse impression on Fuller. "Margaret did not like me," she recalled the same year she delivered her speech to the Society of Philosophical Enquiry, "indeed my presence at her conversations irritated her, and my 'clairvoyance' told me, at one time, that she was on the point of asking me to leave the class." Dall stayed put, however. She valued the talks "too much as a means of culture."[124] She took notes of the 1841 Conversations—the only transcriptions other than Elizabeth's to have survived—and eventually published them, also in 1895, as *Margaret and Her Friends, or Ten Conversations with Margaret Fuller.*

Now she stood before the group of assembled men and women and proposed to trace New England Transcendentalism to its roots. She began with an unexpected choice: Anne Hutchinson. Hutchinson was the Puritan woman banished from the Massachusetts Bay Colony in 1638 for questioning the authority of its ministers. Like Elizabeth Peabody and Margaret Fuller, she had received an unusually good education for a girl, in this case from her clerical father, but her wide reading in theology eventually got her into trouble. She led discussion groups in her home, where she provided exegesis of the sermons of her minister, Joseph Cotton (Lydia Emerson's ancestor on her mother's side). Her insistence on personal revelation at the expense of orthodoxy placed her squarely at odds with the colony's theocracy, prompting a trial and eventual expulsion. For Dall, the spirit of Hutchinson's antinomianism—her belief that the holy spirit freed all people from the strictures of Mosaic law—resurfaced in transcendentalism: "Idealism, which had originated with Anne Hutchinson, was 'now imported in foreign packages from France and Germany.'"[125]

Dall also identified Fuller's adolescent friend, Frederick Henry Hedge, as a crucial medium for German thought and literature in the United States. She considered the adoption of Coleridge's terminology by Elizabeth Peabody's mentor, William Ellery Channing, an especially important event in the formation of transcendentalism. But it was Margaret Fuller who brought the movement to full fruition.

For Dall, Fuller was the direct heir of Anne Hutchinson: a fiercely original voice in a world dominated by men. It was no accident, she said, that both the original spirit of transcendentalism as well as its highest expression had come from women. "The characteristics of the Transcendental movement were shown in the temper of its agitation for the rights of woman and the enlargement of her duties," Dall observed.[126] The movement's insistence on "the inalienable worth of man, and of the immanence of the Divine in the Human" had been embraced by women who desired to think and exist without hindrances.[127]

But even within this context, Fuller was remarkable. "It is hopeless to convey to those who never saw her any idea of Margaret Fuller, to give those who never lived in the circle that she inspired any impression of her being and influence. She was not beautiful, people said; but she was more than beautiful. A sort of glow surrounded her, and warmed those who listened."[128]

Dall was speaking of the Conversations, of course, which she placed at the very center of the transcendentalist movement. The Bright Circle of women who gathered in the parlor of Elizabeth Peabody's bookshop, she believed, had had the most to gain by living up to its ideals. "I consider it the greatest blessing of my life that I was admitted almost as a child to the circle that surrounded [Fuller]," Dall told her audience, "and felt from my first conscious moments the noble atmosphere she diffused. Among the girls of that circle one saw no low, ignoble motives, no vanity, no poor ambitions, no coquetries, no looking to marriage as an end, no proneness to idle gossip."[129]

Not only did the Conversations embody the spirit of transcendentalism, they were also the beginning of the woman's movement. Dall drew a direct line from the talks to the feminist movement in which she was now involved. She could only lament that Fuller had not survived to see the fruits of her efforts, the alteration, however partial, in women's affairs. "I do not think I am mistaken in saying that what is meant by New England Transcendentalism perished with Margaret Fuller," she concluded. "The tragedy of 1850 swallowed carelessly much that we held precious; but it promised more, and the glory of Margaret's life did not perish."[130]

Dall's speech was forgotten almost as soon as it was given. By the time of her death in 1912, the history of the transcendentalist taught in English classes around the country was radically different from the version she delivered. That history was firmly settled around the figures of Emerson and Thoreau. It was based in Concord, not Boston, and its foundational members, thinkers such as Mary Moody Emerson and Elizabeth Palmer Peabody, were reduced to caricatures who stood at the fringes. Even Margaret Fuller was reduced to a minor player, one whose writings were dismissed for being inferior to her talk.

But Dall had made an important point: the nation's first philosophical and literary movement owed its existence as much to a group of women as to the men who confidently assumed the mantle of spokespersons. Those women wished to extend the premises of transcendentalism. They longed to think for themselves, to act upon their inner promptings, to help wherever possible to change the world.

What mattered most to Dall was that they did these things in the spirit of collaboration. The writings of Mary Moody Emerson, Elizabeth and Sophia Peabody, Lydia Emerson, and Margaret Fuller—all were distributed among widening circles of readers, whether published or not. More often their collaborations took the form of conversation: ardent, generous, *feisty* talk, talk that seemed combustible, explosive, charged with new ideas and opportunities, new ways of being.

These conversations, whether occurring in the Maine countryside or the stuffy front room of a Boston rowhouse, helped create a new standard of values for women. And while they may not have immediately changed the condition of every life they encompassed, they continued to reverberate, to ripple into wider circles, reaching ever growing numbers of people. Even now, if you listen carefully, you can hear their voices, the rustle of their speech—the conversations, as Mary Moody Emerson liked to phrase it, that make the soul.

Acknowledgments

This book owes so much to so many. Friends, family, colleagues, scholars, archivists—all inhabit these pages, bestowing them with warmth and generous plenitude. *Bright Circle* would not have been conceived without the formative work of feminist scholars who brought the women portrayed here into the light of serious consideration. I have benefitted from and am ever grateful to Phyllis Cole, Megan Marshall, Noelle A. Baker, Larry J. Reynolds, Nancy Craig Simmons, Delores Bird Carpenter, Patricia Dunlavy Valenti, Charles Capper, Bruce Ronda, Tiffany K. Wayne, Christina Zwarg, and many others.

Fitting for a book about conversations, this one emerged from talks with friends and colleagues who have shaped my thinking in profound and fundamental ways. For their wisdom and considered opinions, I am grateful to Katie Conrad, Phil Drake, Dorice Elliott, Anna Neil, and Paul Outka. Laura Mielke sharpened my argument, supplied sources and expertise, and offered unflagging encouragement through the long process. Ann Rowland is the perfect reader, alert to the textures of narrative and argument. Chris Hanlon provided expert commentary as the project was rounding completion, for which I am ever grateful. The great kindness and intelligence of Lawrence Buell and Robert Gross made bouncing ideas back and forth a pleasure, and I also owe warm thanks to Henry Louis Gates, Jr. for his generosity. As usual, Robert Milder pressed me to think harder about my material—the true gift of a mentor.

I am grateful to the National Endowment for the Humanities' Public Scholars program and its officers for enabling me to work for one year without interruption, thereby making *Bright Circle* possible and timely. A Grant for Works in Progress from the Robert B. Silvers Foundation also helped immeasurably. Other institutions providing invaluable aid include the Kenneth Spencer Research Library at the University of Kansas, the American Antiquarian Society, the Houghton Library at Harvard University, the New York Public Library, the Massachusetts Historical Society, and the Concord Free Public Library.

I would like to thank my agent, Marianne Merola, for her tireless support of this project, from conception to completion, and also Jacqueline Norton at Oxford University Press, who was the first to hear me formulate a vague conception of what eventually became this book. Special thanks are owed to graduate research assistant Hannah Scupham for transcribing the second volume of Sophia Peabody's *Cuba Journals*, and to Helena Cassels for transcribing George

Tolman's renditions of Mary Moody Emerson's Almanacks. Elspeth Healey, Special Collections Curator at KU, first showed me the inscribed copy of *Nature* that Ralph Waldo Emerson gave to his aunt—a crucial spark.

Love and gratitude to the "Moms," a Bright Circle in their own right. And, as always, love to Julie, who makes everything possible.

Abbreviations

People

EPP	Elizabeth Palmer Peabody [daughter]
LJE	Lydia Jackson Emerson
MF	Margaret Fuller
MME	Mary Moody Emerson
Mrs. EPP	Eliza Palmer Peabody [mother]
NH	Nathaniel Hawthorne
RWE	Ralph Waldo Emerson
SPH	Sophia Peabody Hawthorne

Sources

CE	Nathaniel Hawthorne, *Centenary Edition of the Works of Nathaniel Hawthorne*, ed. William Charvat et al., 23 vols. (Columbus: Ohio State University Press, 1962–93).
CJ	*The Cuba Journal 1833–1835, by Sophia Peabody Hawthorne*, vol. 1 ed. Claire Badaracco (Ann Arbor, Mich.: University Microfilms International, 1985). Vols. 2 and 3 transcribed by Hannah Scupham.
CW	Ralph Waldo Emerson, *The Complete Works of Ralph Waldo Emerson*, 10 vols., ed. Joseph Slater, Robert E. Spiller, et al. (Cambridge: Harvard University Press, 1971–2013).
FFP	Fuller Family Papers, Houghton Library, Harvard University.
JMN	Ralph Waldo Emerson, *Journals and Miscellaneous Notebooks of Ralph Waldo Emerson*, ed. William H. Gilman et al., 16 vols. (Cambridge: Harvard University Press, 1960–82).
LEPP	*Letters of Elizabeth Palmer Peabody: American Renaissance Woman*, ed. Bruce A. Ronda (Middletown, Connecticut: Wesleyan University Press, 1984.)
LifeLJE	Ellen Tucker Emerson, *The Life of Lidian Jackson Emerson*, ed. Delores Bird Carpenter (Boston: Twayne Publishers, 1980).
LLJE	*The Selected Letters of Lidian Jackson Emerson*, ed. Delores Bird Carpenter (Columbia: University of Missouri Press, 1987).
LMF	*The Letters of Margaret Fuller*, ed. Robert N. Hudspeth, 6 vols. (Ithaca: Cornell University Press, 1983–94).
LMME	*The Selected Letters of Mary Moody Emerson*, ed. Nancy Craig Simmons (Athens, GA: University of Georgia Press, 1993).

LRWE	*The Letters of Ralph Waldo Emerson*, ed. Ralph L. Rusk (vols. 1–6) and Eleanor M. Tilton (vols. 7–10) (New York: Columbia University Press, 1939, 1990–5).
MVWC	*Biography of Elizabeth Palmer Peabody*, unpublished manuscript, by Mary Van Wyck Church, Massachusetts Historical Society.
NYPL-Berg	Henry W. and Albert A. Berg Collection, the New York Public Library, Astor, Lenox, and Tilden Foundations.
OM	*Memoirs of Margaret Fuller Ossoli*, ed. Ralph Waldo Emerson, James Freeman Clarke, and William Henry Channing, 2 vols. (Boston: Phillips, Sampson, 1852).
WWP	Baker, Noelle A. and Sandra Harbert Petrulionis. *The Almanacks of Mary Moody Emerson: A Scholarly Digital Edition*. Women Writers Project.

List of Illustrations

1. *View of West Street looking toward Boston Common, Boston, Mass. Ca. 1875.* General photographic collection, Historic New England. 2
2. Books from Elizabeth Palmer Peabody's lending library. Concord Free Public Library. 5
3. Bookplate from the lending library. Concord Free Public Library. 6
4. *Boston, 13 West Street, where Hawthorne was married.* Frank Cousins Glass Plate Negatives Collection, Phillips Library, Peabody Essex Museum, Rowley, MA. 10
5. Silhouette of Mary Moody Emerson, Concord Free Public Library. Images © 2020 James E. Coutré. 11
6. A page from Mary Moody Emerson's Almanacks, Houghton Library, Harvard University. 14
7. Frank O. Brazetti, *Old Manse, Monument Street, Concord, Middlesex County, MA,* in *Historic American Buildings Survey* (1941). Prints and Photographs Division, Library of Congress, Washington, DC. 16
8. *Wax Portrait of the Reverend William Emerson. Presented by the Reverend Robert W. Haskins, 1924.* Concord Free Public Library. 17
9. *Portrait of Rev. William Emerson,* artist unknown, published in *Polyanthos,* May 1812. 18
10. John Singleton Copley, *Portrait of Mrs. John Stevens (Judith Sargent, later Mrs. John Murray),* 1770–2. Terra Foundation for American Art, Daniel J. Terra Collection. 23
11. Mary Van Schalkwyck, reproduced from *Memorials of Mary Wilder White: A Century Ago in New England,* by Elizabeth Amelia Dwight; edited by Mary Wilder Tileston. 27
12. Bear Mountain, Maine, *c.*1895. Collections of Maine Historical Society, courtesy of http://www.VintageMaineImages.com. 38
13. *Ralph Waldo Emerson* (*c.*1829). Houghton Library, Harvard University. 42
14. Elizabeth Sherman Hoar. Concord Free Public Library. Images © 2020 James E. Coutré. 45
15. Sarah Goodridge, *Miniature of Ellen Tucker Emerson* (about 1830). Concord Museum Collection, Gift of Dr. Augusta G. Williams; Pi806. 56
16. *Silhouette of the Peabody family.* Peabody Essex Museum. 69

17. *Sophia Peabody Hawthorne, Sketchbook of original pencil drawings. Signed, dated, May 1832–Dec. 6, 1833.* Henry W. and Albert A. Berg Collection of English and American Literature, The New York Public Library. *The New York Public Library Digital Collections.* 1832–3. https://digitalcollections.nypl.org/items/dcf7da70-4af3-0131-c393-58d385a7b928. 73

18. *Bowdoin Square, Boston, 1825.* Boston Public Library, Arts Department. 81

19. "Harvard University, with the procession of the alumni from the church to the pavillion, September 8, 1836." (1840) The Miriam and Ira D. Wallach Division of Art, Prints and Photographs: Print Collection, The New York Public Library. *The New York Public Library Digital Collections.* https://digitalcollections.nypl.org/items/510d47d9-7c31-a3d9-e040-e00a18064a99. 82

20. Charles Fraser, *Washington Allston* (1824). Image courtesy of The Gibbes Museum of Art/Carolina Art Association. 83

21. Washington Allston, *The Reverend William Ellery Channing* (1811). Museum of Fine Arts, Boston. 86

22. *Federal St. Church, 1809–59. Boston* (*c.*1855–9). Boston Public Library, Arts Department. Online. January 16, 2024. https://ark.digitalcommonwealth.org/ark:/50959/2801pk15b. 87

23. Washington Allston, *Samuel Taylor Coleridge, age 42*, engraved by Samuel Cousins. Library of Congress Prints and Photographs Division, Washington, D.C. 90

24. *The Late A. Bronson Alcott* (1888). The Miriam and Ira D. Wallach Division of Art, Prints and Photographs: Print Collection, The New York Public Library. *The New York Public Library Digital Collections.* 1888-03-06. https://digitalcollections.nypl.org/items/510d47dc-442f-a3d9-e040-e00a18064a99. 99

25. George W. Boynton, Masonic Temple, Boston. Detail of 1835 map of Boston, entitled "Plan of Boston with parts of the adjacent towns." Published by Boston Bewick Company. Boston Public Library. 102

26. Title page of Elizabeth Peabody's *Record of a School.* 103

27. Concord town square, engraving, Autobiographical collections of Amos Bronson Alcott. Vol. V, 1840–4. Houghton Library, Harvard University. 109

28. Chester Harding (American, 1792–1866). *Portrait of Sophia Peabody*, 1830. Oil on canvas, 30 1/8×25 1/8 inches (76.454×63.754 cm). Gift of the Estate of Rosamond Mikkelsen, 2016.59.1 Peabody Essex Museum. 128

29. George Washington Felt (1776–1847). *View of Court House Square, Salem*, 1810–20. Oil on wood panel, 34 3/4×52 3/8×1 in. (88.27×133.03×2.54 cm). Gift of the estate of Benjamin F. Brown, 1919. Courtesy of Peabody Essex Museum. Photo by Walter Silver/PEM. 131

30. Nathaniel Peabody, *The Art of Preserving Teeth* (Salem: Joshua and John D. Cushing, 1824). Image by the National Library of Medicine. 133

31. William F. Draper, *Dr. Walter Channing*. Harvard Center for the History of Medicine. 138

32. *Self-portrait of Sarah Goodridge* (1830). Museum of Fine Arts, Boston. 142
33. Thomas Doughty's *View of West Point* (1827). Collection of the Museum of the Shenandoah Valley, Julian Wood Glass Jr. Collection, 0056.2. Photo by Ron Blunt. 143
34. *Self portrait of Chester Harding* (*c*.1825). Andrew W. Mellon Collection, National Portrait Gallery, Washington. 144
35. Marquier, Luis. *El Quitrin (Habana).* 0AD. https://collections.library.yale.edu/catalog/2057438. Beinecke Rare Book and Manuscript Library, Yale University. 151
36. *A representation of the sugar-cane and the art of making sugar* (1749), engraved for the *Universal Magazine.* Popular graphic art print filing series, Library of Congress. 154
37. Jean Alexandre Allais, *Group of Waltzers* (1817). Jerome Robbins Dance Division, The New York Public Library. *The New York Public Library Digital Collections.* 1817-02-01. https://digitalcollections.nypl.org/items/7486bd10-f034-0132-2821-58d385a7b928. 155
38. "Vista de Una Casa de Calderas," *Album Pintoresco de la Isla de Cuba.* B. May y Ca. Oilprinting Storch & Kramer, Berlin, 1855. David Rumsey Map Collection, David Rumsey Map Center, Stanford Libraries. 157
39. Frank Cousins, *Salem, 53 Charter Street, Nathaniel Peabody house* (*c*.1865–1914). Phillips Library at the Peabody Essex Museum. 163
40. "A practitioner of Mesmerism using Animal Magnetism." Wellcome Collection. 166
41. Charles Osgood (1809–1890), United States, *Portrait of Nathaniel Hawthorne* (detail), 1840. Oil on canvas, Salem, Massachusetts, United States. 29 1/2×24 1/2 inches (74.93×62.23 cm). Peabody Essex Museum, Gift of Professor Richard C. Manning, 1933. Photo by Mark Sexton and Jeffrey Dykes. 168
42. Illustration from Nathaniel Hawthorne, *The Gentle Boy: A Thrice Told Tale* (Wiley & Putnam: New York and London 1839). 171
43. Photograph of Sophia Peabody Hawthorne's bas relief (medallion head) of Charles Chauncy Emerson, from Emerson family photograph album; original plaster medallion in Emerson House. Album from the estate of Amelia Forbes Emerson, 1982. Concord Free Public Library. 175
44. Lydia Jackson Emerson in the 1840s. Concord Free Public Library. 192
45. *A view of Plymouth, from the beach east of the harbour-the oldest town in New England and landing place of the Pilgrim fathers (1851).* The Miriam and Ira D. Wallach Division of Art, Prints and Photographs: Print Collection, The New York Public Library. *The New York Public Library Digital Collections.* https://digitalcollections.nypl.org/items/510d47d9-7c8a-a3d9-e040-e00a18064a99. 199
46. Church and hall, Meeting House Hill, Dorchester (*c*.1898). Boston Public Library, Arts Department. 202

47. "Emmanuel Swedenborg." The Miriam and Ira D. Wallach Division of Art, Prints and Photographs: Print Collection, The New York Public Library. *The New York Public Library Digital Collections.* 1800–99. https://digitalcollections.nypl.org/items/deba6c60-4ed2-0130-131f-58d385a7b928. 211

48. Woodcut of Angelina Emily Grimké. Library of Congress Prints and Photographs Division Washington, D.C. 217

49. Woodcut of Sarah Moore Grimké. Library of Congress Prints and Photographs Division Washington, D.C. 218

50. Waldo Emerson. Daguerreotype: sixth plate; oval frame, case, 1841. Houghton Library, Harvard University. 222

51. Ellen Tucker Emerson, Photographed by Elliot and Fry, London (1873). Concord Free Public Library. 226

52. Hiram Powers, *Anna Hazard Barker Ward*, modeled 1837–8, Smithsonian American Art Museum. Museum purchase in memory of Ralph Cross Johnson, 1968.155.35. 229

53. Portrait of Caroline Sturgis Tappan, by Eastman Johnson, *c.*1840s. Courtesy Sturgis Library. 229

54. Margaret Fuller, 1846. Courtesy National Portrait Gallery, Smithsonian Institution. 245

55. John Opie, *Mary Wollstonecraft* (*c.* 1797), National Portrait Gallery, London. 250

56. David Claypoole Johnston, *Washington Allston in His Studio* (date unknown). Bowdoin College Museum of Art, Museum Purchase, Elizabeth B. G. Hamlin Fund, 1965. 252

57. Cambridge Port Private Grammar School, Norris Collection, Cambridge Historical Commission. 256

58. Auguste Edouart, *Lydia Maria Francis Child.* National Portrait Gallery, Smithsonian Institution; gift of Robert L. McNeil, Jr. 259

59. Christopher Cranch, "The Moral Influence of the Dial" (*c.*1841–4). Courtesy Houghton Library, Harvard University. 269

60. *Madame Récamier.* The Miriam and Ira D. Wallach Division of Art, Prints and Photographs: Print Collection, The New York Public Library. *The New York Public Library Digital Collections.* https://digitalcollections.nypl.org/items/98807c86-13c5-f9fe-e040-e00a180639db 275

61. Ellen Sturgis Hooper. Sturgis Library. 281

62. "The Great Lawsuit" as it appeared in *The Dial.* 285

63. Otto Knirsch, "*Horace Greeley and Family*" (1872). National Portrait Gallery, Smithsonian Institution. 291

64. Sarah Freeman Clarke, "Arched Rock from the Water," in Margaret Fuller's *Summer on the Lakes.* 292

65. *Edgar Allan Poe* (1848). American Antiquarian Society. Gift of Mrs. Charles T. Tatman in memory of her husband, 1947. 297

66. Auguste Charpentier, *George Sand* (1837/39). The Fryderyk Chopin Institute, Warsaw. 303

67. *Adam Mickiewicz* (1842). 305

68. H. G. Smith, photographer. *Giovanni Angelo Ossoli with cane, photographic image of a half-length seated portrait* (photograph, undated). Houghton Library, Harvard University. 309

69. "Garibaldi at Rome, 1849, from a sketch made during the siege" (1854). The Miriam and Ira D. Wallach Division of Art, Prints and Photographs: Picture Collection, New York Public Library. *The New York Public Library Digital Collections.* https://digitalcollections.nypl.org/items/510d47e1-3239-a3d9-e040-e00a18064a99. 311

70. "The Death of Margaret Fuller Ossoli." The Miriam and Ira D. Wallach Division of Art, Prints and Photographs: Picture Collection, New York Public Library. *The New York Public Library Digital Collections* (1854). https://digitalcollections.nypl.org/items/a132d2df-b0b6-cfb4-e040-e00a180672ea 315

71. Sophia Peabody Hawthorne, "[Peabody,] Elizabeth [Palmer, sister], AL (incomplete) to. Feb. 8, 1855." Henry W. and Albert A. Berg Collection of English and American Literature, The New York Public Library. *The New York Public Library Digital Collections.* 1855. https://digitalcollections.nypl.org/items/52169a40-3f68-0131-85e2-58d385a7bbd0. 322

72. Harriet Goodhue Hosmer, 1865, albumen print (carte-de-visite) by Black & Case. Department of Image Collections, National Gallery of Art Library, Washington, D.C. 323

73. Louisa Lander, from *Cosmopolitan Art Journal*, vol. 5, no. 1 (March 1861). 324

74. *Paulina Wright Davis.* The Miriam and Ira D. Wallach Division of Art, Prints and Photographs: Print Collection, The New York Public Library. *The New York Public Library Digital Collections.* https://digitalcollections.nypl.org/items/510d47df-7348-a3d9-e040-e00a18064a99 330

75. *Lydia Jackson Emerson* (1866). National Portrait Gallery, Smithsonian Institution; gift of Stephen White. 332

76. John W. Paradis, *Elizabeth Oakes Prince Smith (Mrs. Seba Smith)* (*c.*1845). Chester Dale Collection, National Gallery of Art, Washington, D.C. 336

77. *Mary Moody Emerson*, posthumous tintype. Houghton Library, Harvard University. 339

78. Francis Benjamin Johnston, *Kindergarten in a Vegetable Garden* (*c.* 1899). Library of Congress Prints and Photographs Division, Washington, D.C. 345

79. Photographic portrait of Elizabeth Peabody at mid-life, seated at table, reading book [undated]. Concord Free Public Library. 348

80. J. W. Black, *Caroline Healey Dall* (1870s). Smithsonian Institution Archives, Record Unit 95, Box 6, Folder: 43. 350

List of Plates

1. Thomas Walley, *George Whitfield Preaching in Bolton, June 1850*, from the collections of Bolton Museu.
2. Vladimir Borovikovsky, *Portrait of Madame de Staël* (1812).
3. Elias Martin, *Reading Lesson at a Dame School.* Yale Center for British Art, Paul Mellon Collection.
4. Phillip Harry, *Tremont Street* (ca. 1843). Museum of Fine Arts, Boston. Gift of Maxim Karolik for the M. and M. Karolik Collection of American Paintings, 1815–1865.
5. Chester Harding (American, 1792–1866). *Portrait of Sophia Peabody*, 1830. Oil on canvas, 30 1/8 × 25 1/8 inches (76.454 × 63.754 cm). Gift of the Estate of Rosamond Mikkelsen, 2016.59.1 Peabody Essex Museum.
6. Marquier, Luis. *El Quitrin (Habana)*. 0AD. https://collections.library.yale.edu/catalog/2057438. Beinecke Rare Book and Manuscript Library, Yale University.
7. Sophia Amelia Peabody, *Isola San Giovanni*, 1839–40. Oil on canvas. Gift of Joan D. Ensor, in memory of her mother, Imogen Hawthorne, granddaughter of Sophia and Nathaniel Hawthorne, 2004. 138521. Peabody Essex Museum. Photo by Walter Silver.
8. Twin inkstand at Ralph Waldo Emerson House. Courtesy Ralph Waldo Emerson Memorial Association.
9. Lydia Jackson Emerson with son Edward Waldo Emerson (1844–1930), mid-1840s. Courtesy Houghton Library, Harvard University.
10. Margaret Fuller, 1846. Courtesy National Portrait Gallery, Smithsonian Institution.
11. Richard Evans, *Harriet Martineau* (1834). National Portrait Gallery, London.
12. Michael Seymour, *From the Cambria steamer, starting from Boston, U.S Bunker's Hill Monument* (1846). Library of Congress.

Endnotes

Introduction

1. James Freeman Clarke *Autobiography, Diary and Correspondence*, ed. Edward Everett Hale (Boston: Houghton Mifflin, 1891), pp. 143. For an excellent discussion of the cultural milieu surrounding the West Street bookshop, see Lynn E. Hyde, "West Street: Nexus of Boston Reform, 1835–1845," master's thesis, Harvard Extension School, https://dash.harvard.edu/bitstream/handle/1/42004041/HYDE-DOCUMENT-2018.pdf?sequence=1&isAllowed=y.
2. Elizabeth Palmer Peabody, "A Glimpse of Christ's Idea of Society," *Dial*, 2 (October 1841), p. 222.
3. Clarke, *Autobiography, Diary and Correspondence*, pp. 143.
4. Quoted in George Willis Cooke, "Introduction," *An Historical and Biographical Introduction to Accompany the Dial*, 2 vols. (The Rowfant Club, 1902), 1: 148.
5. *OM*, 1: 332–3.
6. The speaker is Margaret Fuller, *LMF*, 2: 118.
7. *OM*, 1: 339–40.
8. MF to Sophia Ripley, August 27, 1839, *LMF*, 2: 86–9.

Chapter 1

1. Elizabeth Hoar, quoted in *Memorials of Mary Wilder White, by Elizabeth Amelia Dwight*, ed. Mary Tilder Tileston (Boston: Everett Press, 1903), p. 113.
2. RWE, "Mary Moody Emerson," *The Complete Works of Ralph Waldo Emerson: Lectures and Biographical Sketches*, ed. Edward Waldo Emerson, vol. 10 (Boston: Houghton Mifflin, 1911), p. 407. Hereafter cited as "MME."
3. This anecdote appears in *LMME*, p. 546.
4. RWE, "Mary Moody Emerson," *The Atlantic*, December 1883, p. 737. https://www.theatlantic.com/magazine/archive/1883/12/mary-moody-emerson/539490/. Another version of the story, with yellow ribbons instead of pink, can be found in F. B. Sanborn, "The Women of Concord," p. 157.
5. The author is Samuel Purviance, an eighteenth-century Marylander quoted in Mary Beth Norton, *Liberty's Daughters: The Revolutionary Experience of American Women, 1750–1800* (Ithaca: Cornell UP, 1980), p. 3.
6. Quoted in Mary Palmer Tyler, *Grandmother Tyler's Book: The Recollections of Mary Palmer Tyler, 1775–1866* (New York: Putnam's, 1925), p. 9.
7. Quoted in Phyllis Cole, *Mary Moody Emerson and the Origins of Transcendentalism* (NY: Oxford, 1998), p. 195.
8. November 5, 1804, Almanacks, WWP. http://wwo.wwp.northeastern.edu.www2.lib.ku.edu/WWO/search?browse-all=yes#!/view/emerson.almanack.xml. References to the Almanacks are from this source unless otherwise noted.
9. *Memorial to Mary Wilde White*, p. 114.
10. Almanack, November 8, 1804.
11. Ibid.
12. MME to Sarah Alden Bradford, January 1, 1817, *LMME*, p. 98.
13. MME to William Emerson^{2}, March 17, 1795, *LMME*, p. 11.
14. Cole, p. 7; Almanack, March 17, 1829.
15. Cole, p. 8.
16. Almanack, November 7, 1804.
17. Edward Emerson, *A Chaplain of the Revolution* (Boston: n.p., 1922), p. 20.
18. Almanack, May 16, 1826.
19. Quoted in Cole, p. 71.
20. RWE, "MME," p. 414.
21. Quoted in Ellen Tucker Emerson, "What I can remember About Father," in Ralph Waldo Emerson Memorial Association archives, Houghton Library, Harvard University.
22. Almanack, November 22, 1804.

23. MME to RWE, June 13, 1826, *LMME*, p. 214.
24. MME to Charles Chauncy Emerson, July 28, [1833], *LMME*, p. 344.
25. William Emerson, "An Oration in Commemoration of the Anniversary of American Independence," http://consource.org/document/an-oration-in-commemoration-of-the-anniversary-of-american-independence-by-william-emerson-1802.
26. Almanack, November 3, 1804.
27. MME to Charles Chauncy Emerson and Edwards Bliss Emerson, January 1827, *LMME*, p. 224.
28. Almanack, October 5, [1822?].
29. MME to William Emerson², June 24, 1810, *LMME*, p. 55.
30. Jonathan Edwards, *A Faithful Narrative of the Surprising Work of God in the Conversion of Many Hundred Souls in Northampton, Massachusetts, A. D. 1735* (New York: Dunning & Spalding, 1832), pp. 83–4.
31. Quoted in Evelyn Barish, *Emerson: The Roots of Prophecy* (Princeton: Princeton University Press, 1989), p. 41.
32. Edward Young, *The Complaint; or Night-Thoughts on Life, Death, and Immortality, by the Reverend Edward Young, L.L.D.* (Philadelphia: Robert Bell, 1777), p. 25. This is likely the edition Mary Moody Emerson read.
33. Almanack, November 19, 1804.
34. Almanack, 1810. n.d.
35. Quoted in Cole, p. 98.
36. Sophia Ripley, "Woman," *The Dial*, vol. 1 (January 1841), p. 363.
37. Quoted in Ruth Bloch, "The Gendered Meaning of Virtue in Revolutionary America," *Signs*, 13 (Autumn 1987), p. 41.
38. Judith Sargent Murray, *Selected Writing of Judith Sargent Murray* ed. Sharon M. Harris (New York: Oxford University Press, 1995), p. xliii.
39. Judith Murray Sargent, *Massachusetts Magazine*, II (March 1790), p. 133.
40. Quoted in Linda K. Kerber, *Women of the Republic: Intellect and Ideology in Revolutionary America* (Chapel Hill: University of North Carolina Press, 1980), p. 205.
41. MME to Ruth Haskins Emerson, January 20, 1799, *LMME*, p. 24.
42. RWE, "MME," p. 417.
43. MME to William Emerson², August 12, 1795, *LMME*, p. 14.
44. Almanack, July 15, 1853.
45. Almanack, November 6, 1804.
46. Almanack, October 18, 1847.
47. Quoted in M. H. Abram, *The Mirror and the Lamp: Romantic Theory and the Critical Tradition* (New York: Oxford University Press, 1971), p. 173.
48. William Wordsworth, "Preface," *Lyrical Ballads with Other Poems*, vol. 1 (London: Riggs, 1800), p. xiv.
49. Quoted in Claire Tomalin, *Jane Austen: A Life* (New York: Vintage, 1999), p. 217.
50. Quoted in *LMME*, p. xxviii.
51. Almanack, [October?] 17, 1817.
52. *Memorials of Mary Wilder White*, p. 121.
53. Ibid., pp. 13, 22.
54. Ibid., pp. 74, 91.
55. Ibid., pp. 122–3.
56. See Phyllis Cole's "'Conversation that Makes the Soul': Writing the Biography of Mary Moody Emerson," *Lives Out of Letters: Essays in American Biography and Documentation*, ed. Robert Habich (Madison, NJ: Fairleigh Dickinson UP, 2004), pp. 204–24.
57. Quoted in Rosalie Feltenstein, "Mary Moody Emerson: The Gadfly of Concord," *American Quarterly*, vol. 5 (Autumn 1953), p. 236.
58. Ibid., p. 262.
59. Quoted in Franklin Sanborn, *Recollections of Seventy Years*, vol. 2 (Boston: Richard G. Badger, The Gorham Press, 1909), p. 361.
60. *Memorials of Mary Wilder White*, pp. 120–1.
61. Ibid.
62. Ibid., pp. 129–30.
63. Ibid., p. 130.
64. *Monthly Anthology and Boston Review* July (1804), pp. 393–4. As Cole points out, "Though pseudonymous authorship was standard practice in this journal, no other submission began with such an explicit avowal of need for privacy, and none of the other pseudonyms was female" (Cole, p. 114).

65. *Monthly Anthology*, 1 (July 1804), pp. 394–5.
66. Ibid.
67. Ibid., 1 (August 1804), pp. 454–5.
68. Coleridge, "Dejection: An Ode," ll. 51–2.
69. *Memorials of Mary Wilder White*, p. 186.
70. *Monthly Anthology*, 1 (January 1805), p. 72.
71. MME to William Emerson[2], [May 1805], *LMME*, p. 30.
72. Quoted in Cole, p. 113.
73. *Monthly Anthology* 1 (June 1805), p. 343.
74. Quoted in Barish, p. 22.
75. Quoted in Cole, p. 128.
76. Quoted in Ronald A. Bosco and Joel Myerson, *The Emerson Brothers: A Fraternal Biography in Letters* (New York: Oxford University Press, 2005), p. 131.
77. William Emerson Inventory, List of Debts (Suffolk Probate No, 23771), in Ralph L. Rusk, *The Life of Ralph Waldo Emerson* (New York: Charles Scribner's Sons, 1949), p. 30.
78. William Emerson[2] to Phebe Bliss Emerson Ripley, January 11, 1810, Houghton Library bMS Am 1280.226 (2925).
79. RWE, "Domestic Life," *The Complete Works of Ralph Waldo Emerson*, Centenary Edition, 12 vols., ed. Edward Waldo Emerson (Boston: Houghton Mifflin, 1903–4), 2: 133.
80. Quoted in Barish, p. 56.
81. Ibid.
82. *The Emerson Brothers*, pp. 35, 138.
83. Sarah Alden Ripley is quoted in *LMME*, pp. 408–9.
84. Elizabeth Hoar, quoted in Cole, p. 143.
85. Ibid., 119.
86. Almanack, June 18, 1806.
87. Almanack, June 16, 1806.
88. Almanack, July 17, 1806.
89. Cole, p. 172.
90. Almanack, 1811, George Tolman transcription, MS Am 1280.235 (579, folders 1–12), Houghton Library, Harvard University.
91. Quoted in Barish, p. 50.
92. MME to Ruth Haskins Emerson, June 12, [1819], *LMME*, p. 119, emphasis added.
93. Waldo was even more explicit; his aunt believed that her "darling nephews... should be richly & holily qualified & bred to purify the old faith of what narrowness & error adhered to it & import all its fire into the new age." See RWE, *JMN*, 7: 446–7.
94. MME to Edward Bliss Emerson, November 9, 1816, *LMME*, p. 97.
95. *The Emerson Brothers*, p. 217.
96. Ibid., p. 208.
97. MME to Charles Chauncy Emerson, [1812?], *LMME*, p. 66.
98. Almanack, 1815.
99. Anonymous, "Observations on Madame de Stael's Corinna," *Monthly Anthology* 2 (September 1808), p. 467.
100. De Staël, *On Germany* (London: John Murray, 1813), p. 288.
101. Ibid., p. 110.
102. Quoted in Barish, p. 161.
103. MME to Edward Bliss Emerson, October 7, [1823], *LMME*, p. 174.
104. Quoted in *The Emerson Brothers*, p. 220; May 31, 1818.
105. MME to Charles Chauncy Emerson, [May 1827], *LMME*, p. 227.
106. *Worthy Women of Our First Century*, ed. Sarah Butler Wister and Agnes Irwin (Philadelphia: J. B. Lippincott & Co., 1877), p. 115.
107. Sarah Alden Ripley to MME [1813?], Sarah Alden Bradford Ripley Papers, Schlesinger Library, Radcliffe Institute.
108. MME to Sarah Alden Ripley, [1814?], *LMME*, p. 86.
109. Quoted in Cole, p. 156.
110. Sarah Alden Ripley to MME, September 3, 1819, Schlesinger Library.
111. MME to Ann [Brewer] Sargent Gage, October 3, 1854, *LMME*, p. 567.
112. MME to Ann [Brewer] Sargent Gage, December 27, 1820, *LMME*, p. 137.
113. MME to Ann [Brewer] Sargent Gage, January 20, 1820, *LMME*, pp. 134–6.
114. Letter and poem quoted in Joan W. Goodwin, *The Remarkable Mrs. Ripley: The Life of Sarah Alden Bradford Ripley* (Boston: Northeastern University Press, 1998), p. 55.

115. Franklin Sanborn, *The Personality of Emerson* (Boston: Chas. Goodspeed, 1903), pp. 118–19.
116. MME to RWE, September 11, 1826, *LMME*, p. 22.
117. RWE, "MME," p. 594.
118. *LRWE*, 1: 40.
119. MME to RWE, January 18, 1821, *LMME*, p. 139.
120. Cole, p. 177.
121. MME to RWE, March 11, 1820, *LMME*, p. 136.; MME to RWE, November 4 [1817], *LMME*, p. 104.
122. MME to RWE, July 26, 1812, *LMME*, p. 65.
123. Quoted in Cole, p. 170.
124. Ibid.
125. *LRWE*, 1: 54.
126. *JMN*, 7: 442.
127. *LRWE*, 1: 103.
128. MME to RWE, May 26, 1818, *LMME*, pp. 112–13.
129. *JMN*, 1: 5.
130. Quoted in Cole, p. 186.
131. Quoted in Nancy Craig Simmons, "A Calendar of the Letters of Mary Moody Emerson," *Studies in the American Renaissance* (1993), p. 1.
132. *LRWE*, 1: 115.
133. MME to RWE, June 26, 1822, *LMME*, p. 155.
134. Almanack, 1806.
135. MME to RWE, July 19, 1822, *LMME*, p. 160.
136. MME to RWE, [July] 25, [1822], *LMME*, p. 161.
137. MME to RWE, April 13, 1824, *LMME*, p. 182.
138. MME to RWE, January 20, 1824, *LMME*, p. 178.
139. MME to RWE, April 13, 1824, *LMME*, p. 182.
140. MME to RWE, June 26, 1822, *LMME*, pp. 155–7.
141. Almanack [1831–2], Tolman transcription, Houghton Library, Harvard University.
142. MME to RWE, January 18, 1821, *LMME*, p. 224.
143. Quoted in Cole, p. 199.
144. Almanack, 1820. Interestingly, and according to "Intertextual References in the Alamanacks of Mary Moody Emerson: Visualization for Close and Distant Reading," this passage closely follows one from de Staël's *On Germany*.
145. Almanack, circa October 1822.
146. Quoted in Cole, p. 200.
147. *LRWE*, 1: 54.
148. *JMN*, 1: 49.
149. Quoted in James Elliott Cabot, *A Memoir of Ralph Waldo Emerson*, 2 vols. (Boston: Houghton Mifflin, 1895), 1: 117–18.
150. *LRWE*, 1: 208.
151. MME to RWE, June 7, 1830, *LMME*, p. 287.
152. *JMN*, 1: 33.
153. I wish to thank Ann Rowland for prompting me to think about the Mary-Waldo collaboration in these terms.
154. *JMN*, 2: 123.
155. *LRWE*, 1: 174.
156. Ibid., 1: 170.
157. MME to Sarah Alden Ripley, *LMME*, p. 227, fn. 1.
158. Almanack, May 13, 1827.
159. Ibid., May 17, 1827.
160. Ibid., May 12, 1827.
161. Ibid., June 21, 1827.
162. Ibid.
163. Ibid., May 20, 1827, May 8, 1827.
164. Ibid., May 20, 1827.
165. Ibid., May 9, 1827.
166. Ibid., July 15, 1827.
167. Ibid., July 15, 1827.
168. Ibid., September 8, 1828.

169. Ibid., July 3, 1827.
170. Almanack, October 5, 1828, Tolman transcription, Houghton Library, Harvard University.
171. Ibid., October 17, 1827.
172. Ibid., September 10, 1828.
173. Ibid., October 14, 1827.
174. MME to William Emerson[3], June 21, 1826, *LMME*, p. 216.
175. Ellen Tucker Emerson, *One First Love: The Letters of Ellen Louisa Tucker to Ralph Waldo Emerson* ed. By Edith W. Gregg (Cambridge: Harvard University Press, 1962), p. 96.
176. MME to Ellen Louisa Tucker and RWE, January 24, 1829, *LMME*, p. 251.
177. Quoted in Cole, p. 211.
178. MME to Edward Bliss Emerson, March 15, 1830, *LMME*, p. 283.
179. *One First Love*, pp. 116–17.
180. MME to Ellen Louisa Tucker and RWE, January 24, 1829, *LMME*, p. 251.
181. *One First Love*, p. 125.
182. Ibid., p. 136.
183. MME to Charles Chauncy Emerson, January 26, 1831, *LMME*, p. 304.
184. Quoted in *The Emerson Brothers*, p. 266.
185. *One First Love*, pp. 137–8.
186. *LRWE*, 1: 318.
187. *JMN*, 3: 228.
188. Ibid., 3: 226.
189. Quoted in Cole, p. 209.
190. *JMN*, 3: 244.
191. Ibid., 3: 279.
192. Ibid.
193. MME to RWE, September 23, 1831, *LMME*, p. 310.
194. MME to RWE, February 1832, *LMME*, pp. 313–14.
195. Ibid.
196. Quoted in David R. Williams, "The Wilderness Raptures of Mary Moody Emerson: One Calvinist Link to Transcendentalism," *Studies in the American Renaissance* (1986), p. 12.
197. *JMN*, 4: 30.
198. Ibid., 4: 318.
199. Quoted in Cole, p. 220.
200. MME to Charles Chauncy Emerson, January 8, 1833, *LMME*, p. 330.
201. MME to Charles Chauncy Emerson, February 10, 1833, *LMME*, p. 333.
202. MME to Charles Chauncy Emerson, January 8, 1833, *LMME*, p. 330.
203. *JMN*, 4: 335.
204. *JMN*, 5: 64.
205. Ibid., 5: 19–20.
206. *CW*, 1: 10.
207. *JMN*, 5: 53.
208. *CW*, 1: 45.
209. Ibid., 1: 7.
210. Ibid., 1: 38.
211. Ibid., 1: 30.
212. Ibid., 1: 17.
213. Mary Moody Emerson's inscribed copy of *Nature* is in the Spencer Research Library at the University of Kansas. A note from Edith Bardwell, of Napa, California, describes its provenance: "'Aunt Mary Emerson' spent the last years of her life in the home of my grandmother, daughter of Robert and Rebecca (Emerson) Haskins, and died there so long ago that my mother was only a small girl, mystified often by the actions of the old lady in public. Her mind was impaired and she did odd things. You know how sensitive children can be." For this discovery, I am grateful to Elspeth Healey, Special Collections Curator, Spencer Research Library, University of Kansas.
214. *CW*, 1: 9.
215. Some examples: For his senior essay at Harvard, a treatise on "The Present State of Ethical Philosophy," he had copied paragraphs from a letter she wrote about de Staël; he similarly pilfered from the Almanacks for his early sermons, including one delivered in July 1829, when he closed with a stirring address to the congregation: "Scathed and mildewed by age without one illusion of hope left, I unite myself to this first of Beings. Luxury or comfort I do not ask—cold, hungry, sick, I can praise him; the faster the days go by, the more I praise him, waiting till it shall

please him in his high will, to remand my dust to dust, release my spirit into the Communion with him for which it aspires." This expression of steadfast piety had been lifted from passages in Mary's Almanacks from November 13 and 18, 1828: "Scathed and mildewed by age without one illusion of hope even for an easy & felt age I unite myself my very self to this first of Beings. The little comforts—luxuries &c. I don't ask health—cold—hungry—dirty I can praise—the faster the days go thro' ever so torpid in mind & body the more I praise..."

216. *CW*, 1: 9.
217. MME to RWE, November 4, 1817, *LMME*, p. 104.
218. Quoted in Noelle A. Baker and Sandra H Petrulionis, "Mary Moody Was a Scholar, a Thinker, and an Inspiration," *Humanities*, 38 (Winter 2017). https://www.neh.gov/humanities/2017/winter/feature/mary-moody-emerson-was-scholar-thinker-and-inspiration-all-who-knew-her
219. *CW*, 1: 9.
220. Ibid., 1: 13.
221. MME to LJE, September 29, 1836, *LMME*, p. 374.
222. Ibid., pp. 374–5. Mary's response prefigured that of Oliver Wendell Holmes by half a century. *Nature*, he wrote, "has its obscurities, its extravagances, but as a poem it is noble and inspiring." Holmes, *Ralph Waldo Emerson* (Boston, 1885), p. 103.
223. MME to William Emerson[3], September 39, 1838, *LMME*, p. 394.
224. Quoted in *James Freeman Clarke: Autobiography, Diary and Correspondence*, p. 133.
225. Lydia Maria Child, *Letters from New York: Second Series* (New York: C. S. Francis, 1845), p. 125.
226. Nathaniel Hawthorne, *CE*, 10: 31-2.
227. James Freeman Clarke, *Western Messenger*, November 1838, quoted in Arthur S. Bolster, *James Freeman Clarke, Disciple to Advancing Truth* (Boston: Beacon Press, 1954), p. 115.
228. MME to William Emerson[3], September 39, 1838, *LMME*, pp. 394–5.
229. Quoted in Cabot, *A Memoir of Ralph Waldo Emerson*, p. 29.
230. *JMN*, 14: 67.
231. Elizabeth Hoar to MME, April 23, 1839, "Elizabeth of Concord: Selected Letters of Elizabeth Sherman Hoar (1814–1878) to the Emerson Family, and the Emerson Circle (Part Two)," *Studies in the American Renaissance* (1985), p. 153.
232. MF to Sophia Ripley, August 27, 1839, *LMF*, 2: 87.
233. Quoted in Nancy Craig Simmons, "Margaret Fuller's Boston Conversations: The 1839–1840 Series," in *Studies in the American Renaissance*, (1994), p. 197.

Chapter 2

1. MME to Ann Sargent Gage, March 30, 1833; quoted in Bruce A. Ronda, *Elizabeth Palmer Peabody: A Reformer on Her Own Terms* (Cambridge, Mass.: Harvard University Press, 1999), p. 219.
2. Megan Marshall, *the Peabody Sisters: Three Women Who Ignited American Romanticism* (Boston: Houghton Mifflin, 2005), p. 172. Marshall says this this undated comment was made in October 1827.
3. See Julian Hawthorne, *The Memoirs of Julian Hawthorne*, ed. Edith G. Hawthorne (New York: Macmillan, 1938), p. 44.
4. M. Le Baron DeGerando, *Self-Education; or the Means and Art of Moral Progress*, translated by Elizabeth Palmer Peabody, third edition (Boston: T. O. H. O. Burnham, 1860), p. 5.
5. EPP to MME, October 7, 1845, EPP Papers, American Antiquarian Society.
6. MME to Ann Sargent Gage, March 30, 19833, *LMME*, p. 337.
7. MVWC.
8. Ibid., pp. 113–14.
9. Ibid., p. 341.
10. Quoted in Noelle A. Baker, "'Let me do nothing smale:' Mary Moody Emerson's 'Talking' Manuscripts," *ESQ: A Journal of the American Renaissance* 57 (Number 1-2, 2011), p. 25.
11. EPP, "Emerson as Preacher," Franklin B. Sanborn, ed., *The Genius and Character of Emerson: Lectures at the Concord School of Philosophy* (Port Washington, NY: Kennikat Press, 1971; reprint of 1885 edition), pp. 151–2.
12. Almanack, Tolman transcript, June 14, 1826, Houghton Library, Harvard University.
13. EPP, "Mrs. Elizabeth Palmer Peabody," *American Journal of Education*, 34 (1882), p. 739.
14. Elizabeth Hunt Palmer to Mary Smith Cranch, August 13, 1799; Peabody Family Papers 1790–1880, MHS.
15. These poems are quoted in Marshall, *The Peabody Sisters*, p. 44.
16. Mary Peabody Mann to Horace Mann, Horace Mann Papers, MHS. Both this and the following letter can be found in Marshall, "Two Early Poems of Mrs. Elizabeth Palmer Peabody," *Proceedings of the Massachusetts Historical Society*, third series, vol. 100 (1998), p, 42.

17. SPH to Mary Peabody Mann, February 7, 1853, NYPL-Berg.
18. Mrs. Elizabeth Palmer Peabody, "Biographical Sketch of Gen. Joseph Palmer," *The New Englander*, vol. 3 (January 1845), p. 1.
19. Ibid., p. 22.
20. EPP, "Mrs. Elizabeth Palmer Peabody," *American Journal of Education*, p. 742.
21. Quoted in Marshall, p. 49.
22. Mrs. EPP to Nathaniel Peabody, February 1800, Peabody Family Papers, MHS.
23. Megan Marshall, "Two Early Poems," p. 57.
24. Mrs. EPP to Nathaniel Peabody, March 1, 1800, Peabody Family Papers, MHS.
25. Quoted in Marshall, *The Peabody Sisters*, p. 54.
26. Nathaniel Peabody's biographical recollections, transcribed by Ruth M. Baylor, Peabody Family Papers MHS, p. 17.
27. Walter Channing to Mary Peabody Mann, March 2, 1853, typescript by Robert L. Straker, p. 1741, Antiochiana.
28. Mrs. EPP to EPP and Mary Peabody Mann, January 12, 1851, NYPL-Berg.
29. Ibid.
30. Mrs. EPP to SPH, n. d., in Julian Hawthorne, *Nathaniel Hawthorne and His Wife* (Boston: James Osgood, 1885), 1: 71.
31. EPP to Mrs. EPP, February 8, 1847, MVWC, p. 6.
32. Undated letter, Mrs. EPP to EPP, Peabody Family Papers, MHS.
33. From a poem by Mrs. EPP (writing as "Belinda"), "Some Thoughts Occasioned by the Present Juncture," *Haverhill Federal-Gazette*, March 15, 1799.
34. EPP, "Mrs. Elizabeth Palmer Peabody," p. 742.
35. Ibid., p. 721.
36. Mrs. EPP to EPP and Mary Peabody Mann, October 4, 1824, typescript by Robert L. Straker, p. 250, Antiochiana.
37. EPP, *Lectures in the Training School for Kindergartners* (Boston: D. C. Heath, 1886), pp. 102–3.
38. EPP, "Letter from Miss E. P. Peabody," *The American Journal of Education*, vol. 30 (1880), p. 584.
39. EPP to SPH, June 23, 1822, NYPL-Berg.
40. Both quotes are from Barbara Welter's pathbreaking "The Cult of True Womanhood," *American Quarterly*, vol. 18 (Summer 1966), pp. 153, 154.
41. Mrs. EPP to EPP, April 25, 1819, typescript by Robert L. Straker, p. 105, Antiochana.
42. Anna Q. T. Parsons, "Reminiscences of Miss Peabody," *Kindergarten Review*, 14 (1904), p. 539.
43. Octavius Brooks Frothingham, *Memoir of William Henry Channing* (Boston: Houghton Mifflin, 1886), pp. 396–7.
44. MVWC, p. 30, 69.
45. EPP, "Mrs. Elizabeth Palmer Peabody," p. 742.
46. EPP to Sarah Russell Sullivan, November 1827, typescript by Robert L. Straker, p. 454, Antiochiana.
47. Quoted in Marshall, p. 116.
48 EPP to Maria Chase, May 1821, *LEPP*, p. 55.
49. EPP, "Emerson as Preacher," p. 150.
50. EPP, *Last Evening with Allston, and Other Papers* (Boston: D. Lothrop, 1887), p. 1.
51. Quoted in Charlene Avallone, "Elizabeth Palmer Peabody and the 'Art' of Conversation," in *Reinventing the Peabody Sisters*, ed. Monika M. Elbert, Julie E. Hall, and Kathrine Rodier (Iowa City: University of Iowa Press, 2006), p. 23.
52. EPP to SPH, May 15, 1824, NYPL-Berg.
53. EPP to Mary Peabody Mann, April 1834, NYPL-Berg.
54. Nate Peabody to EPP, April 13, 1838, typescript by Robert L. Straker, Antiochiana.
55. EPP to Mrs. EPP, May 1822, in Mrs. EPP's copybook, letter 24, Peabody Family Papers, MHS.
56. Quoted in Marshall, p. 142.
57. EPP to Mary Peabody Mann, July 15, 1834, NYPL-Berg.
58. MVWC, p. 93.
59. EPP, *Reminiscences of Rev. Wm. Ellery Channing, D.D.* (Boston: Roberts Bros., 1880), pp. 37–8.
60. Ibid., p. 13.
61. MVWC, pp. 122–3.
62. Ibid., p. 123.
63. EPP, *Reminiscences of Rev. Wm. Ellery Channing*, pp. 12, iii.
64. William Ellery Channing, "Unitarian Christianity," delivered in Baltimore, May 5, 1819, https://people.wku.edu/jan.garrett/channsht.htm.

65. MVWC, pp. 30–3.
66. Ibid.
67. EPP, *Reminiscences of the Rev. Wm. Ellery Channing*, p. 121.
68. Channing, "Self-Culture," in *William Ellery Channing: Selected Writings*, ed. David Robinson (NY: Paulist Press, 1985), p. 228.
69. Ibid., p. 229.
70. Mary Peabody Mann to Maria Chase, March 8, 1826, Sophia Smith Collection, Smith College Library.
71. EPP, *Reminiscences of the Rev. Wm. Ellery Channing, D.D.*, p. 279.
72. MVWC, p. 30.
73. Ibid., p. 149.
74. Ibid., p. 99.
75. Ibid.
76. EPP to Orestes Brownson [1840], *LEPP*, p. 248.
77. EPP's letters to Wordsworth are printed in Margaret Neussendorfer, "Elizabeth Palmer Peabody to William Wordsworth, 1825–1845," *Studies in the American Renaissance* (1984), pp. 181–211.
78. Ibid., p. 184.
79. Ibid., p. 187.
80. William Ellery Channing, "Lectures on the Elevation of the Labouring Portion of the Community," (Boston: Ticknor, 1840), p. 21.
81. MVWC, p. 341.
82. Quoted in Molly Ridell, "Letters of William Ellery Channing in the *Christian Inquirer*," *The Eagle Feather*, vol. 13, no. 1 (2016), p. 4.
83. J.E.L., "Woman's Rights," *Christian Inquirer*, October 25 (1851), p. 2.
84. EPP to Elizabeth Davis Bliss, July 8, 1830, *LEPP*, p. 94.
85. *Christian Examiner*, May 1834, ibid., p. 190.
86. Ibid., p. 195.
87. *Christian Examiner*, July 1834, p. 317.
88. Ibid., September 1834, p. 78.
89. Ibid., May 1834, p. 190.
90. Moncure Dr. Conway, *Autobiography Memories and Experiences*, 2 vols. (Boston: Houghton Mifflin, 1904), 1: 160.
91. EPP to Orestes Brownson, [ca. 1840], *LEPP*, p. 248.
92. Ibid.
93. EPP to William Wordsworth, March 27, 1829, in Neussendorfer, "Elizabeth Palmer Peabody to William Wordsworth, 1825–1845," pp. 188.
94. EPP, *Reminiscences of the Rev. Wm. Ellery Channing*, p. 148.
95. Quoted in "Literary Notices," *The New-England Magazine*, vol. 4 (1833), p. 81.
96. EPP to Maria Chase, [April 1833] *LEPP*, p. 107.
97. *JMN*, 16: 259.
98. Germaine de Staël, *Germany* (London: John Murray, 1813), p. 77.
99. EPP to Maria Chase [April 1833], *LEPP*, p. 107.
100. Quoted in Ronda, *Elizabeth Palmer Peabody: A Reformer on Her Own Terms*, p. 73.
101. Ibid.
102. Charles Godfrey Leland, *Memoirs* (D. Appleton & Co., 1893), p. 66.
103. EPP to Mary Peabody Mann, July [21?] 1834, "Cuba Journal," NYPL-Berg.
104. EPP, *Record of a School: Exemplifying the General Principles of Spiritual Culture* (Boston: James Munroe, 1835), p. 29.
105. Bronson Alcott, "Life, Speculative and Actual, 1835," p. 21, *59M-308 (8) Houghton Library, Harvard University.
106. EPP to Elizabeth Bliss, [before August 1, 1835], *LEPP*, p. 151.
107. EPP, *Record of a School*, p. 143 (my emphasis).
108. Ibid., p. 20.
109. Ibid., p. 150.
110. Ibid., p. 145.
111. Quoted in Ronda, p. 149.
112. Harriet Martineau, *Society in America*, second edition, vol. III (London: Saunders and Otley, 1839), p. 175.
113. Quoted in Josephine E. Roberts, "Elizabeth Peabody and the Temple School," *New England Quarterly*, 15 (1942), p. 504.

114. EPP, *Record of a School*, pp. 156–7.
115. Ibid., pp. 189, 191.
116. EPP to William Wordsworth, September 7, 1835, Neussendorfer, "Elizabeth Palmer Peabody to William Wordsworth, 1825–1845," p. 194.
117. *LRWE*, 7: 245.
118. Mary Peabody Mann to George Francis Peabody, April 10, 1836, transcript by Robert L. Straker, Antiochiana.
119. EPP, *Record of a School*, p. iii.
120. Ibid., p. vii.
121. Ibid., pp. vi–vii.
122. Ibid., p. vii.
123. Amos Bronson Alcott, *Conversations with Children on the Gospels*, 2 vols. (Boston: James Munroe, 1836), 1: pp. 254–5.
124. Ibid., 1: 232.
125. Ibid., 1: iv.
126. EPP to Mary Peabody Mann, [April 1836], *LEPP*, pp. 157–63.
127. EPP to Amos Bronson Alcott, August 7, 1836, *LEPP*, pp. 180–1.
128. Quoted Franklin B. Sanborn and William T. Harris, *A. Bronson Alcott: His Life and Philosophy*, 2 vols. (Boston: Roberts Brothers, 1893), 1: 216.
129. These responses are reported in *LEPP*, p. 182.
130. "*Record of a School*," *The Knickerbocker*, vol. 7. (February 1836), p. 129.
131. MVWC, p. 106.
132. LJE to EPP, [August 1836], *LLJE*, p. 50.
133. EPP, "Emerson as Preacher," pp. 151–2.
134. Quoted in Philip F. Gura, *American Transcendentalism: A History* (NY: Hill & Wang, 2007), p. 92.
135. Jane Thompson Hallet Pritchard to Amelia M. Prichard, March 20, 1845, Pritchard Family Papers, Concord Free Public Library.
136. MVWC, p. 272.
137. Ibid., p. 276.
138. Ibid., p. 270.
139. EPP to Mary Peabody Mann, February 25, 1835, "Cuba Journal," NYPL-Berg.
140. MVWC, p. 270.
141. Ibid., pp. 280–1.
142. Ibid., pp. 281–2.
143. Ibid., p. 275.
144. Ibid., p. 277.
145. Ibid., pp. 279–80.
146. Ibid., p. 280.
147. Ibid., p. 280.
148. *LRWE*, 1: 449, fn. 70.
149. MVWC, August 5, 1838, p. 360.
150. Ibid.
151. *LEPP*, 188.
152. Ibid., 206.
153. EPP to Horace Mann, September 4, 1836, transcription by Robert L. Straker, Antiochiana.
154. EPP to George Peabody, August 8 [1830], *LEPP*, p. 229.
155. MVWC, p. 305.
156. Quoted in Cabot, *A Memoir of Ralph Waldo Emerson*, 1: 249.
157. Robert D. Richardson, *Emerson: The Mind on Fire* (Berkeley, Calif: University of California Press, 1995), p. 246.
158. MVWC, p. 281.
159. Ibid., p. 306.
160. Ibid., p. 316.
161. EPP to Amelie Boelte, June 30, 1886, *LEPP*, p. 432.
162. MVWC, pp. 312–13.
163. Ibid., p. 314.
164. Quoted in Marshall, p. 162.
165. RWE, *The Early Lectures of Ralph Waldo Emerson*, ed. Robert E. Spiller and Wallace E. Williams, vol. 3 (Cambridge, Mass.: Belknap Press of Harvard University Press, 1972), p. 234.
166. MVWC, pp. 308–9.

167. Ibid., pp. 316–17.
168. Ibid., pp. 320–1.
169. Ibid., p. 360.
170. RWE, *CW*, 1: 90.
171. EPP, "Emerson as Preacher," p. 158.
172. MVWC, p. 362.
173. Quoted in Gura, *American Transcendentalism*, p. 105.
174. Quoted in Octavius Brook Frothingham, *Transcendentalism in New England: A History* (New York: G. P. Putnam's Sons, 1880), p. 125.
175. MVWC, p. 366.
176. EPP to RWE, September 13, 1838, *LEPP*, p. 212.
177. MVWC, p. 320.
178. Ibid., p. 391.
179. Ibid., p. 398.
180. Ibid., p. 390.
181. EPP, "Emerson as Preacher," pp. 159–60.
182. Ibid., p. 151; MVWC, p. 341.
183. MVWC, p. 381.
184. Ibid., pp. 381–2.
185. Ibid., p. 321.
186. EPP to William P. Andrews, November 12, 1880, *LEPP*, p. 405.
187. Both communications are from *Jones Very: The Complete Poems*, ed. Helen R. Deese (Athens, Ga.: University of Georgia Press, 1993), p. xiv.
188. *LRWE*, 2: 154.
189. Edwin Gittelman, *Jones Very: The Effective Years, 1833–1940* (New York: Columbia University Press, 1967), pp. 146–7.
190. *JMN*, 5: 480.
191. *CW*, 1: 90.
192. Barbara Packer, *The Transcendentalists* (Athens, Georgia: University of Georgia Press, 2007), p. 70.
193. Deese, *Poems of Jones Very*, p. xvi.
194. EPP to William P. Andrews, November 12, 1880, *LEPP*, p. 406.
195. Ibid., p. 406.
196. Ibid.
197. Ibid., p. 407.
198. EPP to RWE, September 24, 1838, *LEPP*, p. 208.
199. Ibid., pp. 208–9.
200. Ibid.
201. *LRWE*, 7: 325.
202. EPP to William P. Andrews, November 12, 1880, *LEPP*, p. 408.
203. EPP to RWE, September 24, 1838, *LEPP*, p. 209.
204. Ibid.
205. EPP, *Last Evening with Allston, and Other Essays*, p. 245.
206. Ibid.
207. Orestes Brownson, "The Laboring Classes," in *The Transcendentalists*, ed. Perry Miller (Cambridge, Mass: Harvard University Press, 1950), p. 439.
208. EPP, "A Glimpse of Christ's Idea of Society," *Dial*, vol. 2 (October 1841), p. 217.
209. Quoted in George Willis Cooke, *An Historical and Biographical Introduction to Accompany the "Dial,"* 2 vols. [1902] (New York: Russell and Russell, 1961), 1: 148.
210. EPP to Horace Mann, September 4, 1836, transcript by Robert L. Straker, Antiochiana.
211. EPP to Mary Peabody Mann, [week of May 16, 1836], *LEPP*, p. 175.
212. *13–15 West Street, Elizabeth Peabody Bookstore and Circulating Library: Boston Landmarks Commission Study Report* (2011), p. 16. https://www.cityofboston.gov/images_documents/13-15_West_Street_Study_Report_tcm3-31148.pdf
213. Edward Everett Hale, *A New England Boyhood* (Boston: Little, Brown, 1900), p. 248.
214. EPP to Samuel Ward Gray, as quoted in Ronda, p. 186.
215. EPP, "A Glimpse of Christ's Idea of Society," *The Dial*, vol. II (October 1841), p. 222.
216. George Bradford, quoted in *Memorial History of Boston*, ed. Justin Winsor (Boston: Osgood, 1881–1882), vol. 4, p. 329, fn. 1.
217. MF to Sophia Ripley, August 27, 1839, *LMF*, 2: 86–9.

218. Ibid.
219. Joel Myerson, "Caroline Dall's Reminiscences of Margaret Fuller," *Harvard Library Bulletin*, vol. 22 (October 1974), p. 423.
220. MME to Elizabeth Hoar, April 8, 1841, *LMME*, p. 426.
221. Quoted in Charles Capper, *Margaret Fuller: An American Romantic Life: The Private Years*, 2 vols. (New York: Oxford University Press, 1992), 1: 299.
222. Unidentified woman quoted in *OM*, 1: 332.
223. Thomas Wentworth Higginson, *Cheerful Yesterdays* [1895] (New York: Arno, 1968), p. 86.

Chapter 3

1. Quoted in *Reinventing the Peabody Sisters*, p. x.
2. Quoted in Philip McFarland, *Hawthorne in Concord* (New York: Grove Press, 2004), p. 26.
3. Julian Hawthorne, *Nathaniel Hawthorne and His Wife: A Biography*, 2 vols. (Boston, James R. Osgood, 1885), 1: 43.
4. FFP, dated May 11, 1842.
5. EPP, *Reminiscences of Rev. William Ellery Channing, D.D.*, p. 404; Howe quoted in Charles Capper, *Margaret Fuller: An American Romantic Life: The Private Years* vol. 1 (New York: Oxford University Press, 1992), p. 304.
6. Sarah Hoar to Frances Jane Prichard, December 12, 1829, Frances Jane Prichard Papers, Concord Free Public Library.
7. *OM*, 1: 308.
8. Thomas Wentworth Higginson, *Margaret Fuller Ossoli* (Boston: Houghton Mifflin, 1887), p. 117.
9. Quoted in Megan Marshall, *The Peabody Sisters*, pp. 358–9; SP to EP, no date.
10. Patricia Dunlavy Valenti, *Sophia Peabody Hawthorne: A Life*, 2 vols. (Columbia, Mo.: University of Missouri Press, 2004), 1: 142.
11. Nathaniel Peabody, *The Art of Preserving Teeth* (Salem: Joshua and John D. Cushing, 1824), pp. 6–7.
12. Julian Hawthorne, *Nathaniel Hawthorne and His Wife*, 1: 47.
13. Ibid., 1: 52.
14. SPH to EPP, August 2, 1822, NYPL-Berg.
15. SPH to Mary Wilder White, January 1828, NYPL-Berg.
16. Julian Hawthorne, *Nathaniel Hawthorne and His Wife*, 1: 182.
17. Ibid., 1: 38, 177.
18. EP to SPH, June 23, 1823, NYPL-Berg.
19. EP to SPH, March 31, 1823, LEPP, p. 59.
20. Ibid., p. 61.
21. Valenti, *Sophia Peabody Hawthorne: A Life*, 1: 24.
22. SPH to EPP, July 1833, NYPL-Berg.
23. John Keats, *The Letters of John Keats, 1814–1821*, 2 vols. (Cambridge: Harvard University Press, 2002), 1: 94.
24. Adam Oehlenschlaäger, *Correggio, a Tragedy* translated by Theodore Martin (London: John W. Parker, 1854), iv.
25. EPP to SPH, May 15, 1824, NYPL-Berg.
26. SPH to EPP, November 5, 1824, NYPL-Berg.
27. SPH, diary, 1829, p. 1 NYPL-Berg.
28. SPH, *CJ*, 2: 10; EPP to MPM, April 1–13, 1834, NYPL-Berg.
29. SPH notebook, January–June 1835, NYPL-Berg.
30. Mrs. Peabody to SPH, [Salem?, 1828?]; Mrs. Peabody to SPH, January 8, 1844, NYPL-Berg.
31. Quoted in Marshall, p. 72.
32. Mary Peabody Mann, "Reminiscences," typescript by Robert L. Straker, Antioch, p. 103, Antiochiana.
33. Julian Hawthorne, *Nathaniel Hawthorne and His Wife*, 1: 47.
34. Dr. Nathaniel Peabody to Francis Peabody, June 6, 1826, Dartmouth.
35. SPH, diary, May 11, 1829, NYPL-Berg.
36. Quoted in T. Walter Herbert, *Dearest Beloved: The Hawthornes and the Making of the Middle-Class Family* (Berkeley: University of California Press, 1993), p. 38.
37. Quoted in Megan Marshall, p. 192.
38. SPH, diary, 1830, NYPL-Berg.
39. MVWC, p. 50.

40. Richard H. Millington, "The Letters of Sophia Peabody: A Miniature Edition," *Nathaniel Hawthorne Review*, 2011, p. 17.
41. SPH to EPP, June 17, 1826, NYPL-Berg.
42. Julian Hawthorne, *Nathaniel Hawthorne and His Wife*, 1: 63.
43. Walter Channing to SPH, November 17, 1828, NYPL-Berg; "*habit of being sick,*" according to Mary Peabody Mann, writing to Maria Chase, January 17, 1830, Peabody Family Papers, Smith College.
44. Quoted in Megan Marshall, p. 194; Mrs. Peabody to MPM, n.d., typescript by Robert L. Straker, p. 470, Antiochiana.
45. Nathaniel Cranch Peabody, reminiscences, Antiochiana.
46. SPH, diary, 1829, NYPL-Berg.
47. Mrs. Peabody to SPH, 1828, NYPL-Berg.
48. SPH to EPP, May 3, 1838, NYPL-Berg.
49. SPH to EPP, May and June, 1822, NYPL-Berg.
50. Julian Hawthorne, *Nathaniel Hawthorne and His Wife*, 1: 67.
51. SPH, journal, August 29, 1830, NYPL-Berg.
52. Ibid., my emphasis.
53. SPH, journal, July 1830, NYPL-Berg.
54. Ibid.
55. Mrs. EPP commonplace book 1829–30, June 29, 1830, Peabody Family Papers, MHS; Julian Hawthorne, *Nathaniel Hawthorne and His Wife*, 1: 68.
56. Ibid., 1: 51.
57. James Boswell, *The Life of Samuel Johnson*, 4 vols. (New York: John R. Anderson, 1889), 3: 127.
58. Charles Coleman Sellers, *The Artist of the Revolution: The Early Life of Charles Willson Peale* (Hebron, Conn.: Feather and Good, 1939), p. 80.
59. Quoted material from James F. O'Gorman, "Accomplished in All Departments of Art," *New York Times*, https://archive.nytimes.com/www.nytimes.com/books/first/o/ogorman-art.html.
60. Francis Graeter, *Mary's Journey: A German Tale* (Boston: S. G. Goodrich, 1829), p. 126.
61. Lydia Maria Child was also fond of this statement, citing it in *An Appeal in Favor of That Class of Americans Called Africans* [1833] (Bedford, Ma.: Applewood Books, n.d.). p. 172.
62. SPH, journal, June 8, 1830, NYPL-Berg.
63. SPH, journal, June 12, 1830, NYPL-Berg.
64. SPH, Dedham journal, 1830, NYPL-Berg.
65. Chester Harding, *A Sketch of Chester Harding, Artist, Drawn by His Own Hand*, ed. Margaret E. White (Boston, Houghton Mifflin, 1890), p. 38.
66. Ibid., pp. 63–4.
67. SPH, journal, July 12, 1830, NYPL-Berg.
68. SPH, journal, January–February, 1832; January 10, 1832, NYPL-Berg.
69. Louisa Hall Tharp, *The Peabody Sisters of Salem* (Boston: Little, Brown, 1950), p. 55.
70. SPH, diary, September 12, 1829, NYPL-Berg.
71. SPH to Mary Peabody Mann, November 20, 1832; SPH, journal, February 15, 1832, NYPL-Berg.
72. SPH, journal, January–February, 1832; January 13, 1832, NYPL-Berg.
73. SPH to Mrs. EPP, May 12, 1832, NYPL-Berg.
74. SPH, Holograph Notes on the Uses of Colour in Painting, NYPL-Berg.
75. Julius Caesar Ibetson, *An Accidence, or Gamut, of Oil Painting*, second ed. (London: Harvey and Darton, 1828), p. 2.
76. SPH to EPP, October 22, 1832, in "20 a.l.s. SAP to EPP," NYPL-Berg.
77. Quoted in Valenti, p. 31.
78. SPH diary, February 14–18, 1832, NYPL-Berg.
79. This comment, taken from SPH's journal beginning 1832 and located in the Hawthorne Family Papers, Green Library, Stanford University, is quoted from Marshall, p. 261.
80. Quoted in Patricia Dunlavy Valenti, "Sophia Peabody Hawthorne: A Study of Artistic Influence," *Studies in the American Renaissance* (1990), p. 7.
81. EPP to SP, [1833], NYL-Berg.
82. SPH to EPP, May 21–2 [1833], and SPH to EPP July 18–19, [1833], NYPL-Berg.
83. EPP to Sarah Hale, [May 15, 1833], *LEPP*, p. 109.
84. EPP to SP, [1833], NYPL-Berg.
85. SPH to EPP, May 19, [1836?]; SPH to Mary Peabody Mann and EPP, May 21–2, 1833, NYPL-Berg.
86. SPH to MPM, August 7, 1833, NYPL-Berg.
87. SPH to EPP, n.d., 1833, NYPL-Berg.
88. Quoted in Ronda, p. 103.

89. Ibid.
90. SPH to EPP, n.d., 1833, NYPL-Berg.
91. Mary Peabody Mann to SPH, [September?] [1833?], NYPL-Berg.
92. *CJ*, 1: 5–6.
93. *CJ*, 1: 12.
94. Abiel Abbot, *Letters Written in the Interior of Cuba* (Boston: Bowles and Dearborn, 1829) p. 194.
95. *CJ*, 1: 45.
96. Tharp, *The Peabody Sisters of Salem*, pp. 73–4.
97. *CJ*, 1: xxii.
98. *Rosamond Culbertson: or, A Narrative of the Captivity and Sufferings of an American Female Under the Popish Priests, in the Island of Cuba, with a Full Disclosure of Their Manners and Customs, Written by Herself* (London: Hodson, 1837). The English version of the novel included its putative author's surname.
99. See Louis A. Pérez Jr., *Cuba in the American Imagination: Metaphor and the Imperial Ethos* (Chapel Hill: The University of North Carolina Press, 2008), p. 25. See also Ada Ferrer, *Cuba: An American History* (New York: Scribners, 2022).
100. EPP to Mary Peabody Mann, August 18 [1834], *LEPP*, p. 133.
101. EPP is quoting Mary Peabody Mann in a letter dated August 8–10, 1834, NYPL-Berg.
102. *CJ*, 2: 47.
103. The book was Mme. Celnert, *The Gentleman and the Lady's Book of Politeness and Propriety of Deportment, Dedicated to the Youth of Both Sexes.*
104. Mrs. EPP to SPH, April 27, 1834, NYPL-Berg.
105. Both dreams in *CJ*, 1: 82.
106. Ibid., 1: 125.
107. Ibid., 1: 124.
108. Quoted in Valenti, p. 63.
109. *CJ*, 1: 16, 135.
110. Ibid., 1: 18.
111. Ibid., 1: 60–1.
112. Ibid., 1: 61.
113. Ibid., 2: 52.
114. Ibid., 1: 183.
115. Valenti, p. 60.
116. Quoted in Valenti, p. 56.
117. *CJ* 1: xxxiii.
118. Ibid., 1: 33.
119. Ibid., 1: 18.
120. Ibid., 1: 74.
121. Ibid., 1: 92–3.
122. Ibid., 1: 93.
123. Ibid., 1: 66, 106, 35.
124. Ibid., 1: 163.
125. Ibid., 1: 131.
126. Ibid., 2: 230.
127. Ibid., 2: 14.
128. Ibid., 1: 57.
129. Ibid., 1: 566.
130. RWE, *CW*, 1: 10.
131. *CJ*, 2: 53.
132. Ibid., 1: 470–1.
133. EPP to Mary Peabody Mann, [November] 18 [1834], NYPL-Berg.
134. *CJ*, 3: 90.
135. EPP to SPH, [September 1834?], NYPL-Berg.
136. Mrs. EPP to SPH, November–December 1834, n.d., NYPL-Berg.
137. SPH to Mrs. EPP, March 11, 1835, NYPL-Berg.
138. SPH to Mrs. EPP, April 23, 1835, NYPL-Berg.
139. SPH to NH, December 6, 1838, Peabody Sisters Collection, Clifton Waller Barrett Library of American Literature, University of Virginia.
140. Mary Peabody Mann to Horace Mann, May 30, 1835, typescript by Robert L. Straker, Antiochiana.

141. EPP to Mary Peabody Mann, [July] 15, [1834], NYPL-Berg.
142. SPH to Mary Peabody Mann, June 19, 1835, NYPL-Berg.
143. SPH to EPP, September 29, 1835, NYPL-Berg.
144. Quoted in Marshall, p. 309.
145. SPH to Mary Peabody Mann, June 30, 1835, NYPL-Berg.
146. SPH to EPP, October 15, 1835, NYPL-Berg.
147. For my interpretation of *Lorenzo and Jessica*, I am indebted to the museum talk by Sarah Monks, available at https://www.youtube.com/watch?list=SRArt+in+Focus:+Washington&v=aD-wSU1YQ2E.
148. SPH to EPP, August 12–13, 1835, NYPL-Berg.
149. See Samuel Chase Coale, "Mysteries of Mesmerism: Hawthorne's Haunted House," in *A Historical Guide to Nathaniel Hawthorne*, ed. Larry J. Reynolds (New York: Oxford University Press, 2001), pp. 49–78.
150. EPP to Mary Peabody Mann, June 18, 1836, NYPL-Berg.
151. Quoted in Marshall, p. 354.
152. Norman Holmes Pearson, "Elizabeth Peabody on Hawthorne," *Essex Institute Historical Collections*, 94 (July 1958), p. 264.
153. Elizabeth Hawthorne to James T. Fields, December 12, 1870, Boston Public Library; Mary Peabody to George Peabody, November 16, 1837, NYPL-Berg; Edwin Haviland Miller, *Salem is My Dwelling Place* (Iowa City: University of Iowa Press, 1994), p. 3; Henry W. Longfellow to George Washington Greene, October 22, 1838, *The Letters, 1813–1843* (Cambridge: Harvard University Press, 1967), 1: 277.
154. Mary Peabody Mann to George Peabody, November 16, 1837, NYPL-Berg.
155. Pearson, "Elizabeth Peabody on Hawthorne," p. 264.
156. Ibid., p. 264.
157. In Julian Hawthorne, *Hawthorne and His Wife*, 1: 179.
158. Megan Marshall, "The Peabody Sisters as Sisters," in *Reinventing the Peabody Sisters*, p. 248.
159. *CE*, 15: 252.
160. SPH to EPP, April 23, 1838, NYPL-Berg.
161. Ibid.
162. *CE*, 23: 202.
163. SPH to EPP, [April] 29, 1838, copybook journal letters in unknown hand, NYPL-Berg.
164. Nathaniel Hawthorne, *Tales and Sketches* (New York: Library of America, 1982), p. 641.
165. Ibid., p. 642.
166. NH, *The Complete Writing of Nathaniel Hawthorne*, 2 vols. (Boston: Houghton Mifflin, 1900), 1: 83–4.
167. Quoted in Marshall, pp. 371–2.
168. Quoted in Brenda Wineapple, *Hawthorne: A Life* (New York: Random House, 2003), p. 129.
169. Ibid., 126.
170. SPH to EPP, July [1839], Hawthorne Family Papers, Green Library, Stanford University.
171. NH to SPH, July 24, 1839, *CE*, 15: 330.
172. NH, *CE*, 15: 397–8.
173. Ibid., 15: 339.
174. Quoted in Marshall, p. 390.
175. SPH, Commonplace book, 1839, NYPL-Berg.
176. *CE*, 15: 363.
177. Ibid., 15: 404–5.
178. Rose Hawthorne Lathrop, *Memories of Hawthorne* (Boston: Houghton, Mifflin and Company, 1897), pp. 16–17.
179. RWE to LJE, April 22 and 23, 1836, *LRWE*, 2: 12.
180. *CE*, 15: 443, fn. 3.
181. Ibid., 15: 442.
182. Quoted in Lathrop, *Memories of Hawthorne*, p. 184.
183. RWE to SPH, January 20, 1838, *LRWE*, 7: 294.
184. *CE*, 15: 473–4.
185. Ibid., 15: 476.
186. Ibid., 15: 475.
187. Leslie Perrin Wilson, "'No Worthless Books': Elizabeth Peabody's Foreign Library," *The Papers of the Bibliographical Society of America*, 99 (March 2005): 121.
188. Quoted in Lindsay Swift, *Brook Farm* (New York: Corinth Books, 1961), p. 15.

189. Nathaniel Hawthorne, *Love Letters of Nathaniel Hawthorne* (Chicago: Privately Printed by the Society of the Dofobs, 1907), vol. 1, p. 229.
190. George Ripley to RWE, quoted in Henry W. Sams, *Autobiography of Brook Farm* (New York: Prentice-Hall, 1958), p. 6.
191. *Fuller in Her Own Time*, ed. Joel Myerson (Iowa City: University of Iowa Press, 2008), p. xxii.
192. Higginson, *Margaret Fuller Ossoli*, p. 118.
193. *OM*, 1: 340.
194. Ibid., 1: 339.
195. Ibid., 1: 340.
196. Ibid., 1: 341; quoted in Capper, 1: 304.
197. *OM*, 1: 341.
198. Nancy Craig Simmons, "Margaret Fuller's Boston Conversations: The 1839–1840 Series," *Studies in the American Renaissance* (1994), p. 215.
199. Myerson, *Fuller in Her Own Time*, p. 43.
200. Simmons, "Margaret Fuller's Boston Conversations," p. 215.
201. Ibid., p. 216.
202. *CE*, 15: 511.
203. NH to SPH, April 13, 1841, *CE*, 15: 527.
204. NH to SPH, April 13 and 14, 1841, *CE*, 15: 528.
205. Wineapple, *Hawthorne: A Life*, p. 153.
206. NH to SPH, April 16, 1841, *CE*, 15: 531.
207. Charles Dickens, *American Notes for General Circulation* (London: Chapman and Hall, 1855), p. 22.
208. *CE*, 15: 576.
209. Ibid., 15: 579.
210. Ibid., 15: 578.
211. Ibid., 15: 588.
212. SPH to Elizabeth Hoar, August 28, 1841, Pritchard Collection, Concord Free Public Library.
213. Attributed to Elizabeth Hoar by Megan Marshall, p. 434.
214. SPH to Mary Wilder White Foote, April 6, 1842, Hawthorne Family Papers, Green Library, Stanford University.
215. SPH to Mrs. EPP, July 10, 1842, NYPL-Berg.
216. SPH and NH, *Ordinary Mysteries: The Common Journal of Nathaniel and Sophia Hawthorne, 1842–1843*, ed. Nicholas R. Lawrence and Marta L. Werner (Philadelphia: American Philosophical Society, 2006), pp. 65, 77, 87, 153.
217. Ibid., p. 37.
218. SPH, notebooks [1842–3], Morgan Library.
219. SPH to Mrs. EPP, August 22, 1842, NYPL-Berg.
220. *Ordinary Mysteries*, p. 51.
221. Sophia Hawthorne to Mary Wilder White Foote, July 5, 1842, Hawthorne Family Papers, Green Library, Stanford University.
222. *Ordinary Mysteries*, p. 99.
223. Ibid., p. 49.
224. SPH to EPP, [1838], NYPL-Berg.
225. SPH to Mrs. EPP, September 3, 1842, NYPL-Berg.
226. SPH to Mrs. EPP, August 5–September 9, 1842, NYPL-Berg.
227. SPH to Mrs. EPP, August 30–September 4, 1842, NYPL-Berg.
228. SPH to Mrs. EPP, September 3, 1842, NYPL-Berg.
229. *Ordinary Mysteries*, p. 121.
230. Ibid., p. 41.
231. SPH to Mary Wilder White Foote, December 30, 1842, quoted in McFarland, *Hawthorne in Concord*, p. 55.
232. SPH to Mrs. EPP, February 22–4, 1843, NYPL-Berg.
233. SPH to Mary White, April 6, 1843, Hawthorne Family Papers, Green Library, Stanford University.
234. SPH to Mrs. EPP, February 22–4, 1843, NYPL-Berg.
235. *Ordinary Mysteries*, p. 247.
236. Ibid., p. 243.
237. *Ordinary Mysteries*, p. 251.
238. Mrs. EPP to SPH, August 1843, NYPL-Berg.

239. Rose Hawthorne Lathrop, *Memories of Hawthorne*, p. 72.
240. William Holman Hunt, *Pre-Raphaelitism and the Pre-Raphaelite Brotherhood*, 2 vols. (New York: MacMillan, 1905), 1: 106.
241. Rose Hawthorne Lathrop, *Memories of Hawthorne*, p. 65.
242. *Ordinary Mysteries*, p. 277.
243. SPH, "Sophia Hawthorne Journal," n.d. pp. 18, 19, NYPL-Berg.
244. SPH to James T. Fields, January 1, 1862, Boston Public Library; SPH to Mary Peabody Mann, September 30, 1851, NYPL-Berg.
245. SPH to Mary Peabody Mann, February 6, 1844, NYPL-Berg.
246. SPH to Mrs. EPP, January 21, 1844, NYPL-Berg.
247. *Nathaniel Hawthorne: The Contemporary Reviews*, ed. John L. Idol and Buford Jones (Cambridge: Cambridge University Press, 1994), p. xxxiv.
248. "'The Impulses of Human Nature': Margaret Fuller's Journal from June through October 1844," ed. Martha L. Berg and Alive De V. Perry, *Proceedings of the Massachusetts Historical Society*, 102 (1990), p. 89.
249. MF to SPH, June 4 [1842], NYPL-Berg.
250. MF, *Woman in the Nineteenth Century* (New York: Greeley & McElrath, 1845), p. 74.
251. Jane Prichard to Amelia Prichard, April 11, 1845, Concord Free Public Library.
252. SPH to Mrs. EPP, March 6, 1845, NYPL-Berg.
253. SPH to EPP, February 16, 1851, NYPL-Berg.
254. SPH to Mrs. EPP, September 7, 1845, NYPL-Berg.

Chapter 4

1. Quoted in Ronda, p. 156.
2. LJE to EPP, [late July 1836], *LLJE*, p. 49.
3. Quoted in *The Journal of Unitarian Universalist History*, 29 (2003), p. 81.
4. *LifeLJE*, p. 105.
5. Caroline Healey Dall, *Margaret and Her Friends* (Cambridge, Mass.: University Press, 1895), p. 8.
6. *History of Woman Suffrage*, ed. Elizabeth Cady Stanton, Susan B. Anthony, and Matilda Joslyn Gage, 3 vols. (Rochester, New York: Charles Mann, 1889), p. 32; MF to Sarah Helen Whitman, January 21, 1840, *LMF*, 2: 118.
7. Nancy Craig Simmons, "Margaret Fuller's Boston Conversations: The 1839–1840 Series," p. 205.
8. Ibid., p. 214.
9. *LifeLJE*, p. 43.
10. RWE, *The Complete Sermons of Ralph Waldo Emerson*, ed. Albert J. von Frank, 4 vols. (Columbia: University of Missouri Press, 1989), 4: 229.
11. The friend is unidentified. *LifeLJE*, p. 47.
12. Ibid.
13. RWE, *Journals*, [1910] p. 436.
14. *LLJE*, February 28, 1832, p. 18.
15. *LifeLJE*, p. 47.
16. Ibid., p. 48.
17. Ibid.
18. Ibid.
19. Ibid., p. 15.
20. Ibid., p. 25.
21. Ibid.
22. Ibid.
23. Ibid., p. 8.
24. Anthony Sammarco, "At Dorchester academy, proper young ladies learned needlework," *Dorchester Community News*, November 5, 1993.
25. Quoted in Ralph L. Rusk, *The Life of Ralph Waldo Emerson*, p. 217.
26. *LLJE*, pp. 1–2.
27. *LifeLJE*, p. 13.
28. *LLJE*, June 3, 1822, p. 8.
29. *LifeLJE*, pp. 33, 10.
30. Ibid., p. 23.
31. Ibid., p. 25.
32. Ibid., p. 28.
33. See *LMF*, 1: 108, fn. 5.
34. Quoted in Charles Capper, *Margaret Fuller: An American Romantic Life*, vol. 1, p. 65.

35. *LifeLJE*, p. 37.
36. Virginia Woolf, *A Room of One's Own* (New York: Broadview Press, 2001), p. 6.
37. *LifeLJE*, pp. 37–8.
38. Ibid., p. 29.
39. Ibid.
40. Ibid., p. 19.
41. This portrait of Lidian is gleaned from Carlos Baker, *Emerson among the Eccentrics: A Group Portrait* (New York: Viking, 1996), p. 40.
42. Ibid.
43. *JMN*, 5: 371.
44. *LifeLJE*, p. 23.
45. Ibid., p. 41.
46. Ibid., p. 45.
47. *LLJE*, p. 12.
48. Ibid., p. 5.
49. *LifeLJE*, p. 42.
50. Ibid., p. 48.
51. Ibid.
52. *LRWE*, 1: 434–5.
53. Ibid.
54. *LifeLJE*, p. 50.
55. Quoted in Ronald A. Bosco and Joel Myerson, *The Emerson Brothers*, p. 279; *LLJE*, p. 38.
56. *LifeLJE*, pp. 48–9.
57. LJE to Lucy Jackson Brown, September 16, 1835, *LLJE*, p. 33.
58. *LifeLJE*, p. 48.
59. *LRWE*, 1: 429, n. 33.
60. EPP to Elizabeth Bliss, [March 4, 1835?], *LEPP*, p. 148.
61. *LifeLJE*, pp. 49, 31.
62. *LifeLJE*, p. 49.
63. *LRWE*, 1: 438.
64. Franklin B. Sanborn, *Recollections of Seventy Years*, 2 vols. (Boston: Richard Badger, 1909), 2: 482–3.
65. *LifeLJE*, p. 50.
66. Ibid., p. 51.
67. Ibid., p. 50.
68. LJE to Lucy Jackson Brown, [March 10 or May 10, 1835], *LLJE*, p. 25.
69. July 26, 1833, Elizabeth Hoar to the Prichard family, Prichard Collection, Concord Free Public Library.
70. *LLJE*, p. 26.
71. LJE to Lucy Jackson Brown, May 23, 1835, *LLJE*, p. 27.
72. Quoted in Rusk, *The Life of Ralph Waldo Emerson*, p. 214.
73. *LifeLJE*, p. 51.
74. Ibid.
75. Ibid., p. 52.
76. *LRWE*, 1: 444.
77. *JMN*, 5: 48.
78. *LLJE*, p. xxiii.
79. Ibid., p. xxii.
80. LJE to EPP, July 28, 1835, *LLJE*, pp. 27–8.
81. Emmanuel Swedenborg, *A Compendium of the Writings of the Theological and Spiritual Writings of Emmanuel Swedenborg* (2nd ed. Boston: Crosby and Nichols, and Otis Clapp, 1854), p. 281.
82. LJE to EPP, July 28, 1835, *LLJE*, p. 29.
83. Ibid.
84. *LRWE*, 1: 447.
85. *LifeLJE*, p. 55.
86. Ibid., p. 91.
87. Ibid., p. 92.
88. Ibid.
89. LJE to EPP, August 1836, *LLJE*, p. 50.
90. Quoted in Baker, *Emerson among the Eccentrics*, p. 461.
91. *JMN*, 8: 88.

92. LJE to Lucy Jackson Brown, September 16, 1835, *LLJE*, p. 33.
93. *JMN*, 5: 456.
94. *LifeLJE*, p. 77.
95. LJE to Lucy Jackson Brown, September 30, 1835, *LLJE*, p. 40.
96. *LifeLJE*, p. 71.
97. LJE to EPP, [June 1836], *LLJE*, p. 48.
98. Elizabeth Hoar to MME, June 7, 1836, "The Letters of Elizabeth Hoar (Part Two)," *Studies in the American Renaissance* (1985), p. 142.
99. *LifeLJE*, pp. 72–3.
100. Ibid., p. 73.
101. Len Gougeon, "Abolition, the Emersons, and 1837," *The New England Quarterly*, vol. 54, (September 1981), p. 346.
102. A. E. Grimké, *Appeal to the Christian Women of the South* (n.p., 1836), p. 16.
103. LJE to Lucy Jackson Brown, September 9, 1837, *LLJE*, pp. 60–1.
104. *JMN*, 5: 382.
105. *CW*, 2: 30.
106. *JMN*, 5: 440.
107. Ibid., 12: 181.
108. Ibid., 5: 489–90, and fn. 490.
109. LJE to Lucy Jackson Brown, April 23, 1838, *LLJE*, p. 74.
110. See "The Cherokee Situation, 1838," Concord Free Public Library, https://concordlibrary.org/special-collections/emerson-celebration/Em_Con_37.
111. Quoted in Rusk, *The Life of Ralph Waldo Emerson*, p. 267.
112. LJE to Ellen Tucker Emerson, April 28, 1873, *LLJE*, p. 308.
113. LJE to Lucy Jackson Brown, April 23, 1838, *LLJE*, p. 74.
114. Hooper was the cousin of Elizabeth Davis Bliss Bancroft, Lydia's childhood friend. Ellen Sturgis Hooper, "I Slept, and Dreamed That Life was Beauty," in *The Transcendentalists*, ed. Perry Miller (Cambridge, MA: Harvard University Press, 1950), p. 402.
115. *LifeLJE*, p. 68.
116. LJE to Lucy Jackson Brown, September 2, 1837, *LLJE*, p. 58.
117. LJE to EPP, August 22, 1837, *LLJE*, p. 57.
118. LJE to Lucy Jackson Brown, September 2, 1837, *LLJE*, p. 59.
119. In Richardson, *Emerson: The Mind on Fire*, p. 84.
120. LJE to RWE, July 18, 1841, *LLJE*, p. 96.
121. LJE to Lucy Jackson Brown, September 22, 1835, *LLJE*, p. 35.
122. *JMN*, 5: 454.
123. *LLJE*, p. 70.
124. Ibid., p. 67.
125. Ibid., p. 15.
126. Ibid., p. 69.
127. MVWC, p. 279.
128. *CW*, 1: 9.
129. *JMN*, 5: 234.
130. Ibid., 5: 300.
131. LJE to Sophia Brown, August 19, 1837, *LLJE*, pp. 56–7.
132. LJE to Frank C. Brown, mistakenly dated 1846; Houghton Library, https://iiif.lib.harvard.edu/manifests/view/drs:42970229$183i.
133. *JMN*, 5: 480–1.
134. Ibid., 5: 343.
135. LJE to EPP, *LLJE*, p. 53.
136. LJE to Lucy Jackson Brown, sometime after October 31, 1836, *LLJE*, pp. 50–1.
137. Ibid.
138. *LifeLJE*, pp. 79–80.
139. Ibid., p. 80.
140. Ibid.
141. Henry David Thoreau, *The Writing of Henry David Thoreau*, 10 vols., ed. Horace Elisha Scudder, Harrison Gray Otis Blake, Franklin Sanborn, Ralph Waldo Emerson (Boston: Houghton Mifflin, 1893), 1: 506.
142. In Albert J. von Frank, *An Emerson Chronology* (Boston: G. K. Hall, 1994), p. 129.
143. LJE to Lucy Jackson Brown, April 1838, *LLJE*, p. 73.
144. *LifeLJE*, p. 78.

145. LJE to EPP, January 20, 1839, *LLJE*, p. 82.
146. MF to Caroline Sturgis, May 14, 1837, *LMF*, 1: 273.
147. Capper, *Margaret Fuller: An American Life*, 2: 71.
148. LJE to Lucy Jackson Brown, fragment, 1838, *LLJE*, p. 81.
149. *LifeLJE*, p. 77.
150. *JMN*, 7: 170.
151. Jane Prichard to Amelia Prichard, February 25, 1839, Prichard Family Papers, Concord Free Public Library.
152. *CW*, 2: 99.
153. Ibid., 2: 101.
154. Ibid., 2: 106.
155. *Correspondence of Carlyle and Emerson*, ed. Charles Eliot Norton, 2 vols. (Boston: James E. Osgood, 1883), 1: 161.
156. *LifeLJE*, p. 79.
157. MME to Elizabeth Hoar, April 8, 1841, *LMME*, p. 427.
158. Quoted in Charles Fourier, *The Theory of the Four Movements*, ed. Gareth Stedman Jones and Ian Patterson (Cambridge: Cambridge University Press, 1996), p. 132.
159. Albert Brisbane, *Social Destiny of Man: or, Association and Reorganization of Industry* (Philadelphia: C. F. Stollmeyer, 1840), p. 480.
160. Henry James, *Autobiography*, ed. Frederick Wilcox Dupee (Princeton: Princeton University Press, 1983), p. 364.
161. *LRWE*, 2: 338, n. 364.
162. Kathleen Lawrence, "The 'Dry-Lighted Soul' Ignites: Emerson and His Soul-Mate Caroline Sturgis as Seen in Her Houghton Manuscripts," *Harvard Library Bulletin*, New Series, Volume 16 (Fall 2005), p. 61.
163. Quoted in Joel Myerson, *A Historical Guide to Ralph Waldo Emerson* (New York: Oxford University Press, 2000), p. 226.
164. Ibid., p. 223.
165. *JMN*, 7: 532.
166. Ibid., 8: 144.
167. *LifeLJE*, p. 84.
168. Ibid., p. 83.
169. Ibid., p. 79.
170. Ibid., p. 130.
171. Ibid., p. 128.
172. Ibid., fn. 186, p. 227.
173. Ibid., p. 84.
174. *JMN*, 8: 242.
175. William Blake, *Songs of Innocence and of Experience, Shewing the Two Contrary States of the Human Soul*, ed. James John Garth Wilkinson (London: W. Pickering, 1839), p. xvi.
176. Ibid., p. xviii.
177. The entirety of the "Transcendental Bible" is published in *LifeLJE*, pp. 81–3.
178. *LifeLJE*, p. 83.
179. *CW*, 1: 203–4.
180. When exactly Lydia's "Transcendental Bible" was written is a matter of some speculation. Ellen's recollections are unclear, but she mentions that it was written while Lydia visited her brother Charles T. Jackson. This visit seems to have occurred in 1843.
181. LJE to Lucy Jackson Brown, January 1842, *LLJE*, p. 100.
182. *LifeLJE*, p. 88.
183. Ibid.
184. LJE to Lucy Jackson Brown, February 4, 1842, *LLJE*, p. 104.
185. MME to RWE, Ruth Haskins Emerson, and Elizabeth Hoar, February 1, 1842, *LMME*, p. 439.
186. MF to William Henry Channing, February 1841, *LMF*: 3: 42–3.
187. *OM*, 2: 43.
188. MVWC, p. 382.
189. EPP to Elizabeth Hoar, February 16, 1842, Prichard Family Papers, Concord Free Public Library.
190. *LRWE*, 3: 11–13.
191. Baker, *Emerson among the Eccentrics*, p. 195.
192. SPH to Mrs. EPP, September 1 and 2, 1842, NYPL-Berg.
193. "Margaret Fuller's 1842 Journal: At Concord with the Emersons," ed. Joel Myerson, *Harvard Library Bulletin* (1973), p. 338.

194. Ibid., p. 331.
195. In Bell Gale Chevigny, *The Woman and the Myth: Margaret Fuller's Life and Writings* (Boston: Northeastern University Press, 1994), p. 128.
196. Ibid., pp. 331–2.
197. LJE to RWE, January 10, 1843, *LLJE*, pp. 113–14.
198. *LRWE*, 3: 12, 18, 12.
199. LJE to RWE, March 10, 1842, *LLJE*, p. 109.
200. *LRWE*, 3: 12.
201. LJE to RWE, January 30, 1843, *LLJE*, p. 120.
202. *JMN*, 8: 365.
203. Ibid., 8: 368.
204. RWE, *Ralph Waldo Emerson: The Major Poetry*, ed. Albert J. Von Frank (Cambridge, Mass.: The Belknap Press of Harvard University Press, 2015), p. 121.
205. *CW*, 3: 27.
206. Ibid., 3: 29.
207. Ibid., 3: 49.
208. LJE to RWE, February 17, 1843, *LLJE*, p. 129.
209. LJE to RWE, December 21, 1845, *LLJE*, pp. 134–5.
210. *LRWE*, 3: 129.
211. Ibid., 3: 138.
212. Ibid., 3: 144.
213. Ibid., 3: 129–30.
214. Ibid., 3: 21.
215. LJE to RWE, January 30, 1843, *LLJE*, p. 120.
216. MME to LJE, March 3, 1844, *LMME*, p. 457.
217. MME to LJE, April 12, 1846, *LMME*, p. 486.
218. MME to LJE, March 3, 1844, *LMME*, p. 457.
219. LJE to Edward Waldo Emerson, *LLJE*, p. 228.
220. MME to LJE, January 28, 1848, *LMME*, p. 503.
221. MME to LJE, June 26, 1850, *LMME*, p. 518.
222. MME to LJE, July 26, 1850, *LMME*, p. 521.
223. Emanuel Swedenborg, *The Delights of Wisdom on the Subject of Conjugial Love*, translated by John Chadwick (London: The Swedenborg Society, 1996), p. 173.
224. LJE to MME, August 11, 1850, *LLJE*, p. 174.
225. Ibid., p. xxv.
226. Ibid.
227. LJE to Ellen Tucker Emerson, April 28, 1872, *LLJE*, p. 309.
228. *Life LJE*, p. xiv.
229. Ibid.
230. *CW*, 3: 49.
231. *LLJE*, p. xx.
232. Ibid., p. xxv.
233. LJE to MME, August 11, 1850, *LJE*, p. 173.

Chapter 5

1. [Ca. May 1833], Box 4, FFP, 6.
2. MF, May 5, 1844, "Fragments of Margaret Fuller's Journal, 1844–45," p. 6; Fruitlands Museum, Harvard, Mass.
3. Robert D. Habich, "Margaret Fuller's Journal for October 1842," *Harvard Library Bulletin.* 33 (Summer 1985), p. 290.
4. MF, May 26, 1840, Boston Public Library, Department of Rare Books and Manuscripts.
5. *OM*, 1: 95.
6. Ibid., 1: 337.
7. Ibid., 1: 105; 108.
8. Ibid., 1: 340.
9. Ibid., p. 107.
10. Ibid., 1: 107.
11. MF to Frederic Henry Hedge, January 1, 1840, *LMF*, 2: 113.
12. *OM*, 1: 37.
13. MF to James Freeman Clarke, May 1833, *LMF*, 1: 189.
14. MF, Winter 1839–40, in "Scrapbook," 1838–44, Perry-Clarke Collection, MHS, p. 164.

15. [1839], FFP, Box A.
16. MF to Caroline Sturgis, January 27, 1839, *LMF*, 2: 40.
17. Julia Ward Howell, *Margaret Fuller (Marchesa Ossoli)* (Boston: Roberts Brothers, 1883), p. 186.
18. Lydia Maria Child, review in the *Broadway Journal*, 1 (February 15, 1845), p. 97.; Charles Capper, *Margaret Fuller: An American Romantic Life*, 2 vols. (New York: Oxford University Press, 2007), 2: 186–7.
19. Orestes Brownson, "Miss Fuller and Reformers," *Brownson's Quarterly Review*, April 1845; see http://orestesbrownson.org/63.html.
20. MME to RWE, April 7, 1845, *LMME*, p. 471.
21. *OM*, 1: 105.
22. Quoted in "Notebook Margaret Fuller Ossoli," [1851], *JMN*, 11: 482.
23. Edward D. Hall, "Reminiscences of Dr. John Park," *Proceedings of the American Antiquarian Society*, 7 (1), p. 83.
24. *JMN*, 11: 482.
25. Mary Wollstonecraft, *A Vindication of the Rights of Woman* (New York: Scribner and Welford, 1890), pp. viii, 58, 102.
26. Margarett Crane Fuller to Timothy Fuller, December 23, 1818, FFP, 6: 41.
27. Capper, *Margaret Fuller: An American Romantic Life*, 1: 19.
28. Quoted in Thomas Wentworth Higginson, "Who Was Margaret Fuller?", in *The Magnificent Activist: The Writings of Thomas Wentworth Higginson 1823–1911*, ed. By Howard N. Meyer (New York: Da Capo Press, 2000), p. 284.
29. MF to James Freeman Clarke, July 1, 1833, *LMF*, 1: 186.
30. Timothy Fuller to MF, April 13, 1820; FFP, 5: 6.
31. *OM*, 1: 14.
32. Timothy Fuller to Margarett Crane Fuller, April 28, 1814; FFP, 3: 7.
33. *OM*, 1: 15.
34. *OM*, 2: 52.
35. MF to Caroline Sturgis, July [24?], 1838, *LMF*, 1: 338.
36. MF to Almira Barker, October 6, 1834, *LMF*, 1: 209.
37. "Marine Journal," *Boston Courier*, November 7, 1839, p. 2.
38. Quoted in *LMF*, 2: 89, fn. 1.
39. MF to Sophia Ripley, August 27, 1839, *LMF*, 2: 88.
40. *OM*, 1: 332.
41. Ibid.
42. Ibid., 1: 336.
43. Nancy Craig Simmons, "Margaret Fuller's Boston Conversations: The 1839–1840 Series," *Studies in the American Renaissance* (1994), p. 203.
44. Oliver Wendell Holmes, *The Works of Oliver Wendell Holmes*, 13 vols. (Boston: Houghton Mifflin, 1892), 8: 242–3.
45. *OM*, 2: 5; 1: 92–3.
46. Timothy Fuller to MF, December 15, 1822. FFP, 5: 16.
47. FFP, 5: 16.
48. *OM*, 1: 45–7.
49. MF to Susan Prescott, January 1830, *LMF*, 1: 160.
50. Nancy Craig Simmons, "Margaret Fuller's Boston Conversations," p. 203.
51. Ibid.
52. Ibid.
53. *OM*, 1: 213.
54. MF to James Nathan, April 15, 1845, *LMF*, 4: 76.
55. *OM*, 2: 2.
56. Ibid., 1: 135.
57. Elizabeth Hoar to MME, April 23, 1839, quoted in *Fuller in Her Own Time*, p. 51.
58. *OM*, 1: 135.
59. Ibid., 1: 117.
60. In Carolyn L. Karcher, *The First Woman of the Republic: A Cultural Biography of Lydia Maria Child* (Durham, NC: Duke University Press, 1994), p. 40.
61. *Selected Letters of Lydia Maria Child*, ed. Milton Meltzer and Patricia G. Holland (Amherst: University of Massachusetts Press, 1982), p. 10.
62. Harriet Martineau, *Harriet Martineau's Autobiography*, 3 vols. (London: Smith, Elder, 1877), 2: 72.
63. FFP, 3: 371–5.
64. Quoted in Capper, 2: 101.

65. MF to James Freeman Clarke, August 7, 1832, *LMF*, 6: 187.
66. MF to James Freeman Clarke, [ca. May 20, 1833], *LMF*, 1: 182.
67. James Freeman Clarke, "Journal of the Understanding," December 11, 1832, in James Freeman Clarke Papers, Houghton Library, Harvard University.
68. FFP, Box 4, n. d.
69. William and Mary Wordsworth, *The Love Letters of William and Mary Wordsworth*, ed. Beth Darlington (Ithaca: Cornell University Press, 1981), p. 60.
70. "Tribute to Hon. George T. Davis," *Proceedings of the Massachusetts Historical Society*, vol. 15 (1876–7), pp. 308, 309, 308.
71. MF to James Freeman Clarke, October 11, 1835, *LMF*, 6: 272.
72. MF to [? George T. Davis], [ca. winter] [1829–30], *LMF*, 1: 159.
73. Quoted in Capper, 1: 104.
74. MF to George T. Davis, February 2, 1831, *LMF*, 1: 174.
75. *OM*, 1: 108.
76. Ibid., 2: 167–8.
77. Ibid., 2: 10–11.
78. FFP, Box A.
79. *OM*, 1: 139–41.
80. FFP, 3: 379.
81. Ibid., 3: 377–9.
82. MF to Albert H. Tracy, November 6, 1843, *LMF*, 3: 156.
83. *OM*, 1: 155–6.
84. MF to James Nathan, September 29, 1845, *LMF*, 4: 163.
85. MF to James Freeman Clarke, March 23, 1836, *LMF*, 1: 254.
86. MF to James Nathan, July 22, 1845, *LMF*, 4: 137.
87. MF to unknown correspondent, November 3, 1835, *LMF*, 1: 237.
88. MF to Amos Bronson Alcott, June 27, 1837, *LMF*, 1: 286–7.
89. "Elizabeth of Concord: Selected Letters of Elizabeth Sherman Hoar (1814–1878) to the Emerson, Family, and the Emerson Circle (Part Two)," *Studies in the American Renaissance* (1985), p. 153.
90. *OM*, 1: 202–3.
91. MF to RWE, no date, *LMF*, 3: 96.
92. Simmons, "Margaret Fuller's Boston Conversations," p. 209.
93. MF to LJE, August 19, 1838, *LMF*, 1: 341.
94. *OM* 1: 149.
95. Margaret Fuller, "A Short Essay on Critics," *The Dial* vol. 1 (July 1840), p. 10.
96. MF to RWE, July 5, 1840, *LMF*, 2: 146.
97. Quoted in Capper, 2: 3.
98. Quoted in *JMN*, 8: 211.
99. MF to [?], November 26, 1839, *LMF*, 2: 101.
100. "[*Journal: Reflections*] autograph manuscript, 1839 November 7 and undated, 1839," FFP, 5.
101. MF to RWE, November 1839, *LMF*, 2: 97.
102. MF to [?] [ca. Autumn? 1839?], *LMF*, 2: 97.
103. MF to Sarah Helen Whitman, January 21, 1840, *LMF*, 2: 118.
104. Elizabeth Cady Stanton, *History of Woman Suffrage*, vol. 1, ed. Stanton, Susan B. Anthony, and Matilda Joslyn, preface.
105. MF to Sophia Ripley, August 27, 1839, *LMF*, 2: 86–8.
106. Simmons, "Margaret Fuller's Boston Conversations," p. 204.
107. Ibid.
108. Ibid., p. 208.
109. Lydia Maria Child, *The Family Nurse; or, Companion of The Frugal Housewife* (London: Bentley, 1837), p. 73.
110. Simmons, "Margaret Fuller's Boston Conversations," p. 208.
111. Ibid.
112. Ibid., p. 205.
113. Ibid.
114. Ibid., pp. 206–7.
115. Quoted in John Matteson, *The Lives of Margaret Fuller* (New York: Norton, 2013), p. 96.
116. *OM*, 2: 8.
117. Quoted in Capper, 1: 280.
118. James Freeman Clarke to MF, *LMF*, 1: 251.

119. Robert D. Habich, "Margaret Fuller's Journal for October 1842," *Harvard Library Bulletin*, 33 (Summer 1985), pp. 286–7.
120. *OM*, 2: 103.
121. MF to Samuel Gray Ward, October 15, 1839, *LMF*, 2: 95.
122. MF to [?], January 1832, *LMF*, 1: 175.
123. *OM*, 1: 308.
124. MF to Caroline Sturgis, September 6, 1840, *LMF*, 2: 158.
125. *OM*, 2: 45.
126. Ibid., 1: 308–9.
127. MF to Caroline Sturgis, September 26, 1840, *LMF*, 2: 158–9.
128. MF to RWE, September 29, 1840, *LMF*, 2: 160.
129. MF, "Journal," Margaret Fuller Ossoli Collection, Boston Public Library, p. 119. Emphasis in original.
130. MF to Caroline Sturgis, September 8, 1840, *LMF*, 2: 157–8.
131. MF to Caroline Sturgis, September 26, 1840, *LMF*, 2: 158.
132. MF to RWE, December 4, 1840, *LMF*, 2: 188.
133. MF to William Henry Channing, December 3, 1840, *LMF*, 2: 187.
134. *JMN*, 7: 48.
135. Ibid., 7: 301.
136. MF to RWE September 29, 1840, *LMF*, 2: 159–60.
137. *LMF*, 2: 161, fn. 1.
138. *LRWE*, 2: 325.
139. *JMN*, 7: 509–10.
140. MF to William Henry Channing, October 25 and 28, 1840, *LMF*, 2: 167.
141. Quoted in Capper, 2: 24.
142. MF to John S. Dwight, October 9, 1838, *LMF*, 1: 347.
143. MF, ["Fragments of Margaret Fuller's Journal]," Fruitlands Library, pp. 35–6.
144. Ibid.
145. MF to Elizabeth Hoar, March 20, 1842, *LMF*, 3: 55.
146. MF to RWE, July 11, 1848, *LMF*, 5: 86.
147. MF to Sarah Helen Whitman, January 21, 1840, *LMF*, 2: 118–19.
148. Simmons, "Margaret Fuller's Boston Conversations," p. 214.
149. Ibid.
150. Ibid., p. 215.
151. Quoted in Ronda, *Elizabeth Palmer Peabody: A Reformer on her Own Terms*, p. 147.
152. Simmons, "Margaret Fuller's Boston Conversations," p. 216.
153. Ibid.
154. Ibid., p. 218.
155. MF to Albert H. Tracey, November 6, 1843, *LMF*, 3: 156.
156. MF to George T. Davis, December 17, 1842, *LMF*, 3: 105.
157. MF, *Woman in the Nineteenth Century* (New York: Greeley & McElrath, 1845), p. 4.
158. Ibid., p. 101.
159. Ibid., p. 103.
160. Ibid., p. 27.
161. Ibid., p. 58.
162. Ibid., p. 60.
163. Ibid., p. 69.
164. Ibid.
165. Ibid., pp. 27–8.
166. Ibid., p. 26.
167. Ibid., p. 28.
168. Both letters quoted in Julian Hawthorne, *Nathaniel Hawthorne and His Wife* (Boston: James R. Osgood and Company, 1885), 1: 257–8.
169. George Eliot, "Margaret Fuller and Mary Wollstonecraft," in *The Writings of George Eliot,* 25 vols. (Boston: Houghton Mifflin, 1908), 22: 326. Eliot was one of the first to trace a lineage from Mary Wollstonecraft to MF.
170. Quoted in Margaret Fuller, *Woman in the Nineteenth Century*, ed. Larry J. Reynolds (NY. Norton, 1998), p. 231.
171. Caroline Healey Dall, *Historical Pictures Retouched: A Volume of Miscellanies*, 2 vols. (Boston: Walker, Wise, 1850), 1: 24–49.

172. MF to RWE, May 9, 1843, *LMF*, 3: 124.
173. *LRWE*, 3: 183.
174. Theodore Parker, August, 1843, Houghton Library, Harvard University; HDT, July 8, 1843, *The Correspondence of Henry David Thoreau*, ed. Walter Harding and Carl Bode (New York, 1958), pp. 124–5.
175. Quoted in George Willis Cooke, *An Historical and Biographical Introduction to Accompany the "Dial,"* 2 vols. (Cleveland, 1902), 1: 172.
176. Quoted in Karen Ann Szymanski, "Margaret Fuller: The New York Years," unpublished dissertation, Syracuse University, 1980, p. 49.
177. Emily Dickinson, "Drowning is not so pitiful," #1452, *The Poems of Emily Dickinson: Reading Edition*, ed. R. W. Franklin (Cambridge: Belknap Press, 2005).
178. MF to RWE, August 4, 1843, *LMF*, 3: 138.
179. MF to RWE, August 17, 1843, *LMF*, 3: 143.
180. MF to Richard Fuller, July 29, 1843, *LMF*, 3: 132.
181. Thomas Wentworth Higginson, *Margaret Fuller Ossoli* (Boston: Houghton Mifflin, 1887), p. 194.
182. MF to Jane F. Tuckerman, July 22, 1844, *LMF*, 3: 217.
183. MF to Georgianna Bruce, July 16, 1844, *LMF*, 3: 211.
184. Quoted in Chevigny, p. 556.
185. MF to Georgianna Bruce, October 20, 1844, *LMF*, 3: 236.
186. Quoted in Matteson, *The Lives of Margaret Fuller* (New York: Norton, 2012), p. 264.
187. MF, *Woman in the Nineteenth Century*, p. 119.
188. Ibid., p. 84.
189. Ibid., p. 159.
190. MF to William Henry Channing, November 17, 1844, *LMF*, 3: 241.
191. MF to Richard Fuller, October 15, 1844, *LMF*, 3: 234.
192. MF to Mary Rotch, January 15, 1845, *LMF*, 4: 45.
193. MF to James Nathan, May? 4? 1845, *LMF*, 4: 95.
194. Margaret Fuller, *Margaret Fuller, Critic: Writings from the* New-York Tribune, *1844–1846*, ed. By Judith Mattson Bean and Joel Myerson (New York: Columbia UP, 2000), pp. 233, 238.
195. *The Works of Edgar Alan Poe*, ed. Richard Henry Stoddard, 5 vols. (New York: A. C. Armstrong, 1895), 5: 515–16.
196. LMF to James Nathan, March 15, 1845, *LMF*, 4: 62.
197. MF to James Nathan, April 9, 1845, *LMF*, 4: 72.
198. MF to James Nathan, May? 4?, 1845, *LMF*, 4: 95.
199. MF to James Nathan, April 6, 1845, *LMF*, 4: 68.
200. MF to James Nathan, April 14, 1845, *LMF*, 4: 75.
201. See "Farewell," *Margaret Fuller's New York Journalism: A Biographical Essay and Key Writings*, ed. Catherine C. Mitchell (Knoxville: University of Tennessee Press, 1995), p. 204.
202. MF to Thomas Delf, September 1, 1846, *LMF*, 4: 226–7.
203. MF to Richard Fuller, September 27, 1846, *LMF*, 4: 228.
204. Quoted in Julia Ward Howe, *Margaret Fuller*, p. 81.
205. MF to Evert A. Duyckinck, October 30, 1846, *LMF*, 4: 234.
206. *OM*, 2: 186.
207. MF to Caroline Sturgis, November 16, 1846, *LMF*, 4: 239–40.
208. Ibid.
209. MF to RWE, January 18, 1847, *LMF*, 4: 259.
210. MF to Elizabeth Hoar, January 18, 1847, *LMF*, 4: 256.
211. Ibid.
212. MF to RWE, March 15, 1847, *LMF*, 4; 261.
213. MF to Rebecca Spring, April 10, 1846, *LMF*, 4: 263.
214. Adam Mickiewicz to MF, February 1847, *LMF*, 4: 176 fn.
215. MF to William Henry Channing, May 7, 1847, *LMF*, 4: 271.
216. MF, *Woman in the Nineteenth Century*, p. 163.
217. Putnam, quoted in *Margaret Fuller in Her Own Time*, pp. 79–80.

Epilogue

1. Quoted in *LMF*, 5: 280 fn.
2. MF to Marcus and Rebecca Spring, April 10, 1846, *LMF*, 4: 262.
3. Ibid., 4: 263.
4. *LMF*, 5: 248.
5. MF to RWE, May 19, 1848, *LMF*, 5: 66.

6. MF to RWE, ca. May 1848, *LMF*, 5: 64.
7. MF to William Henry Channing, May 7, 1847, *LMF*, 4: 271.
8. MF, *These Sad but Glorious Days: Dispatches from Europe, 1846–1850*, ed. Larry J. Reynolds and Susan Belasco Smith (New Haven: Yale University Press, 1991), p. 285.
9. MF to RWE, June 10, 1849, *LMF*, 5: 239.
10. MF to Richard Fuller, March 17, 1849, *LMF*, 5: 213.
11. MF to Caroline Sturgis, ca. December 17, 1849, *LMF*, 5: 303; EBB quoted in Capper, *Margaret Fuller: An American Romantic Life*, 2: 485.
12. MF to Richard Fuller, July 8, 1849, *LMF*, 5: 244.
13. MF to unknown, November 29, 1849, *LMF*, 5: 282.
14. MF to Constanza Arconati Visconti, August 1849, *LMF*, 5: 250.
15. MF to RWE, October 21, 1849, *LMF*, 5: 271.
16. MF to E. Hoar? Ca. Autumn 1849, *LMF*, 5: 266.
17. MF to William Henry Channing, December 17, 1849, *LMF*, 5: 300.
18. MF to unknown, November 29, 1849, *LMF*, 5: 282.
19. MF to Emelyn Story, November 1849, *LMF*, 5: 280.
20. MF to Ellen Fuller Channing, July 19, 1849, *LMF*, 5: 242.
21. MF to Costanza Arconati Visconti, October 16, 1849, *LMF*, 5: 269–70.
22. MF to Margarett Crane Fuller, August 31, *LMF*, 5: 259.
23. MF to Ellen Fuller Channing, March 13, 1849, *LMF*, 5: 207.
24. MF to Costanza Arconati Visconti, April 6, 1850, *LMF*, 6: 74.
25. MF to Costanza Arconati Visconti, April 12, 1850, *LMF*, 6: 75.
26. Quoted in Capper, 2: 507.
27. Ibid., 2: 509.
28. In Henry David Thoreau, *The Writings of Henry David Thoreau*, ed. Franklin Sanborn (Boston: Houghton Mifflin, 1906), 6: iii.
29. *Life LJE*, p. 124.
30. *JMN*, July 21[?] 1850.
31. Quoted in Joan Van Mehren, *Minerva and the Muse: A Life of Margaret Fuller* (Amherst: University of Massachusetts Press, 1994), p. 339.
32. Quoted in *LMF*, 6: 8–9.
33. Ibid.
34. Ibid.
35. Marcus Spring to MF, fn., *LMF*, 6: 89.
36. Quoted in Capper, 2: 517.
37. Horace Greeley, "Death of Margaret Fuller," *New York Daily Tribune*, July 23, 1850, p. 4.
38. In Margaret Fuller Ossoli, *At Home and Abroad, or Things and Thoughts in America and Europe*, ed. by Arthur B. Fuller (Boston: Crosby, Nichols, and Company, 1856), p. 456.
39. *OM*, 1: 294.
40. Ibid., 2: 236.
41. Julia Ward Howe, "What the Nineteenth Century Has Done for Women," in *Julia Ward Howe and the Woman Suffrage Movement: A Selection from her Speeches and Essays*, ed. Florence Howe Hall (Boston: Sana Estes, 1913), p. 178.
42. Howe, *Margaret Fuller (Marchesa Ossoli)*, p. 278.
43. Quoted in Patricia Dunlavy Valenti, *Sophia Peabody Hawthorne: A Life*, 2: 23.
44. SPH to Eliza Peabody, August 1, 1850, NYPL-Berg.
45. Mary Peabody Mann to SPH, [August?], 1850, NYPL-Berg.
46. Quoted in Valenti, 2: 20.
47. *CE*, 3: 2.
48. SPH to EPP, 1858, NYPL-Berg; SPH, *Notes in England and Italy* (New York: G. P. Putnam, 1878), p. 198.
49. Robert Milder and Randall Fuller, ed., *The Business of Reflection: Hawthorne in His Notebooks* (Columbus, Ohio: The Ohio State University Press, 2009), pp. 202–4.
50. Ada Shepard to Clay Badge, Ada Shepard Papers, 1857–1859, Box 2, Folder 3, packet 7, dated March 13, 1858–April 9, 1858, Concord Free Public Library.
51. SPH to James T. Fields, November 28, 1859, Boston Public Library.
52. Julian Hawthorne, *Nathaniel Hawthorne and His Wife: A Biography*, 1: 39.
53. Ibid., p. 40.
54. SPH to EPP and Mrs. EPP, December 1850, wrongly dated [1868?], NYPL-Berg.
55. Quoted in Valenti, 2: 275.

56. *A List of the Recent Publications of G. P. Putnam's Sons* (1877), p. 8. https://www.google.com/books/edition/The_Publishers_Trade_List_Annual/vm9fAAAAcAAJ?hl=en&gbpv=1&dq=notes+in+England+and+Italy+mrs.+hawthorne&pg=RA59-PA8&printsec=frontcover
57. Rose Hawthorne Lathrop, *Memories of Hawthorne* (Boston: Houghton Mifflin, 1897), p. 314.
58. LJE to MME, August 11, 1850, *LLJE*, p. 173.
59. *LifeLJE*, p. 124.
60. Ibid.
61. Tiffany K. Wayne, *Woman Thinking: Feminism and Transcendentalism in Nineteenth-Century America* (Lanham, Maryland: Lexington Books, 2005), p. 47.
62. Quoted in Len Gougeon, "Emerson on the Woman Question: The Evolution of His Thought," *New England Quarterly*, 71 (December 1998), p. 575.
63. *LifeLJE*, p. xxxi.
64. LJE to MME, August 11, 1850, *LLJE*, p. 172.
65. *LifeLJE*, P. 141.
66. LJE to her children, [1863], *LLJE*, p. 219.
67. These details of the burning of the Emerson home are in Christopher Hanlon's *Emerson's Memory Loss: Originality, Communality, and the Late Style* (New York: Oxford University Press, 2018), p. 18.
68. *LLJE*, p. 182.
69. Ibid., p. 188.
70. Ibid., p. 199.
71. Ibid., p. 140.
72. LJE to RWE, February 19, 1852, *LLJE*, p. 177.
73. *LifeLJE*, pp. 205–6.
74. Ibid., p. 206.
75. Ibid., p. 210.
76. MME to LJE, December 2, 1851, *LMME*, p. 537.
77. MME to RWE, August 16, 1850, *LMME*, p. 522.
78. MF to Elizabeth Hoar, October [ca. 20?], 1841, *LMF*, 2: 246.
79. MME to RWE, August 16, 1850, *LMME*, p. 522.
80. Quoted in Tiffany K. Wayne, *Woman Thinking: Feminism and Transcendentalism in Nineteenth-Century*, p. 53.
81. Elizabeth Oakes Smith, *Selections from the Autobiography of Elizabeth Oakes Smith*, ed. By Mary Alice Wyman (Lewiston, Maine: Lewiston Journal Company, 1924), p. 135.
82. *LMME*, p. xxxii.
83. Ralph Barton Perry, *The Thought and Character of William James* (Boston: Little, Brown, 1936), 1: 149.
84. Franklin Benjamin Sanborn, *Recollections of Seventy Years*, 2: 384.
85. Quoted in Phyllis Cole, *Mary Moody Emerson and the Origins of Transcendentalism: A Family History*, p. 285.
86. Henry David Thoreau, *The Writings of Henry David Thoreau: Journal, Volume 4: 1851–1852*, ed. Nancy Craig Simmons (Princeton: Princeton University Press, 1993), 4: 183–4.
87. MME, "The Meeting of Two Friends after Long Separation by Death," *Christian Register*, 25 (August 22, 1846), p. 1.
88. Quoted in Cole, p. 282.
89. December 1849 or January 1850, folder 21, Almanacks, Tolman transcription, Houghton Library.
90. MME to LJE, March 18, 1861, *LMME*, p. 597.
91. RWE, *Works*, 12 vols. (Boston: Houghton Mifflin, 1893), 11: 429.
92. *LRWE*, 9: 107.
93. Cole, p. 261.
94. Ellen Tucker Emerson to Edith Emerson Forbes, *The Letters of Ellen Tucker Emerson*, ed. Edith E. W. Gregg, 2 vols. (Kent State University Press, 1982), 1: 224.
95. Cole, p. 290.
96. RWE, *Emerson's Complete Works*, ed. James Elliott Cabot (Boston: Houghton Mifflin, 1883), 6: 374.
97. RWE, "Mary Moody Emerson, *The Atlantic Monthly* (December 1883). https://www.theatlantic.com/magazine/archive/1883/12/mary-moody-emerson/539490/
98. EPP to MME, October 7, 1845, EPP Papers, American Antiquarian Society.
99. MME to Ann Sargent Gage, *LMME*, pp. 565, 587.
100. EPP to Ann Sargent Gage, ca. 1846. American Antiquarian Society.

101. EPP, "Principles and Methods of Education; My Experiences as a Teacher," *American Journal of Education*, 32 (1882), pp. 736–7.
102. Mrs. EPP to EPP, n.d., transcription by Robert L. Straker, Antiochiana.
103. EPP to SPH, January 11–12, 1853, in Julian Hawthorne, 1: 485–7.
104. EPP to Samuel Gray Ward, January 30, 1853, quoted in Bruce Ronda, p. 243.
105. Sarah Clarke to EPP, October 22, 1855; quoted in Ronda, p. 254.
106. EPP to Rawlins Pickman, 1858, Horace Mann II Papers, MHS.
107. EPP, "Prospectus," *Kindergarten Messenger*, 1 (January and February, 1877), p. 1.
108. Lucy Wheelock, "Miss Peabody as I Knew Her," in *Kindergarten and Child Culture: Pioneers of the Kindergarten in America* (New York: Century, 1924), pp. 33–4.
109. Quoted in Ronda, pp. 224–5.
110. "Miss Peabody's Reminiscences of Margaret's Married Life," *Boston Evening Transcript*, June 10, 1885.
111. Ibid.
112. Mary Peabody Mann to Horace Mann, July 20, 1856, transcription by Robert L. Straker, Antiochiana.
113. The anecdote, which was widely reported, appears in Harriet Hosmer to Cornelia Carr, in *Harriet Hosmer, Letters and Memories*, ed. Cornelia Carr (New York: Moffat, Yard, 1912), p. 32.
114. Mark DeWolfe Howe, *The Later Years of the Saturday Club, 1870–1920* (Boston: Houghton Mifflin, 1927), pp. 156–7.
115. Henry James, *The Bostonians*, 2 vols. (London: Macmillan, 1921), p. 216.
116. EPP to Mary Peabody Mann, August 1879, *LEPP*, pp. 388–9.
117. Florence Whiting Brown, "Alcott and the Concord School of Philosophy," in *Concord Harvest, The Later Transcendentalists*, ed. Kenneth Cameron, 2 vols. (Hartford: Transcendental Books, 1970), 2: 169–70.
118. Quoted in Ronda, p. 340.
119. SPH to Mrs. EPP, September 29–October 10, 1850, NYPL-Berg.
120. Sarah Clarke, "This Comes Saluting the Friends of Elizabeth Peabody," ms., Boston Public Library.
121. George Willis Cooke, *Unitarianism in America: A History of Its Origin and Development* (Boston: American Unitarian Association, 1902), p. 371. According to Cooke, the first woman ordained to the Unitarian ministry was Celia C. Burleigh, in 1871.
122. Caroline Healey Dall, in Joel Myerson, "Caroline Dall's Reminiscences of Margaret Fuller," *Harvard Library Bulletin*, 22 (1974), p. 419.
123. Ibid., p. 423.
124. Ibid., p. 416.
125. Caroline Dall, *Transcendentalism in New England: A Lecture Delivered Before the Society of Philosophical Enquiry, Washington, D.C.* (Boston: n.d., n. p.), p. 13.
126. Ibid., p. 24.
127. Ibid., p. 25.
128. Ibid., p. 35.
129. Ibid., pp. 35–6.
130. Ibid., p. 38. This statement is in a note at the end of the lecture; it is not clear whether Dall delivered it during her talk.

Bibliographic Essay

Mary Moody Emerson

Except for Phyllis Cole's groundbreaking, magisterial *Mary Moody Emerson and the Origins of Transcendentalism: A Family History* (New York: Oxford University Press, 1998), the scholarship on Mary Moody Emerson remains comparatively slim. Invaluable is Nancy Craig Simmons' *The Selected Letters of Mary Moody Emerson* (Athens, GA: University of Georgia Press, 1993) as well as the continuing online project presenting authoritative transcriptions of the Almanacks, which can be found at Women Writers Project, https://wwp.northeastern.edu/research/projects/manuscripts/emerson/index.html. Also very fine is Noelle A. Baker's "'Let me do nothing smale': Mary Moody Emerson and Women's 'Talking' Manuscripts," *ESQ: A Journal of the American Renaissance*, vol. 37, no. 1–2, 2011, pp. 21–48, and "'Something more than material': Nonverbal Conversation in Mary Moody Emerson's Almanacks," *Resources for American Literary Study*, vol. 35 (2010), pp. 29–67. Other rounded portraits of MME can be found in Evelyn Barish's *Emerson: The Roots of Prophecy* (Princeton: Princeton University Press, 1989) and Robert D. Richardson's *Emerson: The Mind on Fire* (Berkeley, CA: University of California Press, 1995). See also David R. Williams, "The Wilderness Rapture of Mary Moody Emerson: One Calvinist Link to Transcendentalism," *Studies in the American Renaissance* (1986), pp. 1–16. MME features prominently in *Toward a Female Genealogy of Transcendentalism*, mentioned above.

Older works tend to focus less on MME's thought than her peculiarities, although occasionally a glimpse of the formidable person peek through. Franklin Benjamin Sanborn, who never let a fact get in the way of a good story, provides firsthand testimony in "The Women of Concord," which can be found in *Transcendental Epilogue: Primary Materials for Research in Emerson, Thoreau, Literary New England, the Influence of German Theology, and Higher Biblical Criticism*, ed. Kenneth Walter Cameron (Hartford, CT: Transcendental Books, 1982), pp. 25–47. George Tolman, who transcribed in wonderfully legible handwriting many of the Almanacks around the turn of the century, authored "Mary Moody Emerson" (privately printed by Edward Waldo Emerson in 1929 but now available through print-on-demand) that is based on his close reading of her works. See also Van Wyck Brooks, "The Cassandra of New England," *Scribner's Magazine*, 81 (February 1927), pp. 125–9, and Rosalie Feltenstein, "Mary Moody Emerson: The Gadfly of Concord," *American Quarterly*, 5 (Fall 1953), pp. 231–46. Finally, and of considerable value, is Ralph Waldo Emerson's "Mary Moody Emerson," reprinted in *Lectures and Biographical Sketches* (Boston: Houghton Mifflin, 1884), pp. 371–404.

MME's Almanacks are extraordinarily difficult to interpret, in part because of the damage they have suffered, in part because her handwriting is often barely legible. I have relied on the painstaking work of the editors at the Women Writers Project, as well as the digitized Tolman transcriptions, to make sense of it.

Elizabeth Peabody

Bruce A. Ronda is the author of the only full-fledged biography, *Elizabeth Palmer Peabody: A Reformer on Her Own Terms* (Cambridge, MA: Harvard University Press, 1999). Megan Marshall's excellent *The Peabody Sisters: Three Women Who Ignited American Romanticism* (Boston: Houghton Mifflin, 2005) recounts EPP's life up to the mid-1840s. Articles on Peabody include Nina Baym, "The Ann Sisters: Elizabeth Peabody's Millennial Historicism," *American Literary History*, vol. 3, no. 1 (Spring 1991), pp. 27–45; Diane Brown Jones, "Elizabeth Palmer Peabody's Transcendental Manifesto," *Studies in the American Renaissance* (1992), pp. 195–207; and the collection of essays in *Reinventing the Peabody Sisters*, ed. Monica

M. Elbert, Julie E. Hall, Katherine Rodier (Iowa City: University of Iowa Press, 2006) is a most welcome addition.

Of enormous value is the unpublished manuscript biography of EPP by Mary Van Wyck Church, housed at the Massachusetts Historical Society and containing extracts from journals and other documents available in no other form. The MHS also has letters from EPP's mother, Eliza Peabody, as does the NYPL. Antioch College is the repository of EPP-related material donated through Horace and Mary Peabody Mann's children. EPP's transcriptions of the Margaret Fuller's Conversations are housed at the American Antiquarian Society.

Finally, the most informative work about EPP is her own writing, which ranges widely, sometimes abstrusely, but always with a radiant intelligence.

Sophia Peabody Hawthorne

For many years, Sophia Peabody Hawthorne was a bit player in studies and biographies of her husband. The only full-length biography is Patricia Dunlavy Valenti's two-volume *Sophia Peabody Hawthorne, A Life*, which juxtaposes SPH's upbringing and adult experiences with those of her husband (Columbia, Mo.: University of Missouri Press, 2004). The "Cuba Journal" has begun to attract scholarly interest, including Daniela Ciani Forza, "Sophia Peabody Hawthorne's 'Cuba Journal': A Link Between Cultures," *The Nathaniel Hawthorne Review*, vol. 37 (2011), pp. 73–96; and Ivonne M. Garcia, "Transnational Crossings: Sophia Hawthorne's Authorial Persona from the 'Cuba Journal' to Notes in England and Italy," *The Nathaniel Hawthorne Review*, vol. 37 (2011), pp. 97–120.

A treasure trove of SPH's manuscripts and letters, including the "Cuba Journal," has been digitized by the New York Public Library. SPH, *Notes in England and Italy. By Mrs. Hawthorne* (New York: G P. Putnam's, 1878) and Julian Hawthorne's *Nathaniel Hawthorne and His Wife; a Biography*, 2 vols. (Boston: Houghton Mifflin, 1884) remain indispensable.

Lydia Jackson Emerson

Portraits of LJE generally focus on her poor health and disagreements with her husband. For Ralph L. Rusk, writing in 1949, she was afflicted with "imaginary ills" that were likely the result of "her unconscious protest against a philosophy that she was unable to live up to," while for Megan Marshall, she is best understood as an oppressed housewife who "sought refuge in illness and, when well, in an obsessive attention to the details of housekeeping." These are representative of a much more pervasive tendency. (Rusk, *The Life of Ralph Waldo Emerson* [New York: Columbia University Press, 1949], p. 358, and Marshall, *The Peabody Sisters: Three Women Who Ignited American Romanticism* [Boston: Houghton Mifflin, 2005], p. 335.)

The best alternative to these narratives are the two works I have principally relied on: *LLJE* and *Life LJE*. See also Delores Bird Carpenter, "Lidian Emerson's 'Transcendental Bible,'" *Studies in the American Renaissance* (1980), pp. 91–5, and the interesting unpublished dissertation by Shirley B. Faile, *Children and Education in the Family of Lidian Jackson and Ralph Waldo Emerson*, 1992.

Margaret Fuller

Fuller's life and work has received the most attention from scholars and general readers. Early biographies include *OM*; Julia Ward Howe, *Margaret Fuller (Marchesa Ossoli)* (Boston: Roberts Brothers, 1883); and Thomas Wentworth Higginson, *Margaret Fuller* (Boston: Houghton, Mifflin, 1884). More recent works include Bell Gale Chevigny, *The Woman and the Myth: Margaret Fuller's Life and Writings* (Boston: Northeastern University Press, 1993); Charles Capper, *Margaret Fuller: An American Romantic Life* (New York: Oxford University Press, 1992–2007); Jeffrey Steele, *Transfiguring America: Myth, Ideology, and Mourning in Margaret Fuller's Writing* (Columbia, Mo: University of Missouri Press, 2001); Megan Marshall, *Margaret Fuller: A New American Life* (New York: Houghton Mifflin, 2013); John Matteson, *The Lives of Margaret Fuller* (New York: Norton, 2013). Also especially useful in thinking about MF and RWE is Christina Zwarg, *Feminist Conversations: Fuller, Emerson, and the Play of Reading* (Ithaca: Cornell University Press, 1995). Finally, of enormous interest is *Margaret Fuller and Her Circles*, ed. by Brigitte Bailey, Kathryn P. Viens, and Conrad Edick Wright (Amherst, MA: University of New Hampshire Press, 2013).

Articles and book chapters have proliferated in the last thirty years, including Nancy Craig Simmons, "Margaret Fuller's Boston Conversations: The 1839–1840 Series," *Studies in the American Renaissance* (1994), pp. 95–266; Christina Zwarg, "The Storied Facts of Margaret Fuller," *The New England Quarterly: A Historical Review of New England Life and Letters*, 69 (March 1996), pp. 128–42; Tess Lewis, "Margaret Fuller: The American Mind Writ Large," *American Scholar*, 65 (Spring 1996), pp. 284–92; Phyllis Cole, "The Nineteenth-Century Women's Rights Movement and the Canonization of Margaret Fuller," *ESQ: A Journal of Nineteenth-Century American Literature and Culture*, 44 (1994), pp. 1–33; Judith Mattson Bean, "Margaret Fuller and Julia Ward Howe: A Woman-to-Woman Influence," in Fritz Fleischmann, *Margaret Fuller's Cultural Critique: Her Age and Legacy* (New York: Peter Lang, 2000), pp. 91–108; Colleen Glenney Boggs, "Margaret Fuller's American Translation," *American Literature: A Journal of Literary History, Criticism, and Biography*, 76 (March 2004), pp. 31–58; Charles Capper, "Getting from Here to There: Margaret Fuller's American Transnational Odyssey," in Capper and Cristina Giorcelli, eds., *Margaret Fuller: Transatlantic Crossings in a Revolutionary Age* (Madison, WI: University of Wisconsin Press, 2007), pp. 3–26; Kathleen Ann Lawrence, "Soul Sisters and the Sister Arts: Margaret Fuller, Caroline Sturgis, and Their Private World of Love and Art," 57 (2011), *ESQ: A Journal of Nineteenth-Century American Literature and Culture*, pp. 79–104; Jason Hoppe, "'So Much Soul Here I Do Not Need a Book': Idealization and Aesthetics of Margaret Fuller's Coterie, 1839–1842," 61 (2015) *ESQ: A Journal of Nineteenth-Century American Literature and Culture*, pp. 362–409; and Jeffrey Steele, "Reconfiguring 'Public Attention': Margaret Fuller in New York City," 42 (Fall 2015), *Nineteenth-Century Prose*, pp. 125–54.

Woman in the Nineteenth Century remains widely in print. Other writings by Fuller can be found in the collections of her New York journalism gathered by her brother Arthur Buckminster Fuller: *Life Without and Life Within; or, Reviews, Narratives, Essays, and Poems* (New York: The Tribune Association, 1869); *At Home and Abroad; or, Things and Thoughts in American and Europe* (New York: The Tribune Association, 1869); and *Art, Literature, and the Drama* (New York: The Tribune Association, 1869). See also Jeffrey Steele, *The Essential Margaret Fuller* (Rutgers University Press, 1992) and Larry J. Reynolds, *These Sad But Glorious Days: Dispatches from Europe, 1846–1850* (New Haven: Yale University Press, 1991).

Robert N. Hudspeth's six-volume collection of Fuller's letters is definitive. Harvard's Houghton Library holds the bulk of Fuller's papers (Fuller Family Papers), much of it digitized, much of it not.

Index

Note: Following the page number; 'n.' after a page number indicates the footnote number.

For the benefit of digital users, indexed terms that span two pages (e.g., 52–53) may, on occasion, appear on only one of those pages.

Abbott, Abiel 152
abolition 3
Adams, David Phineas 30
Adams, John Quincy 30–1, 153
Alcott, Abba 100–1, 107
Alcott, Amos Bronson 1, 98–107, 111, 113, 122–3, 224
  writings of:
  Conversations with Children on the Gospels 104–8
  "Orphic Sayings" 267
Alcott, Louisa May 100–1, 137, 341
Alcott, May 341
Allston, Washington 82–3, 86–8, 108, 128–9, 146, 158, 164, 172, 251
American Woman Suffrage Association 318
An Accidence, or Gamut, of Oil Painting (Ibetson) 146–7
Animal Magnetism, or Psychoduamy (Leger) 298
An Enquiry into the Duties of the Female Sex (Gisborne) 27–8
Appeal to the Christian Women of the South (Sarah Grimké) 216
Association of American Women 318
Austen, Jane 255–6

Bancroft, Elizabeth Davis Bliss 125–6, 177, 202, 204, 207–8, 213, 272
Bancroft, George 125–6, 176
Bangs, Henry P. 313
Barker, Anna Hazard, see *Anna Hazard Barker Ward*
Barlow, Almira 316
Bem, Joseph 344
Benjamin, Park 172
Blackwood's Magazine 140–1, 145
Blake, William 32
  writings of:
  "The Marriage of Heaven and Hell" 231–2
  The Songs of Innocence and Experience 232
Bolles, Lucus 121
Boston Daily Transcript 346–7
Bowditch, Nathaniel 77
Bradford, George Partridge 125, 196, 206
Bradford, Sarah Alden, see *Sarah Alden Bradford Ripley*
Brewer, Ann Sargent, see *Ann Sargent Brewer Gage*
Bridgman, Laura 180–1
Brisbane, Albert 227
Brook Farm 4, 125, 176–7
Brown, Charles 205
Brown, Charles Brockden 255–6
Brown, Lucy Jackson (LJE's sister) 195–6, 202
Browning, Elizabeth Barrett 307–8
Browning, Robert 307
Brownson, Orestes 110, 113, 123, 248, 267–8
Bruce, Georgianna 293
Brunton, Mary 26
Bryant, William Cullen 135
Buckminster, Isaac Lyman 84–5, 112
Buckminster, Joseph Stevens 84, 89, 205–6
Burns, Robert 300
Burroughs, James Rice 150–1, 153–4
Byron, Lord George Gordon 12, 36, 49, 135

Calvinism 20
Carlyle, Thomas 140–1, 196–7, 226–7, 248, 301, 307
Channing, Ellen Fuller 185, 187
Channing, Ellery 185, 228, 314–16
Channing, Mary 89, 125–6, 177
Channing, Walter 138
Channing, William Ellery 44, 48, 70, 85–93, 113, 115, 122–3, 130, 138–9, 147
  writings of:
  "Emancipation" 125
  "Self-Culture" 89
Channing, William Henry 258, 267–8, 273, 316–17
Chapman, Maria Weston 125
Child, Lydia Maria 66, 125–6, 177, 248, 258–9, 271, 320
Chopin, Frédéric 302
Christian Examiner 96
Christian Inquirer 94

Clarke, James Freeman 66, 113, 208, 246–7, 258, 291–2
Clarke, Sarah 114, 130, 167, 177–8, 208, 254, 258, 291–2, 316–17, 345, 349
  art of: 292
Cleveland, Dorcas Hiller 149–50
Clevenger, Shobal 172
Cole, Thomas 159
Coleridge, Samuel Taylor 9, 25, 32, 58, 82–3, 89, 92, 110
  Writings of:
  Aids to Reflection 58, 101
  Biographia Literaria 89
  The Friend 97
Columbus, Christopher 52
Concord Female Anti-Slavery Society 216–17
Concord School of Philosophy 332–3, 348–9
Confessions (Rousseau) 255–6
Confessions of an Opium-Eater (De Quincy) 301
conversation, as transcendentalist artform 98
"Conversations," of MF 1, 4–7, 67, 125, 129, 174, 177–9, 194–5, 247, 254–5, 269–73, 280–3, 318
Conversations with Goethe (Eckermann) 267
Conway, Moncure Daniel 346
Cooper, James Fenimore 205–6
Copley, John Singleton 74
Correggio, a Tragedy (Oehlenschläger) 135
Cotton, John 199
Cowper, William 21, 78–9
Cranch, Christopher Pearse 267, 317
Cuba 153
Cudworth, Ralph 241
Cushman, Charlotte 321–4

Dacier, Madame 77
Dall, Caroline Healey 126, 177, 289–90, 349–53
  writings of:
  Margaret and Her Friends, or Ten Conversations with Margaret Fuller 351
Dana, Richard H. 153
Dante 43–4
Darwin, Charles 105–6
Davis, George 261–2, 284
Davis, Paulina Wright 329, 350–1
De Gerando, Joseph 70, 97, 140–1
Democracy in America (De Tocqueville) 91
De Quincy, Thomas 301
De Zayas, Fernando 156, 161
Dial, The 3–4, 123, 125, 264, 267–8
Dickens, Charles 180–1
Dickinson, Emily 24, 26, 62, 149, 245, 291
  writings of:
  "I started Early—Took my Dog" 245
Discourses on the Philosophy of Religion (Ripley) 110
Don Quixote 202
Doughty, Thomas 143–4
Duties of Man, The (Mazzini) 302
Duyckinck, Evert 296–7

Eckermann, Johann Peter 267
Edgeworth, Maria 77, 106, 205–6
Edwards, Jonathan 20
Eichhorn, Johann Gottfried 40–1
Eliot, George 289
Elm Vale (MME's home) 37
Emerson, Charles Chauncey 33–4, 39–42, 44–5, 63–4, 110–11, 175, 210, 215–16, 267
Emerson, Edith 234–5
Emerson, Edward Bliss 33–4, 39, 41, 111
Emerson, Edward Waldo (RWE and LJE's son) 240
Emerson, Ellen Tucker (RWE's first wife) 55–8, 215
Emerson, Ellen Tucker (RWE and LJE's daughter) 194, 225, 314, 331, 340
Emerson, Lydia Jackson 9, 65, 108–11, 114, 118–20, 125–6, 175–6, 187, 192–244, 328–34
  health of 204–5
  love of conversation 194
  writings of:
  "Transcendental Bible" 9, 231–4
Emerson, Mary Caroline 33–4
Emerson, Mary Moody 9, 11–72, 84, 110, 112–13, 116–17, 119–20, 126, 159–60, 194, 208–9, 216, 227, 235, 241–4, 248, 334–41
  appearance and behavior of 11–12
  influence on RWE 46–52
  refusal of marriage 24
  writings of:
  "Almanacks" 9, 13–14, 37–8, 48–53, 340
  "A Meeting of Two Friends after Long Separation by Death" 337–8
  "The Woman" 338
Emerson (Ripley), Phebe Walker 16
Emerson, Ralph Waldo 3, 8–9, 24, 33–5, 42–3, 45–6, 55–61, 82, 98, 106, 108–23, 130, 174, 185–6, 195–8, 206–7, 246–7, 266–7, 277–8, 290, 317
  philosophy of individualism 213, 218
  writings of:
  "The American Scholar" 48 fn, 66–7, 100–1, 220
  "Divinity School Address" 116–17, 120–1, 264
  Essays: First Series 52
  "Experience" 239, 243

"Love" 225–7
"Man the Reformer" 267–8
Nature 8–9, 52, 61, 110–11, 119, 129, 160, 222–3
"The Poet" 48 fn
"Self-Reliance" 3
"Thoughts on the Religion of the Middle Ages" 82
"The Transcendentalist" 233–4
"Threnody" 239
Emerson, Robert Bulkeley 33–5, 39, 44–5
Emerson, Ruth Haskins 15, 33–5, 38–9, 61, 110, 209–10
Emerson, Waldo (LJE and RWE's son) 110–11, 114–15, 221, 234
death of 234–6, 284
Emerson, William (MME's father) 15–16, 55, 184
Emerson, William (MME's brother) 17–19, 30–1, 33–5, 53, 81
Emerson, William (MME's nephew) 33–4, 39–41, 55, 65
Endymion: A Poetic Romance (Keats) 187
Evidences of Christianity (Palen) 134

Fairie Queene, The (Spenser) 77, 189
Family Nurse; or Companion to the Frugal Housewife, A (Child) 271
Fichte, Johann Gottlieb 32
Fields, James T. 326
Fiske, Joseph Emerson 166
Flaxman, John 148
Foote, Caleb 167
Fourier, Charles 227
Francis, Convers 258–9
Friedrich, Caspar David 159
Froebel, Friedrich 344
Fruitlands 240
Fugitive Slave Act 329, 331
Fuller, Ellen, *see* Ellen Fuller Channing
Fuller, Margaret 3, 7–8, 67, 108, 111–13, 129, 178, 193–4, 220, 224–5, 235–7, 244–314, 346–7, 352
conversation of 246–7
"Conversations," see *separate entry*
writings of:
"Asylum for Discharged Female Convicts" 296
"Farewell to New York" 299
"The Great Lawsuit. Man *versus* men; Woman *versus* Women" 284–7
"Lost and Won" 263
"Mariana" 257
reviews for *New-York Tribune* 296
"A Short Essay on Critics" 267–8
Summer on the Lakes 292–3
Woman in the Nineteenth Century 3, 7–8, 189–91, 247, 294–5
"Wrongs of American Women, The" 296
Fuller, Sarah Margarett 76, 250–1
Fuller, Richard 292, 300–1
Fuller, Timothy 76, 249–51, 263–4

Gage, Ann Sargent Brewer 44–5, 65
Gardner, Sally Jackson 282–3
Garrison, William Lloyd 333
Goddard, Lucy 272
Godey's Magazine and Lady's Book 297
Godwin, William 27–8
Goethe, Johann Wolfgang von 12, 21, 40, 115, 247–8, 260–1
writings of:
Faust 248
"Ganymed" 115
Wilheim Meister 206, 274
Goodridge, Eliza 142
Goodridge, Sarah 142
art of:
Beauty Revisited 142
Graeter, Francis 142–3
writings of:
Mary's Journey: A German Tale 142
Great Awakening 20
Greeley, Horace 227, 290, 296–7, 314–17
Greeley, Mary 290
Grimké, Angelina 216
Grimké, Sarah 216

Hall, Ann 142
Harding, Chester 144–5
Haskins, Hannah (MME's niece) 126
Hasty, Catharine 313
Hasty, Seth Libby 307
Hawthorne, Elizabeth Manning "Ebe" 132–4, 167, 172–3
Hawthorne, Julian 129, 326
Hawthorne, Louisa 167
Hawthorne, Nathaniel 3–4, 8–9, 66, 125, 131–4, 167–73, 236, 318–19, 325
writings of:
The Blithedale Romance 170, 321
"Edward Randolph's Painting" 170–1
The House of the Seven Gables 321
"The Gentle Boy" 171
"My Kinsman, Major Molineux" 167
The Marble Faun 325
"The Minister's Veil" 167
Mosses from an Old Manse 188–9

Hawthorne, Nathaniel (*cont.*)
The Scarlet Letter 170, 319
Twice-Told Tales 167–8
Hawthorne, Sophia Peabody 8–9, 69–70, 78, 108, 112, 124–6, 128–91, 193, 236, 287–8, 318–28
aesthetic sense of 132
health 137–40
relationship with EPP 134–5
art of:
Endymion 187–9
Flight into Egypt 165
Isola 174
Jessica and Lorenzo 164
writings of:
Cuba Journal 8–9, 129, 152–3, 159–60, 169
Notes in England and Italy 327
"To a Priestess of the Temple Not Made with Hands" 129
Hawthorne, Una 189
Healey, Caroline, *see* Caroline Healey Dall
Hedge, Frederic Henry 3–4, 101, 113, 351–2
Herder, Johann Gottfried 206
Herschel, Caroline 105
Higginson, Thomas Wentworth 292–3
History of the Corruptions of Christianity (Priestley) 134
History of Philosophy (Enfield) 134
History of the Rise and Fall of the Roman Empire (Gibbon) 37–8, 140
Hoar, Elizabeth 44–5, 67, 110, 113–14, 125–6, 175, 182, 209–10, 216, 258
Holmes, Oliver Wendell 255
Hooper, Ellen Sturgis 125–6, 179, 207–8, 219–20, 267–8, 271–2, 281
Hosmer, Henrietta 321–4
Howe, Julia Ward 130, 153, 318
Howe, Samuel Gridley 180–1
Hume, David 12, 36
writings of:
History of Great Britain 250–1
Hunt, Holman 187
Hutchinson, Anne 351

Institutes of Natural Philosophy (Enfield) 205–6

Jackson, Charles (LJE's father) 137, 203
Jackson, Charles T. (LJE's brother) 142–3, 196
Jackson, Lucy Cotton (LJE's mother) 199–200, 203
James, Alice 341
James, Henry 228
writings of:
The Bostonians 347–8
James, Sr., Henry 337
Johnson, Samuel 141

Kant, Immanuel 40, 58
Keats, John 135, 273
Kemble, Fanny 296–7, 319
Kendal, Sarah 202
King, Samuel 142
Koran 37–8
Kraitsir, Charles 344

Landers, Lois 321–4
Lardner, Nathaniel 71–2
La Recompensa 151–2
Leger, Theodore 298
Liberator, The 216
Longfellow, Fanny 142–3
Longfellow, Henry Wadsworth 135, 142–3, 167–8
Lowell, James Russell 267–8
Lynch, Anne 296–7
Lyrical Ballads 36

Mann, Horace 162–3, 188–9
Mann, Mary Peabody 69–70, 78, 84, 91, 105, 124–6, 136, 320
Martineau, Harriet 104, 109, 162, 215, 259–60, 301
writings of:
"On Female Education" 104
Society in America 104
Marsh, James 101
Massachusetts Society for the Prevention of Cruelty to Animals 331–2
Mather, Cotton 199
Mazzini, Giuseppe 301
Melville, Herman 296–7
Memoir of Margaret Fuller Ossoli 317
Merchant of Venice, The 164
Mesmer, Franz Anton 165
mesmerism 165–6
Metamorphosis (Apuleis) 272
Mickiewicz, Adam 304, 308
Milton, John 13
Modern Painters (Ruskin) 241
Montagu, Elizabeth 77
Monthly Anthology and Boston Review 30
Morrell, Laurette de Tousard 152
Morrell, Robert 152
Mosheim, Johann Lorenz von 37–8
Mott, Lucretia 310
Mozier, Joseph 324–5

Murray, Judith Sargent 22–4, 95, 147, 201
writings of:
The Gleaner 24
"On the Equality of the Sexes" 24, 95
Murillo, Bartolomé Esteban 161–2

Napoleon 192
Nathan, James 298–300
National Women's Rights Convention 329
Natural Theology (Palen) 134
New England Galaxy 263
New England Women's Club 340–1
New England Women's Rights Convention 350–1
New View of Christianity, Society, and the Church (Brownson) 110
New-York Tribune 290
Newton, Isaac 32–3, 37–8
Night Thoughts (Young) 21
North American Review 81
Norton, Andrews 96, 117
Novalis 32

"Ode to Psyche" (Keats) 273
Old Manse 15, 182
Olsen, Tillie 341
"On the Banks of Bonnie Lock Lomond" 300
Ossoli, Angelino (Nino) 312
Ossoli, Giovanni Angelo 308–10
Our Dumb Animals 331–2

Paradise Lost 13
Park, Cornelia Hall 181
Park, John 249
Parker, Theodore 4, 123, 267, 290
writings of:
"Thoughts on Labor" 267–8
Parsons, Anna Q. T. 80
Parsons, Hannah Haskins 338
Peabody, Eliza Palmer (EPP's mother) 72–7, 124, 136, 185, 193, 288–9, 295, 318–19, 344–5
writings of:
"The True Woman" 72–4
Peabody, Elizabeth Palmer 1, 4, 8, 28, 44–5, 69–72, 77–127, 193, 206–8, 224, 235–6, 249, 341–9
bookshop 1–4, 123–7, 176, 193
"historical conferences" of 97–8
and kindergarten 344
writings of:
Aesthetic Papers 343
"A Glimpse of Christ's Idea of Society" 123, 227
"Egotheism, the Atheism of Today" 122–3
The Family School 108
First Lessons in Grammar on the Plan of Pestalozzi 101 fn
First Steps in the Study of History: Being Part First of a Key to History 97
Kindergarten Culture 345–6
The Kindergarten in Italy 345–6
Kindergarten Messenger 345–6
Last Evening with Washington Allston 346
Letters to Kindergarteners 345–6
Record of a School: Exemplifying the General Principles of Self Culture 1, 102–6, 108, 110, 117, 162
Reminiscences of the Rev. William Ellery Channing, D. D. 346
Self-Education: Or the Means and Art of Moral Progress (translation) 70
"The Spirit of the Hebrew Scriptures" 94–7, 162
Peabody, George (EPP's brother) 78, 116
Peabody, Mary Tyler, see *Mary Peabody Mann*
Peabody, Nathaniel (EPP's father) 74–6, 124, 131–2
writings of:
The Art of Preserving Teeth 131–2
Peabody, Nathaniel "Nat" (EPP's brother) 76–7, 84, 116
Peabody, Sophia Amelia, see *Sophia Peabody Hawthorne*
Peabody, Wellington (EPP's brother) 78
Peale, Charles Willson 141–2
Peale, Rembrandt 141–2
Percival, James Gates 135
Pestalozzi, Johann Heinrich 100–1 fn
Pierce, Franklin 321–4
Plotinus 241
Poe, Edgar Allan 189, 296–7
writings of:
"The Literati of New York" 297
Pope, Alexander 36
Portrait of a Lady, The (James) 62
Powers, Hiram 228
Poyen, Charles 165–6
Praxiteles 136
Prelude, The (Wordsworth) 32–3, 36 fn
Pride and Prejudice (Austen) 156
Progress of Animal Magnetism in New England (Poyen) 165–6
Putnam, George Palmer 113, 306

Quincy, Eliza Morton 271
Quincy, Josiah 120

Rachel (actress) 302
Radcliffe, Ann 19
  writings of:
  Mysteries of Udolpho, The 19, 26–8
Rècamier, Madame 274
Report on the Magnetical Experiments (Poyen) 165–6
Richter, Jean Paul 140–1
Ripley, Daniel Bliss 50
Ripley, Ezra 18, 35, 184
Ripley, George 3–4, 110, 113, 176–7
Ripley, Samuel 43, 189
Ripley, Sarah Alden Bradford 12, 52, 114, 196
Ripley, Sophia 125, 177, 271
  writings of:
  "Woman" 267–8
Romanticism 11–12
Romeo and Juliet 47–8
Rosamond: or, A Narrative of the Captivity… (anonymous) 153
Rosetti, Dante Gabriel 187
Rousseau, Jean-Jacques 255–6
Russell, Mary Howland 202

Salem, Mass. 131–2
Sand, George 302–4
Schlegel, Friedrich 32
Schiller, Friedrich 32, 206
Scott, Sir Walter 205–6, 300
Scotus, John 52
Sedgwick, Catherine Maria 108, 319
Shaw, Anna 271
Shepard, Ada 325
Slavery in Cuba 157–8
Smith, Elizabeth Oakes 335–6
Social Destiny of Man (Brisbane) 227–8
Society for Philosophical Inquiry 349–50
Somerville, Mary 77, 105–6
Southey, Robert 89
Sparks, Jared 89
Spinoza, Baruch 12, 36
Spring, Marcus 299
Spring, Rebecca 299, 316–17
Stäel, Madame de 40, 44, 47, 77, 98, 241, 255–6
  writings of:
  Corinne 40, 78–9, 247
  On Germany 40, 206
St. Leon 27–8
Stanton, Elizabeth Cady 194, 270, 289–90, 308
Story, William Wetmore 324
Stray Leaves from a Seamstress's Journal (anonymous) 289
Stuart, Gilbert 142
Sturgis (Tappan), Caroline 125–6, 177, 207–8, 228, 253, 267, 271, 316
Sturgis, Ellen, *see* Ellen Sturgis Hooper
Sumner, Charles 260
Swedenborg, Emmanuel 210–12, 231–2
  writings of:
  Wisdom's Delight in Marriage ("Conjugial") Love 212, 231–2

Tappan, William Aspinwall 310–11
Taylor, Bayard 314–16
Tempest, The 46, 54, 251, 286
Temple School 1, 99, 101–5, 207–8
Thackeray, William Makepeace 261
Thoreau, Cynthia 12
Thoreau, Henry David 3, 8, 113, 182, 185, 224, 267, 290, 314–16, 337
  writings of:
  Walden 12, 62, 129, 184
Thoreau, John 234
Thoughts on Democracy (Mazzini) 302
Ticknor, George 81
Ticknor, William 325–6
The Token 167
Tocqueville, Alexis de 91
Transcendental Club 38–9, 113, 119–20, 125, 176
Transcendentalism 12, 49, 65–6, 97, 338, 351–2
Treatise on Domestic and Agricultural Association (Fourier) 227
Turner, J. M. W. 159

Una, The 329, 350–1
Unitarianism 20–1, 31, 208
Upham, Charles 121

Van Schalkwyck, Mary 26–33, 132, 167
Very, Jones 119–23, 225
Vestiges of the Natural History of Creation (Chambers) 241
Visconti, Costanza Arconati 312

Ward, Anna Barker Hazard 228, 273–6, 319
Ward, Samuel Gray 273, 319
Webster, Daniel 30–1, 42, 48
White, Daniel Appleton 132, 167
White, Eliza 132
White (Foote), Mary Wilder 132, 167, 183
Whitman, Walt 15–16, 62
Wilkinson, J. J. Garth 231–2
Wisdom of the Nine, The 204
Wollaston, William 52

Wollstonecraft, Mary 22–3, 27–8, 104, 194, 249–52, 316
writings of:
Thoughts on the Education of Daughters 249–50
Vindication on the Rights of Woman 22–3, 27–8, 249–50
women in republican U.S. 12
women's rights 3, 7
Woolf, Virginia 204, 341
Wordsworth, Dorothy 301, 341
Wordsworth, William 9, 12, 21, 25, 32, 36, 49, 70, 89, 92, 106, 261, 301
Wyeth, N. C. 313

Young, Edward 21

all that they learn – First their college exercises – their political duties – the exercises of professional studies – the very first action of life
in any direction – calls upon them for reproduction of what they have
learnt. – This is what is most neglected in the education of women
– they learn without any attempt to reproduce – The little reproduction
to which they are called seems mainly for the purposes of idle display.
It is to supply this deficiency that these conversations have been planned.
Miss Fuller guarded against the idea that she was to teach any thing
She merely meant to be the nucleus of conversation – She had had
some experience in conducting such a conversation, – & she proposed
to be one to give her own best thoughts on any subject that was
named, as a means of calling out the thoughts of others. She thought it
would be a good plan to take up subjects on which we knew words – &
had impressions, & vague irregular notions, & compel ourselves to
define those words – to turn these impressions into thoughts, & to systematise these thoughts – We should probably have to go through some mortification in finding how much less we knew than we thought – & on the
other hand we should probably find ourselves encouraged by seeing how
much & how rapidly we should gain by making a simple & clear effort for expression.
These were Miss Fuller's most important thoughts. They were expressed with
much illustration – & many more ideas were mingled with them – & all
was expressed with the most captivating address & grace – & the most beautiful modesty. The position in which she placed herself with respect to
the rest was entirely ladylike [illegible] [illegible]sonable – She said all that
she intended, to express [illegible] [illegible] with which she came, and
expected all who [illegible] [illegible] come & with great tact indicated all
the things she [illegible] [illegible] the meeting.